"A richly textured study of historical continuities in the face of revolutionary change. Lankina's meticulous account of the pre-communist origins of Russia's post-communist society sheds new light on the logics of persistence and resilience in Russian social structure that shape political possibilities in the present day. *Estate Origins* is a rewarding read for anyone interested in the social requisites of democracy."

Bryn Rosenfeld, Assistant Professor, Department of Government, Cornell University

"Elegantly crafted, beautifully written, richly illustrated, and rigorously evidenced, this book provides an axial twist to Soviet and Russian history and an exemplary, landmark study of the resilience and reproduction of social structures, social identities, and social distinctions, and their significance for politics. Lankina's masterpiece is Tolstoyan in its epic breadth of coverage, evocative powers, and intimate unpacking of the lives and times of Russia's *meshchanstvo*."

John Sidel, Sir Patrick Gillam Chair in International and Comparative Politics, London School of Economics and Political Science

The Estate Origins of Democracy in Russia

A devastating challenge to the idea of communism as a "great leveler," this highly original, rigorous, and ambitious book debunks Marxism-inspired accounts of its equalitarian consequences. It is the first study systematically to link the genesis of the "bourgeoisie-cum-middle class" – imperial, Soviet, and post-communist – to the tsarist estate institutions that distinguished between the nobility, clergy, urban merchants and *meshchane*, and peasantry. It demonstrates how the pre-communist bourgeoisie, particularly the merchant and urban commercial strata but also the aristocracy and clergy, with their high human capital, survived and adapted in Soviet Russia. Under both tsarism and communism, the estate system engendered an educated, autonomous bourgeoisie and professional class, along with an oppositional public sphere and persistent social cleavages that continue to plague democratic consensus. This book also shows how the middle class, conventionally bracketed under one generic umbrella, is often two-pronged in nature – one originating among the educated estates of feudal orders and the other fabricated as part of state-induced modernization.

Tomila V. Lankina is Professor of International Relations at the London School of Economics and Political Science. She has previously authored two books and has published widely in leading disciplinary journals on democracy, authoritarianism, mass protests, and historical patterns of human capital and democracy in Russia and other states.

The Estate Origins of Democracy in Russia

From Imperial Bourgeoisie to Post-Communist Middle Class

TOMILA V. LANKINA

London School of Economics and Political Science

CAMBRIDGE
UNIVERSITY PRESS

CAMBRIDGE
UNIVERSITY PRESS

University Printing House, Cambridge CB2 8BS, United Kingdom

One Liberty Plaza, 20th Floor, New York, NY 10006, USA

477 Williamstown Road, Port Melbourne, VIC 3207, Australia

314–321, 3rd Floor, Plot 3, Splendor Forum, Jasola District Centre,
New Delhi – 110025, India

103 Penang Road, #05–06/07, Visioncrest Commercial, Singapore 238467

Cambridge University Press is part of the University of Cambridge.

It furthers the University's mission by disseminating knowledge in the pursuit of
education, learning, and research at the highest international levels of excellence.

www.cambridge.org
Information on this title: www.cambridge.org/9781316512678
DOI: 10.1017/9781009071017

First published 2022

Printed in the United Kingdom by TJ Books Limited, Padstow Cornwall

A catalogue record for this publication is available from the British Library.

ISBN 978-1-316-51267-8 Hardback

To my father, Vladimir Ivanovich Lankin
And to the memory of Yuna Petrovna

Contents

Figures

Tables

Preface

The Soviet system represented the best concealed, longest, and most sustained form of institutional, social, and economic plagiarism in modern history.[1] It collapsed not merely because of the inherent failings of state-directed economic production; the Orwellian fossilization of the bloated party elite detached from society; or mass popular dissatisfaction. It met its dramatic end in 1991 when it was forced to shed the facade that concealed the organic, self-reproducing, and resilient society of pre-Bolshevik Russia. The best that could be taken from this society had been shamelessly appropriated. Thus, entire industries, knowledge-producing infrastructures, professional organizations, and other tangible resources – the "hardware" – along with professionals, from engineers, to schoolteachers, to scientists in universities and research centers, to cultural figures, and farmers – the "software" – became Soviet in name. Once so formally appropriated into the hydra of Soviet institutions, social groups discreetly continued to nurse their dense networks and latent structures of survivalist knowledge – the "good" and the "bad" ones. These structures facilitated the production of human capital as well as societal backwardness; social mobility and advancement as well as the conservation of pre-communist social stratification and inequalities; and institutions and ties driving societal activism as well as those that crowd out oppositional, activist engagement.

The angle on social persistence presented here differs from most historically informed accounts of Russia's politics. A synthesis of these accounts would read something like this. The Revolution of 1917 represented a profound rupture with the *ancien régime*. The Bolsheviks ruthlessly obliterated key features of the past socioeconomic order – from the system of estates to agrarian institutions and illiteracy. Relying on brutal coercion, Soviet leaders secured rapid industrialization. To this end, they built entire cities from scratch, often in

---

[1] A metaphor I deploy to capture Bolshevik claims to constructing a new society rather than building upon old regime foundations.

inhospitable lands. Entire populations were moved at random. The Gulag only exacerbated the dislocation and displacement, uprooting the society of the past. Many of those who managed to survive and thrive in the relatively permissive years of the New Economic Policy (NEP) of the 1920s were exterminated in the purges of the 1930s. Gradually, the Soviets succeeded at building a new society, one in which the party represented the embodiment of the new elite; in which a new Soviet intelligentsia emerged due to the revolutionaries' educational policies; and in which agrarian populations and factory workers, while exploited in collective farms and on the shop floor, enjoyed hitherto unprecedented levels of social mobility. Even now, thirty years after communism's collapse, Russia's political development continues to be strongly influenced by communist legacies. These make their presence felt in anything from voting patterns in the new single-industry "mono-towns," to public expressions of traumas associated with the Gulag, and the political and economic behavior of the former communist *nomenklatura*, KGB operatives, and party elite. Recent historical works on the Gulag have continued to cognitively program the reader with the assumption of cataclysmic destruction wrought by the communist project and not of the latent continuity between the pre-communist past and the post-communist present.

As a child growing up in the Soviet Union, I spent many summers with my grandmother and aunt, who lived in the Black Sea paradise of the Crimea. I have always felt that my grandmother had been somehow different. One observation was that I never saw her indulging in the *semechki* with other women on the bench outside her modest Soviet flat. Those of us who grew up in Russia – and perhaps many a westerner gone native – would know the *semechki* as the simple – and messy – snack of roasted, unprocessed, savory, sunflower seeds. Evading the *semechki* and bench-time gossip, my grandmother spent much of her leisure time playing the piano – Chopin's waltzes and Shatrov's melancholy *On the Hills of Manchuria* (*Na sopkakh Man'chzhurii*) were her favorites – and obsessively pursuing her hobby of assembling newspaper clippings about interesting discoveries, facts, and events in the realms of politics, society, and art. These, she kept saying, will be passed on to us, the next generation. Was it a pure lottery of nature that my grandmother ended up being different from many other babushkas on the bench outside her house? Or was there something peculiar about her background that nurtured certain behaviors, professional choices, and retirement preoccupations? Aside from the subtleties of how she comported herself, nothing would mark her out as anything but a quintessential Soviet citizen, a member of the Soviet intelligentsia. Born in 1913, she grew up in the Soviet Union, pursued humanities training in a Soviet higher educational institution, worked as a teacher, married, had children, suffered the mysterious disappearance of her husband in the 1930s, and lived modestly until she died in the 1980s in a Soviet flat. Some of the other relatives were more like the babushkas on the bench; others, like my mother, had an air of difference. I too occasionally treat myself to the *semechki*.

In pursuing research for this book, I have come to recognize just how typical my family is – not in the sense of its *sovietness* but in the sense of the threads that connected the distant, *pre*-Soviet past with the life paths of future generations. Like with my family, for many Soviet citizens an invisible hand of history continued to nudge one's social standing, education, tastes, and lifestyle choices; and this hand was not one of the many tentacles of the hydra of the communist state. Public policy may have pronounced the dawn of a new society, but past social stratification continued to be discreetly reproduced in the private sphere, in turn conditioning one's eventual position in that of the public. The eclectic familial constellations of class and status were as much products of social change induced by Bolshevik upheaval as they represented longer-term spatially uneven patterns of imperial sociocultural demography, expansion, frontier settlement, and, crucially, state attempts to control, reward, classify, incorporate, conscript, and tax the imperial subject and citizen via the institution of the estate. Contingencies of birth, marriage, and one's profession shaped these processes as did the long-term structural underpinnings of society. Much of the information about these past structures and possibilities has, of course, remained buried in one's consciousness – and ever deeper as the communist decades went by. The bold revelations about the past, the memoirs, and historians' archival research have, for many Russians, brought these unconscious and invisible threads into the realm of consciousness. The observation about the *semechki* ceases to be just that – a mere observation; instead, it has become part of the articulated family narrative of cultivated upbringing in early twentieth-century imperial Russia; of marriage alliances with those of noble ancestry; and of the stigma of illegitimate births.

This book situates the apparently random and contingent individual stories of the stratum that came to be referred to as the *new* Soviet intelligentsia, and in post-Soviet Russia as the *middle class*, within the social-structural context of the Russian Empire. Contrary to widespread myths, communist Russia never abolished – but, in many ways, reinforced – the deep, caste-like inequalities in society. I argue that the system of estates that institutionalized social divisions into the categories of nobility, clergy, merchant, *meshchane*, and peasantry, among other distinctions, was intrinsic not only to the gelling of the modern social stratification but to the deep social cleavages that remained concealed behind superficial nods to egalitarianism. To understand why this is the case, I invite the reader to consider the repercussions of the Great Reforms of the 1860s (notably serf emancipation) and the Bolshevik takeover of 1917. Fundamentally different in nature, context, purpose, and intent, these watershed events facilitated the conversion of the stratification of an estates-based society into one that cleaved the superbly educated professional, entrepreneurial, and enlightened proto-bourgeoisie – or, in modern parlance, the middle class – from the large mass of illiterate and poorly educated citizens and, in the case of manorial peasants, subjects. In both cases, the decimation of material wealth – in the form of the abolition of serfdom in the 1860s and the expropriation of land and possessions post-1917 – would only push the materially well-off even further to embrace and colonize the modern world of education and the professions. In both the 1860s and 1917, the various social groups were not confronting the new era from an equal starting point – the institution of the estate advantaged some over others as Russia embraced modernity; and it continues to shape how Russians position themselves vis-à-vis the state and navigate possibilities for autonomous social action today.

The long journey that brought me to the topic of social persistence comes from my interest in and more than twenty years of research into the drivers of subnational developmental and democratic variations in Russia and beyond. Already in the early 1990s, it became evident to political geographers and political scientists that territories that had been subjected to broadly similar policies of Soviet state-driven developmentalism exhibited pronounced differences in voting patterns, civic activism, and protest; these have endured as the post-communist decades went by. They also feature stark socioeconomic differences and contrasts. Conventionally analyzed with reference to urbanization or per capita income differentials, these variations have serious real-life repercussions for the daily lives of ordinary people. Some localities boast modern health clinics, a superb educational system, and nationally prominent universities and centers of research excellence that provide opportunities for jobs and careers; in others, such possibilities are few and far between, and the youth have few options beyond the local community college followed by factory or farm work. Russia thus has its own equivalent of America's Appalachia or Italy's South – territories apparently left behind in a perpetual cycle of underdevelopment. The political landscapes that characterize the territorial "haves" and "have-nots" also vary – some habitually endorse the "party of power," whatever that may be, while others are islands of democratic resilience.

I locate these contemporary patterns in the social-structural legacies of the imperial caste-like institution of the estate. In some modernizing enclaves, the aristocracy, the clergy, the muscular merchant class, the proto-bourgeois urban estate of the *meshchane*, and segments of the peasantry that had enjoyed greater freedoms even before emancipation reforms capitalized on their comparative freedoms, social ties, and human capital to seize new opportunities in industry, education, and the professions. Because the Bolsheviks reinforced the positional advantage of the empire's educated strata, mass literacy and social uplift campaigns failed to obliterate the deep social divisions that derived from the constellation of estates and concomitant variations in rights, responsibilities, and freedoms. If anything, the Soviet regime has succeeded in creating an inferior "second-class" middle class within the middle class – in the form of a peasant pursuing technical college education; the factory worker taking an evening university course; or a collective farmer finally allowed to escape to the city. The phenomenon of the "second-class middle class" has plagued political scientists' attempts to make sense of politics today, for few scholars have ventured to understand the fine-grained texture of Russian society and go beyond conventional survey research categories. Why do 65–75 percent of citizens endorse Putin in a developed country that enjoys high levels of overall education? Why is the protest movement or civic activism confined to a small minority of "sophisticated urbanites" even as public services crumble and corruption mounts?

My findings have implications for understanding the endurance of patterns of social stratification in modern society and democratic variations within and among nations. They question recent materialist accounts of inequality and policy suggestions for eliminating it. The material foundations of inequities in democracies and autocracies, developed or developing, are of course intricately connected to the intergenerational transfer of educational-professional endowments. The latter, however, are not simply and straightforwardly amenable to the "great leveler" effect as described by Walter Scheidel or the redistributive formulae of Thomas Piketty. Key elements of inequalities that my research exposes are the historical underpinnings of the social cleavage between the professionally incorporated worker – the "organization man and woman" – in a modern knowledge economy and the lower-skilled strata not so incorporated and increasingly "left out" and "left behind" – cleavages that, as we know, have posed grave threats to democracy and liberalism across the globe. Professionals, not classes in a Marxist sense; *society*, not *capital* – these are the categories that I work with in this book.

I am indebted to many colleagues, students, friends, and family who have helped to make this book happen. I received immensely valuable comments when I presented early versions of the research at the German Association for East European Studies (DGO) Economy and Society Group "Shaping Eastern European Societies and Economies: Culture, Religion and Historical Legacies" conference in Berlin in 2018 and at the graduate colloquium at the Ludwig Maximilian University in Munich in 2018. As the manuscript acquired the contours of a rather imperfect book, I subjected it to the scrutiny of leading academic experts on post-communist and comparative politics. Sam Greene at King's College London generously offered to host a book workshop in June 2019. Mark Berenson, Sam Greene, Henry Hale, Alexander Libman, Ed Morgan-Jones, Ola Onuch, Elizabeth Plantan, Grigore Pop-Eleches, Bryn Rosenfeld, and Katerina Tertytchnaya served as lead discussants on each chapter, providing sharp, critical, and, at times, brutally searching comments. Archie Brown, Zeynep Bulutgil, Ian Burgoyne, Yelena Burlina, Volha Charnysh, Vladimir Gel'man, Anna Getmansky, Janet Hartley, Otto Kienitz, Jeff Kopstein, Boris Kozhin, Marcus Kreuzer, Anna Lankina, Rada Lankina, Álvaro Morcillo Laiz, David Pearce, John Sidel, Wolfgang Teckenberg, Guzel Yusupova, Vlad Zubok, and participants at the University of Berkeley's European Politics Working Group read drafts of the entire monograph, or parts of it, or helped with queries on theory and empirics, providing useful insights or comments that pointed to inconsistencies, gaps, and errors in my analysis, as did two anonymous referees. John Sidel not only thoroughly read and commented on the manuscript but did joint brainstorming on the book's title. Álvaro Morcillo Laiz has been also my guide on the works, editions, and translations of Weber. Mark Beissinger, Cathy Boone, Valerie Bunce, Jeff Chwieroth, Jeff Kopstein, and Peter Trubowitz helped me navigate the world of publishers and editors and provided encouragement during the crucial final stages of the project. I will forever retain fond memories of a lunch I had in London with Al and Nancy Stepan, shortly before Al passed away. Sadly, Professor Stepan will not see these expressions of gratitude from one of his many mentees, but both Al's and Nancy's words of wisdom about what I should include in my future book are very much reflected in it: "Tell us stories of real people!" Any errors of course remain solely my own.

I want to add a special word of thanks to the archivists Mary Linn Wernet and Sharon Wolff, whose efforts in guiding me through and obtaining the Constantine Neklutin collection of materials from the Cammie G. Henry Research Center at Northwestern State University of Louisiana have been invaluable. Constantine added a face, a reality, a human drama, to the merchant in imperial and Soviet Russia. Without the Neklutin collection, this would have been a very different book, and I owe a huge debt of gratitude to Mary and Sharon for their patience in digitizing the materials for me and for their incredible efficiency in communications and responses to my incessant email queries. I also wish to thank Irina Kolbintseva, a descendant from the large Neklutin clan, for alerting me to this amazing archive and for sharing moving stories about the family's adaptation in Bolshevik Russia.

The book is a product of many years of research, transcending the narrower preoccupation with the reproduction of social structures across regime types. During those years, I benefited from generous funding from the British Academy, Stanford University, the Woodrow Wilson International Center for Scholars in Washington, DC, the World Resources Institute, De Montfort University, and St. Antony's and Balliol Colleges at Oxford University. I have been blessed with membership on the Program on New Approaches to Research and Security in Eurasia (PONARS) network and with the comments from peers on my work during its various stages. I could not be more grateful to the London School of Economics (LSE), my home institution. At LSE, the Suntory and Toyota International Centres for Economics and Related Disciplines (STICERD); the Centre for International Studies; the Department of International Relations; and the Paulsen fund supplied my project with a steady stream of generous funding over the last decade. A grant from the LSE International Inequalities Institute steered my research toward a deeper exploration of questions of social stratification and why it matters for democracy. I am very lucky to have worked and collaborated with outstanding scholars like Alexander Libman and Katerina Tertytchnaya, whose data contributions and cutting-edge analysis and insight into the political economy of Russia's regions and society are found in our coauthored work, which I cite throughout the book. I am fortunate to have among my LSE colleagues eminent historians of Tsarist and Soviet Russia. The manuscript benefited from conversations with my colleague and friend Vladislav (Vlad) Zubok; from the discussions I have had with Dominic (Chai) Lieven – not least his anecdotes about the escape of his family of Baltic German nobles from revolutionary Russia; and from the insights of the historian of imperial Russia Janet Hartley. Yulia Netesova, Daniel Fitter, and Kohei Watanabe provided superb research assistance. My PhD students Lana Bilalova and Marnie Howlett helped with data analysis. Giovanni Angioni was particularly indispensable as a critic and data analyst, also patiently helping me deal with glitches in formatting and data presentation. To all my students, I owe gratitude for learning from their projects. In Samara, I am grateful to Ul'yana Kulyanina and Zoya Kobozeva for their help with archival research and for their friendship and good company during my many weeks away from my family. Andrey Aref'yev was helpful with conducting interviews and archival work. Archie Brown, my doctoral supervisor, remains a good friend and discerning commentator on my work, as is his wife Pat. Yuna Petrovna, Natasha Lankina, and Vadim Lankin helped gather material that went into this book. My siblings and family scrutinized the book at its various stages and put up patiently with my disappearances into the home office–den, while my son Fyodor, a toddler when I began the project, over time started contributing ideas and suggestions too. Our nanny Lydia not only helped keep the noise down but became an amazing substitute Russian babushka who took charge of the house as I brought the book to completion. The inspiration for the book came from long conversations with my father Vladimir Lankin, who opened my eyes to the details of our family ancestry. These conversations made me realize that the imperial bourgeoisie, whether of the *haute* or *kleiner Mensch* variety, and its reincarnation as the white-collar strata in Soviet and post-Soviet Russia, has remained a neglected subject in both historiography and political science. My sisters Rada and Anna and brother Yegor provided friendship and support, as did my parents-in-law Michael and Diana Burgoyne, whose English humor has been the finest armor against the idiosyncrasies of my Russian character and who have given me the best family I could have hoped for in my adoptive country. Tragically, Yuna Petrovna did not live to see this project completed, but her joyful and life-affirming spirit lives on in the wisdom of the matriarchs found in the pages of this book. Most importantly, having a family of my own opened my eyes to alternative ways of perceiving the long course of Russia's politics. The love and support of my husband Ian, and the wonderful gift and inspiration of our son Fyodor, did as much for bringing this project to fruition as the many hours of research and writing.

Notes on Transliteration

The book uses the US Board of Geographic Names (BGN) and the Permanent Committee on Geographic Names for British Official Use (PCGN) system of Russian transliteration. Exceptions to this usage are when terms employed are conventionally transliterated otherwise (e.g., perestroika, not perestroyka) or names of specific authors publishing in English usually transliterated otherwise (e.g., Nikolai, not Nikolay Petrov). This system renders more accurate transliteration of words like svoi (one's own in plural) as distinct from svoy (one's own in singular). I depart from this system only in transliterating ё as yo as opposed to yё and by transliterating ъ the same ways as ь (') rather than ". For the letter "e," "ye" is used instead of "e" if "e" is at the beginning of a word, after vowels, and after "й," "ъ" and "ь." In citations of other work, the original transliteration is preserved. The transliteration rules are reproduced in the table here.

а – a	к – k	х – kh
б – b	л – l	ц – ts
в – v	м – m	ч – ch
г – g	н – n	ш – sh
д – d	о – o	щ – shch
е – e/ye	п – p	ъ – '
ё – yo	р – r	ы – y
ж – zh	с – s	ь – '
з – z	т – t	э – e
и – i	у – u	ю – yu
й – y	ф – f	я – ya

Abbreviations

ABNY	Amalgamated Bank of New York
ACWA	Amalgamated Clothing Workers of America
CheKa	Extraordinary Commission
d.	*delo*
DPE	Department of Public Education
ed. khr.	*edinitsa khraneniya*
ENC	effective number of candidates
Esery	Party of Socialist Revolutionaries
f.	*fond*
FIDESZ	Alliance of Young Democrats
GFA	Golubkov Family Archive
GULAG	Chief Administration of Camps
Ispolkom	Executive Committee
Kadety	Party of Constitutional Democrats
KDIE	Kazan District Inspectorate of Education
KFPA	Kobozeva Family Photographic Archive
Komsomol	All-Union Leninist Communist Youth League
KOMUCH	Committee of Members of the All-Russian Constituent Assembly
KPRF	Communist Party of the Russian Federation
KWG	Khardina Women's Gymnasium
l. (ll.)	*list, listy*
MVD	Ministry of Internal Affairs
Narkompros	People's Commissariat of Education
NC	Neklutin Collection
NEP	New Economic Policy
NKVD	People's Commissariat of Internal Affairs
ob.	*oborotnyy*
Obkom	Oblast Committee

OGPU	Unified State Political Administration
op.	*opis'*
RAIC	Russian-American Industrial Corporation
RKM	Worker and Peasant Militia
RSFSR	Russian Soviet Federative Socialist Republic
SAHE	Society for Archaeology, History and Ethnography
SGLAC	Samara Guberniya Learned Archive Commission
SGPCFH	Samara Guberniya Patronage of Children's Foster Homes
SM	Samara Museum
SME	small and medium-sized enterprise
SOGASPI	Samara Oblast State Archive of Social-Political History
Sovnarkom	Council of People's Commissars
SSEE	Samara Society for the Encouragement of Education
SSPU	Samara Society of Public Universities
SSUZ	Middle Specialized Educational Establishment
SU	Samara University
TFA	Tikhovidov Family Archive
THPSSS	The Harvard Project on the Soviet Social System
TORGSIN	Trade with Foreigners (organization)
TsGASO	Central State Archive of Samara Oblast
UMC	Universal Match Corporation
UR	United Russia
UT	Union Tours (company)
VI	Vanhanen index
VKPb	All-Union Communist Party, Bolshevik
VTsIk	All-Russian Central Executive Committee
VUZ	Higher Educational Establishment

Note: *Fond, opis', delo, edinitsa khraneniya, list,* and *list oborotnyy* are standard Russian terms referring to a collection within an archive, a subgroup of materials within the collection, file, file designation, leaf, and reverse side of leaf, respectively. Materials from the Neklutin Collection (NC) are listed with folder/item numbers or the folder and exact title of a memoir or essay at first citation. Shortened titles of archival items are mostly employed or they have been simplified.

Dramatis Personae

Pyotr Aref'yev, merchant, "renaissance man," active in civic life of Samara. Son Mitya. Married to Ol'ga Lyakhovskaya, Polish nobility in Samara (second wife and stepmother to Mitya). Property: shop and mansion on Dvoryanskaya; exotic furniture and artifacts acquired on voyages to Asia and Europe; piano with ivory keys. Education: gymnasium.

Anneta Yakovlevna Bass, director of leading modern art museum, descendant of well-off merchant family; family engaged in tea trading; cosmopolitan, European education for children. Education: prestigious school, metropolitan university.

Professor Vera Gol'msten, director of Samara Museum; daughter of Russified Swedish doctor from St. Petersburg. Metropolitan intelligentsia working in Samara. Property: unknown. Education: prestigious *lyceum* in St Petersburg, university, higher academic accolades (doctorate).

The Grinbergs, famous medical dynasty; well-off merchants; active in the civic life of the Jewish community in Samara. Property: landmark mansion rented out to a leading Samara bank. Education: European, other.

The Kavetskiys, estate unknown, possibly Polish nobles, leading medical dynasty; active as medical elite and in the enlightenment sphere of Samara. Property: residence on Dvoryanskaya. Education: prestigious imperial gymnasia and medical schools.

The Kobozev-Kashin family, *meshchane* and peasants working and trading in Samara City. Family includes a proprietor of a hair salon, domestic maids, a store manager (*prikazchik*), and traveling salesman for the Brothers Krestovnikov merchant enterprise. Property: stone and wooden two-story house; country house (*dacha*). Education: possibly accountancy courses.

Olen'ka Konovalova, Samara *meshchane*, grain traders and *rentier*. Daughter marries into the Volodkoviches family of Polish nobility in Samara. Property: two-story house with ground floor rented out to tenants; family ran prosperous grain business before loss of breadwinner. Education: gymnasium, musical conservatory.

The Neklutin family, merchants, owners of large flour mills in Samara. Prominent in urban governance as members of City Duma and elected *gorodskoy golova*. Property: mansions in Samara; one of the first owners of automobile. Education: gymnasium, technical school, university. Intermarried with leading merchant clans; Constantine Neklutin marries educated *meshchanka*.

The Sherstnev-Plotnikov family, merchants and *meshchane*. Active in city governance, ancestor member of City Duma and mayor (*gorodskoy golova*). Property: multiple mansions on Polevaya Street, Khlebnaya Square, and elsewhere. Education: unknown.

Valerian Dmitriyevich Tikhovidov, veterinarian, born into a family of school instructors in Samara. Marries Miss Kokh, of respectable family of Volga German settlers. Estate unknown, possibly clergy. Property: houses in Samara and Stavropol'-on-the-Volga. Education: seminary and higher.

Appearances

Dmitri Shostakovich, composer of cultivated Russian-Polish ancestry; son Maksim patient of Doctor Grinberg.

Aleksey Tolstoy, related to the writer Leo Tolstoy; famous writer of noble ancestry native to Samara; pupil in Samara *real'noye uchilishche*. Family property: mansion in elite quarter of Samara.

Others: teachers at art school, Jewish school, Khardina gymnasium; other gymnasium proprietors and teachers; Samara Museum employees; pupils on archaeological courses; professoriate of Samara University; engineers, enlighteners, moonlighters in shadow economy.

I

Theorizing Post-Revolutionary Social Resilience

How does a society reproduce its latent structures of power, hierarchy, and status under the weight of the revolutionary, transformative, and, indeed, totalizing impulse of a visionary, utopian state? What underpins these "below the waterline" processes of resilience?[1] Moreover, how and why does it matter for political outcomes today, long after the demise of the successive orders that have sought in vain to trample over the innate logic of society? In his classic polemic on the historical method, Carlo Ginzburg eulogizes the power of the subtle trace, the clue, the hidden, and the concealed as key to the unmasking of the fundamental, the significant, and the essential.[2] Clues, he surmises, are seldom found in what is most visible, most public, and most conspicuous but rather are discreetly scattered where one is least prone to look for them. Yet the grand, the monumental, and the visible sphere of the totalizing revolutionary regime has constituted the overwhelming preoccupation of the scholar of communism. Public policy – the rules and regulations of the state, and not the institutions or the inner rationalities of society – has shaped the way we regard politics in communist and post-communist regimes.[3] Scholars analyzing communist systems during the Cold War had, of course, no choice but to work with publicly available policy documents, statistics, and other official data concerning state building, institutionalization, and political socialization. These official records and accounts privileged the leviathan over the silent, societal, drivers of resilience.[4]

[1] "Power is like an iceberg; ... most of it lies below the waterline," Pierson, "Power," 124.
[2] See the essay "Clues: Roots of an Evidential Paradigm" in Ginzburg, Clues, 87–113.
[3] A statist focus has dominated theorizing into development and state building in a variety of settings, prompting scholars to call for grounding analysis "in more macro- and/or more micro-scopic analyses of human context and behavior." Boone, Political Topographies, 12. A related issue is the "decontextual revolution" in the social sciences. Pierson, Politics in Time, 167.
[4] Such was the power of these narratives that leading Western sociologists identified the Communist Party as the Soviet Union's most prescient "differentiator" based on membership or nonmembership. Tilly, Durable Inequality, 12. Western observers who interacted with the

1

The preoccupation with state institutions and the political elite – party apparatchiks, the nomenklatura, and other state functionaries,[5] the political sphere – endowed these actors with an exaggerated aura of agency and importance. Ideological narratives about the inauguration of a new society became internalized in academic discourse on the communist project.[6] These assumptions have continued to cast a shadow over analytical inquiry into post-communist countries. Societies with a legacy of Leninism have been regarded as receptacles, whether enthusiastic or passive, naïve or skeptical, of socialization in schools, the Komsomol, or other official societies and clubs;[7] and the elites, in relation to where they had been positioned in the various agencies of the state or party apparatus.[8] So deeply ingrained has been the revolutionary state-building paradigm as a starting point for analyzing the contemporary polity, economy, and society that efforts to transcend it have been few and far between, remaining scattered on the margins of the mainstream debates on post-communist transformations.[9] Even as new paradigms emerged to analyze Leninist legacies and their present-day imprint on society, and as hitherto hidden data became available, the discreet adaptations of the many to the social order of the futuristic regime – indeed, the role that these many have played in foisting their own institutions, practices, and values onto the state – have often remained concealed behind the shocking and the traumatic, behind the stories of the terror, dislocations, and deportations.[10] Mundane, parochial, and quotidian, these adaptations have frequently escaped the lens of the present-day historian, the sociologist, and the political scientist, driven as he or she is by the indignity to expose the state's totalism, the terror, and the inflicted trauma inscribed on the biography of the distinguished scholar, the grand aristocrat, or the metropolitan patrician *intelligent*.[11]

Soviet intelligentsia were exposed to heterodox views and were aware of social continuities. The problem was how to use this information, since it could be dismissed as "unrepresentative" or "anecdotal"; one had also to be careful about exposing the identity of the interlocutor. I am grateful to Archie Brown for suggesting this qualification, pers. comm., November 30, 2020.

[5] Prominent examples are Djilas, *New Class*; Rigby, *Political Elites*; Voslensky, *Nomenklatura*; Hough and Fainsod, *How the Soviet Union Is Governed*.

[6] For instance, E. H. Carr came to write about the Soviet project in the vein of "a great achievement" despite early reservations in the context of Stalinist repressions. Davies, "Carr's Changing Views," 102.

[7] See studies ascribing agency to Soviet citizens but focusing on everyday Soviet realities rather than broader societal influences transcending communism. Yurchak, *Everything Was Forever*.

[8] E.g., Hanley et al., "Russia-Old Wine in a New Bottle?"; Kryshtanovskaya and White, "From Soviet Nomenklatura"; Gelman et al., *Making and Breaking*; Libman and Obydenkova, "CPSU Legacies."

[9] See Tchuikina, *Dvoryanskaya pamyat'*; and Lankina et al., "Appropriation and Subversion."

[10] Consider the titles of the following influential books: Conquest, *Great Terror*; Applebaum, *Gulag*; Snyder, *Bloodlands*.

[11] See, for instance, Smith, *Former People*; Zubok, *Idea of Russia*.

Yet the possibilities of society's hidden logics of persistence and resilience have become increasingly hard to overlook as new data, archival revelations, and the advanced statistical toolkit of the social scientist have pushed against the artificial straitjacket of the revolutionary paradigm.[12] The new scholarship has raised awareness of the agency of the Gulag inmate, the professional, and the housewife to defy, obstruct, and sabotage the state's policy imperatives and the Moloch of its repressive apparatus.[13] Moreover, we now know[14] that somehow the past, pre-communist, patterns of development,[15] of industry,[16] and of *industriousness*,[17] and of civic values and voting,[18] transcended the ostensibly totalizing grip of the communist state.[19]

These new accounts – based on long-concealed "top secret" archival materials and the possibilities accorded to scholars by the advances in data accumulation and methods of social scientific analysis – beg for a new, overarching, revisionist take on the political implications of the legacies of social resilience in countries undergoing profound state-led attempts to overturn the social structure of the past. My book dissects but one, albeit highly consequential, facet of these legacies: the reproduction of social stratification behind the thin veneer of egalitarianism, with concomitant implications for the legacy of a group variously bracketed as the bourgeoisie or middle class – and prominently featuring in theorizing on democratic origins and resilience.[20] Dissecting how and with what consequences the relatively privileged, propertied, educated, and aspirational groups – the bourgeoisie-cum-middle class of the old regime – manage to reproduce their

---

[12] Both concepts capture adaptation: persistence alludes to the reproduction of the social structure despite the Revolution, and resilience to the modifying tactics, strategies, and behaviors that may include an element of change but are motivated by socially conservative impulses. I am grateful to Marcus Kreuzer for suggesting this clarification, pers. comm., November 15, 2020.

[13] Examples are Alexopoulos, *Stalin's Outcasts*; Fitzpatrick, "Two Faces"; Shearer, "Soviet Gulag"; Hardy, *Gulag after Stalin*.

[14] Gaddis's book title nicely captures the revisionism that emerged after the archives were opened to scholars with the end of communism in Europe. Gaddis, *We Now Know*. On the historical turn in the social sciences, see Capoccia and Ziblatt, "Historical Turn"; Wawro and Katznelson, "Designing"; Lankina et al., "Appropriation and Subversion"; Simpser et al., "Dead but Not Gone"; Kotkin and Beissinger, "Historical Legacies."

[15] Lankina et al., "Appropriation and Subversion"; Acemoglu et al., "Social Structure."

[16] Tomila Lankina and Alexander Libman, "The Jekyll and Hyde of Soviet Policies: Endogenous Modernization, the Gulag and Post-Communist Support for Democracy." Paper presented at the Annual Meeting and Exhibition of the American Political Science Association, San Francisco, August 31 to September 3, 2017 (unpublished).

[17] This term encapsulates the social-cultural underpinnings of the Industrial Revolution. de Vries, *Industrious Revolution*.

[18] I refer to interwar democratic statehood in communist states. For a discussion, see Pop-Eleches, "Historical Legacies."

[19] As late as 1959, leading Sovietologists continued to describe the Soviet Union as a "totalitarian dictatorship." See Inkeles and Bauer, *Soviet Citizen*, 124.

[20] The "bourgeoisie" label does not exclude the wealthiest groups or those occupying leading positions in the professions or industry. See Rosenfeld, *Autocratic Middle Class*, 61.

positional, intergenerational advantage vis-à-vis the less privileged working masses – indeed, their "bourgeois" values even under a most brutal leveling regime – speaks to debates and issues far beyond the communist experience in Europe, since it goes to the root of ongoing polemics concerning the drivers and democratic implications of inequalities in the globalized knowledge economies of the present.[21] In the sections that follow, I provide a summary of the argument about the origins and resilience of social configurations in imperial, Soviet, and post-Soviet Russia; discuss the theoretical underpinnings of the analytical framework; outline a research design; and explain how this account differs from earlier studies on the implications of the communist experience for post-communist social structures and democratic trajectories.

THE ARGUMENT

This book explains post-communist Russia's social stratification and relatedly its democratic fortunes with reference to the social structure predating communism. I locate the genesis of the bourgeoisie-cum-middle class, conventionally regarded as broadly supportive of democratic institutions, in the estate system of imperial Russia, which distinguished between the nobility, the clergy, the urban estates of merchants and the *meshchane*,[22] and the peasantry. The estate – its juridical, material, and symbolic aspects – simultaneously facilitated the gelling of a highly educated, institutionally incorporated autonomous bourgeoisie and professional stratum and engendered social and interregional inequalities that persisted through the communist period and will plague subsequent democratic consolidation. Employing post-communist electoral and public opinion data, and analyzing them in conjunction with historical census records, I demonstrate that the pre-communist social structure has shaped Russia's stark subnational developmental and democratic disparities as well as the overall national outcomes in democratic quality.

The statistical toolkit enables me to establish that the population share of one estate in particular – the urban *meshchane* – strongly covaries with a range of communist and post-communist period developmental outcomes, in education, in the extent of the saturation of the regional workforce with prestigious "bourgeois" professions, and in entrepreneurship – configurations considered

---

[21] On materialist angles, see Piketty, *Capital*. Others contend, "the interests of a class most directly refer to standing and rank, to status and security, that is, they are primarily not economic but social." Polanyi, *Great Transformation*, 160.

[22] The term originates in the Polish *miasto*, city, and *mieszczane* from city residents, also found in other Slavic languages – *myastechko* as city, settlement in Belorussian, and *misto* as city, town, in Ukrainian – usually referring to smaller settlements. Hence, the derogatory Russian word *mestechkovyy* – one exhibiting limited and parochial interests, a symbol of "provincialism" and "narrow-mindedness." The notion of *mestechkovost'* became inscribed in portrayals of *meshchanstvo*. Kobozeva, "Gorod i meshchane," 49–50.

conducive to the building and institutionalization of a democratic political system. The nebulous, fluid, and highly mobile nature of this estate makes the sole reliance on imperial census data conceptually problematic,[23] as would attempts to rigidly delineate the fluid and fuzzy permutations of imperial-cum-Soviet-cum-post-Soviet bourgeoisie turned *Soviet* intelligentsia turned post-Soviet middle class. The challenge is compounded if we take on the task of going beyond an analysis of the *reproduction* of a broad status category and explore heterogeneity in Soviet-era *mobility* among and within the various segments constituting it.[24]

The *meshchanin* or *meshchanka* of the 1897 census – the sole available comprehensive record that we have covering the empire's entire territory – often moved between merchant and *meschane* estate status; their material stature would often be on a par with the clergyman or noble of modest means. Equally, a *meshchanin* may have been a peasant previously but one who abandoned the rural dwelling and pursuits of the past, acquiring solid footing as an urban artisan, a clerk, or a teacher and marrying into the strata of a higher social estate and rank.[25] Religion and ethnicity would not be irrelevant for understanding the makeup of, and social heterogeneity within, this estate, as it absorbed many urban middling residents of "foreign" status and the upwardly mobile communities of Germans and Jews. Uniting these "mixed-title" men and women (*raznochintsy*) would, increasingly, be their education and occupational standing;[26] and the *meshchane* not only faithfully capture the splendid adaptation of the mysterious middling estate but also hint at the trajectories of the more privileged strata discreetly reinventing themselves as Soviet Russia's *new* intelligentsia. For the many reincarnating merchants and *meshchane* in Russia's provincial town, there would be the surviving aristocrat or two making a life as a university professor, a librarian, or an illustrator,[27] leaving a profound imprint on the cultural fabric of society. As Norbert Elias and John L. Scotson once observed, the preoccupation of the statistical method with high numbers often obscures the prestige, the gravitas, and the influence of a few influentials, out of proportion to their numerical weight in a community.[28]

This book situates imperial Russia's fluid estate structure – a *premodern* relic – within the autonomous professional, educational, and civic institutions of a *modern* society. I consider the Great Reforms of the 1860s – the abolition of

---

[23] On the over-time case-transformation dimension of the ontology of cases, see Abbott, *Time Matters*, 142.

[24] I thank Vladimir Gel'man for suggesting I discuss heterogeneity in social mobility trajectories. An important challenge is studying "objects moving through time and being qualitatively transformed." Kreuzer, *Grammar of Time*, in press.

[25] On estate fluidity, see Mironov, *Sotsial'naya istoriya*, 1.

[26] See Wirtschafter, *Social Identity*, esp. 62–99.

[27] See accounts in Smith, *Former People*; Channon, "Tsarist Landowners"; Golitsyn, *Zapiski*.

[28] Elias and Scotson, *Established and Outsiders*, 11.

serfdom but also other progressive initiatives in education, local governance, and economic modernization – as an important moment that structured the social configurations post-1917. These reforms combined the significant uprooting of the economic foundations of the landed gentry's wealth with the preservation of an archaic estates-based order that continued to privilege some over others while also facilitating the material advancement of the propertied and upwardly mobile free urban estates. Furthermore, the reforms only scratched the surface of the highly unequal system of educational access, as I shall explain, which was an important feature of the estates-based society. The gentry, deprived of key sources of income derived from the land, seized opportunities to procure a modern education and a salaried professional station in life, as did the merchant and the high-status *meshchanin* whose children competed for a place at classic gymnasia and technical schools. If we take the above-discussed perspective on the reforms, their consequences for the social structure would be far-reaching. Although, by the early twentieth century, rural Russia had experienced precipitous modernization, a chasm continued to cleave it from urban society. The latter resembled the towns and cities in the developed Western world much more so than the former, the pastoral small farm idyll of England or North America.[29] By the end of the nineteenth century, the modernity unleashed by the Great Reforms transformed urban Russia. Not only did it represent a hive of tightly knit institutions of urban governance, commerce, industry, the professions, and education, but these retained their autonomy or quasi-self-governing stature vis-à-vis the state. Yet the estate structure shaped, and became embedded in, these institutions, which not only aided but also constrained social mobility. As late as 1917, a web of juridical and symbolic privileges and barriers continued to lubricate the status of the estates at the top of the social pyramid, particularly nobles; the mobility of the up-and-coming merchant class based on guild criteria; and access to urban property, the trades, and services favoring the *meshchane*, while constraining those of other groups.[30] Rather than being atomized, the institutional arenas of this society of estates featured strong network ties,[31] again aiding social fluidity but also delineating its possibilities in important ways.

The empire's estate structure is central to understanding the origins, institutional underpinnings, and makeup of the nascent bourgeoisie and professional classes. When the Bolsheviks took power, in developed peripheral towns, not to mention the core metropolitan centers, they did not merely encounter a "bourgeoisie" as an abstract class category but as an institutional

---

[29] See essays in Clowes et al., *Between Tsar and People*. This chasm has been characterized as a cultural conflict between the "people" (*narod*) and the "educated minority." Mironov, *Rossiyskaya imperiya*, 2:844.

[30] On estates, see Mironov, *Rossiyskaya imperiya*, 1:340–443.

[31] See Kaplan, *Historians*; Frieden, *Russian Physicians*.

fact more characteristic of C. Wright Mills's modern organizational society than one of the halcyon days of the country gentleman, the small farmer, and the family business entrepreneur.[32] Axing the imperial police or ministries and the regional branches associated with the core sites of imperial rule would alter, but not shatter, other institutional-bureaucratic arenas and cognate ties. The bourgeois who was incorporated into modern professional, civic, and advocacy institutions enjoyed both the tangible bureaucratic and the symbolic foundations of social distinction. Indeed, they also retained a modicum of autonomy from the state. These institutional artifacts of the modernization of the estates-layered imperial society, I argue, constitute the main drivers of within- and interregional variations in communist and post-communist social, economic, and political development.

Although the inheritors of tsarist Russia's mantle of the relatively privileged strata constitute the focus of my study, their adaptations could be meaningfully explored if contextualized in the overall social structure of imperial and post-revolutionary Russia. Does not the social label of choice – be it the middle, the bourgeoisie, the intelligentsia, the professional, and the like – simultaneously circumscribe what the category *is* and what *it is not*, in relation to others? "We cannot have love without lovers, nor deference without squires and labourers," observes E. P. Thompson in his dynamic and context-sensitive analysis of the making of the working class in England.[33] This perspective is far removed from the narratives about the Soviet Union's well-known Orwellian inequalities. These overwhelmingly focused on the spectacular ascent of the peasant and factory worker – the Khrushchevs, the Brezhnevs, the Gorbachevs of Soviet society – to the pinnacles of power through the party, managerial, and trade union routes.[34] Instead, my ordinary, silent, unsung custodians of the bygone, unequal, social order are the liminal, the descendant, the inheritor of what Harley Balzer quite poignantly referred to as the "missing middle."[35] Balzer was, of course, referring to the understudiedness of this stratum of the educated, propertied, proto-professional, and entrepreneurial groups, in my analysis captured by the statistic of the *meshchane* but also straddling other "educated" estates.[36] These categories are understood here in an intergenerational sense as a *status group*. In the communist period, they came to be referred to as Soviet *intelligentsia*, loosely defined with reference to the occupation of a nonmanual job. In post-communist

---

[32] Mills, *White Collar*.   [33] Thompson, *Making of the English Working Class*, 8.

[34] See Voslensky, *Nomenklatura*; Rigby, *Political Elites*; Rigby, *Communist Party Membership*; Timasheff, *Great Retreat*; Djilas, *New Class*; Fitzpatrick, *Education*; Fainsod, *How Russia Is Ruled*; Hough and Fainsod, *How the Soviet Union Is Governed*.

[35] Balzer, *Russia's Missing Middle Class*. See also Wirtschafter, *Social Identity*.

[36] Encompassing entrepreneurs, professionals, individuals engaged in artistic pursuits, and those deriving income from rent. For stylistic convenience, I refer to them also as the *estates-derived* or *estatist* stratum – capturing the origin among "educated estates" but also alluding to an *estatist* dimension of group construction and maintenance in a Weberian sense of shared values, lifestyle, and status.

Russia, I argue, their descendants constitute the bulk of the *new* bourgeoisie-cum-professional middle classes.[37]

Social Persistence and Resilience across Distinct Political Orders and Regimes

Extant theorizing offers some signposts for us to construct an account of historical continuities but falls far short of explaining them in the context of profound revolutionary transformation. My main concern is to understand the *social-institutional* underpinnings of persistence and resilience in stratification across distinct political orders and regimes, and the implications of these patterns for long-term political outcomes. The temporal frame of the analysis straddles the pivotal moments of, and developments leading up to, the 1860s Great Reforms, the Bolshevik Revolution of 1917, and the end of communism in 1991. Conventionally, these epochs have been analyzed within the paradigm of critical junctures. Eminent works in historical sociology conceptualize critical junctures as institutionally and politically fluid moments during which policy choices are highly contingent but, depending on the specific decisions adopted, could have enduring and often self-replicating effects, conceptualized as *legacies*.[38] This heuristic is not entirely without merit for our analysis and hence is theoretically embedded in the temporal framework adapted here: radical policy solutions for change – in intention, if not execution – are undeniably consequential for society, the economy, and political development. Yet a careful examination of these "junctures" reveals the many continuities – and nondecisions – straddling them and the broader social agency accounting for both the choices made and the successful obstructions of policies promulgated.[39]

One key *nondecision* during the Great Reforms was a failure to create and implement the rudiments of a universal public education system that would have helped to socially elevate the hitherto unfree and otherwise underprivileged strata on the bottom rungs of imperial society;[40] another was

---

[37] The word "intelligentsia" in Soviet Russia "was often used interchangeably (and inconsistently) with *sluzhashchie* (officials, office workers), though 'intelligentsia' tended to refer to writers, teachers, doctors, lawyers, statisticians, and technicians, whereas *sluzhashchie* tended to be applied to clerical workers." Lankina et al., "Appropriation and Subversion," 254. The discussion draws on Rigby, *Political Elites*, 28, 31. On Soviet definitions, see also Zubok, *Zhivago's Children*, 4–5; and Churchward, *Soviet Intelligentsia*, 3–4.

[38] Capoccia and Kelemen, "Study of Critical Junctures"; and Collier and Munck, "Critical Junctures."

[39] For a critique and discussion of combining path-dependence and "punctuated equilibrium" models and sensitivity to contingency and adaptation of extant institutions, see Thelen, "How Institutions Evolve," 212–13. Critical juncture theorizing does not preclude *antecedent conditions* shaping implementation or choices made during fluid periods of reform, but the focus is on high-level political dynamics. See Dunning, "Contingency and Determinism"; Collier and Collier, *Shaping the Political Arena*.

[40] On educational access, see Lyubzhin, *Istoriya russkoy shkoly*, 2. The landed gentry's obstruction of universal schooling – not least due to fears of losing skilled peasants to the urban

the failure to reform the estates-based Petrine Table of Ranks in civil service.[41] The latter reflected the hierarchy of the estates while also incentivizing the acquisition of a superb education as a way of advancing on the highly structured scale of pay, progression, and pension perks embracing both government service and large swathes of occupations from teaching to medicine.[42] The Great Reforms thus combined features that helped further unleash the forces of a merit-based society with those of an antediluvian order where estate ascription continued to matter for one's station in life. Together, the reforms and the non-reforms created incentives and structural opportunities for further colonization of knowledge- and skills-intensive bureaucracies and modern professions by the habitually free – and educated – estates.

The privileged citizens of the estate order were in the best position to seize opportunities in education because of either a habitual emphasis on learning, in the case of the aristocracy and clergy, or the incentives, financial resources, and value proclivities that enabled it and were also characteristic of the urban merchant and *meshchane* estates. Moreover, within what I loosely refer to as the educated estates category, gradations in formal status to a considerable extent shaped one's station as a bourgeois. They influenced, say, whether he or she occupied the pinnacle of professional esteem in the elite occupations or joined the army of the modestly paid "semi-intelligentsia" as a nurse, teaching assistant, or feldsher,[43] the latter category, however, still vastly more privileged than the overwhelming mass of serf subjects in the largely illiterate society.[44] The embourgeoisement of Russia's imperial order would be thus grafted onto the institutional palette of estates. Put simply, an important legacy of the 1860s was the substitution of one type of inequality – serfdom- and estates-originating – for another, the human capital–derived one. The latter pattern anticipates characteristics of the knowledge-privileging demos of the present era.

Consider now the "juncture" of 1917. Here, compromise upon compromise diluted the many pivotal decisions that have preoccupied the scholar of the great revolutionary break.[45] Soviet historiography highlights the Bolsheviks' conscious and tactical choice to work with "old" specialists as it became clear

---

workforce – has been documented in various contexts. Iversen and Soskice, *Democracy and Prosperity*, 70.

[41] The "layering" aspect of policy making, whereby "proponents of change work around institutions that have powerful vested interests," has also been highlighted. Tarrow, "The World Changed Today!," 10. In Russia, the nobility incurred losses due to land reform while retaining their advantage in other policy domains.

[42] Mironov, *Rossiyskaya imperiya*, 2:433–39.

[43] Russian transliteration is *fel'dsher* – medical assistant or paramedic – from the German *Feldscher*. Emmons and Vucinich, *Zemstvo*, xi.

[44] On feldshers as "semi-intelligentsia," see Ramer, "Professionalism and Politics," 118; and on teachers as "low status" intelligentsia, Seregny, "Professional Activism," 169.

[45] As recently as 2015, scholars have argued: "Communism not only leveled incomes in the region but, perhaps more importantly, destroyed the basis of status societies virtually everywhere it ruled." Kopstein and Bernhard, "Post-Communism," 382.

that the goals of swift industrialization and modernization were unattainable when deploying proletarian cadre alone.[46] Mervyn Matthews traces the origins of the entrenched system of inequalities in Soviet society to the early 1920s. Lenin, his credentials of being a "fervent egalitarian" notwithstanding,[47] endorsed the first raft of concessions to the old bourgeoisie to maintain the Bolsheviks' tenuous grip on power. Stalin went on to codify, institutionalize, and enhance the privileges of the white-collar professional elite. Khrushchev only haphazardly and unsuccessfully attempted to undo Stalin's class compromises before Brezhnev restored them with a vengeance.[48]

The volumes of studies in the critical juncture vein that "forensicize" the policy-elite dynamics behind these compromises have relegated to the shadows the social construction of decisions eschewed or abandoned, the concessions made, and the ideology discreetly shelved. Such "eventful analyses"[49] – "*l'histoire événementielle*"[50] – that reduce the historical process to elite decisions, high politics, and national policy tend to background, if not outright ignore, the complexity of the realm of the social that does not neatly converge with overarching political superstructures. As recent critiques have noted, critical juncture perspectives assume the singularity of the historical process; regard change as intrinsic to pivotal decisions of key players; and take as given a relatively clean structural break between epochs that then freezes, as it were, continuity in structures, institutions, and practices unleashed by the pivotal event.[51] Crucially, some caveats notwithstanding, these heuristics largely neglect the complex layering of interconnected processes that follow distinct and often conflicting *temporal logics*. Situating assumptions about change within important political and policy junctures ascribes causal primacy to the immediate time pegged to them while neglecting aspects of the historical process that exhibit very different characteristics in temporal scope, reach, and density of association with the present.[52] Here, "calendric"[53] devices become a descriptive substitute, a justification for, and source of reification of an epoch. Even when not bracketed under the "critical" break rubric, this assumption is implicit in foundational works on 1917 and its consequences. The revolutionary event in these accounts is the starting point and 1991 the end

---

[46] Inkeles, "Social Stratification"; Bailes, *Technology*.   [47] Matthews, *Privilege*, 20.

[48] Ibid., 20.   [49] Kreuzer, *Grammar of Time*, in press.

[50] François Semiand's phrase, cited to distinguish "the instant and the *longue durée*," in Braudel, *On History*, 27.

[51] For some of the critiques highlighting institutional resilience "even in the face of huge historic breaks" like revolutions, see Thelen, "How Institutions Evolve," 209.

[52] In framing the discussion, I draw on Kreuzer, "Varieties of Time"; and Zerubavel, *Hidden Rhythms*. On the dangers of reifying concepts and overdetermined analysis, see also Kreuzer, "Structure of Description," 127.

[53] Kreuzer, "Varieties of Time," 8.

point.[54] The naïve view of Soviet institutional origins is one essentially pegged to these pivotal policies and confirmatory of what may be termed the Bolshevik "founding myths" – the Soviet university, the Soviet school system, the Soviet scientific achievements, the Soviet space project, and so forth. Because everything becomes "Soviet" and dated as bound to 1917, so too do our cognitive assumptions about the nature of the institution, achievement, or milestone in question.

This book, by contrast, has a far broader historical horizon, and it is here that the institutional-social genealogies that I reconstruct – in medicine, education, and industry – come to the aid. We know from the various institutionalist strands in sociology that institutions are often contingent in origin, but hard to reverse once established, and are inertial, adaptable, and subject to increasing returns.[55] Yet the facet of institutions accentuated here is that specific configurations have a self-reproducing and self-amplifying dynamic not just because of embedded resources but also because of the much longer-term process of social investment. Institutions are embedders of the social both in an immediate sense of reflecting societal structures and in the lengthier scope of temporal horizons invested into them as symbolic stages in life and career progression. We may, for example, consider the tiered educational edifices of imperial Russia as important institutions both in the informal sense of structuring and channeling social gradations and in an organizational sense of established routines, modi operandi, and professional and social gatekeeping. The adolescent born in 1910 would not cease to aspire to a place in a gymnasium just because the Bolsheviks have proclaimed it as a bourgeois school; his or her parent, teachers, and social peers would fight to preserve it too.

The alternative *longue durée* and path-dependency perspectives that I opt for loosen up the temporally rigid demarcatory assumptions of critical juncture theory – foregrounding not backgrounding the past even when, superficially, change at the level of political superstructures appears to be deep and profound. They are far more sensitive to the layering of "multiple concurrent processes,"[56] transcending visible structural breaks that "lock," as it were, assumptions about change within rigid periodization frames, and potentially highly consequential for the polity, economy, and society thereafter. While the *longue durée* heuristic attunes us to the towering role of the distant past – including the self-explanatory natural foundations of long-term sociodemographic and economic

---

[54] Such period slicing is also found in statistical analyses of outcomes of Soviet policies, resulting in scholars ascribing causal significance to them. On the pitfalls of the approach in quantitative analyses and on the fallacy of periodization pegged to "great events" in history, see Isaac and Griffin, "Ahistoricism," 885, 877.

[55] Howlett and Goetz, "Introduction," 483.

[56] I am indebted to Marcus Kreuzer for helping me frame this discussion. Personal email correspondence and comments on chapter, November 15, 2020. The *longue durée* perspective is associated with the work of Fernand Braudel. See essay in Braudel, *On History*, 25–54.

trends – in shaping the present, path-dependency helps us make sense of the mechanisms that account for the reproduction of patterns that *do* warrant careful explanation, since they may counterintuitively straddle the apparent, highly visible, structural breaks and turning points in epochs. Both the *longue durée* and path-dependency angles are alert to the heterogeneity of the temporal aspect of change and lethargy in long-established patterns – in Sebastian Conrad's apt characterization, "the synchronicity, of the non-synchronous."[57] Much as the *longue durée* highlights the slow unfolding but often highly resilient socioeconomic dynamics, path-dependency incorporates the multiple temporal logics accounting for *why* apparent structural change may not immediately shatter long-established values, practices, and institutions. Here, the temporal dimension of events itself becomes part of the causal structure.[58]

Path-dependency is best encapsulated in Arthur Stinchcombe's heuristic of "causal loops," whereby "an *effect* created by causes at some previous period *becomes a cause of that same effect* in succeeding periods."[59] The metaphorical prime mover effects creating the "cause" we are most concerned with are the heterogenous structural conditions of various territories over centuries that shape patterns of settlement, land use, frontier colonization, and migration. My main preoccupation, however, is with the effects of these historically protracted *longue durée* processes often of a natural, spontaneous, slow-moving kind, on the more agential, purposeful, policy-institutional dimension of the estate – both a product of state policy and a bottom-up social impulse – which in turn shaped, structured, and even calcified heterogeneity in social possibilities, rights, freedoms, and obligations. This is the "cause" occupying center stage in this book's analysis, effecting the "loops" reverberating across the epochal events of some two centuries considered here. Stinchcombe's framework is also attuned to the cognitive dimension of path-dependencies in institutions – these acquire a self-replicating character not only because, say, bureaucracies, or other formal and informal institutions, once established are hard to reverse but because whole generations grow up with cognitive mindsets pegged as it were to these institutions. Here, institutional resilience is attributed in an agential sense to segments of society that may be as yet outside of organizational sites reflecting wider institutional configurations but have a vested interest in perpetuating them because whole careers, life progression, and aspirations are cognitively mapped onto them. Institutional stability, maturity, and duration, of course, matter, since institutionalization creates the kinds of certainties that individuals crave as do parents for their children. Hence, Stinchcombe asserts that such "institutional self-replicating forces" are most powerful in "modern societies" considering the structured,

---

[57] Conrad, *What Is Global History?*, 141.

[58] For a discussion of time concepts, see Kreuzer, *Grammar of Time*, in press.

[59] Stinchcombe, *Constructing Social Theories*, 103 (emphasis in original). An institution is defined as "a structure in which powerful people are committed to some value or interest." Ibid., 107.

resource-intensive modes of training and socialization into "elite" status. They are also the consequence of greater levels of competition for a position at the top of the social pyramid because "fewer channels are blocked off on ascriptive grounds."[60] Indeed, "in societies with familial or tribal religions, poorly developed educational systems, and little mass media, we would ... expect institutional structures to be much more fragile, much more affected by wars, revolutions, and redistributions of power."[61]

Theorizing Class and Status

Anchoring the discussion on social class and status serves two broad objectives in the analytical framework outlined here.[62] The first is more carefully discerning the *how* dimension of the reproduction of social stratification that straddles a revolutionary juncture. The second is to understand the broader *effects* of social resilience as it impinges on the political proclivities of citizens. Unpacking the *how* of social reproduction goes to the root of debates about what constitutes classes and social groups. I briefly discuss these polemics and

---

[60] Ibid., 115.   [61] Ibid., 113.

[62] I am sympathetic to definitions of the middle class or bourgeoisie couched in occupational terms, but with caveats, given the historically broad scope of my analysis. In occupational terms, these strata are often delineated with reference to nonmanual occupations, including private sector work and self-employment, and the arts, as distinct from manual and routine jobs of so-called blue-collar factory, retail, or agricultural workforce that usually do not require advanced secondary and tertiary education. (See the excellent discussion of the terms in Rosenfeld, *Autocratic Middle Class*, 60–61.) I also bracket imperial small business owners, petty rentiers, and artisans under this rubric, since my analysis is sensitive both to the difference between these strata and, say, unfree peasants and to greater facility of the transformation of the nascent bourgeoisie into the urban professional middle class in the communist decades. I share the concerns that the "traditional" and "old" middle classes of artisans, merchants, petty traders, or small shopkeepers have been unfairly dismissed as not middle class in a modern sense unlike professionals; they are associated with "premodern" or "underdeveloped" economies and are expected to be relegated to the dustbin of history as countries modernize. Davis, *Discipline*, 31. Davis, in my view, rightly ascribes to small producers and entrepreneurs, rural and urban, "a disciplinary ethos which assumes a certain degree of austerity, self-regulation, and self-imposed personal restraint marshalled in the service of an individual producer's output or productivity." Ibid., 11. On the other hand, I also concur with critique of elite competition accounts focusing on land reforms during Europe's democratization as less appropriate for late developing industrial contexts where a focus on the state-dependent middle class as an important actor is warranted. Rosenfeld, *Autocratic Middle Class*, 18–19. I hesitate to rigidly delineate the elite and the petty bourgeoisie alike in the sense of income, property, or top position in a hierarchy, since my study encompasses three regime types and epochs with profound repercussions for the material and formal-professional situation of individuals. The life course angle on social reproduction of the imperial bourgeoisie helps chart how the bulk of elite, middling, and lower proto–middle class segments of imperial society moved into Soviet middle class white-collar occupations. In other words, their cultural, human, and professional capital remained a constant marker that precluded descent into lifelong manual occupations – even if spells of factory or farm work were widespread during class witch hunts.

their relevance for the historical evidence presented here before addressing the question of the implications of social resilience from the perspective of broader democratic theorizing.

Analysts of social structures distinguish materialist accounts of class from those that underscore the nontangible, symbolic, ideational dimension of cleavages among groups.[63] Classic materialist accounts have postulated social divisions as a function of the unequal distribution of material assets and, in the Marxist class schemata favored by Soviet ideologues, as rooted in dependency relationships between those who own the means of production and others whose labor they exploit.[64] In Lenin's formulation, "classes are groups of people, one of which can appropriate the labor of another owing to the different place they occupy in a definite system of social economy."[65] Beginning with Max Weber,[66] and in a tradition most extensively theorized

---

[63] Thus, Rosenfeld distinguishes between theories that focus on social relations of status and power from those highlighting ownership of capital or projecting normative assumptions about classes as carriers of specific values, or as a "unified class actor." *Autocratic Middle Class*, 58.

[64] For a discussion, and on differences with non-Marxist perspectives, see Wright, *Understanding Class*; on Weber, see esp. 21–56.

[65] Cited in Teckenberg, "Social Structure," 28.

[66] Weber, "Class, Status and Party"; *Wirtschaft und Gesellschaft*, 1:78–88. My perspective is Weberian in the significance I attach to both the material and the *Ehre/Lebensführung*, "*amorpher Art*" characteristics of the middle class; in my emphasis on values engendered in both feudal and industrial-capitalist economies; and on bureaucratic incorporation of modern societies. Ibid., 82, 83. I concur with the hunch that "Weber has won whatever Weber-Marx debate there ever was." Glassman et al., *For Democracy*, ix. Marx "was wrong to write off the small-business middle class, and the middle classes in general, in terms of their impact on industrial-capitalist societies." Ibid., 89. Marx considered "wage-labourers, capitalists and landowners" as "the three great classes of modern society based on the capitalist mode of production" Marx, *Capital*, 3:1025. The ending of volume 3, compiled by Friedrich Engels based on Marx's notes, suggests that "doctors and government officials would also form two classes, as they belong to two distinct social groups, the revenue of each group's members flowing from its own source." There is also mention of the "fragmentation of interests" based on the division of labor within the three key classes, anticipating a fuller discussion of professionals and their position in the class triptych. "At this point," however, a note from "F. E." reads, "the manuscript breaks off." Ibid., 1026. The race for mechanized production forms an important element in Marx's analysis of capitalism. See, for instance, ibid., 553–64. However, the logical outgrowth of technological development as necessitating and engendering a large knowledge group of professionals is not incorporated into his class configurations. The question remains as to whether producers of machines are, in Marxist classification, the "exploiter" or the "exploited," the "ruling" or the "oppressed." Marx and Engels, *The Communist Manifesto*, 5. Another source of conceptual muddle is that the French "bourgeoisie" is used synonymously with capitalists; it is "the class of modern capitalists, owners of the means of social production and employers of wage-labor." Ibid., 9n1. This is erroneous, for, as Vivek Chibber discusses, the "bourgeoisie" that ostensibly played a leading role in the "bourgeois" French Revolution was a far more "nebulous" term, encompassing "industrialists, merchants, shopkeepers, urban professionals. In fact, the typical bourgeois in eighteenth century France belong to the last category, simply because of its growing importance in political economy." Chibber, *Postcolonial Theory*, 70. It is only in Marxist analyses, which discounted the professional middle class, many self-employed, and those who

by the French sociologist Pierre Bourdieu,[67] all the way to the present-day polemics into the social underpinnings of inequality,[68] scholars have sought to inject nuance into or otherwise deflate materialist claims on social stratification. Weber famously juxtaposed *status groups* (*Stände*)[69] with *classes*. Class in Weber's analysis is defined in materialist terms:

We may speak of a "class" when 1) a number of people have in common a specific causal component of their life chances, in so far as 2) this component is represented exclusively by economic interests in the possession of goods and opportunities for income, and 3) is represented under the conditions of the commodity or labor markets.[70]

Classes are contrasted with *status groups*, "amorphous communities" characterized by a "status situation" (*ständische Lage*),[71] distinct from a "class situation."[72] Status transcends narrowly material aspects of group formation and maintenance, since it pertains to cultural preferences, tastes, and aspirations, or, in Weber's formulation, *Lebensführung*.[73] These intangible elements of group construction are distinct from features like property ownership, labor exploitation, or the extraction of rent.

Weber's *status groups* found resonance among Western and Soviet sociologists writing in the more permissive period following Premier Nikita

---

did not neatly fit into their class schemata, that bourgeoisie became synonymous with "capitalists."

[67] Bourdieu and Passeron, *Reproduction in Education*; Bourdieu and Passeron, *Inheritors*; Bourdieu, *Distinction*.

[68] Clark, *The Son Also Rises*; Putnam, *Our Kids*.

[69] Weber, *Economy and Society*, 1:305. Weber equates "Klassenlage" to "Marktlage." Ibid., 79. Teckenberg, discussing Soviet social stratification, indicates that "estates" is a more appropriate translation of Weber's *Stände* than the term employed in translations of Weber in American scholarship as "status groups." Teckenberg, "Social Structure," 9. I use "status groups" with reference to social position in post-feudal societies whether derived from formal estate ascription or not, to avoid confusion with the formal category of the estate in imperial Russia. Weber's term *ständische Lage*, by contrast, captures nontangible, "ambiguous" aspects of social position, including in modern societies. Weber, *Economy and Society*, 1:306. The context in which Weber uses the term is important: Weber also refers to estates (*Stände*) as a legal arrangement under feudalism and to *Ständestaat*, translated as "polity of estates," as an arrangement for granting privileges as part of state and alliance building and social control and, with some qualifiers, as an intermediate stage between feudal patrimonialism and development of bureaucracies. Ibid., 1087. In such a context, *Stände* perfectly captures *sosloviya* as indeed the medieval concept of the estate. On usage, translation, and meaning of the estate and *sosloviye*, see also Smith, *For the Common Good*, 5–6.

[70] This formulation comes from a distillation of Weber's concepts in a compilation of works on social stratification. Weber, "Class, Status and Party," 21. I consider this an accurate translation from the original German passages. See *Wirtschaft und Gesellschaft*, 1:78. Elsewhere I also refer to the more recent edition of Weber's compilation of works published as the two-volume *Economy and Society*.

[71] Teckenberg translates it as "social status." Teckenberg, "Social Structure," 9. I believe a more accurate translation is "status situation" or "status position."

[72] Weber, "Class, Status and Party," 21.   [73] Weber, *Wirtschaft und Gesellschaft*, 1:83.

Khrushchev's de-Stalinization campaign known as the Thaw. These works have done much to problematize – indeed, to discredit – Marxist hubris on class and inequality in Russian society. Wolfgang Teckenberg writes that the nonmaterial, cognitive orientations and preferences of *status groups* often trumped material aspects of Soviet *classes* in shaping social identities. Individuals on the same income scale – and theoretically not subjected to the exploitative owner–laborer relationship that is characteristic of capitalist societies but coming from different social-professional groups – tended to exhibit divergent friendship patterns, cultural pursuits, and parental preferences concerning children's education.[74] Teckenberg highlights another useful Weberian angle on classes versus status groups in distinguishing between material wealth and consumption preferences. Both, of course, not infrequently converge: "Property as such is not always recognized as a status qualification, but in the long run it is, and with extraordinary regularity," writes Weber.[75] Yet, while "'classes' are stratified according to their relations to the production and acquisition of goods; ... 'status groups' are stratified according to the principles of their *consumption* of goods as represented by special 'styles of life.'"[76]

In a proto-knowledge economy, one that prizes recognized and regulated professional credentials, specialized skills, and education, formal architectures and infrastructures of proficiency become part of the intergenerational cognitive "stylization" maps. Yet we also know from Bourdieu's theorizing that these cognitive proclivities are not distributed evenly across groups in society.[77] They are reproduced among the like-minded within a stable social "field," encompassing individuals with homologous educational, leisure, and professional pursuits and aspirations, and discursively and symbolically practiced through speech, modes of comport, and cultural markers. The signifiers of belonging are simultaneously exclusionary toward others outside of the field or those representing lower social gradations within it and new entrants.[78]

---

[74] Teckenberg, "Social Structure." Others have described Soviet and post-Soviet Russia as "esta-tist-corporatist society" (*soslovno-korporativnoye obshchestvo*) because citizen rights vary, as when some are disadvantaged due to the *propiska* system of residential registration or because of "incorporation" into professional networks facilitating social advancement. Yastrebov, "Kharakter stratifikatsii," 20; see also Vishnevskiy, *Serp i rubl'*, 101–4. Post-communist countries with an "estate-like" social structure (*soslovnoye*) arguably "stagnate" more in intergener-ational mobility than Western countries with more developed market economies. Yastrebov, "Kharakter stratifikatsii," 29. See also Kordonskiy, *Soslovnaya struktura*.

[75] Weber, "Class, Status and Party," 24.

[76] Ibid., 27 (emphasis in original). In German: "nach den Prinzipien ihres Güter*konsums* in Gestalt spezifischer Arten von 'Lebensführung'" (emphasis in original). *Wirtschaft und Gesellschaft*, 1:86–87.

[77] See also Elias, *Civilizing Process*; Veblen, *Theory of the Leisure Class*.

[78] This is a distillation of concepts found throughout Bourdieu's work. For a summary and critique, see Grenfell, *Pierre Bourdieu*.

In imperial Russia, the *Ständestaat* created not just the material but also the ideational preconditions for the colonization of expertise institutions by the educated estates. Over time, property and capital became tangential to the broader contours of the emerging professional strata, since their qualities as a status group – and the orientations mapping life progression onto the infrastructures of knowledge – helped consolidate their relational position vis-à-vis others.[79] The embeddedness in expertise-intensive institutional infrastructures that is characteristic of modern states facilitates adaptation across regime types, since the status group, and the various substrata that comprise it, possesses prized knowledge and skills and, indeed, the bureaucratic-organizational resources to resist change.

Yet skills, narrowly defined, and broader knowledge, be it cultural, transactional, market, or other, engender individual autonomy beyond the bureaucratic-institutional structures of modernity. Institutional resources provide the status group with clout vis-à-vis the state's bureaucratic and political machinery; but individual perspicacity also enables fluency, fluidity, and occupational hedging, engendering, to use the Hungarian sociologist Iván Szelényi's apt distinction, *autonomy* even when the individual or the group is lacking *authority*. Alternatively, to use the heuristics proposed in another study, Bolshevik social "appropriation" may, of course, lead to some career-motivated party membership and activism, thereby leading to "subversion" of the autonomous potential of some educated members of the old middle class, but others in this group may well avoid the cadre or managerial route, instead joining professions or taking part in pursuits that are relatively free from the oppressions of ideological dogma. In fact, the skills of some would be so highly valued by the regime that it would follow only lax party membership criteria for particular high-demand specialties.[80] Autonomous possibilities would also be available to the strata blessed with socialization in both the knowledge infrastructures of a modern society and the experience of private entrepreneurship and the business acumen intrinsic to the materially defined bourgeoisie as purveyors of property and capital.

My emphasis on the *cognitive* and *institutional* incorporation of feudalism-originating free estates into modern knowledge organizations departs from accounts focusing on class that are couched in exploiter/exploited terms. The broader time reach enables us to perceive how inequitably distributed human capital derived from a feudal order emerges as the *constant* privileging marker that transcends the *variability* of distinct regimes' governing politics, property ownership, and social relations. If anything, the status resilience of the educated estatist group precisely derives from *fluidity* in occupational navigation in

---

[79] As Weber writes, "Auch ein 'Berufsstand' ist 'Stand', d. h. prätendiert mit Erfolg soziale 'Ehre' normalerweise erst kraft der, eventuell durch den Beruf bedingten, spezifischen 'Lebensführung.'" Weber, *Wirtschaft und Gesellschaft*, 1:87.

[80] Szelényi, *Socialist Entrepreneurs*, 75; Lankina et al., "Appropriation and Subversion."

modern knowledge-privileging societies – as when the merchant invests heavily into superb engineering education for his or her son, or the artisan and *rentier* into a future academic career at a public university. Much as with the concept of "generation," not amenable to neat partition,[81] so too do we face difficulties in carving out the professional from the entrepreneur. These observations and the questions they raise are not as self-evident as they seem, since the long shadow of the Marxist chimera has continued to influence the most recent polemics on social distinction and division in society. Thus, Thomas Piketty, in his landmark *Capital in the Twenty-First Century*,[82] drawing on the work of his compatriot Pierre Bourdieu, provides a very cursory discussion of cultural-human capital as relevant to the broader structures of inequality in Western societies. Unfortunately, Bourdieu's insights, relegated to one page, are interpreted in purely materialist terms, since the author alludes to "public money" as pivotal in the distribution of, and correctives to, nontangible capital of various sorts in society.[83] That an esteem for skills, knowledge, and cultural endowment transcends leveling regimes may well also be obscured as analysts focus on the temporally proximate structures of polity and policy without unpacking the fine dynamics of social reproduction in a historically sensitive way. Piketty's work has, for instance, been lauded for the analytical framework that spans at least two centuries – and for his deft analysis of the ostensibly leveling phase associated with the communist project in Europe, warranting subtle calls for peaceable and amicable forms of economic redistribution. Yet evidence from the historically universalist analysis of Pitirim Sorokin – not referenced in *Capital* – reveals the failures of grand social equity schemes and the *cyclical, fluctuating*, and *trendless* nature of inequalities:

Communism is only an additional example in a long series of similar experiments performed on small and large scale, sometimes peacefully ... sometimes violently ... If many forms of stratification were destroyed for a moment, they regularly reappeared again in the old or in a modified form, often being built by the hands of the levelers themselves.[84]

This book dissects some of the bases for these undercurrents – the *lived-in* and *practiced*, daily and *calendrically affirmed* social hierarchies – pegged

---

[81] On this, see Zerubavel, *Time Maps*, 60.   [82] Piketty, *Capital*.

[83] "It would be naïve, however, to think that free higher education would resolve all problems," comments Piketty: "In 1964, Pierre Bourdieu and Jean-Claude Passeron analyzed, in *Les héritiers*, more subtle mechanisms of social and cultural selection, which often do the same work as financial selection. In practice, *the French system of 'grandes écoles' leads to spending more public money on students from more advantaged social backgrounds, while less money is spent on university students who come from more modest backgrounds*. Again, the contrast between the official discourse of 'republican meritocracy' and the reality (in which social spending amplifies inequalities of social origin) is extreme." Ibid., 486 (emphasis added).

[84] Sorokin, *Social Mobility*, 16.

to the aspirations for institutional embedding in a school, career, and profession – and transcending any losses or inflictions of the material "base" of social relations.

The Middle Class and Democracy

Sensitivity to the historical underpinnings of the estates-derived bourgeoisie and their reincarnation as white-collar professionals in Soviet Russia allows us to discern elements of heterogeneity within a stratum conventionally bracketed under one generic middle-class umbrella. Soviet Russia took the credit for engendering a *new* middle class from among the hitherto underprivileged worker and peasant masses, one that shared the designation of an intermediate social layer or *prosloyka* of white-collar employees and intelligentsia with the remnants of the *old* bourgeoisie. The copresence of such distinct substrata within one national setting is nontrivial for democratic theorizing. According to a venerable tradition in political science, modernization processes engender an enlightened, educated, and autonomous demos; and, as the size of this group grows, so does, arguably, a constituency favoring political openness, moderation, and the rule of law.[85] These assumptions have been subjected to scrutiny when applied to "deviant" states that have "modernized" but have failed to live up to expectations of support for a democratic political system among the middle classes.[86] In his seminal work on democracy, Robert Dahl took issue with teleological premises about the political consequences of development that sanitize the national context.[87] Drawing on the work of the University of Chicago economist Bert Hoselitz,[88] Dahl distinguished between a middle class engendered "autonomously" as part of a process of gradual capitalist development and one fabricated speedily consequential to state-led modernization.[89]

Concerns about a weak democratic commitment, if not authoritarian complicity, of the state-dependent middle class in countries sharing a legacy of rapid state-led modernization have been echoed in recent empirical scholarship

---

[85] Lipset, "Some Social Requisites." See also Huntington, *Third Wave*, esp. 59–72. For critiques, see O'Donnell, *Modernization*; Slater, *Ordering Power*. For a devastating account of modernization theory as a failed Cold War intellectual project, see Gilman, *Mandarins*.

[86] See Przeworski et al., *Democracy*; and Foa, "Modernization and Authoritarianism." See also studies of Western white-collar strata supporting authoritarianism. Speier, *German White-Collar Workers*. On alienation, homogenization, and pressures to conform among white-collar employees, see Kracauer, *Die Angestellten*.

[87] Dahl, *Polyarchy*.

[88] An ideal type of "autonomous" development is arguably where "all decisions affecting economic growth are made by individuals other than those holding political power." This is contrasted with hypothetical settings where "all economic growth ... would be strictly induced, that is, provided for and planned by a central authority." Hoselitz, *Sociological Aspects*, 97, 98.

[89] Dahl, *Polyarchy*, 73, citing Hoselitz, *Sociological Aspects*, 74 and 97ff.

on present-day autocracies and developing democracies.[90] Several sets of causal mechanisms have been proposed to account for these patterns. Whether in China, India, or Russia,[91] the democratic ambivalences of a state-fabricated middle class have been linked to widespread state employment and dependencies; loyalty toward incumbent regimes because of the indebtedness of traditionally underprivileged groups to the state for their social elevation; and, in post-communist contexts in particular, fears, dependencies, and pressures among employees of large communist-era industries that make them vulnerable to workplace mobilization during elections.[92]

My analysis advances these debates further insofar as it takes the emphasis away from contingencies pegged to individual orientations within an immediate political context, highlighting instead the temporally far broader processes of social construction. Occupational status is connected to structural possibilities for individual and group autonomy within a diverse employment landscape. The human capital and other value attributes that make such autonomy possible are not easily reducible to state policies of social uplift pursued in a compressed time span. Moreover, assumptions concerning their leveling consequences are questionable in settings with a long legacy of institutionalized social gradations – in Russia, for instance, embodied in the caste-like institution of the estate. Armed with the Dahl–Hoselitz conceptual toolkit, we may appropriately regard societies living through communism from the point of view of the layering of both state-directed, "induced," or "hegemonic" processes as well as the more spontaneous, gradual, and "autonomous" ones in the construction of social groups. The autonomous inputs would include both familial channels and a broader exposure to a capitalist plural, modern, urban society associated with a prior politically distinct and temporally distant order.

Such a perspective would also help us to adjudicate between leading strands in communist-era sociological debates between the so-called *modernizers* versus those in the *Homo sovieticus* camps.[93] While the former argued that

---

[90] Rosenfeld, *Autocratic Middle Class*; Chen, *Middle Class*, esp. 7–20. See also Bell, "After the Tsunami"; and essays in Johnson, *Middle Classes*. Relatedly, following Weber, Kohli juxtaposes the "protracted" development of "state traditions" in Europe with the rapid importation of state institutions in the global periphery, often via colonial rule, to where neither a public "ethos" among the elite nor an "effective public arena" had been strongly in evidence. Kohli, *State-Directed Development*, 395–96. Others highlight how states may dampen or activate social identity, conflict, and political demands. See Evans et al., *Bringing the State Back In*, 253–55.

[91] On Russia, see Rosenfeld, "Reevaluating"; and on employment with state bureaucracies in parts of Asia shaping political preferences, see Bell, "After the Tsunami."

[92] Frye et al., "Political Machines"; Hale, *Patronal Politics*; Lankina and Libman, "Soviet Legacies"; McMann, *Economic Autonomy*; Stokes, "Political Clientelism." On "contingent" support for democracy among both labor and capital due to state dependence and patronage in late developer contexts, see also Bellin, "Contingent Democrats"; and Chen, *Middle Class*, 6.

[93] Term popularized in Zinov'ev, *Gomo sovetikus*. Available from RoyalLib.com: https://royallib.com /book/zinovev_aleksandr/gomo_sovetikus.html (accessed April 7, 2020). See also Sinyavsky, *Soviet Civilization*.

even communist modernization could, over time, nurture a democratic citizen, the latter tended to bring to the fore the indoctrinating aspects of Leninist polities fabricating a brainwashed citizenry.[94] More recently, Grigore Pop-Eleches and Joshua Tucker have systematically analyzed the continued relevance of this aspect of communist societies in understanding differences in public attitudes as compared to contexts that have not experienced communism.[95] Whether through indoctrination in schools, in the professions, or in routinized ideology-impregnated practices of community engagement, citizens in communist societies have arguably internalized values, participatory attitudes, and modi operandi that constitute a hindrance to democratic consolidation. Another strand of theorizing, the "Soviet subjectivity" school of thought,[96] while highlighting citizen agency in navigating, constructing, and interrogating identity in a communist polis, has also privileged the public realm as the core around which these subjectivities – the "self" and "subjecthood" made ostensibly productive by the Soviet experience[97] – are constructed and debated. Scholars link these subjectivities explicitly or implicitly to the apathy, cynicism, or, alternatively, agency of the Soviet and post-Soviet citizen.[98]

The middle ground proposed here takes the emphasis away from the implications of inputs intrinsic to the communist experience and instead highlights the parallel channels of genesis of the middle class, embracing both the more autonomous processes of socialization preceding the communist period and those intrinsic to state-led hegemonic modernization.[99]

---

[94] For a summary of these debates, see Gerber, "Market," 479–80; Parkin, "System Contradiction"; and, concerning intellectual occupations, Lipset and Dobson, "Intellectual as Critic." On generational value differences, notably concerning private enterprise, see Dobson, "Communism's Legacy"; and Silver, "Political Beliefs," 232–35.

[95] Pop-Eleches and Tucker, *Communism's Shadow*. See also Pop-Eleches, "Communist Development."

[96] Hellbeck, *Revolution*; Hellbeck, "Working." For a critique of this approach in cultural history and anthropology, see Fitzpatrick, *Tear Off the Masks!*, 8–9, esp. 8n10. Like Fitzpatrick, I harbor unease about "totalizing theory" – be it Marxist of Foucauldian – and, given that Foucault appears to have displaced Marx as the fashionable thinker of our times (at least in the UK), I eschew deferential references to Foucault. Ibid., 8.

[97] Hellbeck, discussed in Fitzpatrick, *Tear Off the Masks!*, 8.

[98] Hellbeck, *Revolution*; Yurchak, *Everything Was Forever*.

[99] On communist legacies, see Pop-Eleches and Tucker, *Communism's Shadow*; Kotkin and Beissinger, "Historical Legacies"; Kopstein, "Review Article"; LaPorte and Lussier, "What Is the Leninist Legacy?"; Wittenberg, "What Is a Historical Legacy?" University of California at Berkeley, March 25, 2012, 9 (unpublished manuscript); and Danielle N. Lussier and Jody M. LaPorte, "Critical Juncture(s) of Communism and Post-Communism: Identifying and Evaluating Path Dependent Processes in the Post-Soviet Space." Paper presented at The American Political Science Annual Meeting, August 31 to September 3, 2017, San Francisco. Earlier classic works on communist/Leninist legacies are Jowitt, *New World Disorder*; Elster et al., *Institutional Design*; Hanson, "Leninist Legacy"; Ekiert and Hanson, "Time, Space, and Institutional Change."

The question then becomes not whether *communist* regimes helped engender a modern – democratic – citizen, thereby sowing the seeds of their own destruction, or indeed the extent to which they trampled on society's potential for democracy, but whether and how the legacies of the autonomous *pre-communist* demos were able to survive through the decades of hegemonic societal remolding.

MECHANISMS OF REPRODUCTION

I now more precisely articulate hypothesized mechanisms linking the tsarist social structure – specifically, the bourgeoisie – to variations in democratic quality among Russia's regions and over-time national-level fluctuations in political regime type. Succinctly, I define the bourgeois legacy as a set of social endowments that are reproduced, maintained, and survive across time and distinct regimes. Marrying the institutional aspect of the legacy with the cognitional dimension is essential to my framework because institutions alone would fail to engender the bourgeois legacy. I regard professional, bureaucratic, and civic institutions as embedders of a highly unequal and stratified society. Institutions and intra-institutional hierarchies, even if we approach them broadly as practices, values, or rules of entry and exclusion, mirror as well as channel social stratification.[100] Conversely, I do not imagine the bourgeois legacy to manifest itself solely in a value-cognitional sense, outside of the institutions so described. The argument is that cognitions are rooted in tangible and metaphorical institutional architectures that provide goalposts, signposts, roadblocks, and openings; and, of course, they furnish resources and a possibility for the reproduction of values within organizational spaces.

In my account, the bourgeois legacy does not straightforwardly lead individuals to explicitly articulate demands for, struggle for, or protest for democracy.[101] My dual conception of a bourgeois legacy begs for a different causal logic. I regard institutions and institutional pluralism in roughly similar terms as Weber did when he discussed the genesis of European city-states and trading towns as incipient shoots of the participatory autonomy of communes of burghers. The town burghers may actively seek to shelter their communities, rights, and privileges from the encroachment of others, notably via the "monopolization of the economic opportunities offered by the city."[102] These exclusive enclaves, however, also engendered a passionate sense of entitlement to autonomous governance. The professions, museums, universities, and other

---

[100] On occupations traditionally colonized by low-status groups like the military rank-and-file, see, for instance, Davis, *Discipline*, 203.

[101] The book is careful to avoid a naïve view of social processes identifying particular social groups with progressive, democratic, or other sentiments and causes. On the pitfalls of the approach regarding the working class in Nazi Germany, see Eley, "On Your Marx," 502–3.

[102] Weber, *Economy and Society*, 2:1252. See also 1328–29.

such institutions discussed in this book – even when tactically adapted and modified to fit Bolshevik ideological imperatives – are precisely regarded from this perspective. The second prong of my dual, institutional-cognitional perspective, that of values, also warrants elaboration. Far from regarding the fallen aristocrat, merchant, or *meshchanka* as a cohesive group with well-articulated democratic preferences, I regard their values from the point of view of the privileged estatist society's cognitive embeddedness in the institutions of modernity, which of course drives a striving to embrace these arenas in an intergenerational sense. Such cognitive maps incentivize not only superb education perpetuated within families – a reasonable predictor of democratic preferences in a variety of contexts – but also possibilities for careers in sites that permit autonomous thought, sensibility, and action even under the most inquisitional and totalizing regimes. In post-communist countries, such human endowments in turn enable hedging between the market and public sector or self-employment possibilities.

In articulating a causal story linking the bourgeoisie to democracy through seven decades of communism, I identify four interconnected pathways. The first two routes of *education* and *professional incorporation* operate at the juncture of state policy and social structure. I argue that the state reinforced the social status of the pre-communist bourgeoisie by dint of leveraging their human capital and professional skills, the developmental *software*. It also did so by appropriating the developmental *hardware* in the form of professional sites originating within imperial Russia and embedding these individuals into the Soviet polity and institutions. The third channel, which I label *social closure*, we could more appropriately anchor within society in a Bourdieusian sense. It pertains to values that familial, cultural, and community milieus nurture outside of state policy – these may or may not be reinforced through state directives and practice. Finally, I incorporate the various elements of time, already alluded to and echoed in the first three mechanisms, more explicitly into the causal structure of the explanatory framework.

Education

Following a voluminous body of evidence spurred on by the modernization paradigm,[103] I regard education, broadly defined, as a starting point for unpacking the legacies of social structure and their present-day social-political implications. I link the spatially heterogenous patterns of education and professional training to the imperial distribution of estates. The Bolsheviks used extant human capital because it facilitated industrialization and human development. Civil strife, economic collapse, famine, epidemics, and disease engender a *dis-leveler* effect whereby post-revolutionary shocks to regime legitimacy incentivize even further the reliance on – and social elevation

[103] Lerner, *Passing of Traditional Society*; Lipset, "Some Social Requisites."

of – the dietitian, the veterinarian, the medic, and the civil engineer.[104] The implication of the tactical decision to embrace the "bourgeois specialist" is the reproduction of spatial heterogeneity in human capital in Russia's regions. Put simply, territories with a larger pre-revolutionary share of the educated estates are likely to exhibit higher rates of literacy, schooling, and university attendance. Anticipating the results of the statistical analysis, we can confidently say that this is an appropriate starting point for the theory proposed here.

As noted, simply reasserting covariation between education and democracy is problematic. Recent evidence about education and professional training in autocracies has been linked via various pathways – either through ideological indoctrination in schools or via the mechanism of fabricating loyalty and professionally dependent constituencies – to authoritarian values and support rather than democracy. Classic accounts of the Soviet project precisely highlight spectacular achievements in evening out educational access and providing opportunities to those from modest backgrounds and to the illiterate rural residents and semiliterate factory workforce in particular, strata that would then enter the urban white-collar labor force.[105] Generational change would also inevitably interfere with assumptions about straightforward links between the quality and extent of imperial-era, as compared to Soviet-period, education of the strata who may be first-generation literates or secondary school attendees. Analyzing the estate makeup of a territory and its employment structure in late imperial Russia and education as measured by literacy would be one way to explore variations between "autonomously" nurtured bourgeoisie and one engendered consequential to the policies of an authoritarian state. We would expect that territories exhibiting better educational outcomes and professional development would possess not only the infrastructures of modern education that the Bolsheviks appropriated and expanded but also greater availability of a skills base among the educated estates to deliver schooling and professional training. Demand for education, which I hypothesize remained habitual and inertial among imperial Russia's bourgeoisie and proto-bourgeois strata, would also be higher in such territories.

Professional Incorporation and Autonomy

If we were to simply employ literacy or educational attainment statistics – individual-level attributes of citizens residing in districts – our analysis would be insensitive to the broader social contexts in which individuals had been embedded at the time of the Bolshevik Revolution; to nuances of their socialization; and to collective value transmission. Because, as I shall demonstrate, appropriation of the human capital of *individuals* to serve the

---

[104] I am paraphrasing the title of the book by Scheidel, *Great Leveler*.
[105] Fitzpatrick, *Education*.

Bolsheviks' developmental agenda is inseparable from the story of the appropriation of professional *institutions*, my second hypothesized channel of persistence is bureaucratic-social autonomy nurturing islands of social distinction and oppositional orientations vis-à-vis the state.

One pattern that emerges from even a cursory examination of the estate makeup of imperial Russia's professional institutions is that the various estates do not exhibit patterns of random and chance distribution. The Soviet state-appropriated professionals thus maintained a certain *estate* profile, something that nurtured the corporate aspect of professional embeddedness, value, and identity construction. The assimilation of the historically privileged groups' social distinctions into modern institutions of the professions, learning, and quasi-civic enterprise – often with the aid of substantial familial investment – facilitates resilience in social structure, not least because modernizing regimes appropriate such institutions as part of the agenda of hasty state-led development. Moreover, even in a communist context, over time, there would be possibilities to self-select into what Sorokin describes as "deliberative," as distinct from "executive" employment sites, those like academia, research, or the arts where intra-professional gradation is not as "clear cut" nor so "centralized as in purely executive bodies."[106]

In what ways would this pattern of incorporation matter for understanding the social underpinnings of democratic support during and after communism? In addressing this question, I draw attention to professional and civic autonomous action in evidence under the old regime and carried over into the institutions of Bolshevik Russia. This is particularly relevant in the case of cultural institutions where the *haute* bourgeoisie comprised of nobles, educated scions of clergymen, and merchant philanthropists found refuge as the witch hunts against "former people" raged.[107] The autonomous action represents an extension of the legacies of the estate corporation and of impulses nurtured against the background of the enlightened society's evasions and resistance to the encroachments of the tsarist state. Yet autonomous impulses would extend to other arenas that we associate with the large Soviet public sector, notably in education, medicine, and engineering.[108] The appropriation of the empire's professional institutions would be consequential not only for enabling individuals with a particular social-estate profile in their impulse for social distinction but also for endowing them with a modicum of autonomy vis-à-vis the state.[109]

---

[106] Sorokin, *Social Mobility*, 116.
[107] Tchuikina, *Dvoryanskaya pamyat'*; Smith, *Former People*.
[108] On struggles for professional autonomy in imperial Russia, see Balzer, *Russia's Missing Middle Class*.
[109] Discussions of the social structure mapping onto white-collar professions and intra-professional gradations and hierarchies within them and consequences for relationships with political power feature in classic works on twentieth-century dictatorial regimes. Consider the distinction between the "old" bourgeoisie, the *Bildungsbürgertum*, and the "new" white-collar

Social Closure

The third and related channel of social persistence and resilience is social closure. Unlike the other two channels, which operate at the juncture of state policy and society, social reproduction via this route may well operate *despite* state policies not *because of them*. The Bolshevik state may have been eager to even out educational inequalities and obliterate the bourgeoisie, yet I identify values transmitted via the familial and pre-revolutionary social networks as an essential ingredient in the intergenerational reproduction of the social structure. Following Stinchcombe, and drawing on the theorizing of Bourdieu, we would expect to observe a form of inertia in the aspirational dimension of social status, since, even against a radical revolutionary upheaval, the individual would remain embedded within a multigenerational, familial, and social environment or "field" that would have socialized within oneself the expectation of an education, a profession, a cultural status befitting one's station in society. With respect to the urban bourgeoisie, nobility, and clergy, we would expect to observe the reproduction of habitual impulses in learning that could be contrasted with the aspirations of lower status groups targeted as beneficiaries of Bolshevik policies of social uplift. Social closure would also operate at the level of selectivity in social interaction. Again, we would expect socialization to exhibit continuities with past patterns of ties and bonds exhibiting estatist characteristics.

Finally, I expect social closure to operate at the level of values, practices, and networks that could only have originated and functioned *outside* of state policy and sanction. Some – like engagements reflecting familiarity with market production, trade, and finance, as would be the case with merchants who before the Revolution owned mills, bakeries, and farms – in my analytical framework constitute direct channels of maintenance of bourgeois skills and values. Other aspects of values extraneous to Bolshevik policy would be indirectly related to the germination of autonomous social impulses vis-à-vis the state. In the latter category are embeddedness in, and connectedness to,

workers in research charting the rise of support for the far right in interwar Germany. Speier, *German White-Collar Workers*; Kracauer, *Mass Ornament*, esp. 122–27. See also *Die Angestellten*; and Jarausch, "German Professions." The German *Bildungsbürgertum* is similar to the concept of Russia's intelligentsia. Originating in late eighteenth-century Central Europe, it encompassed gymnasium- and university-trained "cultivated middle classes," including civil servants, free professionals, and some entrepreneurs, who "derived their unity from formal neohumanist training and informal student subculture, which established a distinguished style (classical citations), form of communication (literary journals), and manner of sociability (student corporations)." The concept arguably emerged "as a retrospective critical category" in the 1920s. Ibid., 17. Another group, Prussian *Junkers*, were a semi-feudal caste-like group, possessing "politico-intellectual supremacy" within "directive-organizational" political society and the officer class and a "strong consciousness of being an independent social group" until at least 1918. Gramsci, *Selections*, 19. On the social structure embedded in schools in Italy and elsewhere, see also ibid., 40–43; and on that topic, Bourdieu et al., *Reproduction in Education*.

outside sources of information transmitted via correspondence with émigré relatives abroad, remittances, and, via these channels, access to resources facilitating adaptation and shadow market exchange under socialism.

Time: Historical and Clock Aspects

The above-discussed three mechanisms of social persistence are attuned to the complementarities, disjunctures, and clashes between the slow- and long-maturing social and the fast-paced and radical political realms. The various dimensions of time in the analytical framework warrant some further conceptual elaboration. This section dwells at some length on the questions of how and why careful attention to the temporal structure of the causal processes helps further unpack the paradoxical logics of social persistence despite the revolutionary juncture and post-revolutionary societal remolding that spanned seven decades.

Scholars working in the comparative sociology and comparative historical analysis traditions distinguish between the *physical* aspects of *clock time*, as captured in dates, tempo, pace, and duration of policies and events, and the "thick"[110] aspects of *historical time*. As Marcus Kreuzer explains, calendric sequences like hours in a day or weeks are units of time that are not historical: "they are recurring and not tied to a specific context whose comparison across time helps us understand change through time and hence historical time."[111] In the narratives on communism, the physical aspects of clock time have taken primacy in that the project's "duration" neatly overlaps with the calendric milestones of 1917–91, taking precedence over historical time. Yet sensitivity to both the clock and the historical dimensions of time – to variation in the contrasting but co-constituting, "time scales" or *Zeitschichten*, "layers of time" – both those fleeting and the tectonic[112] – warrants simultaneous expansion of our epochal horizons but also calls for the shrinkage, as it were, of notions of physical time – in our case, the duration of communism as a project itself. Let me explain.

Consider a revolutionary situation where the legitimacy of the new power holder hinges on effective delivery of basic public services.[113] Picture the civil strife, the famine, the epidemics, the disease that accompany events of gargantuan historical proportion like the Bolshevik Revolution and that may even be intrinsic to them. These are *fast-paced* happenings incentivizing a fallback on expertise, knowledge, and education, engendered in the long

---

[110] Kreuzer, "Varieties of Time," 13, online copy. On these aspects of temporality, see Grzymala-Busse, "Time Will Tell?" 1268.

[111] Kreuzer, "Varieties of Time," 4.   [112] Conrad, *What Is Global History?*, 142, 147.

[113] Weber poignantly writes: "Even in the case of revolution by force or of occupation by an enemy, the bureaucratic machinery will normally continue to function just as it has for the previous legal government." Weber, *Economy and Society*, 1:224.

historical process of social construction – aspects of "thick" historical time that foil attempts to map human lives, values, and agency neatly onto the revolutionary epoch. Institutional longevity may consequently effect regress, reversals, compromises, or a status quo fallback in policy *in the now*, nurturing, via a causal loop, social-institutional resilience at times of profound change during which we would least expect inertia. In the immediate post-revolutionary period, millions of people not only perished in the Civil War but succumbed to raging epidemics and famine. Typhus furnishes one example. While, in 1913, the country registered 7.3 cases of typhus per 10,000 people, in 1918, the figure rose to 21.9 and to 265.3 in 1919, reaching an "all-time high" of 393.9 per 10,000 people in 1920.[114] "'Typhus,' Lenin declared shortly after the revolution, 'among a population [already] weakened by hunger without bread, soap, fuel, may become such a scourge as not to give us an opportunity to undertake socialist construction … *Either the louse defeats socialism or socialism defeats the louse.*'"[115]

Long-established institutions, whether in medicine, education, or the veterinary sciences – encapsulating the edifices, skills, and horizons in training and experience – acquire urgent resilience in such troubled junctures precisely because no time could be wasted on creating new, properly "communist" institutions, lest millions more people die of starvation or disease and survivors take to the pitchfork to dislodge the opportunists who have seized power. This angle, morbidly prescient in the world of COVID-19, is distinct from perspectives on crisis points as propitious to institutional change.[116] My assumption concerning the *great dis-leveler*[117] effect of fast-based revolutionary whirlwinds precisely derives from sensitivity to the immediate urgency of knowledge as against the temporally far more protracted, stable, and slow intergenerational processes of institutional construction and of intra-institutional social and cognitive embedding. Calamity, in such times of crisis, finds strange bedfellows with stability! The duration, pace, trajectories, and cycles of these overlaying occurrences – key temporal concepts in comparative historical analysis[118] – would of course vary across historical contexts subjected to communism; and the consequences for social resilience would be different too. The confluence of processes with a fast-paced tempo and social currency acquired via slow, protracted, long-maturing, long-horizon – transgenerational – nurturing of expertise creates immense possibilities for the calcification of the social structure, warranting a fresh angle on how we regard

---

[114] Field, *Doctor and Patient*, 15.   [115] Cited in ibid., 15 (emphasis added).
[116] Howlett and Goetz, "Introduction," 485.   [117] Here, I paraphrase Scheidel, *Great Leveler*.
[118] Aminzade, "Historical Sociology," 458. Pace has been defined as a "number of events in a given amount of time," duration as "the amount of time elapsed for a given event or sequence of events. By contrast, cycles and trajectories have a more qualitative nature in that cycles refer to repetitive events marked by ascending/descending sequences, and trajectories invokes cumulativeness and directionality." Ibid., 459.

the social consequences of "social revolutions," and solutions to inequality, in the present.

The professionalization of Russia's estates-derived bourgeoisie, I conjecture, engendered concomitant "life course" progressionary milestones – subjective aspects of the perception of times past, present, and future[119] – the school, the university, the coveted service title, the modern occupation, often organically coexisting with private entrepreneurship, trade, a business. These social identities would be operating at the level of far more expansive temporal frameworks than those enchained to 1917 and Bolshevik policy. Indeed, they would have long become "social facts" in their engrained perception of naturalness and inevitability.[120] A nuanced appreciation of these fluid orientations – of the people "left out"[121] of the macro-historical, Marxian-march-of-history assumptions, or of the political grandee-, events-centered, "eventual"[122] analyses of the social scientist – would thereby help us relativize the comparatively privileged estates' perception of loss when the Bolsheviks confiscated their properties and other possessions. Numerous accounts have prioritized this material shattering in assuming away the old bourgeoisie. Yet scores of documentary records, whether memoirs, letters, or other private papers, reveal that, in fact, overwhelmingly, the sense of disorientation, desperation, and anger is attached to restrictions on the pursuit of habitual trajectories of a nonmaterial essence – the place in the gymnasium for the clever aristocratic boy; the university offer withdrawn from the adolescent merchant girl; the professional possibilities in *service* for the *meshchanin-rentier* circumscribed; the scientific work in a laboratory for the clergyman-veterinarian cut short.[123] To return to comparative historical sociology concepts, in terms of *historical time*, the orientations of the generic bourgeoisie would span the horizons of multiple generations prior to and following 1917; and the *clock time* that has meaning would be, say, the urgency of the beginning of the new school year, and hence the need to enact, to preserve, and to adjust as best as possible the arenas of pedagogic–professional–scientific interaction from before.

Despite the apocalyptic perturbations that occurred in the decade that followed the abdication of Tsar Nicholas II and the Bolshevik coup, we may then consider 1928 as a more appropriate starting point for analyzing socially meaningful communist legacies than 1917 and 1986 – the year that Mikhail Gorbachev commenced his far-reaching reforms and autonomous society emerged from the shadows – as the more appropriate end point. Soviet communism in its most socially shattering forms would have lasted not

---

[119] On this, see ibid., 461.
[120] On the inertial and socially coercive, aspect of "temporal regularities," routines, and schedules, see Zerubavel, *Hidden Rhythms*, 43; he draws on Durkheim.
[121] Conrad, *What Is Global History?*, 157.   [122] Kreuzer, *Grammar of Time*, in press.
[123] To avoid repetition, I cite and discuss these throughout the book.

seventy but fifty-eight years, barely two generations according to this view, and, even so, with many of the caveats that I dissect throughout the book as to what "communism" really meant if we reconsider its purportedly uprooting, modifying, and corrective impacts. Such an adjustment in periodization could be defended on the grounds that social calibration processes in the 1917–28 period, while punctuated with repression, civil war, and "war communism" shocks, were less consequential for the structure of society than those that followed. The Leninist regime inflicted far more draconian projects on the Russian people post-1928, even if "dress rehearsals" for those same policies occurred earlier on a smaller scale. Churches, synagogues, and mosques were destroyed or closed; "bourgeois" university faculties and schools were suspended; professionals were purged; private enterprise was choked and entrepreneurs repressed, exiled, or pushed into the shadows; collectivization was forced upon the peasantry; the Gulag was institutionalized, consolidated, and metastasized across the vast stretches of the Soviet empire; and, eventually, entire peoples were decimated. Reversals, regress, and a relaxation of course followed key "milestones" and policies after 1928. Yet demarcating the 1917–28 period as only vaguely communist would analytically sensitize us both to the radical changes that did occur post-1928 and to the many qualifiers we could add to their effects even after that point, precisely because the "bourgeoisie" would have had a decade under the new regime to solidify old ties; train children and grandchildren in properly tsarist institutions; acquire, retain, or consolidate anchors in a respectable profession; and, crucially, the patriarch and the matriarch, while still alive, would have had a decade to pursue an injunctional agenda vis-à-vis the values of the younger generation.

The analytical framework also warrants linking time to space. Not only does the pace of change vary depending on where you are in the spatial matrix – the metropolitan center or the provinces far removed[124] – but the tempo[125] of happenings in one location shapes strategies of individual and network survival based on perceived havens with a far slower rate of change. Many an aristocrat or merchant spent years, if not decades, sitting out, as it were, the vagaries of class policy in a provincial museum or library only to then reinvent themselves as the cultural aristocracy in the metropolitan Soviet Union. Conventionally periodized slices of time pegged to the New Economic Policy (NEP) or the Great Purge would not capture their predicament.

[124] The sociologist Pitirim Sorokin captured well this contrasting sense of time when briefly departing Petrograd for the provincial town of Veliki Ustyug following the February Revolution of 1917. "What a relief to leave the capital with its constantly moving crowds, its disorder, dirt, and hysteria, and to be again in the tranquil places I love! ... How perfect is the calm of it all! How pure and still the air, as if no revolution exists!" Sorokin, *A Long Journey*, 119.

[125] Or frequency of sub-events in a larger event. Grzymala-Busse, "Time Will Tell?" 1282. Actors during fast-paced change arguably are more likely to rely on "off the shelf" templates and on personal networks. Ibid., 1282.

Spatial separation also enables survival in a temporally broad sense of career progression – for who would recognize in the leading Soviet newspaper editor in Moscow the scion of a provincial merchant family running an empire of bathhouses in imperial Samara?[126] Where could we place such a not-so-hapless descendant of the purveyor of capitalist enterprise turned literatus in the Marxist scheme of things, impoverished as it is of sensitivity to the complexity of time and space and generations in the construction of social identities, professional stations, and behaviors? Space–time matrices in my analysis are also inclusive of fast-paced transnational diasporic–émigré linkages that Soviet policy facilitated as it encouraged remittances as a cash cow for the currency-starved Soviet state. At the same time, the space–time conundrum has the unfortunate role of the conceptual "blinker" in my analysis, since many a scholar would assume away social resilience precisely because of the *time-compressed* and *spatially expansive* human dislocation intrinsic to the Gulag, the exiles, the deportations, and the grand projects to industrialize the frontier. Yet, as will become clear, social ties were energetically reconfiguring and self-correcting *in spite of* and even at times *because of* dislocation, mirroring pre-revolutionary associations among individuals.

RESEARCH DESIGN

To empirically tease out the patterns and mechanisms of the reproduction of the social structure across distinct regimes and orders, I combine large-n statistical analysis of Russia's entire universe of administrative units with an in-depth causal process analysis of one subnational case. I also perform social network analysis to explore the estate, professional, and social ties that structured late imperial society and their alteration, severance, and reproduction after the Revolution. Finally, survey microdata help to chart covariation between self-reported estate ancestry and professional adaptation. Each empirical chapter combines systematic large-n data analysis with an in-depth reading of archival, memoir, and interview-sourced materials to dissect the micro-dynamics and processes of social adaptation. The detailed social ethnography of one region helps to more fully tease out patterns of social-structural continuities revealed in large-n analysis and enables a fine-grained examination of heterogeneity and subtle intragroup hierarchies within the would-be *Soviet intelligentsia*. The added illustrative materials from literary and cinematographic classics documenting the tapestries of values and destinies of various social groups drive home the normalcy of uncovered patterns, possibly surmised otherwise as atypical or uncharacteristic of Russia as a whole. I consider the ontology of, the various aspects of the "making of," the Russian bourgeoisie as an essential analytical step

[126] Reference to Aleksandr Chakovskiy, editor-in-chief of *Literaturnaya gazeta*. For ancestry, see *Yevreyskiy mir Samary* ("Jewish world of Samara"): sites.google.com/site/samaraemir/muzej-naa-ekspozicia/kupcy-i-predprinimateli/m-a-cakovskij (accessed September 21, 2020).

in the deductive process of theory testing, because if we do not get the question right – the origin, nature, and sources of distinction of the bourgeoisie – we would repeat the errors found on the pages of earlier studies, of discursively and analytically reproducing either Leninist categories of class or generic preconceptions about the post-Soviet middle class. Additionally, comparative analysis of other communist countries' late feudal societies and the sequencing of landmark pre-communist social reforms corroborates findings about social structure and political regime variations derived from the Russian case.

Large-n Statistical Analysis

District- and region-level statistical analysis helps tease out the significance of estate constellations as drivers of general variations in socioeconomic development and democratic quality over and above Soviet modernization policies.[127] The regional data, which are supplemented with individual survey data and within-region social network analysis, also allow us to distinguish between the surviving legacies of an "organically" nurtured bourgeoisie/middle class and one "incubated"[128] more recently under a "hegemonic" modernizing order. The units of analysis cover the full developmental-social-political spectrum of territories, from wealthy industrial giants with oppositional voting patterns to economic laggards predictably delivering a pro-Kremlin vote.[129] The spatial and historical underpinnings of development also vary. Unlike the earlier work of economic historians who have deployed data for European Russia only, my universe of observations encompasses the entire gamut of regions as diverse as the Black Earth lands in European Russia, with their historically high density of serfdom, agrarian dominance within the economy, and socioeconomic underdevelopment; the Siberian and Far Eastern frontier regions, with a very different set of historical legacies of development, Soviet and pre-Soviet; and the Middle Volga and North Caucasus territories that combine elements of the frontier with economic characteristics of European Russia. These various territories also featured distinct constellations of estates. Anticipating the results, I find that the imperial-era social structure is a significant predictor of variations in regional occupational patterns and democratic quality over and above communist modernization legacies. The "general linear reality"[130] exposed in my large-n analysis would nevertheless stop short of uncovering the "interactionist"[131] complexity driving the paradoxical reproduction of the social structure underpinning a bourgeois social order in a revolutionary polity that saw

[127] Analyzing all territories helps alleviate selection bias: the observations are not limited to those with extreme values on the dependent variable. King et al., *Designing Social Inquiry*; Collier et al., "Claiming Too Much."

[128] To use the apt characterization in Rosenfeld, "Reevaluating," 637.

[129] On "democratic deficit" in rural areas, see McMann and Petrov, "Survey of Democracy"; McMann, *Economic Autonomy*; Gel'man and Ross, *The Politics*; but see Lankina and Libman, "Soviet Legacies."

[130] Abbott, *Time Matters*, 37–63.   [131] Ibid., 154.

its *raison d'être* as obliterating that very social order.[132] I therefore select one region for an in-depth exploration of the complex mechanisms behind the statistical results.

Single-Case Selection

My "single case within one national context" framework departs from empirical strategies pursued in classic works in historical sociology concerned with radical revolutionary transformations. Studies in the "critical juncture" tradition have often worked with several country cases. This research and, more broadly, landmark books in comparative historical sociology have tended to explicitly rely on secondary historical sources.[133] The strategy of mining published historical monographs is, of course, the only feasible one considering the methodological device of comparison of multiple countries across long time stretches. This approach is not appropriate for advancing the research goals I set for myself in this study. To begin with, I find problematic the assertion that goes something like "historians have already done all the groundwork for us social scientists." Conceptually, this is fraught, considering that historians may ask certain questions while ignoring others. Ideological biases may well creep into the kinds of questions posed and the ways they are answered. Moreover, the availability of sources may simply relegate an important question into the realm of the non-question. Consider the example of social structure – the topic closest to the heart of this book. No single work of history has, as far as I am aware, systematically analyzed the adaptation, destinies, or reproduction of the "bourgeois" estates of merchants and *meshchane* in Soviet Russia.[134] By contrast, we have substantial historical scholarship on the social mobility of the proletariat, which was actually barely emergent in 1917 but accorded high prominence in Marxist visions of

---

[132] One strategy would have been to pursue a controlled case comparison of a small number of cases (regions) carefully selected based on a set of criteria of outcome differences and similarities, while allowing for the control of variations on the key independent variable of interest. A recent excellent book using this approach is Finkel, *Ordinary Jews*.

[133] See the discussion of sources in Skocpol, *States and Social Revolutions*, xiv. See also Collier and Collier, *Shaping the Political Arena*; Kalyvas, *Rise of Christian Democracy*; Slater, *Ordering Power*.

[134] Even leading scholars of Soviet Russia, who acknowledged the role of pre-revolutionary legacies, relegated the urban estates to oblivion. In the questionnaire administered to Soviet refugees as part of The Harvard Project on the Soviet Social System (THPSSS), possible answers to the pre-revolutionary social group of parents include the nobility, the intelligentsia, landowners, officialdom, merchants, craftsmen (artisans), workers, the peasantry, the middle class, the clergy, and the military. It is unclear whether "middle class" refers to *meshchane* or another group; the authors do not specify this. There is no discussion of merchant ancestry in the survey results, which refer to groups in class, status (upper-lower), and occupational terms. Inkeles and Bauer, *Soviet Citizen*, 413.

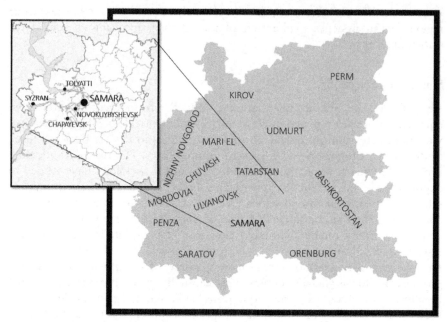

FIGURE 1.1 Map of Samara

the march of history.[135] Simply relying on secondary sources to unpack the estates-related trajectory of inequality and the resulting variations among social groups and within the middle class would not get us very far, as this is not a question that Western, let alone, Soviet historians have concerned themselves with very much. Why might that be the case?

Two sets of works suffice to illustrate the ways that the epoch in which historical tomes are produced may crucially shape both the questions asked and the answers proposed. One is the quasi-hagiographic excursion into Soviet achievements written by Sydney and Beatrice Webb in the 1930s and 1940s.[136] The other, far more nuanced, set of works is by the historian Sheila Fitzpatrick. The Webbs were, of course, working at a time when many left-wing intellectuals embraced the promise of communism before illusions were shattered in the wake of Stalin's show trials and knowledge about the human cost of collectivization and the purges became widespread.[137] Fitzpatrick belonged to a different generation of social historians who wrote Soviet history in the wake of the anti-establishment social upheavals in the West in the late 1960s and 1970s. Against this zeitgeist, the Soviet state's apparently

[135] Fitzpatrick, *Education*; Fitzpatrick, "Cultural Revolution."
[136] Webb and Webb, *Soviet Communism*.
[137] Although many observers even at the time were aware of the show trials and recognized them for what they are. See the discussion of the Webbs in Brown, *Rise and Fall*, 121.

spectacular inroads into social mobility would represent a far more interesting and relevant question than would the possibility of the reproduction of the bourgeoisie that Stalin proclaimed extinct by the mid-1930s but which may logically constitute a legitimate subject of scholarly inquiry in the period after communism collapsed, when scholars began to grapple with questions of the pro-democracy and pro-market orientations of the post-communist citizen. Yet, from the 1990s onward, for many historians – and writers of popular historical jeremiads – the more interesting questions became Stalinist destruction, terror, and uprooting, not continuities and adaptations.[138] Here, again, we observe the phenomenon of the non-question sorely problematizing reliance on secondary historical sources.[139] My chosen empirical strategy is therefore to sacrifice the potential for generating systematic comparative insights from qualitative analysis of several cases and instead reap the benefit of immersing myself into the hitherto underutilized papers from provincial archives and other eclectic troves of materials.[140] Sourcing the archive and validating findings employing new data allow me to form my own impressions about pivotal policy decisions and social antidotes to them. Historians have charged that "quantitative results are trivial, since they prove only what has been known already."[141] This book will hopefully escape that criticism because of the blend of original history and data analysis.

The region of Samara constitutes, in my study, the "pathway" case,[142] which helps test and tease out mechanisms otherwise prone to concerns of spurious correlation between variables like "estates" and "democracy" not only removed in time but straddling three regime types – tsarist monarchy, communism, and post-Soviet failed democracy. Samara typifies Russia's other historically cosmopolitan, trading, and enterprising regions, though it, of course, also exhibits characteristics peculiar to the historical contingencies of the place. Protestants and Catholics, Jews, Germans, and Poles have been as historically constitutive of the social fabric of this region as the Eastern Orthodox, Muslims, ethnic Russians, Ukrainians, Mordovians, and Tatars. Merchants and *meshchane* enjoyed social prominence in the fast-developing towns. A frontier

---

[138] See, for instance, Snyder, *Bloodlands*; Conquest, *Great Terror*; Applebaum, *Gulag*.

[139] On the *new social history* "propelled by radical democratic or Marxist concerns," see Jarausch and Hardy, *Quantitative Methods*, 6. I share the concern with "mute masses" but analyze both the *petite* and *grande bourgeoisie* – notably the understudied, indeed largely forgotten, provincial bourgeoisie – hardly subject of interest, or sympathy, among the Marxism-inspired historians and social scientists analyzing the Soviet project.

[140] On the merits of provincial archives, off limits to Western historians during communism, and which often contain revelations pertaining to nuances of center-regional relations, contingency, and local agency, see Sunderland, *Taming*, 231.

[141] Jarausch and Hardy, *Quantitative Methods*, 3.

[142] Key conditions for selection are that the case is not an extreme outlier and there is strong covariance between the scores on the key variables of interest. Gerring, "Case Selection," 664–68. In the Online Appendix 4 (OA4), I corroborate that Samara is not an outlier. On merits of within-case analysis, see Collier et al., "Claiming Too Much," 95–97.

territory and one with some steppe soils less fertile than in the Black Earth lands, for centuries it served as a haven for peasant escapees, vagabonds, bandits, and rebels.[143] Serfdom never took root as much here as in the Black Earth Central Russian *gubernii*. A significant proportion of peasants were under state or Crown authority, their burdens, writes Orlando Figes, "not as onerous as those of the serfs," a "distinction [that] continued to be true after the Emancipation."[144] Moreover, while not a stellar haven for highbrow education, Samara's overall literacy and education levels were comparatively high. Samara City's location on the Volga facilitated impressive development as Russia industrialized. The river had historically been a natural artery for commercial trade between the Northern industrial and the Southern grain-producing regions as well as the mineral-rich Urals. By the time of the Bolshevik coup, Samara had been connected to virtually all the new railway lines linking the vast swathes of empire from Central Asia to the Caucasus and Siberia and constructed during the nineteenth century's railway boom.[145] The native merchant and foreign capital–driven industrial expansion also led to the flourishing of sophisticated pastimes, civic activism, and philanthropy.[146] During the Civil War, in 1918, Samara briefly became the seat of the anti-Bolshevik Constituent Assembly (*Komitet chlenov vserossiyskogo Uchreditel'nogo sobraniya*, KOMUCH) aided by the mutinous Czech Legion.[147]

Simultaneously, Samara typifies, indeed exemplifies, the Bolsheviks' grandstanding industrialization efforts. If we discern societal resilience even in territories with intense state-driven developmentalism, we may safely debunk received wisdoms about the consequences of revolutionary "social modernization" in areas with less intense forms of restructuring. Aside from Moscow and St. Petersburg, Samara is the only other city that served as Russia's political center when, during World War II, Stalin turned it into a temporary national capital and ordered the relocation there of industries and workforce. A secret underground bunker was built for Stalin in Samara, and foreign embassies were quickly evacuated to the city in the early months of the war. A large penal settlement just outside of the city emerged – the Bezymyanlag camp, part of the "archipelago" of Soviet forced labor. Postwar Samara continued to attract large-scale labor migration, notably of workers and engineers who serviced the sophisticated energy, weapons production, and aerospace industries. The region is home to Tolyatti, a city mythologized as built "from scratch" and named after the Italian Communist Party leader Palmiro Togliatti. Tolyatti underwent population growth on an unprecedented scale owing to migration from other territories in the 1960s and 1970s to man the Volga Automobile Plant and other industries. An overwhelmingly rural region before the Revolution, Samara's countryside also underwent profound change as agriculture was collectivized, and the formerly "backward" territories populated by seminomadic groups were brought into

---

[143] See Hartley, *Volga*, esp. 67–85.   [144] Figes, *Peasant Russia*, 23.
[145] Along with Saratov. Ibid., 21.   [146] Aleksushin, "K tipologii."   [147] Kalyagin, "Komitet."

the fold of Soviet modernity. Societal resilience in a region experiencing economic and social change of this magnitude would constitute an important test of the argument advanced in this book.

Sources

The bulk of historical data came from the 1897 imperial population census – the most comprehensive source of demographic, occupational, and other statistics for the empire; I discuss the census further in the supplementary appendices (Appendix B). I assembled additional data on imperial elections to the State Duma (national representative assembly) and on post-communist elections; on repressions; and on aspects of historical settlement of the frontier. Matching districts with their historical antecedents – something that, as far as I am aware, others have not done for the entire territory of present-day Russia – alone took me more than a year,[148] not least because of having to triangulate historical data for accuracy for each of Russia's present-day 2,000-odd districts. For social network analysis exploring patterns of organizational and social interaction, I created a dataset out of an imperial directory of white-collar professionals in Samara City on the eve of the Revolution, comprising more than 4,000 entries. A large author-commissioned survey from Levada, Russia's top polling agency, helps ascertain not only awareness of ancestral estates but also covariation between self-reported ancestry and occupational positioning in the Soviet labor market.[149]

A wide range of primary sources are jointly deployed to supplement the cross-regional and within-region statistical data. Hundreds of pages of hitherto underutilized documents from Samara's state archives constitute the main source of information on institutions normally associated with Soviet developmental achievements. These materials, discussed further in Appendix A, shed light on the imperial foundations of professional bodies, educational institutions, medical clinics, regional universities, and the network ties that link individuals working there. They also allow us to dissect how these institutions morphed into *Soviet* bodies. Archival records on denunciations and repressions and data illuminating the choices to site a Gulag camp are deployed to shed further light on the appropriation of the tsarist infrastructure and skills base to advance Soviet industrial development. The Bolsheviks abandon the obsessive tracing of citizens' social origins in the 1930s, just as they proclaim the dawn of a classless society. Where archival sources turn silent about citizens'

---

[148] Supplementary Appendices are provided at the end of the book. Additional data tests and research are in the Online Appendices (OA). Replication codes for all tests are in OA5.

[149] Designed with Katerina Tertytchnaya and Alexander Libman. Research summarized in "Social Structure and Attitudes towards Protest: Survey Evidence from Russia." Paper presented at the American Political Science Association Annual National Convention and Exhibition, San Francisco, September 10–13, 2020.

pre-revolutionary social positions, the recollections of the grandmother, the elderly memoirist, or the family archivist pick up and help us weave together the threads of time, illuminating the transmission of social status through the communist decades. Three family archives have aided this part of the analysis: the Constantine Neklutin archive, deposited with the Cammie G. Henry Research Center at Northwestern State University of Louisiana, chronicling the family of a merchant clan; the Zoya Kobozeva archive, which sheds light on the adaptation of the *meshchane* and free peasants in Samara; and the Sergey Golubkov family collection summarized in his published memoirs and illuminating the adaptation of several branches of the extended family of Polish nobles, upwardly mobile peasants, and *meshchane* (see the illustrative genealogies in Appendix E). More than a hundred genealogical essays by Samara's present-day high school and university students, which they wrote as part of a regional historical competition, corroborate intergenerational social continuities in time and space. In turn, some forty-five interviews conducted with materially well-off, high status, and otherwise successful middle-class professionals, the gilded bourgeoisie of present-day Samara, tell us how the descendants of imperial Russia's "missing middle" fared in the context of the tribulations of post-communism (questionnaire reproduced in Appendix D). Their recollections are set against narratives of the rural and blue-collar respondent. The individual accounts are cross-checked against the voices of the Soviet informant, the People's Commissariat of Internal Affairs (NKVD) official, and the regional planner that speak to us from declassified archival sources.

CONCLUSION AND CHAPTER STRUCTURE

This chapter has charted out a theoretical framework guiding the empirical journey in the rest of the book. Drawing on eclectic and interdisciplinary literatures, I have identified where I am indebted to extant studies and where my work represents a departure from purported apodictic accounts of the revolutionary social experience. I have also noted where the book parts with the recent literature that has benefited from scholars' access to a far wider range of sources and methodological tools than those available to the previous generations of writers on communism. I do not negate the socioeconomic changes and value shifts associated with the communist project, but the chapters that follow explore the ways in which Bolshevik policies interacted with, molded, and were shaped by imperial society. Anticipating critiques of an overstatement of the argument about social continuities, I highlight that my objective is to affect a shift in paradigmatic assumptions but without throwing the baby that is the communist impact out of the causal chain bathwater. Rather than entirely negating the significance of post-revolutionary change, the book unpacks the subtle ways in which communism did not matter as much as we thought it did.[150] This in turn should offer food for thought to enthusiasts of

[150] I thank Jeff Kopstein for encouraging me to add these qualifiers.

facile solutions to intractable societal problems today, in this time of rising social inequalities, whatever the national context.

The following chapters proceed as follows. Chapter 2 discusses the juridical structure of the estates and de facto patterns of social rigidity, fluidity, and mobility, as well as the encounter between the Tsarist society of estates and the Bolshevik class project. A social mapping and network exercise for Samara is presented in Chapter 3 to capture the estate aspects of imperial society and their reflection in modern institutions of urban governance, the professions, learning, and the civic sphere. The two chapters on the professions and education, Chapters 4 and 5 respectively, analyze institutional continuities in space and the social logics embedded in the reproduction of social stratification through those very institutions – the public hospitals, the museums, the schools – called on to deliver a new, classless, communist society, and their role in nurturing a quasi-autonomous sphere vis-à-vis the state. Chapter 6 discusses the material dimension of social closure and the ways in which extant social ties within Soviet Russia and outside – encompassing wealthy émigré relatives, friends, former professional and business associates, and their "honor" obligations toward those left behind – perpetuated estate-derived market-supportive and professional possibilities in a post-revolutionary society. The subtle layering of memory, knowledge, and awareness of how the past shapes one's position in the present are questions I then explore in Chapter 7. Chapter 8 links the spatial components of Soviet development, particularly those related to the coercive aspects of industrialization, to imperial-era developmental and social configurations. Chapter 9 analyzes interregional variations in democratic quality as derived from long-term social-structural patterns. The final chapter, Chapter 10, brings in the cases of Hungary and China to explain how the insights help us understand social structure and democratic – and authoritarian – resilience and backsliding in a variety of contexts with experience of communism. An Afterword concludes the book with a summary of findings and some thoughts about future research questions.

2

From Imperial Estates to Estatist Society

And yet in this curious new order the old classes of society continued to exist more or less in their former hierarchy, notwithstanding the disappearance of their legal privileges and disabilities.

Nothing obscures our social vision as effectively as the economistic prejudice.

Karl Polanyi, The Great Transformation[1]

The "specter" of conventional class categories has loomed large over social-political analyses, whether Marxism-inspired or other.[2] Consequently, long-gone institutions foundational for understanding the genesis of social distinction in modern societies have remained in the shadows in classic and present-day polemics about sources of inequality and political contention. One overlooked question is how the peculiarities of feudal state building may create socially heterogenous openings, closures, and opportunities at the juncture where human capital and, specifically, professionally and organizationally incorporated knowledge and know-how begin to take center stage as a social marker. The conventional class paradigm is evident, for instance, in historical political economy works that have accorded pride of place to the categories of "lord," "peasant," or "bourgeois," in unpacking the genesis of modern political orders.[3] These towering classifications obscure what I consider to be the defining elements of the stratification and political orientations in modern societies that originated within feudalism – namely, professional embedding, the possibilities for complex roles and the aspirational multiplexities that straddle the various class-defined groups, and an inequitable public sphere.

---

[1] Polanyi, Great Transformation, 120, 166.
[2] For this critique, see Davis, Discipline, 31–50 and 51.
[3] Moore, Social Origins; Boix, Democracy and Redistribution; Acemoglu and Robinson, Economic Origins.

Max Weber showed a sensitive appreciation for these elements of transition from feudalism to modernity in analyzing the *Ständestaat*. The great sociologist's appreciation for the trans-epochal imprint of the estate has not, however, percolated widely into understandings of this institution's long-term consequences for social configuration, as is evident in the many ambiguities and mistranslations of the word *Stand* in Weber's work.[4] Yet the estate, as

---

[4] In Weber's analysis, estates represent the beginnings of the depersonalization of rule via the corporate autonomy of groups, occupational or otherwise, even if their privileges, positive and negative, historically originate in favors bestowed selectively or in a personalistic way. "Alle Arten ständischer," he writes, "auf mehr oder minder fester Appropriation der Verwaltungsmacht ruhender, Herrschaft stehen im Verhältnis zum Patriarchalismus insofern der legalen Herrschaft näher, als, sie, kraft der Garantien, welche die Zuständigkeiten der Privilegierten umgeben, den Charakter eines besondersartigen 'Rechtsgrundes' haben (Folge der ständischen 'Gewaltenteilung'), der den patriarchalischen Gebilden mit ihren völlig der Willkür des Herrn anheimgegebenen Verwaltungen fehlt." *Wirtschaft und Gesellschaft*, 4:221. ("In relation to patrimonialism, all types of estate rule, based on a more or less solid appropriation of administrative power, are closer to legal rule in that, by virtue of the guarantees surrounding the competences of the privileged, they have the character of a special kind of 'legal foundation' (consequential to the estates' 'separation of powers'), which is missing in the patrimonial orders with their administration completely abandoned to the arbitrariness of the Lord.") Translation my own.

In an acclaimed new translation of Weber, Keith Treibe translates *Stand*, *Stände* as "social rank" and, depending on context, as "social status," "hierarchical," "social hierarchy." Treibe defends his preference for "rank" – in my view, a not very adequate translation that conjures up more formal bureaucratic hierarchies and titles – over Parsonian "status" because the latter is arguably too "diffuse"; he also eschews using "estate" because "early modern England had no such equivalent." This strikes me as an inappropriate, indeed parochial, justification for excluding the more precise concept of the estate as pertaining to institutions of a feudal order in a variety of contexts. See Weber, *Economy and Society*, trans. Treibe, 478. On the difficulties of translating the term, see also Treibe's defense of the translation of *Ständische Herrschaft* as "hierarchical rule," 361n12 – a translation of the concept so vague as to embrace many forms of polity, institution, or organization, modern or premodern – whereas, in fact, Weber's elaboration of this concept makes it clear that the reference is to the estate as a premodern legal arrangement akin to Russian *sosloviye*. The inappropriateness of this translation is evident if we consider passages where Weber discusses the origin of contractual aspects of rights and duties in a feudal *Ständestaat*. See, for instance, *Wirtschaft und Gesellschaft*, 4:111, 220–21; and on estates as an exclusionary corporate arrangement in Western cities under feudalism and in Russia, see *Wirtschaft und Gesellschaft*, 5:17–23. The Fischoff et al. volume provides a more appropriate translation of *Ständische Herrschaft* as "estate-type domination." *Economy and Society*, 2:232. Even in this volume, though, the confusion in translations of Weber's usage of *Stände* is evident in passages where Weber rapidly moves from discussions of status honor and esteem in a modern sense of nonmaterial social markers of inclusion and exclusion and *Stände* referring to medieval estates and their legal monopolization of privileges in the context of "*stark[e]*," "*ständische Gliederungen*." See *Wirtschaft und Gesellschaft*, 1:86. Thus, in the Fischoff et al. translation, we find references to the "status order" where Weber invokes monopolistic tendencies of merchant and craft guilds, whereas the content of the passages makes it clear that a more appropriate translation would have been estates-based order, and indeed the translators refer to "estates of knights, peasants, priests" only to then switch to terms like "stratification by status" with reference to the estates of the Middle Ages. See *Economy and Society*, 2:937. Elsewhere, however, we find a more accurate, context-appropriate, translation of *Ständestaat* as "polity of estates" in the feudal Occident. Ibid., 1086.

a corporate system of governance; as an institution *positively* and *negatively* structuring privileges, rights, and duties; and as an identity-, esteem-, and cognition-molding – Weber's *Ehre* – arrangement, may well have deep repercussions for the social structure long after it has ceased to exist as an institution.

This chapter dissects the estate as pivotal to understanding the long-lasting patterns of social stratification in Russian society and, relatedly, the contours, networks, and fissures within the resultant estatist public and political sphere. In Chapter 3, I use data and archival sources for Samara to analyze the consequences of the cohabitation of the estate with the processes of modernization for the nature, autonomy, and vibrancy of the public sphere and social resilience after the Revolution. Before we proceed to analyze those path-dependencies, we ought to unpack the legal-policy underpinnings of the estate to understand how it is reflected in modern educational, professional, and government institutions. Many readers may be unfamiliar with the estate, so a discussion of this institution at some length is warranted. I try nevertheless to navigate a fine line between digressing into excessive historical detail and presenting a conceptually lucid and parsimonious framework. First, the chapter outlines the peculiarities of old-regime Russia's semi-feudal order as engendering a wedge – or, worse, a chasm – between the estatist, estates-derived, and relatively privileged social group, and the substrata within it, and the unfree peasants.[5] It then reviews historical and sociological sources concerned with the transitioning of society from the imperial to the Soviet era. Finally, it charts how the fragmentary knowledge about the reproduction of latent social distinctions and equally submerged institutional sources of autonomy among the more privileged social groups sets the stage for the subsequent chapters' fine-grained analysis of the persistence of the estatist bourgeoisie as a *legacy* across regime types.

ESTATES UNDER IMPERIAL SOCIAL STRATIFICATION

The historian Boris Mironov defines the estate (*sosloviye*) as "a juridically circumscribed group with hereditary rights and obligations" – a term that became widespread in Russian jurisprudence by the second quarter of the nineteenth century.[6] The 1835 Code of Laws of the Russian Empire (*Svod zakonov Rossiyskoy imperii*), which survived in a modified form until the Bolshevik Revolution, identified the four main estates of the nobility

---

[5] Teckenberg also used "estatist society," but to refer to Soviet status groups in a Weberian sense rather than pointing to an origin in imperial estates. I acknowledge Professor Teckenberg's inspiration for the terms employed here. Teckenberg, "Social Structure."

[6] Mironov, *Sotsial'naya istoriya*, 1:334. Here and elsewhere my translation from the Russian edition.

(*dvoryane/dvoryanstvo*) – the service estate, often referred to as the "gentry";[7] the clergy (*dukhovenstvo*); town dwellers (*gorodskiye obyvateli*); and rural dwellers (*sel'skiye obyvateli*). Within each estate, there were distinctions between, for instance, the hereditary and personal nobility or, within the clergy, those based on religious denomination.[8] The most populous estate after the peasantry and distinct in status from merchants was another urban estate, the *meshchane*.[9] The Great Reforms of the nineteenth century contributed to the erosion of boundaries between the estates.[10] All peasants became citizens, while taxes and other levies led to the impoverishment of portions of the nobility. Nevertheless, "the four-estate paradigm" remained the most widespread classificatory category.[11] The social pyramid in Figure 2.1 features percentage-share distributions of the main estates.[12]

In my analysis, the estate is conceptualized as an institution that will have a profound and long-lasting "lock-in" effect on social stratification. I am sensitive to the following dimensions of the estate: (1) the legal-corporate aspects of property rights, taxation, access to trade, and broader citizenship structuring entitlements and acquisition of capital; (2) the habitual emphasis on learning, which was characteristic of the priestly caste or due to service obligations to the monarchy and state,[13] as well as, relatedly, proto-professional skills that could be transferred into modern occupations; and (3)

---

[7] Unlike in England, where "gentry" referred to a segment of the middle estate or the commons, including merchants and yeoman farmers, as distinct from peers, the Russian term *dvoryanstvo* referred to both those equivalent to English peers and the landed segment of the gentry (not merchants). Legal status, not wealth, differentiated this estate from others. Becker, *Nobility and Privilege*, 15–16. See also Smith, *Former People*, 25. On the misleading nature of the translation of *dvoryane, dvoryanstvo*, as either nobility, aristocracy, or gentry considering that Petrine reforms subsumed both pre-Petrine notables, such as *boyare* and lesser service *dvoryane*, and new nobles that could ascend in status through service or personal imperial favor, see Reyfman, *How Russia Learned to Write*, 5–6.

[8] Mironov, *Rossiyskaya imperiya*, 1:338.

[9] It is also the least studied and most misrepresented of all the estates. Orlovsky, "Lower Middle Strata," 249, 252.

[10] The first phase of the Great Reforms occurred under Alexander I (1801–25); the second under Alexander II (1856–81). During this time, the serfs were liberated; notions of the rule of law were injected into Russian jurisprudence; jury trials and judicial independence were introduced; and self-governing *zemstvo* bodies were set up. Timasheff also refers to the second part of Nicholas II's reign as the third phase, which included the creation of the State Duma in 1905–6; the freeing (in 1906) of peasants from paying fees for land acquired after liberation; and Stolypin reforms, named after Prime Minister Pyotr Stolypin (1906–11), which allowed peasants to separate their land plots from rural communes. *Great Retreat*, 27–30.

[11] Mironov, *Sotsial'naya istoriya*, 1:339.

[12] Troynitskiy, *Obshchiy svod*, 1:xiii. Percentages for European Russia are 0.95 (hereditary nobles) and 0.52 (personal and service nobles); 0.54 (clergy); 10.65 (*meshchane*); 0.33 (hereditary and personal honorary citizens); 0.25 (merchants); and 84.16 (peasants). European Russia excludes Polish territories (*privislinskiye gubernii*) where the *meshchane* constituted 23.53 percent of the population and peasants 72.98 percent. Ibid., 1:xiii.

[13] Smith, *Former People*, 25.

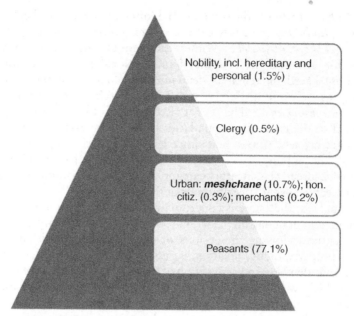

FIGURE 2.1 The estate social pyramid
Source. Image created by author; 1897 census data for the Russian Empire

the estate as a refuge reflecting the social processes of horizontal fluidity, vertical mobility, and population movement but also as a designation that, once bestowed, structures the material and human capital aspects of social positioning and opportunity. Indeed, as recent studies have found, many clung on to their estate, however lowly: it shaped identities and indeed estate loyalties, even among peasants; it provided a structured and highly regimented set of not just legal obligations but also rights; and it fostered devotion to the institutions of governance organized along narrow estate-based rather than broader citizenship lines.[14] In analyzing the third dimension of the estate, I am therefore alert to the estate as both a molder of social status and an indicator of processes outside of the narrow institutional channels of ascription to a particular group, notably those of a more *longue durée* nature and more appropriately bracketed under the rubric of cultural-historical demography. Finally, (4) I detect the significance of the estate in the proto-democratic institutions of local governance dating back to the eighteenth century, and the *zemstvo* reforms of the nineteenth, and highlight the co-constitutive nature of these as well as the educational, professional, and

---

[14] Burbank, *Russian Peasants*, 12–14, 261–65. Estates, of course, did not encompass "the totality" of all groups in Russia. Confino, "Soslovie," 693. Nevertheless, the state made efforts to ascribe most individuals to an estate; and individuals knew the power of having an estate designation. "No estate, no rights." Burbank, *Russian Peasants*, 13.

corporate-estate institutions in the production of an estates-enmeshed public sphere. Although anchored in late imperial Russia, my analysis dissects the processes of embourgeoisement with highly inequitable social-political consequences that I conjecture are also found in other societies experiencing a transition from feudalism to knowledge-intensive modern economies. In turn, such a perspective helps us transcend the conceptualization of class in a situational, temporally restricted sense and perceive it as an intergenerational concept that straddles distinct property, institutional, social, and political regimes.

The Estate As a Legal Category: Rights, Obligations, and Freedoms

In the Russian Empire, the estate represented a fundamental juridical category delineating social groups – their legal identity, rights, and obligations – much as it did in feudal orders that had experienced erosion somewhat earlier elsewhere in Europe. While individuals in post-feudal societies – at least in theory – derive rights from more general conceptions of citizenship, in estate-based orders social status is contingent on juridically and institutionally regimented, often hereditary, belonging to a category in a caste-like structure.[15] In Russia, estate designation to various degrees determined or influenced personal and economic independence; freedom of choice of residence; social mobility; a limited or unlimited personal right to the ownership of private property and movable and immovable assets; choice of occupation; and social and legal protections.[16] The estate also regimented the application of, and exemptions from, corporal punishment.[17]

The hereditary nobility (*dvoryanstvo*) occupied the top layer of institutional entitlements, citizenship, and privileges not bestowed on other estates. Already in 1785, Catherine II's Charter to the Nobility (*Zhalovannaya gramota*) confirmed the nobility's "freedom and liberty ... in perpetuity."[18] Nobles also enjoyed privileges in entering military or state service and with foreign travel; they were exempt from corporal punishment; and they were endowed with special protections against any violation of "dignity."[19] The clergy occupied second place in legal status and prestige under the estates hierarchy, straddling Russia's urban and rural worlds and acquiring the juridical imprimatur of a separate "free" estate simultaneously with nobles. Other estates remained bound by corporate constraints to various extents even as the Crown gradually eroded or abolished them over the nineteenth century.

The estate also bestowed inequitable duties and obligations with implications for economic standing and status – tax burdens and other fees

---

[15] For a discussion, see Mousnier et al., "Problems." [16] Mironov, *Rossiyskaya imperiya*, 2:38.
[17] On application to peasant and urban estates, see ibid., 22, 48. [18] Ibid., 39.
[19] A reference to recourse to the courts and imperial sanction in depriving individuals of noble titles. Ibid., 39.

and levies, trading rights, property ownership, and, until the 1860s, the right to own serfs. The Crown's 1785 charter freed the hereditary nobility from payment of any taxes; the nobility also enjoyed exclusive rights to own land and serfs.[20] By contrast, the so-called personal nobles (*lichnyye dvoryane*) – those not in state service long enough to acquire hereditary status – could not own serfs. The Great Reforms progressively shifted the tax burdens from the lower estates to the well-off nobility – notably as new state taxes were introduced on urban and other property.[21] The *haute* aristocracy, however, were well positioned to offset the new tax burdens against their privileged access to salaried income through state service.

The clergy (*dukhovenstvo*) did not have serf ownership rights but enjoyed special tax status. Like nobles, already in the eighteenth century they progressively secured freedom from personal taxation (*podushnaya podat'*).[22] Even though clergymen's work had been extraneous to the salaried structure of state service and progression, priests and monks received the right to obtain prestigious awards such as the Order of St. Stanislaus, entitling one to hereditary nobility status along with serf ownership rights.[23] Even as a "free" estate, all the way up until 1917 parish clergy nevertheless lacked the right to engage in entrepreneurship or own factories, plants, or other production facilities. The Crown also restricted clergymen's rights to land ownership, sale, and purchase. These prohibitions were a source of considerable resentment; many clergymen, particularly in deprived rural areas, lacked the stable income of state titled officials (*chinovniki*).[24] Only in the empire's waning years did the clergy secure entitlement to state salaries commensurate with the status of other educated strata in state service.[25]

Within the urban estate category, merchants (*kuptsy*) occupied the top rank in the hierarchy of prestige, wealth, and status. This began to change toward the twentieth century as the title of "honored/ honorable citizen" (*pochyotnyy grazhdanin*) – bestowed on those who had distinguished themselves in urban governance, service, or philanthropy – displaced that of merchant in desirability and prestige.[26] The 1775 imperial legal code divided merchants into three guilds based on declared capital – the first guild constituted the wealthiest merchants. Initially hereditary, from 1785 onward other urban strata could buy the title subject to availability of capital. Conversely, a merchant unable to pay the dues would fall back into the *meshchane* estate. Merchants were exempt from the payment of a direct head tax (*podushnyy nalog*), in lieu of which they were obliged to transfer a share of their declared capital to the state's coffers.[27] Along with personal, or nonhereditary, nobles and the children of Orthodox

---

[20] Mironov, *Rossiyskaya imperiya*, 1:341.   [21] Ibid., 355.

[22] As well as from corporal punishment (excluding lower-ranking clergymen). By the start of the nineteenth century, the clergy had rights similar to those of personal nobles. Mironov, *Rossiyskaya imperiya*, 2:44.

[23] Ibid.   [24] Ibid., 45.   [25] Ibid., 1:381.   [26] Ibid., 387–90.   [27] Ibid., 386–87, 395.

priests who completed a seminary or spiritual academy, a merchant who had been in the guild for ten years could apply for hereditary *pochyotnyy grazhdanin* status. This position carried an exemption from the payment of poll tax, which *meshchane* had to pay, as well as military service and corporal punishment. The Crown abolished the third guild in 1863 and opened up further opportunities for any estate to obtain merchant status, while bestowing new privileges on first-guild merchants.[28]

Until the 1860s, the main rationale for aspiring to join the merchantry was the status and tax privileges, but guild payments were large. Accordingly, considerable fluidity characterized merchant and *meshchane* estates, mirroring the financial circumstances of individual families.[29] The father of the medical doctor turned playwright Anton Chekhov, who began his life as a serf on a noble's estate,[30] fought hard to procure merchant status – he owned a grocery business in the southern city of Taganrog – only to be relegated to the *meshchane* estate when business fortunes soured.[31] It is true that contingencies – luck, self-selection, individual inheritance – could catapult one into a merchant guild. Once in, however, the merchant enjoyed considerable privileges in the geographical scope of trade, the taxation regime governing property, and the sanctioned size of trading or manufacturing enterprises.[32]

The corporate rights of the *meshchane* were likewise nontrivial, however, considering their implications for the generation of urban rent, enterprise, and access to public services. Until the second quarter of the nineteenth century, the *meshchane* shared with merchants virtually exclusive rights to trade and industry within town boundaries.[33] Urban burghers capitalized on their privileged status to consolidate and protect economic advantages vis-à-vis those of outsiders. Would-be peasant entrepreneurs in towns ended up paying "exorbitant fees to 'borrow' a townsperson's trading rights"; the inventory of goods they could trade in small shops was strictly regimented; and, as rural people's commercial rights expanded in the nineteenth century, they confronted urban interests and opposition.[34] Serfs who aspired to become land speculators likewise found their possibilities circumscribed – for town status was a sure way to avoid fee-charging "intermediaries."[35]

[28] Ibid., 388, 386–89; Bartlett, *Chekhov*, 37.

[29] Mironov, *Rossiyskaya imperiya*, 1:386–97. See also Makitrin and Barinova, "Samarskoye kupechestvo," 44, 56.

[30] Anton Chekhov's grandfather bought his way out of serfdom in 1841. Bartlett, *Chekhov*, 35.

[31] Ibid., 32–33.   [32] Smith, *For the Common Good*, 23–28; Dowler, "Merchants," esp. 49–52.

[33] Mironov, *Rossiyskaya imperiya*, 1:384–85. See also Kobozeva, "Meshchanskaya povsednev-nost'," 164.

[34] Smith, *For the Common Good*, 24–25.

[35] Ibid., 25. On the disadvantages of "extralegal" status for land, property, and credit market access, even in accounts highlighting serf and emancipated peasant opportunities for entrepreneurship and accumulation of wealth, see also Dennison, *Russian Serfdom*, 217, 213–33. Others have noted that "in many areas pseudo-serf relations had continued [after emancipation], until by way of formal education and more importantly education by the market and by the

Although the Great Reforms opened up new avenues of social mobility for peasants, the *meshchane* were best placed to attain merchant or honorary citizen status. The historian Alison Smith finds that in provincial towns the merchant community overwhelmingly derived from the *meshchane* or artisans.[36] The *meshchane*'s material status as a propertied bourgeois is reflected in census records listing significant numbers as "employers of labor," running a "one person enterprise," "employers using only family members," and "rentiers."[37] Although materially less well off than merchants, the *meshchane* frequently owned multiple urban properties even if often of a squalid kind, renting out a "corner" or a room to students, migrants, or peasant seasonal laborers in towns (*otkhodniki*).[38] Social mobility from a peasant to *meshchanin* and higher was widespread but often involved considerable costs, took decades, or crossed generations.[39]

Historically, the peasant estate (*krest'yanstvo*) not only was the most deprived in a material and socioeconomic sense but remained outside of the citizenship status that other estates enjoyed. By the seventeenth century, it acquired the contours of the least privileged hereditary caste, deprived of free movement, the right to unauthorized departure from the commune, and exemption from corporal punishment; it was also shackled with material dues and work in kind. In Gregory Freeze's classic account of the estate paradigm, peasants represented "by far the most rigid, separate, and distinctive component in the whole social order, in good measure because of their strict segregation from the rest of the administrative, judicial, and economic system."[40] Not coincidentally, in Russian jurisprudence and public discussions, we find references to town dwellers as citizenry (*grazhdanstvo*),

experience of the fair operations of the law collectivist mentality began to give way to individualism." Crisp, *Studies*, 20. In a groundbreaking study, Burbank sees peasants in post-emancipation Russia as citizens actively exercising their legal rights in courts, but until 1917 these, as she emphasizes, remained inextricably linked to their estate as peasants. Unequal as these rights might have been in the estate scheme of things, "they [peasants] took their estate-based rights for granted, as the ordinary way of things." Burbank, *Russian Peasants*, 13.

[36] Towns surveyed for the years 1804–1913 were Iaroslavl', Riazan', Saratov, and Tver'. In Moscow, by contrast, new merchants were largely peasants by origin. Smith, *For the Common Good*, 40.

[37] Orlovsky, "Lower Middle Strata," 252. See tables 16.2 and 16.3, 251.

[38] On *meshchane*'s real estate ownership, see Dolgopyatov, "Domovladeniye," esp. 348 on "corner" properties.

[39] Patterns varied from city to city. One Petr Chulkov, the son of a freed serf Makar Chulkov who entered Moscow urban society in 1863, became a hereditary honored citizen in 1911 – some fifty years later. Smith, *For the Common Good*, 200. Serfs were prepared to pay considerable fees to the tune of 100 rubles to lords for the right to marry off their daughters to someone from "a higher legal estate," a merchant or *meshchanin*. Dennison, *Russian Serfdom*, 225. On the desirability of a change of estate from peasant to townsperson among peasants, see also Burbank, *Russian Peasants*, 14.

[40] Freeze, "*Soslovie*," 30. Freeze notes the coexistence of the plasticity of the estate system with resilience to change. Ibid.

a designation distinguishing them from peasants.[41] As Petr Struve, a leading member of the liberal Constitutional Democrats Party (*kadety*), poignantly observed, the 1917 Russian Revolution came about because of "the lack of political rights [*politicheskoe bespravie*] of the gentry and the lack of civil rights [*grazhdanskoe bespravie*] of the peasantry."[42]

Unlike merchants and the *meshchane*, peasants, particularly former serfs, had little experience of legally protected property rights, property ownership, or entrepreneurship.[43] As Struve noted, peasants lacked the "spirit of property"; the "peasant allotment," not "peasant property," remained the defining characteristic in Russian agriculture. Even after emancipation, attitudes concerning private property among peasants remained underdeveloped, and the Revolution arguably substituted one form of collective ownership for another.[44] State peasants, however, enjoyed rights distinct from those of manorial serfs and freed serfs, notably in the fertile Black Earth lands of European Russia, with its historical prevalence of serfdom. The so-called state- or Crown-owned peasants from the late eighteenth century enjoyed personal freedoms and property rights.[45] Many of the peasants who were encouraged to settle in frontier territories as part of Crown policy had the designation of state peasants and therefore habitually enjoyed greater liberties than manorial serfs.[46]

Estates and Human Capital

Another aspect of the estate order of note in the account of social resilience presented here pertains to the human capital dimension of status differentials. The priestly caste, for instance, in traditional societies carries knowledge otherwise inaccessible to the masses. Although the priestly estate's redundant wisdom is not equivalent to modern expertise dispersed via wide-access or universal schooling, Russia's clergy – much like the Brahmin caste in India – seamlessly transitioned into modern professional realms.[47] As an educated

---

[41] Mironov, *Rossiyskaya imperiya*, 1:338; Kobozeva, "Meshchanskaya povsednevnost'," 163; and Freeze, "*Soslovie.*" See 16–17n18. The 1860s reforms placed all peasants in the category of "free rural dwellers." Mironov, *Sotsial'naya istoriya*, 1:399.

[42] Cited in Burbank, *Intelligentsia*, 134.

[43] "Legally protected" is an important distinction. Even on serf estates, notably in the Central Industrial Region, a rural property market developed among serfs, but enforcement was extra-legal in nature, customary, and governed by the lord and not by state law. Dennison, *Russian Serfdom*, esp. 213–33. To join the merchant estate, even the wealthy serfs had to purchase their freedom first. Ibid., 214. See also on serf manufactories Crisp, *Studies*, 12–17.

[44] Cited and discussed in Burbank, *Intelligentsia*, 148.

[45] Mironov, *Rossiyskaya imperiya*, 1:398–99.

[46] The Central Industrial Region with its less fertile lands was also distinctive in that many serfs fulfilled duties in cash or kind (*obrok*) and less with corvée labor (*barshchina*). Dennison, *Russian Serfdom*, 32.

[47] On the embedding of caste in the construction of India's middle class, and the imprint of colonial-era "classificatory practices" in relationships within and among groups, see

estate, often personifying the sole enlightened authority in the countryside, the clergy performed a variety of state functions – from civil registration, to the dissemination of state laws and edicts, and providing basic schooling, medical, and veterinary care within the community.[48] The clergy became a major supplier of educated youth, who abandoned the calling of the hereditary estate in droves and joined the professions and, indeed, the revolutionary movement.[49] The modesty of household wealth among this estate notwithstanding, a large proportion habitually attended seminaries and theological academies equivalent to secondary and higher educational institutions, which provided education of a quality that was out of reach to most citizens and subjects alike.[50]

The aristocracy and nobility's status as a high human capital estate derived from their state service – as courtiers, civil administrators, and military servicemen.[51] The Crown did not automatically bestow service titles on scions of the hereditary aristocracy and gentry. These were conditional on success in a highly regimented system of merit-based schooling, with entry points as early as age seven and examinations and assessments governing entry, progression, and graduation at each stage.

In turn, the wealthier segments among the urban estates were incentivized to join state service and the professions. For the merchant and *meshchane* upstarts lacking hereditary titles, state service – and the education required to access positions in government, bureaucracy, and the professions – enabled entry into the echelon of the personal, nonhereditary nobility. The urban estates' commercial and other rights endowed them with significant "early riser"–type advantages, accounting for easily traceable patterns of social mobility through service in the pre-revolutionary decades.[52]

Fernandes, "Hegemony," 61. India's first prime minister, Jawaharlal Nehru, a self-described "middle-class person," was the son of a Brahmin lawyer and educated at England's elite Harrow School. Baviskar et al., "Introduction," 5.

[48] On the role of seminary graduates in the development of agricultural sciences, see Moon, *The Plough*, 49.

[49] The clergy supplied many members of the "radical intelligentsia" – in the 1870s, 22 percent of *narodniki* hailed from this estate. Mironov, *Sotsial'naya istoriya*, 1:377. The *narodniki* (from the word *narod*, people) were populists seeking to mobilize peasant masses against the tzarist regime and around socialist causes.

[50] Mironov, *Rossiyskaya imperiya*, 1:372.   [51] Smith, *Former People*, 25.

[52] New evidence problematizes earlier portrayals of the educational-occupational profile of *meshchane*. One early account juxtaposes the *meshchanstvo* to the burgher of medieval and modern Europe based on a socioeconomic profile of this estate in the late eighteenth and early-to-mid nineteenth centuries. The stark juxtaposition in my view is unjustified as applied particularly to the later imperial period, which the study does not encompass. Based on analysis of individual towns, large segments of *meshchane* are placed in the categories of *"gering qualifizierte,"* as *"Gelegenheitsarbeiter,"* and as engaged in *"Saisonarbeit."* Hildermeier, "Was war das Mescanstvo?" 37. See also Wirtschafter, *Social Identity*, 130. On stigmatization of *meshchanstvo* in Stalin's Russia, see Dunham, *In Stalin's Time*, esp. 19–23; on images of "greed," see Tavrina, "Obraz"; and on squalor, Dostoevsky's *Crime and Punishment* (*Prestupleniye i nakazaniye*); and *Poor People* (*Bednyye lyudi*). See also, on squalor as a literary device,

Peasants, particularly manorial former serfs, remained overwhelmingly illiterate; and the penetration of formal education beyond primary schooling remained weak. Literacy and access to schooling steadily rose toward the final years of empire, a process that accelerated with the introduction of the early twentieth-century agrarian reforms under Pyotr Stolypin that completed peasant emancipation. Upwardly mobile peasants became, as Ben Eklof finds, an important supplier of primary school teachers.[53] Literacy statistics reveal, however, the gulf between peasants and other estates. Even in 1917, the bulk of citizens, mostly peasants, remained illiterate.[54] Table 2.1 illustrates that, in European Russia for instance, whether urban or rural dwellers, citizens belonging to the urban estates were considerably more literate than peasants; urban peasants on average had a 64 percent literacy rate as compared to the *meshchane* and the other urban estates, at 73 percent.

TABLE 2.1 *Literacy in European Russia by estate in the years 1847–1917, above age nine (%)*

Estate	1847	1857	1867	1877	1887	1897	1907	1917
Nobility	76	77	80	82	84	86	88	90
Town	89	91	92	94	95	95	97	98
Village	59	62	64	67	68	71	73	76
Clergy	68	72	77	81	85	89	92	95
Town	82	85	88	91	93	95	97	98
Village	59	64	70	76	82	86	91	94
Urban estate	30	37	39	44	48	54	59	64
Town	33	36	41	47	54	60	66	73
Village	30	32	34	37	44	47	51	56
Peasant	10	12	14	18	21	27	30	32
Town	25	27	31	36	43	50	57	64
Village	9	11	13	16	20	22	27	32

Note. Includes territories outside of present-day Russia.
Source. Mironov, *Rossiyskaya imperiya*, 3:483, table 12.16.

Bakhtin, *Problems of Dostoevsky's Poetics*, 115, notably on the role of "slum naturalism" and its Hellenistic and Roman literary origins in Dostoevsky's genre and plot construction.
[53] Eklof, *Russian Peasant Schools*, 189–90.
[54] In European Russia, only 42.3 percent of the population aged nine and above in 1917 were literate. Mironov, *Rossiyskaya imperiya*, 3:482, table 12.15. See also Brooks, *When Russia Learned to Read*, 4.

The Estate As a Reflection of Society, and the State's Attempts to Manage Social Complexity

Finally, I consider the estate as an institution reflecting both social impulses and those of the state as it looked to restrict, channel, or otherwise influence population mobility, movement, and settlement. The *meshchane* poignantly illustrate how the estate reflected and simultaneously structured, inhibited, or liberated groups in society. The *meshchane* were not simply urban residents who did not fit into the other estate categories of noblemen, clergymen, or peasants. Nor should we simply appropriate as typical the caricaturized portrayals of the *meshchane* in the philippics of the pre-revolutionary intelligentsia, some of whose illustrious spokespersons precisely originated within the *meshchanstvo*, hence their disdain for the petty bourgeois milieus of their upbringing.[55] Rather, I emphasize how, whatever the origin, the *meshchane*'s corporate institutions, tax status, trading, and property rights configure possibilities, incentives, and cognitive maps. This perspective enables us to delineate the broad social contours of the *meshchanstvo* itself and retain sensitivity to the status heterogeneity within it.

On the one hand, the *meshchane* absorbed all kinds of groups, as the state, much like the Bolsheviks some decades later, scrambled to categorize an ever more complex society into antiquated categories of a caste-like order. Sponginess, perhaps more so than is the case with the other estates, characterized this social stratum, which over the course of the nineteenth century expanded pursuant to successive edicts, struggling as the authorities were to cope with labor migration and the population movement of political exiles and ethnic and religious groups.[56] Considerable self-selection characterized the *meshchanstvo*. Scores of adventurous peasants abandoned rural occupations to become urban artisans, maids, or clerks. Yet, once the status of a *meshchanin* had been acquired, one would conform, enact, and aspire to the full palette of the social entitlements of this estate.[57]

Segments within the *meshchane* also embodied the social deviant, who was instrumental in effecting a shift from feudalism to capitalism – one who "engages in behavior which constitutes in a certain sense a breach of the existing order and is either contrary to, or at least not positively weighted in, the hierarchy of existing social values."[58] In medieval Europe, the deviant would be the moneylender held in disdain by the official church,[59] much like in Russia the peasant *mir* regarded urban freedoms and mercantile individualism as suspect. The philosopher Nikolai Berdyaev captured this sentiment in characterizing the "Russian people" as the "least *meshchanskiy*"

---

[55] Kobozeva, "Meshchanskaya povsednevnost'," 118–19.

[56] Kobozeva, "Gorod i meshchane," 51–52.

[57] Ibid. On the peasant transition into towns in post-emancipation Russia, see Ryndzyunskiy, *Krest'yane i gorod*.

[58] Hoselitz, *Sociological Aspects*, 62.   [59] Ibid., 62.

of all peoples, one self-consciously, out of choice, adhering the least to "bourgeois" values, lifestyle, and ethos – even when indulging in "bourgeois sins [*poroki*]."[60] Segments of the *meshchane* were culturally distinct – Russia's answer to medieval Europe's Syrian, Byzantine, or Jewish communities who were instrumental in the gradual "domestication" of entrepreneurial practices among native groups.[61] The Russian Orthodox peasant commune may be sluggish in making this transition, but the German peasant settler turned *meshchanin* would be well ahead in embracing the values of individualism, universal literacy, schooling, and enterprise.[62] Likewise, the culturally marginal Jews and Greeks were entrepreneurial urban pioneers, outsiders whose practices – and lifestyle – became the envy and model for native merchants to emulate, something that Rosamund Bartlett discerns in Taganrog's Greek traders, among whom the young Chekhov grew up.[63] Typifying the native deviant pattern were also the Old Believers – their industry, industriousness, and mutual credit support likewise effected admirable economic success.[64]

The peculiarities of the spatial distribution of estates reflected these processes and in addition derived from patterns of a more *longue durée* nature such as (1) the prevalence of serfdom as opposed to institutions with looser forms of peasant bondage – notably state peasant ownership, obligations, and rights, something that led to varied spatial configurations depending on land quality and location on the frontier; (2) the historical settlement of dispossessed communities fleeing persecution or otherwise encouraged to settle in uninhabited frontier lands – Jews, Old Believers, settlers from Europe's Germanic lands, often designated, or attaining, *meshchane* and merchant status; (3) settlement in territories with historically established trading outposts on major natural transportation routes and access points with

---

[60] Cited in Vishnevskiy, *Serp i rubl'*, 107.

[61] Hoselitz, *Sociological Aspects*, 63, 66–67. On Jewish entrepreneurship, see Armstrong, "Socializing for Modernization," 95–98; and for restrictions on opportunities beyond the Pale of Settlement, see Kahan, "Notes on Jewish Entrepreneurship."

[62] Not to be confused with Baltic Germans – *mamluks* rather than *pariahs* given their privileges as the administrative, political, and commercial elite. Blackwell, "Russian Entrepreneur," 25. On divisions within Russia's German community, see Armstrong, "Socializing for Modernization," esp. 98–103. The community expanded after the Polish partition, which also added Jewish populations, enhancing the contingent of native or other subjugated entrepreneurial groups like Old Believers and Volga Tatars. Ibid., 87. Armstrong notes "disdain for economic activities among the Russian intelligentsia" and temptation to join the nobility among other native economically affluent groups. Ibid., 89.

[63] Bartlett, *Chekhov*. In 1897, 39 percent of the empire's Jews engaged in commerce and trade and 35.4 percent in manufacturing and crafts. Jews faced restrictions on residence in rural areas. Altshuler, *Soviet Jewry*, 7, 8.

[64] See Blackwell, "Old Believers"; Buss, "Economic Ethics." In a famous eyewitness treatise on pre-reform Russia, one observer wrote: "The Old Believers are in general much more simple, moral, sober, and reliable than the other Russian peasants." In education, they are "far superior to the other Russians ... They sharpen their minds with theological subtleties." Haxthausen, *Studies*, 136.

a historical presence of Greek (in the south), Baltic German (in the northwest), and Jewish (in the empire's western reaches) communities where merchant enterprise thrived; (4) settlement in territories that served as penal colonies, particularly in Siberia, where not only individual political exiles like the writer Fyodor Dostoevsky, as well as many rebellious aristocrats, were sent but also members of specific ethnic communities who settled and established colonies in large numbers – like the Poles in Siberia, often belonging to *meshchane* and noble estates; (5) patterns of colonization of territories into which individuals of nonmainstream beliefs self-selected – including those communities already listed – namely schismatics, members of sects like the Molokans,[65] and those seeking to disappear into the wilderness because of looming persecution and to establish a new life as respectable bourgeois – one such group would be Poles in the Middle Volga or Siberia who were exiled or escaping persecution for national liberation impulses; (6) the imperatives of establishing an imperial footprint in sparsely populated lands in Siberia and the Far East where the Orthodox clergy had a marked population share; and (7), of course, particularly after emancipation, the movement of peasants either engaged as seasonal workers while maintaining attachment to the land or establishing urban status through property ownership and trade in their own *gubernii*, as well as those state peasants before and after emancipation who settled in faraway *gubernii* to help consolidate state control over the frontier and who enjoyed the concomitant freedoms not bestowed on serfs.[66]

Estates, Education, and Professional Institutions

Up to now, I have focused on how the estate as a legal category and social practice shaped popular responses to, and opportunities and restrictions in the context of, imperial Russia's statecraft, development, and expansion. I here provide further detail on the human capital dimension of the estate. Table 2.2 reports the estate composition of the pupil body of secondary educational establishments in 1914. In male gymnasia, nobles dominate all other groups, in a far higher proportion to their population share (1.5 percent in 1917 as per

---

[65] On this sect, influenced by European Protestant teachings, see *Studies*, 150–56.

[66] On steppe colonization in the North Caucasus, Lower and Middle Volga, and Trans-Ural regions, see Sunderland, *Taming*. On Siberian settlement, land tenure, and penal exile, see Treadgold, *Great Siberian Migration*. On exile and colonies, see also Kennan, *Siberia*, 1; and Hartley, *Siberia*, 115–30. On internal migration, spatial variations in land tenure, and restrictions on movement, see also Moon, *The Plough*; and Moon, "Peasant Migration." On German settlers, see Schippan and Striegnitz, *Wolgadeutsche*; and Koch, *Volga Germans*. For a concise history of Mennonites, descendants of Germanized Dutch Anabaptists, regarded as model settlers, see Sunderland, *Taming*, 117–18; and on Jewish farmer frontier colonies and state policy encouraging resettlement from formerly Polish lands, see ibid., 118–22. On post-emancipation peasant migration, see Burds, *Peasant Dreams*.

TABLE 2.2 *Shares of the different estates in the pupil body, 1914*

	Middle (*srednye*) Technical Colleges	Men's Gymnasia	*Real'nyye uchilishcha*	Women's Gymnasia
Total pupils	8,272	147,751	80,800	311,637
Nobility	10.71% Hereditary: 259 (3.13%)/ Personal and officials: 627 (7.6%)	32.67% Hereditary: 12,618 (8.54%)/ Personal and officials: 35,659 (24.13%)	22.57% Hereditary: 4,776 (5.9%)/ Personal and officials: 13,465 (16.66%)	21.9 % Hereditary: 17,005 (5.45%)/ Personal and officials: 51,250 (16.44%)
Clergy	1.85% 153	5.66% 8,360	2.84% 2,296	4.85% 15,114
Merchants and honorary citizens	5.31% 440	10.03% 14,832	9.54% 7,715	9.6% 29,889
Meshchane and artisans	35% 2,892	26.82% 39,625	29.6% 23,953	35.23% 109,787
Peasants	42% 3,471	19.74% 29,167	27.34% 22,094	23.17% 72,220

Note. Includes territories outside of present-day Russia.
Source. Data based on Ministry of Public Enlightenment reports for 1913; compiled by Anfimov and Korelin, "Rossiya 1913 god," 332–33; table 5. Percentages calculated by author.

the social pyramid presented in Figure 2.1), but *meshchane* are not far behind and are in fact also proportionately *overrepresented*.

The figures are also suggestive of the embeddedness of the estate in professional bodies, which, as I shall discuss in Chapters 4 and 5, were appropriated as *Soviet* after 1917. The *meshchane* estate is noticeable in the practically oriented technical colleges and "real schools" (*real'nyye uchilishcha*) that offered modern and practical subjects – these fed pupils into engineering and other technical professions. In women's gymnasia, while the share of nobles is high, the *meshchane* predominate as the single largest estate category. In the first decades of Bolshevik rule, the Soviet teaching profession, overwhelmingly feminized, would be heavily made up of the *meshchane*. The gender aspect of estatism in educational institutions is noteworthy. Education is among the professions least subjected to Stalinist purges; women were also less likely than men to suffer repressions.[67] Typically, the *meshchane* constituted between a quarter and a third of the pupil body across the different types of secondary and higher institutions, bar veterinary colleges where learners of clerical origin predominated.[68] The evidence that we possess about this estate also strongly indicates social heterogeneity – the more privileged segment of the *meshchane* opted for gymnasia over technical colleges. The share of merchants in elite secondary institutions – male and female – appears to be modest, at 10 percent, but, as with nobles, it constitutes a dramatic *overrepresentation*, in proportion to their population. Modern professional and educational institutions absorbed the society of the estates and nurtured the estatist society of post-imperial Russia.

Understanding the Inter-temporal Resilience of the Four-Estate Paradigm

Why did the social gradations of a bygone feudal order continue to find reflection in education and professions considering the far-reaching changes in the institution of estates following the Great Reforms? To answer this question, we need to go back to the Petrine-era policy initiatives that were designed to inject achievement into social advancement. Peter the Great's creation, the Table of Ranks (*Tabel' o rangakh*), represented a hierarchical structure of civil service progression based on merit. Everyone, including hereditary nobles, had to ascend it from the bottom rank upward, with material rewards and elevated esteem at every rung on the ladder. Inaugurated in 1722, the system survived with modifications until 1917.[69] During the reign of Tsar Alexander I (1801–25), professionals outside of administrative and ministerial service – engineers, teachers, librarians, medics – joined Crown civil servants.

---

[67] See Ilic, "The Forgotten." The gender dimension of the legacy warrants separate research.
[68] See Pykhalov, "Obrazovaniye," table 5, 199.
[69] In practice, connections and patronage also played a role. Mironov, *Rossiyskaya imperiya*, 2:499–500, 508.

Comprising some 10 percent of officialdom, these professionals became employees under the authority of ministerial agencies, enjoying a stable salaried income and pensions on a par with bureaucratic functionaries.[70]

The Table of Ranks meshed with the classification of estates – indeed, the "noble" category signified crown achievement in the structure of progression for the non-noble. Fourteen ranks detailed an elaborate hierarchical structure of titles – *Kantsler*, (chancellor), *Deystvitel'nyy taynyy sovetnik* (actual privy councilor), *Deystvitel'nyy statskiy sovetnik* (actual state councilor), *Kollezhskiy assessor* (collegiate assessor), and so forth – as well as their rights, duties, and criteria for admission.[71] It represented a system open at the stage of entry – anyone, regardless of origin, could begin ascending the ladder to reach the highest point on something like the "spine" of a modern civil service bureaucracy. By the end of the nineteenth century, the "new nobility" of *chinovniki*, who obtained the status of noble through service, constituted 66 percent of the estate.[72] Peculiar to these reforms was a combination of merit as an essential criterion of progression and the ascriptive aspect of estate titles. Reaching a certain level on the "spine" earned one the title of a personal noble, while advancing higher earned a hereditary one. Crown service had been largely an urban occupation – 75 percent of officials and professionals were based and employed in cities, although only 13 percent of the population resided in urban areas according to the 1897 census.[73]

At the outset, education was *the* key criterion for admission and ascent, and educational restructuring went hand in hand with civil service reforms. If merit, not birth, determined career advancement, systematic criteria were urgently needed to evaluate the quality of entrants. According to a 1737 imperial stipulation, even before entering service, children of nobles were to undergo a rigorous system of assessments at ages seven, twelve, sixteen, and twenty; from age twelve, pupils were required to take exams in reading, writing, religious teachings, arithmetic, geometry, geography, history, and fortifications.[74] Even as Peter III with his February 18, 1762 manifesto freed nobles from obligatory state service, the injunction to pursue education remained "such that no one would dare to raise their children without teaching them science [*nauka*]."[75] Because aristocratic education – in specialized institutions and in the home, with tutors – became a *sine qua non*

[70] Ibid., 434.
[71] Speranskiy, *Polnoye sobraniye*, 486–93, available from the online portal of the Russian National Library: nlr.ru/e-res/law_r/search.php?part=28&regim=3 (accessed May 28, 2020). On service ranks and social obsession with them, see also Reyfman, *How Russia Learned to Write*.
[72] Mironov, *Rossiyskaya imperiya*, 2:295.   [73] Ibid., 434.
[74] Ibid., 38. On the rigid system of examinations preparing for service, and the obsession with education to secure coveted service positions, see also Raeff, *Origins*, 131–35.
[75] Discussed and cited in Mironov, *Rossiyskaya imperiya*, 2:39. Put differently, "the obligation to serve also implied the obligation to be educated." Raeff, *Origins*, 131.

for a service career and material comforts, it conserved extant social structures inhering within the system of estates.

The Great Reforms are evocative of a shattering effect on the landed gentry's wealth. Yet, while serfdom disappeared, the Table of Ranks endured. As Mironov notes, although free from obligatory state service, "for many nobles state service was proving to be essential due to material difficulties (since the vast majority of nobles were poor and existed only on salary), for a few – due to considerations of honor [*chestolyubiye*]."[76] It is precisely when serfdom was abolished that civil service and education, providing an entry ticket into both traditional service and modern occupations, acquired increased significance as sources of stable income. The hitherto privileged estates – due to birth, prior serf ownership, or achievement – were most advantaged at this juncture,[77] since they could convert the remnants of their wealth into paid-for education for their children or could afford to pay for it if they were already blessed with a salaried *chin* (bureaucratic title), enabling human capital investment.

While nobles, already habitually practicing classical education, could buy their way into the modern trades, hedging against the financial vagaries of the zenith of serfdom, the merchant, already numerate and literate, could invest their newly acquired wealth in the education of their offspring, and the clergy would typically sail through the gymnasium entrance exam because of the habitual education that began in the home. The resulting education patterns were heavily skewed toward these free estates. As the pyramid in Figure 2.1 shows, for instance, merchants may have nationally constituted 0.2 percent of the population, but, in 1914, 10 percent of male and female gymnasia and *real'nyye uchilishcha* pupils were merchants or honorary citizens – the latter often of merchant background who had distinguished themselves in civic affairs or philanthropy. The merchant estate also featured an increasing trend of intergenerational material wealth transfer at the start of the twentieth century.[78]

At its zenith, the imperial state pursued a series of educational reforms. These conserved the combination of exam-based selection and wealth as the two pillars that structured access, since Russia never set up a universal system of *free* gymnasium education even if it made it legally accessible to all irrespective of estate. Indeed, the estate found its way into the Enlightenment Ministry's Charter on Gymnasia and Pro-gymnasia of 1864, which stipulated that these institutions "are maintained either at government expense or that of communities [*obshchestva*], estates or private persons."[79] According to item

---

[76] Mironov, *Rossiyskaya imperiya*, 2:40. See also Raeff, *Origins*, who argued that even after elimination of the compulsory aspect, "state service remained the most popular way of life for the nobility," 11–12.

[77] Among the nonserving lesser gentry "degradation" and "lumpenization" after emancipation exacerbated issues of estate fragmentation that stemmed from equal inheritance for male heirs. Mironov, *Rossiyskaya imperiya*, 1:359–60.

[78] Ibid., 395.   [79] Lyubzhin, *Istoriya russkoy shkoly*, 283.

79 detailing residential "pensions" (*pansiony*), "children of all estates were to be admitted, but in the pension maintained with funding from one estate, boarders of other estates were to be accepted only subject to consent of the representative of the estate maintaining the pension."[80]

The Charter recognized both state authority over gymnasia and their autonomy – in effect, conserving the estate in modern institutions of learning. Gymnasium teachers were to be part of the bureaucratic structure of the Table of Ranks. Headmasters and inspectors were to be approved by the minister of public enlightenment and the district overseer, respectively. Once appointed, these individuals would have freedom and discretion in hiring teachers and other staff, subject to the superintendent's approval.[81] The bureaucratization of a modern system of education thus remained embedded in the self-governing institutions of the estates; educational bodies retained considerable leeway in hiring and admissions; and, reliant as they were largely on private funding, were incentivized to maintain paid-for instruction accessible to the wealthy estates. Essentially, we observe the investment of wealth derivative of the estates-based social order into human capital at key junctures of progressive reforms. The juridical rights of privileged estates continued to be embedded in elements of educational access;[82] even at the apogee of the Russian empire, the nobility tried to block, derail, or otherwise water down policies to broaden social access to secondary schooling.[83]

Estates and the Public Sphere

The institution of the estate would have consequences for the political sphere or, more accurately, the public sphere as it functioned as an intermediating domain between the social and the political. A bimodal society cleaved the educated free from the illiterate unfree and engendered a bimodal public sphere, one in which certain estates had received *early entry* to the channels of access to political, economic, and social resources, and one which facilitated individual and group autonomy within an otherwise autocratic state. Fluidity, heterogeneity, and complexity in the interpenetration and permutation of the estate and the social groups and institutions that governed their relationships and freedoms of course matter in my analysis. Even within the highly fluid, spatially, and horizontally heterogenous processes, we may discern estates-derived social cleavages that spilled out into the arenas of the public domain.

The estate corporation or society (*obshchestvo*), which governed the various estates' rights, duties, and obligations, epitomized the inequitable hierarchy of

---

[80] Ibid., 292.   [81] Ibid., 284.

[82] Elite military *kadet* schools catered to the aristocracy; seminaries mostly trained children of clergy. Mironov, *Rossiyskaya imperiya*, 1:343. Home tutors and elite boarding schools were habitual in nobles' upbringing, since at least the late eighteenth century. Raeff, *Origins*, 122–47.

[83] Becker, *Nobility and Privilege*, 120–29.

status, with both material and symbolic implications, something evident in the various estate corporations' distinct participatory and decision-making prerogatives and autonomy. The nobles' corporate assemblies (*dvoryanskiye obshchestva*) were endowed with superior privileges as compared to those of the urban estates – not least in the area of tax obligations.[84] The corporations did not cease to matter after the Great Reforms, since new self-governance institutions that were set up to expand citizen, including peasant, autonomy in deciding on matters of local welfare coexisted with, and were coconstitutive of, the estate societies.[85] Further, by many accounts, the aristocracy continued to derive esteem, material welfare, and communal support from their service in provincial nobles' assemblies;[86] and the urban corporations drew renewed vigor from the mounting responsibilities for social services provision as the population of towns increased.[87] Smith sources new archival evidence of vigilance in the merchant and *meshchane*-run urban societies as late as 1914 in dictating the rules of entry and exclusion for urban citizenship. The corporation evolved from one "based primarily in individual obligation to the society, to something based primarily in the society's obligation to its members,"[88] a proto-civic aspect that others perusing papers of provincial *meshchane* corporations also observed – one, however, that was inseparable from the institution of the estate.[89] Reminiscent of Weberian church communities and their screening practices, these bodies assessed "moral worth" and creditworthiness – new entrants were asked to supply certificates from others in the community vouching for these credentials.[90] Urban corporations in the most developed cities and towns devised ever more stringent criteria for initiation into the *Bürgertum* to cope with the influx of peasants and other groups, some offloaded by ministerial agencies seeking to ensure that everyone had an estate designation for classificatory, taxation, and other purposes.[91] The exclusionary practices of estate corporations helped

---

[84] Mironov, *Rossiyskaya imperiya*, 2:40; 1:341. Personal nobles were also de facto excluded from the nobles' communities/corporations. Ibid., 344–45.

[85] Kobozeva, "Meshchanskaya povsednevnost'," 168–72.

[86] Even young nobles often preferred estate service over state and military service. Leadership of local nobles' assemblies also served as a springboard to *guberniya* and metropolitan positions in government. Kabytov et al., *Zhizn' i sud'ba*, esp. 43–73.

[87] The *meshchane*'s estate corporation (*meshchanskoye obshchestvo*) arguably provided a glue that united disparate individuals within an urban setting. Kobozeva, "Gorod i meshchane," 52.

[88] Smith, *For the Common Good*, 150.

[89] On complaints against post-emancipation "external elements" (*prishlyye elementy*) "lacking knowledge," "imposed" on the community, and as a drain on budgets, notably medical costs, of *meshchane uprava*, which has to take money away from needy *meshchane* to pay for the costs of undeserving peasant and decommissioned soldier newcomers, see the 1885 example of the petition in Samara in Kobozeva, *Meshchanskoye sosoloviye*, 188–90.

[90] Weber, "'Churches' and 'Sects.'"

[91] Petrine laws freed nobles and clergy from military draft and soul tax associated with low status. Smith, *For the Common Good*, 34–35. By the end of the nineteenth century, the soul

further accentuate the social distinction between the more privileged estates – the proto-middle class in class parlance – and the peasant, a cleavage that remained as toilers of the soil and low-paid laborers streamed into the cities in the 1920s and onward.

Let us now consider the more generic, all-encompassing, institutions of self-rule that evolved in the eighteenth and nineteenth centuries, the precursors to inclusive, citizenship-based, rather than estate ascription-based, democratic governance. The *zemstvo* bodies of province and district self-government established as part of the Great Reforms have received disproportionate attention in the literature on imperial Russia's political liberalization and, to an extent, justifiably so.[92] As Thomas Pearson notes, state attempts to control them notwithstanding, notably via a special statute adapted in 1890, the *zemstva* "remained relatively autonomous institutions that became cells of political opposition to the autocracy."[93] Yet foundational local governance institutions established for the benefit of the "citizen" (*grazhdanstvo*) segment of the bimodal society date back to the last quarter of the eighteenth century – these institutions

tax to the central state was no longer collected and local corporations only collected local taxes. Writes Smith: "The responsibilities of *soslovie* societies had shifted from facing outward – from acting as a conduit for the payment of the soul tax to the center – to facing inward, dealing with local taxes and providing services." Ibid., 151. On citizenship implications of the tax reforms, whereby individual tax responsibility displaced the collective one, see Kotsonis, "Face-to-Face."

[92] See essays in Emmons and Vucinich, *Zemstvo*. On *zemstvo* reforms, see Pearson, *Russian Officialdom in Crisis*, 21–59; and Starr, *Decentralization*. The two volumes largely focus on policy debates and key lobby groups and both skirt over the parallel estate-based institutions of urban governance. Starr, for instance, refers to "the so-called urban classes" whose "political significance ... was minimal." Ibid., 7. There is no discussion of the *meshchane* as an estate. For pioneering analysis of the social composition of *zemstva* and allocation of public goods employing panel data, see Nafziger, "Did Ivan's Vote Matter?." Elections were based on curia: rural and urban property owners and peasant village communes elected local assembly (*sobranie*) members; the executive arm was the *uprava*. Peasants were allocated a minority of seats and landlords, mostly nobles, ended up with the majority of seats in the assemblies. Ibid., 394. On the spatial distribution of *zemstva*, which were initially established in thirty-four provinces only, see ibid., 397. The paper focuses on landlord and peasant curia while eschewing discussion of the second curia of merchant and urban "classes," which is in my view indicative of the general scholarly neglect of *meshchanstvo*. Interestingly, Nafziger finds that the "new" nobility of small landholders ennobled through service – which we may surmise included honored citizens originating in the merchant and *meshchane* urban estates and wealthy enough to buy land – are considered as the *zemstvo*'s liberal wing – these groups opposed conservative gentry in assembly proceedings. Ibid., 428.

[93] Pearson, *Russian Officialdom in Crisis*, 212. For division of opinion on the *zemstvo*'s political significance, see Nafziger, "Did Ivan's Vote Matter?" 395; and on the 1890 statute, ibid., 405. The conservative reforms increased the curia of landlords and urban property owners while reducing those of peasant communities. Ibid., 405–6. For a breakdown in representation by estate in district assemblies and executive boards, see table 3b, 406. The figures indicate that, in the district assemblies for 1890–93, nobles were significantly overrepresented (55.2 percent), merchants and "urban classes" somewhat overrepresented (13.8 percent), and peasants significantly underrepresented (31 percent) if we consider their overall population share. Ibid., 406.

continued to function parallel to the *zemstvo* and estate societies; they "collected their own taxes and acted as alternative suppliers of public goods and services."[94] The contours of Catherine's 1775 decentralization reforms remained basically intact until the fall of the monarchy.[95] Within rural settings, local administration remained in the hands of the landed gentry, not peasants, while the free urban estates gradually developed autonomy, civic consciousness, and a concern for the common good of the city, township, or hamlet.[96] As Zoya Kobozeva writes,

> Contrary to what is established from a historiographical point of view that before the 1860s the state appropriated part of the functions of local self-government and only in the reform period delegated them to local society [*obshchestvennost'*], it is precisely in the pre-reform period that the urban *meshchane* and merchants created their own model of "urban citizenship" "from below" regarding a city's needs as their own, from the position of work ethic and the psychology of "the proprietor" [*khozyain*].[97]

Catherine's urban charter sanctioned the formation of "civic society" (*obshchestvo grazhdanskoye*) with its own meeting place, an archive, seal, and mandate to form generic and estates-based, citywide, or intra-urban district assemblies. A study of mid-nineteenth-century Samara sheds light on the implementation of the charter in practice. Electors were citizens aged twenty-five and over who owned capital with interest at a set level. Those eligible to vote selected the city head (*gorodskoy golova*), burgomasters, executive members to the city magistrate (*ratmany*), merchant and *meshchane* "elders" (*starosty*), and judges (*slovesnyye sud'yi*).[98] Each city district was entitled to elect elders and deputies charged with making entries to the urban register (*obyvatel'skaya kniga*) confirming residence, property ownership, and inheritance. The general urban assembly (*obshchaya duma*) that met once every three years elected a six-member *duma* (*shestiglasnaya duma*) made up of the urban estates that was to meet at least once weekly. Aside from basic public order and record-keeping functions, the *duma* was also charged with general welfare, trade, and enterprise. Revenue and expenditures, including for the foundation of schools and public buildings, and comprising customs dues, fees, levies from property, and income from the merchant and *meshchane* trades, were also within the purview of the *dumy*.[99]

---

[94] Nafziger, "Did Ivan's Vote Matter?" 417.

[95] Instead of eleven, fifty provinces subdivided into twenty districts were established with the Tsar-appointee governor-general as provincial chief executive. Pearson, *Russian Officialdom in Crisis*, 2.

[96] Ibid., 3.   [97] Kobozeva, "Meshchanskaya povsednevnost'," 173. Author's translation.

[98] A large fire in 1850 destroyed many of Samara's urban chronicles. Surviving records describe how ballots in election every three years to the urban assembly, the *golova*, magistrates, *ratmany*, *meshchane* and merchant elders, among other officials, were carried out using special ballot "balls." Ibid., 182–83. Qualities like "good behavior" and no record of "sins" or of unsettled penalties were criteria for candidacy. Ibid., 183.

[99] Ibid., 166–67.

The estate, as is evident from stipulations concerning the urban bodies, remained formally embedded in the "civic" *obshchestva* and continued to be relevant for the de facto, informal, aspects of their day-to-day operations. In that sense, these precursors to autonomous civic–public domains that were institutionally separate or quasi-independent from Crown power exhibited very similar characteristics to the bifurcations that scholars have come to associate with the *zemstva*.[100] Thus, the "elders" (*starosty*), formally subordinate to the urban head (*gorodskoy golova*), represented and pursued the corporate interests of the urban estate on whose behalf they acted.[101] Within the generic structure of urban self-governance, the lower-level clerks, debt collectors, surveyors, and the like were elected by, and maintained authority over the affairs of, the specific urban estate – merchants, artisans, and *meshchane*.[102]

Institutions, identities, and resources intrinsic to the estate also shaped opportunities and restrictions alike, as to how far the various groups sought to engage in, take advantage of, or eschew participation in these bodies. Thus, in many provincial towns, nobles often avoided membership on the all-estate local assemblies, considering public association with the lower free estates of merchants, artisanry, and *meshchane* beneath them and preferring to restrict

---

[100] Pearson, *Russian Officialdom in Crisis*. For an excellent discussion of the continued role of the estate in local governance after the Great Reforms, see Starr, "Local Initiative." I disagree with Starr's broad-brush dismissal of the substantive role of urban assemblies before and after the Great Reforms, but many of the insights corroborate my angle on estate. Starr argues that the institutionalization of the estate under Catherine II strengthened corporate interests and identities of the three estates of peasants, townsmen, and nobles. The powers, resources, and revenue-generating possibilities in pre-*zemstvo* estate-corporate and urban assemblies were limited, but an impulse to better their own members was not absent, and practices to subvert state authority and dodge corporate tax levies developed. Estate institutions fostered distinct identities, conflicts, and cleavages, "pitting town against countryside," but also town against gentry, as when the gentry were allowed to own manufacturing and trading enterprises, which "nullified the privilege that had defined the urban estate as a group," as did the right granted to the urban gentry to membership in urban guilds and via the guilds in elected town government granted in 1807. Ibid., 18. Rather than the role of the estate being diminished after emancipation, each estate now had "ample grounds for asserting its needs and interests more vigorously than before." Ibid., 26. Some estates were clearly more privileged in the substantive aspects of local governance. Whether gentry or urban estate, "both were accustomed to deal with larger sums of money than was the peasantry." These patterns resulted in distinct estate-related "political cultures" and "differing corporate sense" that was then brought into the *zemstvo*. Ibid., 20. Here, too, one's estate mattered. Thus, as a service estate, "a status that continued de facto long after it had been eliminated de juris in 1762, the gentry could boast thousands of members with a good knowledge of both state law and bureaucratic procedure, skills that they were able to apply to their advantage in the zemstvos." Ibid., 21. And "gentry marshalls, urban magistrates, and peasant elders inevitably felt somehow beholden to the members of the estate that had elected them to office." Ibid., 23. Because ministerial agencies were not replicated locally and there was limited integration among state and estate institutions, provincial officials often felt "a sense of utter powerlessness." Ibid., 25.

[101] Kobozeva, "Meshchanskaya povsednevnost'," 167–68.   [102] Ibid., 168.

their activities to the narrowly estate-based nobles' corporations or the more prestigious state service.[103] In turn, urban estates often showed resistance to the aristocrats' and state bureaucrats' influence on urban affairs.[104] Local governance bore the stamp of the merchant–*meshchane* alliance in many provincial towns as a result. Aside from the times and settings when the prestige and significance of the town dictated otherwise, much like work in the *zemstvo* for the already overworked *meshchanin* or artisan, the "civic" duties, usually unpaid, were often regarded as an onerous imposition on scarce time.[105]

Yet these institutions were proto-democratic. They were proto-democratic because of their elective essence and because they carried the expectation of moral worth, trustworthiness, and social respectability, attached to service therein as well as provided experiences of working for the broader public good. Property criteria made it clear that only *free* burghers who made a defined contribution to the public purse in terms of taxation, and hence those, presumably, with an interest in how dues were levied and monies spent, were eligible. However modest the estate corporation as a representation of a democratic institution – the Crown-appointed *guberniya* governors maintained formal control over them – their significance is again revealed in the contrast with social groups and estates on which meaningful local autonomy had not been bestowed. The question of self-governance for former serfs resembling the already long-established quasi-assemblies benefiting the free urban estates only arose during the 1860s reforms; and, even with the rural *zemstva* in place, local assemblies came to be dominated by landlords, that is, the gentry, not the peasant.[106] Of course, all the estates – including serfs – enjoyed some form of estate-based or communal self-governance even at the height of absolutism, not least because there were too few state functionaries to micromanage the localities across the empire's vast reaches.[107] The difference is that some, like the nobles, clergy, and merchants, obtained the status of free citizens with more substantive autonomy to govern their estate and localities early on, followed by the *meshchane*, while manorial peasants, who, unlike the other estates had not just the state as a layer of authority over them but also the lord – with a lag of nearly a hundred years after the *meshchane*. As Mironov notes, "the trading-industrial population of cities, more than any other social group of Russian society, understood the importance of individual rights for successful economic activity in the sphere of commerce, artisan pursuits and industry." It therefore fought tooth and nail to curb state expropriations of urban property, demanded respect for private property, and secured the

---

[103] Also true for rural assemblies. Pearson, *Russian Officialdom in Crisis*, 7–8.

[104] Kobozeva, "Meshchanskaya povsednevnost'," 170, 173. The study covers the 1850s and 1860s.

[105] Ibid., 169, 174.   [106] Pearson, *Russian Officialdom in Crisis*, 95.

[107] Particularly on the serf commune, see Dennison, *Russian Serfdom*, esp. 98–127.

establishment of special estate courts governed by law.[108] By the end of the eighteenth century, urban communes of elected burghers acquired juridical person status, while the state peasants' communes obtained these rights in the 1840s, and manorial peasants did so only in the 1860s.[109]

The time–space dimension of how we ought to regard the autonomy, meaningfulness, and *estatism* of local self-government is important here of course.[110] The *Gorodovoye ulozheniye* (urban code) of 1870 was a milestone in local governance reforms, since it endowed all urban residents with voting rights based on property ownership and tax contributions rather than their estate.[111] Broader conceptions of citizenship animated the new urban local self-governing assemblies and their executive bodies. We also observe regional variations in the configurations, extent, and practices of local governance. While in some urban settings state authority determined local affairs, elsewhere citizen initiative was paramount.[112] The significance of partaking in urban bodies from the perspective of the allocation, distribution, and spread of resources (or rent) among the various social groups also rose as the empire industrialized, effecting a concomitant shift toward a – albeit at times uneasy, awkward, or conversely, highly fruitful – cohabitation among the most wealthy and powerful estates, with the merchants and the nobles as the agenda setters and power holders. This was the case in Moscow, where merchants had come to run the city but with the participation of leading aristocrats;[113] and this is what we observe in Samara, as I discuss in Chapter 3.

Whether in the *zemstvo* or the urban *duma* and *uprava*, officials, elected or appointed, were simultaneously embedded concentrically in the equally if not more significant institutional domains of *service* and the professions and indeed the estate corporation – and these, as discussed, had been circumscribed in terms of the estate. Indeed, historians continue to mull over the question as to whether it was the *zemstvo* as an institution or the "third element" of hired "physicians, teachers, statisticians," who displaced the gentry in influence, that account for the *zemstva*'s success in public service provision in the last two or

[108] Mironov, *Rossiyskaya imperiya*, 2:47.   [109] Ibid., 249.

[110] Some scholars contend that only in the last quarter of the nineteenth century did local government bodies begin to play a meaningful role in urban affairs. See the discussion in Kobozeva, "Meshchanskaya povsednevnost'," 181.

[111] On the reforms' implications for the *meshchane*, see ibid. Kobozeva sees the "golden era" of the *meshchane*'s contribution to urban governance in the preceding period, when local assemblies retained a corporatist, estate-based, character. Ibid., 110. Concerning urban property rights and the exclusion of farming townspeople as councils sought to establish control over urban land, see also Wirtschafter, *Social Identity*, 138–39.

[112] Kobozeva, "Meshchanskaya povsednevnost'," 168. Thus, in Simbirsk, the *guberniya* administration "fully controlled the work of city dumas [and] interfered with urban affairs." Ibid., 177.

[113] On merchants supporting the mayoralty of Prince V. M. Golitsyn in 1897, see Rieber, *Merchants*, 109; and Golitsyn, *Zapiski*, 22–23.

three decades of empire.[114] By the beginning of the twentieth century, Russia's professions acquired the contours of modern corporate identities, resources, and resourcefulness as well as a civic and public consciousness – all conducive to the mutual embeddedness of institutions of local governance, old and new, and the occupational service realms. Yet these mutually networked and embedded spheres showed fissures along estate lines.[115]

Finally, sensitivity to the estate as configurating social status as well as the concomitant embeddedness of the institutions of the public sphere allows us to begin to explain the bimodal polity's resilience in the Bolshevik state. The co-constitutive nature of the estates, state service, local governance and the educational and professional institutions in the making of the public citizen is just as significant for understanding the structures of opportunity in the various public, civic, professional, and educational realms in tsarist Russia as it is for appreciating sources of survival under the Bolshevik regime.

OLD SOCIETY MEETS THE NEW BOLSHEVIK STATE

At the outset, I should say that there are no systematic analyses of the estate in the context of the Soviet project, bar the peasantry, which scholars usually approach as a class category and not with reference to the estates. The accounts that we have in the vein of "old-regime educated society meets new Bolshevik state" are overwhelmingly couched in references to the "bourgeoisie," "intelligentsia" or "former people," with a sprinkling of highly fragmented and unsystematic mentions of the aristocracy, clergy, or merchants.[116] Usually, references to the estates feature in accounts of Bolshevik attempts at co-optation or targeted repression and elimination. The *meshchane*, the most sizeable group after the peasantry, are virtually ignored beyond their passing significance as targets of the Bolsheviks' derision of the old, moneyed, and propertied bourgeoisie.[117] This is really astonishing considering the extent to which the estate permeated all aspects of life in

---

[114] Pearson, *Russian Officialdom in Crisis*, 240. Improvements in *zemstvo* work were also attributed to the 1890 *zemstvo* statute, which fostered greater coordination, professionalization, and commitment to service. Ibid., 240–42.

[115] Pedagogic professional associations featured divisions between primary school and rural teachers of peasant or lower middle-class origin and those in secondary schools, notably gymnasium teachers of noble, elite civil service, and clergy backgrounds: "As one teacher commented, the division of the profession into castes proved impossible to overcome." Ruane, *Gender*, 193. On the estate profile of historical societies, see Kaplan, *Historians*, 4–5. On fissures among merchants and *meshchane* along "caste" lines precluding broader coalescence of "class" interests among entrepreneurs, see Rieber, *Merchants*, 415, 280. On the "condescending" attitude of merchants toward *meshchane*, see ibid., 332; and on condescension of nobles toward merchants, see ibid., 45.

[116] References to the literature are in the discussion in this section and in the section "Conceptual Approaches to Society."

[117] See Dunham, *In Stalin's Time*.

imperial Russia – something that I hope to have conveyed to the reader in the earlier passages of this chapter.

Established accounts therefore suffer from two broad limitations that have hitherto obstructed the generation of theory concerning the reproduction of social structures in regimes seeking to exterminate and obliterate – once and for all – the bourgeoisie, capitalism, and inequalities. The first limitation has been discussed in Chapter 1 and concerns the fallacy of "rupture," whereby theoretically important questions like social stratification, inequalities, or the political system are analyzed within the paradigmatic framework of the new state, its ideology, and regime. The second limitation stems from the first, namely that any deviations, inadequacies, or departures are pegged to the happenings – policies, elite conflicts, institutional-bureaucratic dynamics – within the conceptual container of the triumphant regime and system – the political-elite realms that are detached from the social. It is thus that we have ceased to question what "Soviet" and "communist" really mean and whether such labels are appropriate – labels that essentialize the full palette of the societal-human experience with reference to the political system that neatly partitions the past from the present. Nevertheless, historical studies supply useful guideposts for understanding the general political frameworks within which imperial society reincarnated and functioned. Moreover, micro-level sociological studies, even if they rely on conventional sociodemographic categories devoid of operationalizations and measures anchored in the pre-communist past, provide a systematic portrait of resilience in social stratification that is equally valuable. This corroborating evidence, however, cries out for a systematic link to imperial society.

Stages in Bolshevik Policy on Class

As a starting point for dissecting inter-epoch social resilience, I faithfully reproduce what we know about the general contours of Bolshevik policy on class and the key social "milestones" of the immediate post-revolutionary period. I provide but a brief synopsis here both with the purpose of outlining factual reminders and to convey the flavor of how earlier analyses approached the question. The Bolsheviks, as is well known, saw society's key divisions as between the two antagonistic classes of the proletariat and the bourgeoisie. At the vanguard were the proletariat comprised of industrial workers allied with the landless and impoverished peasant class. The bourgeoisie encompassed industrialists, private traders, wealthy peasants, former nobles, and "bourgeois" intelligentsia, including members of the professions.[118] The expropriation and nationalization of land, banks, industrial holdings, real estate, and large and small merchant-run retail outlets in towns and in the countryside, as well as smaller properties, had immediate and profound

---

[118] Fitzpatrick, *Tear Off the Masks!*, 32.

effects on the material foundations of social stratification.[119] An October 1917 decree targeting the gentry and the well-off peasant alike revoked private land ownership.[120] Draconian policies of "class war" against prosperous peasants reached their crescendo with grain, cattle, and other requisitions as well as coerced collectivization in 1928–32.[121] In the towns, "consolidation" (*uplotneniye*) limited how much space the "bourgeois" could occupy in his or her own property; the rest was to be handed over to the new "proletarian" dwellers. Residents were expelled should they show resistance to communalization and the expropriation of private property and material possessions.[122] Another strategy to eliminate the bourgeoisie and the Revolution's other enemies, including the clergy, was to create a category of "the disenfranchised" (*lishentsy*), derived from the word *lishit'*, to deprive.[123] The *lishentsy* were not only robbed of the "quite platonic"[124] right to vote – as Moshe Lewin sarcastically writes – but also opportunities for public employment and housing, healthcare, or subsistence aid.[125]

Within less than a decade, the Bolsheviks relaxed and then abandoned key elements of the class vigilance that targeted the hitherto stigmatized groups. Regarding "old specialists" in particular, not only did the witch hunts ease off as a matter of state policy but overtures were made "inviting" them to work for the new regime. The most severe and targeted persecution of thousands of professionals occurred in the late 1920s. It began with the Shakhty affair in 1927–29 – the alleged infiltration of industry by "bourgeois" technical specialists.[126] Expulsions of pupils with a clergy, "kulak" (wealthy peasant), merchant, or tsarist official background from educational and professional institutions were also carried out.[127] The anti-bourgeois element of the "cultural revolution" ended with Stalin's 1931 speech about the need to end the "baiting of specialists."[128] A radical policy U-turn against "equality-mongering,"[129] it was attributed in large measure to the dissatisfaction with the results of the first five-year plan of 1928–32.[130] By 1931, the regime resolutely began to abandon its wholesale hostility toward the old

---

[119] Lewin, "Society," 58–59.   [120] Smith, *Former People*, 133–34.
[121] Fitzpatrick, "Cultural Revolution," 9. For a concise summary of the policy and recent estimates on deportees and excess deaths from collectivization, see Edele, *Stalinist Society*, 40–7.
[122] Smith, *Former People*, 132–33; 134.
[123] Alexopoulos, *Stalin's Outcasts*, 1. See also Lewin, "Society," 58–59.
[124] Lewin, "Society," 59.   [125] Alexopoulos, *Stalin's Outcasts*, 2–3.
[126] For details, see Bailes, *Technology*, 69–94. The Shakhty trial took place in 1928, but Bailes notes that the case began to develop toward the end of 1927. Bailes, *Technology*, 73.
[127] Fitzpatrick, "Cultural Revolution," 23.
[128] Inkeles, "Social Stratification," 256. On early Soviet class policy, see also Inkeles and Bauer, *Soviet Citizen*, 67–76.
[129] Inkeles, "Social Stratification," 256.
[130] Ibid., 256. Education also underwent reversal toward an emphasis on technical expertise. Bailes, *Technology*, 223.

intelligentsia in the institutions of the Bolshevik state;[131] and as the Soviet state discreetly dropped its obsessive record-keeping concerning the survival, reincarnation, and adaptation of the "bourgeoisie," so too vanished references to the old society, which were progressively displaced as scholars, both Soviet and Western, appropriated Soviet rhetoric on class.

Conceptual Approaches to Society

In discussing extant knowledge about the encounter of old-regime Russia with the Bolshevik project, I discern several influential perspectives at variance with my proposed analytical framework: the *Marxist class* perspective; the *Weberian bureaucratic* angle; and the *new elite* perspective.[132] Marxism-inspired accounts married assumptions about fundamental cleavages in society – as derived from the ownership of productive assets and the exploitation of labor – with Bolshevik class schemata where the proletariat is the vanguard stratum, the peasantry another exploited class, and the intelligentsia a *layer* lacking class attributes – neither an exploiter nor an exploited stratum. Accounts that I loosely group under the Weberian bureaucratic rubric shy away from Marxist class categories, highlighting instead the bureaucratic apparatus and its employees as engendering a new class of managers and professionals. What I label the *new elite* perspective became dominant in analyses of the communist polity, viewing social stratification through the prism of distinctions between the so-called new class of communist apparatchiks – party and managerial nomenklatura – and the rest of society. By way of offering a succinct critique of these three broad approaches, I discern how they dealt with questions fundamental to understanding the extent, nature, and magnitude of social change. Specifically: (1) How did scholars working from the vantage points of these broad paradigms see society? (2) How did they regard the transition of the old society into the new? (3) What implications do earlier paradigmatic perspectives have for understanding the values and interests of the various strata? Finally, (4) what evidence do we have at hand to allow us to interrogate these perspectives, justifying thereby the alternative paradigm presented in this book?

Marxism-inspired scholarship tended to embrace soviet categories of class and explored social transformation from the point of view of progress in the relational status of the "working class," "peasants," and "intelligentsia."[133] Serious historians, whose work remains foundational for understanding soviet social mobility – notably that of Sheila Fitzpatrick – exposed the trials of

---

[131] Bailes, *Technology*, 186.
[132] For an overview of Soviet-period literature on mobility and stratification, see Gerber and Hout, "Tightening Up."
[133] For a recent discussion of the Marxist class paradigm in relation to estates, see Confino, "Soslovie."

applying Marxist class schemata to old-regime Russia.[134] Yet Fitzpatrick's own analysis became solidly anchored in these same class configurations – a reflection of the internalization of Soviet discourse among scholars analyzing communist political systems across a variety of cognate disciplines. Classic work in this field is Fitzpatrick's account of mobility among the "proletarian" cadre of thousands of promoted workers (*vydvizhentsy*)[135] – via affirmative action quotas and other policies in a highly compressed time span.[136] In reading this work, one cannot help but perceive the ideological leanings of even the most serious and well-regarded scholars in interpreting – and exaggerating – the Bolsheviks' socially transformative achievements.[137] Fitzpatrick celebrated "the mass promotion of former workers and peasants into the Soviet political and social elite" as evidence of "a fulfilment of the promises of the revolution."[138] In this account, official statistics, with some caveats, are presented as evidence of the "spectacular" ascent of youth from "*working-class and peasant families*" into the ranks of "qualified specialists" trained in higher and specialized educational institutions in the 1930s.[139]

Underpinning the *Weberian bureaucratic* perspective is the emphasis on social status, rewards, and the agency of the technocratic intelligentsia and managerial apparatus. These groups ostensibly emerged consequential to the drive for industrialization and modernization more broadly.[140] The emphasis is on the corporate dimension of class construction – and specifically on the institutions, resources, skills, and leverage vis-à-vis the state and the Communist Party apparatus. The "old specialist" is present in research emphasizing the rising power of the bureaucratic class in the early post-revolutionary years.[141] Yet, because much of the relevant research – particularly in sociology – emerged during the later decades of communism, what is notable by its absence is the lack of systematic analysis of the social underpinnings of the prior social order in giving rise to the networks that might have sustained this apparatus; or indeed of the values *outside* of the narrow bureaucratic ones that fed, sustained, and reproduced those *within* a bureaucratic-corporate setting. The perspectives are technocratic, not society-centered in the sense proposed here; that is, they do not marry social structures with the institutions of the public sphere or public sector. The interests, values,

---

[134] Fitzpatrick, *Tear Off the Masks!*, 34.

[135] On the "Brezhnev generation" *vydvizhentsy*, see Fitzpatrick, "Cultural Revolution," 38–39.

[136] Ibid., 32–33. Fitzpatrick considers it "the positive corollary of the campaign against 'bourgeois' intelligentsia and the social purging of the bureaucracy," 32. As others rightly suggest, it is problematic to generalize about social mobility based on this one "Brezhnev generation" cohort of proletarian cadre catapulted into Soviet leadership positions from humble backgrounds via training in higher technical schools. David-Fox, *Revolution of the Mind*, 16.

[137] For a similar observation, see David-Fox, *Revolution of the Mind*, 16.

[138] Fitzpatrick, *Education*, 254.   [139] Ibid., 240–41 (emphasis added).

[140] See, for instance, Nove, "Is There."   [141] Bailes, *Technology*.

and incentives of the high-status group thus conceptualized are couched in terms of professional position and bureaucratic imperatives rather than as anchored in intergenerational estatist milieus that nurtured the ascent into these structures in the first instance.

Finally, what I label the *new elite* perspective – another variant of the *new class* view[142] – is preoccupied with the rise of the party-managerial stratum as the top layer in the social stratification pyramid – essentially embracing the values of the caste-like monarchical order of imperial Russia, along with the trappings of palatial residences, gourmet food, and privileges for the few. This perspective is associated with Milovan Djilas, himself a member of the inner circle of leadership in communist Yugoslavia; with the polemics of the exiled revolutionary Leon Trotsky about the "betrayal" of revolutionary ideals;[143] and with subsequent scholarly analyses of the ways in which the party and managerial apparatus became the embodiment of privilege and high status.[144] The émigré scholar Nicholas Timasheff famously represented these dynamics in the form of an inversion of the prior social pyramid – with the new ruling elite of revolutionaries at the top and the "former upper class" finding themselves at the bottom of the scale of power, status, and privilege.[145] Although Timasheff, like other detached observers of the subversion of communist ideals of social egalitarianism, remained deeply skeptical of the turgid claims by communist propagandists about their achievements, implicit in his analysis is the association between the immediate *material* aspects of the downfall of the formerly high-status groups and their de facto status in soviet society. While accepting that there were some "fellow-travelers" from among tsarism's relatively privileged strata at the top of the new class pyramid, which, he admits, had not been limited to the Communist Party machine but also included "leadership in cultural activity," these, he argues, mostly consisted of "the semi-intellectuals" from among "the former middle class."[146] Even after the adoption of the Stalin 1936 Constitution, which proclaimed a classless society, those disenfranchised in the 1920s, Timasheff insists, "continue to rest at the bottom of the social pyramid."[147] The author eschews analyzing how the new clique of political rulers may well coexist with a parallel world of

---

[142] A perspective that sees bureaucracies, technocrats, and intellectuals as a new class. Konrád and Szelényi, *Intellectuals*, xiv–xv. See also Gouldner, *Future of Intellectuals*; and Furaker, "Review Essay."

[143] Djilas saw "the roots of the new class ... in a special party, the Bolshevik type," with "professional revolutionaries" and "the party" as "the core of that class," and invoked Trotsky's argument of the mutation of the professional revolutionary into "Stalinist bureaucrat." Djilas, *New Class*, 39; Trotsky, *Revolution Betrayed*, e.g., 39–43; 187–93.

[144] Rigby, *Political Elites*, esp. 412–53. See also Timasheff, *Great Retreat*; Matthews, *Privilege*.

[145] Timasheff, *Great Retreat*, 296; on social changes captured in the pyramid, see ibid., 295–311. As to the future of the disenfranchised former upper class, "the group will disappear when the last individuals now belonging to it die." Ibid., 309.

[146] Ibid., 300–1.   [147] Ibid., 309.

the self-reproducing and organic old-regime society embedded in a vast network of knowledge institutions – and as such endowed with the resources, values, autonomy, and leverage to shape, mold, and subvert policy not just in the realm of the social but also in the political.

Whatever the perspective, we observe an abrupt shift in scholarly narratives from old-regime legacies toward new paradigms solidly anchored in the vocabulary of the revolutionizing state; and, even while proposing new ways of studying communist societies, or indeed even when critical of Marxist class categories, the theorizing overlooks and remains detached from pre-revolutionary social legacies. Preoccupied as they are with the formal architectures of political systems and bureaucratic apparatuses, these accounts are oblivious to the parallel, interlocking, or conflicting dynamics within the realm of the *social*. The temporal frame of the post-revolutionary order renders these analyses insensitive to the question of how social experience transcends the narrow time frame of the new regime's architecture and policies; or how segments of the old society may have colonized the ostensibly new institutions – their ethos may well have transcended the narrowly "bureaucratic" one to embrace the values of the social networks, groups, and individuals embedded within them; or, indeed, how we may think about institutionally incorporated knowledge enclaves harboring groups with a particular estate profile, as islands of social autonomy or even an oppositional public sphere. Moreover, they are insensitive to how society, even when not formally incorporated into the hydra of "communist" institutions, may impose its own rules, logic, and constraints on the official realm of policy.

To what extent did mainstream analyses of the communist social structure consider its implications for the political realm? As noted in Chapter 1, in sociological scholarship, this question featured in the paradigmatic wars between the so-called *modernizers* and the *Homo sovieticus* camps – these too were detached from old-regime social legacies.[148] The *modernizers* claimed victory in this debate as communist regimes crumbled – in a process led by professionals, intellectuals, and reformist communist elites. Their victory was short-lived as, soon thereafter, several formerly communist states came to hover

---

[148] This summary is based on Gerber, "Market." On Sovietology debates on the *exposure* versus the potentially "intellectually liberating effects" of Soviet schooling, see also Silver, "Political Beliefs," 101. Silver finds support for the "liberating effects" thesis: the better-educated respondents within every age cohort among Soviet Union émigrés to the United States in the 1970s were less supportive of the Soviet regime. Ibid., 116–18. The youngest cohort born in 1946–60 were "distinctly less supportive of the regime than older cohorts." Ibid., 118. Nevertheless, the finding that education holds as a predictor of regime norms across all cohorts, including for those born in the years 1916–25 (the oldest groups surveyed), may be interpreted as partly an artifact of the pre-communist social structure, something that Silver does not consider. The analytical referents are Soviet education, material satisfaction with public services and well-being, and the ways in which different generational cohorts experience the Soviet project.

on the precipice of illiberalism – their fragile embrace of democracy pinned to precisely the kinds of "legacies of communism"[149] that the *Homo sovieticus* camp had been highlighting some decades earlier – manifested in anti-market, illiberal, and anti-democratic attitudes.

Couched as they are in terms of *communist* policies – be that their modernizing or indoctrinating aspects – these debates about the democratic potential of Leninist societies are a poor guide for gauging the imprint of *old-regime* legacies as they make their way through the discursive fog of communist class jargon. My account underlines the significance of *cognitional*[150] aspects of a social legacy or the intergenerational maps that structure a well-charted progression through long-established institutions of learning and the professions and affecting positioning within the public sphere. I therefore consider the available evidence concerning the vibrancy of "below the waterline"[151] processes of social resilience beneath the thin veneer of the proclaimed new society.

Social Resilience: Extant Evidence

I distinguish between micro-evidence of social resilience – as revealed in the 1937 census and subsequent surveys concerning social mobility, evidence that most closely mirrors my own approach of identifying the estate as a marker that structures social-professional networks and hence adaptations, resilience, and reproduction within the confines of the soviet project – and corroborating data that speak to the nexus between bureaucratic-institutional and social-estate legacies.

Let us examine first individual-level data. Because the Soviet state abandoned references to old social categories of the estate and proclaimed the dawn of a new, classless, order, I discern social resilience via other markers of the old-regime society. One systematic source supplying individual-level data for the late 1930s is the long-concealed "Stalin" census. Leading statisticians and demographers were involved in designing the census, "carried out in line with the best traditions of Russian pre-revolutionary statistics."[152] The census was held on the eve of the Orthodox New Year, on January 6, 1937.[153] The whereabouts of the records remained unknown until researchers unearthed a portion of the files in the Russian State Archive of the Economy in the 1980s. Only a few dozen generic data tables survived; the detailed records that were to be published in roughly one hundred tomes, possibly containing

[149] Pop-Eleches and Tucker, *Communism's Shadow.*   [150] Simpser et al., "Dead but Not Gone."
[151] Pierson, "Power," 124.
[152] Zhiromskaya et al., *Polveka*, 143. On accessibility and quality of Soviet statistics, see Wheatcroft and Davies, "Crooked Mirror"; and on perceptions and doubts among Soviet statisticians of Soviet statistics, see Herrera, *Mirrors*, 144–45.
[153] Old-style Russian calendar. Zhiromskaya et al., *Polveka*, 5.

more than a million data tables, were not recovered.[154] What remains of the census – some aggregate tables and data and records of official discussions of the census results – indicates that the Soviet Union's high-level decision-makers did not anticipate, and were in fact aghast at, the results. After hectic discussions about massaging the data, the "defective" results were classified as "top secret."[155] Another census was held in 1939, one far more concerned about producing the "right" statistics than with revealing the population's true sociodemographic characteristics.[156] The intensification of repressions in 1937 could be seen in the light of attempts to destroy the elements of the old society that the surveys revealed to be alive and flourishing, and thereby bring the *real* society further into alignment with the *imaginary* society proclaimed in Stalin's constitution.[157]

So, what did Stalin not like about the census results? Much has been made of the fact that it exposed severe demographic problems caused by the excesses of collectivization, famine, and repressions. A less familiar fact is that the census contained detailed questions on occupations and sources of income; it is evident that the drafters sought to reflect the reality of the soviet occupational structure as accurately as possible. Many categories faithfully characterizing the full palette of occupational and income experience – including proprietor of a tavern, subsistence from renting out properties, rural property owner (*sel'skiy khozyain*), governess, lackey, and so on – were replicated from the dictionary of occupations from the first Soviet census in 1926, held only a few years after the Revolution.[158] The census revealed that, among women in particular, many derived their income from being *rentiers*.[159] The questionnaire prepared for the 1939 census contained fewer such categories, virtually eliminating the free, unofficial professions, proprietors of small eateries and tea rooms, and the clergy.[160] In the 1939 surveys, the figure for "nonworkers" (*ne-trudyashchiyesya*) is ten times(!) higher than in 1937 – presumably because various nonconventional occupations, the clergy, rentiers, paupers, prostitutes, and so on were grouped under this rubric.[161]

The data also corroborated that a significant share of the population remained illiterate or barely literate – contrary to propaganda that, by the mid-1930s, the Soviet Union reached virtual "universal literacy." Some 14 percent of all men and 33.8 percent of women at and over the age of nine were illiterate, although the criteria for "literacy" were very liberal. The census-takers entered anyone who claimed to be able to write one's surname and read letter to letter (*po slogam*) as literate. While among women of the 12–14 and

---

[154] Ibid., 3.   [155] Ibid., 136.   [156] Ibid., 136–39.
[157] I am grateful to Ul'yana Kulyanina for raising this point.
[158] Zhiromskaya et al., *Polveka*, 23, 24.
[159] Ibid., 76. The word "rentier" was not used. The questionnaire asked about living off of renting out properties. Ibid., 23, 19, 72, 142.
[160] Ibid., 24.   [161] Ibid., 72.

18–19 age groups only 5 percent and 11.5 percent, respectively, were illiterate, older women showed particularly low literacy levels. Among women aged 40–44, close to half, and 83 percent of those aged 60–64, were illiterate. Formal education beyond secondary school remained the exception not the rule. Nearly 60 percent of citizens aged sixteen claimed to be literate but lacked formal education. Only 4.3 percent of the population had completed high school (*sredneye obrazovaniye*) and only 0.6 percent had degrees from higher educational institutions.[162]

Subsequent scholarship documented the significance of education – of prior generations – in accounting for the enduring stratification.[163] Pioneering sociological studies of social structure and mobility were conducted in the Siberian region of Novosibirsk in the 1950s and 1960s. Researchers examined the social makeup of the 1962–65 cohorts of school leavers. The findings were laced with obligatory references to Soviet achievements in eradicating inequalities in society: "Establishment of the social relationships of socialism led to enormous social shifts in our society and made for an extraordinarily high social mobility," claimed the authors. "*This process continues energetically.*"[164] The data nevertheless served to deflate those very claims.[165] In what is corroborated in repeated series of surveys elsewhere in the Soviet Union, already at secondary school levels, "there are certain differentiating factors, the result of which is a certain filtering out of children of workers after completing the obligatory eight-year school instruction and an increase in the graduating year of the share of children of specialists and *sluzhashchiye* (white-collar employees) with higher education."[166] These broad patterns were confirmed in a recent study employing retrospective surveys of different age cohorts for a Russia-wide nationally representative population sample. The panel data cover the years 1994–2011, with a question on parental education inserted in 2006.[167] The surveys revealed that, among respondents born in the period 1946–60, 22 percent graduated from a "higher school." Among this cohort, the percentage with higher education rose to 67.4 percent if the mother had a university diploma, to 40.4 percent if she possessed secondary professional education, and to 31.1 percent if she had a high

[162] Ibid., 94–95.
[163] Scholars have taken up Sorokin's concept of "trendless fluctuation" (also "goalless fluctuation") and developed further in analyses of relative aspects of social mobility as opposed to those measured in absolute terms. Erikson and Goldthorpe, *Class Mobility*; Sorokin, *Social Mobility*. For a discussion, see Gordey Yastrebov, "Intergenerational Social Mobility in Soviet and Post-Soviet Russia." National Research University Higher School of Economics Basic Research Program Working Paper No. WP BRP 69/SOC/2016, February 3, 2016. ideas .repec.org/p/hig/wpaper/69-soc-2016.html (accessed November 9, 2020).
[164] Shubkin et al., "Quantitative Methods," 14 (emphasis added).   [165] Ibid.
[166] Astafyev and Shubkin, "Sotsiologiya obrazovaniya," 169.
[167] National Research University Higher School of Economics Russia Longitudinal Monitoring Survey (RLMS-HSE). hse.ru/rlms and www.cpc.unc.edu/projects/rlms (accessed April 11, 2020).

school diploma.[168] Thus, the educational chances of the offspring of mothers born around 1920–25 were significantly higher if the parent had been university educated. The discussion in the section "Estates and Human Capital" in this chapter makes evident that the probability of a semiliterate female worker or peasant possessing even a record of more than four years of schooling, let alone gymnasium or university education, was extremely low in the immediate post-revolutionary period. It is therefore not very plausible that these educated mothers hailed from the peasantry, as opposed to the urban, clergy, or nobility estates.

Studies that linked Soviet to post-Soviet waves of surveys essentially confirmed these broader trends in social mobility, notably with regard to the familial and particularly maternal education and occupational imprint on the status of future generations.[169] In an influential study, Theodore Gerber and Michael Hout argued that evidence of an accelerating transmission of intergenerational social status advantage emerged immediately in the post–World War II period;[170] and, analyzing post-Soviet social stratification, Ovsey Shkaratan and Gordey Yastrebov point to the "prevalence of estate [*soslovnyye*] forms of inequalities over class ones" as a "direct continuation" of Soviet patterns.[171] Thus, for the sons or daughters of peasants, "mobility" represented factory work in the city and, occasionally, in the sphere of retail services; and considerable stability characterized the intergenerational status of well-qualified manual workers.[172]

While, in the earlier decades, children of well-qualified factory workers often became urban white-collar professionals, this became rarer by the 1970s and 1980s – the implication being that most white-collar professionals hailed from that same group. My own interpretation of these temporal differences is that, for those reporting parental origin from the 1920s to 1940s, there is a likelihood of an overreporting of "worker" and "peasant" backgrounds, so the accuracy of these statistics is in any case questionable – for who would willingly report *meshchane* or merchant ancestry at the height of Stalin's rule? In contrast, by the 1950s, everyone, moreover, begins to operate within Soviet class categories, and listing a *sluzhashchiye* background would not carry the same kinds of risks as would admitting to a "bourgeois" estate in 1937.[173] In another study, Alexey Bessudnov documents, based on a meta-analysis of surveys conducted between 1991 and 2011, that even when controlling for formal educational credentials, parental occupational status matters for that of respondents.[174] The findings

---

[168] Roshchina, "Intergeneration Educational Mobility," 1412. The author uses "higher school" to refer to tertiary education.

[169] Shkaratan and Yastrebov, "Sravnitel'nyy analiz."

[170] Gerber and Hout, "Educational Stratification," 624.

[171] Shkaratan and Yastrebov, "Sravnitel'nyy analiz," 6.   [172] Ibid., 22, 25.

[173] Inkeles and Bauer, *Soviet Citizen*, 83. For an overview of historical work on stratification, see van Leeuwen and Maas, "Historical Studies."

[174] Bessudnov, "Effects," 157.

concerning the payoffs from formal education are more ambiguous, however[175] – something that is indicative of variation in social prestige among institutions and degrees and not easily captured in surveys. The Harvard Project on the Soviet Social System (THPSSS), which surveyed Soviet refugees, is revealing of patterns already observable in the mid-to-late 1940s. In a scenario of "absolute equality of opportunity," 2 percent of the children of professionals and administrators would become members of the Soviet intelligentsia, while, in reality, 65 percent did; and rather than 33 percent becoming workers, merely 14 percent "moved down to that level." "By contrast," the study found, "the child of a peasant had a chance for ultimate placement at any given occupational level that was fairly close to what the random assignment of people to jobs would have decreed."[176] These revelations confirm the many cross-national studies concerning covariation between origin and destination (OD) even if the nuances and magnitude of these patterns vary from country to country.[177]

The OD statistics could be fruitfully contextualized with reference to data on the social-demographic aspects of Soviet urbanization compiled by Anatoliy Vishnevskiy. By 1990, urbanization reached 66 percent in the Soviet Union, yet among those aged sixty, only roughly 15–17 percent had been born in the city (*korennyye gorozhane*); 40 percent among those aged forty; and among those aged twenty and younger, more than 50 percent were native urbanites, constituting only 37 percent of the population. "By the time of the USSR's collapse," concludes Vishnevskiy,

one could not contend that Soviet society became a solidly and overwhelmingly urban society. The USSR citizens in their majority remained urbanites in the first generation, with half to three quarters comprised of urbanites and half or a quarter of peasants – bearing the stamp of transient status, of marginality. To a certain extent, this stamp will be inherited by their children.[178]

While the micro-evidence suggestive of inter-temporal resilience in the social structure is considerable, even if couched in mainstream categories of class, we lack a proportionately rich account of the horizontal network–institutional– organizational spaces as contributing to, facilitating, and nurturing the resilience patterns that are evident from the microdata. Yet, as we know from the account of the estate in tsarist Russia discussed in this chapter, educated society had been a densely networked one, incorporated into a web of civic, professional, educational, and local governance institutions that assumed the function of a quasi-public sphere and one, at times, overtly oppositional toward

---

[175] Ibid., 162.   [176] Inkeles and Bauer, *Soviet Citizen*, 83.

[177] Socialist interventions favoring lower class mobility "typically created persisting differences in the subsequent life chances of the affected cohorts." Nevertheless, "policies favoring or dis-favoring particular classes are strongest at the outset and then fade or disappear completely." Hout and DiPrete, "What We Have Learned," 12.

[178] Vishnevskiy, *Serp i rubl'*, 94. See also Mironov, *Rossiyskaya imperiya*, 1:856–57.

the monarchy. Here, membership, participation, fissures, frictions, and indeed the distribution of public and private occupations and identities, however, strongly bore the stamp of the estate. Detailed historical works on isolated islands of social conservation in Soviet Russia are available for institutions like the Academy of Sciences in Leningrad and the metropolitan universities. Here, we are told that the aristocracy continued to make their influence felt not just before but also after Stalin's purges and witch hunts.[179] Historical accounts of the professions – in medicine, education, and engineering – also hint at their continued colonization by estates that we would expect to find in those spaces.[180] Indeed, some studies, like THPSSS, even managed to obtain limited information on the prior estate ascription of Soviet medics;[181] and revisionist historiography has hinted at the pervasiveness of clandestine private enterprise, one that coexists with the public–professional roles of communist citizens.[182]

Finally, works in history and those straddling history and political science have painted a portrait of a quasi-public sphere, notably beginning with Khrushchev's Thaw and onward, channeled via official think tanks, research and development outlets and cultural societies, the informal café, and the club scene.[183] Numerous accounts have concerned themselves with the leading dissidents, intellectuals, and intelligentsia in Moscow and St. Petersburg. The preoccupation with this narrow segment of metropolitan elite society complicates theorizing into the reproduction of the estatist bourgeoisie, its within-group heterogeneity, and its connectedness across time and in space. Like the micro-sociological survey-based data, these accounts have eschewed embedding theory – if there is one – in the broader institutions, networks, and structures dating to the imperial period. Furthermore, they have not systematically told us in what ways the estate, social heterogeneity within the estates, and the linkages among the various groups might matter for one's ideational-positional predicament in the Soviet and post-Soviet Russian polity.

Figure 2.2 provides a visual summary of the historical argument and proposed mechanisms of social persistence. The social ladder at the bottom third of the triangle helps visualize the channels and stages of mobility from the peasantry to the nobility. The positioning of the "clergy" box signifies its separate status as a relatively free hereditary estate. Of course, those in families already on a particular rung of the ladder prior to the Petrine reforms – notably the hereditary aristocracy – were able to retain their status, if they could prove their pedigree, in an intergenerational sense, even if material fortunes soured; by contrast, for instance, merchants would fall back into

[179] Graham, *Soviet Academy of Sciences*; Tromly, *Making the Soviet Intelligentsia*.
[180] Bailes, *Technology*; Field, *Doctor and Patient*; Ewing, *Teachers of Stalinism*.
[181] Inkeles and Bauer, *Soviet Citizen*; Field, *Doctor and Patient*.
[182] Edele, *Stalinist Society*; Osokina, *Our Daily Bread*.
[183] Zubok, *Zhivago's Children*; Churchward, *Soviet Intelligentsia*; Shlapentokh, *Soviet Intellectuals*. For more recent treatment of metropolitan elite society, see Slezkine, *House of Government*.

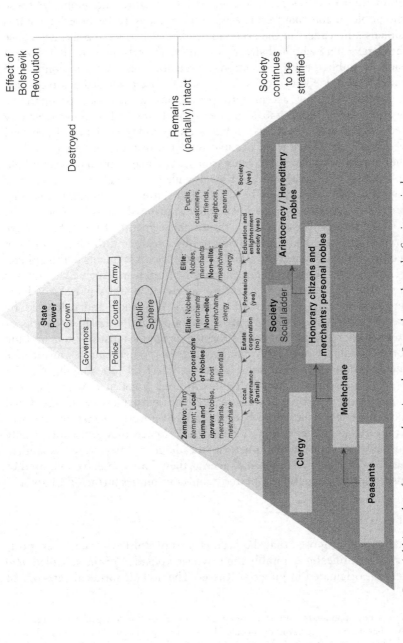

FIGURE 2.2 Imperial hierarchy of power and society, late 1800s through to the Soviet period

meshchane status for failure to pay guild fees. The annotation to the right of this section points to the significance of social stratification at the time of the Revolution for the subsequent, *Soviet*, social structure and mobility: those from the noble or merchant estates were more likely to become high-status professionals and leaders in the arts and academia than were peasants. Those from the clergy estate who had already discarded the robe in favor of a modern profession, in public health, education, or scientific research – in contrast to priests who were immediate targets of repression – also possessed relatively high human capital, enabling ascent into prestigious white-collar occupations. Moreover, the *meshchane* had a greater probability of becoming relatively esteemed white-collar communist public sector employees than did peasants who were likely to stay in rural occupations or transition into factory labor. Over the communist decades and generations, of course, many a peasant would become a public sector employee, but meanwhile the *meshchane* would not be standing still either – they would be ahead of the latter-day peasant in reaching the more prestigious provincial or metropolitan professional roles. The middle section of the triangle presents the institutional segments of the public sphere that survived after the Revolution (denoted by "yes") and those that did not (denoted by "no"), as indeed the estate composition of segments in this sphere. For instance, professional and educational institutions in which civic pursuits originated and flourished during tzarism survived, as did segments of local government structures dealing with culture or education and colonized by cultivated groups, while the corporate estate bodies did not. The networks of peers, service clients, and friendships formed around estatist pursuits and life trajectories – ordinary but highly educated citizens, potentially re-constitutive of a new, communist, autonomous society – survived too. Finally, the top section of the diagram shows those institutions associated with the core metropolitan sites of Crown power that were not particularly well networked with local societies, their estate bodies, and self-governing institutions over which they ruled in the various provinces,[184] hence they are conceptually distinguished from the public sphere in the diagram; they were disbanded, decimated, or radically reconfigured, even if their staff may have migrated to other institutions. I unpack these patterns and continuities further in Chapter 3.

CONCLUSION

This chapter has proposed that the peculiarities of Bolshevik and, later, post-Soviet social stratification, notably the privileged position of the so-called *new* intelligentsia, originated in imperial Russia. The archaic juridical category of

---

[184] As Starr writes, appointed governors with no local roots envied "the degree of attachment to the locality that the estate representatives could claim," viewing estate institutions "as a kind of state within a state ... Retained intact until the end of serfdom, the clash of state and estate (or 'society') was then perpetuated down to the end of the old regime." Starr, "Local Initiative," 24.

the estates coexisted in tsarist Russia with the emerging professions, a middle class, and some social mobility within the lower strata of society. Weberian insights into the corporate aspects of the estate were invoked to frame the discussion of historical evidence for the deep institutionalization of caste-like gradations that permeated all aspects of social life. This neglected institution illuminates the sources of opportunity for social, civic, and corporate autonomy, professionalization, and embourgeoisement of society, as much as it anticipates the calcification of social distinctions. When it comes to the legacies of the estate in communist, let alone post-communist, Russia, there is a lacuna of historical knowledge. Monographs on the early years of communism supply a substantial repository of the material concerning the Bolsheviks' social dilemmas in pursuing class vigilance, yet implicit in most accounts is profound rupture. Furthermore, the utility of these sources for understanding longer-term patterns of social resilience and change diminishes along with the drying up of Soviet data that would shed light on any continuity between the tsarist and Soviet polity. Subsequent sociological explorations into social inequalities and mobility, while deploying conventional categories of class, as indeed the handful of studies into islands of social reproduction within specific public institutions, nevertheless help us begin to discern path-dependencies that transcend the revolutionary juncture.

Chapter 3 provides a systematic portrait of the social structure of a large trading city on the Volga. It sets the stage for a more systematic exploration of how society would find reflection in the institutions that the Bolsheviks demonized and then appropriated in the service of progress; and of how networks, skills, values, know-how, and the expertise of old-regime Russia constitute a "bourgeois" legacy that we could link to both broader long-term outcomes in the political sphere – across space and in time – and social inequities that transcend the distinct epochs.

3

Mapping Society and the Public Sphere in Imperial Russia

How did the society of estates perpetuate its latent hierarchies, closure, and autonomy in the modernizing context of tsarist Russia? What are the key professional arenas that embodied the tension between bureaucratic incorporation into the state and the maintenance of autonomous sphere of initiative? And how and in what ways did the social networks, professional, and civic institutions continue to constitute quasi-free social arenas and, indeed, in some instances embed themselves in the institutions of the new Bolshevik state? Finally, to the extent that the estates-enmeshed society found its reflection in the professional and cultural institutions of the new regime, in what ways would these social continuities reinforce the material, resource, and cognitional aspects of the social structure and channel the construction of the autonomously nurtured element of the *Soviet* middle class and orientations toward the state among this stratum? To begin to answer these questions, we ought to outline the contours of social stratification as it mapped onto professional institutions and the public sphere. A social network analysis exercise would also allow us to begin to situate elements of path-dependency in the density of ties and social engagements of a stratum that I conceptualize interchangeably as the bourgeoisie and the middle class.

Jürgen Habermas is known for conceiving the public sphere as spaces, engagements, and practices that involve the deliberation of public issues by private people, that is, individuals not formally associated with the institutions of the state or incorporated into political society. "The bourgeois public sphere," writes Habermas, "may be conceived above all as the sphere of private people come together as a public," one defined in relation to "public authorities."[1] Habermas deplored what he saw as the erosion of the bourgeois

---

[1] Habermas, *Structural Transformation*, 27.

public sphere of the "waning nineteenth century" with the advent of the interventionist state of the twentieth.[2]

A public sphere so delineated would, however, exclude large and vibrant arenas of societal engagement within institutions in one way or another, if even tangentially they were associated with state power.[3] Joel Migdal writes: "All societies, democratic and nondemocratic alike, have broad dimensions of public life – life outside the walls of one's home – where social interaction is frequent and largely ungoverned by state law."[4] Yet, in contexts with a "totalizing" ideology, virtually every activity outside the home is state governed, regimented, and controlled; indeed, there is no public sphere outside of state institutions, at least in intention. The Table of Ranks also placed a vast chunk of the public sphere into arenas that are within state purview. The gymnasium may be funded by private individuals, who deliberated publicly the common good of the new educational institution; they engaged in fundraising; and they lobbied state authority. Yet the institution would be within the juridical purview of a state body, the Ministry of Enlightenment. School heads and lay teachers would be part of the *Tabel'* state system of pay and progression; and much of the school activity would be regulated by state exam boards and other oversight bodies. Yet the public sphere within which the school originated would not cease with the formal establishment of the institution. Far from it, for it may well become yet another arena of public debate, one where participants subvert state laws, purview, and sanction for the benefit of the "common good." The gymnasium would become the proverbial coffee house and the *salon* – the embodiment of the Habermasian bourgeois public sphere.

These patterns not only failed to lose their relevance in Bolshevik Russia but acquired added salience. It would be facile to assume that a lack of state sanction meant the withering of the public sphere in Soviet Russia. Studies of individual institutions – from the Academy of Sciences in the 1920s and 1930s[5] to the policy think tanks of the 1970s and 1980s, the *institutional amphibians* of the Gorbachev era,[6] institutions embedded within, or funded and controlled by, state power – point precisely to the kinds of arenas where individuals found safe

---

[2] Ibid., 142.

[3] For a similar point, see Balzer, "Conclusion," 300–1. Balzer critiques the implicit simplistic state/society dualism, highlighting the state's role in the maintenance of a legal order that makes autonomous participation possible. America-centered assumptions that the professions are entirely autonomous from the state have also been discussed as inapplicable to continental Europe or Russia where state involvement does not preclude professional autonomy. See Ruane, *Gender*, 6–12. Relatedly, others underline Russia's similarity to the more developed old-regime France and Germany, in both the pervasiveness of state control, surveillance, and suspicion of autonomous society and the role of the state as an enabler, collaborator, and facilitator of the public sphere. Bradley, *Voluntary Associations*, 18–27.

[4] Migdal, *State in Society*, 164.   [5] Graham, *Soviet Academy of Sciences*.

[6] See the discussion of the concept in the section "Institutional Amphibiousness or Civil Society?" in Brown, *Seven Years*, 157–89; and the original term that comes from "amphibious" as "leading a double life" in Ding, "Institutional Amphibiousness," 298. See also Checkel, "Ideas."

havens to debate, deliberate, and conceive public issues, and in the process often subverting state policy.[7]

This chapter and those that follow show that, before the Revolution, Russia had a public sphere partially embedded in the institutional apparatus of the tsarist state. Autonomy, however, characterized the relevant bodies – either as consequential to explicit state sanction or as informal mechanisms for the maintenance of social initiative that may or may not have enjoyed official imprimatur. The *zemstvo* local governance reforms have been well covered in recent studies in political science and economic history as an illustration of the delegation of state authority to local social enterprise.[8] Yet societal autonomous action in urban Russia outside of the *zemstvo* extended to virtually every area of social activity. Merchant entrepreneurs set up mutual credit and insurance societies; local dignitaries and intelligentsia debated together to open charities and hospices; and individuals and groups of citizens set up schools catering to a wide clientele and social base.[9]

Whatever the cause embraced, the institutionalization of society into a dense web of autonomous or semiautonomous public and private institutions followed the contours of estate. Social enterprise provided opportunities to build network ties outside of one's estate and class but also to solidify bonds with those from one's own narrower stratum. The estate continued to matter in the consolidation or extension of these networks, both formal organizational and social.[10] The Bolsheviks decimated segments of the state apparatus associated with police sanction, surveillance, and repression. However, as becomes clear from my social network analysis, a large chunk of the autonomous, highly networked, and enterprising society survived the Revolution. The dense ties linking professional organizations like schools and hospitals, and the civic arena that embraced museums, historical conservation

---

[7] On Soviet intelligentsia salons, see Shlapentokh, *Soviet Intellectuals*, 85–86. Even when under KGB surveillance, these were influential fora for debate. See also material on satirical discussions and polemics in the Club of Writers, Club of Actors, and the Library of Social Literature of the Academy of Sciences during Khrushchev's Thaw; on art museums and exhibitions with political overtones, notably in Novosibirsk, see ibid., 114, 116; and on the mass bard movement and performances in the late 1960s in cult clubs, see ibid., 125–27. Even funerals of dissidents and intellectuals became political events. Ibid., 140.

[8] Nafziger, "Did Ivan's Vote Matter?"; Finkel et al., "Does Reform Prevent Rebellion?"; Dower et al., "Collective Action." For earlier challenges to assumptions about Russia's underdeveloped participatory institutions, suffrage, legal system, and comparative referents in Europe, see White, "Soviet Political Culture," esp. 65–77.

[9] On Russia-wide trends and metropolitan civil society and public sphere, see Bradley, *Voluntary Associations*; and Pravilova, *Public Empire*. On Samara, see Barinova, "Blagotvoritel'naya deyatel'nost'." On charitable deeds of *meshchane* of modest means, see Kobozeva, *Meshchanskoye sosoloviye*, 297–99.

[10] As other critics of Habermas's work note, the Western bourgeois public sphere too had always been structured in exclusionary ways, featuring gender- and class-based dominance and inequalities. Baviskar and Ray, "Introduction," esp. 17–19.

bureaus, and archaeological interest groups, helped cushion and eventually catapult segments of the estatist bourgeoisie into the elite or otherwise comfortably well-off "intelligentsia" substratum of Soviet society. The autonomous agency of these institutions and the actors embedded within them, nurtured in their own tensions, evasions, and complications of dealing with the tsarist state, facilitated adaptation and survival under the new regime, something that I conceptualize as one element of the democratic legacy of educated estates.

The chapter begins with a descriptive account of the social character of the urban bourgeoisie in late imperial Samara. Next, I perform a systematic social network analysis employing material from pre-revolutionary directories of the city's white-collar strata and civil society and give an account of the patterns of adaptation seen in the bourgeoisie after the Revolution. The analysis, sensitive to the "enmeshing" of society in both "social time" and "social space,"[11] sets the stage for a more systematic exploration of the reproduction of the social structure and autonomy vis-à-vis the Soviet state among the various shades of the estatist bourgeoisie.

A TRADING CITY ON THE VOLGA

In 2017, when Samara was preparing to host the FIFA World Cup, a debate unfolded in the pages of local newspapers, in blogs, and on television screens. Is Samara a merchant or *meshchane* city? The Samara tourism board touted the merchant brand as historically the most exact – and image boosting – representation of the booming grain trading center on the Volga. To others, like the Samara University historian Zoya Kobozeva, it exemplified a *meshchane* city, what with the far more sizeable population of this estate and its contribution to enterprise, trade, and the professions, as indeed its peculiar cultural fabric. Still others considered the debate moot, since they identified, inaccurately, the *meshchane* as equivalent to "urban," something not particularly evocative of the unique identity of their native town.[12] These debates and ambivalences in point of fact nicely capture the social tapestry of the city that became something like the grain Eldorado, in a span of a mere five

---

[11] Abbott, *Time Matters*, 124.

[12] A summary of the debates is provided by Zoya Kobozeva. Interview, June 19, 2017. Unless otherwise specified, interviews were carried out by the author and took place in Samara. Samara-based researchers Zoya Kobozeva (ZK), Ul'yana Kulyanina (UK), and Andrey Aref'yev (AA) carried out additional interviews; I list their initials where they conducted the interview. On polemics about Samara's merchant versus *meshchane* identity, see Zoya Kobozeva, "Trendy i brendy i 'plat'ya iz sitsa' . . ." *SamKul't*, November 18, 2015. Available online at: samcult.ru/heritage/5502 (accessed April 18, 2020). Official 2018 Football Championship websites and promotional materials highlight Samara's merchant legacy: kp.ru/putevoditel/chm-2018/samara/; and samddn.ru/novosti/novosti/v-samare-otkrylas-vystavka-posvyashchennaya-prodvizheniyu-oblastnogo-tsentra-kak-goroda-organizatora/ (accessed April 17, 2020).

decades, emerging out of the sleepy semirural outpost where pigs and cattle grazed on the dusty town square, lazily shrugging off flies. The pigs, even in the early 1900s, continued to deface Samara's squares and courtyards; and the perennial dust lining its roads led many a metropolitan *intelligent* passing through the town to pin a scathing epitaph of the cesspit that was Samara for posterity.[13] Yet these images of provincial Russian gloom and backwardness coexisted with art nouveau architecture of stunning elegance, opulence, and beauty; the classically designed gymnasia; tramlines; modern plumbing; electricity; and the towering signs of industrializing Russia – of mills and granaries, plants, factories, and large steamships claiming the Volga.

Merchants, a mere fraction of the city's population, had come to play an outsized role in the trade and industrial boom. Samara's merchant stratum was comprised overwhelmingly of the descendants of state peasants, who enjoyed greater liberties as compared to serfs. These "peasants of yesterday" were already making a mark in urban Russia as owners of small shops, traders, and eventually prosperous entrepreneurs in the late eighteenth century, a process that accelerated in the second half of the nineteenth. They were also amassing large tracts of farmland. The Shikhobalov clan of Samara's wealthy grain traders personified this pattern.[14] Their descendants trace the family's origins in Samara to the Old Believer community who fled the Orthodox Church reforms of Patriarch Nikon in the late seventeenth century and established the village of Kol'tsovka. They brought with them scores of banned religious books and insisted on performing religious rituals in the old way.[15] The Shikhobalovs well into the nineteenth century maintained the estate designation as state peasants and, to underscore their disdain for the nobility's contempt for peasants, preserved "a stubborn attachment to peasant dress and manners."[16]

[13] On dust and urban cattle grazing, see Kobozeva, "Meshchanskaya povsednevnost'," 471–72. On farm animal grazing, puddles on the square adjoining the railway station, and provincialism, see Yerofeyev, "Yakovlev Fyodor Timofeyevich," available online at *Istoricheskaya Samara* ("Historical Samara"): Историческая-самара.рф/каталог/самарская-персоналия/я/яковлев-фёдор-тимофеевич.html (accessed December 17, 2019); and Mikhaylova, "Golovkin Konstantin Pavlovich," December 17, 2014. Available online at *Samarskiye sud'by* ("Samara Destinies"): samsud.ru/blogs/hroniki-samarochki/golovkin-konstantin-pavlovich.html (accessed May 4, 2018).

[14] Neklutin uses the spelling Shikhobaloff. Constantine Neklutin, "My Mother: Anastasia M. Neklutin," 1976. Constantine Neklutin Collection. Cammie G. Henry Research Center at Northwestern State University of Louisiana (hereafter NC), file (hereafter "f.") 228, 2.

[15] "My Mother," 1–2. Here and elsewhere in this chapter, "My mother" is the short version of the family history; a longer discussion appears in a note "To Vadim Constantine Neklutin," 1933. NC, f. 232. For an excellent overview of the cultural and social underpinnings of entrepreneurship, charitable giving, transition to professional roles and education among merchant sons, and impulses to maintain autonomy vis-à-vis the state among Old Believers, see Rieber, *Merchants*, 139–48. For a brief overview of the community in historiography, see Rogers, *Old Faith*, 35–26.

[16] "My Mother," 4. On the dynasty, see also Goncharenko, "Kupecheskaya dinastiya."

Yet they were "millionaires" some twenty-five years before serf emancipation, free as they had been from attachment to the commune and the gentry estate.[17]

We have detailed accounts of the business empire of the extended clan from the merchant Constantine Neklutin, whose father married into the Shikhobalov tree. The family, on the eve of the Bolshevik Revolution owned 90,000 acres of farmland, which produced grain and fed the profitable enterprise of horse and cattle breeding. The Shikhobalov-Neklutins also owned a large, mechanized, flour mill processing 120 tons of grain daily and, reportedly, Russia's first mechanized bakery with a daily capacity of processing forty tons of flour.[18] These Volga merchants were among the pioneers in exporting flour to Europe: Italy was one destination, and in 1911 Constantine traveled to London to procure contracts.[19]

The merchant entrepreneur, however, also presented a profile that does not make Samara's ostensible *meshchane* identity unfit for purpose. Many had risen within one or two generations from the modesty of *meshchanstvo* to merchant and then personal noble or honored citizen status. Intermarriage among wealthy merchants was of course encouraged since it would consolidate their influence over the enterprise and governance in the city and *guberniya*. Marriage ties linked the most notable merchant families – the Neklutins, Subbotins, Suroshnikovs, Kurliny, and Shikhobalovs. The rising merchant of comparatively modest wealth, Nicolai Gavrilovich Neklutin, went on to marry Anastasia Shikhobalova, the granddaughter of Nicolai (Nicholas)[20] Shikhobalov(ff), one of the original Old Believer settlers[21] and daughter of one of his sons Matvey (Mathew) Nikolayevich Shikhobalov. Yet merchants also married *meshchane*, even if they scrutinized their prospective partner's provenance. When, in 1916, the young Constantine announced his plans to marry the educated *meshchanka* Pelageia (Polia) Egorova, whose family, typically for *meshchane*, ran a grocery shop,[22] the response of his mother Anastasia, *née* Shikhobalova, was: "Do you know that she belongs to an entirely different circle – our relatives and friends have no connections, even by

---

[17] "My Mother," 4.
[18] Neklutin, "Notes Made at Different Times, Mostly about Russia and USSR, April 1920–circa January 1926." Handwritten notes, NC, f. 196, 2.
[19] Ibid., 3.   [20] In notes written in English, Neklutin also uses anglicized names.
[21] "My Mother."
[22] Polia's mother Elena married a widower with family connections to a prosperous merchant enterprise from his first marriage. Neklutin, "Changes in Relation between Different Classes in Russia." NC, f. 234, 215. A record of transaction dated March 16, 1916 states: "I, the below-signing Samara *meshchanin* Konstantin Petrovich Yegorov, issued the present receipt to my mother the Samara *meshchanka* Yelena Avtonomovna Yegorova." The transaction concerned the lending of money to purchase a property. The notary cited Yegorov's identification documents supplied by the Samara Meshchanskaya Uprava. Another notary document, a will from March 26, 1916, confirms that the *meshchanka* Pelageya Petrovna Yegorova will inherit mobile and immobile assets of the Samara *meshchanka* Yelena Avtonomovna Yegorova, her mother, also citing documents supplied by the Samara Meshchanskaya Uprava. NC, f. 5.

Elena Avtonomovna
&
Alexandre Avtonomovich
Egoroff
Mother & Uncle
of Mrs C. Neklutin

1868

FIGURE 3.1 Elena Egorova, *meshchanka*
Mother of Constantine's future wife Polia. NC, f. 207, 13.

marriage, with relatives of her family?"[23] Constantine reminded his mother that her father too, the merchant Mathew Shikhobalov, did not grant a blessing for her marriage union with the up-and-coming merchant Neklutin. Anastasia then revealed that she had done research on Polia's family, noting the noble credentials of one of the ancestors of the bride-to-be, the merchant provenance of a relative of hers, and the professional status of Polia herself. (See Figures 3.1 and 3.2 for photographic records of the two families.) Constantine recalls,

I understood that she [mother] referred to the fact that Polia lived at the northern edge of the city. So I said that I was not marrying her relatives and I reminded my mother that after her marriage she lived for a long time just a couple of blocks from Egorova's house. Mother knew that and mentioned that my father bought groceries from the Egorova store. Then she told me that Polia's grandfather belonged to the nobility and was the manager of the Nobility Club, that her mother married a merchant Egorova [*sic*] who was many years

[23] "My Mother," 37. Elsewhere, he lists the position of Polia's maternal grandfather Avtonom Egoroff as "Dvorianskoe sobranie," which he translates as "Club for Nobility." "Changes," 213. Family documents also indicate that the Egoroffs were serf owners, hereditary nobles from the Moscow region, and that Avtonom married a serf girl from the estate. "Changes," 214.

FIGURE 3.2 The Neklutin-Shikhobalov family of wealthy merchants
With annotations from Constantine. Anastasia, Neklutin's mother (née Shikhobalova), seated in the middle, surrounded by children, grandchildren, and in-laws. Constantine is in the top row, third from the right. NC, f. 207, 13.

older than she and that she was a very religious person, and that Polia worked at the railroad office and had a responsible position.[24]

Merchants came to shape, and colonize, the institutions of urban governance. Several generations of the Neklutin clan were elected to, and maintained considerable influence on, Samara's municipal bodies. In the 1880s, Constantine's father Nicolai Gavrilovich occupied a position on the city's executive arm (*uprava*); in 1885, and then again in 1889, he served as elected representative to the city's council (*duma*). By 1893, Nicolai's leadership skills, integrity, and wide respect among the propertied strata propelled him to the elected position of city head (*gorodskoy golova*). Constantine followed in his father's footsteps to become an elected city councilor in later years. A neglected institution in studies of provincial Russia's public sphere as compared to the *zemstvo*, the city *duma* and its executive arm represented in that period the pulse of urban life. Here, pivotal decisions about enterprise, urban infrastructure, and public services were made; and merchant rivals locked

[24] "My Mother," 38.

horns over issues of land reclamation and redevelopment. By all accounts, this had been an autonomous sphere of urban decision-making epitomizing the dictum about the "undermanaged" empire – in the sense of the thin imperial presence in the provinces and the delegation of developmental initiative to local elected institutions. Constantine left a detailed account of the elaborate procedure of election of deputies based on his own experience of being a nominee and representative in 1913:

Only property owners, paying direct property taxes to the city, could vote. Every taxpayer had one vote and it didn't matter if he paid 10 roubles or 10,000 per year. There might be 1500 names on the tax list.

On election day they would come to the municipal theater and would stay there until 54 members were elected.

On the stage there were 10 to 12 small voting boxes. Nominations were made from the floor; nominee should be present and consent to putting his name on one of the voting boxes.

Then all the voters walked onto the stage. At each box they received a ball. Each voter put his hand with the ball through a fabric sleeve and placed the ball into the left (no) or right (yes) hole. The ball triggered the counter and then rolled out from a single channel. The same ball was used by all the voters at each box; so every candidate was voted for or against by every voter.

After the election of 30 to 35 members, voters would begin to drift out and it would become more difficult to find a full set of candidates. Eventually, an owner of a large brewery came to the box where Victor [Neklutin's brother] and I were siting (one of us represented the Neklutin property and the other the flour mill corporation) and insisted on putting up our names for the election. Victor refused and I claimed nobody knew me. He insisted and I finally agreed.[25]

Merchant wealth also enabled entry into, and influence within, the habitual province of the aristocracy – the public sphere that not only extended into the elected institutions of urban governance but also embraced civic activism outside of it. Samara's eminent gentry families of aristocratic, hereditary, pedigree, included a branch of the Tolstoy family, related to the famous writer Leo Tolstoy. The Tolstoy who grew up in Samara, Aleksey, left vivid portraits of the city's aristocracy, merchants, and *meshchane*, in his short stories and novels.[26] Tolstoy's writing betrays the aristocracy's scurrilous disdain for the urban estates. Yet merchants eventually joined and even displaced hereditary landowners as powerful voices in municipal affairs. Although, at

---

[25] "My Mother," 34. After the February Revolution, anyone aged twenty-one years and older could vote in urban *duma* elections, which brought to power the Socialist Revolutionary Party. Constantine was also reelected but, by January 2018, the Bolsheviks "closed City Hall by forcing everyone out and nailing down all the doors." "My Mother," 49, 53.

[26] See, for instance, references to provincialism in the character Dasha's reflections on her home town of Samara in Tolstoy's trilogy, including to dust and flies, as well as unflattering images of *meshchane* women spitting out husks of sunflower seeds (*semechki*) that Dasha spots on another boat while on a trip on the Volga. Tolstoy, *Khozhdeniye*, 79, 96, 83.

the turn of the twentieth century, Neklutin writes that "in social life these two groups [nobles and merchant entrepreneurs], as a rule, did not mix," participation in joint charitable and other events was gradually eroding the barriers and indeed often hostility among these strata.[27] Privately initiated and funded schools, hospices, and boarding institutions for the blind and deaf mushroomed in sync with the rise of the muscular merchant stratum and the wealth that merchant enterprise fueled.[28] The beneficiaries may have been the lower urban strata, the unfortunate, and the dispossessed, but the informal and formal associations, clubs, and societies running and debating these pursuits, were largely of noble and merchant makeup.

Foreign enterprise organically blended with, and in important ways shaped, local enterprise and civic life. The von Vakano family of entrepreneurs of aristocratic Austrian background illustrates this pattern. Renowned for the breweries and beer that they produced from locally sourced grains and exported throughout Russia, locally they are remembered also for their civic pursuits. The von Vakanos founded one of Russia's oldest tennis clubs, attached to the Samara Yacht and Boating Club, another elite establishment. The records of tennis tournaments in the club in the first decade of the 1900s provide a snapshot of the makeup and ties of the bourgeoisie – a blend of nobles, merchants, and professionals like doctors, gymnasium teachers, and academics.[29] The family also initiated urban development projects, including modern plumbing in the city. Together with other industrialists and merchants, they set up and sponsored schools, hospices, and other institutions, helping the socially disadvantaged.[30]

Wealth creation among the newly affluent fed the privileged estates' habitual impulse to set up gymnasia, in turn fueling demand for schooling among the lower urban strata. The moneyed groups aspired to access superb medical clinics and the celebrity doctor nurtured his public persona with charitable engagements that transcended the paying client. This characterized the Grinberg dynasty of medics of merchant background, whose medical engagements coexisted with private enterprise in real estate development and who not only catered to the medical needs of the wealthy clientele but also kept their clinics open to the city's poor.[31] Rail and shipping fueled demand for

[27] "To Vadim Constantine Neklutin," 22. See also "Changes," 207–8. When the noble Aleksandr Nikolayevich Naumov (1868–1950), future chairman of the *guberniya* nobles' assembly, married the daughter of a distinguished merchant, Anna Konstantinovna Ushkova (1878–1962) in 1898, this was initially frowned upon by other nobles – "not a person of our circle." Kabytov et al., *Zhizn' i sud'ba*, 122, 131, 132.

[28] Aleksushin, "K tipologii." Listings of charitable bodies are available from SGSC, *Pamyatnaya knizhka*.

[29] Aleksushin and Sinin, *Pervyy vek*, 37–50.

[30] Savchenko and Dubinin, *Rossiyskiye nemtsy*, 88, 90. Aleksushin, "K tipologii," 21, 22, 25; Aleksushina, "Von Vakano A," 239–41.

[31] *Yevreyskiy mir Samary* ("Jewish world of Samara"). See the virtual museum site: sites.google.com/site/samaraemir/muzejnaa-ekspozicia/kupcy-i-predprinimateli/m-a-grinberg (accessed April 17, 2020).

engineers trained in the secondary schools with a practical bent, the *real'nyye uchilishcha*, and encouraged local dignitaries to get together to conceive the long overdue polytechnic institute and eventually the university. At inception, the privately initiated, funded, and managed institutions of learning and the professions were subjected to the state's legal scrutiny, sanction, approval, and oversight. Nina Andreyevna Khardina, the noblewoman who founded the fee-paying Khardina Women's Gymnasium (KWG), had to comply with onerous paperwork requirements concerning anything from the quality of teaching to the pupils' legal right to reside in Samara. Yet her gymnasium, like other similar educational institutions, retained considerable autonomy in hiring and firing, in fundraising, and in the day-to-day operations of paid staff otherwise formally under state authority. Local initiative also invited the engagement of the metropolitan cultural and professional elite. In setting up new educational institutions, academicians from St. Petersburg, Moscow, and Kiev worked together with native Samara enlightenment figures trained in the metropolitan universities or in the Middle Volga area regional university of Kazan.

The lower urban echelons, notably the *meshchane*, benefited from, but also drove, the embourgeoisement of Samara society. By the end of the nineteenth century, a wide range of schools – and scholarships – catered to pupils of heterogenous social stature and means. Because of the status of towns like Samara as magnet cities for the education of sons and daughters of the gentry and aspirational rural smallholders and traders, native *meshchane* profited as rentiers from the demand for rental dwellings, which allowed them to put their own children through private schooling. Supplying digs to gentry boys who attended prestigious urban gymnasia and whose parents remained in the countryside constituted a steady source of income for many *meshchane*. The urban estate also engaged in food catering services. An arrangement whereby cooked meals were provided on order was common in urban Russia at the time; a type of "small business" activity, the customers were often single men who lived nearby or rented premises in the same house.[32] Accounts from Russian literary classics suggest that *meshchane* occupied the niche position of urban rentiers and small business entrepreneurs in services that they often combined with other trades. The writer Ivan Bunin became a lodger in the house of a *meshchanin* when, in 1881, his gentry family sent the eleven-year Ivan to attend a gymnasium in the town of Yeletsk in Tula *guberniya* – something recorded in his autobiographical novel *The Life of Arsen'yev*. Compared to the child's privileged upbringing on his ancestral gentry estate, the dwellings of the *meshchanin* Rostovtsev – in real-life *meshchanin* Byakin[33] – who "engaged in buying and re-selling bread [and] cattle," appeared as "a petty and poor

---

[32] Sergey Golubkov, referring to his great-grandmother's income-generating activities. Interview, October 25, 2018.
[33] Baboreko, *I. A. Bunin*, 9. There is also mention of a *meshchanka* A. O. Rostovtseva from whom Bunin rented. Ibid., 10.

milieu," for "rich city dwellers had no need for renters [*nakhlebniki*]." Simultaneously, Rostovtsev, who sent his own son to the gymnasium, is portrayed as a bourgeois whom the spoiled gentry boy greatly admires, one with "a once and for all developed code of a respectable [*blagopristoynoy*] life, domestic as well as public."[34]

Many such gymnasium-trained rentiers joined the urban professional bourgeoisie or married into it. Olen'ka Konovalova, a descendant of the extended multigenerational clan of the Barsukovs, Konovalovs, Shanins, and Zarubalovs – *meshchane* families engaged in grain production and commerce – personified this trajectory.[35] Born in 1900, Olen'ka completed the prestigious First Women's Gymnasium in 1917, where leisure pastimes involved joint socials with the *realisty*[36] – boys from the nearby *real'noye uchilishche* that the young Alyosha (Aleksey) Tolstoy had earlier attended. The death of Olen'ka's father in 1907 encouraged his widow to look for alternative sources of income. To make ends meet, Olen'ka's mother, Yelena Stepanovna Konovalova, rented out spare rooms on the ground floor of the house, while also supplementing her income with sewing made-to-order clothes and selling cooked meals.[37] One of Konovalova's tenants in 1915 is the engineer Aleksey Fyodorovich Yevteyev, who had been stationed temporarily with the artillery regiment during the Great War. Aleksey and Olen'ka fall in love, but their romance is interrupted as the engineer's sojourn in Samara comes to an end. Through World War I, the Revolution, and the Civil War, Aleksey and Olen'ka continue their correspondence. In 1920, Yevteyev, by then deputy head of a factory producing artillery supplies in the Moscow region, marries his muse and the young family reestablish a life as intelligentsia in Soviet Samara.[38]

Many of the unsung members of the lower to middling bourgeoisie, while lacking prominence in the civic arenas colonized by the aristocracy and merchants, played an important role in setting the boundaries of autonomy

---

[34] Bunin, "Zhizn' Arsen'yeva," 363, 364. The Marxist writer Maxim Gorky ascribed similar characteristics to the *meshchane* – of thrift, moderation, yearning for a stable life, relative affluence, property ownership, and educational aspirations for their children – but famously derided them in his 1901 play *Meshchane* precisely for those reasons. Anticipating the naïve and crude schemata of socialist realism, the positive hero in the play is the mechanic Nil, who extols the moral virtues of manual work. The negative character is Bessemenov, Nil's foster father, an "affluent [*zazhitochnyy*] *meshchanin*," the manager of a decorating enterprise simultaneously deriving income from renting out rooms in his house. The family employ a cook (*kukharka*), doubling as a cleaner, in case we entertain any doubt that *meshchane* are the exploiting class. Repeatedly, we are exposed to Bessemenov's miserliness (*krokhoborstvo*); moderation (*v meru*) in everything from sentiment to intelligence, to bravery, ostensibly characteristics of a "model [*obraztsovyy*] *meshchanin*"; vulgarity (*poshlost'*); exactitude in collecting every single kopeck in rent from lodgers (*akkuratnyy*); greed (*zhaden*); and dismay at workers "drinking away their earnings [*propili zarobotok*]." M. *Gorky*, 273, 300, 313, 339.

[35] Biography narrated by her grandson. Golubkov, *Portfel'*; and interview, ZK, February 26, 2017.

[36] Interview with Sergey Golubkov, October 25, 2018.

[37] Golubkov, *Portfel'*; and interview, October 25, 2018. [38] Ibid., 26–31.

vis-à-vis the state, as purveyors of technical knowledge and expertise. Valerian Dmitriyevich Tikhovidov was one such professional. Born in 1878 into a family of Samara-based primary school and *uchilishcha* (specialized schools) teachers, Valerian attended *uchilishche* No. 1 and then pursued "spiritual" training at a seminary – an educational trajectory typical of the clergy estate – completing it in 1902. After graduating from Kazan Veterinary Institute with a diploma in veterinary medicine, Valerian Dmitriyevich worked for *zemstvo* bodies of self-government as a district vet. In this role, he fought epidemics, supervised quarantine regimes, and developed modern veterinary laboratories and breeding stations, specifically the famous Bezenchuk agricultural experimental station.[39] Professionals like Tikhovidov were largely given free rein to get on with their work, considering their pivotal role in safeguarding public health and urban and rural food supply chains; the shortage of expertise; and the state's tenuous reach in the provinces.

This impressionistic account of a provincial metropolis provides a flavor of the various shades of provincial Russia's bourgeoisie. Samara's bourgeoisie had been nurtured within the milieu of a largely self-governing city, where the wealthiest honed his skills in oratory and policy making in the *duma*; where the noble and merchant banded together – and bonded in the process – to debate the founding of a new school; where one obtained education within the self-governing gymnasia and technical colleges, often paid for through the private enterprise of the *meshchanin* and *meshchanka* as rentiers or entrepreneurs; and where the profession, largely colonized by the educated estates, increasingly represented a well-institutionalized arena of free social engagements.

SOCIAL STRUCTURE, NETWORKS, AND TIES

To provide a more systematic portrait of Samara society, I draw on a precious source of information on social structure: the *pamyatnyye knizhki* (memorial books), also called the *adres-kalendari* (address-calendars), of individual *gubernii*. These were directories with comprehensive listings of key public and private institutions, along with their staff, addresses, and, where available, telephone numbers. Olen'ka Konovalova's grandson, for instance, was able to locate one such private telephone number for his great-grandfather.[40] Names of employees, their service rank, and their position within the institution, as well as often their estate, were detailed in the *knizhki*. As discussed in Chapter 2, positions in government formed part of the Petrine nomenclature of ranks. Under Tsar Alexander I, engineers, teachers, librarians, doctors, and other professionals joined the listings of Crown civil servants; they took an oath,

[39] Pneumonia, bacterial skin infections, and Siberian ulcer were common diseases affecting farm animals in the Middle Volga region. Popov, "Vernost' professii," 4th Annual Essay Competition "Family History – 2012," Tolyatti. See also SGSC, *Pamyatnaya knizhka*. Statistical sec., 32–35.
[40] Golubkov, *Portfel'*, 17–16; SGSC, *Pamyatnaya knizhka*.

wore uniforms, and received state remuneration, pensions, and perks.[41] One indicator of the high professionalization of local *chinovniki* as a group is their educational credentials: in 1897, 40.8 percent of Crown officials in local bodies had received higher education and 20.7 percent had a high school (*sredneye*) education.[42]

The *knizhki*, compiled and published by the *guberniya* Statistical Committee, are available for several years, but I chose to analyze information from the 1916 yearbook, the year preceding the Revolution.[43] I wanted to understand what Samara society looked like just a few months before the fall of the Romanovs and the Bolshevik coup that followed. In turn, the listings of names and occupational positions allow me to trace social continuities and ruptures in the 1920s and 1930s. The yearbook covers the entire *guberniya*, but to make the analysis manageable, I focus on Samara, the *guberniya* center, and which, in any case, already before the Revolution housed most state and public institutions. Mironov notes that state penetration into rural areas had been low;[44] most Crown civil servants were based in *guberniya* capitals.[45] Tables 3.1 and 3.2 provide basic statistics for the regional population, estate, religious, and demographic makeup.[46] As had been typical, the bulk of the population of close to 4 million people, 92.7 percent, belonged to the peasant estate, with the next sizeable estate being the *meshchane*, at 5.7 percent (43 percent in Samara City). Table 3.2 shows that a large share of the population – more than one out of ten residents – belonged to Christian faiths, comprising Lutherans, Catholics, and Old Believers – something that shaped mobility from the peasantry to the *meshchane* and to merchants.

Entries for Samara City alone – in 1916 a fast-growing conurbation with a population approaching 100,000 citizens – come to more than 4,000.[47] The directory leads with the itemization of Crown appointees – the governor and senior locally based imperial ministerial staff, overwhelmingly of noble makeup. Directory listings also cover institutions under the authority of the nine imperial

---

[41] Mironov, *Rossiyskaya imperiya*, 2:434. The 1722 Table of Ranks divided the bureaucracy into four groups: (1) lowest ranking civil servants (*kantselyarskiye sluzhashchiye* or *kantslyaristy*), who did not or could not have a noble title; (2) civil servants of IX–XIV rank; (3) those of VI–VIII rank; (4) and those of the highest bureaucratic (I–V) rank as well as generals. Ibid., 494.

[42] Ibid., table 8.16, 493.   [43] SGSC, *Pamyatnaya knizhka*.

[44] Immediately before World War I, there were 253,000 *chinovniki* in the 50 European Russian *gubernii* with a total population of 103.2 million people, or 1.5 per 1,000 people. Comparative ratios for Britain, Germany, France, and Austro-Hungary were 8.2, 6.1, 7.3, and 5.1, respectively. Mironov, *Rossiyskaya imperiya*, 2:441, table 8.6.

[45] Ibid., 435.

[46] In 1910, in Russia, excluding the Caucasus, Poland, Finland, and Central Asia, there were 43 towns and cities with a population of 50 to 99,900 people, and 19, with 100,000 to 499,900 people comprising 6.1 and 2.7 percent, respectively, among some 700 towns and cities. Only 4 cities had more than 500,000 people. Mironov, *Sotsial'naya istoriya*, 1:287, tables v.1 and v.2.

[47] A small minority of persons appear multiple times because they held several professional or civic positions.

TABLE 3.1 *City of Samara and the* guberniya *population*

Samara *guberniya* population, 1914	
Male	1,924,148
Female	1,970,435
Total	3,894,583
Samara City population, 1914	
Male	46,839
Female	52,390
Total	99,229
Samara City estates, 1897	
Hereditary and personal nobles	5,319
Clergy	1,560
Merchants	1,259
Meshchane	39,254
Peasants	39,826
Foreign nationals	317
Other estates	2,464
Total	89,999

Note. The 1914 data are for the period immediately prior to World War I, which affected populations and demographics.
Source. 1916 yearbook, Statistical sec., 2–3; *Samarskaya guberniya.* Data from 1897 census.

ministries – the 141 schools in the regional center under the Ministry of Enlightenment's jurisdiction;[48] those within the purview of sectoral bodies of State Control, the *Konnozavodstva* (cultivation of horse breeds) and the *Dukhovnoye vedomstvo* (spiritual authority); listings of eight major private credit organizations; thirty-five charitable and public welfare bodies; some 200 practicing doctors, midwives, feldshers, and dentists; four veterinary doctors; roughly fifty private insurance societies; and the major Emperor Alexander Museum and the public library attached to it.[49] Editorial boards and staff of the seven Samara-based periodical press outlets – *Guberniskiye vedomosti, Gordskoy*

---

[48] Interior, Justice, Finance, Trade and Industry, Agriculture, Imperial Court and Landholding (*udely*), Transport and Communications, Military Affairs, Public Enlightenment. In 1914, in the region, 381 new schools were opened with an additional 32,161 pupils, bringing the pupil total to 256,323 (168,667 male and 87,656 female). SGSC, *Pamyatnaya knizhka.* Statistical sec., 36.

[49] In 1914, the *guberniya* had 298 registered doctors, including 31 female; 609 male and female feldshers; 56 midwives (*povival'nyye babki*); 18 inoculators (*osnovoprivivateli*); 21 dentists; 2

TABLE 3.2 *Samara* guberniya *estate structure and religion, 1897 (%)*

Estate		Religion	
Hereditary nobles	0.2	Orthodox and *yedinovertsy* (coreligionists)	77.3
Personal nobles and *chinovniki* (civil servants)	0.2	*Raskol'niki* (Old Believers)	3.4
Clergy	0.4	Catholics	2.1
Honorary citizens and merchants	0.3	Lutherans	6.4
Meshchane	5.7	Other Christian faiths	0.2
Peasants	92.7	Jews	0.1
Inorodtsy (non-natives)	0.3	*Magometane* (Muslims)	10.3
Others, incl. foreigners	0.2	Other faiths	0.2
Total	100	Total	100

Note. I reproduce Russian terms as listed in the yearbook. *Yedinovertsy* are Old Believers formally part of the Orthodox Church.
Source. 1916 yearbook, Statistical sec., 3. Data from 1897 census.

vestnik, Volzhskoye slovo, Volzhskiy den', Samarskiy zemledelets, Nash golos, Samarskiye yeparkhal'nyye vedomosti – are also included.

Only white-collar positions are listed. Thus, gymnasium employee records would encompass senior personnel from the head teacher – and the merchants and public officials patronizing the institution – to junior staff like a matron or school nurse. Manual occupations, including cleaners, guards, or couriers, are not among the entries. Laborers in the city's 59 factories and plants, a 4,939-strong workforce, are likewise omitted.[50] Evening and part-time courses are excluded from the listings of educational institutions, but appendices containing private advertisements provide a flavor of additional sources of training – and employment – for urban residents. "Persons of both genders, literate and illiterate are accepted," proclaims the advertisement for "Courses of accounting, commercial arithmetic, correspondence, Russian, German, French, English languages, stenography, calligraphy, typing, computing using abacus and computing machines, work with cashier and reprographic equipment ... There is no limit to the duration of studies – study until you learn [*uchatsya do tekh por, poka vyuchatsya*]."[51] If we consider the listings in "class" terms, the directory thus covers virtually the entire palette of the upper-class citizenry in professional occupations or those who were public figures and the broad spectrum of middle-class jobs – from lower middle-class semiprofessionals

---

masseurs; 173 pharmacists; 75 pharmacy apprentices; 94 approved pharmacies, of which 13 in Samara City; and 30 pharmacies attached to hospitals and clinics. Ibid., Statistical sec., 31.
[50] Ibid., Statistical sec., 11.   [51] Ibid., Advertisements sec., 3.

like nurses, midwives, or railways clerks to upper middle-class ones such as senior doctors running their own private clinics – as indeed voluntary groups almost exclusively patronized by high-status elites and professionals.

Considering that most institutions and occupations, bar teaching and medicine, were almost exclusively male, the directory thus covers a significant slice of those in the public eye and professional society. A proportion of adult male professionals would have been supporting a family of three to five people,[52] so we have a combined portrait of the various gradations of the elite and middling segments of white-collar professionals and entrepreneurs who plausibly comprised some 10–20 percent of the city's population. This is a conservative estimate. While I was able to find some residents who feature in memoirs of descendants as residing in Samara at the time, others are missing. Professor Zoya Mikhaylovna Kobozeva hails from an extended family of several generations of local *meshchane* (the Yegorovs, Grigor'yevs, and Termans), which also included urban dwellers who, for one reason or another, maintained formal ascription to the peasant estate (the Kashins) but acquired the trappings of urban living and intermarried with *meshchane*. (For photographic records, see Figures 3.3 and 3.4.) Kobozeva's great-grandfather, Mikhail Nikanorovich Kashin, had been a traveling salesman for the Brothers Krestovnikov merchant trading empire, a white-collar occupation as is evidenced in the photographic representations and numerous postcards that the paterfamilias regularly sent to his family while on his many travels.[53] Although the Krestovnikovs were among Russia's most famous trading families,[54] their sales office is not listed in the 1916 directory. Samara trading agencies and branches of metropolitan companies were evidently too numerous to list and are therefore omitted from the *knizhki*. Likewise, although comprehensive listings of doctors, midwives, dentists, and dental technicians are available, such information is lacking for the small businesses of hairdressers, florists, and grocery stores, or for the scores of Samara's rentiers. The *meshchanin*

---

[52] On the difficulties of estimating "typical" family size for different estates considering age, mortality, infanticide, abortion, cohabitation in one household with members of different generations, family/household size depending on life stages, and so on, see Mironov, *Sotsial'naya istoriya*, 1: 219–36. On estimates of the size of clergy families in the mid-nineteenth century, see 223, table iv.3. Among rural households in European Russia, including among those ascribed to estates other than peasants, according to a 1917 survey, the average family size was 6.1 people. Ibid., 226; urban households had an average family size of 4.3 in European Russia already in 1897, though Mironov suggests that rural migration had the effect of changing family and demographic patterns. Ibid., 232; 323–36. The nuclear family became the predominant type of household among urban dwellers: "in shedding archaic forms of family organization the city was ahead of the village by some 50 years, i.e., by two … and possibly by three generations." Ibid., 236.

[53] After the Revolution, Kashin worked as a supplies and estate manager (*zavkhoz*) at the Institute of Physics. Interviews with Zoya Kobozeva, October 5, 2016; October 25, 2018; KFPA; and Mikhail B. Kashin, "Rucheyki slivayutsya v reki," unpublished manuscript, Samara 2005.

[54] Rieber, *Merchants*, 163–64.

FIGURE 3.3 Samara *meshchane*
Ivan Yakovlevich Lebedev, left, proprietor of a hair salon, and ancestral relation of Zoya
Kobozeva. Kobozeva family photographic archive and annotations (hereafter KFPA),
image 154.1

Dorofey Romanovich Grigor'yev, proprietor of a grocery shop (*bakaleynaya
lavka*) and distributor of farm appliances for the Kaskov Firm, whose
descendants are found in present-day Samara, did not have a mention in the
listings.[55]

The yearbook's advertisements section provides a flavor of the booming
buy-to-let and rental markets that some present-day Samara residents report
as having provided income, if not substantial wealth, for their forbears:

Furnished Home San-Remo: 45 luxuriously furnished suites, electric lighting, running
water, sewage, courier services...

[55] Interview with Zoya Kobozeva, October 25, 2018.

FIGURE 3.4 Yekaterina Ignat'yevna Kashina
Wife of the manager of the Samara office of the Brothers Krestovnikov Trading House Mikhail Nikanorovich Kashin, originally from the peasant estate and hailing from the village of Bol'shaya Glushitsa of Samara guberniya. Great-grandmother of Zoya Kobozeva. KFPA, image 12.1

Furnished House Nice [*Nitsa*]: Suites newly renovated and sumptuously furnished; lifts and electric lighting available, baths, couriers and first-rate cuisine...

Volga-Siberia Suites: electric lighting, splendid cuisine. Please ignore the nay-say of coachmen [*na vymysly izvozchikov proshu ne obrashchat' vnimaniye*].[56]

To provide examples from other *gubernii*, the doctor-turned-playwright Anton Chekhov would have been listed in the *knizhki* when working in the Moscow *guberniya* as a *zemstvo* doctor. His father, the erstwhile "pillar of the community" who ran a grocery store in the southern city of Taganrog – a city in

---

[56] SGSC, *Pamyatnaya knizhka.* Advertisements sec., 5, 4.

the *oblast' Voyska donskogo* administrative region – may not have had a mention in the yearbook, particularly after his business collapsed, something that would compromise participation in the many philanthropic and other public engagements preoccupying wealthy merchants.[57]

The estate is conspicuous in the listings of senior public figures, as are indications of rank. Hereditary nobles predominated at the apex of *guberniya* power. This would be typical for other provinces – in 1917, 73 percent of top national and provincial administrators came from this group.[58] The vice-governor, for instance, is recorded as "Kamer-Junker of the Court of His Imperial Highness, *Nadvornyy sovetnik*, Prince [*knyaz'*] Sergey Vasil'yevch Gorchakov"; the chairman of the Samara Guberniya Learned Archive Commission (SGLAC) is recorded as "The Samara *Uyezd* Chairman [*predvoditel'*] of the Nobility, Kamer-Junker of the Court of His Imperial Highness Count [*graf*] Mstislav Nikolayevich Tolstoy;" the City Public Bank chief executive features as "merchant, Ivan Yefimovich Il'yin";[59] and so on.

For lower-ranked professionals, the usage of one's estate is indicative of an impulse to show off their prestigious credentials while downplaying those betraying the modest origins of the position holder. The City Public Bank also lists a *meshchanin* as an accountant and a hereditary honored citizen as a member of the oversight committee. In another organization, an employee is listed as a merchant or honorary citizen, that is, with their estate designation, alongside their occupational position of assistant or engineer. Simultaneously, a colleague with a similar or more junior occupational position does not include their estate. Thus, in the Chancellery of the Management of the Samara-Zlatoustovskaya Railways, one *deloproizvoditel'* (scribe) is listed simply as Arkhip Fyodorovich Belov; another as "son of the Senior Officer [*ober-ofitser*] Mikhail Mikhaylovich Izvozchikov"; and one of the aides of the *deloproizvoditel'* is recorded as a "Personal Honored Citizen Andrey Andreyevich Preobrazhenskiy." The manager of the Samara City Butchery appears modestly as "Veterinary doctor, Valerian Yul'yevich Volferts." Rather than being to "all educated Russians" an "embarrassing anachronism"[60] – an argument that the historian Sheila Fitzpatrick advanced when discussing the imperial estate system – I consider the omission of one's estate designation as evidence of its continued role as a signifier of social status. The absence of an estate listing for some is an indicator of its continued relevance, not irrelevance, since those with merchant or honored citizen status were clearly keen to publicize these accolades; and the highest positioned, likely the *most educated* strata among Crown officials, evidently ensured that their estate and the *chin* (title) signifying their estate were scrupulously recorded.

---

[57] Bartlett, *Chekhov*, 32, 33, 35.   [58] Mironov, *Rossiyskaya imperiya*, 2:504, table 8.19.
[59] SGSC, *Pamyatnaya knizhka*. Samara *guberniya* organizations and titles (*chin*) sec. 5, 8.
[60] Fitzpatrick, *Tear Off the Masks!*, 72.

Religion and ethnicity are not listed in the directory, but there is some indication of a niche dimension to occupations. Cultural, religious, or other factors often incentivized or facilitated ascription to an estate. Thus, the children of German farmers were well-placed to become urban professionals – with *meshchane*, honorary citizen, or personal noble status – because of their habitual literacy and schooling; and Jews shackled with residential restrictions and paperwork requirements – like the family of First Guild merchant Lev Filippovich Heyfets, grandfather of Anneta Bass, an eminent figure in Soviet Samara's art circles – were eager to join the merchant or honored citizen estates through service and enterprise.[61] Individuals of Polish ancestry – a small but professionally esteemed community in Samara, which included many nobles – feature as shipping, railway, and communications employees.[62] Members of the German community are frequently listed as gymnasium teachers, engineers, and medics in the yearbook as well as government employees.[63] Jewish professionals were robustly represented in the medical sphere, something that is corroborated in family histories and genealogies of Samara's Jewish community.[64] By contrast, government bodies and leading state banks tend to feature Russian Orthodox and Old Believer, noble and merchant, respectively, family names at their helm.[65]

Social Networks and Ties: Formal Social Network Analysis

I now turn to charting out the contours of networks of professionals and their social and estate composition. A static organizational-professional-civic map would only take us so far in understanding the social structure as reflected in *interactions* among individuals and groups. Powerful or otherwise socially influential individuals – even when not in positions of power – are often those

---

[61] On Heyfets, see Burlina, *Yevreyi*, 51. I use Russian transliteration of the family name; in English-speaking countries it is likely Heifetz. New legislation sanctioning trade and entrepreneurship without ascription to the merchant estate and changes in tax laws whereby taxes were levied on enterprises, not on individuals, made merchant status less attractive to Orthodox Christian entrepreneurs. For Jews, the merchant estate meant elevation of one's social status against the background of discriminatory laws. On the implications of the 1898 new trade tax (*promyslovyy nalog*), see Makitrin and Barinova, "Samarskoye kupechestvo," 44.

[62] Foreign proprietors of large industries often engaged in positive discrimination, opting for engineers and other skilled professionals of German, Polish, French, or other European non-Russian origin. Rieber, *Merchants*, 219, 223, 225, 226.

[63] Well into the first half of the nineteenth century, some 30 percent of top-ranked *chinovniki* were also of German ancestry. Mironov, *Rossiyskaya imperiya*, 2:509. On German pedagogues and officials in Samara, see Savchenko and Dubinin, *Rossiyskiye nemtsy*, 92–93.

[64] Burlina, "Imya?" 120, 123.

[65] Jews, however, were becoming more prominent in entrepreneurship by the end of the nineteenth century. Samara's merchant families, overwhelmingly Orthodox Christian, were a dominant, but shrinking, community, reduced in numbers from 141 to 71 between 1895 and 1916. The Jewish merchant community rose from eight families in 1895 to twenty-five in 1916. Makitrin and Barinova, "Samarskoye kupechestvo," 51 and 52, table 6.

who keep a presence in leading institutions of government and in the public and civic sphere. They are the Boosters of Sinclair Lewis's American small town, the doers and shakers in the community who personally know the governor – and his wife – while also frequently seen to deliver a well-timed and well-publicized speech in the soup kitchen of the town's urban slum. A historical ethnography of society of the kind presented here does not allow me to sit in, or listen in on, the ladies' gossip in the governor's parlor or interrogate the community's influencers concerning the other well-networked individuals in the group.[66] The listings of invitees – and of those who turn up or fail to show – at the social bridge session, the community ball, and the school charity event are of necessity an unrealistic source for establishing social networks that far back in time. Nevertheless, the 1916 yearbook allows us to record the multiple affiliations of government figures, local governance officials, professionals, schoolteachers, and civic activists. Which are the best connected and networked organizations? Who is the most networked notable? Which organizations is he or she affiliated with or patronizes? And, by extension, who are the people he or she is likely to know and interact with? What are the shared characteristics of those people when we consider their estate, organizational embeddedness, and pursuits in the public and civic arenas of Samara? And are these the kinds of organizations that the Bolsheviks disbanded and whose key executives they subjected to violence and persecution, like the police force and the governor's office? A networking exercise such as this would then allow us to analyze the reproduction of organizational-network structures and ties after the Revolution. A portrait of these ties in turn aids us in ascertaining elements of social closure or porousness; of organizational resources; of skills and capital. These could potentially not only aid survival in the Soviet state but in fundamental ways help preserve islands of social autonomy, even if circumscribed in an estatist way.

For the social networking exercise, I created a dataset listing the city's organizations and associated individuals. I first perform analysis employing organizations, and then turn to individuals, as nodes. Figure 3.5 is a sociogram of the entire organizational network,[67] generated using Cytoscape and Gephi software and providing a visual illustration of the scope and magnitude of the ties linking organizations through individuals. Clearly visible are large circles at the center pointing to a high degree of what social network theorists refer to as network centrality: they represent nodes pivotal to connecting the network. Many other nodes are but tiny dots on the image, far removed from the "core" featuring dense network ties. Each node stands for an organization, with a total of 290 nodes corresponding to all organizations,

---

[66] See the discussion of informal rules of entry and exclusion in homes of powerful people in Hunter, *Community Power Structure*, 36–38; and on "social cliques" in Davis et al., *Deep South*, 128–60.

[67] I am grateful to Giovanni Angioni for the social network analysis. The discussion of concepts is based on Kadushin, *Understanding Social Networks*.

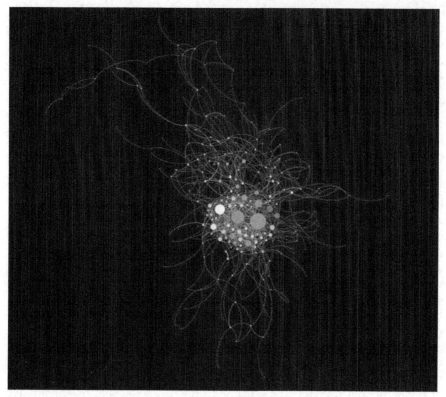

FIGURE 3.5 Professional and civic network ties, City of Samara, 1916
Source. Produced based on author analysis of data from the 1916 yearbook

state, and non-state, in the directory. Altogether, the directory includes 3,412 individuals, of whom a number are associated with several organizations. There are 1,025 "edges," or connections, in the network. We observe high concentration toward the core, whereby the top ten organizations modulate the entirety of the network. Indeed, within a degree range going from 104 to 0, only 3 organizations are above 50, featuring strong "betweenness" and "closeness" centrality. These institutions have comparatively high numbers of connections while also supplying links to other organizational "nodes." Looking at network periphery, we observe that many nodes are poorly connected in terms of both distance from the core and degree in absolute terms. The network's assorted shades stand for different clusters.

The three most networked organizations are the representative institutions that reflected bottom-up democratic impulses – the *gorodskaya duma* (city council/assembly), as noted in the section "A Trading City on the Volga," an elected body overwhelmingly of privileged makeup; the SGLAC, a civic grouping par excellence and embracing some of the individuals who were also engaged in urban governance; and a civic body epitomizing the philanthropic impulse of old-regime Russia, the Samara Guberniya Patronage of Children's Foster Homes (SGPCFH). The latter two, like the *duma*, feature high-status nobles and merchants. Chapter 2 has illuminated how the nobility's affluence and habitually acquired formal education, as indeed the facilitating enterprise of the *dvoryanskoye sobraniye*, the self-governing assembly of corporations of nobles; merchants' wealth, enabling educational investment; and the philanthropy that eased the acquisition of the title of honored citizen, all facilitated progression and ascent into the highest service ranks. The three institutions thus embody the archaic character of Russian society – insofar as one's estate apparently continued to be a predictor of status – and the modern, proto-democratic, aspect manifested in participatory elected institutions, as indeed a thriving public sphere. The high-status, well-networked, urban society had been one that was self-constituting and self-initiating; and autonomy, as I shall unpack in the following chapters, would not come easily but would be continuously negotiated and defended vis-à-vis the imperial Russian state. As such, the public sphere prepared individuals and their networks for the necessary struggles of carving out a semi-sovereign space under the Bolsheviks.

When we expand the range of "most networked" sites beyond the top three, the following picture appears. In Table 3.3, I first isolate the top and bottom ten organizations by "centrality" – a concept that network theorists break into (1) "degree" or number of connections radiating from one node; (2) "betweenness" or the extent to which nodes represent connectors linking other nodes; and (3) "closeness," or length of the shortest path linking the binary connections between nodes. As in Figure 3.5, we observe that Samara's most connected organizations and associated individuals are the institutions of elected government and its executive bodies – the *duma* and *uprava*; those in the enlightenment sphere – like the SGLAC and the Samara Society of Public Universities (SSPU); other civil society organizations, namely the Patronage of Foster Homes, the Red Cross, and the Promotion of Sobriety societies; as well as gymnasia and other secondary schools, like the Women's Gymnasium No. 2, the Countess Khovanskaya Gymnasium, and the Commercial *uchilishche*. The summary presented here and in Figure 3.5 points to a well-networked society but also one where *networkedness* is heavily skewed toward a small set of organizations and individuals. Some professional organizations, particularly in medicine and education, not straightforwardly conceptualized as high status, also feature as well-networked.

To make sense of these patterns, I distinguish between "luxury" and "occupational" networks. The "luxury" networks included leading noble and merchant families. Individuals belonging to them not only owned and ran banks and credit societies and occupied quasi-professional positions as board members on state bodies but simultaneously patronized, funded, ran, and participated in the work of scores of charities and philanthropic activities; they also socialized in expensive leisure venues like the von Vakano Yacht and Tennis Club.[68] The wealthy Samara First Guild merchant Pyotr Nikolayevich Aref'yev, who housed his business and family on the elite Dvoryanskaya Street (boulevard of nobles), was one such figure. Aref'yev's main professional entry in the 1916 directory is under the rubric of Managers of Insurance, Shipping and other Societies, Banks, and Trading Houses in Samara City. We find his name in addition on six other public and charitable bodies, as either affiliate or patron. Consistent with his renaissance man persona,[69] the erudite Aref'yev appears as a board member or patron of SGLAC; the local Chapter of Society of Patronage over the Blind; SSPU; the Society for the Encouragement of Education; and the Council of Russia's Imperial Theatre Society. An accomplished amateur photographer, Aref'yev also appears on the records for the Samara Photographic Society.[70]

The "occupational" networks feature one individual as an employee of multiple institutions in broadly similar positions. This pattern is particularly interesting given that social network analysis draws our attention to "role sets" or "status" relationships linking individuals *within* and *outside* a professional organization but also engendering friendship and other personal ties and information flows – the "content multiplexity" aspect of ties.[71] While superior–subordinate is a classic status dyad within an organization that may also involve friendship, in some professions like teaching the role set involves multiple formal organizations and informal connections, including the school board, the parent, the pupil, and the public education board.[72] Employment with multiple cognate professional organizations is likely to intensify the "multiplexity" effect, particularly in professions featuring service roles to wider society. In Samara, education and medicine featured dense networks. It would not be uncommon for a teacher to make her rounds giving lessons at three or four different schools or for a doctor to be in the employ of multiple medical institutions. These patterns were less common for senior employees in the city's most prestigious institutions, for instance the leading private gymnasia. There, a teacher's pay would be commensurate with their prestige though some pedagogues taught in several institutions of equal stature. Directors of gymnasia earned high incomes by the standards of the professions at the time. In 1917, Nina Andreyevna, the founding principal of KWG, earned an annual salary of 2,400 rubles, the top bracket for late imperial professional wages.[73] Lay teachers in schools, however, were often employed

---

[68] Aleksushin and Sinin, *Pervyy vek.*   [69] Myakisheva, "Istoriya," 142.
[70] Listed as a hereditary honorary citizen. SGSC, *Pamyatnaya knizhka.*
[71] Kadushin, *Understanding Social Networks*, 36.   [72] Ibid., 36.
[73] Estimates of the average annual pay for teachers in 1911 in city schools are 528 rubles for men and 447 for women. Brooks, *When Russia Learned to Read*, 46. On average, the annual income of a Russian "intelligent" with higher education was 1,058 rubles in 1913. Mironov,

part-time and earned modest salaries. The *statskiy sovetnik* Pavel Aleksandrovich Preobrazhenskiy, for instance, a clergyman by estate and Nina Andreyevna's close family friend, gave only two lessons a week, earning an annual salary of 200 rubles from KWG. He additionally received an annual premium of 900 rubles as chairman of the school's Pedagogical Council. We also know from the 1916 yearbook that Preobrazhenskiy taught at the Commercial *uchilishche*.[74] Furthermore, high-status pedagogues cultivated links with elite society in ways other than employment at multiple prestigious schools. They sat on the *duma*, deliberated on the Learned Archive Commission or other such bodies, and pursued philanthropic activities. Preobrazhenskiy typified this pattern. A notable "enlightenment" figure, he was active in the work of SSPU and SGLAC.[75]

Some evidence of intra-occupational differentiation is found in the types of institutions individuals tended to be associated and networked with. For instance, a Mariya Aleksandrovna Smolich taught at two institutions, both private: the Private Women's Gymnasium of V. A. Arsen'yeva and the Private *real'noye uchilishche* of A. T. Maksheeva. Vladimir Dmitriyevich Tikhovidov is listed with only one institution, the Romanov Gymnasium for boys. By contrast, the instructor of religion Ioann Petrovich Dobrokhotov, a clergyman by estate, is listed for three public schools, namely two parish schools for poorer children and a religious female *uchilishche*.[76]

Like teachers, physicians were often affiliated with multiple institutions. Nancy Mandelker Frieden's account of the medical profession sheds light on the material imperatives – indeed, sheer poverty – that drove many junior doctors to pursue multiple jobs to make ends meet.[77] As the biography of the medical doctor Liya Samuilovna Pasternak, a descendant of a Jewish *cantonist* who settled in Samara in the nineteenth century, illustrates, medical professionals often came from modest, not infrequently *meshchane*, backgrounds: Liya's grandfather had been

---

Sotsial'naya istoriya, 1: 156–57n178. There were considerable variations and earnings fluctuations among even the secondary school teachers in elite schools. The Ministry of Education defined the salary of women school directors at 2,000 rubles per year plus housing, which could be supplemented with teaching income. Teacher salaries fluctuated because directors used discretion to assign additional contact hours beyond the mandated minimum of instruction per week. Although gymnasium teachers complained of low pay, this was in part a consequence of the desire "to live as equals among the educated classes. In late nineteenth-century Russia, this meant a comfortable apartment with a servant and money to spend on certain amenities such as books, theatre, and travel." By contrast, primary schoolteachers' salaries were on a par with those of skilled workers and they, "like their pupils' parents, struggled to make ends meet." One Moscow University Pedagogical Society report in 1900 estimated the cost of living in the city for a childless single secondary schoolteacher at 1,800 rubles per year. Many gave lessons outside the classroom, privately, during the summer months, or at several other schools. Ruane, *Gender*, 57, 56, 58, 59. Costs in the provinces like Samara would have, of course, been lower.

[74] Authorization for payment of salaries for September 1917. Khardina papers. Tsentral'nyy Gosudarstvennyy arkhiv Samarskoy oblasti (hereafter TsGASO), f. 300, op. 1, d. 46.

[75] SGSC, *Pamyatnaya knizhka*. [76] Ibid. [77] Frieden, *Russian Physicians*.

a shoemaker.[78] By contrast, the most sought-after medics running private clinics – those whom Frieden would categorize as comfortably well-off – are not always so networked with multiple medical hospitals and clinics. Various sources allow us to piece together the engagements of medics at the pinnacle of the profession. Isolated physicians feature among the luxury networks, rubbing elbows with leading merchants and industrialists at elite leisure venues. Moisey Abramovich Grinberg, one among a dynasty of medics, ran his own private clinic. The mansion that he built for his family in the then fashionable art nouveau style, which doubled as his private practice, is a telling representation of the affluence of this Samara family.[79] The extended Grinberg family also had the means to enjoy membership with the Yacht Boating and Tennis Club – a province of the Samara elite[80] – and were active in the public affairs of Samara's Jewish community.[81]

Intra- and extra-occupational status differentiation is evident when medics transcend their narrow professional role and assume managerial positions, essentially attaining the status, remuneration, and networks of the elite. Consider the example of Yevgeniy Leopol'dovich Kavetskiy, one of imperial Samara's leading medics.[82] Already in 1898, Kavetskiy headed the city's Pathology and Anatomy Services, a managerial post that transcended his narrow occupational role as a practicing doctor. Kavetskiy is in addition listed as an employee of the Guberniya Zemstvo Hospital; as a doctor working in the Lazaret for Evacuated Soldiers attached to the Samara Ol'ginskaya Community; and as an employee of the Zemstvo Midwifery School. Simultaneously, he is privy to the luxury networks, engaged as he is with the Samara Society for the Encouragement of Education (SSEE) and the charitable institution the Committee of Samara Community of Sisters of Mercy. Only a handful of the directory's dozens of doctors and teachers feature as patrons or activists on charitable, public enlightenment, or other civic bodies – a province of the upper echelons of Samara's bourgeoisie.[83]

Finally, I identify academia, and, more broadly, enlightenment spheres, as representing a broader concentric network, encompassing high-status public figures; professionals in medicine, engineering, and teaching; amateur enlightenment figures; patrons of the arts and sciences; professional and lay classicists; historians; and archaeologists. Aside from Doctor Kavetskiy, in this network we find the landowner Vladimir Petrovich Arapov, a *kollezhskiy assessor*. A senior expert with the Samara-Ural Management of Agriculture and State

---

[78] Burlina, "Imya?" 124.

[79] *Yevreyskiy mir Samary.* Virtual museum site: sites.google.com/site/samaraemir/muzejnaa-ekspozicia/kupcy-i-predprinimateli/m-a-grinberg (accessed December 23, 2020).

[80] The son of Dr. Moisey Abramovich Grinberg was a participant in a 1912 tennis tournament. Aleksushin and Sinin, *Pervyy vek*, 42.

[81] Burlina, "Iz istorii," 41–42.

[82] For a summary of Kavetskiy's bio, see the Wikipedia entry: ru.wikipedia.org/wiki/ Кавецкий,_ Евгений_Леопольдович (accessed April 17, 2020).

[83] SGSC, *Pamyatnaya knizhka.*

Property, Vladimir Petrovich had also been a prolific participant in a variety of causes, as a member of SGLAC, SSPU, the Samara Chapter of Imperial Russian Society of Gardeners, and the Bureau of Aid to Rural Cooperatives attached to the Samara Society for the Improvement of the Peasant Economy. Pyotr Aleksandrovich Shcherbachyov, employed as a city architect with the Samara City *uprava*, and his extended family, were also linked to the academy networks. A merchant family related to Samara's feted mayor Pyotr V. Alabin, the Shcherbachyov family had been active in various civic initiatives.[84]

Table 3.3 presents the ten most connected organizations by degree, betweenness centrality, and closeness centrality. The concept of betweenness centrality captures the position of a node – in our case, organization – as lying in between other nodes and hence playing a "facilitator" role. We see that SGLAC, the *duma*, and the Spiritual Seminary, for instance, play a vital role in connecting other organizations.[85]

Let us now explore organizations and networks outside of the core network cites. In what ways did these differ from the most-connected sites of social-professional interaction? One notable observation is that institutions associated with Crown or state power – the governor's office, the Ministry of Interior (MVD), procuracy agencies – are among the *least* networked. Not only did these institutions constitute prime targets for Bolshevik destruction but individuals embedded within them featured fewer network ties to local enlightenment and professional notables that would have enabled adaptation under the new regime. Another striking pattern in Table 3.4 is the predominance of parish schools in the list of *least* connected organizations. These attracted poorer students; and teaching would not have been as prestigious a vocation as being a gymnasium instructor and pay would have been lower. Individuals working for these schools were not part of the elite or enlightenment networks overlapping with bodies of self-governance – the *duma* and its executive body. As such, they are distinct from the gymnasia appearing among the most connected sites. In the latter case, directors, patrons, and teachers, often of noble, merchant, or high-status *meshchane* background,

[84] Ibid. Mikhaylova, "Zastyvshaya muzyka …. kakaya ona, arkhitektura Samary?" *Samarskiye sud'by* ("Samara Destinies"): samsud.ru/blogs/hroniki-samarochki/zastyvshaja-muzyka-kakaja-ona-arhitektur.html (accessed April 17, 2020); Yerofeyev, "Shcherbachyov Aleksandr Aleksandrovich," *Istoricheskaya Samara*, ("Historical Samara"): историческая-самара.рф/каталог/самарская-персоналия/щ/щербачёв-александр-александрович.html (accessed April 17, 2020).
[85] These are crossroads, organizations through which people move and connect to other organizations. Thus, the Spiritual Seminary, which does not appear as particularly important based on other network indicators, helps link other organizations. Although not as well connected as, say, the *duma*, without their mediation, or bridging function, the well-connected organizations would not play the same role in the network. On the other hand, closeness centrality tells us that a node is "closer" to other nodes. A real-life pattern would be facility of connection with, and movement to or from, an institution where common acquaintances are also likely to be encountered.

TABLE 3.3 *Top ten most connected organizations, 1916*

Ranking	Degree	Betweenness Centrality	Closeness Centrality
1	Samara City Duma	SGLAC	SGLAC
2	SGLAC	Samara City Duma	Samara City Duma
3	SGPCFH	Spiritual Seminary	Women's Gymnasium No. 2
4	Women's Gymnasium No. 2*	SGPCFH	SSPU
5	Gubernskoye Zemskoye Sobraniye	Samara City Uprava	SGPCFH
6	SSPU	Women's Gymnasium No. 2	Samara City Uprava
7	Samara Local Chapter of Russian Society of Red Cross	SSPU	Samara Commercial Uchilishche
8	Samara Commercial Uchilishche	Yeparkhiya Female Uchilishche	Yeparkhiya Uchilishche Council
9	Samara Guberniya Agency for Insurance of Workers	Spiritual Uchilishche	Guberniya Committee for Propagating Public Sobriety**
10	Samara City Uprava	City Parish Uchilishcha	Countess Khovanskaya Women's Gymnasium No. 3

Note. * The gymnasium featured individuals like Mariya Preobrazhenskaya, whose close family relations taught at KWG and were among the most connected individuals in the enlightenment sphere; and Nikolay Osorgin, a noble and member of SGLAC. SGSC, *Pamyatnaya knizhka*; TsGASO, f. 300, op. 2, ed khr. 9. ** *Gubernskiy Komitet popechitel'stva o narodnoy trezvosti.*

combined school-connected work with civic or urban governance engagements. The historian Scott Seregny situates the lay teacher of the "culture pioneer" variety as a socially isolated figure, a semiprofessional of vastly superior training to that of the unschooled target masses, who is nevertheless perceived as a social inferior by enlightened society.[86]

Unlike doctors, urban or rural, who could impress on the tsarist government the need for professional autonomy, given the more pressing demands of

---

[86] Seregny, "Professional Activism," 169–71. On pre-revolutionary discussions of *polu-intelligentsia* as those with only secondary specialized education like primary school teachers, nurses, or technicians as distinct from university-educated "*intelligentsia* proper," see also Churchward, *Soviet Intelligentsia*, 5.

TABLE 3.4 *Bottom ten least connected organizations, 1916*

Ranking	Degree	Betweenness Centrality	Closeness Centrality
1	143rd Infantry Spare Battalion	Men's Primary Uchilishche attached to workhouse	CPU, mixed, 19th
2	CPU, mixed, 48th	Governor Office, MVD	CPU, mixed, 39th
3	CPU, mixed, 27th	Samara Evangelical-Lutheran Parish	CPU, mixed, 37th
4	Prayer House	Uchilshche for Blind Children	CPU, mixed, 38th
5	Samara District Evacuation Point	Samara City Agency for Trade Tax	143rd Infantry Spare Battalion
6	CPU, Male, 1st	Council of Russian Imperial Theatre Society	CPU, mixed, 48th
7	Men's Gymnasium No. 3	Prison Church	CPU, mixed, 27th
8	Krestovozdvizhenskaya Church	Samara River Yacht Boating Club*	CPU, mixed, 44th
9	Guberniya Excise Duty Management	Procuracy Monitoring of Samara District Court	Prayer House
10	Accounting Courses, Board of Mutual Aid Society for Prikazchiki (shop managers, sales agents) in the City of Samara	Guberniya Agency for Factory and Mining Industry Affairs	CPU, mixed, 17-25th

Note. CPU stands for city parish *uchilishcha*. * Erich von Vakano, who ran the club, was wounded in 1915, fighting on the Russian side in World War I; his father and brother were accused of "spying" and sent to Buzuluk town as Russia joined the war against Austria. In 1916, the club virtually closed, hence its appearance as a weakly networked node. Aleksushin et al., *Pervyy vek*, 50.

epidemics, lay teachers were also less successful at organizing professionally.[87] This pattern is not insignificant, since, by many accounts, individuals working with these less esteemed institutions constituted the foot soldiers of enlightenment in post-revolutionary Russia and were less conspicuous targets of class-based

[87] Seregny, "Professional Activism," 175. On medical associations, see Hutchinson, "Politics," 89; and, on the connection between epidemics and medical professional associations and autonomy, see Frieden, *Russian Physicians*, esp. 135. Ruane, however, argues that the issue was not so much weak organization, which she disputes, but divisions between the primary school and rural teachers of peasant or lower middle-class origin and those in secondary schools, notably gymnasium teachers of largely noble, elite civil service, and clergy backgrounds. "As one teacher commented, the division of the profession into castes proved impossible to overcome." Ruane, *Gender*, 193.

witch hunts and scrutiny. By contrast, individuals in the well-networked arenas of the more high-status public sphere would be far more likely targets for persecution. Their embeddedness in formal and informal institutions of elite learning and routinized interactions, however, would aid survival and adaptation. Social network theory approaches the real-world consequences of role multiplexity from the perspective of organizational or corporate performance, transparency, and efficiency. Kadushin thus summarizes the ambiguous effects of close ties: "Multiple flows between positions as well as multiple simultaneous positions can enhance a relationship and build trust ... On the other hand, depending on the circumstances, the same friendship can create a conflict of interest or even the possibility of fraud."[88] As I shall discuss in the following chapters, the fusion between personal friendship and professional roles and ties helped not only the survival but also the maintenance of the autonomous professional sphere in Soviet Russia. Prevarications, various forms of sheltering of colleagues from persecution, fabrication of documents – or "fraud" as in the Kadushin quote – became "weapons"[89] in the arsenal of the status-maintenance impulses of communist Russia's suspect bourgeoisie.

Analysis of Individuals As Nodes

Here, I extend the analysis presented in Figure 3.5 by employing individuals, rather than organizations, as nodes. The assumption is that one "focal node" connecting others directly creates what network theorists refer to as an "interpersonal environment": individuals so connected are likely to know each other, meet, and interact personally, in contrast to nodes more distant in terms of the multiple other nodes one has to "traverse" to link up with the focal node.[90] In this exercise, each node represents an individual, while organizations are links connecting individuals. If two or more individuals worked for the same organization, I assume that they had a reasonable chance of being in contact with each other. That organization therefore becomes a link, "an edge," between the two nodes. As is clear from Figure 3.6, we have a much higher number of nodes (3,410) as compared to the analysis in which organizations were nodes. We also see a very substantial number of connections: almost 104,000. This is clear from the overview snapshot: a large, densely connected network.

The second most striking characteristic is the clear division in clusters, which are recognizable through the assorted shades. Indeed, the value of overall

---

[88] Kadushin, *Understanding Social Networks*, 37.

[89] The metaphor underlines the resistance of underprivileged groups. Scott, *Weapons*.

[90] Kadushin, *Understanding Social Networks*, 27–28. Note: these clusters should not be interpreted as key organizations. By design, organizations here represent links among individuals – individuals belonging to an important cluster are well connected, not the other way around. Instead of showing the most connected organizations, this part of the analysis discerns the most "connecting" ones.

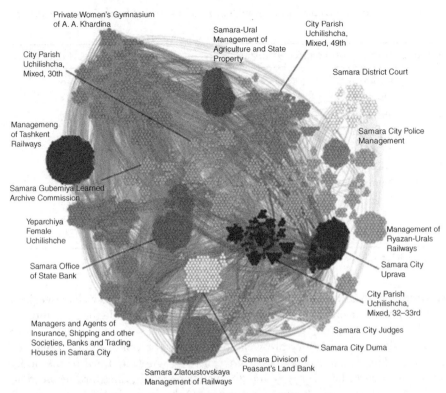

FIGURE 3.6 Network overview with individuals as nodes, 1916

modularity or the extent to which a network is divided into clusters, is remarkably high: almost 0.9 on a [−1; +1] range. Clusters are generally large and well connected, as the edges show; their shade matches that of the corresponding node. There are nonetheless clusters that are less connected and appear peripheral in their location vis-à-vis other, more connected, ones. For instance, the clusters corresponding to the police authority and the offices of the Tashkent Railways and Peasants' Land Bank feature poor links with other organizational settings. Hardly any lines connecting certain clusters to other sites implies a lack of ties to other clusters among individuals working within these settings. Generally, what is striking, but unsurprising, is that the least connected clusters are imperial bureaucracies with authority over operations of railways, police forces, and the courts. By contrast, the more connected sites are educational and urban governance institutions. Often established consequential to private philanthropy and civic initiative, the prestigious educational institutions like gymnasia especially maintained a character of participation in the thriving urban public sphere, even though they were subjected to imperial educational authority and sanction. Likewise, the Duma, a representative

TABLE 3.5 *Individuals and estate ascription. Edges (links) between organizations, 1916*

Ranking	Name (most connected)	Estate	Edges Count
1	Bashkirov, V.	HHC	46
2	Osorgin, N.	noble	45
3	Sheshlov, A.	HHC	45
4	Yurin, Ye.	*titulyarnyy sovetnik* (personal noble)	36
5	Smirnov, S.	*nadvornyy sovetnik* (personal noble)	28
6	Suroshnikov, V.	HHC	28
7	Naumova, A.	noble	21
8	Yegorov, A.	HHC	18
9	Aref'yev, P.	HHC	16
10	Arapov, V.	*kollezhskiy assessor* (personal noble)	15

Note. HHC stands for hereditary honored citizen.

institution packed with civic notables and leading merchants, is well networked, linking philanthropists and civic personnel outside and inside the assembly.

The network presents a balanced distribution of connections. Most individuals in the directory are well connected – the opposite of a polarized network. The degree range goes from 379 to 0, with one-third of the nodes showing a degree between 379 and 80 (well connected), one-third between 80 and 20, and one-third between 20 and 0. Only fifteen individuals have no connection. We can say the same for closeness centrality, which is on average high: for one-third of nodes, it is equal to one (maximum). The distinction between the core and periphery is significantly less marked in this case. Table 3.5 illustrates how the most connected individuals are nobles and honored citizens. Recall that citizens were awarded personal noble status due to distinction or length in service, community engagements, or philanthropy. The same applies to honored citizen status, something that the *meshchane* and merchants aspired to for material and symbolic reasons.[91]

SAMARA SOCIETY AFTER THE REVOLUTION

The fall of the Romanovs and the witch hunts and persecution of leading aristocratic families have come to be associated with the destruction of an entire

---

[91] In 1870–97, there was a more than fivefold rise in honored citizens in European Russia (excluding Poland and Finland) and an almost 50 percent reduction in guild merchants. The honored citizen title accorded similar privileges as the merchant estate, but hereditary honored citizens did not have to pay annual dues to retain the title. The number of *meshchane* almost doubled in that period. Mironov, *Sotsial'naya istoriya*, 1:115, table II.9, and discussion, 116.

social order. I do not seek to diminish the significance of social change following the Bolshevik Revolution and the ensuing Civil War; in Samara, it mirrored the dislocation characterizing the top layers of the aristocracy and the industrial tycoons elsewhere in Russia. The city briefly, for four months, became the seat of KOMUCH. After retaking Samara from KOMUCH, the Bolsheviks disbanded the institutions of elected government and nationalized private enterprises.[92] Many families belonging to the governing and economic elite faded away from the social map of Samara, their properties expropriated; many had the means to emigrate and scores did – a route taken by some members of the Shikhobalov clan and another leading merchant family, the Ardzhanovs.[93] The merchant and public figure Constantine Neklutin emigrated to America, taking his immediate family with him; others from the extended clan remained in Samara; and individual family members suffered exile, privations, and repression in the late 1920s and 1930s.[94] Some, like the leading merchant socialite Aleksandra Pavlovna ("Sandi") Kurlina (b. 1876), spent the rest of their lives in discreet self-exile. Kurlina remained in a communal flat in Moscow, albeit residing on Myaskovskogo Street, located in the vicinity of the prestigious Arbat district and the iconic Prague restaurant. Kurlina kept a low profile until her death (ca. 1970).[95]

Transcending the tiny group of renowned notables were scores of lesser aristocrats, professionals or proto-professionals, and civic old-timers who were embedded in the occupational networks in the realms of culture, education, medicine, engineering, and public service. They boasted a dynastic pedigree of education in superb institutions of learning, a habitual trajectory of nobles' upbringing whether they entered the world of the modern salaried professional or not; and they were in the best position to colonize professions that involved the production of new knowledge or that required high-level and specialist skills. Among this group increasingly were also scions of merchant families whose wealth allowed the acquisition of the same kinds of educational accolades that cleaved the elite and middling bourgeoisie from the overwhelmingly illiterate and undereducated masses of society. Finally, the *new joiners* were a rising upwardly mobile cohort of would-be middling professionals – often of *meshchane*, clergy, and mixed-title origin – for example, the Olen'ka Konovalovs. They too were completing or already possessed diplomas from prestigious secondary schools and universities or

[92] The von Vakano beer factory was nationalized in the 1920s. Savchenko and Dubinin, *Rossiyskiye nemtsy*, 91.

[93] Estimates of Russia's post-revolutionary émigrés range from 800,000 to 3 million. Bessudnov, "Effects," 150; Vishnevskiy, *Demografcheskaya modernizatsiya*, 404–5. On Lenin's exile of intellectuals, see Chamberlain, *Lenin's Private War*.

[94] Author personal interview with a descendant, Irina Kolbintseva, Samara, October 25, 2018; NC.

[95] Exact date unknown. For a fascinating photographic collection of the family and biographical sketches, see Yerofeyev, "Kurliny, kupecheskiy rod," on the *Istoricheskaya Samara* ("Historical Samara") website: Историческая-самара.рф/каталог/самарская-персоналия/к/курлины,-купеческий-род.html (accessed April 18, 2020).

from less prestigious ones that bestowed narrow sought-after specialties. These individuals belonged to a different generation and as such would not feature among the most highly networked elite and professionals in the 1916 directory. They were, however, already active in many of the same social arenas as the prior generation of nobles and wealthier merchants – acquiring the contacts and ties, as indeed the human capital, skills, and social "mattering maps,"[96] of the more established estatist bourgeoisie. In what follows, I chart out continuities and shifts in the social-organizational embeddedness of individuals whose careers traversed the tsarist and Bolshevik regimes.

Charting Middle-Class Adaptation after the Revolution

Social network analysis of Samara society in 1916 suggests that several of the "most networked" interlocking sites of autonomous social enterprise also maintained a strong estatist character, comprised as they had been overwhelmingly of nobles and merchants. We do not possess an equivalent of the 1916 directory that would allow us to chart out systematically the contours of decimation, or, alternatively, reconstitution, of social-professional ties and arenas of social enterprise and interaction. The task would be particularly daunting when it comes to mid-level professionals who do not have obituaries or Wikipedia pages dedicated to them and individuals who preferred to maintain a low profile while essentially resuming their previous work. The evidence that we do have concerning the *vertical* career progression of individual middling professionals is strongly indicative of continuities in the embeddedness of occupational *horizontal* ties and networks. Consider the *Soviet* résumé of the veterinary professional Valerian Dmitriyevich Tikhovidov. The Revolution brings uncertainty into Tikhovidov's professional life, yet his career picks up after only a brief interlude. As Tikhovidov's great-great-grandson narrates, "there was no feldsher in Yekaterinovka and so on 1 May 1918 the Samara Guberniya Veterinary Administration ... appointed him to the position that he previously occupied as head of the Yekaterinovka Veterinary District."[97] Over the years, even after the Bolsheviks took power from KOMUCH, Tikhovidov's professional engagements included teaching veterinary science to trainee vets and work at the Bezenchuk Experimental Cattle Breeding and other veterinary stations that also feature on his imperial CV.[98]

The more systematic evidence concerning high-status professionals, academics, and cultural dignitaries allows us to further probe the perpetuity of those professional networks and ties. In Figure 3.7 and Table 3.6, I present findings from a structured analysis of the enlightenment network. The data underpinning the exercise are highly skewed toward individuals for whom

---

[96] Citation from Goldstein, *The Mind-Body Problem* in Migdal, *State in Society*, 113–14.
[97] Popov, "Vernost' professii," 2012, chap. 4.   [98] Ibid.

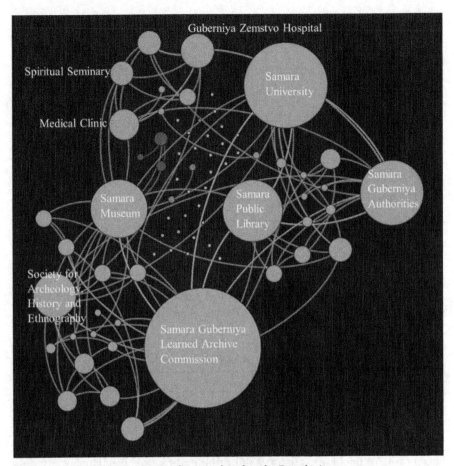

FIGURE 3.7 Enlightenment social networks after the Revolution

information is available from archival sources and additional scattered and unsystematic records. These sources include webpages of academic and research institutes in which the professionals enjoyed successful careers in the Soviet period, obituaries, Wikipedia entries, and family genealogical records from popular ancestry discussion sites. Information is cross-checked across a range of sources, but by its very nature it does not supply a comprehensive picture of social-organizational ties. Despite the strong information availability bias, the exercise promises to be revealing. Even if leading members of the pre-communist educated estates-derived bourgeoisie, Samara and metropolitan, resumed their professional engagements and network ties, then there is a very strong possibility of similar patterns among the *kleiner Mensch* not so tarnished.

TABLE 3.6 *Top ten most connected organizations, 1920s*

Ranking	Degree	Betweenness Centrality	Closeness Centrality
1	SGLAC	SGLAC	Private school of 3rd grade of Arsen'yeva
2	Samara Museum	Samara University	Arsen'yeva Private Women's Gymnasium
3	Samara University	SSPU	SGPCFH
4	SAHE	Samara Museum	Uchilishche for Blind Children
5	SSPU	SAHE	SGLAC
6	SSEE	SSEE	SSPU
7	Guberniya Zemstvo Hospital	Medical Clinic	Samara Museum
8	Medical Clinic	Spiritual Seminary	SSEE
9	Samara Chapter of Imperial Russian Society of Gardeners	Countess Khovanskaya Women's Gymnasium No. 3	Samara University
10	Spiritual Seminary	City Parish School	SAHE

Table 3.6 suggests that the top three most networked organizations in terms of degree centrality are, again, SGLAC, the Samara Museum, and Samara University. One addition to the list of well-networked institutions is the Society for Archaeology, History, and Ethnography (SAHE). The Society does not feature in the 1916 social network data, but as I shall discuss in Chapter 4, it became a newly constituted arena of autonomous social action, embracing many of the same individuals, from SGLAC, the Museum, the Samara City *duma*, and the university as patrons and students, the next generation of the status group. Individuals working in the gymnasium educational sector and in medicine also appear to be linked to the high-status enlightenment networks associated with the museum and the university. When it comes to estates, as Table 3.7 reveals, merchants, or rather, individuals of merchant background, predominate in this network. This observation applies both to the metropolitan and native enlightenment figures and to professionals. In identifying an individual's estate origin, the criterion I applied was the highest estate designation in the family background, which may have included a mix of estate titles. There are forty-two merchants on the list compared to thirty-nine nobles, including the titled aristocracy of princes and counts. Seven individuals feature clergy backgrounds; there is only one *meshchanin*. I was unable to find

TABLE 3.7 *Individuals and estate characteristics, 1917–1920s. Edges (links) between organizations*

Most Connected Individuals		
Ranking	Name	Edges Count
1	Aref'yev, P. (dies shortly after Revolution)	15
2	Arapov, V.	10
3	Klykov, L.	10
4	Perets, V.	10
5	Smirnov, A.	10
6	Kavetskiy, Ye.	6
7	Khovanskiy, S.	6
8	Permyakov, S.	6
9	Golovkin, K.	3
10	Gundobin, V.	3
Estate/Designation	Edges Count	Cumulative
merchant	42	42
noble	30	72
clergy	7	79
prince	6	85
Cossack	4	89
count	3	92
sluzhashchiy	3	95
foreign national	1	96
meshchanin	1	97
unknown	22	119

Note. Individuals stand for connections between organizations, or edges. The table links individuals to their estate, using the latter to count the edges. Merchants connect to more organizations than nobles, followed by the clergy – including key sites like SGLAC, SSPU, Samara Museum, and SAHE.

any information on estate origins beyond a reference to *sluzhashchiy* for three individuals; this label most likely masked privileged ancestry where the more ideologically palatable peasant or worker background was unavailable as material to write into one's new Soviet biography. Finally, I was unable to find information on the pre-revolutionary estate for twenty-two individuals on the list.

Let me now step back and consider how the rudimentary social network exercise provides signposts for a more fine-grained investigation of social adaptation after the Revolution. Both Figure 3.7 and the descriptive data in Tables 3.6 and 3.7 are suggestive of interconnected organizational sites that also feature network links to other, in some ways formally constituted, bureaucratic or civic organizations. Conspicuous among these are enlightenment institutions, like the museum, the university, and affiliate institutions for the propagation of knowledge. These, however, are linked also to elite secondary schools. A sprinkling of parish and other lower order primary institutions also features, which is suggestive of the copresence of persons affiliated with lower-level education and highbrow enlightenment sphere. The organizational arms of the medical profession – hospitals and clinics – also feature ties to civil society groups concerned with the propagation of enlightenment organizations. Finally, there is some sign of linkages between peripheral bodies associated with state power – executive divisions of imperial authorities – and other arenas of professional-civic-social interaction. The sprinkling of seminarians among networked individuals is indicative of the embeddedness of the hereditary clergy in the professions and in civic life. The odd *meshchanin* also makes an appearance in the otherwise overwhelmingly merchant and noble networks of professional-civic society. These patterns are indicative of the resilience of subterranean structures of governance and social networks – those positioned between the bureaucratic apparatus of the state and broader society. Distinct from core sites of imperial power that have preoccupied earlier scholars of the Revolution's state-building consequences, they deserve far greater scrutiny as carriers of the pre-revolutionary social structure, autonomous organization, and resources.[99]

CONCLUSION

This chapter has outlined the contours of a slice of urban bourgeois society before and after the Revolution. Far more developed than mainstream accounts of Russian backwardness would suggest, Samara exhibited patterns of social stratification and mobility characteristic of other flourishing centers of industry, commerce, and trades. It featured well-developed institutions and traditions of urban governance and was teaming with philanthropic, charitable, educational, and cultural initiative. It was also a region where economic modernization processes, the development of professions, structures of local governance, and the enlightenment drive engendered a highly networked society, one, however, where the estate continued to shape an individual's social position and ties. The noble, merchant, and industrialist rubbed elbows in the yacht club and the city hall; and the gymnasium teacher shared honorary membership of the school management board with the governor or bank magnate. Merchants,

---

[99] Interestingly, THPSSS found that high-status groups were the likeliest to report strong and extensive friendship ties, more so than workers and peasants. Peasants said they have no friends "almost three times as often as the members of the intelligentsia," perhaps due to their larger networks of relatives. Inkeles and Bauer, *Soviet Citizen*, 200, and 199, table 51. Friendships were also usually formed among those with similar social characteristics. Ibid., 201.

meshchane, and nobles intermarried, though parental blessing for such a union might come reluctantly; far less likely were marital ties between nobles and factory laborers or peasants. Importantly, social closure found reflection in the well-networked, institutionally dense, arenas of social action poised between the apparatus of the state and wider society.

These patterns help us reconsider theoretical assumptions about a partially state-embedded and state-dependent public sphere, its inauthenticity dismissed in the Habermasian notions of a wholly "private" society come public.[100] Experience of semi-attachment to the clutches of state power precisely engenders resilience that could only come from the tactical arsenal of resistance, something that helps us understand the significance of the role of the old public under the new political-systemic order. Further, this discussion not only brings to light the simultaneously broad reach and stratified insularity of the civic networks but anticipates how these features could preserve and relaunch both the status relations and the possibilities for autonomous or even defiant-oppositional engagement against state power under the most totalizing and socially leveling regimes. The imperative to conserve the extant status relationships of an estatist society fuses with hostility toward, and hence a desire to resist, a state ideologically bent on destroying them as vestiges of a bygone order. Simultaneously, the resources and resourcefulness derived from embeddedness in a highly networked group equips some of our well-placed protagonists in the professional arm of the public sphere with the tools to impress their indispensability as experts on the leveling state, again, paradoxically, engendering autonomy and status conservation through a symbiotic relationship with state power. This angle on the public sphere brings to the fore the twin dimensions of social inequities and the simultaneous capacity of the high-status strata to preserve, renew, and regenerate a private stand against the utopian, oppressive, state.

Chapter 4 explores the continuities in the social-professional-network tapestries of the post-revolutionary period. An analytical framework is proposed that is sensitive to the reproduction of the old professional and the enlightenment arenas of social autonomy from the state, and indeed to the platforms that the Soviet regime itself made available for the educated estates to build new network ties and consolidate old ones.

---

[100] Habermas, *Structural Transformation*, 142.

4

The Professions in the Making of Estatist Society

> The old professor was on guard, ensuring that [such] a charlatan is not allowed to practice if he is for whatever reason unsuitable for this trade. The students knew this well ... no ambivalence, no hints could exist in a trade where all was clear and precise, like a clock, like the somber professor himself, the representative of the Western scientist, the image of whom will be forever linked with the Medical-Chirurgical Academy, the professor, who instilled simultaneously fear and adulation, as one could only adulate a person who is a bearer of pure truth. *And so when the professor, a world authority, sternly told the student, gently immersing his hands into the entrails of a corpse: "Gentleman, please take off your gloves," – the student would be ready to immerse not just his hands, but his entire body into the decaying intestines of the putrid corpse.*
>
> Nikolay Garin-Mikhaylovskiy, *Studenty*[1]

In Mikhail Bulgakov's novel *Heart of a Dog*, Professor Filipp Filippovich Preobrazhenskiy sets out to perform a hitherto unknown medical experiment. Part of the brain (the *hypophysis*) and the male sexual glands of a human, a declassee drunkard Klim Chugunkin found dead on the streets of 1920s Moscow, are transplanted into the body of a street dog called Sharik. The canine quickly develops into a human, adapting the name of Poligraf Poligrafovich Sharikov, yet never fulfills the promise of continued blossoming into Man. The professor and his aide, Dr. Bormenthal, desperately seek to dislodge Sharikov from their plush living quarters, seven rooms in total serviced by domestic maids, a guard, and a cook. Yet Sharikov expends considerable energy seeking to retain, which he successfully does with the help of Bolshevik vigilantes, his living space in Preobrazhenskiy's home. Eventually, the guinea pig's binge-drinking, debauchery, robbery, sloppiness, and sexual promiscuity lead the exasperated professor to reengineer Sharikov into a dog.

---

[1] Author's translation. Garin-Mikhaylovskiy, *Studenty; Inzhenery*, 114–15 (emphasis added).

The ending, much as the metaphoric references running through it, is a powerful indictment on the ideology and practice of class vigilance. The final scene depicts the professor contentedly ensconced in his plush office and, at the feet of his desk, Sharik the dog. Sharik may surmise that he has finally arrived, since his appropriation of the bourgeois home is now solid and unshakable. Yet the real winner here is Preobrazhenskiy, who has shown Sharik his place in Soviet society.[2]

Preobrazhenskiy's story is one of resilience – of the propertied, superbly educated, and expert bourgeoisie. The clinic could be also construed as an alternative public space to the metaphoric political space embodied in the Bolsheviks' housing committee, which is lodged in another apartment. In the eminent medic's quarters, public matters are debated and negotiated in both explicit and subtle ways. Preobrazhenskiy's refusal to be dislodged from his residence, which doubles as his clinic, is also a public stand against the encroachments on private property, professional autonomy, and individual liberty. The clinic is a site where the process of procuring and negotiating professional autonomy vis-à-vis state authority is inseparable from the negotiation of autonomy as a citizen. Not only is the professor besieged by a stream of wealthy "bourgeois" patients, embodying the Russia of the *old regime* but he is also enjoying the patronage of *new* Russia, the Bolshevik political elite, reliant as they are on his medical prowess – in curing impotence, a likely pun on Bolshevik authority.

To what extent did the Preobrazhenskiys represent a mass phenomenon that transcends the vignettes of individuals immortalized in highbrow literature and popular culture? Moreover, how can they help us tease out the significance of the bourgeoisie as an intergenerational category in animating the space between the state and the ostensibly atomized society? The story presented here goes beyond exploring professional persistence transcending the revolutionary juncture. The professional or proto-professional is contextualized here in imperial Russia's highly unequal, albeit fluid, estates-fractured society. In the following sections, I provide a conceptual framework that is sensitive both to the formal professional channels of social reproduction and to alternative proto-professional arenas peculiar to a revolutionary, inquisitional, state with a radical social agenda; I substantiate my argument about channels of professional-social persistence employing original data; and, finally, I deploy insights from social network analysis to explore the horizontal and spatial aspects of the social ties that facilitated the educated estates' professional adaptation.

---

[2] Bulgakov, *Sobach'ye serdtse*. Written in 1925, the book was published after Bulgakov's death. A film version was released in 1988.

CONCEPTUAL FRAMEWORK

My analysis is sensitive to the logics of the expertise-derived autonomy, leverage, and agency of the professional, the scholar, and the torchbearer of the enlightenment that are characteristic of modern societies broadly and narrowly of a totalizing revolutionary order where those very agents of knowledge are subjected to ideological stigma. A full-variance cross-regional analysis provides baseline evidence of a self-reproducing nature of professional knowledge – in space and in time. While this exercise helps us partially account for regional heterogeneity in the social structure, a linear account would not do justice to the nuances of professional–personal life cycles given the checkered nature of professional reproduction; the heterogeneity in adaptation within employment sites and among social groups; and the horizontal network ties aiding social possibilities and effecting shifts within networks. Studies in comparative historical analysis distinguish between "self-reproducing" sequences and those lacking consistency in direction – a period of self-reproducing and "self-amplifying" dynamics may be followed by "backlashes" and "reversals" in ways that erode an otherwise advantageous starting point.[3] The Bolsheviks never set out to mimic the old regime's social hierarchies. Yet the immediate contingencies of the power grab amid the simultaneously unfolding and socially engulfing tragedies of gargantuan proportions – famine, disease, civil war – forced concessions to be made for institutions that were fundamental to the reproduction of society embedded within them, notably the professions. Scholars analyzing the twentieth century's wars and revolutions have tended to underline their social *leveler* effects – the rising power of the working class in Europe after World War I; the decimation of wealth after World War II;[4] and, of course, the equalitarian achievements of the great "social" Revolution of 1917 itself.[5] Alternatively, "actor-based functionalist"[6] perspectives regarded Soviet Russia's inequalities from the vantage point of the "new class" paradigm, that is, as consequential to what the historical drama's most powerful thespians, the Bolsheviks, wanted for themselves.[7]

The theory here parts with these established notions of post-revolutionary social outcomes in that I focus on completely different sets of actors and institutions – the well-networked liminal sites of professional, quasi-professional, and civic enterprise – helping the dismantled regime's privileged to *retain*, or, with some time digression, *regain*, their status in society. Following Pierson,[8] I am sensitive to the "conjunctural" aspect of social processes, their unfolding at the intersection of "realms" with "different historical roots"

---

[3] Faletti and Mahoney, "Comparative," 220–21, 222.   [4] Scheidel, *Great Leveler*.
[5] Fitzpatrick, *Education*.   [6] Pierson, *Politics in Time*, 14.   [7] Djilas, *New Class*.
[8] Pierson, *Politics in Time*, 56–57, discussing critiques of formalism of periodization in Orren and Skowronek, "Beyond the Iconography of Order," 315, 317, 320.

during dynamic processes of social change.[9] Chapter 3 discussed those subterranean institutions with a pronounced estatist makeup that were positioned between the apparatus of the state and broader society as among urban Samara's most networked. Individuals embedded within them constituted ties linking institutions of urban governance, professions like medicine and teaching, and the more nebulous enlightenment domain that drew on, and fed, these various arenas of network ties. The agency of these institutions and networks in my account helps us take stock of post-revolutionary outcomes in the social structure and the persistence of their autonomy.

The three concepts that I propose as encompassing the distinct sets of the subterranean *old* institutions that structured the bourgeoisie's possibilities for professional adaptation and status reproduction – as well as the *new* regime-engineered or regime-supported arenas that tied distinct professional or quasi-professional sites together – are (1) the *organization man* route, capturing established professions; (2) the *pop-up society* channel of quasi-professional social elevation and network reach; and (3) the *museum society* of cultivated bourgeoisie congregating in islands of social closure such as historical preservation societies, art galleries, libraries, and the like. These arenas are by no means mutually exclusive. To the contrary, I am sensitive both to the individual opportunities for *switching* roles and *hedging* in a fluid marketplace of options, where repression could be imminent, and to those intrinsic to the policy demands of the revolutionizing state itself, which also tend to exhibit considerable flux. Nurturing the various types of professional are also social inputs – the long-in-the-making intergenerational aspirations and deference. I distinguish between temporal wavelengths of various duration to draw attention to the disjuncture between long-maturing social values, goalposts, gravity, deference, and the top-down quickly promulgated policies of recognition or misrecognition of the professional. The account is thus sensitive not only to the significance of intermediating institutions as pivotal to understanding resilience in the social structure but also to the bottom-up and top-down channels of lethargy or change, positioned as these subterranean arenas are between the state and broader society.

I do not purport to provide an exhaustive account of the full palette of professional adaptation. Such an exercise is beyond the scope of this book, as every profession itself warrants careful sociological study – indeed some, like engineering, have been explored elsewhere, in historical accounts, albeit from a different angle to the one taken here.[10] Rather, I unearth new evidence that allows me to situate concrete individuals, networks, and organizations within pre-revolutionary professional milieus, in ways that are sensitive to the estate. This in turn helps dissect the organizational-professional-social networks and

[9] Pierson, *Politics in Time*, 56.
[10] Graham, *Ghost of the Executed Engineer*; Bailes, *Technology*.

concomitant resources; to chart out institutional path-dependencies; and to trace the progression or genesis of the positioning of individuals so embedded within the Soviet labor market. This analysis in turn will set the stage for unpacking heterogeneity in the social profile, values, and autonomy among the distinct substrata of the post-Soviet middle class and their orientations toward the political realm.

STATISTICAL ANALYSIS

I first provide some baseline analysis of covariation between estate structure, literacy as a proxy for imperial education, and Soviet regional occupational characteristics. Two caveats about this exercise are in order. The occupational data encompass but one channel of the reproduction of the broad-reach network of institutions harboring hierarchically stratified estatist groups: the organization man arenas. To the extent that it covers established professions, this dimension of social-institutional reproduction is distinct from the other two interlinked – pop-up and museum society – channels. The statistical exercise is here regarded as a preliminary step in ascertaining institutional-professional resilience. Specifically, I employ the measure of the share of engineers and doctors with a university education in regional populations in 1960, 1965, and 1970, controlling for variables conventionally employed in analyses of Russia's regional developmental variations. The statistical analysis reported in Table 4.1 and Figure 4.1 reveals that professions mythologized as Soviet achievements – medicine and engineering – are significantly related to both the spatial distribution of human capital and the size of the educated estates and *meshchane* group in tsarist Russia's territories. Note that the coefficients for engineers increase over time while remaining stable for doctors. Considering aggregated "educated estates," we find an even more statistically significant positive relationship, confirming the magnitude and signs of the effect on university-trained professionals over time. I now unpack the causal mechanisms that account for professional resilience with reference to three stylized arenas: the organization man; the pop-up society; and the museum society.

ARENAS OF PROFESSIONAL-SOCIAL REPRODUCTION

The Organization Man

The "organization man" trajectory of adaptation is the most straightforward, highly institutionalized, and structured channel of reproduction in social stratification. I borrow this term from William H. Whyte for the catchiness of the title, though his preoccupation was somewhat different.[11] The organization

---

[11] Specifically, the rise of large organizations as America's predominant employer, emphasizing the collectivist ethos undermining personal initiative. Whyte, *Organization Man*.

TABLE 4.1 *Effect of pre-communist literacy and social structure on communist-era professional education and social structure (oblast-level), OLS*

Dep. Var.: Share of Engineers (Eng.) and Doctors (Doc.) with University Education	Eng. 1960	Eng. 1965	Eng. 1970	Doc. 1960	Doc. 1965	Doc 1970
Effect of pre-revolutionary literacy						
Literacy rate	0.032**	0.042**	0.051**	0.006***	0.006***	0.006***
	(0.013)	(0.017)	(0.020)	(0.002)	(0.002)	(0.002)
Effect of pre-revolutionary social structure						
Share of *meshchane*	0.0448*	0.0605	0.0748*	0.0104***	0.0115***	0.0113***
	(0.0268)	(0.0350)	(0.0426)	(0.00391)	(0.00425)	(0.00425)
Share of educated estates	0.0452**	0.0605**	0.0741**	0.0096***	0.0106***	0.0104***
	(0.0218)	(0.0279)	(0.0335)	(0.00298)	(0.00320)	(0.00319)
Observations	71	71	71	71	71	71

Note. Dep. Var = dependent variable; OLS = Ordinary Least Squares Regression. The table summarizes the results of three sets of regressions, all controlling for a binary variable for ethnic regions (autonomous republics) and distance from Moscow. Effects of control variables suppressed. * $p<0.1$; ** $p<0.05$; *** $p<0.01$. Robust standard errors in parentheses.
Source. Data based on Lankina and Libman, "Two-Pronged Middle Class." Analysis reproduced and expanded with permission of the coauthor.

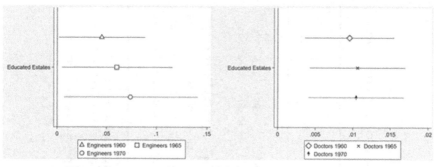

FIGURE 4.1 Educated estates and Soviet professions

man embodies the early riser advantage, given the incurrence of significant "start-up" costs in large modern bureaucracies. Organizational analysis expects such groups to marshal considerable resources to perpetuate their advantages even in challenging political environments.[12] The medical profession encapsulates these dimensions of professional institutionalization. As Frieden writes, late imperial medicine had come to exhibit the classic characteristics of a modern profession, one with entry stringently regulated via protracted, rigorous, and often expensive training in institutions of the highest caliber, at home and abroad; one in which professional associations, medical journals, and public debate ensured not only striving for but achievement of genuine autonomy from the state; and one that was already on the way to shedding the stigma of being a low-paid, low-status, and unrewarding occupation.[13] It also captured the horizons of multiple generations, if we consider the long-term planning for entry into educational institutions in preparing for a medical career.[14] Medicine in Russia, by dint of being networked with, and embedded within, the European medical profession, and because of progression through the same kinds of intra- and extra-professional struggles around access and exclusion, also featured established, solid, and structured hierarchies as well as careful gatekeeping against unwanted trespassing into the ivory tower of medical practice and status. In 1904, there were more than 5,000 medical students studying at seven university medical faculties and a specialist school, the Imperial Military Medical Academy.[15] Established in 1798 originally as the Medical and Surgical Academy, it became a leading educational institution. Frieden writes that "some of its graduates achieved acclaim throughout Europe and many

---

[12] Pierson, *Politics in Time*, 73.   [13] Frieden, *Russian Physicians*, 4–5, 201–28, 30–31.
[14] The state sought to make the profession attractive to commoners via perks, studentships, scholarships, and civil service progression on the Table of Ranks. Ibid., 21–52.
[15] Moscow, Dorpat, Khar'kov, Kiev, Kazan', Warsaw, Tomsk. Ibid., 50, table 2.6.

became outstanding professors of medicine."[16] Even these data are an incomplete picture of the hardware – the institutional architecture of the profession and professional training – and software – the human dimension – of medical practice. The data in the years leading up to the Revolution would not include Samara University's (SU) Medical Faculty; conceived before World War I, it only formally opened its doors to the first student cohort in the autumn of 1918. In dissecting *post*-revolutionary appropriation of the profession, the most systematic account to my knowledge is Stephen Wheatcroft's, who attributes the massive expansion of medical cadres in the 1920s and 1930s to the training of future medics "dating back to at least a decade before the revolution."[17] As late as 1930, of the 68,037 doctors, 22,248, nearly a third, had qualified before 1918.[18]

While these records are a valuable starting point for tracing the reproduction of the *professional*, we have yet to discern the reincarnation of the organization man behind them, that is, one embedded within a network of hierarchical, bureaucratic structures where professional rules of incorporation are also inevitably impregnated with a social character. One official account obtained from archival sources helps us begin to chart continuities in organizational and status blueprints straddling the pre- and post-revolutionary profession. In a highly publicized ceremony commemorating five years of the establishment of Samara's *Soviet* medical profession, in 1923 nearly fifty professionals in hospitals, medical clinics, surgeries, x-ray facilities, psychiatric wards, physiotherapy clinics, and scores of specialized medical facilities, as well as a sprinkling of pharmacy workers, were feted. Virtually all medical professionals among the laureates had completed training and pursued much of their medical career under the old regime. Their estate, which otherwise featured as a social descriptor in the witch hunts against the bourgeoisie that accompanied the consolidation of Bolshevik rule, is discreetly omitted from these accounts. The one exception is a certain Mikhaylov, born in 1873, who had worked in the medical profession for twenty-four years, beginning his career in the employ of a private pharmacist. Much is made in the celebrations of Mikhaylov's "peasant" origins. Over his twenty-four years of service as an urban resident and professional, Mikhailov would have likely transitioned to the estate of *meshchanin*, plausibly also the estate of his employer, the pharmacy manager.[19]

Medics' educational credentials reflect intra-occupational differentiation between doctors or consultants and junior employees such as nurses and feldshers. Possessing higher education is characteristic of doctors on the list. Aside from a generic reference to a university degree, consultants' academic

---

[16] Ibid., 31.   [17] Wheatcroft, "Doctors," 22.   [18] Ibid., 23.
[19] Protocols of Education Department and other agencies, 1923–24, Samarskiy oblastnoy gosudarstvennyy arkhiv sotsial'noy i politicheskoy istorii (hereafter SOGASPI), f. 1, op. 1116, ed. khr. 1, ll. 70–73.

résumés also feature elite institutions like the Imperial Medical and Surgical Academy. By contrast, the educational trajectory of nurses appears limited to specialized secondary quasi-vocational institutions like schools for feldshers. After the Revolution, those medical doctors who had trained in elite metropolitan higher educational institutions retained the status of consultants; those qualified as nurses remained nurses; and so on. The consultant Pyotr Aleksandrovich Pokrovskiy, for instance (b. 1852), after graduating from the elite Medical and Surgical Academy, served as a specialist war doctor in 1877 during the Russo-Turkish War, the 1904–5 Russo-Japanese War, and the 1914–18 Great War, only to become a Red Army doctor. Of the feldsher Vasiliy Maksimovich Kazakov (b. 1867), whose medical career spanned thirty-two years, we know that, after finishing training at a feldsher school in 1890, he worked in a *zemstvo* hospital and the *guberniya*'s various other medical institutions before transitioning to the status of a Soviet feldsher with the medical facilities of the regional *militsiya* (police) forces. A similarly smooth conversion into Soviet nursing is observed for sister Pyatova (b. 1878), likewise a graduate of a feldsher school. A sister Ivanova, who boasted twenty-five years' experience in nursing, continued working as a nurse at the House of Mother and Child in Soviet Samara. Finally, of the "peasant" pharmacist Mikhaylov, we know that, after his pharmacy was nationalized, he secured employment in the warehouses of the *guberniya* department of health and the medical trade bureau (*medtorg*).[20] These are just a handful of examples. These early records may not be representative of intra-professional positional continuities, given that they precede several waves of repressions. Nevertheless, they anticipate a pattern distinct from the more fluid channels of professional adaptation that characterized occupations requiring lower levels of technical specialization and training.

In analyzing the organization man route of social reproduction, my concern is to go beyond documenting islands of institutional incorporation and to sketch out a fuller institutional tapestry of autonomous occupational sites of medical practice. I am also sensitive to the social relationships between the professional and the broader public and to what I label *dynastic* pedigree, which not only structures aspirations within families but also augments the social aspect of reverence and prestige for the practitioner.

The Kavetskiys As Organization Men

The institutional, personal, and dynastic history of Yevgeniy Leopol'dovich Kavetskiy, Samara's leading medical practitioner and scholar, helps us analyze these various dimensions of professional reproduction. Additional sources concerning the battle over the preservation of SU's Medical Faculty situate Kavetskiy's unblemished accolades within the black box of institutional struggles of an established profession vis-à-vis the Bolshevik state. Yevgeniy

---

[20] Protocols, 1923–24, SOGASPI, f. 1, op. 1116, ed. khr. 1, ll. 70–73.

Leopol'dovich was born in 1865 into a Polish family in the city of Poltava. After graduating from the gymnasium, Kavetskiy obtained a degree with distinction from the Medical Faculty of Kharkov University.[21] In 1898, Kavetskiy, already an experienced practitioner specializing in epidemiology, moved to Samara where he became the founding executive of the city's first clinical laboratory attached to the *guberniya zemstvo* hospital, Soviet Samara's future Central Hospital.[22] His post-revolutionary career spans the deanship of SU's Medical Faculty, the vice-chancellorship of SU, and directorships at the Research Institute of Epidemiology and Microbiology, which emerged after SU's closure in 1927, and the Faculty of Pathological Anatomy at the Samara Medical Institute, which essentially became the heir to SU's Medical Faculty. Kavetskiy also made his mark within the wider universe of professional associations, congresses, and journals – carried over into the *Soviet* profession even as old associations acquired new names with a revolutionary flavor.[23] Although Kavetskiy's career included spells of practice in Siberia in the years coinciding with post-revolutionary strife and famine – a trajectory characteristic of the population movement in that period – most of his professional work is tied to Samara.[24]

Kavetskiy's stature as a real person-cum-ideal type in our analysis of the organization man also emerges if we regard his dynastic professional-educational capital. Both of Kavetskiy's sons became medics at the pinnacle of the profession, one of whom, Nikolay Yevgen'yevich, in Samara. Born in 1896, in 1915 Nikolay completed Samara's Second Men's Gymnasium with a silver medal. "Already in the 5th year of gymnasium," he wrote in his CV, he "decid[ed] to be a doctor."[25] Although Kavetskiy junior pursued a medical degree at Tomsk University, when his father returned to Samara to resume his work there, so did Nikolay, acquiring the status of assistant in 1923 with SU's Medical Faculty and in 1926 defending the title of *privat-docent* (lecturer) for his work on infectious diseases. Nikolay enjoyed a stellar career as a *Soviet* medic, sustaining leading positions in research institutes and medical facilities in the late 1920s, practicing medicine, and teaching at the Medical Institute in the 1930s and 1940s. Like his father, Nikolay served on multiple professional bodies. Over a span of twenty-nine years, he chaired the Kuybyshev

---

[21] Kavetskiy's son Nikolay lists Kharkov medical faculty as his father's alma mater; and his granddaughter, the daughter of Kavetskiy's other son Rostislav Yevgen'yevich, Natal'ya Kavetskaya-Mazepa, who published a memoir about her father and his family, also the Odessa medical school. Biography of Nikolay Kavetskiy, June 21, 1968. Kavetskiy papers, 1916–74. TsGASO, f. P-4135, op. 3, ed. khr., 438, l. 1; Kavetskaya-Mazepa, *O moyom ottse*, 8.

[22] Biography, ll. 1–2.

[23] In 1905–18 and 1923–24, Kavetskiy chaired the Samara Guberniya Society of Doctors. Ibid.

[24] Kavetskiy senior, sympathizer with the *kadety* party, left Samara for Siberia after the Bolsheviks took power. Kavetskaya-Mazepa, *O moyom ottse*, 18.

[25] Biography, l. 2.

(Samara)[26] Oblast Scientific Society of Therapy professionals in addition to holding at least fifteen different quasi-civic roles in a long list of professional associations, regional and national, as chairman, secretary, treasurer, and member of the International Organization for External Medicine. Kavetskiy also became a prolific contributor to the scientific outlets of the specialty: the journal *Therapeutical Archive*, where he also served on the editorial board, as well as *Healthcare of the Russian Federation, Clinical Medicine*, and *Kazan Medical Journal*, in addition to his many edited, authored, and coauthored volumes.[27] Nikolay's brother Rostislav Yevgen'yevich likewise attended the Samara Men's Gymnasium, following which he completed studies at SU's Medical Faculty in 1925. Rostislav rose to the positions of academician with the Ukrainian Academy of Sciences and director of the Kiev Scientific Research Institute of Experimental and Clinical Oncology.[28] The Kavetskiys also made their mark on the sphere of university-level elite medical training. This arena of social-professional reproduction illuminates the struggles to safeguard and preserve professional autonomy concealed behind the unblemished résumés of Samara's medical elite. A brief sketch of the hidden battles concerning the preservation of this important channel of continuities in the profession is therefore in order.

The University and Medical Faculty As Sites of Struggle for Professional Survival and Autonomy

As noted in the "Conceptual Framework" section, self-reproducing dynamics in professional adaptation were punctuated with setbacks, reversals, and regress. The corporate aspect of professionalization enabled the organization man arenas to survive temporary ideology-driven witch hunts; and the fast-paced tempo of unfolding human catastrophes placed significant limits on the policy enactments of Bolshevik class dogma. As is clear from the Kavetskiys' professional careers, they became inextricably linked to university-level pedagogy, research, and training. Little-perused historical sources concerning the founding, closure, and eventual reopening under a new name of SU and its Medical Faculty provide a glimpse into the black box of the micro-dynamics of struggles for institutional-professional survival after the closure of SU's Medical Faculty.[29] They reveal the hydra-like propinquities of the reconstitution of the same old institutions,[30] as well as the proclivities of the same pre-revolutionary

[26] Samara was renamed after the Old Bolshevik Valerian Kuybyshev's death in 1935. I use Samara for the sake of consistency unless Kuybyshev features in citations of other work.
[27] Biography, ll. 2–22.   [28] Biography, l. 17; Kavetskaya-Mazepa, *O moyom ottse*, 29.
[29] An estimated 600 students were transferred to Voronezh University after closure in 1923. The faculty continued to function for some time, but admissions ceased in 1923. Kuz'minykh et al., *Vera Vladimirovna Gol'msten*, 26.
[30] University faculty raised concerns about planned new institutions like the Institute of Medical Knowledge in place of SU and its Medical Faculty: "New institutions emerging out of the ruins of the old may require more funding than the maintenance of the erstwhile University." Protocol,

professionals and civic personages to reenact the engagements of the pre-revolutionary public sphere. The university will be mythologized as a creation of the Soviet government, a mythology so ingrained that even a monograph employing archival sources and published in 2001 referred to it as founded pursuant to the January 21, 1918 "Decree of the Sovnarkom [Council of People's Deputies] of the RSFSR."[31] Documentary sources not only suggest otherwise but reveal that the new Soviet government targeted the establishment as a haven for the bourgeoisie. A letter from Professor P. Smirnov, a member of the imperial professoriate, conveys the dismay at Bolshevik policy considering the university's perceived importance in the eyes of Samara's enlightened public: "In the Samara *kray*, an event of immense significance is taking place ... the closure of a University ... This event ought to be taken with the utmost seriousness, such that every citizen living in the *kray* ought to consider it," read the opening lines of his handwritten address to the Bolshevik functionary, Comrade Antonov-Ovseyenko, in 1922.[32]

Although SU was founded in the empire's twilight years,[33] it had been long in the making as *guberniya* bodies, *zemstvo* authorities, and city notables lobbied for higher educational institutions commensurate with Samara's status as a hub of industry and commerce. The authorities conceived the university as a two-stage process. In the first stage, polytechnical and pedagogical institutes were to be established, followed in the second stage with the setting up of medical, history, and Oriental studies departments.[34] When KOMUCH – the "counter-revolutionary" forces associated with the remnants of the Constituent Assembly – briefly took power in Samara, this event was recorded in the minutes of the faculty's joint deliberations with the new authorities as "rare and fortuitous."[35] In 1918, under KOMUCH rule, and enjoying support from the city head (*golova*) A. M. Smirnov,[36] the university's status was formally recognized "with all the concomitant rights and privileges."[37] Astonishingly, neither the imposition of Bolshevik rule in Samara, as the "counter-revolutionaries" fled, nor the strife and famine that followed stopped the efforts to develop the core faculties in their tracks. By the start of the

Commission for the Liquidation of Samara State University," June 15, 1922. TsGASO, f. 81, op. 1, ed. khr. 533, l. 173 ob.

[31] Kuz'min, *Zdravookhraneniye*, 82. See, however, Kuz'minykh et al., *Vera Vladimirovna Gol'msten*, 17.

[32] TsGASO, f. 81, op. 1, ed. khr. 533, l. 222, papers 1922, hereafter "Professor Smirnov's letter." See also concerns regarding the Bolshevik decision to close SU, letter to Samara *gubispolkom* from the SU Professoriate-Teaching Collegium, May 8, 1922. TsGASO, f. 81, op. 1, ed. khr. 533, ll. 155–56 ob. On SU "Liquidation Commission," see TsGASO, f. 81, op. 1, ed. khr. 533, ll. 173–73 ob.

[33] KOMUCH Order, July 14, 1918, TsGASO, f. 3931m1, op. 1, ed. khr. 30, l. 7; Protocol of joint session of Guberniya *zemstvo uprava* and council of Professors of the Samara Pedagogical Institute, July 27, 1918. TsGASO, f. 3931m1, op. 1, ed. hr. 30, ll. 12–14.

[34] Professor Smirnov's letter, ll. 222 and 222 ob.; Protocol, ll. 12–14.   [35] Protocol, l. 12 ob.

[36] Protocol, l. 12 ob.   [37] Order, TsGASO, f. 3931m1, op. 1, ed. khr. 30, l. 1.

academic year, on September 1, 1918, academics from Samara, Petrograd (St. Petersburg), Kiev, and Kazan were ready to commence teaching subjects ranging from classical philology, psychology and philosophy, to history, Russian language and literature, and medicine.[38] University staff worked unpaid or on patched-up financial arrangements; many succumbed to exhaustion, disease, and famine.[39] Yet academic instruction continued apace; entrants to each subsequent academic cohort were dutifully examined; and teaching, extracurricular opportunities, library resources, including from the faculty's personal collections, and pastoral care were provided to students.[40]

The university and its medical school faced an uphill battle in self-preservation as soon as the Bolsheviks took power in Samara. A common line of attack on SU was that it provided refuge for the "former people" and their children. These individuals had reportedly escaped persecution elsewhere, seeking shelter in the *guberniya*'s politically permissive environment in the uncertainty of the Civil War – a "clique [*kuchka*] of hungry professors, who had come to eat in the then well-fed [*sytaya*] Samara."[41] To this, the professoriate replied that many academics had in fact joined prior to the two revolutions; that not a few hailed from the *guberniya* and had dedicated their lives to promoting enlightenment in Samara; and that the university's day-to-day activities provided evidence of high-quality educational processes.[42]

The authorities also repeatedly raised concerns about sustainability in the context of civil strife, famine, and economic ruin.[43] In response, the professoriate supplied detailed estimates of funding sources. These included charity donations, additional employment that sustained the livelihoods of some faculty, business–private partnership-type arrangements, and university tuition fees. The Medical Faculty emerged as the best endowed, drawing as it

---

[38] Handwritten letter, August 10, 2018, signed by SU rector A. Nechayev, to Head of DPE, KOMUCH member, Yegor Lazarev. TsGASO, f. 3931 M. 1, op. 1, ed. khr. 30, ll. 10–11 ob.; and handwritten note "On the Pedagogic Institute's professoriate," n.d. TsGASO, f. 3931m1, op. 1, ed. khr. 30, ll. 15–16.

[39] Professor Smirnov's letter, l. 223.

[40] "Report on the activities of the Faculty of History and Philology of Samara State University," written by Acting Dean Prof. V. Perets and Faculty Secretary V. Andrianova. TsGASO, f. 81, op. 1, ed. khr. 419, part 1, ll. 49–56 ob. Covers the 1918–19 academic year, n.d.; and "On the professoriate." See also SU letter to *gubispolkom*, May 8, 1922. TsGASO, f. 81, op. 1, ed. khr. 533, ll. 155–56 ob.

[41] Professor Smirnov's letter, l. 222.   [42] Ibid., ll. 222, 222 ob., 223.

[43] Liquidation Protocol, May 13, 1922; and Note on the Preservation and Support for Scientific Activities in the Samara Kray. Papers of *gubispolkom*, TsGASO, f. 81, op. 1, ed. khr. 533, ll. 226–32 ob.; Samara Guberniya DPE document, detailing reasons for closure and for focusing instead the available stretched resources on agricultural and pedagogical institutes, September 1, 1923. SOGASPI, f. 1, ed. khr. 1, op. 1116, ll. 74–75. The Academician M. N. Tikhomirov, who worked in the Samara *uyezd* DPE, part of the *uyezd ispolkom* (executive committee), recalls the "libertarian" (*vol'nyye*) ethos there at that time: "Towards the non-party colleagues who worked with the soviet authorities our managerial staff had a positive attitude, not just formally positive but in a heartfelt way." Tikhomirov, "Samara," 43.

did on income from the fee-paying monied segment of Samara society. The student body in years 2–5, for instance, comprised 215 students in category I who were completely exempt from having to pay for education; the 234 students in the second category of *serednyaki* (middling income) students paid 50 million; and 274 – category III and the largest cohort of students – listed as *imushchiye* (propertied, well-off) paid fees to the tune of 100 million per year. The university's defense of the fee structure underscored the high competition for places. "The total sum for instruction ... is clearly warranted, for students obviously find it more cost-effective to pay 50–100 million for training at Samara University than to be transferred to another one incurring relocation costs not lower but higher than these fees and *where it would be absolutely impossible to obtain a place.*"[44]

Another way to safeguard professional autonomy was to bow to the Bolsheviks' social agenda, while leaving professional standards and gatekeeping intact – especially in scientific research. This practice embodies an element of what scholars in comparative historical analysis have termed institutional "drift," while bowing to the inevitable pressures for a degree of "conversion" when faced with Bolshevik policy demands. Drift is an adaptive process whereby institutional inertia defies the preferences of powerful policy actors. Conversion, another strategy of institutional survival, is the absorption of a new agenda even when original institutional edifices stay largely intact.[45] As Smirnov notes,

Of course, *no one has the right to dictate and order to the scientist tackling great problems the direction of scientific endeavor* ... But the destitute [*nishchaya*] land has the right to expect help from scientists in restoring normality and in getting the country's economy functioning, and to ask for such help. No need to speculate concerning the answer of the scientists of Samara University to the request of the *kray* [to provide help]: it is clear.[46]

In theorizing the significance of calamities for shifts in the social structure, Pitirim Sorokin has highlighted both their shattering effects on extant institutions and their restorative and regenerative role. "Calamities," he writes, "promote scientific and technological progress also by creating new situations for experimentation and observation ... Pestilence affords rare opportunities for the study of various biological and medical problems; famine, for the investigation of a host of biological, psychological, and sociological questions."[47] We may conceptualize the famine and epidemics that raged, just as the revolutionaries sought to develop new institutions and

[44] "Explanatory Note to Estimates of the Maintenance of the Medical Faculty of Samara State University for 1922–1923." Guberniya *ispolkom* papers, TsGASO, f. 81, op. 1, ed. khr. 533, l. 232 (emphasis added). This period coincides with hyperinflation, which was brought under control after the state adopted the gold ruble in 1924.
[45] Hacker et al., "Drift and Conversion," 195.
[46] Professor Smirnov's letter, l. 225 (emphasis added). [47] Sorokin, *Man and Society*, 244.

shatter the old, as a crisis within a crisis. These shocks also encouraged political actors to "eschew experimentation and instead fall back on familiar formulas – resulting in institutional reproduction, not change."[48]

The medical school took the lead in fulfilling the pledge of working with the state toward "restoring normality." The medical professional craftily negotiated his or her adherence to the new regime's agenda by inserting, incrementally, demands for recognition, funding, and resources. Aside from the 1921–22 famine that claimed hundreds of thousands of lives,[49] Samara also experienced raging epidemics as it became a transit and destination point for civilians fleeing strife and bloodshed. In the regional capital alone, 116,004, out of a population of 182,372, or some 63 percent of residents, succumbed to highly infectious diseases – including cholera, Siberian ulcer, and smallpox.[50] In 1923, the region registered the largest number of malaria infections among Russia's *gubernii* – 660,367; of dysentery – 12,429; and scurvy – 3,229.[51] Although many of the most experienced doctors reportedly refused to man the so-called medical-nutrition stations that the government hastily set up as it scrambled to fight epidemics and malnutrition,[52] even the modest skills of the medical trainee were invaluable in the morgues, clinics, and hospitals.[53] The university constituted a core site of civic and state-organized famine and disease relief. The rector, Professor Fridolin, initiated the establishment of the Museum of Famine with the proviso that SU host it as a hub of information dissemination to prevent and treat future outbreaks of disease and malnutrition. The political authorities agreed to support and fund this initiative;[54] and the Medical Faculty's anatomists responded to the urgent public healthcare need to examine the corpses of those who had fallen victim to disease, as well as to treat survivors, and successfully lobbied for the provision of 8 million rubles to equip anatomical research laboratories.[55] The "acute shortage of specialists of the highest qualifications" led the nascent regime to mobilize, as sanitary doctors, "students of the upper years of the medical faculty, practically quite experienced to perform medical procedures."[56] Local authorities requested that seasoned medics and student trainees alike engage in "propaganda of sanitary awareness" among the public.[57] A "Militant epidemic squad," half of which was comprised of the Medical Faculty's senior students, was mobilized;[58] and the main regional press outlet *Samarskaya*

[48] Thelen, *How Institutions Evolve*, 292.
[49] On famine statistics, see Vishnevskiy, *Demograficheskaya modernizatsiya*, 401, 442–44.
[50] Kuz'min, *Zdravookhraneniye*, 102. Some estimates of excess deaths from epidemics alone across Russia for 1918–22 are as high as 7 million. Vishnevskiy, *Demograficheskaya modernizatsiya*, 402.
[51] Kuz'min, *Zdravookhraneniye*, 104.   [52] Ibid., 139.   [53] Ibid., 95, 139.
[54] Ibid., 120. On lobbying for the creation of the museum and requests for state funding in connection with the faculty's famine aid, see also "Note on the Maintenance of Scientific Forces." TsGASO, 1922, f. 81, op. 1, ed. khr. 533, l. 230.
[55] Ibid., 126.   [56] Ibid., 95.   [57] Ibid., 101.   [58] Ibid., 97.

kommuna featured urgent appeals to doctors and senior medical students to join the "lecturing group" instructing junior medics in vocational schools.[59]

These circumstances provided a temporal opening for institutional preservation before the faculty's closure in 1927. During this period, the first cohorts of trained doctors graduated; foundations were laid for medics like the Kavetskiys to reconstruct and configure the hardware and software of the *Soviet* profession; and opportunities were seized to procure and negotiate a modicum of autonomy. In other words, they enabled the survival of established status quo coalitions among the professoriate and medics and the engendering of *new constituencies favoring it – several cohorts of trained professionals.* I now discuss how professional reproduction also derived momentum from "bottom-up" sources of deference outside of the formal channels of sanction and recognition.

Society As a Source of Professional Reproduction

Aside from underscoring how the urgency of demand for expertise enabled the medical profession to safeguard its institutional independence, I also situate occupational avatars and the professional in a dynastic sense more broadly in terms of social reverence and esteem. Sociologists of the professions juxtapose *extra*-professional with *intra*-professional sources of reproduction, a contrast that does not always imply they are not co-constitutive and mutually reinforcing. I shall argue that, in totalizing regimes with an agenda of social transformation, *extra*-professional esteem acquires added salience for three reasons. One is the cultivation of the "high-status" client.[60] In our case, it would be political leadership, top nomenklatura cadre, and the new cultural, scientific, and artistic aristocracy – actors bestowing not only the same kinds of rewards obtainable in politically open settings but also "protection" from the vagaries of witch hunts and persecutions. The second logic of the value of extra-professional esteem in socially totalizing regimes is related to bottom-up societal reverence, which may be particularly instrumental in sheltering the professional even when he or she is out of favor with the cadre apparatchik on grounds of ideology and class. Grassroots esteem may well operate outside of, or go against, the logic of the political aspect of professional recognition. The communist regime may have hounded the individual "bourgeois" specialist or downplayed his or her training, but popular knowledge and "word of mouth" bestow the halo over the head of the "old" professional as against the new. The third, related, reason, is state dysfunction, as when the *sovietness* of the public sector conceals the informality in the provision of what society perceives to be "quality" as distinct from shoddiness in frontline services. In Soviet – much like in post-Soviet – Russia, people got by not because public services were outstanding but because a vast informal economy sprang up to fill the gaps in welfare provision. Jeremy Morris and Abel Polese highlight how the frontline,

---

[59] Ibid., 101.   [60] Abbott, *System of Professions,* 122–24; Abbott, "Status."

street-level, professionals operate in an economy of favors where the state is akin to an "absentee landlord" unable to live up to its own awesome proclamations and where professional-social interaction acquires its own logic of expectations of roles, morality, and norms.[61]

In our analysis, Dr. Kavetskiy and the Kavetskiys as a dynasty embody *intra-professional* esteem: Nikolay mentions 175 scientific publications produced over 45 years of an illustrious medical career. To unpack the extra-professional element of deference, I bring in Dr. Samuil Abramovich Grinberg, the pediatrician and member of the Grinberg medical dynasty encountered already in Chapter 3. Grinberg had also been acquainted with the Kavetskiys, co-participating in medical associations, congresses, and other occupational venues, even if likely enjoying less intra-professional regard associated with being at the cutting edge of scientific research. Grinberg's social circle included local and metropolitan intelligentsia exercising their choice as consumers by opting to be treated by the pedigree medic over and above a lesser professional. Boris Kozhin, a Samara old-timer and documentary filmmaker, who had been exposed to professional medical networks as a child – his mother attended Kavetskiy's Medical Faculty – thus reminisces about Grinberg. When the composer Dmitry Shostakovich and family evacuated to Samara in the early 1940s, his son fell gravely ill. On learning about the family's misfortune, Shostakovich was told: "Go and see Samuil Abramovich." A friendship ensues in the process of the protracted and eventually successful treatment of the sick child. The favor will be repaid. Kozhin recalls being shown tickets that the composer personally signed inviting Dr. Grinberg to the iconic performance of the Leningrad Symphony, in wartime Samara.[62]

While Grinberg's relations with Shostakovich speak to the question of celebrity clientele, an account of the medic's appearance at a premiere of a new circus show in Samara's Strukovskiy Garden – the city's prime spot for leisure then and now – conveys prestige, deference, and respect among the wider society. Recalls Boris Kozhin, then a sixth-grade pupil whom Grinberg, a family friend, invited along to the circus:

We took two steps, two people came up, shook his hand. He addresses everyone by name, they were younger than him: "Dima how is your leg? I recall you used to complain when you were little." He asks another boy whether he had been rinsing his throat. He has angina ... And so slowly by seven pm we arrived in Strukovskiy Garden. When we arrived, the hall was [already] full. It was an invitation-only event. And then, everyone rises from their seats. Dr. Grinberg walked in. Can you believe it? Dr. Grinberg walked in. And everyone, everyone started to shake his hand. And as for those who sat far in the stalls, he pointed his walking stick at them and they shook his walking stick, Dr. Grinberg walks in. *This is what it means to be an old doctor. You understand? He looked after the entire City of Samara.*[63]

---

[61] Morris and Polese, "Informal Health and Education," 492.
[62] Interview with Boris Kozhin, June 20, 2017 and October 24, 2018.
[63] Interview, June 20, 2017 (emphasis added).

Grinberg's reception at the theater represents what Paul Connerton labels the "choreography of authority."[64] That everyone "came up to him" and sought to shake his hand embodied the "identifiable" range of "repertoires" in the reenactment of professional standing. Grinberg here emerges as the "performer" indulging his social status: he gregariously extends his cane to the mass of "observers" as would a saint bestowing the sign of the cross on the distant pilgrim who was unfortunate not to have touched the sacred man himself. And why would Grinberg behave otherwise? Even the social intercourse with Shostakovich, a composer of global acclaim, reflected those same elements of "postural" status:[65] "If you have the wish, the energy and time, please come," allegedly read the note from the musician,[66] as one would plead the deity's descent from the high mount of divinity into society.

In empirical work on post-communist electoral machines, doctors have been portrayed as accomplices in the delivery of the "right" vote – precisely because of their influence and authority over patients and, if they work in state clinics, their dependence on state salary and institutional funding.[67] My account suggests another angle to the professional: the trappings of status were convertible into a form of autonomy vis-à-vis the state and, under market conditions, material wealth enables one to move outside of state-dependent professional sites. In unpacking the various dimensions of status and autonomy that reproduce deference, it is useful to recall Joel Migdal's observation about the coexistence of multiple "moral orders" that clash with stylized understandings of the power of the socially transformative state.[68] The moral order that many a historian and social scientist analyzing Soviet life assumed existed was one prizing social equality and uplift. Yet, when it comes to society's relationship with the "bourgeois" professional, we observe a picture of an alternative or parallel world coexisting or even conflicting with the regime's leveling agenda. This would be especially true for what I term the pedigree professional whose social veneration derived from his or her local knowledge and reputation, which transcended the Soviet era, and from a form of hedging whereby, deep down, Russian people remained highly skeptical of the credentials of the swiftly trained peasant upstart, while genuflecting to the professional of imperial caliber. As Migdal observes, it is common for individuals and groups to assume positions in various situations that may appear conflicting and contradictory.[69] In public life, the Soviet citizen would profess loyalty to ideals of social egalitarianism; yet, in private, that same individual not only would vaguely aspire to have an old-school medic treat his or her sick child rather than the newly minted one but would go to considerable lengths to procure such services, through connections, bribes, or gifts. These

---

[64] Connerton, *How Societies Remember*, 74.   [65] Ibid.

[66] Interview with Boris Kozhin, June 20, 2017.

[67] Lankina, *Governing the Locals*, 122–24; and Rosenfeld, *Autocratic Middle Class*, esp. 86–88.

[68] Migdal, *State in Society*, 132.   [69] Ibid., 185–86.

choices endow society with a regenerative agency of patterns of social stratification and, at the same time, autonomy, transcending the different regimes that span professional life cycles.

The Pop-Up Society

While medicine illustrates the reincarnation of the professionally incorporated estates-derived bourgeoisie via the organization man route, we also observe a more nebulous and fluid occupational domain, characterized here as the pop-up sphere. This is the kind of terrain that captures dynamism during a period of flux, ultimately resulting in institutional reproduction but with an element of change and adaptation to the realities of a new order.[70] The pop-up arena enabled the maintenance and elevation of the positional status of the middling and lower-middling white-collar strata, as indeed for the higher-status individuals otherwise discriminated against in the context of the witch hunts that befell the former bourgeoisie. The lower-status individuals may not have had the material, educational, and social credentials to rise to the top positions and professions that required higher education under the old regime – or they were simply too young and only beginning their careers when the Bolshevik coup happened – nor were they well placed to immediately ascend into senior positions like heads of medical clinics or prestigious university vice-chancellorships under the new one. The pop-up sphere constituted an opportunity for the educated nonprofessional to gradually reinvent themselves as an organization figure and for the true professionals to sit out, as it were, the vagaries of the persecutions and, over time, return to their true calling – and status position – as esteemed organization men and women. It also created possibilities for forging "weak" network ties among what would have been distinct institutional-social spaces – those nevertheless largely encompassing the educated estates – that may have intersected only tangentially, if at all, in the past.

In the pop-up arenas, professional boundaries were fluid and blurred. Much has been written about the social uplift that resulted from activities therein.[71] Instead, I highlight their role in facilitating the rise of the educated nonprofessional and in helping, albeit in a trajectory full of zigzags, the high-status organization man and woman to eventually resume normal careers. The sociologist of professions Andrew Abbott discusses fluid processes of this kind, deploying the concept of "workplace assimilation": "If a professional is incompetent, organizational function demands that his or her work be done by someone else who is probably not officially qualified to do it. Or if there is

---

[70] For a discussion, see Thelen, *How Institutions Evolve*, 292–93.

[71] See, for instance, the healthcare and education passages in the section "The Remaking of Man" in Webb and Webb, *Soviet Communism*, 749; and on volunteer labor in the traveling culture (*kul'tpokhod*) campaigns in Fitzpatrick, *Education*, s172–74.

too much professional work, nonprofessionals do it."[72] When it comes to famine relief, cram campaigns of mass literacy,[73] or the propagation of "culture," there was indeed too much work for only the professional to do. School-age girls who had not yet completed the gymnasium assumed vicarious roles for which their diplomas were not yet at hand but who were far more qualified than the newly minted semiliterate product of the "brigade mode of instruction."[74] In turn, the much-decorated professor assumed – and practiced, if only part-time – the "craft" version of their teaching,[75] however many anxieties they may have had about professional "proletarianization" tasked as they were with carrying out essentially "social work."[76]

In Bolshevik Samara – mirroring processes that were unfolding across the nation – pop-up campaigns targeted sprawling industrial plants, factories, settlements, and the residential dormitories around them in the outlying districts. Industrial laborers were often seasonal rural dwellers; and the factory workforce swelled as peasants fled famine in the countryside and, in the late 1920s, collectivization. "Traveling" (*vyyezdnyye*) enlightenment brigades were dispatched to these locales tasked with gathering statistics and information on attitudes and the social mores of the peasant-proletarian inhabitants; and "on-site" cultural facilities, in the form of the factory "club," were hastily set up to promote culture for the masses. The pop-up society also became lodged in extant institutions of learning. The noblewoman Khardina's gymnasium, for instance, housed the "done with illiteracy!" (*doloy negramotnost'!*) circle in which pupils of higher grades taught the rudiments of literacy.[77]

Some of the leading enlightenment lights, both metropolitan and native to Samara, compensated for the precarity of their position, as they battled to preserve established professional institutions, hierarchies, and their position within them, by moonlighting in the pop-up society. They invoked these items on their CVs in their correspondence with the Bolshevik authorities to negotiate for the retention and recognition of the university and its academic research. Professor Perets combined teaching classics and literature at SU with research of

---

[72] Abbott, *System of Professions*, 65.

[73] As distinct from slowly accumulated knowledge, "cram" and "crash" types of learning in and of themselves reproduce domination because of the "stigmata of 'catching up'" among target or beneficiary groups. Bourdieu, *Language*, 55.

[74] Group method of assessing students to promote disadvantaged strata: if one student gave the right answer, the whole class received a high mark. See the discussion in Tchuikina, *Dvoryanskaya pamyat'*, 169; and Volkov, *Intellektual'nyy sloy*, chap. 4. Unpublished manuscript, available online at Sayt istorika Sergeya Vladimirovicha Volkova (the website of the historian Sergey Vladimirovich Volkov): swolkov.org/ins/index.htm (accessed April 22, 2020).

[75] Abbott, *System of Professions*, 65.   [76] On this point, see ibid., 318.

[77] These accomplishments are listed on websites of schools considered direct institutional "descendants" of the gymnasia: KWG is now Middle School No. 15 named after N. A. Khardina: www.samaraschool15.ru/information/basic-information/school-history/ (accessed April 22, 2020).

the repositories of seventeenth-century monasteries in the Russian North. He also gave a lecture at the Higher People's School (HPS) of the University's Enlightenment Association "on general questions of literary history."[78] This would be a common topic of interest typifying lectures that academics gave as apologia for the university's "bourgeois" credentials. Professor Bashkirov's research at the History and Philology Faculty encompassed "surveying the territories of ancient Bulgars." Bashkirov also lectured at HPS.[79] Professor A. P. Barannikov, a notable authority on Sanskrit, had been preoccupied with translating the ancient Hindu text *Savitri* as the Revolution dawned. Around that time, Barannikov contributed at least one "visiting" lecture to the social calendar of the Railway Workers' Club, a lecture on Taras G. Shevchenko, the Soviet regime–feted Ukrainian poet.[80] Barannikov's conversion from the savant of the ancient Hindu text to perspicacity in matters of Ukrainian verse would not be dissimilar from the engagements of many a high-status *intelligent* as a jack of all trades in the enlightenment drive.

To the extent that "enlightenment" featured broadly as activities bringing knowledge to the masses, Perets, Bashkirov, and other members of the professoriate would share the podium, as it were, with gymnasium-educated lower-status segments of estatist society from among the *meshchane* who may be staging amateur drama performances or lecturing on the benefits of eradicating illiteracy. One such coproducer of enlightenment was Olen'ka Konovalova, who had barely completed the First Women's Gymnasium when the Revolution broke out. Unlike her husband, an engineer – the organization man – Olen'ka lacked specialized higher education; she gained admission into the Samara People's Conservatory to study music but suspended studies after the birth of her child. Her claim to expertise – if she even had one to make – would be her music skills and knowledge of the theater acquired in the gymnasium and the home. Playing the piano for Artillery Factory's "social club," creating mood music during political events, and participating in amateur drama productions were some of Olen'ka's engagements in the pop-up sphere.[81]

Similar professional adaptation features in the employment biographies of the branch of the Neklutin extended family of wealthy merchants and *meshchane*. Several family members were deprived of basic citizenship rights and became *lishentsy*. Like Konovalova, Mariya Aleksandrovna Neklutina (b. 1901), had been completing her gymnasium education just as the Revolution broke out – her gymnasium diploma survives in the family archive. Mariya Aleksandrovna was engaged in the 1920s as a "pedagogue" during *likbez* campaigns, although, due to her *lishentsy* status, not on a salaried basis. Eventually, she moved to the neighboring Ulyanovsk region, where she

[78] "Report." Papers for 1918–19, likely issued in 1919, n.d. TsGASO, f. 81, op. 1, ed. khr. 419, part 1, l. 53.
[79] "Report," l. 52. [80] Ibid. [81] Interview with Sergey Golubkov, October 25, 2018.

converted her pop-up experiences into a salaried occupation, first as a junior instructor and then as a head teacher in a rural school, before retiring in native Samara. As someone who was gymnasium-trained but lacked a specialized pedagogical education, Mariya Aleksandrovna typified first the profile of a habitué of the pop-up society and later that of a professional transitioning into the organization sphere.[82] Mariya Aleksandrovna's sojourn in a rural school where she could better conceal her ancestry is also an example of a trajectory typical of *lishentsy* gradually reinventing their social identity by temporarily withdrawing into the margins of the Soviet professions, often in a rural area or outside of the native region.[83]

The pop-up enlightenment society may take some years to reengineer its way back into organized professions or to institutionalize new ones, but official discourse surrounding the awesome roles of the proto-professionals working within the pop-up society amply compensated for the disadvantages of being outside, or on the margins of, the corporate structure of an established occupation. The teacher–pupil essence of these activities in a compressed time span constructed the kinds of edifices of status that professionals elsewhere, like American doctors crowding out medicine men and quacks, took decades to achieve.[84] The writer Aleksey Tolstoy in his *Road of Suffering* trilogy, which mixes fictional protagonists with documentary accounts of pre-revolutionary politics, painted telling portraits of the genesis of the pop-up proto-professional. The young Alyosha, a scion of Samara's aristocratic family and a relation of the writer Lev Nikolayevich Tolstoy, attended Samara's *real'noye uchilishche* and later recorded many portraits of the *guberniya*'s various estates and social groups. In his famous trilogy, the leading protagonist Katya, by some accounts modeled on Tolstoy's wife, comes from the family of a Samara-based *zemstvo* doctor, a noble. Katya's character development involves transition from an anxious, idling, society lady trapped in a loveless marriage to a tsarist civil servant, like her, a noble, into the bearer of cultural enlightenment to the masses. Not only is Katya in phenomenally high demand in this role but the party apparatchiks at the highest levels of Soviet bureaucracy articulate her superiority vis-à-vis the masses. On inquiring about job opportunities in Moscow,

Katya immediately received an assignment to serve as a pedagogue at a primary school in Presnya. At another desk, she was mobilized by way of public duties for the evening course for the liquidation of illiteracy. At the third desk she was accosted by an exceptionally thin, olive person, with anxious, enormous eyes – he led Katya via corridors and stairways to the department of propaganda of art. There she was loaded with materials for traveling lectures at factories.

---

[82] Interview with Irina Kolbintseva, October 25, 2018.
[83] See Golitsyn, *Zapiski*; and Tchuikina, *Dvoryanskaya pamyat'*, 83.
[84] Tilly, *Durable Inequality*, 181–89.

By way of reassurance, the "olive man" adds:

As for the content of the lectures, we will specify those later … You will be given appropriate literature and a plan. No need to panic, *you are a cultured person – this is enough.*[85]

The problem is not Katya's origins or her deficiencies in professional qualifications or training; the problem is that not enough people with her background had put themselves forward on the altar of the cause of bringing knowledge to the public: "Our tragedy is that we have too few cultured people – more than half of the intelligentsia are sabotaging [the effort], they will come to regret bitterly this," says the "olive man."[86]

While lacking a vocation, specialized skills, or, at times, any real-world employment experience, the gilded or otherwise well-educated imperial strata had been amply endowed with what Bourdieu refers to as nontangible forms of capital, highly convertible in the Bolsheviks' market of "progressive agendas."[87] As Bourdieu writes in *Distinction*, unlike the established professions that require specialization or technical skills, cultural production – both of a highbrow nature and related to matters of everyday taste and lifestyle – is an area where inherited cultural capital and indeed the social connections that come with high status often suffice in the absence of narrowly defined occupational skills.[88]

Even if individual participants in the pop-up arena were harassed and persecuted because of their "bourgeois" origins, the pressing exigencies of effecting the proclaimed revolutionary ideals forced the Bolsheviks to bestow agency and recognition on the educated bourgeoisie. Discussions about the extent to which the working masses embraced activities aimed at cultural uplift – as expressed in a love of reading, enthusiasm for theater attendance, or appreciation of the arts – routinely featured in official press outlets. One party report, after an observation mission dispatched to the worker dormitories of a factory, quoted with indignation the sentiment of a female employee, apparently representative of the wider collective: "On weekends often boredom sets in [*toska beryot*]: the whole day is spent sleeping, there is nowhere to go. We do not read books. The girls [*devchata*] are mourning their fate: there is nothing to wear. And in this way the hours go by." This sentiment was not limited to the female sex. The inspectors discovered that "even one of the most conscientious of workers [*udarnik*] does not read newspapers or literature."[89]

Another report noted that the Theater of Working Youth and the Theater of Young Viewer, which staged plays on topics of "everyday relevance," proved

[85] Tolstoy, *Khozhdeniye*, 750, author's translation (emphasis added). The novel has been translated into English as *Road to Calvary*.
[86] Ibid., 750.   [87] See Tchuikina, *Dvoryanskaya pamyat'*, esp. 58–85.
[88] Bourdieu, *Distinction*, 139–50. See also Tchuikina, *Dvoryanskaya pamyat'*, 58.
[89] Klimochkina, "Povsednevnaya zhizn'," 201.

"particularly popular," in 1936 "overdoing" the plan. The highbrow "classical" theatre productions staged in established cultural venues featured ticket sales 10 percent below the planned target, however.[90] A lack of enthusiasm for the theater contrasted with a philistine taste for the movies, which was undented by high ticket costs. Consequently, regional authorities instructed the Opera Theater to establish close links with trade union clubs; encourage artists to arrange lectures and "exchanges of opinion" concerning operatic art; delegate professional actors as coaches to amateur clubs or *kruzhki* (circles); and organize traveling performances at enterprises to popularize theater among workers.[91]

The Museum Society

In Chapter 3, I drew attention to the energetic enlightenment activities of pre-revolutionary provincial Russia, which united cultural figures, local government officials, elected councilors, and professionals. Simultaneously, I argued that these activities had an estatist character, circumscribed and largely limited as they had been to the nobility and wealthy merchant strata. In the early post-revolutionary years, many high-placed individuals, even when maintaining their network ties, moved in the shadows of the Soviet enlightenment sphere, relegated to it margins. The aristocracy; those outside of the service estate who possessed substantial industrial assets, property, and land, including many merchants and wealthier *meshchane*; and the otherwise tarnished in the eyes of the new regime, such as senior tsarist government employees, police, or political figures opposed to Bolshevism, were most vulnerable to persecution. In 1931, an estimated 7,904 *lishentsy* resided in Samara City alone – traders from the *meshchane* and *kupechestvo* estates and other "undesirables." In 1932–34, many so-called former people, whose rights to reside in Moscow or Leningrad were rescinded, joined the ranks of Samara's *lishentsy*, including a large share of the 10,000 citizens blacklisted after the assassination of Sergey Kirov, the head of Leningrad's party organization, in 1934.[92]

Because, in composition, practices, and values, Russia's enlightenment society reenacted the pre-revolutionary public sphere, I regard it as an important channel of both the social structure and the maintenance of autonomous civic spaces.[93] This, as noted in the "Conceptual Framework" section of this chapter, had been a perilous strategy but one derived from routinized understandings of what constitutes a good life, which idols are to be worshipped, and what goals and milestones are to be achieved. These

[90] Ibid., 213–14.   [91] Ibid., 209–11, 212.   [92] Ibid., 48–49.
[93] The 1960s bard movement "born and developed within officially endorsed institutions – clubs, cafés, libraries and so on," is an example of such spaces, as indeed "semilegal activity" in "weak organizations ... under loose official control." Shlapentokh, *Soviet Intellectuals*, 78, 79.

cognitive maps had been formed in the slow-moving wavelengths exhibiting disjuncture with the superstructural realities of the Bolsheviks' lightning-speed radical agenda. The pursuit of incentives animating the fraught survival strategies of the remnants of the top layers of the estatist bourgeoisie would have both immediate and long-term payoffs. A web of reciprocal arrangements simultaneously preserved the group's core outlook, by delineating the subjects of inclusion and exclusion, and helped percolate through the public arenas of an otherwise hostile regime.

This perspective nuances theoretical understandings of social-structural lethargy by injecting scenarios from repressive contexts where a revolutionary ideology may not easily penetrate long-internalized assumptions about social gravity and exclusion. I propose the term "museum society" for this field of social reproduction. Embeddedness in this arena often formed part of a long-term process of the reinvention of the highest echelons of tsarist society as successful Soviet professionals or even as members of what may be construed as the cultural-scientific aristocracy. As we shall see, survival encompassed day-to-day subtle resistance to the social contamination of the self-anointed custodian of high culture as opposed to the philistine; and it meant continued support for secure havens and arenas of civic debate, deliberation, and autonomy. I have already noted how the metropolitan equivalents of these hives of oppositional social thought and action among elite society received the prominence that they deserve in the writings on political stirrings in a regime that was to write out politics for seven decades. Yet their spatial range transcended Russia's core cities and would be just as significant in provincial hubs with a history of vibrant civic communities.

The museum society rubric includes provincial museums, archives, historical preservation groups and agencies, and similar outfits, some of which retained their status as repositories of cultural artifacts for the public, while others consolidated their institutional status as think tanks and research institutions as the regime matured. I regard these arenas as marginal to the Soviet enlightenment drive in the early post-revolutionary years; as distinct from the pop-up sphere, which had been more ideologically aligned with regime proclamations; and as contrasting in perceived importance from the organization man arenas, which were pivotal in the consolidation of Bolshevik rule, desperate as the Bolsheviks were to retain a modicum of public services provision. Here labored the self-appointed custodians of the heritage that was being destroyed, not one that was being produced and digested for the masses. In practice, this meant curating, cataloguing, and safeguarding from looting those same repositories of cultural artifacts that the aristocracy and wealthy merchants once owned but that were now in state possession. These sites also represented safe havens for a broader stratum of the high-profile "bourgeois" intelligentsia. Despite their superior education and cultural capital, many found themselves outside of the enlightenment, pop-up channel of social reproduction, becoming suspect in the eyes of the regime or because of honestly listing their past origins in lieu of the prevarications that were widespread at the time in the form of ascribing the past within the Soviet category of a *sluzhashchiy* or of downgrading one's origins to more humble ones in job applications. As the passage from the Tolstoy's trilogy illustrates, scores simply refused to serve the new regime. The Russian historian Sergey Volkov collected statistics on the professional adaptation of Russia's pre-revolutionary "intellectual layer." He notes the significant rise of librarians and museum workers in Moscow, for instance, from 467 to 1,149 in the years 1918–1920 and a simultaneous sharp decline in the number of news editors, literary figures, and journalists whose high-profile names were associated with the past regime, from 994 to 329, representing a decline of 66.6 percent;[94] these losses are only partially accounted for by immigration and Civil War deaths and repressions.[95]

The Samara Museum As a Public Sphere and Arena of Social Reproduction

The Samara Museum embodies the established, institutionalized, autonomous, and highly networked aspect of pre-revolutionary society. Broad in its network reach, encompassing as it did progressive officialdom, local government representatives, the academy, the arts, and the literati, it had been a bona fide estatist social body, largely made up of nobles and merchants. Samara was the first of Russia's Middle Volga *gubernii* to establish a public museum. An initiative of city councilor and future mayor Pyotr Vladimirovich Alabin, it enjoyed the robust support of elected representatives when proposed to the City *duma* on January 29, 1880. The museum officially opened its doors to the public in 1886, complete with research divisions in history, archaeology, numismatics, minerals, geology, paleontology, zoology, botany, technology, and ethnography. Over time, it became a research, cultural, and philanthropic hub for the educated stratum of Samara society. Close links were forged with the nascent SU – in 1919, the museum agreed to house the collections of the university's Natural History Museum.[96]

---

[94] Sergey V. Volkov, "Intellektual'nyy sloy v sovetskom obshchestve," chap. 3. I cite these data as estimates; further evidence is needed to substantiate the exact numbers, though the general gist of the argument about transfer and application of skills to the domains of library and museum work is consistent with other studies of adaptation. The scholar Dmitry Likhachev, after spending time in the concentration camp in Solovetsky Islands and penal labor on Belomor Canal, found employment as a proofreader in the Academy of Sciences Press, where "all the staff members were people from 'former classes' who could not find better employment." Zubok, *Zhivago's Children*, 7. In his memoirs, Prince Sergey Golitsyn writes that relatives like Count Pavel Sergeyevich Sheremetev embedded themselves in one or another museum as staff, some with the patronage of leading Soviet officials. Golitsyn, *Zapiski*, 242–43. On family acquaintances who became dynastic museum workers, see also ibid., 366.
[95] Volkov, "Intellektual'nyy sloy."
[96] The discussion in this section is based on the webpage of the Samara *oblast* history and local knowledge museum named after P. V. Alabin: www.alabin.ru/o-muzee/ (accessed March 10, 2021). The local artist, a scion of a merchant family, Konstantin Golovkin, established the

Repressions toward staff began shortly after the Bolsheviks took power. The museum was ordered to suspend its activities; exhibits were closed to the public; and staff harassed. In practice, the museum society – the institution and the informal civic groups that formed around it – did not cease to function. A Museum Collegium was established at the initiative of SAHE, charged with ensuring the preservation and safeguarding of museum treasures in the interim.[97] By 1923, the museum reopened its doors to the public under the directorship of Vera Vladimirovna Gol'msten, a leading archaeologist from St. Petersburg, who helped salvage the museum, along with its vast collections, and kept alive the many scientific and research activities pursued under its auspices.[98] The museum also maintained network ties to other organizational sites of enlightenment society, notably municipal bodies hitherto part of the imperial architecture of government, which remained embedded in the organizational chart, as it were, of Bolshevik Samara. Often, these offices represented socially homogeneous spaces, akin to those of the museum, except that, by dint of being part of the formal Soviet governance architecture, they provided opportunities for the "bourgeois" elite to interact more with the socially distinct sites of Bolshevik rule.[99] These were liminal spaces straddling the organization man and museum society refuge arenas. One such transient site was the *guberniya*'s Archive Division and Fund. The expertise of staff and affiliates was relied on to catalogue expropriated artworks, rare manuscripts, and artifacts.[100]

museum's art section and in 1907 sought to create a dedicated space for art galleries and free public exhibitions, pledging 600,000 rubles for a "Palace of science and art," but the project remained unrealized. Ol'ga Mikhaylova, "Golovkin, Konstantin Pavlovich," December 17, 2014. Available online at Samarskiye sud'by ("Samara Destinies"): samsud.ru/blogs/hroniki-samarochki/golovkin-konstantin-pavlovich.html (accessed May 4, 2018); Ryadchenko, "Samarskiy publichnyy muzey."

[97] The Society's activities in the 1920s are recorded in Tikhomirov, "Samara," 65–66. Tikhomirov worked as librarian and lectured on history at the archaeological courses taught there.

[98] Biography available from Kuz'minykh et al., *Vera Vladimirovna Gol'msten*. On the history of the museum and its affiliates who were, or became, noted archaeologists, see the website of the Samara Archaeological Society: archsamara.ru/history/ (accessed May 12, 2018). Other materials in this passage are based on archival records, memoirs, and other sources.

[99] As such, my emphasis on networks as a mechanism of survival and autonomy is different from similar conceptions of *lost intelligentsia* or even "integral émigré" "fully alienated from the Soviet system" that seeks "individual solutions by 'opting out' of the system" and by dint of "liv[ing] in a private, family or sectarian world of their own, although they will often give competent and loyal service as specialists or skilled workers during working hours." Churchward distinguishes this type from the three other stylized Soviet intelligentsia subtypes of *careerist professionals*, *humanist intelligentsia*, and *open oppositionists*. See *Soviet Intelligentsia*, 139.

[100] Employment with this public body featured in the résumé of Aleksandr Aleksandrovich Marushchenko (1904–76), a student of Gol'msten, who went on to become a "distinguished soviet archaeologist." Professor Aleksey Stepanovich Bashkirov (1885–1963), one of the first tenured appointees at SU's Faculty of History and Philology, one-time Samara Museum director, and eventually a professor at Moscow State University, was likewise an affiliate. See

While the general history of the institution and its many distinguished affiliates are publicly known, my objective is to transcend the institutional biography and to gaze into the black box of social dynamics within it. The social ethnography of one institution, including a rudimentary reconstruction of social network ties, allows us to draw tentative generalizations about some of the ways in which the museum society constituted both an arena of social reproduction and one regenerative of tsarist Russia's enlightenment public sphere.

The Museum As a Socially Exclusive Space

The Samara State Archive of Social and Political History contains "top secret" denunciations, some pertaining to the comings and goings within the museum and the personalities, practices, friendships, and professional networks of its staff. The main accusations in the informers' reports were leveled at the director Vera Gol'msten and her alleged patronage of former people to the exclusion of colleagues with more ideologically pure credentials. The museum, reportedly, "is practically a bastion and a hotbed for the local counter-revolutionary intelligentsia [one that] first and foremost provides them with means for existence."[101] The denunciations list the employees' estate and occupational characteristics – former workers of tsarist police forces; landowners (*pomeshchiki*); a general; and a *zemstvo* functionary. The informers maintained that Gol'msten had significant freedom in hiring and firing staff, ostensibly opting for people of her own social circle: "The museum staffs are selected exclusively from among the anti-Soviet public and former bourgeoisie." In some cases, she hired individuals who had worked for a Soviet institution but may have been dismissed due to their origins – outcasts from the organization man arenas. This was apparently the case with the landowner Arapov, an erstwhile employee of the *guberniya Gubplan* (state planning bureau), who allegedly then secured a position at the museum "with the help of Gol'msten."[102]

The reports go further than simply listing the undesirable origins of employees, since we also get a glimpse into their and their children's patterns of socialization, education, and leisure pursuits. Gol'msten reportedly exploited her connections among the highest echelons of the tsarist academy to secure the admission of the fallen strata's offspring into prestigious institutions of higher learning in St. Petersburg and the Middle Volga city of Kazan, another leading center of excellence in higher education. There is some indication that she

the website of the Samara Archaeological Society: archsamara.ru/history/ (accessed May 12, 2018).
[101] "Top secret, other secret materials, file No. 12, Characteristics of scientific associates of the museum, Samara gubkom VKPb." Papers for 1928, SOGASPI, f. 1, op. 4, ed. khr. 13, l. 20.
[102] Ibid., l. 18.

ХАРАКТЕРИСТИКА

научных сотрудников Самарского музея.

1. Профессор-археолог ГОЛЬМСТЕН Вера Владимировна – Заведующая музеем /хранитель музея/ в Самару прибыла в первые годы революции из Москвы, помимо музея занимает платную должность – ученого секретаря в Обществе археологии, личность не советская, придерживается старых народнических взглядов, имеет тесную связь со старой Самарской буржуазией, быв. миллионерами ШИХОБАЛОВЫМИ и их родственниками, как член об-ва археологии тесно связана с реакционной профессурой, состоящей в об-ве, как-то: с БЕЗСОНОВЫМ, А.Н./б. помещик/, ПРЕОБРАЖЕНСКИМ, П.А./член партии "К-Д"/ быв. генерал-майором ЗВЕРЕВЫМ/, Председателем об-ва археологии АРАПОВЫМ, В.П./член ТНСП-быв. помещик/ и др. штат служащих в музей подбирает исключительно из а/советской публики и быв. буржуазии.

2. Стар. пом. хранителя музея АРАПОВ Владимир Петрович, б. помещик-дворянин, по профессии агроном, быв. преподаватель и ректор Сам. СХИ, председатель Сам. Об-ва археологии, быв. гласный Самарской Губернской Земской Управы и член ТНСП. личность а/советская, имеет тесную связь с реакционной

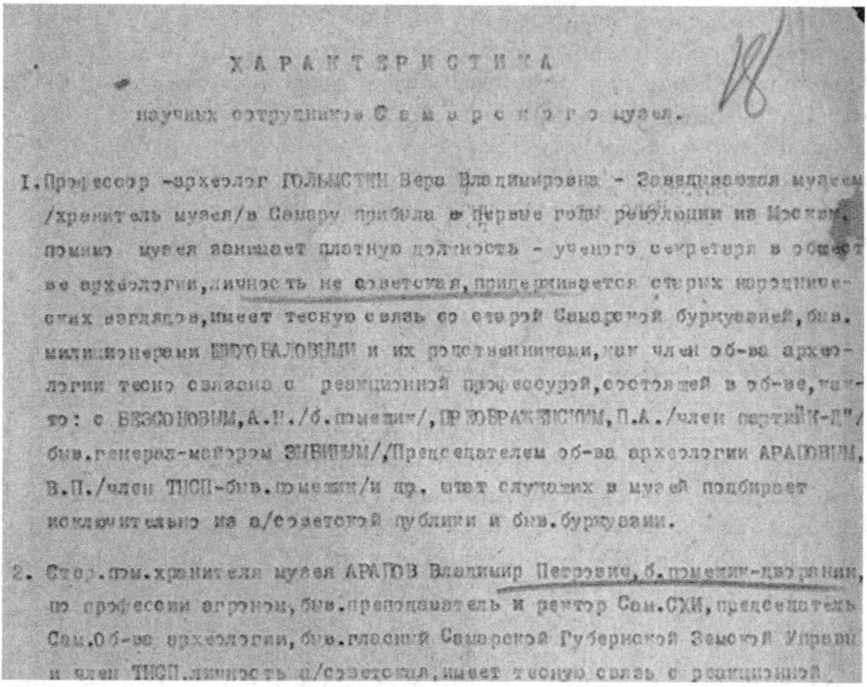

FIGURE 4.2 Informers' reports on museum staff in a "top secret" file, 1928
Source. SOGASPI, f. 1, op. 4, ed. khr. 13, l. 18

prevaricated in vouching for the formal academic credentials of her adolescent referees aspiring to a university place.

The local history (*krayevedcheskiye*) courses organized under the auspices of the Archaeological Society, which met through the 1920s, may well have served the purpose of providing formal instruction, or paper credentials, to university-place *refuseniks*. An informer claimed that most attendees "are unable to gain admission into VUZy."[103] Evening or day courses were known avenues in the circuitous route of former people to eventual redemption as *Soviet* intelligentsia.[104] Others were hired without the credentials required by *Glavnauka*, the ministry dealing with science and the academy. This was the predicament of Aleksandr Vasil'yevich Surchakov, the "son of a Samara guberniya *kulak*," hired as assistant museum curator despite lacking a university degree, which was reportedly a prerequisite for the museum position. Gol'msten allegedly rubber-stamped the employment of the likes of

[103] "Top Secret," l. 21.

[104] Tchuikina, *Dvoryanskaya pamyat'*, 85–91. Alumni of the archaeology courses where Gol'msten taught, and which continued to function after SU's closure, became notable archaeologists following admission to Moscow University. See Kuz'minykh et al., *Vera Vladimirovna Gol'msten*, 27.

Surchakov by "supplying false information" to the effect that "Surchakov completed courses that are equivalent to a VUZ."[105] The extended families of individuals from Gol'msten's and her employees' social circle, whether formally employed at the museum or not, benefited from her help in other ways. One of Gol'msten's "protégés," a certain Vladimir Petrovich Arapov, a member of the "former landholding nobility" (*pomeshchik-dvoryanin*) allegedly provided access to "scientific instruments" belonging to the museum, as indeed his office, "for the perusal of children and relatives of prominent bourgeoisie."[106] A certain Nina Mumortseva, "daughter of the former well-known bourgeoisie [*burzhui*], is presently using the microscope. Her work has no relation to the museum whatsoever."[107]

Conversely, individuals not belonging to Gol'msten's circle were reportedly marginalized, demoted, or stigmatized. This was the fate of Ol'ga Leont'yevna Sinitsina and Fyodor Timofeyevich Yakovlev, the only affiliates presented in a positive light and plausible authors of detailed accounts of the museum's inner workings left for posterity. The social origins of the two – wife of an "army serviceman" and "railway employee" – would set them apart from the scions of industrialists, large landowners, and imperial professoriate with whom Gol'msten ostensibly surrounded herself.[108] Sinitsina's and Yyakovlev's relationships with other employees illustrate subtle dynamics of intraorganizational social exclusion. Sinitsina allegedly "keeps separate from the company of Arapov and Gol'msten, does not enjoy the trust of the latter."[109] Furthermore, she is nudged toward embracing pop-up enlightenment functions, activities clearly shunned among those of Gol'msten's circle. "Most of the museum work is being dumped on the scientific worker Sinitsina, *specifically it is she who almost invariably accompanies visitors doing excursions from various public organizations.*"[110] Yakovlev is likewise presented in a flattering light:

An old museum worker, amateur collector, a railway *sluzhashchiy* by profession, former superintendent of a railway station, works in the museum from the first days of the Revolution, took active part in the preservation of archival and museum treasures, labors in the museum because of his calling.[111]

Like Sinitsina, Yakovlev clearly also suffers from a form of intraorganizational professional and social marginalization: "He is stigmatized by Gol'msten and Arapov [*v opale*]. All along he had the position of scientific worker, but to employ her own people [*svoikh*] – Arapov, Surchakov and others – professor Gol'msten at first offered Yakovlev to combine his work with role of museum treasurer, and then replaced him with another scientific worker."[112]

---

[105] "Top Secret," l. 19. [106] "Top Secret," ll. 18, 20. [107] "Top Secret," l. 20
[108] "Top Secret," ll. 18–21. On the other hand, the son of a "kulak" – Surchakov – was also patronized. Ibid., l. 19.
[109] Ibid., l. 20. [110] Ibid. l. 21 (emphasis added). [111] Ibid., l. 20. [112] Ibid., l. 20.

Outside of the informers' reports, several additional historical records illuminate Yakovlev's predicament in the Samara Museum and Soviet society.[113] From a biographical note,[114] we know that he had been an amateur collector, archaeologist, and advocate for cultural preservation. An apt Russian-language characterization of someone like Yakovlev is *samorodok*, a talented self-made man: his formal education consisted of a few years of primary schooling. At an early age, Yakovlev married a woman from a working family who served as a maid to a St. Petersburg ballerina. By the time of the Bolshevik Revolution, he already possessed a substantial record of *zemstvo* activism and was known in Samara's educated circles. Two of his sons went on to fight for the Whites – the anti-Bolshevik forces – in the Civil War. When the Bolsheviks took power in Samara, Yakovlev was arrested and briefly held in custody; the museum was also shut. When it reopened, Yakovlev, by virtue of being in the eyes of the new authorities as close as it gets to the desperately sought-after "proletarian" cadre, is anointed as the new museum director; his appointment, however, is short-lived. The identity of the informers who wrote the reports on the Samara museum remains unknown; but, given that Yakovlev had been earlier arrested only to be reappointed as museum head and that the questionable political loyalties of his sons made his family vulnerable to repression, it is conceivable that some form of collaboration with the new regime would have ensued.

Yakovlev's personal correspondence, his descendants' recollections, and the memoirs of archaeologists who knew him personally illuminate the subtle estatist dynamics contributing to the social alienation of the self-made man. In the eyes of the communist regime's new foot soldiers, Yakovlev remained a "bourgeois," a label not entirely inappropriate in the quasi-Marxist class schemata, since he had been neither factory worker nor peasant and had been privy to, or at least aspired to membership in, Samara's enlightenment circles. Yakovlev's wife reminisced about an incident that occurred during his short-lived spell as museum director, which entitled the family to reside in the elite quarters attached to the workplace:

Suddenly they [Bolshevik authorities] come – and he had a decent appearance [*intelligentnyy vid*], he wore a top hat [*kotelok*], and he is told: "You are a bourgeois, get out of here. You have no place here." And so, from the 1920s onwards the Yakovlev family permanently resided in a small, cramped apartment, located on the second floor of a wooden house on Ural'skaya [a less prestigious] Street.[115]

Yakovlev, however, is equally an outsider among the cultural glitterati. The historian Mikhail Nikolayevich Tikhomirov, who had been dispatched by the Samara *uyezd* Education Department to salvage the ancient manuscripts of Old

[113] Tikhomirov, "Samara"; Valeriy Yerofeyev, "Yakovlev."   [114] "Yakovlev."
[115] "Yakovlev."

Believer monasteries, thus describes "the unforgettable Fyodor Timofeyevich Yakovlev," his companion on the journey:

In his past life, Fyodor Timofeyevich used to be the head of some railway station or another. Simultaneously, he dealt with, by way of a hobby, archaeological and other matters. This was not a very well-educated person, and in history, frankly speaking, someone who understood nothing. But at the start of the Revolution such people not infrequently ended up occupying various positions, among whom was also Fyodor Timofeyevich ... Even the personal appearance of Fyodor Timofeyevich was curious. A short man of slim build, he used to wear some strange suit with coattails [*faldy*]. On his head was perched an old-fashioned *kotelok* [top hat], in which he presented a portrait of a provincial dandy of our century with the obligatory tendency to try to appeal to the ladies.[116]

The *kotelok* conveyed in the recollections of Yakovlev's descendants as an indicator of respectability and status is in Tikhomirov's memoirs ridiculed as the trappings of an antediluvian social parvenu. Yakovlev's bitterness at his marginality is revealed in his persistent complaints of not being taken seriously by the more learned members of the arts establishment. Although Yakovlev had amassed valuable archaeological artifacts and was keen to preserve them for *guberniya*'s public collections, he found himself excluded from invitations to professional and social events bubbling around the museum. This sentiment emerges in a letter addressed to Konstantin Pavlovich Golovkin, the elite member of "enlightenment" society. In one letter dated February 1917, Yakovlev bitterly alludes to the affront that he experienced at the hands of the then head of the museum, Aleksandr Aleksandrovich Smirnov, and one of its associates, Sergey Yefremovich Permyakov – a high-profile civic personage in pre-revolutionary Samara.[117]

Your Honorable Konstantin Pavlovich!
    ... These days, I have been preoccupied with assembling the collections [for the museum] and have not been out much. As to the museum's misfortunes, I know nothing, and it is to the better that I have been refraining from going there until the matter is finally resolved, for even from Permyakov I had no letters. *You and others like A. G. Yelshin* [listed in the 1916 yearbook as an attorney] *were invited, and as for me for the time being in the eyes of Permyakov and Smirnov I am an unknown entity doing dirty work* [*neizvestnyy rabotnik chyornoy raboty*].
    Respectfully Yours, Yakovlev, 9/II-1919.[118]

---

[116] Tikhomirov, "Samara," 55–56.
[117] The 1916 yearbook lists Sergey Yefremovich Permyakov as a member of the city *uprava* and several civic bodies – the board of Samara Society of Public Universities, the Samara Guberniya Learned Archive Commission, the Samara Chapter of Imperial Russian Society of Gardeners, among others.
[118] "Yakovlev" (emphasis added).

The Samara Museum and the Public Sphere

If we piece together the eclectic documentary fragments, the museum emerges as a hub held together by many invisible threads, the concentric circles of the upper-status intelligentsia, or, in informer-speak, "a convenient place for arranging social dates with members of own circle [*udobnym mestom dlya svidaniy so svoyey publikoy*]."[119] The museum, and museum society, however, is here regarded also as an engine for the maintenance of pre-revolutionary autonomous public spaces. Very little of what emerges from its activities exhibits a revolutionary break with the social engagements of the past. Much as before, archaeological digs are organized and carried out; debating and discussion events are held ("Arapov is frequently visited by personal acquaintances, Bazhanov, Bessonov, etc. who together hold long deliberations; these individuals have no relation to the museum whatsoever");[120] new initiatives are conceived, some carried out and others buried – an informer notes the deliberations about the setting up of a "Gerbarium Society," which "never materialized;"[121] and, much as before, the virtual red carpet is placed at the feet of high-status philanthropists – notables such as nobles, merchants, and industrialists – the Shikhobalovs, the Kurliny, and the Ardzhanovs – the difference being that now their possessions in the museum's safe custody are expropriations, not donations:

On 16 February of this year [1927], the former millionairess Shikhobalova, now Ardzhanova by her husband's name, made a visitation to the Museum, with the aim of inspecting paintings expropriated from the Shikhobalovs during the first years of the Revolution. Shikhobalova was received in the Museum very warmly and cordially. The head of the art division Gundobin personally accompanied her during her inspection tour.[122]

The contours of the museum society that emerge from the archival records echo the historian Vera Kaplan's observations about aspects of imperial Russia's voluntary associational life. The burgeoning historical preservation initiatives represented particularly socially insular spaces with an element of outreach. Kaplan traces the origins of voluntary societies back to the late eighteenth century, precisely the temporal point of the consolidation of the estates along with the more formal institutions of nobles' assemblies and urban corporations. "Although encompassing only the small educated elite," writes Kaplan, "these voluntary associations played a significant role in fashioning the *modus vivendi* of the new estate institutions ... Regardless of their particular goals, the voluntary societies became a kind of greenhouse for promoting and refining the norms of educated sociability, which became essential for the nobles."[123] By the end of the nineteenth century, associational life experienced significant transformation. The historical

---

[119] "Top Secret," l. 20.   [120] Ibid., l. 20.   [121] Ibid., l. 20.   [122] Ibid., ll. 20–21.
[123] Kaplan, *Historians*, 4–5.

associations specifically had come to "provide[d] a meeting place for people belonging to different social strata and with different levels of education and ways of life but with a shared interest in history."[124] These groups simultaneously, however, preserved the conservative, insular features that characterized the earlier period's proto-associational life. The *Kulturträgers'*[125] impulse for enlightenment and inclusivity was "fraught with tension" in a society that continued to be highly unequal, stratified, and hierarchical. Belonging to particular voluntary associations "also meant entering into a sophisticated network of personal connections."[126] These were relied on to obtain employment in academia and the civil service; and appeals were made on behalf of sons aspiring to a desirable job, as indeed were insistent requests to aid one or another public cause.[127] "A voluntary association" thus "provided an institutional framework not only for creating new social arrangements, but also preserving the existing ones."[128]

The Samara Museum of the surveillance-rife society of the 1920s represents continuity with Kaplan's cultural spaces as sites of mutual aid as much as it anticipates patterns of what Morris discusses as "imbrication" in post-communist Russia. Formal professional embeddedness and resources are inextricably enmeshed with "licit and illicit, legal and illegal aspects of economic life ... entangled in a way that makes their disaggregation problematic."[129] These enabled survival in an environment of precarity and marginality, amid an urgency for the preservation of one's self-worth by individuals made worthless and for the absorption of the "surplus" of enlightened outcasts.[130] The imbrication template also enables the diversification of a "portfolio" of tangible and intangible resources.[131] These range from the microscope aiding exam preparation to secure that coveted place at a medical school, to the vital metropolitan connection reanchoring the outcasts from one region in the same social space elsewhere, to the provision of a salaried post for "one's own." Imbrication within a formal institution may not yield immediate monetary payoffs or ones easily "commodified."[132] Yet, what Abbott discusses as a "life cycle" or "life course" perspective sensitive to zigzags, contingencies, and the layering of distinct cohort experiences,[133] suggests long-term advantages in the Soviet labor market. These are evidenced in the stellar careers of individuals enmeshed in Samara's museum network, some decades later. Morris's insights are prescient for making sense of the embeddedness of informality within formal employment arenas and, indeed, for seeing how elements of state-ness could be reconstituted in an atmosphere of

---

[124] Ibid., 2.   [125] Ibid., 155.   [126] Ibid., 208.   [127] Ibid., 208.
[128] Ibid., 212. On the "the search for a provincialist past" and the emergence of a historically conscious public sphere in the context of Russia's Great Reforms, see also Starr, *Decentralization*, 90–106.
[129] Morris, "Informal Economy," 17.   [130] Ibid., 19.   [131] Ibid., 17.   [132] Ibid., 21.
[133] Abbott, "Life Cycles."

the ostensible widespread ruin and collapse of public services. My analysis in addition highlights how heterogeneity in imperial social standing provides unequal starting points for various social groups and situates their resources within their estatist origin and milieu.

Social network theory, however, suggests that such forms of insularity are not particularly conducive to the professional advancement of individuals and groups. If anything, given the already precarious position of the *haute* estates-derived "bourgeoisie," such "strong ties" would only exacerbate their vulnerabilities as they navigate their way under the new regime. It is now time to bring together the three stylized arenas of professional reproduction to illustrate how all three are facilitators in the status maintenance of educated society, while also engendering new opportunities for network ties.

FROM STRONG TO WEAK TIES

The three professional arenas outlined in this chapter are here regarded from the point of view of proclivities toward engendering social relationships that simultaneously connect and establish boundaries, formal and informal, between groups. The pop-up arena would be most porous, facilitating the emergence of ties among individuals originating from distinct milieus and backgrounds within estatist society, who now co-participe "as equals." The organization man sphere would occupy an intermediate place in terms of network openness. In medicine, for instance, it exhibits rigid intra-professional hierarchies and gatekeeping, but one, by dint of wide social contact, rife with possibilities for drawing on old, and engendering new, social ties aiding adaptation. The museum society, on the other end of the scale of network openness, constitutes a highly insular social space involving strong ties, those, in Mark Granovetter's classic framework,[134] not particularly conducive to building bridges with other networks or, relatedly, to advancement in the Bolshevik labor market. Yet a closer look at engagements outside the "black box" of this insular arena has revealed individuals' tangential association with core service-delivery public institutions, as instructors in quasi-vocational courses for the masses or as consultants on matters of cultural and historical preservation to *guberniya* authorities.[135] The biography of the academician Tikhomirov typifies the multiplexity of employment and informal engagement sites – and hats worn – of just one individual imbricated within the enlightenment sphere of Soviet Samara. Tikhomirov's roles encompassed work within official political bodies, the *ispolkom* and its education branch, the university, the museum, and the archaeology society, among others. "Back then there were no laws concerning

---

[134] Granovetter, "Strength of Weak Ties."
[135] Here, I draw on "Report on the activities." TsGASO, f. 81, op. 1, ed. khr. 419, part 1, ll. 49–56 ob.

combining positions [*po sovmestitel'stvu*] and each of us [at SU] could have as many positions as they pleased. It is true that the pay for those positions was not very high ... *I ended up being the most modest combiner* [*sovmestitel'*], *having 7 positions.*"[136] The "weak" ties of the reluctant fellow traveler with Bolshevism aided others in the network who may have chosen to completely shun the new regime.

Another useful approach to analyzing network ties is to identify differences among networks. Organizations within established professions like the medical clinic or insular cultural establishments like the museum in our framework represent "socio-centric" "closed-system" networks. "Open-system" networks would be those where boundaries between insiders and outsiders are not as clear-cut. The pop-up society of proto-professionals constitutes an open-system-type network. Individuals not formally employed in a Soviet public organization or lacking formal educational credentials characteristic of those in established professions would co-participate in ad hoc activities that also embraced the organization personnel and the otherwise insular museum society.

These various networks would have generated a cohort effect. Sociologists refer to this effect as propinquity, in that individuals would tend to find themselves "in the same place at the same time."[137] A pedagogue of *meshchane* background engaging in pop-up lectures alongside the metropolitan professor of gilded ancestry would embody a relationship of "colocation." The gatherings of the museum society in Arapov's office featuring individuals from his circle but not formally employed in the museum would constitute a relationship of social "copresence" in that these contacts tended to mirror "the framework of a social institution or social structure," embracing individuals with shared interests gravitating toward "common arenas or foci for meeting."[138] Interactions of a copresence variety would represent stronger social bonds; yet colocation would be the weaker type of tie that would connect otherwise socially more distant individuals and networks.

Within these sets of relationships – some based on old professional ties and informal interests, others state-engineered as part of the pop-up society – is what network analysts refer to as "homophily";[139] this influences the strength of ties that develop among some individuals or social groups over others. Among several individuals engaged in an activity together, those with higher levels of homophily – shared social, cultural, and status characteristics – tend to form even stronger bonds than co-participants lacking such similarities.[140] Thus, weak individual-level and group-level homophily between Yakovlev and others in the museum society would represent a barrier to interaction

---

[136] Tikhomirov, "Samara," 76 (emphasis added).
[137] Kadushin, *Understanding Social Networks*, 18.   [138] Ibid., 18.   [139] Ibid., 18.
[140] Ibid., 18.

even though, organizationally, Yakovlev is connected to Professors Gol'msten and Smirnov or the artist Gundobin. Over time, as interactions are routinized we would expect homophily to develop between those hitherto lacking shared network membership; yet the process may be gradual. It may take a generation or two before patterns of homophily, derivative of childhood socialization, schooling, and upbringing, are reconfigured.

The geographical separation of network members may have hampered routinized interactions; yet, counterintuitively, it facilitated the maintenance of an individual's social status in an otherwise precarious and ideologically hostile environment. Some individuals became conduits of support for those whose mobility would be blocked locally because of noble, merchant, industrialist, or other "bourgeois" origins, which would have been common knowledge in Samara but not in a metropolitan professional or educational setting. Professor Bashkirov became one such figure facilitating the circulation of estatist society between Samara and metropolitan centers of learning.[141]

The extant institutional architecture is pivotal for the maintenance and reconfiguration of network ties. Social networks are indispensable for the preservation of institutions in an ideologically hostile environment, but so are institutions intrinsic to the sustenance of networks. The tapestries of professional, enlightenment, and civic bodies constitute anchors for the safeguarding of the old institutional and estatist networks imbricated within them, and indeed for the reconstruction of the old after a period of temporal cessation of operation. As the stories of the museum, the medical faculty, and the university make clear, the "above-the-surface" event or threat of formal closure, deprivation of funding, and witch hunts do not put an end to the professional activities, networking, lobbying, and fundraising bubbling beneath the surface. Tsarist subterranean institutions – the medical clinics, the university faculties, the archaeological groups – also represented springboards from which the pop-up society fanned out across the region to spread the gospel of socialism. The ties forged between the upper echelons of imperial society high up on the ladder of an institutionally embedded career, the young *meshchanka* barely out of the gymnasium, and the fallen merchant entrepreneur accelerated the gelling of the socially nebulous but simultaneously firmly estatist middle class that had already been some decades in the making, long before the Revolution.

---

[141] Bashkirov's role in nurturing archaeology in Samara is recorded in celebratory accounts of the profession: the website of the Samara Archaeological Society: archsamara.ru/history/ (accessed April 22, 2020). On the persona of Bashkirov, see also Tikhomirov, "Samara." Tikhomirov emphasizes his "organizational talents" over his scientific accomplishments. Ibid., 68. In personal letters to colleagues, Gol'msten mentions Bashkirov in connection with his efforts to support the activities of archaeologists in Samara, including by seeking to procure funding from Moscow. Letter to V. A. Gorodtsov from Samara, August 1, 1922. Kuz'minykh et al., *Vera Vladimirovna Gol'msten*, 80.

CONCLUSION

In analyzing the reproduction of sites of agential social action in professional institutions, and the engendering of new ones, this chapter identified the professional-organizational route to social status maintenance; the pop-up arena; and the adaptation on the margins of the Soviet public sector of some of the most privileged tsarist burghers. The analysis makes clear that the continued embeddedness of the professional or the proto-professional in highly institutionalized arenas and informal networks and sites of public agency played a facilitating role in social resilience and indeed in the continued practice of autonomous action. The organization man domain explains how established vocations maintained intra-professional hierarchies, intrinsic to which is education in elite institutions of learning. The pop-up arena absorbed a variety of distinct groups broadly, however, drawn from the educated estates. The museum society represented the most socially exclusive and insular professional space, one, though, that featured "weak" survival-aiding ties to the pop-up society; to the organization man arenas of academia in the region and metropolitan centers; and even to local government bodies, institutions that formed part of the Soviet state apparatus. The cognate institutions and networks absorbed the shocks of the attempted social destruction. As public health and services emergencies mounted, the regime's own exigencies privileged the estatist society by bestowing both institutional and symbolic recognition.[142] Furthermore, social deference for, as well as the personal intergenerational milestones of, the estatist society nurtured bottom-up support for extant professions and institutions.

This account has benefited from theories of drivers of institutional resilience and change in comparative historical analysis. The empirics animating the earlier research, however, are largely derived from far more stable political regime settings, even if undergoing profound restructuring.[143] My account provides an extension of these theories by bringing in the agency of wider society, its networks, resources, and legacies of public engagement, in shaping institutional resilience, which, in a causal loop, consolidates extant patterns of social status and stratification. This is not to say that the broader social agency of "the ordinary man" is absent in accounts derived from established Western democracies. Rather, by bringing a post-revolutionary context into theories of institutional durability and change, I underline a far greater urgency of society, and not just actors formally embedded in institutions undergoing reform, in shaping the extent to which adjustments are likely to occur. For the whole fabric of social relations is at stake and not just the existence of one cherished institution or the vested interests of one lobby group. The Stinchcombian long-horizon view,[144] sensitive as it is to social

---

[142] On the practical implications of recognition and misrecognition by the state or other powerful actors, see Ribot et al., "Introduction."
[143] See, for instance, Hacker et al., "Drift and Conversion"; and Thelen, *How Institutions Evolve*.
[144] Stinchcombe, *Constructing Social Theories*.

interest in institutional preservation, as well as insights from the sociology of time that are considerate of the multiple "non-synchronous,"[145] "conjunctural"[146] wavelengths – those of the political realm and of the social – enrich our analysis of institutional dynamics. The cradle-to-grave perspective on institutional reproduction takes heed of the concern for the future career of the adolescent as much as it considers his or her parents' informal admiration and esteem for the professional who teaches, medically treats, or enlightens their offspring and who embodies the old institutions' best. Again, extant tapestries of status and stratification, aided by old intra- and inter-institutional and social ties – those same relations that were meant to have been destroyed in the revolutionary inferno – emerge as potent and often highly successful agents of institutional conservation. In turn, in circular ways, institutional lethargy is as much a preserver of the bureaucratic shell as it is of the prior configurations of the wider society. Chapter 5 extends the analysis of these processes to education, another platform for the conservation of extant social networks and an institutional arena that socializes subsequent generations of Soviet citizens.

---

[145] Conrad, *What Is Global History?*, 141.   [146] Pierson, *Politics in Time*, 56.

5

Education, Socialization, and Social Structure

None of us inherited anything ... except for education.

Russian billionaire[1]

Our teachers were of old, pre-war vintage ... The school was cold. But the classes of Anna Yasnopolskaya, the best literature teacher in all Moscow, were warming to the mind and heart.

Svetlana Alliluyeva, Letters to a Friend[2]

I here extend the insights about the channels of professional continuity discerned in Chapter 4 to focus on institutions that socialized the next generation of Soviet citizens. In the following sections, I present Russia-wide data on resilience in education as related to the estates and follow data analysis with a qualitative mapping account of imperial schooling. Next, I borrow insights from comparative historical analysis into institutional path-dependencies to dissect how the eclectic tapestry of schools catering to Samara's educated society found its phoenix-like reincarnation in Soviet pedagogy even when punctuated with closures and reforms. An exercise in historical forensics concerning the Samara Jewish school allows me to dissect some of the ways in which lower-status pedagogic old-timers capitalized on their new status as *Soviet* school headmasters. Finally, like the patterns observed in Samara City, I dissect heterogeneity in demand for, and supply of, schooling within rural areas.

---

[1] Cited in Schimpfössl, *Rich Russians*, 30.
[2] Stalin's daughter. Alliluyeva, *Letters to a Friend*, 184. The original Russian reads: "Учителя были наши старые, довоенные." Alliluyeva, *Doch' Stalina*, 134. I use "pedigree," "old," or "heritage" with reference to individuals, and "vintage" to inanimate objects like buildings or artifacts.

STATISTICAL ANALYSIS

As the first step in unpacking the legacies of heterogenous demand for, and institutional appropriation in, education, I draw on earlier work with Alexander Libman and ascertain covariation between pre-revolutionary education, social structure, and Soviet and post-Soviet educational attainment in the provinces.[3] In the absence of district-level data on schools that could be aggregated to the regional level, we employ literacy as a proxy for educational development.[4] Figures 5.1–5.3 contain scatterplots of education indicators in 2010 (sourced from the Russian census) vis-à-vis literacy and the educated estates, respectively, in 1897; they illustrate that high literacy *rayony* (districts) and those with a comparatively high share of the educated estates continue to feature greater educational achievement as measured by university attainment per 1,000 people in 2010.

The correlation coefficient for the variable captured in Figure 5.1 is equal to 0.331 and is significant at any reasonable level, even with the inclusion of

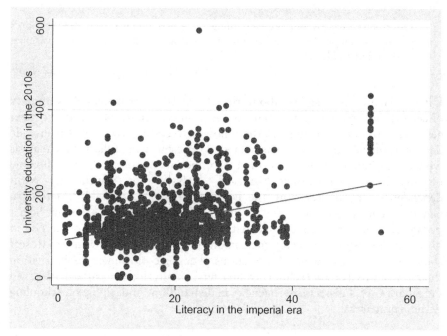

FIGURE 5.1 Imperial literacy (%) and university education (per 1,000 people), 2010

---

[3] This section is based on Lankina and Libman, "Two-Pronged Middle Class." Here and in Figures 5.2–5.3 analysis reproduced with permission of co-author.
[4] Literacy and schooling became virtually universal by the 1950s.

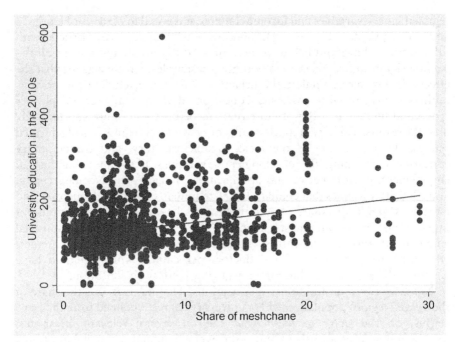

FIGURE 5.2 Share of *meshchane* in 1897 and university education (per 1,000 people), 2010

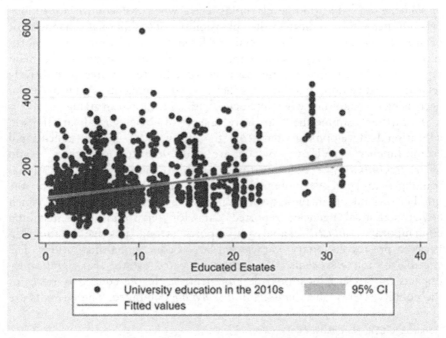

FIGURE 5.3 Share of educated estates in 1897 and university education (per 1,000 people), 2010

regional binary variables and income controls; it is equal to 0.287 for Figure 5.2 and to 0.323 for Figure 5.3). Splitting the sample into districts with urbanization above and below 50 percent – mostly urban and mostly rural – we find significant correlation in both the subsamples, which suggests that the effects do not merely reflect the urban/rural divide. Excluding the obvious outliers – *rayony* with university education of more than 400 people per 1,000 and literacy in 1897 of more than 40 percent – does not substantively alter the results. Table 5.1 reports results of *rayon*-level regressions of educated estates, the *meshchane* as the most sizeable category, and contemporary education controlling for developmental variables like imperial industrial employment, doctors per capita, urbanization, housing, and income; religion and ethnicity variables that could be linked to human capital; and longitude and latitude. Overall, the share of educated estates has a positive and significant impact on post-communist education levels. Imperial-era industrial employment appears not entirely significant, particularly when it interacts with urbanization, housing, and doctors per capita, which seem to have a statistically significant – but rather negligible – effect on education.

Next, we run four additional specifications. The first regresses the share of the *oblast* (region) population with a university degree, obtained from the 2010 census, on the share of *meshchane* and on several relevant covariates. The second adds as a further control the average annual regional educational spending in 2003–12. Table 5.2 demonstrates strong and significant relationship between *meshchane* and educational spending. The effect of *meshchane* on education levels holds even when we control for public expenditures; this indicates the plausibility of additional channels of persistence associated with social preferences. The third and fourth specifications report regression outputs with educated estates as the main regressor. Like *meshchane*, the variable of educated estates is positively related to education, with the coefficient maintaining its significance but decreasing in magnitude when interacted with educational spending.

To further examine the "hardware" aspect of Soviet spatial variations in educational development, data on the number of higher educational establishments or VUZy – which are equivalent to universities – and SSUZy/*tekhnikumy* – or educational establishments offering vocational training – in 1976 were obtained. We also include regional data on the number of students in these institutions in 1940, the earliest year in which Soviet statistical agencies reported data for territorial units matching contemporary *oblasti*.[5] Table 5.3 reports strong positive relationship between pre-revolutionary literacy and Soviet educational institutions. The variable of the *meshchane*, the largest educated estate, also significantly impacts on Soviet educational development, as do the educated estates of the nobility, clergy, merchants, and *meshchane* combined. These results are

---

[5] Source: RSFSR, *Narodnoye khozyaystvo*.

TABLE 5.1 Regressions, share of educated estates and contemporary education, as measured by share of population with university degree in 2010 (rayon-level), OLS

	(1)	(2)	(3)	(4)	(5)	(6)	(7)	(8)
Meshchane	3.063***	2.696***	2.329***	1.206***				
	(0.346)	(0.399)	(0.347)	(0.301)				
Educated estates					2.757***	2.544***	2.175***	1.167***
					(0.293)	(0.340)	(0.295)	(0.267)
Industrial employment (imperial era)		0.458***	-0.0380	0.0612		0.379**	-0.0967	0.0260
		(0.171)	(0.153)	(0.148)		(0.170)	(0.153)	(0.150)
Old Believers		-0.0471	-0.198	-0.0438		0.0282	-0.134	-0.00974
		(0.188)	(0.194)	(0.186)		(0.190)	(0.201)	(0.191)
Catholics		2.828	1.720	0.652		1.362	0.494	-0.0325
		(3.667)	(2.942)	(2.605)		(3.570)	(2.864)	(2.567)
Protestants		-0.810	-0.396	-0.125		-0.353	-0.0140	0.0937
		(1.213)	(0.975)	(0.883)		(1.174)	(0.942)	(0.869)
Jews		-1.792	-1.787	-1.910*		-2.056	-1.962	-2.042**
		(1.551)	(1.346)	(1.034)		(1.490)	(1.303)	(1.011)
Urbanization			0.786***	0.565***			0.781***	0.563***
			(0.386)	(0.351)			(0.384)	(0.351)
Housing				0.000***				0.000121***
				(0.000)				(2.76e-05)

(continued)

TABLE 5.1 (continued)

	(1)	(2)	(3)	(4)	(5)	(6)	(7)	(8)
Doctors per capita				0.012***				0.0118***
				(0.003)				(0.00293)
Latitude				-1.157				-1.128
				(0.979)				(0.965)
Longitude				-0.501				-0.440
				(0.502)				(0.500)
Constant	129.1***	108.1***	63.18***	218.4***	130.9***	114.3***	68.62***	210.6***
	(15.938)	(27.144)	(23.349)	(72.064)	(15.74)	(26.65)	(22.96)	(71.18)
R^2	0.47	0.47	0.63	0.74	0.477	0.479	0.630	0.743
N	1,630	1,629	1,629	1,458	1,630	1,629	1,629	1,458
Oblast fixed effects	Yes	Yes	Yes	Yes	Yes	Yes	Yes	Yes

Note. * $p<0.1$; ** $p<0.05$; *** $p<0.01$. Robust standard errors in parentheses. The sample size decreases with the inclusion of housing and doctors per capita due to missing values.
Source. Data based on Lankina and Libman, "Two-Pronged Middle Class." Here and in Tables 5.2–5.3, analysis reproduced and expanded with permission of coauthor.

TABLE 5.2 *Regressions, share of educated estates and post-communist education attainment, as measured by share of population with university degree in 2010 (oblast-level), OLS*

	(1)	(2)	(3)	(4)
Share of *meshchane*	0.315***	0.196*		
	(0.118)	(0.112)		
Share of educated estates			0.300***	0.208**
			(0.0936)	(0.0967)
Income per capita	0.000***	0.000***	0.000381***	0.000194***
	(0.000)	(0.000)	(0.000116)	(7.05e-05)
Resource extraction share	−0.125***	−0.093***	−0.110***	−0.0843***
	(0.034)	(0.028)	(0.0328)	(0.0272)
Share of ethnic Russians	−0.089***	−0.078***	−0.0894***	−0.0794***
	(0.021)	(0.024)	(0.0197)	(0.0218)
Urbanization	0.114**	0.095**	0.0969**	0.0842**
	(0.050)	(0.046)	(0.0416)	(0.0386)
Distance from Moscow	−0.079	0.107	−0.0658	0.109
	(0.178)	(0.157)	(0.177)	(0.160)
Average annual educational expenditures, 2003–12		0.114***		0.106***
		(0.021)		(0.0216)
Constant	14.901***	18.191***	15.74***	18.52***
	(2.810)	(2.771)	(2.455)	(2.502)
R^2	0.57	0.65	0.600	0.672
N	77	77	77	77

Note. * $p<0.1$; ** $p<0.05$; *** $p<0.01$. Robust standard errors in parentheses.
Source. Lankina and Libman, "Two-Pronged Middle Class."

strongly suggestive of developmental path-dependencies in that the Bolsheviks harnessed the extant educational infrastructure and human capital in the allocation of regional education resources.

PRE-REVOLUTIONARY INSTITUTIONAL AND SOCIAL MAP OF SCHOOLING

Literacy is but a crude proxy for the varied institutional architectures in education; and the estate as a generic category does not capture the complex ways in which the old social structure continued to find reflection in the Soviet school. A more systematic mapping exercise charting the contours of the supply

TABLE 5.3 *Effects of pre-communist literacy and social structure on communist-era development of educational facilities (oblast-level), OLS*

Dep. Var.	Number of universities and equivalent institutions (VUZ), 1976	Number of university (VUZ) students, 1940	Number of professional colleges (SSUZ), 1976	Number of SSUZ students, 1940
	Effect of pre-revolutionary literacy			
Literacy rate	0.610**	1.292**	0.887*	0.346**
	(0.301)	(0.584)	(0.493)	(0.134)
	Effect of pre-revolutionary social structure			
Share of meshchane	1.053*	2.117*	1.694*	0.597**
	(0.583)	(1.160)	(0.982)	(0.291)
Share of educated estates	0.980**	2.026**	1.457*	0.544**
	(0.468)	(0.927)	(0.759)	(0.219)
Observations	70	70	70	70

Note. The table summarizes the results of three sets of regressions, all controlling for a binary variable for ethnically defined regions and distance from Moscow. Effects of control variables suppressed. * $p<0.1$; ** $p<0.05$; *** $p<0.01$. Robust standard errors in parentheses. The difference in sample size compared to Table 5.2 is due to missing values in control variables. *Source.* Lankina and Libman, "Two-Pronged Middle Class."

side, the schooling infrastructure as it relates to social stratification before the Revolution, and the variations in the demand side of education is therefore warranted.

By the time the Bolsheviks took power, Samara boasted an impressive range of schools providing anything from elementary instruction, to classical gymnasium education, and training focused on specific vocational trades – state-run, private, and philanthropic. Schools for artisans, construction/engineering courses, and adult electrical engineering programs coexisted with painting, drawing, art, and music schools and evening hobby classes. The 1916 yearbook, under the rubric of institutions within the purview of the Ministry of Public Enlightenment, lists dozens of public and private schools, including a Teacher Training Institute; two gymnasia for boys; two *real'nyye uchilishcha* (secondary schools or colleges), one of them private; five gymnasia for girls; a city gymnasium; three higher primary *uchilishcha*; a two-class *zemstvo uchilishche* for girls; another one for boys; and a one-class mixed *uchilishche*. The city also administered eight parish schools for boys and eight for girls as well as forty-nine mixed parish schools. Seventeen "third-grade" private and preparatory schools – like the Jewish *uchilishche* or the Russian-Tatar *uchilishche*, or those affiliated with religious institutions like the Roman Catholic Church – which were attached to foster homes were also operative. The Imperial Ministry of Trade and Industry maintained authority over more specialized institutions, notably the Commercial *uchilishche* and the Trade School.

As elsewhere in the Russian Empire, being socially eclectic even among the most prestigious gymnasia and lyceums, the educational system mirrored social stratification – both when it came to the teaching cadre and the pupil body.[6] Gymnasia and increasingly commercial schools favored by merchants occupied the apex of educational prestige. The gymnasium, along with the practices, institutions, and teachers prepping students for entry, had been an urban phenomenon – and increasingly one characteristic of even the small town. Both penetration of the institution and aspiration remained low in the world of the Russian peasant. Bureaucratic regulation of quality went hand in hand with the growth of the private educational sector, which was detached from the state even if subjected to state regulation.[7] Competition among institutions and stringent quality controls incentivized high standards. They also stimulated a marketplace of training that catered to niche professional aspirations and to specific demographic, ethnic, and religious groups.

An organic and highly adaptive process of selectivity, exclusivity, and formal rules for inclusion and exclusion on ascriptive and other grounds coexisted with an expansion of access for the less privileged groups. The noble looked to limit the entry of the non-noble into prestigious institutions; and the state placed restrictions on the movement of Jews, who were shackled with onerous requirements to procure paperwork proving their right of residence beyond the Pale of Settlement when enrolling their son or daughter into a gymnasium. These were just some of the curbs, even if they were breached at the discretion of head teachers eager to accept pupils. Scions of the aristocracy and gentry were now entering in greater numbers institutions that secured a professional career of a specialized kind, just as the merchant, the *meshchanin*, and increasingly the peasant were elbowing their way into them as well. Given the crowded field, securing a place at each point of access warranted schooling in the home initially – the role of domestic tutor was a certified and regulated occupation[8] – to secure a place in the preparatory class or first grade of a gymnasium or *real'noye uchilishche*. This was followed by rigorous secondary school instruction not

---

[6] On social exclusivity in imperial schools, see Ruane, *Gender*, 12–15.

[7] Samara gymnasia were under the authority of the Kazan District Inspectorate of Education (KDIE). TsGASO, Khardina papers, f. 300, op. 1, ed. khr. 4, l.1.

[8] A. Khardina, founder of a women's gymnasium, held a certificate granted by KDIE, authorizing work as a home instructor (*domashnyaya nastavnitsa*) teaching French and history. The 1834 stipulation on home instructors mandated the certificate holder to acquire, at the end of each year, references from the beneficiaries of home instruction and the *uyezd* chairmen of nobles' assemblies (*predvoditely dvoryanstva*). TsGASO, f. 300, op. 3, ed. khr. 3. Khardina completed an eight-year gymnasium course and an additional "pedagogy class" in her gymnasium. Her permit was based on the 1870 MPE Edict (*polozheniye*) on women's gymnasia and pro-gymnasia. Certificate, March 6, 1890, Kazan. TsGASO, f. 300, op. 3, ed. khr. 3, l. 1.

just in the classics but also in modern languages and the hard sciences. The final or extra year in the gymnasium would often be dedicated to study for entry into university to pursue narrow specializations.

Samara illustrates educational patterns that were typical for midsize to large rapidly developing centers of industry and commerce. By the time of the Revolution, this and other towns within the *guberniya* possessed a developed system of education that prepared pupils for entry into the gymnasium, the university, and the professions. We also observe an intergenerational transmission of aspirations, if not inertia – a set of routinized and socially sanctioned expectations about a desirable, indeed what was a "must," trajectory of learning. This was, of course, a fluid process in a fast-changing society. We can distinguish between the social "core" that exhibited such expectations pretty much en masse and the "periphery" of new entrants, the sons and daughters of enterprising peasants and the rural intelligentsia. In the hierarchy of educational prestige, metropolitan boarding institutions were distinct from regional gymnasia and *real'nyye uchilishcha*. These were in turn greater in stature than a range of lesser provincial institutions. Olen'ka Konovalova, who came from the family of Samara's *meshchane* engaging in *rentier* and small business activities, attended the First Women's Gymnasium,[9] as did Riva Mikhaylovna Malinskaya, the granddaughter of a Jewish *cantonist* and daughter of a shoemaker.[10] The wealthy merchant Pyotr Aref'yev attended the same technical school as the noble Alyosha Tolstoy, in Samara, but sent his son Mitya to a gymnasium in St. Petersburg – something likely out of the reach of Samara's *meshchane* of modest means.[11] For pupils, gymnasium or commercial *uchilishche* instruction provided a ticket into university. Kostya Neklutin enrolled at the competitive St. Petersburg Polytechnic Institute;[12] Riva Malinskaya went on to study dentistry at the university in Kazan;[13] and Mitya Aref'yev pursued a degree in chemistry at one of the higher educational institutions in St. Petersburg.[14] This is not to say that only students whose parents could afford university fees studied in prestigious regional and metropolitan schools. Scholarships were available to study in Moscow, St. Petersburg, or Kiev.[15] Someone like Olen'ka could have, if she so wished, continued her instruction in St. Petersburg, like the wealthy merchant boy Mitya. Others had jobs during their time at university because their family could not afford the fees. Evening work and summer internships helped students save for tuition charges and maintenance at metropolitan centers of learning. This was the route taken by Mariya Ivanovna Volodkovich, a future

---

[9] Interview with Sergey Golubkov, October 25, 2018.   [10] Burlina, "Imya?" 124.

[11] Myakisheva, "Istoriya," 148–52.

[12] Neklutin, *Ot Samary do Siettla*; Neklutin, "My Mother," short version.

[13] Burlina, "Imya?" 124.

[14] Conjecture of a memoirist based on Mitya's interest in chemistry. All traces of him disappear after the Revolution. Myakisheva, "Istoriya," 152.

[15] The state encouraged lower-status students to apply. Frieden, *Russian Physicians*, 21–52.

FIGURE 5.4 Family portrait, boys wearing gymnasium uniforms
Antonina Pavlovna (née Novokreshchenova), widow of Matvey N. Neklutin,
Constantine's brother, with her children. NC, f. 207, 13.

relation of Olen'ka through her daughter's marriage.[16] Volodkovich, who hailed
from a Samara-based family of impoverished Polish nobles, attended Moscow's
Prince Golitsyn Higher Agronomy Courses, just as the Revolution broke out.[17]
Figures 5.4 and 5.5, respectively, show children (boys) wearing gymnasium
uniforms and pictures from a school album of a women's gymnasium.

So ingrained became the expectation of a profession or specialism requiring
a university degree that even the wealthiest merchants, otherwise engaged in
running private mills, bakeries, and shipping companies, were hedging their
bets on a professional career – in engineering, science, or medicine. The
Neklutin family papers and memoirs corroborate these patterns. By the late
nineteenth century, *everyone* in Samara among Neklutin's family and social
circle of friends, relatives, and acquaintances were reportedly expected to attend
the gymnasium and many went on to obtain university degrees. Writing about
the persistence of the nobles' unjustified prejudice against the merchant

[16] Great aunt of Sergey Golubkov. Golubkov, *Portfel'*, 40–44.
[17] Written responses to questionnaire. Sergey Golubkov, Samara, February 27, 2017; ibid.

FIGURE 5.5 Pictures from school album
Pupils in private gymnasium of Princess Khovanskaya with picture of Polia Egorova
(Neklutin's future wife) and other family photos. CN annotations. NC, f. 207, 13

"peasants of yesterday" – who were, by the end of the nineteenth century, increasingly influential in commerce, industry, and urban governance – Neklutin recalls:[18]

> It should be mentioned that most of the newcomers to the city quickly understood defects of their upbringing and tried to give their children the best obtainable education.
> The graduation from middle schools (high school in USA) was a "must" for the younger generation and many of them went to institutions for higher education.
> So there were youngsters of merchants and of their employees studying in many fields – law, economics, medicine, agriculture, engineering, forestry and so on.[19]

The young Kostya was sent to the Commercial *uchilishche* in Moscow, an establishment that merchant families patronized. There, aside from the classics and German, French, and English, he studied political economy, economic geography, technology of raw materials, commercial law, and

---

[18] Original English style and clarification of US school equivalent preserved.
[19] Neklutin, "Changes in Relation between Different Classes in Russia." NC, f. 234, 208–9.

accounting.[20] These subjects, the Neklutin elders believed, would be useful in running the family business. Although Constantine, like the other boys in the extended merchant clan, was being groomed to manage the family's business empire, his training was to leave the vistas open for prestigious professions:[21]

My parents wanted to give every member of the family the best available education; they selected a school in Moscow which had opened only ten years before. It was a private school supported by the Moscow Stock Exchange and accepted boys outside of Moscow ... Graduates could go to the Universities and Technical Institutes ...

When I was almost 17, two years before graduation from the School of Commerce, I asked my mother if I should quit and take over part of the business.

She rejected my suggestion and told me to select a University or some other school so I could get the best possible education.[22]

The educational and social profile of instructors contributed to the high academic standing and regard for prestigious secondary schools. University graduates often pursued a stint teaching in a private gymnasium only to then go on to complete an academic doctorate. The biographies of Samara University's professoriate illustrate these patterns. Yefim Ivanovich Tarasov, Professor of History and Philosophy, taught at a women's gymnasium in Penza before becoming a *privat-docent* at the University of St. Petersburg and then SU. Yevgeniy Antonovich Rykhlik, Professor of Slavic Studies, began his career teaching at a private gymnasium in Kiev.[23] Pyotr Petrovich Fridolin taught at the Imperial Russian Aleksandrovskiy *Litsey* (lycée), one of the preeminent schools for nobles, along with instructing at the Smolny Institute, before becoming a *docent* (associate professor) at the History Faculty and eventually

---

[20] "My Mother." Long version. NC, f. 232, 33.

[21] My findings contradict Ruane's argument that "Russian merchants were particularly bound by traditional attitudes toward their place in society and were not interested in becoming members of the new professions" and that "townspeople," because they "were occupied in trade and commerce," did not constitute a proper middle class and one of the sources for new professional groups in Russia. Ruane, *Gender*, 8. In the appendix tables that Ruane provides, *meshchane* prominently feature among teachers. Among male teachers in secondary schools in St. Petersburg in Moscow 12.2 and 4.9 percent were listed as "son of" *meshchane* and merchants, respectively; together, these groups approximate the share of sons of nobles, at 18.3 percent and are higher than for the clergy, at 15.9 percent (202, table 2). The figure for merchants is significantly higher than their overall empire-wide population share. These statistics support my thesis of the professionalization of the two urban estates. Likewise, the Neklutin archive challenges the argument of Armstrong, who writes, including concerning the Old Believer merchants, ostensibly attracted to bureaucratic positions in imitation of the nobility: "Ethnic Russian entrepreneurial families also tended to reject professionalism. Few considered it necessary for their sons to obtain higher engineering education." Armstrong, "Socializing for Modernization," 95.

[22] "My Mother." Short version, 21, 26.

[23] On Rykhlik, see Vlad Kaganov, "Kiev. Chastnaya Gimnaziya Ye. Se. Yevseyevoy," October 9, 2016, *proza.ru*. Available online at: proza.ru/2016/09/10/1573 (accessed April 29, 2020).

rector.[24] Specialized post-secondary school training had also been common among gymnasium instructors. In 1887, Nina (Antonina) Andreyevna Khardina (b. 1871) completed the Samara Women's Gymnasium with a "gold medal" (equivalent to a mark of distinction). There, she studied mathematics, geography, natural history, physics, French, embroidery, and pedagogy, among other subjects. Khardina took advantage of the possibility to take an extra year-long gymnasium course in pedagogy followed by studies at the Higher Women's Bestuzhev Courses in St. Petersburg, which were tailored to aspiring female teachers.[25] She then went on to establish a private gymnasium in Samara.[26]

Gymnasia paid well and often attracted career pedagogues from the upper levels of society. The First Women's Gymnasium, for instance, was representative of the niche position of the scholar of German origin as schoolmaster and teacher of specialized subjects. The school's headmistress was a Yekaterina Vasil'yevna Jungmeister. An Isidor Eduardovich Schiffler was chair of the teaching council (*pedagogicheskiy sovet*). A Wilhelm Nikolayevich Anderson taught physics. Several matrons were also of European ancestry. The gymnasium, like the lyceum in Bourdieu's France, thus featured teachers of high social status and academic caliber, along with a pupil body likewise heavily drawn from the well-off strata. Daughters of aristocrats – women constituted an increasingly high share of gymnasium instructors – were just as likely to teach in a gymnasium as the educated "mixed title" men and women coming from educated urban backgrounds.[27]

The *real'nyye* and commercial *uchilishcha* were secondary schools historically less gilded than gymnasia in terms of their makeup. They were, however, increasingly attracting both nobles and aspirational members of the urban estates as privileged society embraced the modern professions and the arts as a career. The Samara Museum associate Vasiliy Vasil'yevich Gundobin,

---

[24] On Fridolin, see *Biografika* at: bioslovhist.spbu.ru/person/1682-fridolin-petr-petrovich.html (accessed April 29, 2020).

[25] "Certificate," TsGASO, f. 300, op. 3, ed. khr. 3, l. 1. On the specialized pedagogic training for female gymnasium teachers, introduced in 1859, which included a focus on the "science of pedagogy" and the encouragement of child curiosity and moral development, see Ruane, *Gender*, 31. The Bestuzhev courses, opened in 1878, provided "young women with a university-type degree without allowing them into the already-established universities, then exclusively for men." Ibid., 32. They were more prestigious than teachers' institutes, which attracted lower-class students and peasants, many of whose trainees taught in rural schools. Ibid., 36.

[26] During the Soviet period, Khardina de-emphasized this record, highlighting instead experience of teaching Russian language and literature in Sunday schools. Khardina papers, "Working record." TsGASO, f. 300, op. 3, ed. khr. 4.

[27] On the feminization of teaching, see Ewing, *Teachers of Stalinism*, 126–27. In Samara's women's gymnasia, women predominated as instructors, and men in male gymnasia. SGSC, *Pamyatnaya knizhka*. The tradition that began in the late eighteenth century of staffing elite Russian schools by predominantly German and "occasionally English" teachers who were "protestant and bourgeois" instilled in pupils – including among the nobility – "a self-image and social ethic much more like those of the Western bourgeoisie than of the feudal aristocracy," paving the way for a "socially conscious, progressive intelligentsia in the modern sense." Raeff, *Origins*, 140.

whom we encountered in Chapter 4, aside from his position at the City Gymnasium, was also employed as a part-time teacher with the Samara Commercial *Uchilishche*; both he and his mother, an Englishwoman, also taught at Samara's private art school. The *uchilishche*'s board of directors featured recognizable names from Samara's merchant society and included honored citizens. Similarly, Samara's *real'noye uchilishche* educated pupils like the future writer Aleksey Tolstoy, of gentry pedigree. In the 1916 yearbook, the *uchilishche*'s headmaster features with the title of *statskiy sovetnik* – one of the top and best paid ranks in the Petrine system of state service positions.[28]

Then there were parish and artisan schools, which often, though not exclusively, catered to the least privileged urban dwellers. These lower-grade institutions were the limit of formal schooling that many children received in their lifetime. Few of their headmasters and teaching staff, heavily drawn from the clergy and *meshchane* estates, boasted the formal status ranks characteristic of gymnasium and *real'noye uchilishche* instructors. Finally, religious schools occupied a middle position between the more prestigious institutions and the parish school. They supplied instruction that was alternative, or supplementary, to mainstream private and state schooling. The descriptive statistics presented in Chapter 2 (Table 2.2) speak to the estate character of prestigious educational institutions.

The Khardina Gymnasium corroborates the general imperial statistics on the social makeup of schools, although, known for its "progressive" bent, it featured a comparatively high share of pupils of peasant origins. Among the nineteen grade-7 candidates that sat their exam in 1914, seven (37 percent) were of merchant or *meshchane* paternal origin. An equal number, seven, listed their paternal origin as "peasant." Four pupils (21 percent), precisely mirroring the empire-wide statistics for female gymnasia, were in the category of noble or hereditary noble or listed a paternal title indicative of nobility. One appears with the paternal origin of "doctor."[29] However public-spirited in intent, this was not an inexpensive school. In 1915, KWG charged 80 rubles per year to be paid in two installments, which included the right to study two foreign languages, and 60 rubles for the preparatory classes also accessible to boys. Pupils were liable to expulsion if fees were not paid, and those who withdrew from the school before the end of term were not refunded their term payments.[30] The gymnasium nevertheless provided support to girls from poor

[28] SGSC, *Pamyatnaya knizhka*. We know of Alyosha's time at the *uchilishche* from fellow pupil Yevgeniy Gan, future *docent* at Samara Polytechnic. Valeriy Yerofeyev, "Tolstoy Aleksey Nikolayevich," *Istoricheskaya Samara*. Available online at: историческая-Самара.рф//каталог/самарская-персоналия/т/толстой-алексей-николаевич.html (accessed December 18, 2019).

[29] Information on seventh-grade examinations. Khardina papers, TsGASO, f. 300, op. 1, ed. khr. 66 (multiple *listy*).

[30] Terms listed on standard application form in 1915. Khardina papers, TsGASO, f. 300, op. 1, d. 6 (multiple *listy*).

families, with funding from charitable literary events and concerts. This had been widely practiced and was indeed fashionable at the time.[31]

Autonomy in Gymnasia

Let us now ascertain pedagogic autonomy within the architecture of imperial schooling. We know that the Bolsheviks were determined not only to obliterate the estatist society of the past but also to deploy pedagogues and schools as pivotal enablers in the coercive toolkit of societal transformation. To what extent did schools as institutions and pedagogues as professionals enjoy autonomy in matters of educational processes, ethos, and values? Further, how can we begin to analyze the ways in which these elements of institutional agency helped institutional-social reproduction via the channel of the _Soviet_ school? I contend that the social embeddedness of the institutional architecture of schools and the elements of institutional autonomy vis-à-vis the state are intrinsic to understanding social reproduction under a very different political order.

Although subjected to state regulation, I regard imperial Russia's gymnasia as representing arenas of public action outside of state sanction.[32] Scores of gymnasium teachers, like other members of the intelligentsia, harbored left-wing or otherwise progressive liberal sympathies during the twilight of the Romanov Empire.[33] Archival documents from KWG illustrate some of the

---

[31] There is a reference to "charitable drama performances to support pupils at the gymnasium" requiring KDIE approval. Khardina papers, November 9, 1913, TsGASO, f. 300, op. 2, ed. khr. 5, l. 1. The list of "banned plays" included one called "The Power of the Flesh." Ibid., l. 3. The poet Fyodor Sologub recalls one event that Khardina organized as a member of the Society of Public Universities: "The lecture was in Pushkin house. The prices were double [sic], from 10 kopeks to 2 rubles. The hall was packed. Even on the stage there were no less than one hundred of sitting and standing people. The public was very varied. The lecture was difficult for many, but the applause was enthusiastic; at the end I read poems." Letter from Fyodor Sologub to Anastasia Chebotarevskaya, February 8, 1914. Available online at: fsologub.ru/doc/letter1/letter1_187.html (accessed April 27, 2020).

[32] A study of educated and relatively privileged women – overwhelmingly of noble origin but also with a mix of clergy, merchant, and _meshchane_ (referred to as petty bourgeoisie, see 159, unnumbered table) backgrounds – indicates that late nineteenth-century educational institutions – "products of feminist victories – provided meetingplaces [sic] and stimulus for thought." They gave support to independent women and a platform for social influence. Engel, _Mothers and Daughters_, 115. On informal associational life within educational institutions and formal professional organizations and unions and their networks, see also Ruane, _Gender_. "In a country where political parties were illegal, professional organizations and meetings became substitutes for them." Ibid., 91. Because informal associational and civic life among elite teachers was not always regarded as "political" many pedagogues were able to organize, meet, and debate social and political issues of the day. Ibid., 90.

[33] Thus, Pavel Preobrazhenskiy who taught at KWG, was a _kadety_ member. Memoirs of Shchukina Avgusta Ignat'yevna, _née_ Pyrovich. Khardina papers, 15 September 1967–, TsGASO, f. 300, op. 1, ed. khr. 142, ll. 1–3. A Khardina relation also reminisced: "The family was highly cultured;

ways in which school headmistresses and pedagogues defied state authority; subverted state sanction to propagate elements essential to imperial conceptions of nationhood; and resorted to day-to-day practices of mutual aid and support among pupils and teachers engaged in tacit and often symbolically poignant "acts of resistance."[34] In annotations to the gymnasium papers submitted to TsGASO in the 1960s, Khardina's permissive attitude to subversive literature accessible to schoolgirls is presented as evidence of the gymnasium as a *rassadnik* (propagator) of "free thought and revolutionary sentiments among the youth in Samara"; and, more implausibly, that it "was possibly even opened with those aims in mind."[35] Memoirs of individual pupils written during the Soviet period, even when likely dosed with ideologically appropriate interpretations, indeed convey Khardina's permissive sentiment toward leftist and even revolutionary sympathies among pupils. One memoirist wrote:

Many pupils came from the village, hailed from "burnt by destiny" backgrounds, had been expelled from other educational institutions as politically suspect ... One pupil, Anastasiya (Nastya) Vasil'yevna Soboleva ... had been expelled from Stavropol' gymnasium. Had links with the revolutionaries in Samara, specifically with a worker from a furniture factory. [She] had been arrested in 1908 or 1909. Had been incarcerated in the Samara *guberniya* jail for two weeks. I came to visit her with a friend, spoke to Nastya through the bars in the window, and Nastya from the window sang revolutionary songs.

Khardina knew about this. She did not talk about this to other pupils. After release from jail, Nastya continued to study in the gymnasium.[36]

narodniki, Marxists (depending on who would be exiled to Samara at the time), left *kadety* in 1905, pedagogues in the later years in the evenings would debate in the welcoming dining room of the Khardiny, over a glass of strong tea with homemade jam. Not many families in Samara enjoyed such respect." Memoirs of Borisyuk. Khardina papers, TsGASO, f. 300, op. 2, ed. khr. 10, l. 10. In one letter, Lenin urges officials to look into the matter of Preobrazhenskiy's arrest: "Please ... inform me whether it would be possible to release Preobrazhenskiy." Preobrazhenskiy was released. Telegram by V. I. Lenin to Chairman of Samara Extraordinary Commission (CheKa), November 25, 2018. Suris, *V. I. Lenin i VeCheKa*, 133.

[34] Scott, *Weapons*.
[35] Note written by local history scholar (*krayeved*) Strukov, September 15, 1967. Khardina papers. TsGASO, f. 300, op. 1, ed. khr. 142, l. 7. A note on Khardina's biography also mentions that V. I. Lenin in 1892–93 worked as an aide to her father in the Samara district attorney's office. Khardina papers, TsGASO, f. 300, op. 2, ed. khr. 10, l. 2. Secondary school teachers were reportedly less politically radical than primary school teachers whose sympathies and often origins lay with the less privileged working groups and peasants. Social divisions between the secondary and primary school teachers plagued a unified teacher movement whether in matters of professional-associational aims or political demands on the state. During the 1905 revolutionary period, many primary school teachers sympathized with the radical Social Revolutionary Party. Ruane, *Gender*, 128–63. "For city teachers, class and hierarchy remained important distinctions in attempts to reform Russia. Unlike the radicals, they did not advocate sweeping away all vestiges of status and privilege, but were interested instead in redefining the criteria necessary to achieve them." Ibid., 145.
[36] Khardina papers, September 15, 1967 (emphasis added). Memoirs of Shchukina. TsGASO, f. 300, op. 1, ed. khr. 142, l. 2.

Another aspect of Khardina's pre-revolutionary biography eagerly conveyed in notes annotating the KWG archive is her anti-clerical sentiment. One former student wrote:

Teaching and upbringing in the gymnasium were by no means in a disciplinary [*verno-poddannom*], but in a liberal fashion. In the gymnasium, in violation of the order of the time, the hymn "God save the king" was never sung. The religious law teacher, the priest I. I. Andreyev ... coming to the lesson, would be blabbing about anything with the pupils. During lessons pupils did embroidery, crafts, etc., would sit on desks with feet on chairs. The *Batyushka* [father priest] as a matter of fact taught nothing. *Khardina knew about this, but did not take any measures, evidently considering* zakon bozhiy [*divine laws] to be a redundant subject, imposed upon the school by the laws at the time.* During preparations for graduation examinations, in the presence of representatives of the Kazan educational district, the *Batyushka* would distribute tickets with questions, on which the beginnings of answers would be also written, that is, what is called "*shpar-galki*" [cheat-sheets]. Other subjects were, however, taught in an exemplary way.[37]

Expeditious from the point of view of Khardina's future role as a Soviet pedagogue, the anti-clerical, politically, and legally subversive practices could be alternatively regarded as enactments of the quasi-public sphere in a monarchist, "absolutist," state. Hiring a pliant, complacent, and evidently complicit *Batyushka* speaks to the headmistress's subtle ideological subversions, much like the pupil's feet on the chair symbolize political agency in the classroom. The teacher's "permissive" and "liberal" persona and the school's flouting of the tsarist regime's doctrinaire prescriptions provide a space that invites interrogation of political authority, whatever Khardina's ideological proclivities might have been. Moreover, "exemplary" practices in the instruction of literature, history, or art may well refer to critique, scrutiny, and the development of an interrogating and searching mind.[38]

Another source of agency and autonomy were the tightknit networks of school pedagogues and affiliates who also maintained ties to Samara's leading enlightenment and professional arenas. Khardina's niece thus reminisces about the network, alluding also to the professional trajectories of teachers after the Revolution:

Among the pedagogues, the closest to Khardina was the Preobrazhenskiye family ... The mother is a very old woman, the widow of a priest. The eldest children, now completely

---

[37] Ibid., l. 1 (emphasis added). Further, there were no uniforms – "an infringement on the personality [of the pupil]." Marks and exams were limited to a bare minimum "to the extent it was possible to wriggle the way between ministry circulars." Ibid., l. 14.

[38] I agree with Ruane's perception of teachers' resentment of state interference. In contrast to revolutionary idealists working to overthrow the system, teachers and the professions generally "undermined the autocratic system in less dramatic ways by offering another vision of a new Russia and the relationship between state and society." Ruane, *Gender*, 43. "[T]he government," writes Ruane, "expected teachers to instill the traditional values of loyalty and service to the tsar in their pupils. Instead, teachers had been trained to encourage individualism and autonomy through the use of newer teaching methodologies." Ibid., 44.

white, are always very courteous with her, referring to her using "thou." Eldest daughter, Mariya Aleksandrovna, similarly white like her mother, is a pedagogue. The middle one – doctor. The youngest one – beginning pedagogue, teaches at the Khardina gymnasium. The head of the family – the oldest son Pavel Aleksandrovich. Completed a seminary and spiritual academy (?) [original punctuation]. Taught at seminaries (evidently, he had to work to repay his stipend), then he moved to a general education school. He is one of the main pillars of the gymnasium, a member of the *tovarishchestvo* [cooperative board] overseeing the school, friend and counsellor to Nina Andreyevna . . . after the Revolution he became professor at Samara Agricultural Institute.

Middle son, Aleksandr Aleksandrovich, with immobile legs due to tuberculosis . . . despite his illness he too works, does something for the [school?] magazine. Youngest brother, Ivan Aleksandrovich, junior teacher, also in the Khardina gymnasium. Later he became geologist, Doctor of Sciences, member of the USSR Academy of Sciences.

Now they would say – in the gymnasium semeystvennost' [familism] flourished. And that is good, I would say. Could, for instance, the junior teacher Sofya Aleksandrovna shirk her work, knowing that the gymnasium is a blood child of her respected and beloved elder brother. Several people sharing the same spirit and vision very well unite a collective.[39]

To summarize, the imperial school, however socially eclectic, reflected the gradations of estatist society, one where the most privileged estates were marked with social and familial expectations of a certain trajectory of learning and professional careers. The elite gymnasium and technical schools at the apex of educational prestige not only were imbricated within autonomous sites and networks of imperial enlightenment milieus but represented long-established familial, kin, and friendship structures of trust and reciprocity. Gymnasia became meeting sites for political debate outside of school hours; and the school matron took chances to shelter her students, relying on discretion and silences that could only be safe in the context of embeddedness within a network of the like-minded, the trusted, and the tested. The gymnasium represented an engine for the conservation of the microcosm of an educated society of pedagogues, professoriate, and enlighteners. It also provided a forum for transmitting a particular ethos to the pupil, even if at odds with the ideology, policy, and sanction of the state, which retained formal authority over the establishment. As I shall discuss, the pedagogic network, while nested within a core educational institution, would also weather phases of punctuated vulnerability, when old schools became subject to the capricious policy vagaries of a new regime. In fact, it may even have eased elements of reconstitution of the original establishment – along with the erstwhile trappings of social distinction. I now turn to discussing these transformations under the new order.

---

[39] Memoirs of Borisyuk, ll. 12–13 (emphasis added).

SCHOOLS UNDER THE BOLSHEVIK REGIME

To explore institutional reproduction, mutation, and change, as embedded in the social structure, during the pivotal years of the gelling of Bolshevik policy in education, I deploy insights from comparative sociology; these add conceptual weight to the narrative histories of post-revolutionary transformation and continuity in schools. Kathleen Thelen highlights how critical juncture moments, rather than leading to the dismantlement of old institutions and their replacement with new ones, result in a "recalibrated" or "functionally reconverted," "in part or in whole," set of institutional configurations.[40] I here follow other scholars in referring to institutions broadly as a set of durable arrangements structuring practices or policy. This lens is distinct from their narrower conception as particular organizations or sites. Institutions so defined pertaining to education would be imperial-era architectures of learning with socially pronounced channels of educational progression and university access, embodied notably in the gymnasium as distinct from vocational or quasi-vocational channels of training. To understand the processes of "recalibration" of the institution so defined, I dissect organizational, policy, and personnel battles within sites of education. I am also looking for evidence of a willingness of actors vested with an incentive for institutional survival to pursue change and reform at the margins, whether in hiring or shifts in the curriculum, without shattering the historically entrenched patterns in education. Finally, unlike other scholars who have exclusively focused on high-level policy debates in education, I am also sensitive to the *social inputs* into institutional resilience during pivotal moments of would-be "revolutionary" change. These inputs allow the institution to cushion the blows of radical attempts at remolding. Put simply, the hero in my analysis is the ordinary teacher, the parent, the pupil, and not the revolutionary cadre conceiving policy in the Kremlin.

In emphasizing societal inputs, I am alert to divergences between the long-maturing educational goalposts of families that have a multigenerational span and radical and quick policy change. How would parents react when such change befalls them and their children? What is the role of social groups in institutional reproduction? These processes of pedagogic-social-institutional continuity and adaptation could again be fruitfully dissected with reference to the concepts of "drift" and "conversion," which I introduced in Chapter 4. "Drift is a strategy of holding firm while the world changes," while "conversion ... [is] actively altering what institutions do. If the possibility of drift arises when contexts change, opportunities for conversion typically arise when the players change – when political actors inherit institutions not of their own making and inconsistent with their ends."[41] The "holding firm" strategy of drift does not necessarily conflict with conversionary dynamics, since the latter

---

[40] Thelen, *How Institutions Evolve*, 34.   [41] Hacker et al., "Drift and Conversion," 195.

becomes instrumental in the propagation of the former. This counterintuitive pattern becomes evident if we consider the coexistence of a parallel set of actors: (1) political commissars who replaced and purged the old political overlords and who pressed for large-scale institutional reform; (2) the army of well-organized, well-networked "street-level" pedagogues *who remain in place* and who resist policies encroaching on their authority;[42] and (3) something relevant particularly with regard to the tactics of these street-level public sector professionals, the "society" that established teachers routinely encounter, interact with, and are enmeshed in, over the course of their work.[43] Society is here understood as a stratified public with distinct and heterogenous educational preferences formed over a long stretch of time. These would not immediately shift as social groups woke up to the sudden onset of a revolutionary new dawn. Rostislav (Rostya) Kavetskiy, the son of the medical notable Yevgeniy Kavetskiy, was one such pupil caught up in the tsunami of events just as he was completing an elite Samara boys' gymnasium. Yevgeniy, a sympathizer of the *kadety* (Constitutional Democrats) party, decided to take the family temporarily to Siberia after the Bolsheviks took power in Samara. His wife confided in a letter to her relations that Rostya

---

[42] Official reports for 1926–27 noted pedagogues' "corporate" and "narrow-bureaucratic" tendencies; low party membership and "low communist influence on pedagogues by communist organizations working in schools and party organizations"; and a tendency to "attribute all inadequacies to the pupil," making statements like "the pupils are poorly prepared, they are not well brought up, and even 'they are defective, what can I do with them'" (l. 7). Report on the higher (secondary) schools of the City of Samara, SOGASPI, f. 1, op. 1, d. 2764, ll. 6–12. There were also conflicts between "old" and "young" pedagogues, with old pedagogues appearing "inaccessible due to their substantial experience and dignity" (l. 7). Officials alluded to patronizing attitudes whereby new pedagogues lacked the confidence to impress their opinions on the old (l. 7). Draft resolution on the state of pedagogic collectives in secondary schools in the City of Samara, papers for 1928–. SOGASPI, f. 1, op. 1, d. 2764, ll. 3–5; and Report, ll. 6–12. Many pedagogues reportedly did not possess a "Marxist worldview" and were incapable of developing one among pupils. Report, ll. 11–12. As to the social composition of grades 5–7 and 8–9 in Samara City schools, 46.9 and 59.9 percent, respectively, were children of *sluzhashchiye*. The figures for the share of children of workers were 21.7 and 15.1 percent; for peasants, 5.2 and 6 percent; and for artisans and *kustari* (small producers), 9.1 and 7 percent, respectively. Report, ll. 7–8.

[43] Lipsky famously captured the predicament of street-level bureaucracy: "The decisions of street-level bureaucrats, the routines they establish, and the devices they invent to cope with uncertainties and work pressures, effectively *become* the public policies they carry out" (emphasis in original). Lipsky, *Street-Level Bureaucracy*, xii. I additionally emphasize the enmeshing of street-level functionaries with society – an angle different from Lipsky's where the distinction between officials and welfare recipients – "clients" – is more clear-cut. Ibid., 117–25, 59–70. Nevertheless, the insights apply to Russia where discretion and "subtle determinations of who is teachable" would result in a spiral of socially consequential "self-fulfilling prophecies." Ibid., 13, 9. "To designate or treat someone as a welfare recipient, a juvenile delinquent, or a high achiever," writes Lipsky, "affects the relationships of others to that person and . . . the person's self-evaluation." Ibid., 9. Such classificatory practices were intrinsic to the Soviet class project with not dissimilar consequences.

"dedicated every spare minute to sit and drill, all that he is meant to learn in grade 8 . . . the fragile, gentle child, forever shivering, in his thin gymnasium coat [shinel'ka] in the Siberian freezing temperatures, would sit all free evenings, next to the kerosene lamp, immersed in his textbooks." In spring, he passed his gymnasium exams, gaining his entry ticket to university.[44]

Institutional Adaptation: Heterogeneity in Schools and Fees

Our analysis of institutional adaptation begins with canvasing the congruence between state intention – a possible state-centered functional take on education – and outcomes on the ground, in Samara. A good place to start is with Bolshevik policy and practice concerning paid-for instruction. For what kind of a *social* revolutionary whose *raison d'être* is radical egalitarian transformation would condone, retain, or tolerate private schooling – in any society, then as now, the embodiment of social privilege, exclusion, and inequity? The intention to root out this pernicious tsarist relic emerges in the deluge of bureaucratic correspondence between the Kremlin and street-level commissars. Despite these pressures, we observe strong evidence of institutional drift in paid-for education, ultimately accepted in the Soviet school and remaining in place until the 1950s.[45] Directive after directive urgently called for rooting out the practice of charging school fees and private schooling. Although the documents cover the period coinciding with the NEP when private initiative was briefly allowed and blossomed, education was not an area where privatization would be condoned at the level of policy. Regional party documents sought to combat "rumors that are being circulated that in some *uyezdy* of our *guberniya* supposedly there is permission to maintain private schools."[46] Another party report on the state of primary and secondary education in Samara noted the "out-of-control" nature of solicitations for funding (*samo-oblozheniye*).[47] While "categorically" denying that such schools with "paid-for instruction" enjoy official sanction and protesting that they would be beyond the pale "whatever pretext, whatever flag they [school workers] may use to justify their existence," party ideologues noted that the sole motive for such practices are the "limits of state funding." Apparently imposing sanctions on quasi-private or private schools to root them out of existence with one hand, the directive simultaneously created loopholes in the form of an acknowledgment of charges (*oblozheniye*), which,

---

[44] Kavetskaya-Mazepa, *O moyom ottse*, 17.

[45] Private schools returned with a vengeance in post-Soviet Russia. By 1992, 306 "gymnasiums," 198 "lycées," and 85 private schools were opened. There were 69,700 general schools. Matthews, "Elitism," 325. On Soviet elite and specialized schools for "gifted children" and periodic attempts to dismantle or reform them, see Shlapentokh, *Soviet Intellectuals*, 24–26.

[46] Circular "Concerning the private school." Papers for 1922. TsGASO, f. 81, op. 1, ed. khr. 533, l. 52.

[47] Guberniya DPE report for January to March 1922. TsGASO, f. 81, op. 1, ed. khr. 533, l. 93.

nevertheless, "need not be turned into mandatory payments for the right to education."[48] In contemporary public administration speak, the central state liberally showered on schools and local authorities "unfunded mandates." The pedagogic institutions discreetly fudged these, unsupported as they were with national moneys.[49]

Survival in an environment of rampant school closures presupposes the existence of a social clientele with an unyielding demand for private education. With the destruction of the wealth of the industrialist, the merchant magnate, and the gentry squire, we would expect the shattering of the material foundations on which the stratification system in learning rested. Furthermore, the emigration that is often invoked to justify the "great leveler" paradigm and that certainly touched the lives of our protagonist Kostya Neklutin, to give one example, decimated a significant chunk of the social base that underpinned such demand for high-status education. Archival evidence does not corroborate the potential leveling out of social heterogeneity in the demand for schooling, however. The Bolshevik authorities reported that, five years after the Revolution, acute shortages of personnel and funding forced school closures and mergers. Attendance dropped to 70 percent of the pupil body, largely due to "poor food and lack of shoes among school-children."[50] Simultaneously, the catalogue of inherited educational institutions that the Bolsheviks copiously assembled recorded the tapestry of old schools and the profusion of new ones catering not only to elementary school pupils but also to cultural sensibilities going beyond rudimentary instruction. In 1922, the city's musical school (*tekhnikum*), for instance, featured 200 pupils and 25 instructors, continued to charge fees, and remained entirely self-funded. Meanwhile, the art school (*tekhnikum*), though struggling, featured 100 pupils and 16 instructors.[51] These institutions continued to be patronized by the upper layers of estatist society, featuring continuity at the level of pedagogic networks. The artist Gundobin, also an affiliate of the Samara Museum, continued to teach in one such art school in the 1920s, for instance, as did his English mother. An official *guberniya* directive alluded to these patterns:

You [*uyezd* authorities] need not be confused by the reference [in a central circular] to the introduction of paid instruction in art and music schools: the least number of students

---

[48] Circular "Concerning the private school," l. 52.

[49] This would be a classic example of perceived illegitimacy, unreasonableness, overload, and lack of funding or incentive in meeting the policy demands of higher-level organizational authorities. Lipsky, *Street-Level Bureaucracy*, 16–25.

[50] DPE report, l. 93.

[51] Appendix, Gubprofobr (1921–22). TsGASO, f. 81, op. 1, ed. khr. 419, part 1, l. 30 ob. For aristocratic families, a background in the arts facilitated Soviet professional careers. Golitsyn's brother Vladimir, a well-known Soviet artist, attended a private art school. Golitsyn, *Zapiski*, 262.

come from the ranks of the proletariat in such schools and we are not only freeing those students from the need to pay for education, but will be also offering [financial] aid.[52]

Such practices were obfuscated and explained away on the grounds that "private initiative could only generate an insignificant number of establishments that would cater to only a small group of the wealthiest layers of the population," while "our task is to establish foundations for targeting the proletarian strata."[53] As late as 1928, however, one report recorded the existence of "a variety of private schools, which have been opened without the knowledge of Uono [state education body]."[54]

The Pedagogic Marketplace

If post-revolutionary Samara continued to feature heterogeneity in patterns of institutional resilience and demand for private schools, do we observe continuities in the personnel of the various institutions that had under the old regime exhibited a pronounced estatist profile? In the section "Pre-revolutionary Institutional and Social Map of Schooling," I discerned traces of something akin to a pedagogic marketplace in imperial Russia's pedagogy. A high social status not only aided in the acquisition of a teaching post in a prestigious gymnasium but allowed one to set up, run, or otherwise patronize such an institution. Not only were elite pedagogues well networked – they often taught at several prestigious schools, intermarried, and had extended family members in institutions of a similar caliber – but they were imbricated within core sites of imperial enlightenment society, if not within those in the metropolitan capitals where they pursued university degrees. Furthermore, they would have taught boys from gentry, noble, merchant, and high-status professional families – boys like Aleksey (Alyosha) Tolstoy, Mitya Aref'yev, and the brothers Kavetskiy. These pupils were, of course, part of an expanding social mix. The scions of rural entrepreneurs and well-off agriculturalists were also making a steady transition into urban life in Samara. At the other end of the spectrum of pedagogic prestige were teachers in parish schools, who were not so nested, in multiple and complex ways, within the elite and newly rich segments of Samara society.

For a number or reasons, we would expect the Revolution to have destroyed pedagogic hierarchies rooted in imperial institutions of learning. The museum society, for instance, as we have seen, included pedagogues from elite schools like Gundobin who were spied on and otherwise harassed as the Bolsheviks

---

[52] Circular "Concerning the private school," l. 52 ob.   [53] Ibid., l. 52.

[54] Protocol of the Congress of Instructors of Samara *uyezd*, January 4, 1923. TsGASO, f. 2364, op. 1, d. 77, l .9. Professional characteristics of staff indicate prior careers as *zemstvo* workers or instructors. One report for 1927–28 noted that 53 percent of secondary school teachers in Samara City began careers before the Revolution and an unspecified share of teachers received training in that period. SOGASPI, f. 1, op. 1, d. 2764, l. 7.

unleashed witch hunts against the bourgeoisie. By contrast, we would expect low-status pedagogues to fare best in the quasi-marketplace of the Soviet pedagogic profession. Their credentials unblemished, many a low-status *meshchanin*, for instance, could invoke "peasant" ancestry even if such ideologically palatable pedigree would have taken us one or two generations back. Both the functionalist explanations accentuating the *intentions* of policy makers as opposed to social lethargy and those that fall back on the tropes of emigration, social dislocation, and material ruin, however, fall apart if we consider the de facto realities of something akin to a new marketplace in the nascent Soviet pedagogic profession.[55] The Samara records corroborate teacher agency in navigating recruitment in schools. Whether employed in the same school or transitioning into a new one, teachers trained under the old regime were the most sought-after professionals. The rapidly expanding public education sector would not in a fleeting time span compensate for the sound secondary- and often university-level instruction that teachers would have received in the imperial academy. The authorities made desperate attempts to retain educators in state schools who were prepared to work on reduced salaries and with significantly higher teaching loads. One report in 1923 noted that, in Samara, teacher unemployment had been virtually nonexistent considering the high demand for such a cadre.[56] Calls to raise teacher salaries were made, "or else we run the risk of having no workers at all, since they can all simply run away (*razbezhatsya*), a tendency already in evidence now."[57]

Institutional Forensics: The Samara Jewish School

Beyond conveying the agony of the regime's impotence that speaks to us from official reports, documentary evidence of the kind that we possess for the late imperial period illuminating the subtleties of intra- and extra-institutional network ties, pedagogic autonomy, and ethos, is highly fragmentary. Khardina's gymnasium, which supplies detailed information for the imperial period, mutated into the Vocational School for Railway Studies No. 1 in 1919, only to be resurrected in 1930 as the elite and desirable Gymnasium No. 15.[58]

---

[55] On demand for teachers, see Ewing, *Teachers of Stalinism*, 132–49.
[56] Report, Guberniya DPE, September 1, 1923. SOGASPI, f. 1, op. 1, d. 1116, l. 75.
[57] Protocol of the Congress of Instructors. TsGASO, f. 2364, op. 1, d. 77, l. 9 ob.
[58] Prince Sergey Golitsyn provides insights into the pedagogic and social aspects of elite gymnasia through the 1920s. Sergey sat tough competitive exams to get into the former women's Alfyorov gymnasium in Moscow, though the family name also helped. Golitsyn, *Zapiski*, 239. This was an elite gymnasium were daughters of the singer Fyodor Shalyapin studied, as did the poet Marina Tsvetaeva. Ibid., 249. Like KWG it is described as a tight-knit community with the "bulk of pedagogues *alfyorovskiye*, who knew well and worshipped the gymnasium founders – Aleksandra Samsonovna and her husband Aleksandr Danilovich Alfyorovs." Ibid., 249. The Bolsheviks executed the couple without trial in the winter of 1918–19, sending shockwaves through Moscow, but the school continued to operate. Ibid., 250.

Unfortunately, I do not possess information about the happenings within the resurrected school beyond scattered evidence for the stellar *Soviet* alma mater of the string of pupils who became outstanding artistic, scientific, and engineering cadre. This trajectory would mirror that of other prestigious gymnasia turned *Soviet* schools, which were overwhelmingly of an estatist makeup.[59] Following the closure of her gymnasium, Khardina's career exhibited characteristics of the upward trajectory of highly educated individuals familiar to us from the imperial period. She transitioned into the professional sphere of academic research, as did other teachers from her gymnasium, such as Pavel Preobrazhenskiy. Memoirs and letters reveal that the career highs were punctuated with the urgencies of procuring papers testifying to sound social credentials.

In the absence of intra-institutional details on the "subterranean politics" of resurrected gymnasia,[60] I heed Carlo Ginzburg's advice and seek out clues as to continuities in the pedagogic history of institutions that may not otherwise be obvious candidates from the point of view of questions of interest here. These, however, would hopefully, with some sociological imagination, speculation, and conjecture, animate the imperial school and society beneath the Soviet edifice. Our discussion of the medical profession has illustrated how the urgencies of fighting disease, epidemics, and malnutrition enhanced the agency of an already highly institutionalized, networked, and autonomous high-status society. These urgencies emerge also in the *likbez* (elimination of illiteracy) campaigns and those pertaining to expanding, if not simply maintaining at pre-war and pre-revolutionary levels, *primary schooling* – that is, policies concerning the target ideological allies that are the poorly educated workers and peasants. The gymnasia were elitist institutions catering to groups aspiring to university entrance. The most prestigious ones would have been vulnerable to punctuated spells of precariousness. This would be true at least during the temporal frame in which high-level policy debates unfolded over vocationalizing secondary schools as opposed to the maintenance of the university stream of gymnasia-type upper-level programs. This debate was ultimately resolved in favor of the latter, as has been well covered in historiography. The earlier works' emphasis on policy – and divisions among Old Bolsheviks as to the direction of education reform – underlines the relative neglect of the social underpinnings of pedagogic-institutional life cycles as embedded in the demand structures of socially heterogenous societies.[61] This scholarship leaves unanswered pertinent questions like: If a school is "closed down," what happens to the pedagogues and their networks? What about the demands of groups for gymnasium education that have coalesced over years if

---

[59] On the school of Stalin's daughter Svetlana, a former gymnasium founded in the nineteenth century and patronized by merchants, see *Mel* ("Chalk"): mel.fm/istoriya/238145-kreiman_gymnasium (accessed April 27, 2020).
[60] Pierson, "Power," 129.   [61] Fitzpatrick, *Education*; Bailes, *Technology*.

not generations? Will they simply disappear? What would be the strategies of pedagogues when faced with institutional closure, and those of parents and pupils? What configurations do we expect to emerge from these shifting institutional landscapes? How can elements of drift and conversion dissected at a general level for education allow us to unpack the processes that are at work? How wedded would a bourgeois pedagogue be to the ideologically indoctrinating function in *Soviet* pedagogy? If we cannot with any degree of certainty address the question of ideological indoctrination, where should we look for clues in a Ginzburgian sense, tantalizing our imagination as to the discreet reproduction of the ethos of the bourgeois gymnasium?

A plausible ethnographic site for unpacking these questions, one for which some information is available, would of necessity suffer from the issue of selection bias – and it may not be the most obvious case for us. While the straightforward sites would be ones like KWG, for which we have details until 1917, professionals like Nina Andreyevna were seeking to conceal their bourgeois connections, not openly, effusively, and prolifically reminiscing about them during the height of Stalinist rule. One school, however, has been a topic of documentary plaudits and memoirs. These allow us to dissect traces of patterns, if not generate concepts, that may be fruitful for understanding the reconstitution of pedagogic institutions as a site of social persistence in a totalizing state. In the late Soviet period corresponding to Gorbachev's perestroika and early post-Soviet years, diasporic ties aided the publication of memoirs – notably among Jewish and German communities. The urgency to generate oral and written histories, funded often by external philanthropists and governments, came from the large waves of emigration that inevitably eroded the fabric of these historically rooted communities in Samara. Researchers recorded these histories in the late 1980s and 1990s, at a time when pupils who attended the early post-revolutionary vintage schools were still alive.[62]

The educational institution I dwell on is the *Soviet* Jewish School No. 21, which was active in the years 1925–38 and reportedly founded pursuant to a Bolshevik directive.[63] The 1916 yearbook lists only one Jewish school in Samara, the Jewish *uchilishche*, with Tslaf Zel'man-Yankel' Polomov as head teacher. Among the educational institutions that the Bolsheviks catalogued in 1922, seven Jewish schools in Samara City alone feature. Some presumably were excluded from the 1916 yearbook because they were informal homeschooling groups outside of the Ministry of Public Enlightenment's

---

[62] Burlina, "Ya uchilas'." See also Zaslavskaya, *Yeshchyo odno*, 4–5. Available online at: iki.rssi.ru /events/2017/zaslavskaya_book.pdf (accessed April 27, 2020).

[63] Housed in a two-story mansion, it had the capacity to teach 200 children. *Yevreyskiy mir Samary*. Virtual museum site: sites.google.com/site/samaraemir/muzejnaa-ekspozicia/zal-9-evrejskie-skoly/stend-evrejskaa-skola-no-21 (accessed April 17, 2020).

authority.[64] We do not know which of these subsequently became *the* Soviet Jewish School; most likely it was the Jewish *uchilishche*. The memoirs of Tslaf's pupils and other records lack references to his pre-revolutionary teaching career – something typical of professionals adapting to the new Soviet class realities. These silences helped perpetuate the notion of a Soviet school founded in the context of Soviet nationalities policies and taught by a Soviet teacher.[65]

While some of the high-profile gymnasia were airbrushed out of *Soviet* pedagogy, this school survived, even if it was presented as a feat of *Soviet* policy in education. It did so, I conjecture, because of convergence with the tactical exigencies of courting various "nationalities." In this case, it became one of the "national" schools sanctioned to promote and celebrate the culture of a minority group. As a seven-year school, the erstwhile *uchilishche*, which was less prestigious than a gymnasium, represented one of the intermediate – between primary and upper schools – institutions not tarnished with a gymnasium label and one befitting the emphasis on the maintenance of lower-level schooling. Here, we dissect elements of institutional lethargy because of an at least superficial convergence with the ideological precepts of an urgent need for primary schooling. Further, this prestigious school did not have as its head teacher a high-status pedagogue of aristocratic, merchant, or clergy background, the equivalent of a Khardina, Khovanskiy, or one of the Preobrazhenskiys. Instead, we find at its helm an individual who, if we peruse the 1916 yearbook, does not appear to have connections to the high-status pedagogic or enlightenment networks. This is not because Jews had a marginal position in late imperial Samara. Some of the most eminent architects, engineers, jurists, doctors, and entrepreneurs embedded in high-status networks were Jewish, often with the estate ascription of merchant or honored citizen, Dr. Grinberg being one of them.[66] I have already alluded to

---

[64] Six schools and one preschool catering to the 20,000-strong Jewish population. Guberniya DPE report for January to March 1922. TsGASO, f. 81, op. 1, ed. khr. 533, l. 101.

[65] Biographical details available online at:
rujen.ru/index.php/ЦІАФ_Яков_Наумович (Rossiyskaya yevreyskaya entsiklopediya, Russian Jewish Encyclopaedia) (accessed April 27, 2020). KOMUCH rule in Samara was from June 8 to November 18, 1918.

[66] Samara is reportedly the only Middle Volga city that avoided pogroms during the 1905 wave of violence. Il'ya Karpenko, "Volzhskaya zhemchyuzhina," *Lechaim*, Vol. 8, no. 196, 2008. Available online at: lechaim.ru/ARHIV/196/karpenko.htm (accessed October 21, 2020). "Samara, as we remember, avoided pogroms, her residents did not run away into evacuation." Burlina, *Yevreyi*, 49. List of pogroms in 1905–7 is given in "From Kishineff to Bialystok: A Table of Pogroms from 1903 to 1906," The Museum of Family History. Available online at: museum offamilyhistory.com/ajc-yb-v08-pogroms.htm (accessed April 26, 2020). In a memoir, Khardina's relation recalls that, in the autumn of 1905, Khardina sheltered Jewish girls, who appeared very disturbed and anxious, some "crying." "Only many years later," she wrote, "I guessed, and Nina Andreyevna confirmed to me, that these were girls from Jewish families, not even very well acquainted [with Khardina], whom she thus would hide in the days when the pogroms were expected." Memoirs of Borisyak. Khardina papers. TsGASO, f. 300, op. 2, ed. khr. 10, l. 5. There are also records of violations of stipulations concerning the acceptance of

the anticipated rise of the *meshchanin* as Bolshevik Russia's street-level white-collar functionary in a provincial context. A numerically large estate that colonized technical schools, gymnasia, and universities, it was also one less ideologically tarnished than the high-profile merchant industrialist or aristocrat; and many *meshchane* were blessed with the trappings of superior human capital, which was needed to deliver public services. Tslaf's opaque and inconspicuous background would position him well for the kind of status-switching that is likely to have occurred in professional institutions that did not require a highly specialized knowledge of the kind observed in medicine, even though he boasted imperial training in physics and mathematics. The *meshchanin* temporally replaced the noble as someone with more sound biographic credentials.[67]

New archival sources allow us to situate Tslaf in the liminal spaces of Jewish religious pedagogy. Catering to the niche demand for Jewish religious instruction, these schools were neither elite nor entirely marginal like the parish school. Their pedagogues often originated within the educated *meshchanstvo* of the western Pale of Settlement. An entry in the Jewish encyclopedia based on pre-revolutionary records, which are unlikely to have been publicly available during the Soviet period, sheds light on Tslaf's biography. Tslaf was born in 1880 in Vitebskaya *guberniya* in the western reaches of the Russian Empire, where he obtained a traditional Jewish education. In 1907, Tslaf was granted the certificate of a Melamed or teacher in Jewish schools.[68] A well-developed network of schools providing traditional Jewish instruction existed across Russia's provinces. The Melameds taught either in a private school or at home,[69] and they were licensed pursuant to a special government 1893 directive – licenses were reviewed by the *guberniya* directorates of *uchilishchi*.[70] After a spell teaching in the Siberian city of Tomsk,

---

Jewish pupils without right of residence in Samara and admonitions to take responsibility for compliance with appropriate regulations failing which the school could be closed. Letter to Khardina from Director of Public *uchilishcha*, KED, 1910. Khardina papers, TsGASO, f. 300, op. 2, ed. khr 3, l. 88. Parents of Jewish pupils, applicants to Khardina gymnasium, supplied evidence of a police permit of right of residence in Samara. Khardina papers, TsGASO, f. 300, op. 1, d. 36, l. 2.

[67] Golitsyn writes that his Alfyorov gymnasium in Moscow retained old teachers until the end of the 1920s, "living old traditions as well as having pupils who loved and respected old teachers." Some were dismissed, others moved to other schools. "The three sisters Zolotaryov survived, since in their employment papers they called themselves *meshchanki*." Golitsyn, *Zapiski*, 336. One principled teacher, a noble, refused to lie on papers and was denied employment everywhere but gave private lessons. When she died in 1931, "over one hundred former Alfyorovtsy came to her funeral." Ibid., 337.

[68] Kizhner and Chernova, "Tomskiye melamedy," 299.   [69] Ibid.

[70] Ibid., 294. Lay regional authorities inspected sanitary conditions, police, and political records (possible "Zionist-socialist" links) and "morals" – to ensure that the teacher did not lead a promiscuous life (*besputnaya zhizn'*) – though not the substance of Jewish teaching. The local Rabbi ensured the overall quality of teaching processes. Ibid., 294–96, 298.

Tslaf did a degree in physics and mathematics at the Samara Pedagogical Institute. From at least 1913, he worked as head teacher in a Jewish primary school in Samara and became founder of a Jewish library.[71] Concerning the specific school where Tslaf taught, we observe direct institutional transfer, albeit with some forensic speculation inherent in such an exercise, what with the Soviet labels bandaged onto the surviving school.[72]

Tslaf's hiring policies as a *Soviet* appointee indicate that he exercised considerable agency and may well have run an elaborate operation of constructing and sheltering something akin to the museum society, a group of high-status pedagogues maintaining strong personal and friendship ties as indeed "weak" links to other professional sites. In the sellers' market of pedagogues, the best knew their value and likely negotiated their way into the top schools. Memoirists invoke the superior competence of these teachers. Their embeddedness in pedagogic and professional networks that transcended the seven-year school also makes likely the kinds of facilitating roles that the metropolitan ties played for the archaeologist or historian in the networks of Vera Gol'msten in the museum. Indeed, by all accounts, pupils were streamed into the most prestigious higher educational institutions that required knowledge of the kinds of technical subjects – physics, mathematics, and chemistry – that Tslaf superbly taught or catered to in the Jewish school. Pupils were fed into the "bourgeois" engineering, medical, and science university departments in Samara, Kazan, Moscow, Kiev, and St. Petersburg. As with the medical school, the temporal frame of the school's operations, which may have been quite short, need not detract from the longer-term life cycle aspects of institutional-social reproduction. School leavers from the 1925–38 cohorts became professionals who made their living as part of the high-status intelligentsia in later decades.

Memoirists highlight how, as school director, Tslaf took great care to secure the employment of "top" teachers. One of Tslaf's hires was a Sofya Mikhaylovna Vasil'yeva. In the 1916 yearbook, Vasil'yeva features as a teacher at KWG. This affiliation would have connected her to institutions and public bodies that emerged as among the most highly networked, "core" sites in the social network analysis I performed outlining the contours of Samara society immediately before the Bolsheviks took power. Pavel Aleksandrovich Preobrazhenskiy, "the pillar of the gymnasium," for instance, had been a member of the Samara Society for Public Universities and the Samara Guberniya Learned Archive Commission and went on to teach at higher educational institutions after the Revolution. Another of the school's teachers,

---

[71] Ibid., 299–300.

[72] Many Jews in private businesses, industry, and employed with Jewish public and religious institutions joined the Soviet public sector and "filled the void left by the aftermath of the revolution, when the traditional clerical, administrative, and intellectual classes boycotted the Soviet regime or were kept out of these positions." Altshuler, *Soviet Jewry*, 9.

who had been employed at the Khardina Gymnasium at the same time as the old teacher Vasil'yeva, was a Mariya Veniaminovna Portugalova.[73] The Portugalovs were a well-connected and highly respected family in pre-revolutionary Samara. Mariya Veniaminovna's father, the medical doctor Veniamin Osipovich Portugalov, made his name campaigning to promote sobriety in the *guberniya*. Her brother, Yuliy Veniaminovich, went on to become Professor and Head of the Psychiatry Faculty at SU.[74] The Portugalovs–Vasil'yeva connection would have thus constituted a network tie linking the most sought-after school and university-level academics in prestigious faculties. The elite school illustrates the limitations of social uplift, specifically the possibility of the displacement of the broad category of the estates-derived bourgeoisie from well-institutionalized and networked arenas associated with a high social status.

Let me now turn to the question of indoctrination, or rather propose a more appropriate lens, for analyzing the subtleties of socialization in schools – more aptly described in semiotic terms. The emphasis here is on the conservation of the social distinction of the educated estatist society through the communicative intricacies practiced and propagated within social networks.[75] Distinction is something that even in Bourdieu's open society of France is expressed, conveyed, and practiced in discreet, hard-to-grasp ways, through modes of comport, speech, and refinement of the pedagogue and the pupil, processes that also create markers for exclusion.[76] Let us dissect the significance of the mere apparition, the sole utterance, the fleeting allusions to the past, of Sofya Mikhaylovna Vasil'yeva, in the recollections of a pupil:

Small, with short, cropped hair, stooping, and very advanced in age . . . Everything in her amazed us from her first appearance in the class – her personal appearance, and the fact that she by mistake called the diary a *conduit*, and that they were saying that she had been abroad. Back then it stirred the imagination more than now – a flight to the moon. In my mind I still hear her voice, low, slightly dull, I hear her speech – unhurried, paced, subordinating to itself our quite temperamental audience. Only later did I appreciate the beauty of her pure Russian language, fed from some deep sources.[77]

The *conduit* in Vasil'yeva's speech act is an expression of what I term *evocative semantics*, something that marks out status. Pupils wrote of the purity, propriety, and correctness of her language. With what were they juxtaposing

---

[73] SGSC, *Pamyatnaya knizhka*.

[74] For a biography of V. I. Portugalov, see "Portugalov, Veniamin Osipovich." *Yevreyskaya entsiklopediya Brokgauza i Yefrona*. Available online at: https://ru.wikisource.org/ЕЭБЕ/Португалов,_Вениамин_Осипович (accessed December 31, 2020). On Yu. V. Portugalov, see history of Samara State Medical University. Available online at: http://psyhosp.ru/department/ (accessed December 31, 2020).

[75] Gould, "Uses of Network Tools," 264–65.

[76] On this, see, for instance, Bourdieu, *State Nobility*, 32–35.

[77] Recollections of Yeva Markovna Tsvetayeva. Burlina, "Ya uchilas'," 82.

these qualities – with characteristics of teachers not of an imperial pedigree? She had been "abroad," a route by now virtually closed to the awed pupil. Would she have told the pupil about those times? What would she say, and how would that gel with her function of molding the imperial into the Soviet citizen?

Beyond evidence of institutional drift, Tslaf and his hires speak to the disjunctures between the social wavelength – the bottom-up sources of institutional resilience – and the shifting vagaries of official state ideology and policy – the top-down sources of *recognition* and *misrecognition*. The extra-professional social esteem is earned, enacted, and reproduced day-to-day vis-à-vis the client and broader society. This dimension of status imbues individuals with an agency to bestow deference selectively and autonomously from the punctuated processes of state recognition or demotion. Moreover, it illustrates how apparent institutional rupture does not immediately puncture these "slow-moving" and long-acquired dimensions of status and esteem.[78] One's pedigree became the proverbial inferential shortcut as families navigated their way through the Soviet education reforms, a dynamic extending into the highest echelons of Soviet power. No matter how fast the "tempo" of the production of the new teacher,[79] their credentials would not match the hereditary – if we take it to understand not material assets but superior training under the old regime, the emotions, the loyalty bestowed – aspect of the persona of the old teacher:[80]

Almost everyone in the city knew Yakov Naumovich [Tslaf]. Meeting him on the street, the residents would always take off their hat and bow![81]

I studied in the Jewish school, in the famous School No. 21. Our director was Yakov Naumovich Tslaf.

From our school numerous scientists, doctors, and pedagogues emerged.[82]

And how he [Tslaf] taught mathematics! Those who studied with him remember his lessons: wonderful, amazing, creative![83]

The semiotics of *vintageness* are also discerned in the immortality of the architectural edifice of the school surviving the pedigree teacher. The "school No. X that used to be the gymnasium Y" nurtured the day-to-day affirmation of social boundaries and closure – among the children of nomenklatura and the professional class originating in Samara's estatist bourgeoisie who attended these vintage schools. Professor Natalya Borisovna Ivanova,[84] a historian, moved to Samara with her parents, metropolitan professionals, in the 1950s. She recalls attending the School No. 6, the former Samara Second Men's Gymnasium that the Kavetskiy brothers from the medical dynasty attended

---

[78] Pierson, "Power," 82.
[79] On tempo-shaping causal processes and outcomes, see Grzymala-Busse, "Time Will Tell?"
[80] On aspects of social closure endowed with an "inherited" character, see Weber, *Economy and Society*, 1:44.
[81] See *Yevreyskiy mir Samary* ("Jewish world of Samara"): sites.google.com/site/samaraemir/muzej-naa-ekspozicia/zal-9-evrejskie-skoly/stend-evrejskaa-skola-no-21 (accessed April 17, 2020).
[82] Burlina, "Imya?" 120.   [83] *Yevreyskiy mir Samary*.   [84] Name changed.

before the Revolution.[85] Subsequently, it continued to be housed in the same building as the original gymnasium, in the center of "old" Samara.[86] "There were no such schools in the Soviet times: with grand staircases, enormous classrooms, and so forth ... In my class one could say the entire elite of the city studied."[87]

Spatial Heterogeneity in Schools

If punctuated continuities characterized urban schooling, were patterns different in rural schools? We anticipate Bolshevik policy to have been particularly consequential in the countryside, given the ideological and policy commitment to root out widespread illiteracy and promote mass education. The official regime tribune in the region, the *Kommuna*, branded those who eschewed learning as evil persons (*zlostnyye litsa*). Draconian measures of forcible enrolments in courses to end illiteracy were promulgated. Failure to attend *likbez* training or evidence that family members were obstructing attendance was made punishable with deprivation of income and even considered a criminal offense.[88] Official dispatches threatened the imposition of monitoring processes. Inspections revealing less than adequate provisions to root out illiteracy led to high-profile and well-publicized cases of the removal of isolated village soviet chairmen. The state threatened to take tough measures not just against the organizers of the campaign who failed to deliver but also *"against the population subjected to education."* The local Department of Public Education (DPE) reported: "In addition to mass explanatory work ... vis-a-vis *zlostnyye litsa* not attending lessons or shying away from studies ... [the directive is] *to use punitive measures including fines and forcible works*, and to apply these measures to individuals responsible for sabotaging instruction."[89]

Yet, if the Bolsheviks' main objective was to reach the masses hitherto untouched, or only feebly affected, by formal schooling, then this is the area that also exhibited the most pronounced policy failings. State penetration in imperial Russia had been spatially uneven, varying even within one *guberniya*. Remote villages were cut off from regional centers and the capital in the absence of rail and road connections. The concept of state penetration ought to be in any case qualified. State agents on the ground often hailed from local communities. Indeed, the traditional *commune* form of rural governance performed state functions even after the abolition of serfdom and the implementation of other

---

[85] A. Chakovskiy, future Editor-in-Chief of a leading national press outlet, *Literaturnaya Gazeta*, whose ancestors were merchants, also attended this school. See *Samarskiye sud'by* (Samara Destinies): samsud.ru/litadres/address/writers/writers_27.html (accessed April 12, 2019).

[86] It now houses the Institute of Culture. On the gymnasium and successor School No. 6, see: muzeysamobr.ru/obrazovatelnye-uchrezhdeniya-samary/shkoly (accessed April 27, 2020).

[87] Interview, June 22, 2017.   [88] Petrova, "Likbez," 532.

[89] Cited in ibid., 533 (emphases added).

reforms in rural economies and society.[90] Furthermore, as already noted, educational institutions that did exist – as well as their quality – were not always the product of state fiat. They were endogenous to autonomous impulses within society. In thriving urban centers of commerce and industry, like Samara, the upper echelons of the pedagogic profession were embedded in the highly networked sites of the enlightened public sphere. By contrast, the urban teacher parachuted into the village cut a lonely figure. In turn, the teacher native to village society had formed part of the structures of the rural social hierarchy. The Muslim clergy and their familial-social reciprocal networks illustrate this. Habitual expectations of tangible gain derived from learning and the imperative of social status maintenance – material and symbolic incentives of social closure – accounted for heterogenous preferences and outcomes *within* the village. These patterns complicated the implementation of the official policy of targeting the least advantaged groups for enlightenment and uplift.

In dissecting elements of continuity and rupture, I am again sensitive to the heterogeneity in the formal tapestry of schools across and within communities and against a background of widespread socioeconomic dislocation and hardships; the possibility of rural actors with an "early riser" institutional-pedagogic advantage perpetuating intra-rural social gradations; and the inputs from the community shaping, maintaining, reinforcing, or, alternatively, modifying extant patterns of heterogeneity. I also discern inadvertent complicity within official policy in reinforcing rather than rooting out extant patterns of schooling. Specifically, I am alert to the context of the fast-paced tempo of expectations for the delivery of reform as against the realities of weak state penetration and a limited resource base, as well as an obdurate society.

As in Samara City, the dislocation brought about by the Civil War, famine, and disease had catastrophic consequences for education. In Stavropol' *uyezd*, between 1919 and 1922, schooling declined by 40 percent; and forty out of the eighty-nine schools closed. In Melekes *uyezd*, out of the 204 schools that still functioned at the start of the 1922 academic year, only 93 remained open, with a total staff, including teachers, of 178. Schools thus had an average of fewer than two instructors and service personnel. In Buzuluk *uyezd*, the 147 primary (level I) schools with a total of 20,676 pupils were serviced by a total of 393 pedagogues.[91]

Policy documents repeatedly allude to sources of resilience in the maintenance of educational processes, with reference to local agency working outside of the channels of state support and funding. The few functioning schools often relied on "local sources, and the forces of those living in the

[90] Mironov, *Rossiyskaya imperiya*, 2:436–37.
[91] Guberniya DPE report for January to March 1922. TsGASO, f. 81, op. 1, ed. khr. 533, 9–12, l. 94 ob.

respective localities."[92] We find evidence of institutional drift specifically in predominantly Muslim areas with a well-developed network of religious schools. Not only did these schools boast a superior record of continuity in educational process, even when others closed their doors due to lack of funding, but they also featured decent, if not outstanding, infrastructure and resources maintained via community channels of support. To sustain their legitimate status as bona fide educational rather than religious institutions, the pedagogic personnel downplayed the narrowly religious dimension of instruction, succumbing to conversionary pressures coming from above. The regime's sensitivity regarding the national question facilitated habitual practices in schooling;[93] apprehension of losing teachers aside, desperate as the Bolsheviks were to retain them, national and religious minorities were not to be alienated. Even those teachers who had completed higher educational establishments of a "spiritual" kind were acceptable insofar as they possessed a "significant pedagogical record."[94] This was the case with Tatar teachers who had completed the *medrese* (Islamic religious school). Superficial expressions of a profession of loyalty often sufficed, while the structure, the substance, and practices of everyday schooling did not experience fundamental change.

The children of *mullahs* (Muslim clerics) were preponderant among the best educated segments of rural society in Samara's predominantly Muslim areas, something perhaps reflective of the blossoming of enlightenment among a segment of Tatar clergy in the late Romanov Empire. As John Sidel writes, the Volga Basin had been the seat of the *jadidi* reformist movement spearheaded by Tatar intellectuals. Islamic reformist schools combined "classical scholastic tradition" with modern subjects of history, arithmetic, geography, and the Tatar and Russian languages; their alumni went on to study in elite secular graduate schools that prepared youth for modern professional careers.[95] The Bolsheviks, ever vigilant in matters of the class origins of pupils, noted with alarm that significant dropout rates characterized the poor peasant strata, the *bednyaki*, while children of *kulaks*, traders, artisans, Muslim clerics, priests, and the rural intelligentsia were disproportionately represented among pupils in higher grades. A report on schools in the Buguruslan *uyezd*, which had significant populations of ethnic Chuvash, Tatars, and Bashkirs, recorded conscientiousness in school attendance of Tatar children, many of whom were listed as sons and daughters of *mullahs*: "Children of *mullahs* are usually the most literate in the village and actively seek to be admitted into educational institutions . . .; they bring certificates from the local authorities that they belong to the peasantry."[96] More than one in ten of all pupils of a Tatar–Bashkir pedagogical *tekhnikum* in 1924–25 were children of clergy.[97]

---

[92] Ibid.   [93] On this question, see Martin, *Affirmative Action Empire*.

[94] RSFSR People's Commissariat of Worker-Peasant Inspection, report on pedagogic education. TsGASO, f. 81, op. 1, ed. khr. 992, 19, l. 21.

[95] Sidel, *Republicanism*, 77.   [96] Ibid., l. 40.   [97] Ibid., l. 40.

Consider now the contrast with rural areas where the co-constitutive dimensions of both institutional and social drivers of schooling quality had but a weak foundation. To what extent did the Bolshevik state, aggressive in eradicating the vestiges of illiteracy, fill the void in social demand for education? Dissecting these patterns for the early post-revolutionary period is crucial, since this is when the foundations were laid for the trajectory of schooling and professional skills and the possibility of a successful transition into the urban white-collar jobs market when mobility restrictions were lifted in the 1950s. The patterns of tepid social demand for schooling anticipate the rural proletariat and urban precariat that emerged from the peasant estate in worker conurbations on the margins of Samara City some decades later. By contrast, the institutional drift that characterized territories with high demand for education would create a temporal opening, enabling transition into the white-collar professional stratum. This transition occurred before the anti-clerical repressive machinery of the "Great Break" and the collectivization that targeted the rural bourgeoisie of the late 1920s.

Despite the *force majeure* nature of the *likbez* campaigns, in 1920–22, less than 1 percent (17,200) of the illiterate population took part in training. In 1924, there were still 420,000 illiterates aged 18–35 in the Samara *guberniya*.[98] A detailed inspection report concerning the education system in a multiethnic village in the Buguruslan *uyezd* contains as many statistics as it does ethnographic detail about the mores, moral lapses, and everyday practices of the population, which served to derail the Bolsheviks' education campaign. A shortage of teaching staff and their reluctance to engage in – as well as their tacit obstruction of – the higher authorities' attempts to introduce "progressive" elements into the educational process compounded the issues of the villagers' ambivalent attitude and the local *soviet* authorities' passive complicity with communal opposition toward the diktat of outside Bolshevik education managers.[99] Religious observance, superstitions, rural labor responsibilities, and cultural attitudes toward education accounted for high rates of leakage of school pupils by the time they reached the fourth year of primary school. The inspection commission report noted with great satisfaction that, at the beginning of the school year, most pupils were of middling (*serednyaki*) peasant origins (69.5 percent), with 16 percent of pupils coming from the poorest peasant strata (*bednyaki*) and only 13.6 percent from the wealthiest (*zazhitochnyye*) peasantry. To the commission's disappointment, however, a "somewhat different" picture appeared at the time of the survey – that is, later in the school year. The poorest peasants registered 41.9 percent

---

[98] Petrova, "Likbez," 524, 526.

[99] Report on cultural-enlightenment situation, Shantalinskaya *volost'*, Buguruslan *uyezd*, Samara *guberniya*. TsGASO, f. 81, op. 1, ed. khr. 926, part 1. The survey for 1923–24 recorded that the entire *volost'* had thirty-six teachers. Only two were members of RKP/b and two candidates or members of VLKSM. ll. 96, 96 ob.

dropout rates; the middling, 9.4 percent; and the wealthy peasants, only 6.9 percent. After accounting for leakage statistics, only 11.4 percent of pupils came from the poorest strata, 73.7 from the middling strata, and 14.8 percent from among the wealthiest peasants.[100]

Because local officials were embedded in local societies, they often made only perfunctory attempts to improve the quality of schooling. Teachers complained about the onerous constraints on their movement and reporting requirements. They were forbidden to travel outside of their place of residence even during school holidays and required the permission of the village soviet (*sel'sovet*) authorities to do so. This made them feel like a "caged bird within the walls of the school" (*nevol'noy ptashechkoy v stenakh shkoly*). The *sel'sovet* also had to report to the district educational boards about such absences and days away from the village. Fortunately, for teachers, "although this provision ties the hands and feet of the teacher, the only thing that saves him is the fact that the village soviets are always not particularly vigilant in performing these responsibilities."[101]

The rare appearances of *guberniya* nomenklatura in the village became events of immense local significance, testifying to the tenuous reach of the state into localities. During one such appearance, the whole village trailed behind the visiting notables, much as would be the case with an alien descending from another planet. One functionary parachuted from outside for a day observed:

We had to come to the Afon'kino village during the Blagoveshcheniye day, old style calendar [religious holiday]. We walked along the road and entered the office of the *sel'sovet*, and we see that all people are following us from the street into the office. Nobody asked them to come in, no one called them in. This testifies to how much the local population wants to hear, to find out something from the comrades who arrived in their village.[102]

According to another inspection report, although visits from party authorities were becoming more frequent, "no direct link with the center exists, bar receipt of subventions and of reports on their expenditure ... The *tekhnikum* had a casual visitation from two representatives of the Sovnatsmen VTsIK [council of national minorities executive committee], en route to another destination [*proyezdom*], but neither instructions were given, nor inspections were carried out."[103] Both teachers and the regional authorities appeared to be content with the state of affairs whereby much of the contact between the two remained of an epistolary nature in the form of "circulars [and] reports."[104] Intricate social and family relationships linking pupils and their families,

---

[100] Ibid., l. 102 ob.   [101] Ibid., l. 98.
[102] Ibid., l. 107. The report also mentions binge drinking – even the village soviet chairman of Afon'kino himself was intoxicated (*byl p'yan ot golovy do nog*) during the inspection (l. 107).
[103] Report concerning pedagogic education. TsGASO, f. 81, op. 1, ed. khr. 992, l. 27.
[104] Ibid.

teachers, and soviets – and the local soviet bodies in rural areas were often far and wide apart – facilitated habitual patterns in schooling. The peasant Alfey Kichilin's address to the powers-that-be, riddled with spelling and style errors, conveyed the prevailing sentiment among the most socially disadvantaged segments of Samara's peasantry:

The peasant who remains at the grains faces ever greater hardships for fewer laborers are left to do the physical work, while there are more mental laborers. Of course, enlightenment is not bad even for the peasant . . . but no matter how hard the soviet power tries to educate soviet Russia, it has been six years now, but it [Russia] is just as dirty and ignorant, and it is only the sufferings that have multiplied.[105]

CONCLUSION

In this chapter, I charted out both the social and the institutional underpinnings of reproduction in education. Statistical analysis is strongly suggestive of the interconnected human capital and estate drivers of spatial variations in educational attainment and institutions during the communist period and in the present. To unpack the causal mechanisms behind the statistical patterns, I adapted concepts of institutional drift and conversion to Russia's post-revolutionary context.[106] Extending this heuristic framework beyond conventional applications to far more politically stable contexts, I proposed to analyze drift and conversionary dynamics through the lens of the disjuncture between the social wavelengths – heterogenous preferences for education that reflect the intergenerational accumulation of slow-moving processes that do not change overnight – and the shifting state-led policy. The preservation of paid-for instruction against a background of the widespread collapse of public services and the state's incapacity to meet its own awesome and urgent revolutionary proclamations illustrates how socially cataclysmic events may in fact have a built-in *dis-leveler* dimension. Compromises made during these early periods of change could adumbrate lasting socially conserving processes. In Russia's schooling, they worked to empower the expert and the moneyed bourgeois capable of paying tuition fees. The analysis has also been sensitive to role-switching, as when the lower-status members of the educated estates obtained leadership positions. This, I conjecture, is an element of conversionary pressures that counterintuitively enables the reassemblage of high-status pedagogic networks within elite *Soviet* schools.

The contrasting evidence from the rural school accentuates both the urban/rural variations and the within-rural dimensions of the demand and supply side of instruction. The status of the rural clergyman as the predominant supplier of an educated secular workforce underlines the limitations of the materialist lens on status reproduction, accentuating the estate as structuring a habitual

---

[105] Petrova, "Likbez."   [106] Hacker et al., "Drift and Conversion."

emphasis on learning. Throughout this analysis, the state emerges as akin to the flailing wounded bird, flapping its ominous wings over an organic and self-reproducing society. The leviathan appears as such whether in issuing stern directives that are ignored, subverted, or discarded on the ground; in selectively and highly ineffectively applying symbolic and actual violence against the unwilling teacher or beneficiary of the anti-illiteracy campaign; or, indeed, after much frustration in securing a qualified cadre from among the worker and peasant masses, in embracing the "bourgeois" instructor.

6

Market Values and the Economy of Survival

Christ be resurrected! My darling far away Polia! I would like to wish you in this happy bright holiday all that is possible in life that is light and happy. And this light is only possible with His resurrection, for He brought it into this world, is that not true? How are people celebrating this holiday in that country where fate has thrown you? Do they have the same kind of solemn morning service [*torzhestvennaya zautrenya*] there, does the cheerful ringing of the bells roll around, do people walk around with such similarly lit up faces? ...

But ... This was before, and now ... [original punctuation], a shadow has descended, harmony has been broken, a biting sound [*rezhushchiy slukh*] has crept in. This sound, this moaning, is heard everywhere, everywhere and one cannot run away from it. This sound – is the moaning, moaning of hungry families, roaming in rows down the streets! Ah Polia if only you could see this ... the little children around chanting "give us a penny" ["*podayte kopeyechku*"] ... barely moving their feet and barely whispering from exhaustion, "please give." And there one sees corpses under the wall, and here is a black coffin coming out of the gates of a child foster home, and here is a father with orphans – children foraging through piles of garbage! Give, give, give! These crying, monotonous moans, even in the night ... Yes, darkened is the bright happy holiday. The bright rays of light have hit some barrier and a shadow descended on the land. What is this barrier? What is the reason for this shadow? Of these misfortunes? Here is the hard, heavy question.[1]

Letter from Samara to Neklutin family members in America (1920–22)

Your letter, darling aunt Peychika, is steeped with such sadness, that the heart shrinks and your tears and sadness are transmitted through whole oceans, waters, and lands. Why? You keep being sad about something. Perhaps about the days of the past? ... That is needless, if you are longing for your motherland, then I advise you to retain of it all the best that remains in the soul, and for longer, for if you ever

---

[1] Letter, 4 April. Year unclear, possibly 1920–22. NC, f. 16_19.

visit here, you would not find that what has drawn you here and your soul would be filled with disappointment – and accordingly emptiness too.[2]

Letter from Samara to Neklutin family members in America (1927)

The earlier chapters have explored how the well-networked public sphere and the proto-knowledge economy found their embodiment in the Soviet institutions of the professions, in the civic enlightenment arenas, and in education. One objection to the emphasis on the institutional-network path-dependencies that I anticipate is the plausibility of disentangling outcomes consequential to Soviet industrialization and social uplift drives, as distinct from mechanisms intrinsic to the self-preservation and reconfiguration of imperial-era, institutionally embedded estatist networks. Our task here is to explore the counterfactual of the reproduction of values and network ties, if not institutions, far more *misaligned* with Bolshevik policy. If we can discern not only resilience in position within estatist society but also practices intrinsically at odds with Marxist-Leninist dogma, we would have far greater confidence in the plausibility of the account of social autonomy presented in this book. This chapter locates this possibility in the market-reproducing values and networks among the most persecuted strata. Materials from the Neklutin archive, along with records from other merchant and *meshchane* families, allow me to discern adaptation processes among such groups. These communities tarnished themselves not only because of their high-profile entrepreneurship in imperial Samara but also by dint of association with the anti-Bolshevik political-military struggles during the Civil War.[3]

As before, I am alert to the multiple network spaces that wealthy merchants and *meshchane* occupied in pre-revolutionary Russia. This would be true if we take the temporal snapshot of 1916 and an intergenerational perspective that is sensitive to aspirations and educational and professional positioning at the start of the century. The reader may recall that the network spaces of parents and grandparents straddled the political engagements of the public sphere – mayors, councilors, executives in the city *duma*; the enlightenment society; and, of course, private entrepreneurship. Even if parents were not sitting on the boards of elite gymnasia, their children were attending these schools – something that would represent an intergenerational network link to the educated higher-status society. Simultaneously, even when aspiring to attain a modern education and profession, the next generation would have been exposed to routinized practices of familial

---

[2] Letter, December 25, 1927, NC, f. 16_14.

[3] Blackwell suggests why the Russian entrepreneur had been understudied in Soviet-period historiography: "A broader interest in the Russian entrepreneur – his origins, motivations, functions, achievements, society, culture, and politics – was overshadowed by a political and ideological preconcern with the bourgeoisie as it played its appointed role on the Russian road to socialism." Blackwell, "Russian Entrepreneur," 15. Blackwell notes the dearth of biographical studies of Russian entrepreneurs: "The greatest need in the field of Russian entrepreneurial history is to probe inside the mind, family life, and social and cultural experience of the individual entrepreneur." Ibid., 25. To me, the Neklutin archive helps achieve just that.

entrepreneurship and cognate values and discussions in the home. I here introduce the hitherto neglected element of diasporic transnational ties that not only aid survival but sustain, nurture, and engender specific sets of practices and knowledge. Rather than regarding population movement, emigration, and relocation from the perspective of the decimation of social networks, communities, and institutions, as most accounts before mine have done, I precisely dissect the group-reaffirming and value-reproducing aspect of dislocation. Further, I link the cross-regional and transnational ties to those multiple local network and institutional anchors that the *lishentsy* would keep, cast, or look to reanchor within their native region. I hypothesize that heterogeneity within one discernible dimension of social values – attitude toward the market and entrepreneurship – is a vestige of the spatially distinct sets of constellations of the estate. This legacy was sustained as the left-behind merchants but also the wealthy *meshchane* and a sprinkling of entrepreneurial nobles navigated distinct and interconnected spaces in the professions, private enterprise, and the global instruments of banking and finance.[4]

Consistent with the template adapted in the earlier empirical chapters, I first perform cross-regional statistical analysis of market legacies as linked to the urban estates. Archival, interview, and memoir materials then help tease out the mechanisms of the transmission of market-supporting human capital and values. An analysis of transnational–local ties, which the state itself facilitated as it sought to replenish currency reserves, helps dissect their role in both generating "one-off" survival infusions of wealth and sustaining the links to private banking and enterprise via more temporally protracted flows of remittances. The private wealth and market aspects of the bourgeois legacy are also seen as facilitating what I call hedging, encompassing both private enterprise and public sector professions, a career risk-minimizing strategy of the educated estates in evidence long before the Revolution.

STATISTICAL ANALYSIS

Unlike official data on education and the professions, which are easier to come by, private entrepreneurship presents notorious problems for the researcher of communism. This is particularly true for the period before perestroika when the state finally permitted some forms of private enterprise beyond the very narrow realm of rural trading in homegrown produce. Viewed from another perspective, however, activities that the state itself brands and legislates as *illegal* are an even more reliable source on the residue of estates than are education and the professions that the Bolsheviks welcomed and expanded. Private enterprise, bar the period of the NEP, became illegal all the way up to Mikhail Gorbachev's 1987–88 amendments to the relevant laws, which injected market possibilities into the

---

[4] On politically subversive effects of private enterprise under communism, see Róna-Tas, "Second Economy."

Soviet economy. "Speculation" – the reselling of goods to obtain a profit margin – was made a felony punishable by law;[5] the regime kept a tab on and recorded these activities.[6]

Such "felonies" may be regarded as reasonable proxies for proto-entrepreneurial activity, but with caveats. Not all cases of "speculation" resulted in convictions. The widespread deficit in goods and services made black market activities a virtual necessity for many Soviet citizens;[7] and shadow market pursuits in an economy of scarcity may well be driven by factors distinct from those that motivate entrepreneurship in market economies. With these caveats in mind, as part of an earlier collaborative project with this author, Alexander Libman compiled data on "speculation" convictions in 1987, the last year in which the "speculation" code was still being enforced.[8] Do these activities covary with the spatial distribution of estates conceptualized as the bourgeoisie here, notably the most sizeable, the *meshchane*? We find that the correlation coefficient with the *meshchane* is positive and significant (0.309), but the effect disappears when we substitute aggregate convictions with a per capita measure.

Armed with this very tentative evidence, let us now tease out covariation respectively between estate and Gorbachev-period legal entrepreneurial activities and, later, post-communist small and medium business ownership. The cooperative movement is a good place to begin in exploring the entrepreneurial legacy as it encompasses the so-called 1910 generation.[9] Born before the Revolution, this cohort witnessed the NEP, when the Bolsheviks allowed private entrepreneurship that, by many accounts, blossomed precisely in areas formerly known as thriving centers of commerce and enterprise. Members of that generation would be roughly seventy-five years old when Gorbachev unveiled his far-reaching reforms in 1985; many retained vivid memories of life in imperial and early post-revolutionary Russia.[10] Considering what we know about the involvement of grandparents in the upbringing and socializing of Soviet children, and the common residence patterns of three generations sharing an apartment,[11] intergenerational transmission of values is highly plausible.

During perestroika, cooperatives were the first legally permitted form of entrepreneurial activity, beginning in 1987 with the services sector and followed quickly in 1988 with the Law on Cooperatives, which significantly broadened opportunities for enterprise. "Worker cooperatives," owned and managed by the workforce, may have been more ideologically palatable but their ownership features mirrored classic small and medium-size enterprises in capitalist countries.[12] Many successful businessmen of the 1990s began their

---

[5] Klinova, "Spekulyatsiya," 78.   [6] Ibid., 78.

[7] Ledeneva, *Russia's Economy of Favours*, 23–24, 49; Edele, *Stalinist Society*, 209–10; Osokina, *Our Daily Bread*, 106–8, 118–21.

[8] Source: MVDRF and MYuRF, *Prestupnost'*. Data gathered and analyzed as part of a joint project; the discussion presented in this "Statistical Analysis," section of this chapter also draws on this. Lankina and Libman, "Two-Pronged Middle Class."

[9] Tchuikina, *Dvoryanskaya pamyat'*, 11.   [10] Ibid.   [11] Figes, *Whisperers*.

[12] Bim et al., "Hybrid Forms," 3.

ascent to wealth as managers of such collectives. The "oligarchs" Boris
Berezovsky and Mikhail Khodorkovsky are but two best known examples.
Importantly, cooperative owners could hire personnel, easing business
expansion and growth.[13]

Employing *oblast* statistics on the number of cooperatives and employees,[14]
and controlling for several Soviet-period regional developmental indicators, we
find (Table 6.1) that the *meshchane* significantly impact on perestroika-era
proto-entrepreneurship. Put simply, if we take two regions with very similar
developmental characteristics as measured by urbanization and wealth in the
1980s, the region significantly more likely to feature entrepreneurial activity in
1987 would also be the one with a higher population share of the *meshchane* in
1897, nearly 100 years earlier.

The *meshchane*, in absolute terms, appear less relevant than merchants and
nobles, if we compare the coefficients in Table 6.1. Merchants alone represent the
bulk of the educated estates' effect on the number of cooperatives, showing
a coefficient significantly exceeding that of all the other estates. When
interpreting the results, however, we are cognizant of the fact that, in relative
terms, the impact on the outcome variable would be influenced by each estate's
respective share. Thus, the *meshchane* constituted a much larger proportion of the
regional populations, showing greater variation on this measure across regions;
consequently, their weight in determining the outcome would be more substantial.
Indeed, combining merchants and *meshchane* makes the coefficient comparable to
that for the *meshchane* alone. The variable of the nobility also appears to have
a sizeable positive impact, which, nonetheless, ought to be interpreted with
reference to the minuscule population share of this estate.[15] By contrast, as one
would expect given the restrictions on the priestly estate's entrepreneurship in

---

[13] Aven, *Vremya Berezovskogo.*   [14] Source: Goskomstat, *Rossiyskaya Federatsiya.*

[15] Golitsyn corroborates the involvement of nobles as quasi-entrepreneurs during the NEP. In
Moscow, "tradespeople were members of old merchant families – such was, for instance, the
Sveshnikov's furs shop on Okhotnyy Ryad and other *okhotnoryadskiye* stores." Golitsyn,
Zapiski, 229. Aristocrats eschewed trading, associating it with "Nepmen," but served as intermediaries or "maklers." Sergey's cousin Georgiy Osorgin became an intermediary between sellers and
buyers. "Known for his impeccable honesty, he took a certain amount of commission for the
brokerage [*posrednichestvo*], and the former people, entrusting him with brooches, golden spoons
and five-ruble coins, believed in his aristocratic honor [*dvoryanskaya chestnost'*]." Golitsyn asks:
"Why did some aristocrats engage in such non-habitual for their estate pursuits?" "This is because, –
they themselves explained. – In our time we swore allegiance to the tsar, and do not want to serve the
Soviet power." Ibid., 229–30. Attempts by others to perform market transactions were clumsy.
When Sergey's father sought to exchange the monthly $10 remittances sent to his father (Sergey's
grandfather) in a Soviet bank – and official exchange rates were extortionate – it "took a lot of effort
to dissuade him" on the grounds that "everyone was doing it [using the black market]" for he was
adamant he did not want to "perform illegal transactions right on the street." Ibid., 230. On the
other hand, some aristocrats, like Golitsyn's "Uncle Vovik," gained employment with the official
Soviet foreign trade bank, something that would be in sync with the aristocracy's traditional service
occupations. Ibid., 274. Young women also served as au pairs or privately taught French to children
of "Nepmen" families. Ibid., 330, 352.

TABLE 6.1 *Cooperative movement and imperial legacies (oblast-level), OLS*

Dep. var:	Nr coop	Coop empl.	Nr coop	Coop empl.	Nr coop	Coop empl.	Nr coop	Coop empl.	Nr coop	Coop empl.	Nr coop	Coop empl.	Nr coop	Coop empl.
Literacy rate	58.177* (33.894)	1.924* (1.109)												
Meshchane			138.760** (64.365)	4.433** (1.943)										
Merchants					3,050** (1,368)	104.2** (43.99)								
Merchants and meshchane							136.7** (62.97)	4.386** (1.916)						
Nobles									392.8** (180.7)	13.07** (6.037)				
Clergy											−1,917*** (464.6)	−61.37*** (14.91)		
Educated estates													111.3** (49.53)	3.602** (1.551)
Income per capita (1990)	7,608.591 (7,982.254)	286.026 (271.153)	6,516.569 (7,290.112)	249.239 (250.542)	5,288 (5,678)	208.6 (195.8)	6,480 (7,186)	248.1 (247.0)	7,704 (7,726)	289.6 (265.4)	11,624 (8,933)	412.8 (307.7)	6,550 (7,163)	250.6 (246.1)
Urbanization (1990)	30.111 (25.358)	1.250* (0.669)	45.899** (21.798)	1.791*** (0.575)	32.00 (21.19)	1.279** (0.556)	44.77** (21.67)	1.753*** (0.568)	38.50* (20.94)	1.522** (0.561)	74.58*** (22.53)	2.708*** (0.663)	40.55* (22.03)	1.611*** (0.571)
Distance from Moscow	−98.933	−4.545	−98.126	−4.588	−72.82	−3.586	−95.12	−4.483	−154.4	−6.377	−299.2*	−11.02**	−97.49	−4.542

(continued)

TABLE 6.1 *(continued)*

Dep. var:	Nr coop	Coop empl.	Nr coop	Coop empl.	Nr coop	Coop empl.	Nr coop	Coop empl.	Nr coop	Coop empl.	Nr coop	Coop empl.	Nr coop	Coop empl.
	(104.485)	(3.419)	(113.398)	(3.649)	(87.37)	(2.564)	(110.9)	(3.553)	(122.7)	(4.038)	(156.8)	(5.237)	(108.0)	(3.468)
Constant	-2,954.536	-133.174**	-3,696.665	-157.514**	-2,296	-110.0**	-3,639	-155.7**	-2,793	-127.7**	-4,018	-167.8**	-3,382	-147.4**
	(2,141.369)	(65.052)	(2,244.455)	(70.821)	(1,584)	(43.38)	(2,204)	(69.30)	(2,042)	(62.15)	(2,430)	(77.23)	(2,138)	(66.40)
R^2	0.28	0.37	0.33	0.41	0.377	0.475	0.337	0.416	0.312	0.398	0.349	0.427	0.334	0.414
N	70	70	70	70	70	70	70	70	70	70	70	70	70	70

Note. * $p<0.1$; ** $p<0.05$; *** $p<0.01$. Robust standard errors in parentheses.
Source. Lankina and Libman, "Two-Pronged Middle Class." Here and in Table 6.2 analysis reproduced and expanded with permission of coauthor.

tsarist Russia, the clergy exhibits a negative relationship with both the number of cooperatives and employees. Again, given the clergy's relative share, their overall impact on the outcome variable is smaller when compared to the *meshchane*. Nevertheless, the interpretation of the sign still holds.

Next, to estimate the *meshchane*'s effect on post-communist entrepreneurship, we first examine actual small and medium-sized enterprise (SME) activity employing data for 2012: the number of small enterprises, employment, and business turnover. Because Russian data on SMEs are notoriously noisy, we deploy a complementary indicator from the 2012 survey by the Public Opinion Foundation (*Fond obshchestvennogo mneniya*, FOM), Russia's well-respected polling agency. The survey covered most regions and included, among other items, a question about respondents' willingness to run their own business. Because region-representative samples were employed, it is suitable for our analysis. Table 6.2 reports the results for the *meshchane* and literacy legacies and private business activity. We control for variables conventionally used to capture Russia's regional development: income per capita, urbanization, and resource extraction share. The share of ethnic

TABLE 6.2 *Entrepreneurship and imperial legacies (oblast-level), OLS*

Dep. var.:	Able to run one's own business, 2012	Number of SMEs, 2012	SME employment, 2012	SME turnover, 2012	Private sector employment share, 2012
Meshchane	0.257**	2.762**	11.582**	36.207**	0.245*
	(0.099)	(1.130)	(4.606)	(15.163)	(0.135)
Merchants	4.655*	68.24***	289.2**	997.2**	2.865
	(2.356)	(23.20)	(110.5)	(401.6)	(2.774)
Merchants and *meshchane*	0.249**	2.723**	11.42**	35.93**	0.234*
	(0.0961)	(1.102)	(4.530)	(15.04)	(0.129)
Nobles	0.343	12.05***	37.87***	107.3**	0.713
	(0.306)	(3.545)	(13.05)	(48.88)	(0.452)
Clergy	−1.602	−38.38***	−167.6***	−400.2***	−5.516*
	(1.098)	(10.89)	(35.10)	(91.90)	(3.095)
Educated estates	0.191**	2.488**	9.676**	30.20**	0.187*
	(0.0801)	(0.976)	(3.706)	(12.54)	(0.107)

Note. * $p<0.1$; ** $p<0.05$; *** $p<0.01$. Robust standard errors in parentheses. Each educated estate represents the main regressor of a different specification. All specifications include controls for regional developmental variations. Replication codes in OA5 include full models.
Source. Analysis based on Lankina and Libman, "Two-Pronged Middle Class."

Russians, a variable that is used here as a proxy for cultural differences, is also added as well as a control variable of the distance between Moscow and the regional capitals, an indicator of remoteness from metropolitan developmental hubs.

The results are unambiguous. In regions with a history of a larger *meshchane* stratum, more citizens in 2012 responded positively to the question about their ability to run their own business. This effect is associated narrowly with the pre-communist urban estate; higher literacy does not produce similar effects. In other words, we are justified in conceptually distinguishing between the human capital legacy of the estates, which the Bolsheviks augmented, and market values, which they sought to suppress. Furthermore, the *meshchane* also covary with higher SME activity as recorded by Rosstat, the Russian Federal State Statistics Service, and captured in the number of small businesses, volume of employment, and business turnover.[16] Higher employment in the private sector in general, including with SMEs and larger companies, is, again, associated with the *meshchane* and not literacy. Merchants and nobles are also significant in all specifications. Again, we interpret these estates' relative impact on entrepreneurship with caution, considering their modest population share. Mirroring results for the cooperative movement, the clergy estate is negatively related to all forms of entrepreneurial activity.

TRANSNATIONAL TIES AND PUBLIC–PRIVATE SECTOR NETWORKS

In dissecting the causal mechanisms behind the statistical results, I am sensitive to social heterogeneity in market experiences. I also consider the institutional architecture of the Soviet state that structures possibilities, incentives, and constraints for the reproduction of market legacies during the period of consolidation of Bolshevik rule. I am also alert to the adaptive responses of merchant–*meshchane* families embedded in multiple social and institutional spaces, local, transregional, and transnational.

Theorizing Transnational Ties and Network Spaces

The museum society has already alerted us to the shadowy significance of the metropolitan contact as the "weak" tie facilitating survival of the individual – indeed, entire – "bourgeois" network of professional-enlightenment groups in the provinces. Commonly, however, the well-off regional merchant and *meshchanin* had been, or became, nested within an elaborate network of *transnational*, and not just cross-regional, ties. I draw on Peggy Levitt's

---

[16] See the Russian Federal State Statistics Service (Rostat) website: https://eng.rosstat.gov.ru/. Data on SMEs are available in the section "Maloye i sredneye predprinimatel'stvo v Rossii" ("Small and medium entrepreneurship in Russia"): https://rosstat.gov.ru/folder/210/document/13223 (accessed July 28, 2021).

conceptualization of the diasporic left-behind ties as engendering a transnational social field comprised of interlinked and interlocking spaces.[17] Several such spaces with distinct sets of consequences for the "staying" communities may be discerned. One is the universe of émigrés themselves, the "leaving" groups. They are embedded in multinational diasporic communities that are far from being atomized. These feature not only the kinds of support structures that aid material survival of the left-behind but also the nontangible impulse encapsulated best in the concept of honor. The latter is a reputational dimension intrinsic to sitedness in a network where your actions are known to others. The second set of spaces comprises the regional institutional structures of the totalizing state sandwiched between metropolitan coercive and bureaucratic principal figures and the local society and, as such, potentially espousing distinct nativist preferences. The third terrain is populated by the left-behind who navigate, hedge, and juggle a plurality of institutional-social network arenas in ways that exhibit intrafamilial role division and multiplexity. As will become clear, the latter set of processes unfolding within the narrow fields of local professional, educational, familial networks are nevertheless also shaped by the transnational spaces and ties.

The position occupied in the imperial estate structure is consequential for these spaces and their interactionist dynamics in multiple ways. One straightforward factor is the material stature of both the "sending" and the "remaining" communities. Those who managed to leave Russia in the 1920s were overwhelmingly of noble, merchant, and other wealthy backgrounds, not only because of their ideological distaste for Bolshevism or persecution but because they could afford to do so. Émigrés, like migrants today, also tended to quickly set up tightly knit communities. Whether in Harbin, Paris, or Los Angeles, these retained a pronounced estatist profile. Another, not inconsequential, dimension of the estates is human capital, which, as we know, was distributed inequitably within the imperial estate structure. It too heterogeneously affected one's immediate social, and material, position at the point of destination. Human capital also features here as awareness, experience, and knowledge of the institutions, spaces, and practices of banking, commerce, and finance. Remittances derived from positioning in the émigré field shape not only the material but also the professional-educational status of those on the receiving end, since they enable hedging between the private and public sector in employment possibilities. Yet another dimension of transnational spaces is what Levitt loosely terms "social capital."[18] Images, records, and narrations of the world beyond not only animate mental "cartographies"[19] in *new* ways but consolidate the values of the *old* because emigrant nostalgia elicits affirmations of a semblance of a bygone life among those families left behind.[20]

---

[17] Levitt, *Transnational Villagers*, 9.   [18] Ibid., 241.   [19] Ibid., 11.
[20] Ibid., 241; and letters cited in this chapter.

These processes unfolded concurrently just as the Bolsheviks dropped the virtual iron curtain between the Soviet citizen and the outside world for all but a few. The kinds of messages transmitted – as well as the values that émigrés sought reassurance that those left behind still preserved – are best grasped from the perspective of their positioning within the socioeconomic structure of imperial Russia. Finally, the estate matters because the considerable multiplexity of life expectations had been in evidence in merchant–*meshchane* milieus but also among nobles, straddling the market and professional institutions of a knowledge economy. The Neklutin family, both in an intergenerational sense and within one cohort, encapsulates the stages of development of the middle classes in the West. These progressed from the artisan and free farmer during the early stages of capitalist development (seventeenth and eighteenth centuries); to the small shopkeeper, entrepreneurial businessman, and emergent urban professional during industrial capitalism (late nineteenth and early twentieth centuries); to a "new type of middle class" of "technocrats, professionals, managers, bureaucrats, and white-collar office workers" that have become numerically predominant since World War II.[21] The various generations of the Neklutin clan and individuals *within* one temporal snapshot of the late nineteenth and early twentieth centuries straddled the proto-middle class, the industrial magnate elite, and professionals in a modern sense. Furthermore, the spatial permutations of the merchant–*meshchane* extended family, as reflected in occupational positional shifts in the "sending" country (Russia) and the "receiving" country (America), likewise speak to this broad conception of the middle class having its genesis among the trading, artisanal, and farming milieus of Russia's relatively free estates. This perspective, of course, further defies explanations of social outcomes and preferences couched in terms of positioning in the class structure in a Marxist sense.

Émigré Networks and Honor

The Neklutin-Shikhobalov family shared the tragic fate of the high-profile aristocracy and merchants hitherto occupying core positions in structures of urban governance, civic life, industry, and commerce. Constantine scrambled to assemble a coalition of the like-minded within the city *duma*, in vain looking to restore urban governance before the Bolsheviks forcibly evicted councilors from the city hall. Along with other male members of the extended clan, he fled to Siberia, becoming an important figure in the anti-Bolshevik operations headed by Admiral A. V. Kolchak. Eventually, as hopes faded of a restoration of the Provisional Government, Constantine, now a father, took his wife Pelageia and

---

[21] Discussed in Chen, *Middle Class*, 55. By contrast, in China "free farmers or merchant farmers never became an important part of the new middle class." Ibid., 55. Russia also lagged behind Western Europe, but the Neklutin archive corroborates the genesis of the free farmer turned entrepreneur turned professional from among the eighteenth-century's Old Believer agriculturalists.

FIGURE 6.1 Constantine, Pelageia (Polia), and Vadim Neklutin
Photos taken in Harbin for visas to the United States. Annotations from C. N. below.
NC, f. 38, 005

infant son Dima (Vadim) to the Chinese city of Harbin where they temporarily decamped before setting sail for America's West Coast. (See Figure 6.1 for photos of the Neklutin family before their departure for America.)[22] This is, however, as much a story of decimation as of the consolidation of ties to loved ones left behind – some thirty extended family members[23] – and to new fellow émigrés from among the decimated Whites.[24] Constantine's carefully preserved correspondence with a network of relatives, friends, and business partners allows us to discern a web of reciprocal obligations to Russia-based relatives and

---

[22] "My Mother," short version, 49–55; 57–64.   [23] Close family are listed in ibid., 61–63.
[24] I analyzed hundreds of pages of the Neklutin archive extending into the 1970s. Around the 1950s, correspondence with relatives in Russia dries up, but we have records concerning networks of families, friends, and associates from the Samara years who established new lives in the United States. We may also discern the influence of Constantine on the mores of the next two generations of Americans. These questions are beyond the scope of this study.

acquaintances, which I conceptualize, drawing on Weber's notion of group-specific "conventions,"[25] as *honor networks*.[26] These networks were instrumental in pooling together resources and coordinating sophisticated financial operations across four continents.

The voluminous correspondence between Neklutin and the engineer Strol'man allows us to begin to discern commitments, obligations, and the honorable discharge thereof. Before the Revolution, Sergey Alekseyevich Strol'man (b. 1854) had been a well-known mining engineer.[27] His daughter Ol'ga Sergeyevna married General Vladimir Oskarovich Kappel, feted as a hero among White forces fighting the Bolsheviks in Siberia. Ol'ga Sergeyevna was a distant relative of Neklutin. After the Bolsheviks took Ol'ga Sergeyevna hostage, she separated from the general – he was eventually captured and executed by the Red forces – to save her children Tanya and Kirill, changed her name back to Strol'man, and moved in with her parents. In September 1921, the family temporarily settled in the town of Motovilikha in Perm, where the elderly Strol'man, his wife, and the two grandchildren shared a tiny flat.

Neklutin arranged to pool Kappel's assets and the donations that the White forces and would-be émigrés assembled as aid for his widow and children. He relied on his business acumen to convert the funds first into a high-interest account in Japanese yen and then into US dollars. Neklutin kept the money in a trust for Kappel's family and paced the transfers to Russia until the account dried up in 1926. A letter from Peking, dated December 12, 1922, to C. N. Neklutin from his brother-in-law V. Vyrypayev alludes to the background for financial aid to the family:

I confirm receipt of Your respected letter from 6 Dec. of this year in which You write that 1680 gold rubles belonging to the family of Gen. Kappel You sold for yen, which You placed in a current account with a 5 and a half % annual interest, etc.. I from my end can only welcome this rational solution and as a friend of the deceased Vladimir Oskarovich, thank You for looking after his family... I remain respectfully Yours, V. Vyrypayev.[28]

From another letter, we learn that the 1,680 gold rubles had been collected "as donations to the benefit of the family of the deceased General Kappel," "which we request you [Neklutin] to dispense, following our conversation, as

---

[25] Weber, "Class, Status and Party," 26.

[26] Golitsyn's memoirs are an encyclopedic repository of facts concerning émigré and left-behind ties and practices. Many aristocrats emigrated; some married US relief and other aid workers and moved abroad; and letters, remittances, and packages to Russia flowed until at least the 1940s. After Stalin's death and during the Thaw and after, professionals could visit their relatives abroad, in Paris and other places. Golitsyn, *Zapiski*, 268–70. Left-behind relatives also professionally benefited from information sent by émigré relations – Golitsyn's father asked his brother, a US émigré, to send him financial magazines, which he used to write articles on foreign finances for the Soviet newspaper *Finansovaya gazeta*. Ibid., 302. When the *gazeta* was closed, Golitsyn gained employment with *Vsemirnyy sledopyt* (global trekker) and so he then requested and received copies of *Geographical Magazine* from America. Ibid., 332.

[27] For a biography, see Gagkuyev, *Kappel' i kappelevtsy*.   [28] December 12, 1922, NC, f. 19.

you see best, when possible to send or hand them in to the beneficiary. A list of benefactors is being sent in addition."[29] A letter sent from Mr. Vyrypayev from Queensland in Australia, where the Vyrypayevs emigrated, details the financial transaction further:

I send my gratitude for Your letter about the move to America and the money of the late V. O. Keppel. Your conversion of this money into American dollars and the opening of an account in Your name in an American bank, I can only welcome ... I am convinced that the moneys under Your care are kept in conditions of the greatest and quickest readiness to arrive, if need be, to the destination, irrespective of where You happen to be.[30]

Finally, a note accompanying Constantine's papers with the letters to Strol'man reads:

gold rubles in the amount of 1500 were collected in Harbin, I converted that into yens at high price and accumulated interest from the bank; eventually I converted the money into $900 when we left Harbin. I found address of Strolman in Sept. 1923 and I was sending money while we were in Seattle 1923-1926 and the last money was sent from Ferguson, Mo.[31]

The Neklutin–Strol'man correspondence speaks to the status group's honor support network, linking émigrés in Australia, the United States, and Harbin in China. As is evident from a close reading of the frequent and energetic exchange of letters between the two families, Strol'man became something of a nuisance. At one point, his reproach to Neklutin about delay in dispatching funds is rebuffed with a discreet reminder that Constantine is performing a favor to the Strol'man family and is doing so honorably and dutifully.[32] Strol'man's desperation, of course, stemmed from the family's horrific material privations in Soviet Russia, which he describes in great detail to encourage Neklutin to dispatch the funds as expeditiously as

[29] Letter from Tientsin, January 12, 1921, countersigned by "Neklutiny." NC, f. 19.
[30] August 28, 1923, NC, f. 19.
[31] In another, handwritten, note, Neklutin mentions 1,650 rubles converted into more than $900. "I was able to locate the family only in Oct 1923, after 2 year search, so the contact was established only after my arrival to U.S.A. on Nov 2, 1923. All money was sent to the family; it was done gradually, because the delivery of money was not certain." NC, f. 19. In 1925, $900 amounted to a present-day buying power of $12,978, as of May 3, 2020. See the online Historical Currency Conversions tool: futureboy.us/fsp/dollar.fsp?quantity=900&currency=dollars&fromYear=1925.
    The Soviet exchange rate was extortionate, however. In one Vneshtorgbank (foreign trade bank) bank postal record dated November 9, 1925, a $200 transfer from Neklutin is "estimated" (*otseneno*) as 200 rubles. NC, f. 19.
[32] Strol'man alludes to Neklutin's correspondence on this matter in a letter dated September 23, 1925: "I regret greatly that you apparently took so much to heart my requests to you concerning the transfer that I mentioned. I was far from the thought of any reproaches concerning the timing of the dispatch of transfers, but only, being concerned about our resources, wanted to notify You about our wishes concerning the timing of receipt. I could not express anything but gratitude for Your efforts and care about our family." NC, f. 17.

possible: lack of shoes or school accessories for the children; food barely enough to survive; his status as an "invalid" (*kaleka*),[33] dismissed from one job only to obtain another, an equally precarious one, and then to lose it again, because of his bourgeois origins.[34]

Strol'man had, of course, been aware that émigrés pooled funds to support the family of the executed and feted White Army general. Neklutin himself took on the obligation to keep these funds in a trust and disburse them in instalments. He could have eschewed taking on the multiple complicated sets of banking transactions – his own situation as a recent émigré supporting a family in America itself very fragile – or he could have simply disappeared with the funds. Again, these would have come in handy as he settled his family in America; but let us not forget that Neklutin, a man of the utmost integrity, had himself been embedded in a dense transnational network of émigrés, family members, fellow Whites, and acquaintances from his days as a merchant entrepreneur in Samara. The scores of letters dispatched between Seattle, Ferguson (Missouri), Paris, Budapest, Sydney, and Harbin in the 1920s, and until his death in the early 1970s, testify to this embeddedness. His honorable obligations toward those left behind did not cease with the revolutionary juncture and the severance of other ties. The businesslike transactional nature of the Neklutin–Strol'man correspondence is evident given that, bar the cursory preliminaries about family affairs, as well as graphic descriptions of the family's privations, the sole purpose of exchange is about money: date of arrival, delays, shortages. Strol'man's family members generally did not bother to write to Neklutin, apart from the odd letter, a note from the grandson – "Kika Strol'man sends his best to uncle Kostya [*dyade Koste poklon ot Kiki Strol'man*]" – or a "greeting" from his wife and daughter.[35] Yet, for some three years, the correspondence ground on. These honor networks and obligations persisted vis-à-vis a family associated with a notorious anti-Red, old-regime general well into the first decade of Bolshevik rule. That they were not an isolated instance of sophisticated transnational banking operations in aid is clear from the exchanges with other family members through the 1920s and at least until the 1940s. Before I turn to those exchanges, some context is provided illuminating the institutional architecture making such transactions possible.

---

[33] Letter from Perm, September 23, 1925. NC, f. 17.
[34] Letters dated December 31, 1923; 30 (month unclear) 1924 (letters from Strol'man and his daughter); April 5, 1924; September 21, 1924; October 31, 1924; January 7, 1925 (letters from Strol'man and his daughter); February 15, 1925; March 4, 1925; April 14, 1925; April 27, 1925; July 11–13, 1925; July 24, 1925; September 23, 1925; October 14, 1925; December 21, 1925; December 25, 1925; April 5, 1926; October 15, 1926. NC, f. 17; and July 7, 1926. NC, f. 19.
[35] Letters dated December 31, 1923; and October 14, 1925. NC, f. 17.

Meso-level Institutional Spaces: Between Central State Apparatus and Local Society

The Neklutin–Strol'man correspondence revolves around monetary transactions between an individual enmeshed within a transnational network of émigrés and a citizen in Soviet Russia. How were transactions of this kind possible given the revolutionary regime's ideological hostility toward the remnants of the bourgeoisie whether abroad or at home? Furthermore, were they an isolated instance rather than a mass phenomenon? New archival materials allow us not only to put on the hat of the historian and shed some light on the question of intrinsic historical interest but to further extend our conceptual apparatus. The transnationalization of citizens' financial exposure in Soviet Russia features in an important monograph by Yelena Osokina, a Russian historian who, in the early 1990s, came across a large trove of "top secret" documents concerning the operation of a mysterious organization called Torgsin.[36] Torgsin emerged when Stalin's Russia was precipitously depleting the imperial gold fund and when import-driven industrialization dictated a desperate need for hard currency infusions. It is against this background that the Soviet state conspired to mop up the wealth of ordinary citizens, which was stashed in vaults or matrasses or treasured as the one remaining relic of the past – a wedding ring, a cross, a spoon from grandmother's kitchenware. The relics were to be exchanged for vouchers, enabling the purchase of anything from basic foodstuffs to luxury goods; and relatives abroad were encouraged to make currency transfers that could be converted into vouchers. The famine that raged in Russia in the early 1930s allowed the regime to exploit hunger and desperation to obtain precious metals. Torgsin shops opened doors even to peasants where they could exchange small items like coins for bread to avoid certain death. Volga Germans and Jews, whether moneyed or poor, also became target communities considering that many had relatives or concerned fellow co-ethnics and co-religionists abroad.

At its inception, however, Torgsin was designed to exploit the rich; and the treasures that it managed to harvest exceeded the Bolsheviks' wildest expectations. Before opening a shop, Torgsin would send dispatches to local secret police (OGPU) agents and other functionaries to scope the locale for "harvest potential." Emissaries were asked to target territories with "large industry and trade bourgeoisie, gentry estates, hereditary aristocracy, prominent bureaucracy and wealthy *meshchanstvo*, which had been the main holders of household gold, silver, precious gemstones, and so forth."[37] Those with weak evidence of pre-revolutionary wealth were to be avoided as potential Torgsin sites.[38] "Household gold and silver" were referred to as the "whims of

---

[36] Osokina, *Zoloto*, 11. The word is also used as an acronym with all letters capitalized. On how ordinary people experienced Torgsin, see Golitsyn, *Zapiski*, 464–66.
[37] Osokina, *Zoloto*, 57.　　[38] Ibid., 55.

meshchanstvo [*meshchanskiye prikhoti*]" of "old times, thanks to which people used to achieve the known position in the everyday life of times past"; and "in these, Soviet citizens have no need anymore, and their gold and silver items ought to be in a short period of time exchanged for better goods in the department store 'TORGSIN.'"[39]

Osokina was only able to source materials in the Moscow-based central archives and a handful of other regions.[40] Her injunction to researchers was to obtain access to regional archives, which she surmised would provide further details on Torgsin operations and would vary depending on the local bureaucratic-institutional and social peculiarities. I obtained Torgsin "top secret" files from the Samara archives, which corroborate Osokina's account but provide added utility in that they describe the region-specific social structure, bureaucratic infighting, graft, and inefficiencies, as well as the informal economy that sprang up around Torgsin in Samara. Official accounts specifically allude to merchant legacies, and the influx of *lishentsy* from Moscow and St. Petersburg, as corroborating the region's revenue-generating potential. "Considering the former trading-merchant significance of the City of Samara and some large *rayony* ... and the mass relocation from capital cities of former wealthy individuals," stated one letter, "there is a supposition that there should be precious gemstones in our region."[41]

The archival records invite a conceptual distinction between the central apparatus of the state and mid-tier, meso-level, subaltern institutions. The latter came to advocate their own turf interests and imperatives, also by virtue of being perched amidst the local social milieus, helping their agenda as advocates, as it were, for local society. Osokina's colorful biographies of Torgsin operatives paint backgrounds strongly suggestive of merchant–*meshchane* milieus that engender the qualities of financial savviness, perspicacity in navigating commerce and banking, and at times the ruthlessness required to mop up the remittances, gold, and assets of the remnants of the bourgeoise. The same qualities were, however, deployed in the arsenal of battles with the central state apparatus, whether in castigating the OGPU for engaging in surveillance of local citizens, and thereby discouraging them from trading in goods at Torgsin outlets, or in seeking to strike hard bargains furthering nativist advantages to the region. A state outfit, it also featured social imbrication: the infrastructure, the resources, and the time of the bona fide state agent charged with a nationally important task were used for personal gain, if not enrichment, while simultaneously furnishing useful services to the local public, be it in catering, transportation, or leisure.

Streams of bureaucratic correspondence allude to turf wars among OGPU, Torgsin, other "financial organs," and various service agencies. "From the very

---

[39] Advertisement for Torgsin store, cited in ibid., 62.
[40] Moscow, Leningrad, Smolensk *oblasti*, and Uzbekistan. Ibid., 576–77.
[41] Torgsin papers. Report on the bureau's activities for January to July 1933. TsGASO, f. 1078, op. 1, d. 31, l. 5.

first days of my work in Samara," complained an A. Merzoyev in a personal letter to the Torgsin chairman in Moscow, comrade Stashevskiy, "there has not been a single day when I did not encounter breaks [*tormozov*] in my work and unnecessary pressures, since up to now due to *reasons of a subjective character (peculiar solely to Samara)* certain comrades from various organizations do not carefully consider my requests."[42] Merzoyev continued, alluding to the regional aspect of turf wars and anecdotally reiterating Samara's image as a city of *meshchane*–merchant traders (*torgashi*) prone to striking hard bargains: "*I was directly asked the question: And what exactly, aside from rental payments, will TORGSIN give to the city?* My response was that Torgsin creates value for the whole of the Union, including for Samara."[43]

Torgsin's imperative was to justify its existence through replenishing the state gold fund and currency reserves. That of OGPU was to spy on and otherwise harass "bourgeois elements" who revealed their suspect origins and Western contacts on approaching Torgsin. In one account, a German resident, a certain Fast Yakov Abramovich, from the Mariental' village, reported witnessing the arrest of a recipient of 500 US dollars, inheritance from a deceased relative abroad. Torgsin then sent panicked accounts to Moscow complaining that funds had since dried up, as the German community had instructed their relatives in Europe to refrain from sending funds because the authorities would confiscate them anyway. A tailspin of mutual recriminations between Torgsin and OGPU ensued:

According to the report of citizen Fast it is evident that presently there is propaganda among the population such that they should write abroad and ask not to send from there transfers via Torgsin, for fear of being persecuted. From further conversations with comrade Fast it became clear that the individual arrested by the militia of Koshkinskiy *rayon* is citizen Rode Yulius Andreyevich …

Upon making inquiries it was ascertained that Citizen Rode on 14 October deposited to the account of Gosbank 30 US dollars for which he obtained from the Torgsin department store 91 kg of sugar for 45 r. 50 kopeks and for 12 r. 7 kopeks – 2 blankets, 5 kg of pepper, 4 kg of buckwheat, 100 grams of tea and 2 pieces of soap and 1 kg of caramel.

This same individual is arrested in Koshki by the militia organs, in which circumstances – we don't know.

After all this, the Torgsin operations sharply deteriorated, revenue [*vyruchka*] plummeted by 70%.[44]

Other agencies like the unspecified "financial organs" attempted to lay claim to the lucrative stream of resources going through Torgsin, in turn sabotaging the latter's operations. "There are instances," stated one report, "when the agents of financial organs are on duty by the doors of Torgsin department stores and monitor those bringing valuables and receiving goods, which they confiscate

---

[42] Torgsin papers. Secret correspondence, April 1933. TsGASO, f. 1078, op. 1, d. 6, ll. 8–9 (emphasis added).
[43] Ibid., ll. 8–9 (emphasis added).   [44] Torgsin papers. TsGASO, f. 1078, op. 1, d. 15, l. 75.

upon the customer exiting the shop premises."[45] The Samara Torgsin also complained to OGPU about "frequent instances of rail management agencies denying permits to passengers to transport goods purchased in the Torgsin stores. We inform you that the main clients of Torgsin are urban residents, as well as rural dwellers who come to the city to make essential purchases. Both sets of customers purchase goods in limited amounts which do not exceed the norm."[46]

Graft and corruption were widespread. Theft involving Torgsin employees, the strange disappearances of goods, as well as indeed of staff with goods, vouchers, and currency, and bribery were rampant:

The head of the manufactured goods sector of the Torgsin No. 1 shop steals goods, sells them and is a drunkard [*p'yanstvuyet*].[47]

Citizen Afanasyev P. G., VLKSM [Komsomol] member since 1927, b. in 1912, after completing the three-month training course for would-be Torgsin department store directors, having been appointed to the job, deserted it and disappeared in an unknown direction.[48]

Concerning the head of the store in Chapayevsk: ... undeserving of material trust.[49]

Yesterday, in a private conversation our main accountant Rappoport let it slip that we too had "blat" [use of connections for private gain], following the initiative of comrade Shatrov, deficit goods were processed without registering them [*bez buhgalterskogo oformleniya*].[50]

The Samara Torgsin files also explain how citizens engaged in what our statistical analysis captures as "speculation" and, generally, illegal entrepreneurship. The word features often and in fact pervades bureaucratic correspondence regarding the operation of this agency. Youth thugs were a perennial presence around Torgsin outlets, buying up currency and vouchers:

There are many speculators in the vicinity of Torgsin shops ... Among buyers [*perekupshchiki*] feature large numbers of adolescents of 15–18 years, who block entry to the shops [*ne dayut prokhoda v magazine*], contrive to wreak havoc ... [*zavodyat debosh*], the hooligans grab the briefcases and run off.[51]

[45] Torgsin papers. Secret correspondence, 1933. TsGASO, f. 1078, op. 1, d. 1, l. 79.
[46] Torgsin papers. Information about clients of Torgsin addressed to OGPU, secret. The letter ends with an intriguing note: "Needless to say, this consideration does not apply to certain individuals purchasing goods from us in excessive amounts." TsGASO, f. 1078, op. 1, d. 1, l. 3.
[47] Torgsin papers. Correspondence with organs of OGPU, militia, and procuracy. TsGASO, f. 1078, op. 1, d. 77, l. 48.
[48] Torgsin papers. File of secret correspondence for Buguruslan *uyezd*, 1933–34. TsGASO, f. 1078, op. 1, d. 29, l. 8.
[49] Torgsin papers. Correspondence with organs of OGPU, RKM (Raboche-krest'yanskaya militsiya, or Worker and Peasant Militia), and procuracy and judicial-investigative organs. TsGASO, f. 1078, op. 1, d. 4, l. 2.
[50] Torgsin papers. Secret correspondence, 1933. TsGASO, f. 1078, op. 1, d. 6, l. 69.
[51] Torgsin papers. Correspondence with organs of OGPU, militia, procuracy. TsGASO, f. 1078, op. 1, d. 77, l. 17.

Yet the sellers, also "speculators," were often those respectable ordinary citizens who had something to bring to or exchange with Torgsin. Given the highly unfavorable – indeed, extortionate – official exchange rates imposed on vouchers and purchases, many citizens opted to sell, obtain, and exchange on the black markets that sprang up around Torgsin. The Neklutin family, who received regular remittances from the United States, which I discuss in the section "Beneficiaries of Remittances: Family," may well have been among both Torgsin's "official" and black market customers.

The Samara Torgsin files also provide a flavor of the shadow economy of services that entrepreneurial natives joined with apparent impunity. Aside from consumer goods, Torgsin traded holiday vouchers (*putyovki*), although local officials lamented that nobody bothered to buy them. This is unsurprising considering the deprivation and day-to-day struggle for survival in a region that had just experienced famine.[52] One optimistic account noted that "with the objective of more expansive and better service provision to foreign tourists arriving on ships, the Middle Volga office has opened a store on the Samara embankment."[53] In another report, however, the "floating store" is reproached for feeding the monetary instincts of the employee, not the needs of Torgsin and the consumer: "The floating store – is not a prayer house! You need to expend all your energies and mobilize all forces of the entire collective, which costs us a lot of money, *but instead of that you were letting him on escapades to earn money on the side [zarabotki na storone] – boat trips for a fee for random citizens.*"[54]

Having sketched out the wider institutional architecture in ways that are sensitive to the preferential and behavioral ambivalences that stemmed from the *street-level* state functionary's positioning between the central bureaucratic apparatus and its coercive institutions on the one hand and local society on the other, I now explore the dynamics of the transnationalization of financial exposure from the point of view of those on the receiving end – the ideologically suspect merchant–*meshchane* families.

Beneficiaries of Remittances: Family

The eclectic archival papers are strongly suggestive of social heterogeneity in access to outside help, which begs the question of implications, material and

---

[52] The available goods speak to privations of the time, considering that citizens were willing to trade gold and hard currency for them: "flour, groats, bread, sugar, sausage and cured meats, butter, fish, conserves, vodka, confectionery, cooking oil, pasta, tea, [other] groceries, shoes, underwear [*bel'yo*], cloth." Torgsin papers. Syzran Torgsin store report. TsGASO, f. 1078, op. 2, d. 369, l. 8.

[53] Torgsin papers. Bureau report for January to July 1933. TsGASO, f. 1078, op. 1, d. 31, l. 61.

[54] Torgsin papers. Secret correspondence, 1933. TsGASO, f. 1078, op. 1, d. 6, l. 104 (emphasis added). Tourist "packaged" cruises on the Volga were already popular in the late 1800s. Sunderland, *Taming*, 197.

cognitive, for those blessed with it. The Neklutin papers go beyond enumerating the wealth left behind in Russia and the itemization and locational mapping of the various hiding places that concealed vast riches. They also point to the peculiarities of the transnational spaces that Constantine levitated over. Assimilation into the networks of the high-status, well-paid professional *receiving* society is consequential for both the material and the nontangible value transmission processes of those on the *sending* end. In Bolshevik Russia, it had the effect of compensating for the ideologically charged witch hunts that were leveled against those same merchant entrepreneur–*meshchane* families that the national state desperately sought to milk as gold reserves were drying up. These possibilities enabled material survival through the dark years that coincided with famine, civil strife, repression, and dislocation. The family letters also underline the significance of positioning in transnational status spaces for ideational and normative exchanges between the emigrant and family in the native land. Not only is Constantine himself held up as an exemplar of the successful engineering professional but his son Dima too is seen as akin to a Russian-born Horatio Alger–type character. Dima's studiousness, hard work, and pocket money (earned by delivering newspapers in the affluent neighborhood where the Neklutins decamped in their new country) are applauded by family in Russia.[55]

Within five years of emigrating to America, Neklutin rose from a junior position to Chief Engineer in charge of technological development with the Ferguson-based Universal Match Corporation (UMC).[56] Neklutin attributed his professional success to the ethics of industriousness, hard work, and achievement instilled by his mother, who also encouraged him to pursue modern education. "I immediately wrote my mother a letter (in care of Anna) and I claimed that my success in the new country was possible because I followed her advice about the attitude to duties."[57] Neklutin's fondness for his mother, who came from Samara's notable merchant family, the Shikhobalovs, is revealed in the many letters in which touching expressions of concern for her well-being, including material sustenance, were raised and offers of help repeatedly made and, at the other end, gratefully accepted. In turn, Anastasia became the key source of news about other relatives and for the diffusion of financial support to the neediest: the widow, the unemployed civil servant, the critically ill nephew.

After his promotion to Chief Engineer, Neklutin made regular cash transfers to Anastasia: "By the middle of 1926 [I] was able to send my mother $30 a month. That was sufficient for her to support Vladimir's [CN's brother]

---

[55] Latter dated February 7, 1929. NC, f. 166. Anastasia, Constantine's mother, thanks Dima for sending her cash. From Neklutin's notes we know that Dima earned money delivering newspapers.

[56] A successful company. "Universal Match Corp.," April 16, 1964, *New York Times*. Available online at: nytimes.com/1964/04/16/archives/universal-match-corp.html (accessed May 3, 2020).

[57] "My Mother," short version, 63.

family."[58] An electronic historical currency converter allows us to estimate the present-day monetary equivalent of remittances in the 1920s and 1930s. The sum of $30 equals $437.48,[59] an amount higher than the US dollar value of the standard state pension in Moscow in 2021. In the roughly five years from 1926 until his mother's death in 1930 at the age of eighty-five, Neklutin would have transferred the present-day equivalent of more than $26,250 in regular monthly payments only, aside from other cash and parcel injections to Anastasia and the other family members.[60] Excerpts from the letters cited in what follows include annotations from Constantine, elucidating how funds were channeled and diffused; the intermediaries and third-country "transit" options used; and the rough ruble value of the US dollar cash infusions at the time. Often, Neklutin avoided sending remittances via official Soviet channels due to extortionate fees and exchange rates, preferring to conceal cash in letters, referred to surreptitiously as "packages" or "presents." I preserve the style in Neklutin's translations of letters from Russian into English:

> My dear darling Kostya and Polia,
>   Many, many thanks to you for money sent to me for Christmas – I received 20 dollars; then through Sasha [CN's sister Alexandra Ermolaeff in Moscow who received money from the wife of a professor, to whose mother in Paris CN sent a monthly remittance of $30. CN] 60 roubles, which were brought [to Samara. CN] by Maria Stepanovna [Kiseleff, CN's niece – granddaughter of CN's father's sister]. More 60 roubles from you on January 23rd and 10 roubles from my darling grandson Dima, which were brought by Nastia [Anastasia, oldest daughter of CN's brother Vladimir]... My dear darling grandson Dima, many, many thanks for your present [money, CN]. I am glad and happy to have such grandson, – hardworking and who gives me, in my old age, a consolation by your care of me.[61]

---

58 He adds: "The soviets needed the influx of hard money, so there were no formal obstacles." "My Mother," short version, 63.

59 Online Historical Currency Conversions tool: futureboy.us/fsp/dollar.fsp?quantity=30&currency=dollars&fromYear=1926 (estimate made May 4, 2020).

60 By way of comparison, one of Golitsyn's émigré relatives dispatched monthly remittances of $10 from the United States to his father, Sergey's grandfather, Prince Vladimir Mikhaylovich Golitsyn, who moved with family to the Moscow region (Dmitrov). The money paid for grains and cooking oil "as well as the special [treats] for grandfather, the cookies and confectionery." Golitsyn, *Zapiski*, 558. One of Golitsyn's uncles, Vladimir Trubetskoy, secured low-paying employment as a piano player with a small-town cinema theatre in Sergiyev Posad and eventually with a better-paying restaurant orchestra. Vladimir's measly salary notwithstanding, he was able to enjoy a decent quality of life because of remittances from his sister Mariya Sergeyevna, the wife of a Polish magnate, and his brother Nikolay Sergeyevich, the world-renowned émigré linguist and academician employed with the Austrian Academy of Sciences. Ibid., 269, 302. Another relative, residing in a palazzo in Florence, on a monthly basis sent "to something like fifty relations various sums of money." Ibid., 281.

61 Letter, February 7, 1929. C. N. translation and annotations. NC, f. 166.

My dear and darling Kostya and Polia,
    Three packages through Sasha [CN's sister Alexandra Ermolaeff] were received, the last one on March 12th. Many, many thanks for not forgetting me. If it were not for the help from you, I would not know how I could live.[62]

That same letter dated March 19, 1929 alludes to the comparative value of the monetary infusions from America. A relation who moved to the vicinity of Moscow was earning 80 rubles in the first month of employment and the anticipation was that "in summer they will make more." "The main thing is, the life and the apartment are cheap: 7 pounds of milk 40 kopek, meat 20 kop. for .9 pounds, apartment 15 roubles per month." Neklutin's annotation to this passage reads:

Explanation: before I was sending $30 per month, but that was dangerous to send dollars to a private person; the wife of a professor at Moscow University was supporting her mother in Paris and it was dangerous, so I made an agreement with her – I met her at Danielsen's in St Louis – I will send her mother $30 and she will deliver 60 roubles to my sister Alexandra in Moscow. My mother refers to each payment as a 'package.' At that time $1 = 2 roubles.[63]

My dear, darling Kostya and Polia,
    On May 7th I received from you 58.24 roubles, many huge thanks ... we changed our apartment, the old one was damp and the owner was drunkard, he spent on alcohol everything he earned; we occupied 2 rooms for 15 roubles per month and even that was difficult to find on the city edge ... The last money from Sasha [C. N.'s sister Alexandra Ermolaeff in Moscow] I received on March 12th.[64]

A mechanic earned an official wage of 45–65 rubles per month in Samara roughly at the time of the letter.[65] Constantine's mother would be thus receiving at least the equivalent of a modest salary, from US sources alone. Furthermore, state wage reform in 1930 resulted in a reduction in incomes by one and a half to two times in real terms, even for the "vanguard" workers in heavy industry who received comparatively high salaries. Thus, the wage of a lathe operator in a mechanical shop would

---

[62] Letter, March 19, 1929; and C. N. annotations. NC, f. 166.   [63] Ibid.

[64] Letter, May 11, 1930; and C. N. annotations. Anastasia's letters are difficult to decipher due to a lack of punctuation and unclear handwriting. C. N.'s translation helps verify accuracy of my reading of the text. In a "Special remarks" note attached to the letter C. N. wrote: "She was born in 1845, there were no schools (Samara was a small town), so she took lessons at the church from a deacon, only for two months; that explain mistakes and the absence of punctuations." NC, f. 166. Original C. N. writing style preserved.

[65] Letter, August 23, 1930. NC, f. 166. In 1926, Sergei Golitsyn described as "solid income" the roughly 70 rubles per month he earned drawing maps for magazines in Moscow. Golitsyn, *Zapiski*, 345. Sergey's father in 1929 earned 200 rubles, a "solid amount by the standards of the time" as an economist for Gosplan (state planning committee), but the income had to be stretched to feed seven dependents. Ibid., 383.

be 48 rubles under the new system, instead of 100; foundry workers received 56 rubles instead of 90.[66]

Aside from cash infusions, Constantine and Polia sent frequent packages with goods to Russian friends and relatives, until at least the mid-1940s. The Soviet Union's wartime alliances with Western nations and the pre–Lend-Lease loans (1941) and Lend-Lease policies operating in 1941–45 opened up channels of aid and banking transactions, a lifeline for a government starved of cash and foreign reserves as war progressed.[67] Numerous packages were sent to Russian relatives using the services of a company called Union Tours (UT), located on 261 Fifth Avenue (between 28th and 29th Streets) in New York City:[68]

PROMPT DISPATCH AND DELIVERY GUARANTEED. You may now order CLOTHING, SHOES, UNDERWEAR and other goods to be shipped to any person in any part of the U.S.S.R.

Every shipment is made by us under a special import permit issued by the Soviet Authorities. Duty, customs charges and all shipping expenses are prepaid by us and *every shipment is received by the addressee free from any charges.*[69]

Another of the company's leaflets thus advertised its services:

Many people who are not in constant correspondence with their Russian relatives are not in a position to determine just what is best to send. We wish to give you the benefit of our experience *with many thousands of shipments.*[70]

In one letter dated April 15, 1940, a UT company official apologized to Mrs. P. P. Egorova for delays in the delivery of parcels:

---

[66] Osokina, *Our Daily Bread*, 46. [67] Munting, "Lend-Lease."
[68] NC, f. 227. Osokina describes UT, a joint US–Soviet Union venture, as dependent on the Soviet state and pursuing currency exchange and remittances for Torgsin from abroad. Osokina, *Zoloto*, 151, 437n633. The Soviet Union imposed a monopoly; only licensed companies were authorized to ship packages and remittances. Customs duties, postal dues, and other commissions were an important source of currency infusions. "Because of high customs dues, the general cost of packages exceeded by several times the cost of the goods contained within the packages." Ibid., 152. Many packages would have "contraband" currency inside, complicating assessment of the volume of de facto remittances to Soviet citizens. Ibid., 161. Osokina only estimates the volume for Torgsin operations, which initiated currency transfers in 1931. In September 1932, 700–800 transfers from abroad to citizens were made daily, via Torgsin only, with the bulk remitted from the United States. Ibid., 162. "The geography of transfers was determined not only by the geography of famine but to a large extent by emigration flows from Russia, for the money mostly came from relatives." Ibid., 163. Close to 47 million rubles were estimated to have been channeled to the Soviet Union via Torgsin alone. Torgsin ceased to exist in February 1936, while remittances continued to flow via Gosbank and Vneshtorgbank. Ibid., 165, 147. Before Torgsin, remittances approached the value of 30 million rubles in 1928 alone. Ibid., 147.
[69] NC, f. 227 (emphasis in original).
[70] The list included woolen cloth, buttons, coat lining, thread, socks, woolens for ladies' dresses, and the like. NC, f. 227 (emphasis added).

Dear Madam,

In reply to an inquiry received from Mr. Neklutin about the above mentioned order, we wish to advise that it was dispatched promptly and there is no doubt that it has already been received by your relative. Due to conditions in Europe, shipments can only be made in around-about [sic] way and it takes 3 to 4 months for a parcel to arrive in Sverdlovsk. We would suggest that you write to your relative by registered mail asking her to let you know whether or not she received this parcel. We are certain that she will reply that she received it some time ago. For your convenience, we enclose an envelope addressed for registered mail.[71]

The Amalgamated Bank of New York (ABNY) became a leading source of transactions – a bank founded by American trade unions and maintaining links with the Soviet government.[72] Bank-affiliated companies offered a range of stock or bespoke options for what might be sent in a package. Deliveries came with a guarantee and letters confirming receipt of a package suggest that most did make their way to the intended recipient. In one exchange of letters dated November 9, 1944 between Neklutin and an ABNY company official, who had been instructed to process the payment for a package to Mrs. Nasedkina (Bogoyavlenskaya),[73] careful consideration was given to the size of a clothing item – eventually gratefully

---

[71] NC, f. 227.

[72] On relations between US organized labor, notably the Amalgamated Clothing Workers of America (ACWA), and the Soviet Union in the 1920s, see Foner, *History*, 9, chap. 17, 311–22. The Russian-American Industrial Corporation (RAIC) emerged in 1922 after consultations between Lenin, Trotsky, and Kamenev, among other officials, and Sidney Hillman, ACWA President, for "assist[ing] in the economic reconstruction of Soviet Russia." Ibid., 311–12. Although RAIC only lasted until 1925, aside from acting as the Soviet Union's "purchasing agent" in America, it "was the means of opening a medium for transmitting millions of dollars from persons in the United States to their relatives and friends in the Soviet Union." Ibid., 321. The Amalgamated Trust and Savings Bank of Chicago, and ABNY, the two banks owned by ACWA, pioneered US dollar transfers to Russia. By 1925, these outfits processed more than 9 million US dollars destined for the Soviet Union. The ABNY boasted: "As a result of the money transactions thousands of persons who would almost certainly have starved for their want, were enabled to survive the critical period in Russia, and are now back on their feet and self-supporting." Ibid., 321–22. The original 1922 RAIC prospectus is available online at: archive .org/details/22RaicProspectus/page/n13/mode/2up; and en.wikipedia.org/wiki/Amtorg_Trading_ Corporation (accessed November 16, 2020).

[73] Sister of Viktor M. Nasedkin, accountant at Samara branch of the Russian State Bank and close friend of Neklutins, who joined Kappel's forces in Siberia. Nasedkin emigrated to St. Louis, United States, becoming treasurer to the Russian Club and eventually obtaining employment as an accountant at UMC. C. N. handwritten notes for his obituary dated September 17, 1936. NC, f. 226. C. N. became executor to Nasedkin's will and sent remittances from his inheritance to his sister, also an accountant, until the 1940s. Letters provide a window into day-to-day life in Stalin's Russia – from contemplating the services of private doctors and healers to treat Verochka, Nasedkina's daughter who had a serious neurodevelopmental condition (a hypnotist charging 500–700 rubles, letter dated February 19, 1937), to consumer goods scarcity ("here in the city there have been no stockings for sale whatsoever," letter dated February 21, 1937). Letters (sixteen) from Nasedkina to Polina Petrovna sent between 1936 and 1944. NC, f. 226.

received: "We are sorry that we cannot tell you the size of the shoes. However, we wish to state that in case the shoes which she will receive will not fit her, she may be able to exchange them for something else. Hoping to be of further service to you, we are, Yours very truly, Edward Cohen, Asst. Vice-President."[74]

On November 5, 1936, UT were instructed to dispatch a package to Sverdlovsk at a cost of $72.98 (present value of $1,345)[75] with the following items:

1	Lady's light coat, navy-blue
1	Lady's Dress, black
1	Lady's knitted suit, brown
1	Lady's Sweater jacket, navy-blue
3	pair Lady's Stockings
1	pair Lady's Woollen Stockings (2 kinds, black and tan)
1	Lady's Beret, white
1	pair Lady's Shoes, brown
1	piece Goods for Lady's Dress, blue
3	pounds of cocoa[76]

A package to the value of $20.86 postmarked April 17, 1937 to Bogoyavlenskaya lists:

1	pound of tea
2	pounds of cocoa
3	pounds of coffee
2	pounds of chocolate
3	pounds of spry
3	cans of condensed milk
3	pounds of salami[77]

On 7 October 1937, another package valued at $36.68 followed, this time containing:

Lady's Bloomers, 2 pairs
Lady's Stockings, 2 pairs
Lady's Patent Leather Pumps, 1 (length of the foot 9.5, Russian size 37)
Lady's Arctics, 1
Lady's Berets, 3

---

[74] NC, f. 227.

[75] NC, f. 227. Online Historical Currency Conversions tool used: futureboy.us/fsp/dollar.fsp?quantity=72.98&currency=dollars&fromYear=1936 (estimated May 4, 2020).

[76] NC, f. 227. One refugee interviewed for THPSSS commented thus on consumer goods scarcity: "I could buy a suit for 200 rubles, but it was poorly made and of very bad material ... So what I would do was to buy English or Japanese material and pay 1,600 rubles for a suit." Inkeles and Bauer, *Soviet Citizen*, 123.

[77] NC, f. 227.

Goods for Lady's dress (2 types)
Bath Towels, 2
Cocoa, 3 pounds[78]

A receipt dated October 13, 1938 confirmed the dispatch of a similar mix of food and clothing items to the total value of $112.08 to Bogoyavlenskaya. In the following year, a receipt dated November 30, 1939 enumerated items sent to the same recipient to the value of $60.84, including shipping charges, this time also including sheets, pillowcases, bath towels, a lady's handbag, manicure scissors, and, again, several pairs of stockings.[79]

Packages continued to flow to Russia as war raged in Europe:

We are pleased to advise that now you can make your own selection of some food products to be sent to your relatives and friends in Soviet Russia. Other American goods (woollens, shoes, etc.) are shipped by us from New York, but it is not possible to send American foods because of spoilage in transit which now takes twice as long. We, therefore, made arrangements for sending FOODS from Balkan countries ... DELIVERY IS GUARANTEED.[80]

A confirmation of receipt of one such package was sent to Mrs. P. P. Egorova on June 26, 1940. "We are pleased to inform you that merchandise shipment No. 76860 has been received by your relatives." On October 31, 1944, Edward Cohen of ABNY confirmed to Constantine:

We have arranged a list of six different kinds of packages which we can ship to the Soviet Union.

You can select any of the packages on the attached list, and send us the full amount of money, which we will forward to the "Peltours" (Palestinian Egypt Lloyd in Jerusalem), which organization will ship the parcel to your relatives. It usually takes between two to three months, depending on the location of the beneficiary. Our previous parcel transactions have proven to be quite satisfactory.

Three days later, on November 3, 1944, Neklutin replied:

GENTLEMEN: I enclose a check for $26 for parcel No. 1, described in your letter of Oct. 31 [fats, sugar, milk, soup, soap] ...

For the next parcel Mrs. Egorova would like to send No. 4 or No. 5 [food like milk, fats, soup, sugar and 1 pair of shoes or blanket], but all that she knows about the shoes for Mrs. Nasedkin is that her size is No. 37 (Russian).

Please advise if anybody in your organization knows the meaning of No. 37.[81]

Another outlet, the publication called *Novoye Russkoye Slovo* located on 243 West 56th Street, New York City, tailored advertisements specifically to Russian émigrés and their families. On one leaflet advertising "Three New Parcels from the Finest Products," including "Amourette" chocolate bars, honey, soap, California figs, toffees, and tea, with combinations of items ranging in price from $7.67 to $9.13, were listed. Destinations ranged from

[78] Ibid.   [79] Ibid.   [80] Ibid. (emphasis in original).   [81] Ibid.

Western Europe to European Russia to the Asiatic Soviet Union.[82] The availability of registered mail ensured that the most pressing requests were fulfilled quickly. A letter sent via the US postal service postmarked February 28, 1938 arrived on March 16, 1938. Banks and postal agencies found ways to ensure delivery, avoiding territories of military combat in Europe. On September 11, 1944, ABNY was instructed to send a remittance to the value of $18 to Nasedkina-Bogoyavlenskaia in Sverdlovsk, via Peltours, Teheran, Iran ("money for food package").[83] On October 11, 1946, the Manager of the Foreign Department of the Bank wrote:

> We recently wrote by airmail to Palestine Egypt Lloyd, requesting either beneficiary's signed receipt or refund of the amount involved. As soon as we are in possession of any news we shall not fail to notify you.
>
> We assure you in our pleasure in serving your interests.[84]

Let me now step back from the morass of transactions to discern patterns of conceptual interest to the analysis presented here. Together, records of remittances and packages indicate a *routinization of exposure* to assets, goods, and commodities potentially traded on the black market;[85] to the images, tastes, and smells of the extra-Soviet realm, out of the reach of most Soviet citizens; and to what may be termed structures of *market efficiency*, namely concern for consumer satisfaction, promptness in service, and so on. Communication was relatively fast and services expeditious; and the ties between the transnational spaces of the émigré high-status professional and Russian contacts extended to at least until the second half of the 1940s.[86] The speed of communication in turn allowed meaningful feedback loops, linking social demand and the supply side of at first the official – during the NEP – and then the shadow economy of Soviet Russia. The Neklutins knew their family's needs and could respond to demand promptly via the fast channels of

---

[82] Ibid.   [83] Ibid.

[84] NC. Packages were also sent to Iraida (Raia) Sebeko in Budapest in the 1940s and 1950s. NC, f. 227. Neklutin had seven siblings. Iraida was the daughter of Viktor, Constantine's brother, who maintained contact with her sister in Moscow as late as the 1970s. Some packages were possibly intended to make their way to other relations in Russia, via Sebeko, though there are no records in NC. Handwritten note, "Description of the presentation 3th, 4th, 5th, etc. generation of Neklutin family." NC. In another note, C. N. wrote: "All correspondence with Soviet Union stopped in 1935 and it was restored where [*sic*] Raia ... moved to Budapest, Hungary at about 1948." NC, f. 166.

[85] The contents match deficit goods in subsequent years. See Zakharova, "Soviet Fashion," 411–13. Some evidence underlines how remittances may affect political preferences, via the channel of economic satisfaction with political regimes, or increased autonomy and hence lower dependence on state power. See Tertytchnaya et al., "When the Money Stops"; Escribà-Folch et al., "Remittances."

[86] Citizens' faith in their system was shattered, amplifying anti-Soviet feelings, when they were exposed to superior consumer goods and lifestyles in Western Europe as soldiers or refugees. See Inkeles and Bauer, *Soviet Citizen*, 277.

communication in the banking and postal and packaging services. Yet exposure to such transnational social, financial, and retail spaces not only enabled the reproduction of market legacies reflected in values, skills, and know-how but also facilitated a complex set of hedging strategies aimed at status retention, reacquisition, and restitution as Soviet Russia's *professionals* and not just *shadow entrepreneurs*.

Role Multiplexity in Familial Networks

I have already alluded to the positioning of notables in a plurality of institutional-network spaces corresponding to imperial Russia's distinct public and private domains. Merchants not only ran successful enterprises but engaged in city governance as mayors, aldermen, and part-time administrators. They also sat on boards of enlightenment, charitable, and other bodies of the *bien pensant* public sphere. The educational profile of the early twentieth-century merchant and well-off *meshchanka*, and certainly that of their children, who were groomed for the realities of twentieth-century Russia, also opened up avenues into the professions, as engineers, medics, economists, or pedagogues. Emigration and the emergence of a new set of transnational ties sustained and consolidated the possibilities of role multiplexity and hedging in a fluid and often ideologically hostile marketplace of occupational and income-generating options in Bolshevik Russia.[87] Both the external material and the less tangible ideational infusions facilitated the juggling of, and switching between, these multiple adaptations within and among families.

The Neklutin correspondence points to an insular and simultaneously extensive network of relations and ties in Samara City and in other regions in Siberia, the Caucasus, and Ukraine. Beyond a preoccupation with happenings within the multiple nuclear and extended families, we may discern intrafamilial diversity of ties to distinct arenas of public life in Bolshevik Russia. Within one family, role multiplexity was evident during the NEP when male, and some female, family members were preoccupied at first with salvaging, then restoring to prosperity, and then seeking to salvage again the remnants of the business empire until the NEP finally folded. Other family members, however, simultaneously not only engaged in service (*sluzhba*) but were obsessing about retaining or procuring a position within the public sector. This preoccupation may not be solely explained by shrunken possibilities in private enterprise. Rather, it represents an extension of the hedging strategies already in evidence before the Revolution – indeed, something that enabled Constantine himself, the successful merchant émigré, to reinvent himself as an engineering professional in America. Women specifically found the market for *sluzhba* positions less hostile because of their lack of a hands-on association with the

---

[87] Scholars have noted the significance of small "bosses" for middle-class development, even if they were subjected to "self-exploitation." Davis, *Discipline*, 229–31.

business; on account of changing their prominent merchant family name through marriage; or indeed by concealing the old one as had been the case with General Kappel's wife Ol'ga, Strol'man's daughter. Within the same family, one finds a husband or son struggling to salvage the family business only to then fall into precarity and unemployment and the wife or daughter becoming the "sole breadwinner" via a service job, however measly the pay.[88] We may regard the family in similar terms to the museum society – an inward-looking tight-knit network, but one whose reach and possibilities expanded via the association of the odd individual member with the pop-up or the organization man professional arenas. Simultaneously, the relegation of private enterprise into the shadows, once the NEP folded, enabled the preservation of the low-paid *service* tie while generating an undercover income that supported a dignified existence that service alone would not be able to procure. Here, women, not men, emerge as the weavers of the society of the shadow, small entrepreneur engaging in, by all accounts, the lucrative enterprise of sewing, embroidering, and mending.[89]

Hedging

The semantic nuances in references to occupations found in the Neklutin correspondence reflect the habituation, in equal measure, of distinct sets of possibilities for work trajectories and income generation. One term that disappeared from Soviet discourse and only reemerged as Gorbachev sanctioned private markets in the late 1980s is *delo*. In imperial Russia and in the Neklutin correspondence of the 1920s, *delo* refers to business and entrepreneurship. Family members continued to run, or aspired to run, their own business, *delo*. They rarely use the word in its broader meaning of occupation. The *delo* is a continued business pursuit, but more references are found to the word *sluzhba*, or service, after the NEP. Not to be confused with *rabota* (work) – which covers the entire spectrum of occupations and any effort, manual or nonmanual – *sluzhba* refers to the narrower realm of nonmanual work. The word faded away from Soviet occupational jargon but finds echoes in the semantics concerning nonmanual employees as *sluzhashchiye*. Not coincidentally, this became the Bolsheviks' own preferred designation of the stratum that did not fit within the Marxian class labels of proletariat and

---

[88] In the 1926 census, the "unemployed" and those in "other" occupations "apparently often engaged in commerce on a part-time basis." Many former merchants or smaller traders became peddlers, craftsmen, or artisans during the NEP. Altshuler, *Soviet Jewry*, 9. Altshuler discusses Soviet Jews, but the observations likely apply widely to the new private and informal economy.

[89] Amplifying the shadow(y) role of women, Cohen writes that, in the late 1960s to mid-1980s, in something "overlooked in most accounts, women formed the infrastructure of the Soviet dissident movement ... They typed the *samizdat*, organized its distribution, arranged havens for materials and people on the move, and tried to keep the men from drinking too much." Cohen, *The Victims*, 14.

peasants, as *sluzhashchiye* became a social "layer," *prosloyka*. Finally, the word "work," *rabota*, would be employed both in the generic sense of applying effort, manual or nonmanual, and, more frequently, as a reference to manual work of a non-service, non-*delo* kind. Constantine's relations fed their families by practicing *delo* during the NEP; many practiced, or desperately aspired to, *sluzhba*; and particularly during periods of the most severe discrimination and hardships, and only as a temporary resort, they pursued work, *rabota*, in construction. Occasionally, women's handwork also invited the usage of the word, though not when *teaching embroidery*, referred to as *sluzhba*. These excerpts illustrate the usage of *delo* with reference to family business pursuits:

The Bukhvalovs are now living very-very poorly, since all the brothers are unemployed. And the reason for this is that the new economic policy only gives way to cooperation and strangles private businessmen [*chastniki*], and they with Karasevs in the company with one other person (maybe you know, Chemodorov), possessed a mill (the former Karayev plant which they renovated) they spent a huge amount of money repairing it, though at first it worked very well, but in the summer it had been closed down [*yeyo prikokoshili*]. And so now they with the Karasevs are without business [*delo*].[90]

Lamenting the death of a breadwinner in a family, one relative wrote:

Though Kolya [son] is now 23, he still cannot lead the [family] business [*delo*] and Seryozha and Zachariy are still studying.[91]

On the other hand, a thread that also runs through the correspondence flowing between Russia and America is service, or *sluzhba*:

Vera still serves [*sluzhit*] ... Kazimirovich serves [*sluzhit*] in a laboratory ... Vanya serves [*sluzhit*], his wife serves [*sluzhit*] in Buzuluk ...[92]

Nastya is entering service [*sluzhit'*] in an *artel'*, as scientific worker.[93]

Kolia just entered service [*sluzhba*] and continues to study for the same specialty which the nephew of Polina Petrovna had [radio communications], as she often told me.[94]

Ivan with wife both serve [*sluzhat*], though do not help very much [relatives?] and find it in the order of things evidently.[95]

She has just entered the Literature and Art Faculty of Samara University and now comes across as a true philologist, such that I fear even speaking to her ... We both at present are studying, not serving [*ne sluzhim*]. Lyolya was studying last year too, and I was studying and serving [*sluzhila*]. Combining studies and *sluzhba* is frightfully difficult.[96]

[90] Letter, December 25, 1927. NC, f. 16_14; and C. N. annotations, NC, f. 166.
[91] Letter, February 9, 1927, NC, f. 16_16.
[92] Letter, February 7, 1929; and C. N. annotations. NC, f. 166.
[93] Letter, circa October 1930. In annotations, C. N. speculates that Nastya did manual work. NC, f. 166.
[94] Letter, June 1930; and C. N. annotations, NC, f. 166.
[95] Letter, August 23, 1930; and C. N. annotations. NC, f. 166.
[96] Letter, October 17, 1922. NC, f. 16_5.

P. F. serves [*sluzhit*], also Oleg [their son] and she herself serves [*sluzhit*] teaching embroidery [*rukodeliye*].[97]

The boys are all grown-up: 2 are serving [*sluzhat*], one is studying in the Agricultural Institute.[98]

In turn, a letter from a school-aged child to Constantin's son Dima (Vadim) – a cousin in America – conveys the semantic differences in usage of the words "work" (*rabota*) and "service" (*sluzhba*):

Write me how your studies go and what program [you are studying] is in your school. Already a year passed since I stopped my studies. I finished the school, but due to some circumstances [not allowed to enter university due to class origins] I cannot continue my studies. This summer I worked [*rabotal*] as a common worker [*chernorabochim*] on a construction site ... Anya [sister] finished an Arts School in Moscow and soon will enter service [*skoro ustroitsya na sluzhbu*].[99]

THE INDUSTRIOUS SOCIETY

The epistolary exchange paints in equal measure a portrait of the *temporal* succession of private enterprise, as well as public sector *sluzhba*, and intrafamilial differences in role sets within one temporal *sequence* or snapshot. In fact, intrafamilial role-set multiplexity became the norm, not the exception, something that is of consequence if we recall the significance of the "weak" tie to the Soviet state's public sector. Consider the following excerpt from a letter, where service coexists with enterprise within one family and where others take on commissions – sewing and embroidery – coinciding with the dismissal of the breadwinner from a service job:

The Bukhvalov girls – one is working as a doctor in Buzuluk, the other as a nurse here and 2 others are sewing and embroidering. Karasevs, as you know, 2 are married, and the 3rd is studying at the conservatory ... About your brother we know also only through hearsay, that he is dashing from one *delo* to the next; she [name not indicated] started to sew ... The Gagarinskiye lived fabulously. Anya and Zhenya are working as doctors, are earning well and with us little nobodies [*soshki*] of course do not want to have anything to do ... As they say now, Nikolay Mikh. has been made redundant, so he is also unemployed now.[100]

Our earlier exploration of the professional and educational-pedagogic realms provided some fuel to our sociological imagination concerning the adaptative possibilities for even the most hounded bourgeois. Rather than entering

---

[97] Letter, August 23, 1930; and C. N. annotations. NC, f. 166.
[98] Letter, December 25, 1927. NC, f. 16_14.
[99] Letter, February 18, 1930, from Nicholas, son of C. N.'s brother Vladimir; and C. N. annotations. NC, f. 166. C. N. translates passage on *sluzhba* as "soon will have some work."
[100] Letter, December 25, 1927. NC, f. 16_14.

a hornet's nest of ideologically hostile workers and peasants catapulted into the Soviet middle-classdom, the educated estates habituated the organization man, the pop-up, and even the museum society arenas that were saturated with homologous networks of pupils they had shared a desk with at the gymnasium, their former teachers, and the family doctor they knew from visitations to the home. The obsession with *sluzhba* reflected shared impulses within the merchant–*meshchane* communities – something that others of their ilk habituated and that others from their social network aspired to join.

The private entrepreneurship officially sanctioned during the NEP and that then became clandestine, however, constituted the shadow underbelly of a society anxious to keep up with the lifestyles, the aspirations, and the milestones of the past. Moreover, families were eager to sustain continuity in their careers when faced with job, university, and school dismissals due to their class origins. Consider the standard income of a Soviet citizen in a service occupation, one simultaneously paying fees for the coveted medical degree, the private school, or the home tutor. In the mid-to-late 1920s, the salary of an office worker with a large enterprise could reach 45–65 rubles per month. Although referenced in correspondence as a decent income, it often had to be stretched to feed and clothe several other able-bodied, as well as often ill, adults living under the same roof, often in one room, in addition to small children. Others reported a typical service income of as low as 20 rubles a month. Far more earnings could be made on the side, in the economy of production and trade. One of Constantine's in-laws, Marusya, contrasts "work" with "service" when she justifies taking on embroidery, providing not only income but autonomy after being dismissed from university on class grounds. "I am doing embroidery and needlework and consider this work [*rabota*] far more pleasant than some petty service [*sluzhbenki*] for which I would not get more than 20 rubles a month. And here I am free, do not depend on anyone and earn 3–4 times more.[101]

The discreet adaptations of the estates-derived bourgeoisie via practices of market production and exchange are best conceptualized as "industrious society." Jan de Vries thus accentuates cottage industry–type pursuits – many of them from the home and many involving women – as spurring wealth accumulation, market exchange, and ultimately the values characterizing the bourgeoise and the middle classes in Europe.[102] The "industrious society" encompassed vast swathes of *meshchane* – men and women habitually engaged in catering and dry cleaning, as well as rentiers, embroiderers, and seamstresses. In Soviet Russia, it encompassed merchant wives and daughters carrying skills hitherto used for domestic consumption but now deployed in the service of the post-revolutionary bourgeoisie's household economy. These abilities and habitual pursuits, combined with the infusion of remittances and modest luxuries from abroad, fueled the wider shadow economy, which helped

---

[101] Letter, November 9, 1925. NC, f. 16_7.   [102] de Vries, *Industrious Revolution*.

to not just sustain the material aspects of status but also indulge the fallen strata's estatist, *ständische Lage* sensibilities.

The genesis of the industrious society against the background of late imperial fluid estate structure could be pinned to the marriage between cottage industry skills – and mores of the rural world and the commercial possibilities – and the desires of urban society. The older generation in the Neklutin–Shikhobalov family illustrate this transient urban–rural state – the transition into an urban way of life in matters of aspiration and taste, as well as the commercial deployment of home skills and their transfer to the generation of post-revolutionary youth. Constantine wrote thus about the background and utility of his mother Anastasia's sewing skills as against a new preoccupation with the ability to keep up with urban fashions, as well as the grudging acceptance of the former peasant turned prosperous merchant Mathew Shikhobalov of his daughter's indulgences:

Almost every household employed a seamstress for sewing underwear and dresses and capable to knit stockings and socks and do artistic embroideries. Anastasia liked this type of work and became quite proficient in doing all kinds of needlework.

Mathew approved [of] his daughter's interest in this work because in villages this knowledge was important for women. Gradually he accepted frills and decorations on Anastasia's dresses. Probably the change in his attitude was caused by the dresses the neighborhood girls wore when they were visiting Anastasia.

In this part of Samara the houses were owned exclusively by "peasants of yesterday" who were prosperous owners of business enterprises such as retail stores, shops, butcheries and grain brokers ... They accepted the manners, dresses and customs of the city, including some traditions, as promenades on the main street during early afternoon on Sundays, though their youngsters did not mix with younger generations of the nobility.[103]

One of the first accessories to go when Anastasia turned fifteen was the peasant headkerchief. When Anastasia bought a straw hat decorated with flowers, her father's reaction was lukewarm at first but eventually accepting:

"Girl, what is on your head?"
With her breathing stopped she said "It is a hat, papa."
"Is it better than a headkerchief?"
"Yes, it protects my face from sunburn"
"That is reasonable" and after a few seconds,
"I like how it looks on you."[104]

When the seventeen-year-old Anastasia marries the up-and-coming merchant Nikolay Neklutin, he presents her with a "foot-operated Singer sewing machine which just appeared in Russia and a very elaborate sewing box. My mother was delighted and immediately started to learn how to operate the sewing machine."[105]

---

[103] "My Mother," short version, 5–6. Here and elsewhere, original style preserved.
[104] Ibid., 7.   [105] Ibid., 9.

Embroidery and tailoring run through the correspondence of the female sex as they describe adaptation during the first Soviet decade:

Does Kostya live in his mother's house? Yes, living poorly, Inna takes orders for embroidery.[106]

Lately, I had been taking tailoring and embroidery orders, I had lots of orders, so we lived quite well ...[107]

Oh, Polia, after all, you are good at handicraft [*rukodel'nitsa*], at least that is the impression I retained of you ... if you find a spare moment, could you please send me in an envelope some drawings of underwear or dresses or small items [*veshchits kakikh-nibud'*], I would be hugely, hugely grateful.[108]

Sergei is afraid of communist "clean up" [as a former businessman] ... Nastya works on embroideries, Kazimirovich [her husband] serves [*sluzhit*] ...[109]

I also work sewing undergarments for a shop ... The Karasevs were given back their mill and they work in the company of course otherwise they lived very poorly.[110]

Marika is now thankfully again studying works by day and in the evening rushes to the lectures it is hard but cannot do otherwise Lyolya also works, embroiders and sews hats. The archaeological courses she had to leave.[111]

Facilitating Role of Transnational Ties in Market Practices

Finally, I approach the question of the sustenance of market values from the perspective of the broader society of consumers in an economy of scarcity. The linkages between those embedded in the contrasting political, economic, and social spaces, sustained in letters, images, and representations, accentuated the material contrasts between the social spaces of the émigrés and of those left behind. These incentivize impulses to catch up, emulate, and stand out; these same impulses are attributed to fashion as an engine of market production.[112] Simultaneously, these connections of the few to external markets feed and fuel the demands of the many lacking such access. In letters to Constantine's wife Polia, references to hardships are interspersed with gossip about personal appearances, hairstyles, weight, clothes, and fashion – and even evidently a desire to look chic. Written during the NEP, these sentiments reflect relative market freedoms; yet, as the contents of packages for the 1930s and 1940s reveal, fashionable and luxury items continued to flow – these could be exchanged on the black market for other goods, serve as social status enhancers, or both:

---

[106] Letter, April 14, 1926. NC, f. 16_8; and Annotation. NC, f. 166.
[107] Annotation. NC, f. 166. Letter, April 14, 1926. NC, f. 16_8.
[108] Letter, April 14, 1926. NC, f. 16_8
[109] Letter, March 19, 1929; and C. N. annotations. NC, f. 166.
[110] Letter, date unclear, probably 1925–26. NC, f. 16_11.
[111] Letter, December 29, 1926. Punctuation as in letter. NC, f. 16_15.
[112] Bayly, *Birth*, 16, 52, 368.

PS: I wrote a lot, but missed the main things: Olga [Novokreshenoff, closest friend of Polia] does not look nice, with hair colored ginger [*ryzhiy*]; besides she uses cosmetics; but that is her business, evidently she likes that.[113]

As for Inna, I met her at some point on the street she has put on weight and is dressed well.[114]

The Gagarinskiye and living, evidently, well, even very well ... Anya has completed [university] – is looking proud, inaccessible, cold and *chic* (for the present time) woman.[115]

To provide some context to the material privations and possibilities, consider the reminiscences of American and European engineers, thousands of whom were invited to come to the Soviet Union to develop heavy industry in the 1930s. Writes one American witness: "Now it is really cold, but there are thousands of people in Stalingrad who do not have boots, not to mention warm coats. They dress in rags and are shabbier than anything one would see in a rag carnival." "Clothing worn by our Russian friends," comments another US observer, "was generally some odd combination of coats, vests, and trousers, so difficult it was to obtain a whole suit of clothes ... Anything we could offer them in the way of clothing was eagerly accepted and highly prized."[116] If we can speak of "fashion in Soviet society," well into the postwar decades, it remained an indulgence powerfully dependent on handwork; "moonlighting at home"; "acquiring clothes from speculators and black marketeers"; "private craftsmen" templates obtained from abroad; and the possession of the prized Singer sewing machine.[117]

The energetic bubble of the subterranean economy of supply and demand in fashion could be usefully combined with evidence from those likely on the receiving end of the supply chain. Zoya Kobozeva's family archive of middling *meshchane*, for instance, contains no evidence of exposure to the same kinds of transnational émigré spaces that structured privilege, material and symbolic, in Soviet Russia. Lower in wealth and status, their relatives would have also lacked the means to emigrate. We find, however, evidence of an obsessive preoccupation with the procurement and resale of fashion items on the black market. Itemized listings from the Neklutin packages allude to the possibility of continued home production, possibly for sale, of clothing. Constantine's Soviet contacts sought out fabric, buttons, and lining; and these are the items that may well have found their way into the wardrobes of *meshchane* writing letters in the early 1950s:

---

[113] Letter, August 23, 1930; and C. N. annotations. NC, f. 166.
[114] Letter, June 8, n. y. NC, f. 16. [115] Letter, November 8, 1925. NC, f. 16_7.
[116] Cited in Osokina, *Our Daily Bread*, 92.
[117] Zakharova, "Soviet Fashion," 409, 417, 419. The RSFSR Criminal Code Article 99 on "engagement in unlawful crafts" criminalized private, commercially motivated, garment making as an offense punishable by up to two years in jail. Ibid., 421. Given the scope of the shadow economy in garment making and state-inflicted consumer deficits, the deterrent effect is unclear.

My dear Kisa (Kitty)! ... Very pleased that you bought the coat and the berets for the aunts ... Not sure what to write about necklaces, *at the bazaar the gypsy women sell them* for 50 and 60 Rubles each ... How much did you end up paying for the coat? Does it have fur or not?[118]

Took out my dress and shoes from the pawn shop. Sold the shoes and bought a muff, and as for my dress, they [the shopkeepers] had worn it, stained it with red wine blot and generally left it tattered [*zataskali*], awful ...[119]

My dear baby chick [*tsyplyonok*]! Writing to you bathed in champagne vapers, toasting now to the car only a *moskvich* [simple brand] for now since the turn for *pobeda* [luxury brand] has not arrived yet ... Sold your skirt for 115 rubles 5 October 1954.[120]

CONCLUSION

This chapter has analyzed the legacies underpinning the market-supporting practices, behaviors, and values of Russia's estates-derived bourgeoisie. I first presented baseline evidence of covariation between the tsarist estates and entrepreneurial engagements and values long after the demise of the estate as an institution. The Neklutin archive then helped me tease out the complex causal mechanisms underpinning the statistical relationship between the urban trading estates and market values and practices. State policies aided the reproduction of entrepreneurial material and human capital during the NEP and after, as the Bolsheviks sought to replenish the gold fund and currency reserves. In so doing, however, they drew on the wealth generated via market experiences intrinsic to the structure of the estates. Furthermore, I distinguished between the apparatus of the central state – the principals – and the mid-tier agents on the ground – who exhibited characteristics of bureaucratic or turf autonomy, advocacy for the local society, and social imbrication.

During the NEP, merchants and *meshchane* were well-placed to seize opportunities to resume the operation of family businesses or start new ones. Extant know-how, infrastructure, and capital lubricated these processes. These strata also constituted the "industrious society" of producers of cottage industry goods for sale and exchange. Those with émigré relatives abroad became part of a global network of support structures navigating currencies, banking, and exchange rates. These complex and interconnected sets of processes sustained entrepreneurial human capital. They also generated wealth-supporting investments, easing hedging strategies and the embrace of schooling and the acquisition of paid-for education that enabled entry into high-status *sluzhba* jobs. Access to packages and remittances from abroad thus aided the formalization of Soviet public sector roles for those who had found themselves persecuted under Bolshevik authority. Such exposure also provided resources of

[118] Kobozeva, "Samarskaya meshchanka," 76 (emphasis added). Here and in subsequent citations, the punctuation follows that in the original.
[119] Ibid., 76.   [120] Ibid., 77.

monetary value, allowing people to feed and clothe the elderly, the disabled, the children, and the family members temporarily dismissed from their jobs. Statistical analysis suggests that, as the Soviet state made the first steps toward economic liberalization in the 1980s, familial legacies of entrepreneurship helped early market entry; and, after communism, these legacies likely expanded the range of choices available to citizens as they navigated the changing social, economic, and political contexts – as families, employees, and citizens.

The findings further enrich theoretical insights derived from the previous chapters' analysis of professional and educational adaptation. They bring to life the "tectonic" layers of skills, values, and occupational complexity of one family and within one snapshot of an epoch,[121] further interrogating simplistic Marxist understandings of class. Furthermore, they extend the utilitarian reach of extant endowments far beyond one national setting. The zigzags, reversals, and regress emanating from the wider political realm that may temporally dislodge the "bourgeois" from a solid occupation or effect temporary institutional change, familiar to us from the previous chapters, ultimately fail to shatter the structural core of society and the institutions that it sustains, in education or occupations. Like a magician drawing out objects from a top hat, the citizen fashions yet another response out of the toolbox of the endowments from the past – the banking skills, the tailoring trade, or the experiences of a profession. The empirical material alone opens up new avenues of research into communist societies, hitherto absent from recent analyses of what remittances and messages describing the worlds beyond can do to consolidate old, or impart new, values among those left behind.[122] Clearly, even at the height of Stalinist rule, Russia had been a densely globalized and transnationalized nation – one, however, where such exposure had been heavily shaped by path-dependencies in the social structure. It is now time to explore more fully how the legacies of the estate and social structure were sustained beyond the period of the 1920s and 1940s that supplies much of the material in the preceding chapters.

---

[121] Conrad, *What Is Global History?*, 142, 147.
[122] Tertytchnaya et al., "When the Money Stops"; Escribà-Folch et al., "Remittances"; Levitt, *Transnational Villagers*.

7

Family Matters: Looking Back – and Forward – in Time

Our past is unpredictable.

Boris Kozhin[1]

In the Soviet cinematic classic *Pokrovskiye vorota*,[2] we find a motley assemblage of Moscow's intelligentsia sharing a communal apartment (*kommunalka*).[3] The main protagonist is Kostik Ryumin, who, in the 1950s, moves with his aunt Alisa Vital'yevna to pursue postgraduate studies at the prestigious Moscow State University. The film's plot revolves around Kostik's daily encounters with the *kommunalka*'s other dwellers – a poet, a literary critic, a musician, and the professional engraver Savva Ignat'yevich, who is also a teacher at a technical school (*remeslennoye uchilishche*); and it is around Savva that much of the humor revolves. For Savva, as the film makes clear, is a common man. Savva shares not only the *kommunalka* but essentially his wife with the publicist Lev Yevgen'yevich – the epitome of a somewhat absent-minded, or high-minded, intellectual. While Savva solidly has his feet on the ground, Lev Yevgen'yevich levitates in a world of his own, of highbrow culture. Margarita Pavlovna, a scholar, while committed to Savva, does not let go of her husband of fifteen years, Lev Yevgen'yevich, since it is with him that she shares her tastes and outlook. In Savva, she finds the practical, of-this-worldliness, raw masculinity that is somewhat lacking in Lev Yevgen'yevich.

The Soviet project fails Margarita Pavlovna, for, despite the potent ideological pronouncements about the New Soviet Man, she must make do with two men – the man of the plow and the city *intelligent*. Margarita Pavlovna

---

[1] Interview, Samara, October 24, 2018.
[2] Film directed by Mikhail Kazakov based on a play by Leonid Zorin. For a discussion of the plot, see "Pokrovskiye vorota," vokrug.tv/product/show/pokrovskie_vorota/ (accessed May 6, 2020).
[3] On *komunalki*, see Pitelina, "Fenomen."

238

is keen to present Savva as inhabiting her own world – an artist and pedagogue. Yet the cultural snobs from her social circle inevitably rebuff these efforts. At a dinner party, where Savva makes his first public introductions to Margarita's friends, they mutter approvingly: "There is certainly something *authentic* [*podlinnoye*] about him." The subtle derision continues. In the face of Margarita Pavlovna's efforts to present Savva as an artist, he is ridiculed as an "engraver of names on the trophies of champions." The champions are, of course, those who have made it under the Soviet system versus those who have not – the Savvas, the purveyors of vocational professions, fresh into the city from the rural world whence the Soviet project catapulted them. Superficially, Savva's material world is not much different, as all the characters embody the spirit of egalitarianism, occupying as they do a communal flat. Yet Savva's shibboleths are but awkward attempts to polish and engrave a country bumpkin. Savva's answer to the intelligentsia's insertions of French idioms in their speech is to pepper his talk with the Germanisms (*natürlich, alles gemacht, jawohl!*) he picked up as a Soviet soldier in Berlin. The final act of ridicule against the Soviet mobility project is to dress Savva like the premier, Nikita Khrushchev, himself a man of the plow, sporting a panama hat and an embroidered peasant shirt underneath a jacket. Khrushchev's ascent to the pinnacle of Soviet power did not spare him from the derision of estatist society.

Like with any social satire, the film's effectiveness derives from its raw authenticity. The plot is based on the true story of Leonid Zorin, who, as a young student, moves to Moscow in 1948 and encounters a string of characters in his *kommunalka*. Says Zorin:

> *Pokrovskiye vorota* is that rare case when I wrote an entirely autobiographical plot … There is no difference between the young Leonid Zorin and Kostik Ryumin. I came to Moscow from Baku, rented a room on Petrovskiy Boulevard, and there I lived. I camouflaged Petrovskiy Boulevard with *Pokrovskiye vorota* because all protagonists were still alive, and, naturally, I felt a bit awkward.[4]

Soviet propaganda led us to believe that the Kostiks and the rest of the inhabitants of *Pokrovskiye vorota*'s *kommunalka* were the *new* soviet intelligentsia, fashioned all from the same fabric. Why, then, the wall of cognitive distinction between the different characters, if, as Sheila Fitzpatrick writes in her classic account of Soviet social mobility, "the mass promotion of former workers and peasants into the Soviet political and social elite" represented an important facet of "a successful social revolution," indeed, a "fulfilment of the promises of the revolution"?[5]

In its analysis, this chapter breaks with the typical detachment of chroniclers of Russian politics from the social wavelengths that in so many ways defy conventional periodization. These narratives, in Zygmunt Bauman's apt

---

[4] Author trans. "Pokrovskiye vorota," *Vokrug.kino*.   [5] Fitzpatrick, *Education*, 254.

characterization a product of the malaise of the modern epoch to inscribe, delineate, and classify,[6] negate the collective experience of the society that transcends, in a temporal sense, the neat "filing cabinet" of public policy.[7] Periodization atomizes the historical process, obscuring the connectedness of epochs at the level of society.[8] Sharp institutional, policy, or ideological breaks may not immediately penetrate the inner sanctum of the family and the day-to-day subtle mechanisms of value reproduction. Stalin may have proclaimed a classless society, and inconvenient memories were "frozen" out of discourse,[9] yet social distinctions continued to be cognitively programmed among future generations in families and in the realm of the professional, educational, and social institutions to which they were exposed.

One objection to the empirical material presented in Chapters 3–6 that I anticipate is that archival sources largely cover the pivotal juncture of state consolidation and, accordingly, societal adaptation in the 1920s and 1940s. To obtain a portrait of the legacy of the estate as transmitted within the familial-social realm, we need to establish a sense of the intergenerational continuity, or rupture where it occurs, encompassing the late Soviet and post-Soviet decades. In discussing familial channels of status transmission, sociologists employ the concept of *inheritance*.[10] Yet how social lethargy operates via this channel in societies that survive totalizing regimes remains under-researched. Indeed, the few relevant groundbreaking works on communist countries have focused on temporally short and mild forms of regime-attempted totalism.[11] Those interpretive accounts that have focused on cognitive adjustments to the Soviet

---

[6] Bauman, *Modernity*, 2.   [7] Ibid., 2.

[8] One study nicely summarizes the Soviet-era scholarly consensus on periodization. While in classic theorizing on generational change by Mannheim, "in the absence of major changes in the social or political environment, not every cohort emerges with a distinctive outlook; and even when one does, the exact boundaries between generations may still be difficult to identify without a well-defined theory," the Soviet experience is arguably different, for "in the Soviet case, political upheavals have been so pronounced that researchers are in substantial agreement on the basic cut points, diverging chiefly on the *number* of age groups they identify and the group with which they begin." Bahry, "Politics," 74 (emphasis in original). The study invoked is Mannheim, "Problem of Generations." In one essay, Fitzpatrick discusses generational and social aspects of the Thaw. Pre-revolutionary referents are conspicuously absent. Fitzpatrick, "Afterword." Another classic study reports: "To avoid doubts about the influence of prerevolutionary values and experience we have for the investigation of this topic constituted a special subsample which represents *postrevolutionary, purely Soviet conditions and values as fully as possible*, while still retaining a reasonable number of cases. In this analysis we therefore consider only those who were between twenty-one and forty in 1940. The oldest persons in this group were no more than seventeen years old at the time of the Revolution, and the youngest were born in 1919. This means that the majority grew up and were educated under Soviet conditions." Inkeles and Bauer, *Soviet Citizen*, 79 (emphasis added). Despite the methodological setup, the authors then go on precisely to find strong resilience in pre-revolutionary values, preferences, and even contours of the social structure.

[9] Assmann, "Memory," 210.   [10] Erikson and Goldthorpe, *Class Mobility*, 125–27.

[11] Wittenberg, *Crucibles*.

realm in the new subjectivity school among historians have approached this question from the perspective of the strivings to bring one's old cognitions into line with the demands, ideology, and expectations of the new, revolutionary, state.[12] In my account, by contrast, subjective orientations are analyzed from the perspective of being anchored in the institutional tapestry of possibilities originating in imperial Russia, be it in the professions, in education, or in the civic sphere. How, though, are these anchors transmitted from one generation to the next, from one that felt unsafe reminiscing about ancestry to one that had no experience of imperial Russia? How would the projected life trajectory cartographies of one era map, as it were, onto those of another one? What implications would these shifts, continuities, or ruptures in cognitive processes have for the long-term orientational dimension of social, educational, and occupational choices? Moreover, in what ways could this evidence help us anticipate value orientations that at the same time produce the germination of the openness, enlightenment, and civility of a cultivated society and those potentially containing the seeds of intolerance, social segregation, and distance?

The empirical materials – a large Russia-wide survey and, in Samara, interviews with members of the present-day middle class, essays by adolescents composed as part of a historical competition in the 2000s, and written memoirs and other documentary materials of older family members and ancestors – have been assembled and analyzed here with three objectives in mind. One is to address possible ecological fallacies in the district-level statistical analysis and to pinpoint more conclusively ancestral awareness and identity as linked to social status across three distinct regime types and orders. I begin by teasing this out with the help of micro-evidence from the survey. My second objective is to trace the intangible ways in which past social status and values associated with the estate profile of one's forefathers were transmitted via familial socialization. The communist regime claimed, as did scholars analyzing the social implications of communism, that a new society was fabricated and past distinctions obliterated;[13] or, as the historian Sergey Volkov surmised, the "intellectual layer" comprised of the former aristocracy and other educated members of imperial society had been largely "dissolved" in the socialist mass.[14] The Soviet educator N. I. Boldyrev pontificated, "we cannot allow the family to raise [children] as it pleases."[15] If we are able to trace elements of positional distinction to estatist features of the tsarist polis as reproduced within families, this would provide some evidence of social resilience and persistence. Third, I look for evidence of active construction of one's social and public identity, deploying signposts anchored in the imperial past. The factual artifact of the birth

[12] Hellbeck, *Revolution.*   [13] Voslensky, *Nomenklatura.*
[14] See the discussion in Volkov, "Intellektual'nyy sloy," n.p., chap. 4.
[15] Boldyrev, *Rol' shkoly*, 10. On Soviet family policy, see Inkeles and Bauer, *Soviet Citizen*, 189–93. "Our data strongly suggest," write the authors, "that most Soviet families were relatively unaffected in any direct way by the swing of Soviet family legislation." Ibid., 193.

certificate, the gymnasium diploma, the marriage record unearthed in the archives, or something as solid as the family home passed on from one generation to the next, provides some forensic clues. It then falls on the descendant, the "paleontologist," to construct a coherent body out of these "fragmentary fossil remains" – even if with a dose of imagination concerning the colors of the relic's metaphoric feathers.[16]

I am upfront about the methodological issues that plague this type of analysis. The representative survey commissioned by Russia's leading polling agency, Levada, provides an indication of the links between *self-reported* estate ancestry – and therefore to be interpreted with caution – and Soviet as well as post-Soviet educational and occupational trajectories. For the qualitative data-gathering part, interview respondents were identified through snowball sampling by well-connected members of Samara's middle class. The respondents representing the urban intelligentsia, professionals, thinkers, and creatives of twenty-first-century Samara – the jazz musician, the medic, the engineer, the teacher, the proprietor of a PR firm, the dynastic artist, the university professor, the museum curator, the archivist, the producer at a trendy news outlet, the student at a leading university – retrospectively reconstruct the social status of their pre-revolutionary ancestors: the forms, the permutations, or stabilities of their avatars in the post-revolutionary epoch. Selection bias is inherent in the approach to gathering evidence for the qualitative part of the study. To minimize skewing the interview sample toward those who are successful, but also claim ancestry among the educated estates, researchers selected respondents based on their generic present-day status as intelligentsia, not just ancestry.

By their very essence, post hoc reconstructions are often subjective, selective, and unreliable.[17] They, of course, do not provide us with rigorous and robust factual evidence of past status or watertight proof of the cognitional dimension of the reproduction of the estates-derived society. Yet, as becomes evident from the interview material, the qualitative analysis is a good fallback option, complementing survey data, given the many Stalin-era taboos on revealing family backgrounds. Some respondents simply recited tropes that their parents inscribed habitually on university or job applications – "peasant," "worker," "*sluzhashchiy*" – only to reveal aspects of a "bourgeois" background. The interviewee may report "peasant" ancestry, only to indulge in reminiscences about the discovery of a long-buried record of gymnasium instruction or urban *rentier*-type activities of their grandmother or great-aunt.

I partition the empirical journey as follows. First, I discuss theorizing on historical memory. This helps us distinguish between articulated injunctions and situational staging on the one hand and unarticulated silences on the other, as expressed in choices, symbols, or artifacts. The semiotics of quietude are, of course, prescient in a society of "the whisperers";[18] these, however, likewise in

---

[16] Discussion in Schacter, "Memory Distortion," 10.

[17] For a discussion, see ibid. as well as other chapters in this volume.   [18] Figes, *Whisperers*.

subtle ways, may provide an intergenerational orientational compass. Next, I present survey results, which corroborate not only hypothesized covariation between educated estate ancestry and white-collar occupations but, intriguingly, *awareness* of the placement of respondents' forbears in the imperial estate structure. In the remaining sections, I make sense of these patterns by discussing our protagonists' journey of ancestral reconstruction; tapping into reminiscences of private spaces and public-oriented practices within them; exploring familial injunctions and artifacts that create mental cartographies and ties structuring exclusion and belonging; and, finally, discerning the descendants' instrumentalizations of ancestry to actively delineate their place in society.

MEMORY AND THE DELINEATION OF SOCIAL SPACE

In generating theoretical expectations about the *inheritance* dimension of cognitive social mapping in settings with an experience of political-social totalism, I combine insights from theorizing into historical memory with Bourdieu's discernments of familial sources of "distinction."[19] Maurice Halbwachs, most strongly associated with the sociology of memory, postulated that all memory is collective.[20] From early childhood, we absorb the language, the images, and the smells derivative of our wider sets of relationships with others. Collective memory is also transgenerational: early on, we are exposed to communications from the witnesses to and participants in this world for many decades – our grandparents, great-aunts, the octogenarian "friend of the family," the nanny. Our indirect experience of past events therefore does not become ephemeral simply because we had not been privy to them.[21] Rather than focusing on historical events of national magnitude that often motivate studies of collective memory, I concentrate on memory construction as anchored in the household and broader social networks. In my analysis, central to the production of social place, the scripted and the unscripted, is the elderly witness to the pre-revolutionary past: the myopic grandmother; the bearer of the family "legend"; the portrait of the man (*dyad'ka*) on the wall. We would expect the "1910 generation," the last to have been born and to have experienced early adolescence before the Revolution, to retain vivid memories of the past and to idealize it. Studies in social psychology corroborate this proposition.[22] The exact

---

[19] Bourdieu, *Distinction*.   [20] Halbwachs, *On Collective Memory*.
[21] For "in the arrangements that we call social structure lie all the influences of the past." Abbott, *Time Matters*, 258.
[22] Tchuikina, *Dvoryanskaya pamyat'*, 11. I adapt the definition of generation as age cohorts "representing a group of people born at a similar time." "Cohort originates as a demographic term, referring to people born in the same year (or group of years) who then age together and experience specific transitions or societal changes (such as the Second World War) at approximately the same chronological age." Attias-Donfut and Arber, "Equity and Solidarity," 2. Here see also the discussion on alternative conceptualizations of generation.

age at which memory is at its most receptive, in what is known as the "reminiscence bump" of the 10–25 years age bracket,[23] is culturally specific of course.[24] The logic behind these general findings is that this is the age range when our identity, our sense of self, is being formed and our impressions, happenings, and achievements are most vivid; subsequent events are less intensely felt as life's key milestones are left behind and experiences become repetitive.[25] In musical tastes, the late teens and twenties are most "impressionable," for instance. In experimental studies, subjects in their seventies and eighties report as most "liked" music savored in their youth.[26] The 1910 generation's experiences are revelatory not only by virtue of capturing the pre-revolutionary period but because the impressionable peak coincides with the 1920s and early 1930s. The earlier chapters have highlighted significant continuity in the reproduction of networks and ties in this period dating back to the pre-revolutionary era. During such times of flux and forcible adjustments, the choices made, the new practices initiated, and the old ones adapted to suit new realities are crucial pivots in the cognitions of youngsters exposed to them. Moreover, they may have wider significance because they engender informal social institutions that become routinized and intergenerationally reproduced. It is this optic that I embrace, unlike much of the historical-sociological scholarship that has tended to underline the experiences of the 1920s and 1930s intrinsic to the Bolshevik project as constitutive of the mentalities of the generation.[27]

Recent experiments in social psychology also highlight a human propensity to share impressions, something essential for understanding how subsequent cohorts become aware of particular practices, values, and goalposts and may even internalize them.[28] Painful and traumatic memories are often suppressed. This has been documented in research into the memory of Soviet repressions

---

[23] Conway, "Inventory," 32–35.
[24] Depending on constructions of childhood in various societies. Ibid., 33.   [25] Ibid., 32–35.
[26] Schuman et al., "Generational Basis," 73.
[27] Thus, Bahry conceptualizes the generation born between 1910 and 1918 as the "purge generation" because members "entered the schools in time to face the more stringent and rigorous demands of the educational system during Stalin's 'Great Retreat' but began their careers too late to benefit from the political dislocations of the purges." The other generations are the "Brezhnev generation" born in 1900–9 that "benefitted from dizzying career mobility during the purges, often with formal but hardly rigorous schooling"; and those who came of age during World War II (born in 1919–25) and "experienced both the wartime sacrifices and the limited opportunities for education they caused." In other words, the referents for generational change are happenings in the Soviet period. Bahry, "Politics," 71. Zubok argues that "the unintended result of the Stalinist education system" was the creation of a new intelligentsia, "Zhivago's children" born in the 1930s and early 1940s, metaphorically picking up the baton from Yuri, the protagonist of Boris Pasternak's novel *Doctor Zhivago*, embodying the "old intelligentsia" in its death throes after Stalin's purges. Zubok, *Zhivago's Children*, 21. Zubok captures the break between old and new in discussing the fate of Tania, Yuri and Lara's only child, who, growing up among peasants, "has no opportunity to inherit the tradition of freethinking, spirituality, and creativity that her father embodied." Ibid., 17.
[28] Rimé and Christophe, "Emotional Episodes."

and of torture, disappearances, executions, and other traumas inflicted on citizens in other inquisitorial regimes.[29] Beyond extreme trauma, there is a considerable degree of intergenerational sharing of memories. Overhearing family talk is but one of the many transmission channels. Consider the admission of a descendant of the Golubkov-Volodkovich family of nobles and *meshchane* that "within the family" they "talked freely" about pre-revolutionary roots; "only about Vasiliy Ivanovich Golubkov [a repressed relative] they preferred to keep silent."[30] If we refocus the analytical lens on the *memory* of the loss, and the surviving fragments of bygone days that aid reconstruction of the submerged worlds, we can better illuminate the nuances of social reproduction among the fallen strata.

Status transmission is not merely reducible to an awareness of one's family's past standing, since it is effected through subtle exposure to referents that could be broadly subsumed under the rubric of cultural capital. In Bourdieu's analysis, even those exposed to similar levels of formal education in public schools exhibit variable cultural sensibilities derived from parental or other domestic inputs. Scholastic aspects of learning are distinguished from "unintentional,"[31] eclectic ones, nurturing tastes which then serve a classificatory role of "practical affirmation of an inevitable difference."[32] As with other matters of social distinction, these are expressed through juxtaposition and negation, "by the refusal of other tastes." "Aesthetic intolerance," writes Bourdieu, "can be terribly violent."[33] Social distinction is reaffirmed beyond immediate families through embeddedness in carefully maintained and cognitively, discursively, and, in a practice sense, reproduced social "fields."[34] Bourdieu's theorizing cries out, however, for refinements when applied to settings of severe conflict, extreme violence, terror, and attempted shattering of the entire society – a sharp contrast with the prime research sites producing material for his fecund writings.[35] It is one matter to discern how Republican France's *héritiers* sail into *les grandes écoles*,[36] because they have absorbed the educational, cultural, and social capital inherited and nurtured by their parents, themselves solidly anchored within a stable social field, and completely another to anticipate behaviors and responses within a terrorizing context where the regime's *raison d'être* is to dissolve the society of the past in the epic visions of the future. Further, we need more research into the interaction between experiences of repression,

---

[29] Cohen, *The Victims*; Figes, *Whisperers*.
[30] Interview, ZK, February 26, 2017. Golubkov's relative had been repressed in the context of the Prompartiya case (the so-called Industrial Party case against the technical intelligentsia) and died in exile. Golubkov, *Portfel'*, 49–50.
[31] Bourdieu, *Distinction*, 20.   [32] Ibid., 49.   [33] Ibid., 49.
[34] For key Bourdieusian concepts like field, habitus, and cultural capital, see Bourdieu and Passeron, *Reproduction in Education*; Bourdieu et al., *Bourdieu*; Bourdieu, *Language*; *Distinction*.
[35] The nexus between trauma and social preservation is, in Bourdieu's work on migrants and precarity, a different topic.
[36] Bourdieu et al., *Inheritors*.

position in a social hierarchy, and attitudinal consequences. Would the upper layers of estatist society exhibit greater or lesser conservationist impulses when targets of repression as compared to, say, the subjugated *kulak*, similarly pursued but embedded in a different social field? Would they atomize, dissolve, or reconfigure, and with what consequences for the values of the future generation? More broadly, does communist-style class-based repression solidify or shatter social bonds, values, and traditions? As I shall demonstrate, in a totalizing, leveling context incentivizing negation of distinction, particularly if it hazards exposing oneself as a bourgeois, familial nostalgia serves as a discreet conduit for the transmission of tastes – for even the bittersweet memory of the cultural object or pursuit cognitively imprints and delineates desirable "aesthetic positions" as against the "foil" to be derided and avoided.[37]

Although the instinctive element of memory construction in myriad ways shapes inputs into our sense of self, there is also the purposeful, instrumental, agential aspect of *active* fabrication of a social identity. The spontaneity of the confession of the grandmother about the gymnasium girl's attendance of the *realisty*'s balls in the boys' *uchilishche* across the road may be fruitfully contrasted with the manufacturing of situations, and private sites, in which cultural capital could be fashioned. I shall argue that such purposeful cognitive imprints are particularly important in situations of social flux, triggering impulses for status preservation when the group is under threat. An erudite uncle or aunt may be deliberately engaged in the generation of injunctions or role models for the nephew; and the gymnasium-trained grandmother assumes the role of cultivator, bearer as she is of the highbrow idiom of the estatist group. The exoticism of the glittering relative parachuted from Moscow or Leningrad into the provinces for a rare extended family gathering would linger far more in the memory of a child than would the nuclear family's day-to-day routines of meals, chats, and social pastimes. The status perception aspect of such apparitions within the group may endow the speech act, the articulated, and the unarticulated with an aura of significance, a desire to emulate, live up to, and impress.

STATISTICAL ANALYSIS

I begin the paleontological excurse by statistically ascertaining linkages between self-reported educated estates ancestry and professional placement based on earlier research with Alexander Libman and Katerina Tertytchnaya. The analysis is also sensitive to heterogeneity within this category: as I discussed in Chapter 2, estate ascription shaped the nuances of positioning within the imperial *Bürgertum*, much as it did the proclivities to opt for, or be hired into, specific institutions of the Soviet public sector. Table 7.1 reports the distribution of reporting of ancestry in the Levada survey. Because respondents were given the option of identifying multiple estate categories, the total does not add up to 100 percent.

---

[37] Bourdieu, *Distinction*, 50.

TABLE 7.1 *Distribution of respondents by social origin*

Nobility	8%
Merchants	6%
Clergy	2%
Meshchane	7%
Peasants	51%
Foreigners	1%
Cossack	7%
Other	3%
Does not know	23%
Refuse to respond	1%

Note. Survey fielded July 18–24, 2019, in 140 settlements of 51 regions based on probability sampling of adult population; sample size of 1,602 respondents aged 18 and older; representative by gender, age, education, region, and settlement size. Hard-to-reach and sparsely populated areas, small settlements with fewer than 50 people, active military servicemen, prisoners and detainees, residents in closed administrative entities, and the homeless, together comprising 0.8–1.5 percent of adult population, were excluded.
Source. Levada polling agency survey jointly commissioned by Katerina Tertytchnaya, Alexander Libman, and the author in 2019. Results summarized in Tomila Lankina, Alexander Libman, and Katerina Tertytchnaya. "Social Structure and Attitudes Towards Protest: Survey Evidence from Russia." Paper presented at the American Political Science Association Annual National Convention and Exhibition. Virtual Meeting, September 9–13, 2020, San Francisco (unpublished paper).

I do not have a demographic model estimating the probability of the population distribution of descendants that takes into account population changes, intermarriage, and mixed ancestry. Note also that the proportion of self-reported *meshchane* by origin is roughly equivalent to this estate's population in imperial Russia. At the same time, we observe a massively larger proportion of nobility and merchants. These high-status estates may well account for a degree of misreporting. The results, again, highlight that we ought to decipher the meaning of self-reported ancestry with caution and should draw our inferences based on consideration of the survey evidence together with findings from other materials.

Table 7.2 reports regressions including self-reported origin and Soviet social status. We regress the "educated estate" of (great-)grandparents on the human capital-intensive Soviet-period occupations of parents: civil servants (*gosudarstvennyye sluzhashchiye*); high human-capital occupations (teachers,

TABLE 7.2 *Self-reported ancestry and Soviet occupation of descendants, logit, survey evidence*

Dep. var.: Binary variable for ...	Civil servants	Civil servants	Intellectual occupations	Intellectual occupations	High-ranked officials	High-ranked officials
Meshchane	1.202***	1.266***	0.712**	0.792**	0.500	0.532
	(0.219)	(0.223)	(0.326)	(0.329)	(0.444)	(0.437)
Nobility		0.890***		0.968***		1.061***
		(0.224)		(0.300)		(0.355)
Merchants		0.898***		0.647*		0.622
		(0.258)		(0.360)		(0.424)
Clergy		0.062		1.102**		2.309***
		(0.415)		(0.465)		(0.400)
Foreigners				2.128***		1.350
				(0.764)		(0.989)
Constant	−2.003***	−2.175***	−2.842***	−3.093***	−3.381***	−3.746***
	(0.080)	(0.092)	(0.114)	(0.133)	(0.145)	(0.184)
N	1,602	1,593	1,602	1,602	1,602	1,602

Note. * $p<0.1$; ** $p<0.05$; *** $p<0.01$. Robust standard errors in parentheses. "Foreigners" dropped in one regression due to perfect prediction.
Source. Levada survey 2019, Lankina et al., "Social Structure."

doctors, engineers); and high-level state officials. We run two regressions in each case: one employing a binary variable for those with *meshchane* origin as the largest "educated" estate, hypothesized as constituting the backbone of the professional stratum and white-collar employees generally in Soviet Russia; and one with binary variables for the other educated estates. The residual category comprises peasants, Cossacks, and smaller estates. Self-reported descendants of the "educated estates" appear significantly more likely to report Soviet-period civil service or "intellectual" occupations, but there is no link between *meshchane* and merchant origin and high-level state positions. This is consistent with the argument advanced here, namely that the urban estates became the backbone of the professional middle class, a status distinct from positioning in the highest ranks of the state and party apparatuses. It also corroborates earlier accounts of heterogeneity among old-regime educated groups when it comes to their "appropriation" into the party-cadre trajectories of social status and mobility.[38]

[38] Lankina et al., "Appropriation and Subversion." A modification of these regressions with a binary variable for peasant descendants is also estimated, but it is insignificant.

MENTAL CARTOGRAPHIES: QUALITATIVE EVIDENCE

Ancestry Hunting and Surreptitious Discoveries

The survey points to intriguing patterns of *awareness* of estate and perhaps less surprising – given the earlier macro, or regional, statistical evidence provided – of covariation between the estate and Soviet professional pathways. To tease out the mechanisms engendering cognitive-cartographic self-placement within the estate structure of imperial Russia, I discern citizens' mental anchors *backwards in time* vis-à-vis imperial Russia's social spaces. The 1990s saw a profusion of evidence on estate origins in the genre of memoirs as families became less apprehensive about lifting the taboos of their ancestry. Moshe Lewin's reference to the early years of Bolshevism as a "'quicksand' society" is a misnomer given the intergenerational social awareness and sense of social place that I found among numerous respondents and memoirists.[39] Some had difficulty identifying their forbears' estate. Others had pursued extensive research into their family ancestry, unearthing archival evidence of ascription to an estate, transfer between estates, and often eclecticism in estate origin. The merchant–*meshchane* background is conspicuous in family records of the present-day bourgeoisie, as are traces of nobility, usually Polish. While references to merchant accolades may be interpreted as prevarications, given the status aura of "old money," I cast this aside as implausible considering that Russians would have taken great pride in noble ancestry, often engaging in a largely futile search for one in the 1990s. We would expect even more hesitancy in broadcasting one's estate "pedigree" – if we could use that term – as *meshchane*, since the *meshchanstvo* never lost its derogatory connotations. A few examples of ancestry-hunting among some of the eminent merchant and *meshchane* families, from among a myriad we have at hand, are illuminating.

The historian Galina Sergeyevna Sherstneva, a docent at Samara University, and her cousin Vladimir Gennad'yevich Sherstnev, a successful entrepreneur and civic activist, assembled considerable documentary records for two lines of their family, the Plotnikovs and Sherstnevs. Despite some awareness of their ancestry, the family remained largely in the dark about their forbears' estate, occupations, material wealth, and the whereabouts of heritage properties.[40] Only in the mid-1980s, when Gorbachev's glasnost made possible public discussions of legacies hitherto constituting taboos, Sherstnev was able to visualize the dynasty's many properties before the Bolsheviks took power in Samara:

---

[39] Lewin, "Society," 56.
[40] Some family members in the immediate pre-revolutionary period derived income from the property rental market. In the 1920s and 1950s, the state reportedly offered the family to take charge of the maintenance of one of the houses; the family refused due to the costs involved. Interview, ZK, 2017.

In 1986, I drive my eighty-three-year-old sick grandma past Polevaya Street ... By then, she was virtually blind. She says: "Are we on Polevaya?" I say: "Yes." "You see the two-story house?" "Yes." "Do you see the arch in the middle?" I say: "Yes." "Look inside into the courtyard, what do you see?" I say: "I see some garages with wooden gates in the form of a semicircle." She says: "These are not garages, these are stables and entryway, which had been kept by our relatives. This is the place that belonged to our Sherstnev clan, here our Sherstnev relatives lived. There are many such places." I was thirty-six back then, and surmised that due to her illness, something is wrong with my grandma, I was her only grandson, she never told me anything about it before. In other words, she had been self-evidently scarred by past happenings in her life. I did not believe her.[41]

Some years later, Sherstnev asked a local historian to explore the records concerning the history of the house on Polevaya and this is what he found:

Two weeks later I got a call. They said: "We are going to disappoint you. There the Sherstnevs lived indeed, but they were no princes [*knyaz'ya*]." In the early 1990s everyone was crazy about – especially those with money like me – [establishing descent from] princes, counts, and courtiers. And there he goes: "... there are no princes among your ancestors, there are merchants."[42]

Subsequent research revealed that Sherstnev's earliest known ancestors were peasants who bought themselves out of serfdom before the emancipation reforms, established a successful grain trading enterprise, and, already as Second Guild merchants, in 1855 moved from Vladimir *oblast* to Samara. In what typified the ebbs and flows in merchants' material fortunes, the Sherstnevs moved between the estates of *meshchane* and merchant. Dr. Sherstneva's grandfather Aleksey became an industrialist and the proprietor of iron manufacturing plants. On the eve of the Revolution, Sherstnev housed his family in a large mansion around Khlebnaya Square, the trading quarter of Samara. Another marker of affluence was that each of the four Sherstnev children were provided with a house, a substantial two-story stone mansion.[43] The Plotnikov branch, it turned out, also counts among its ancestors the urban notable Fyodor Semyonovich Plotnikov. Born in 1797 into a family of state peasants in the town of Buguruslan, Plotnikov quickly rose to the status of Second Guild merchant with the aid of his wealthy relatives, traders in grain. Beginning his public career as a *ratman*, a title approximating in status as a city council member, his subsequent election as Samara's *gorodskoy golova* (head of city government) signified achievement considering the status of *gubernskiy gorod* (city of *guberniya* significance) that the town acquired in the second half of the nineteenth century.[44]

Others who did not pursue research in public archives were made aware of their estate through the transmission of a "family legend," oral recollections, or other unpublished records. Julia Braun,[45] the chief editor and news anchor at

---

[41] Interview, ZK, 2017.   [42] Ibid.   [43] Ibid.

[44] A publicist, Plotnikov made his residence available for printing one of Samara's earliest news-papers, *Samarskaya gazeta*. Interview, ZK, 2017.

[45] Name changed.

a Samara TV station, comes from a mixed ancestry of ethnic Russians and *Wolgadeutche*, German settlers in the Middle Volga region. Virtually the entire German side of her family shared the fate of the community: they were deported, exiled, and suffered emotional trauma and material privations in the 1940s. Survivors, however, were able to return to their old places of residence and resumed normal lives following rehabilitation. Braun possesses scarce knowledge of the Samara estate of her forbears beyond the "family legend" concerning a residence on Polevaya street, which she distinguishes from the Bezymyanka worker quarters and which also appears in the epiphanous revelations of Sherstnev's grandmother:

My paternal grandmother, they lived, I know, on Polevaya in a two-story house. *As the family legend goes, the previous generations also lived in that house. How they ended up there, why, and who they were I don't know ... Regarding my grandmother there are some doubts – meshchane?* Otherwise how else would they find themselves on Polevaya Street in that two-story house which they inherited? I don't know how they ended up there. But as for grandfather [we know for sure], it is the workers' outskirts, it is Bezymyanka.[46]

Alternatively, the "family legend" triggered extensive genealogical research. Consider the urgency with which the adolescent Daniil Popov desires to animate his parental home with the presence of the veterinarian Valerian Dmitriyevich Tikhovidov, his great-great-grandfather:

In the largest room hung the portrait of some man [*dyad'ka*] with a large moustache, and so I once asked: "Grandma, who is this?" And she answered that, it turns out, this is my great-great grandfather. *And so, it is that I have grown up, but my curiosity increased more and more* [*razozhglos'*]. I started doing research: I searched through the entire house, scoured for clues beneath all the floorboards [*obsharil vse podpoly*], kept asking grandma about him.[47]

Sofya Polikarpovna Bortnik, who enjoyed a career as a mid-level functionary dealing with matters of youth culture in Samara, on her mother's side is a direct descendant of the wealthiest merchant notability of Shikhobalovs – proprietors of mills, factories, land, and mansions.[48] Born in 1926 and living through the Stalinist repressions, Bortnik remained publicly silent on her ancestry only to become a prolific supplier of memoirs, interviews, and recollections about the Shikhobalovs in the 2000s. Unlike some other distant relatives – such as the Neklutins – who fled Russia, Bortnik never left Samara. Sofya Polikarpovna likely acquired details about the Shikhobalovs from post-Soviet periodicals mulling over the theme of "merchant Samara." Yet her account also betrays the many experiential clues about the family's "secret," absorbed – subconsciously – and constructed into a coherent whole as part of a conscious

---

[46] Name changed. Interview, ZK, 2017 (emphasis added).
[47] Popov, Daniil, "Vernost' professii," 2012 (emphasis added).
[48] Great-granddaughter of Mikhey Shikhobalov, brother of Mathew, father of Anastasia, Constantine Neklutin's mother.

journey of self-awareness – from prayers, to the many conversations about the mysterious Shikhobalovs, to parental directives to the young Sofya about the family's work ethic – an allusion to the Old Believer pedigree of her illustrious merchant ancestors. "When I meet other Shikhobalovs from Moscow or St Petersburg," says Sofya Polikarpovna, "we express surprise at how similar our upbringing was. We were not allowed to get up later than 6 am. Children were not only meant to study ... We had to do something also around the house, embroider, knit."[49]

Some would explore, organize, and study a family treasure chest of a deceased relative, complete with epistolary, photographic, and other mementos, allowing them to reconstruct and piece together the tapestries of their family's pre-revolutionary lives. These allow us to cross-validate the familial finds against complementary documentary evidence. Such is the story of the treasures of Ol'ga Ivanovna Lyakhovskaya, the widow of the eminent merchant Pyotr Aref'yev. One of her relatives in Soviet Samara inherited Aref'yev's artifacts and discussed them in a memoir published in the early 2000s.[50] Aref'yev's many private letters allow the memoirist to represent him as a renaissance man and talented photographer; and, indeed, he is clearly one, if we are to trust the 1916 yearbook. On the other hand, the family treasure chest adds flesh to the dry, inanimate, listings of the yearbook. Not only do we learn about Aref'yev's complicated love life and adoration of his son Mitya by the estranged first wife; we also learn of the Soviet fate of Ol'ga herself, Aref'yev's second muse. Ol'ga came to embody the cultivator figure of a French tutor to her grandson within the family home,[51] reminiscing evocatively about the engineering prowess of her father, Captain Lyakhovskiy, the talented but destitute Polish noble. Ol'ga and her second husband, a university-trained engineer, had been on friendly terms with the merchant Sandi Kurlina and therefore, likely, the family of Bortnik-Shikhobalova, something that allows us to connect distinct families even if their descendants themselves were not aware of such ties.[52]

Still others like Professor Zoya Kobozeva grew up in a solidly bourgeois, though modest, *meshchane* family where ancestry had been openly discussed, indeed celebrated. Kobozeva dedicated an academic career to methodically, systematically, and publicly interrogating the *meshchanstvo* as fodder for derision, deploying materials from public and family archives.[53] These records add texture to our understanding of heterogeneity within the Soviet social, educational, and professional journeys of various substrata among the broad category of the educated estates. Whether concerning the fortunes of *meshchane*

---

[49] "Oni lyubili Rossiyu," *Drugoy gorod*, September 19, 2016. Available online at: drugoigorod.ru /bortnic/ (accessed October 24, 2020).

[50] Myakisheva, "Istoriya."   [51] Ibid., 155.   [52] Ibid., 154–55.

[53] See Kobozeva, "Samarskaya meshchanka." Although Kobozeva concurs with some of the portrayals of *meshchanstvo*, supplying in her publications colorful characters from her own family that correspond to images of lowbrow culture, she regards *meshchane* as urban middle class.

of various means – the Sokolovs-Grigor'yevs-Yegorovs among Kobozeva's ancestors – or the phenomenally rich Shikhobalov and Neklutin merchant clans – post-Soviet archival openings and historical revisionism created a space for scrutinizing the Soviet version of social history concerning what is essentially the bulk of the pre-revolutionary bourgeoisie. Kobozeva's account would be cross validated, as it were, when scores of other *meshchane* independently published works in the memoir genre or publicized documentary relics.

The Family Home

To dissect the role of the previous generation in erecting the metaphorical scaffolding that shaped one's social place and help make sense of it based on clues from the past, I contextualize self-placement within the broader social-familial sites and networks. As we know from the discussion of memory, whether spontaneously or purposefully transmitted, it is a collective construct. Who placed the *dyad'ka* on the wall and why?[54] What was the role of the grandmother besides pointing out the mansions in the 1980s? What was the significance of an Uncle Misha and his cherubim-studded guitar? (I introduce this character in the section "Artifactual Exposure").

The intimacy of the family home is approached here from the perspective of peculiar mental maps. These are shaped in the process of consolidation of within-group ties, practices, and values as well as through home tutoring, contact with insiders and fleeting contact with outsiders, and routinized exposure to artifacts and artifactual practices. These intimate cartographies do not lose their relevance when the social experiment forces families to share communal dwellings with those perceived to be socially inferior. Indeed, by many accounts, physical proximity within even the most cramped communal space spurred ingenious acts of daily resistance against mingling – or at least a striving to place limits on it – aimed at preserving the shrinking private space.[55] The estatist order's elder custodians may have been powerless to sanction against social transgressions like the marriage of an aristocrat to a peasant, or the daughter of a merchant magnate to a factory shop-floor boy, or the lady aristocrat to a *meshchanin*, yet new mechanisms of closure secured an identity that made social gravitation toward the right kind of partner, friend, or colleague natural, habitual, and routine.[56]

---

[54] "Photographs," writes Susan Sontag, "furnish evidence … The picture may distort; but there is always a presumption that something exists, or did exist, which is like what's in the picture." Sontag, *On Photography*, 5. On photographs as expressions of "familial ideology," see also Hirsch, *Family Frames*, 12.

[55] Tchuikina, *Dvoryanskaya pamyat'*, 139–40.

[56] Golitsyn, *Zapiski*, 17. For matrimonial practices among nobles, see Tchuikina, *Dvoryanskaya pamyat'*, 146–47, 147–51. In Soviet Russia, *meshchane* feature as undesirable marriage partners in Prince Golitsyn's memoirs. Golitsyn's aunt and cousin "vehemently objected to this [their son and brother's] marriage to the daughter of a Tambov *meshchanin*." Golitsyn, *Zapiski*, 338.

The insular, even backward-looking, practices and enactments enhanced group cohesion, in ways that go against the revolutionary state's socially dissolving impulses. Simultaneously, they consolidated the possibilities of successful status roles within that very state's public sector, in education and the professions. Bourdieu's concept of habitus is a useful angle for making sense of these patterns. "The *habitus*," writes Bourdieu, is "embodied history, internalized as a second nature and so forgotten as history ... the active presence of the whole past of which it is the product. As such, it is what gives practices their relative autonomy with respect to external determinations of the immediate present."[57] The utility of this heuristic for illuminating and explaining structured, patterned lethargy-in-practice and subjective processes as set against group perceptions of threat is yet to be ascertained, however. In other words, it is unclear how it applies to settings where the "external determinations" are the attempted obliteration of the bourgeoisie as a class, along with this group's symbols of and connections to the past. Evidence from conflict studies suggests that violence and other forms of group threat may in fact engender social motivation expressed in "bottom-up" altruistic acts of giving, contributions toward public goods within families and neighborhoods, and trust-based transactions, as well as their reciprocation. Recent studies of post-conflict societies challenge the widely held assumption that human brutality tends to have a fragmenting, atomizing, effect on communities. In fact, violence incentivizes individuals to "band" with others in the group as a mechanism of coping with out-group threats and trauma.[58] Interviews with Soviet refugees in the early 1950s revealed that, particularly when the regime persecuted kin members, families tended to "rally to each other's support and

When Sergey attends the wedding party, he discusses getting drunk on Tambov moonshine (*braga*) "the color of urine." Ibid., 339. The *meshchane* ascription of Viktor Meyyen, a suitor to Golitsyn's sister in 1927 – the descendant of Dutch shipbuilding craftsmen invited by Peter the Great, son of a co-owner of elite rental homes (*dokhodnyye doma*) in a prime spot in Moscow – also invited the concern of family members for whom "origin was the most important thing." The wedding took place nevertheless. Ibid., 425. As late as 1932, Golitsyn wrote "noble" in answer to a question about his social origins on an employment form. "In-spite of everything, I continued to be proud of the estate [*sosloviye*] to which I belonged the first eight years of my life." Ibid., 569. Only 25 percent or less of marriages among interviewed Soviet wartime refugees "represented a crossing of the manual/nonmanual line, and [that] both the manual and white-collar classes have shown very high rates of class endogamy." Inkeles and Bauer, *Soviet Citizen*, 195. "Despite the official fanfare of the regime ... the patterns of marriage across class lines in recent times are very much what they were before the revolution and during the earlier years of the Soviet regime." Ibid., 195.

57 Bourdieu, *Logic of Practice*, 56 (italicization in original). For a discussion, see Maton, "Habitus."
58 Gilligan et al., "Civil War," 604–5. Conflict studies also suggest that group threat may engender support for hawkish parties with a conservative, hardline bent though findings are context-specific. Getmansky and Zeitzoff, "Terrorism."

strengthen the ties of mutual solidarity."[59] Recent archival revelations about the crimes of Stalinism debunk the "atomized" assumptions about Soviet family when a member is arrested or repressed. Instead, relatives went to considerable lengths to save, shelter, or defend the victim, risking their own lives in the process. "Apparently, family ties became stronger, not weaker, under repression," writes Oleg Khlevniuk.[60] Although not all families among our protagonists experienced repressions, many were indirectly exposed to distressing happenings; their relatives fought on the side of the Whites, were exiled, executed, or incarcerated because of their "bourgeois" origins. The older generation in particular, because of a lower propensity for relocation than the more mobile youngsters, would have been more likely to invest their efforts in group cohesion practices.[61]

Home Tutoring

Agential aspects of group preservation are here discerned in practices of routinization of social closure – a backward-looking aspect of the process – that also have consequences for status positioning in the new society – a forward-looking adaptive component. One such practice of consequence is home tutoring. A private, group-preserving activity, and a form of domestication in the provision of public goods, home tutoring is anchored in the aspirational, cognitive palette of the past that is simultaneously oriented toward success in the new public. Recall how the museum society evidenced imbrication of private-serving practices within a public institution: the usage of the microscope for private needs of the aspiring medical student or the authority of the museum head leveraged to procure references for applicants otherwise denied places in higher institutions of learning. Public-oriented practices, and

[59] Inkeles and Bauer, *Soviet Citizen*, 212. Bonding, however, in response to repressions mostly characterized the intelligentsia; the pattern was the reverse for lower-status groups. "Among families in the intelligentsia, for every one reported to have grown apart there were eight which came closer together, whereas in the peasantry the ratio was a mere 1:1.5." Ibid., 213. The authors speculate about a material cushion that protected higher-status families, since as per capita incomes fell, so did the likelihood of reporting that family members were drawn apart. Ibid., 213. They note remarkable occupational continuity of educated groups: "Among the fathers of our respondents more than two thirds of those who were in the intelligentsia *before* the revolution continued in that occupational group *after* the revolution." Ibid., 214 (emphasis original). By contrast, many peasants were forced to flee collectivization and flock into towns with consequences for family cohesion and traditional rural values. Even so, most rural respondents did not report families disintegrating. Ibid., 214–18.

[60] Khlevniuk, *History of the Gulag*, 342. Golitsyn writes: "We, former people . . . in the years of the revolution became tightly bonded to each other, misfortunes drove us closer to each other. We all without hesitation were ready to offer help materially or morally in whatever way possible even to a cousin four times removed if her husband was arrested. We derived strength from our unity [*splochyonnost'*]." Golitsyn, *Zapiski*, 307.

[61] Those with modest options to "flee" from conflict tend to exhibit such behaviors. Gilligan et al., "Civil War," 605.

the resources that consolidated them, become embedded within the private domain. The deeply engrained routine of domestic tutoring could be linked to imperial legacies of the institutionalization of the home instructor via training, special diplomas, and state sanction. Aside from serving the function of prepping for the bona fide Soviet educational and labor market, the routinization of such practices embodies a striving to map individual life progression onto extensions of the imperial pedagogic and professional sites. The tension between backward- and forward-looking impulses is found in Tchuikina's oral history project, which surveys the values of the fallen aristocrats in Soviet Russia. Not only do the cantankerous semantics of reaction to the changes wrought by the new regime convey hostility; they also convey carefully thought-out strategies for active resistance and subversion.[62] As one aristocrat stated: "It was considered necessary to isolate adolescents from undesirable influences and to form for them a circle of socializing from amongst acquaintances, to teach them to react appropriately to propaganda at educational establishments."[63] In response to such group threat, the antidote was to domesticate education even further than what would have been habitual. An obsession with placing children in the best vintage public schools (the former gymnasia) – when such options were precipitously shrinking as the state pursued educational reorganization – is also discerned.[64] Fears, insularity, and the domestication of education are thus simultaneously embedded within the cognitive horizons charting long-term formal educational progression outside the home. The sentiment behind and the strategic responses concerning schooling also run through the Neklutin correspondence. Here, a fixation on gaining a place for one's child in a desirable institution is interlaced with disdain, derision, and a perception of the inferiority of Soviet education.[65]

---

[62] Tchuikina, *Dvoryanskaya pamyat'*, 135. Golitsyn recalls family gatherings in the 1920s and specifically a visit to a "famous actress Fedotova," "an old woman [*starukha*] with paralyzed legs, surrounded by cats, all the walls in her room plastered with icons and photographs, large and small." "I was used to the fact that our guests castigate Soviet power left and right, but the speeches of Glikeriya Nikolayevna, burning with such vicious hatred, left me stunned. One of her cats left a lot of fur on grandma's dress, and so Fedotova exclaimed that only under the Bolsheviks such fur-shedding cats have proliferated." Golitsyn, *Zapiski*, 258.

[63] Tchuikina, *Dvoryanskaya pamyat'*, 135. For similar evidence, see Inkeles and Bauer, *Soviet Citizen*, 220.

[64] Tchuikina, *Dvoryanskaya pamyat'*, 135. See also Golitsyn, *Zapiski*.

[65] One Samara relation wrote: "It is good that your boy [Dima] will receive his upbringing not in our schools where they only damage [*koverkayut*] children, awful to look at children studying in the first level [*stupeni*] of schools." Date unclear, likely 1920s. NC, f. 16_9; and in another letter: "It is obvious that Dimochka is growing up as a fine boy it is a consolation for the parents and it is good that he is studying there will come out as a man [*chelovek*] out of it and here the youth is all broken [*izlomana*], no one has any moral studies my heart breaks from looking at this." Letter dated December 6, 1929. NC, f. 16_17 (original punctuation).

Faced with the urgency of the start of the next school year, rather than passively succumbing to the altered institutions and content in public education, the cultivated noble, the merchant, and the *meshchanin* would devise first ad hoc and then more structured practices of routinized pedagogic informality. These featured similar kinds of networks as in late imperial Russia's public domain. Indeed, the truncated nodes of a network morphed to constitute new ones, featuring some of the same individuals from the erstwhile network. Here, the public strivings, however, would be embedded within the domain of the private. Whether articulated or not, we observe an aspiration for humanitarianism or, in other words, the cultivation of sensibilities in the arts, languages, and classics. These were implicitly juxtaposed with the impulse of vocationalism that was unfolding within the Soviet school, quite aside from other aspects of indoctrination. A high-status widow of an imperial army colonel – Mariya Aleksandrovna Smolich – was productively engaged to tutor a group of children of gymnasium-educated estatist families of Samara, some of whom were simultaneously employed as pedagogues in the Soviet public school;[66] and the cultivated *meshchanka* Olen'ka Konovalova, aside from contriving to create a home-based convivial pedagogic space for the Smolich-taught group, later ensured that her grandson Sergey was an early, avid, and fluent reader and was exposed to European languages. "When I was still a preschooler," narrates Golubkov, "grandmother taught me to read fluently, tried to teach me German and French languages, gave music lessons. This had been all dictated by her deep conviction about the necessity of education in humanities, whatever professional job one had in life."[67] (See Figure 7.1 for a photograph of Konovalova as a gymnasium pupil.) Meanwhile, Ol'ga Lyakhovskaya, the widow of the merchant magnate and renaissance man Pyotr Aref'yev, took upon herself the education of her step-grandson in the rudiments of French.[68] Surrounded by poverty and squalor, the engineer Strol'man home tutored the offspring of the fallen White General Kappel,[69] unwilling or unable as he had been to take on the honorable offer of concerned émigrés to place the children in a *pension* in Hankou or Peking;[70] and not only

---

[66] "In the house of my great-grandmother," recalls Sergey Golubkov, "Mariya Aleksandrovna [Smolich, a gymnasium teacher] gave lessons to a small group, which included my mother, her cousins . . . and children of pedagogues who rented premises [in the house]." Golubkov, *Portfel'*, 31. Here, Golubkov refers to the private two-story wooden house of Yelena Stepanovna Konovalova, Olen'ka's mother, which her young family occupied in 1926 after returning from Moscow where her husband, the engineer Yevteyev, served. Ibid., 31. Smolich, a widow of a tzarist colonel, continued to teach foreign languages all her life. Interview, October 25, 2018.

[67] Golubkov, *Portfel'*, 32. [68] Myakisheva, "Istoriya," 155.

[69] Strol'man mentions the home schooling (*domashneye ucheniye*) of his preschool-age grandson Kirill. Letters, December 31, 1923. NC, f. 17_01; and April 5, 1936. NC, f. 17_01.

[70] Letter to Neklutin in Harbin, from Peking, from V. Vyrypayev, December 12, 1922. NC, f. 19. Hankou is a city in China's Hubei Province. Before the Revolution it already had a sizeable Russian diaspora due to trade ties, in 1914 numbering more than 200 people, mostly merchants. Sharonova, "Russkaya emigratsiya," 220.

FIGURE 7.1 Ol'ga Nikolayevna Konovalova
Gymnasium Pupil, Samara, 1909.
Source. Sergey Golubkov Family Archive (hereafter SGFA).

was the granddaughter of the First Guild merchant Lev Filippovich Heyfets
given the French name Anneta, by way of symbolizing the family's
cosmopolitan reach, but the future long-time director of Samara Art Museum
had also been exposed to the language in the family's domestic space.[71]

These patterns represented a form of institutional drift:[72] practices
institutionalized within late imperial Russia's pedagogy such as domestic
tutoring and prepping – hitherto accessible and sanctioned via well-charted
routes of professional training, diplomas, and state imprimatur – were
channeled, and perhaps became even more widespread, against a
background of group vulnerability.[73] Insularity in the domestication of

---

[71] Burlina, "Staryye." See discussion and family pictures, 49, 50, 51; Nataliya Mikhaylova, "Yeyo
sud'ba – Samara," *Samara i guberniya*, May 2003. Available online at: www.sgubern.ru/articles/
4849/6759/ (accessed May 9, 2020).

[72] Hacker et al., "Drift and Conversion."

[73] Golitsyn, for instance, writes: "Modest though our expenses were back then, my parents decided
together with parents of several other boys and girls that the children should be definitely taught
dancing. Where? Well, in our house of course, in the big lounge." The lessons, which included
some twenty pupils, were taught by a "real ballerina." Golitsyn, *Zapiski*, 261. One relation
"initiated a study group for girls of roughly the same age, whose parents did not want to send
them to a Soviet school." The girls were successfully prepped for entry to secondary school. Ibid.,
287. Private group tutoring involving leading gymnasium instructors, as a substitute for

FIGURE 7.2 Mariya Ivanovna Volodkovich and Aleksey Alekseyevich Golubkov
No date. M. I. Volodkovich, a Polish noble, was the aunt of Aleksey (Sergey Golubkov's
father), who raised him after his mother's death. She enrolled in 1911 and in 1921
completed the Women's Higher Agricultural (Golitsyn) Courses in Moscow and became
a professional agronomist. Golubkov, *Portfel'*, 34–44.
Source: SGFA

practices of the pedagogic sector thus coexisted with the daily exposure of the
new generation of citizen to the Soviet school. The implications of the
subtleties of these responses are nontrivial for social adaptation. One major
concern about a project such as mine is a neglect of the fears, intimidation,
and terror that were unfolding across the public arenas of the Stalinist state.

attendance of Soviet primary schools, was widespread at least until the end of the 1920s when
Soviet authorities started to clamp down on such practices. Ibid., 383.

These horrors would arguably make it imperative to adopt a strategy of dignified social absorption into the broader society or, indeed, if we are to believe the new subjectivity historicism,[74] an enthusiastic and self-inflicted one. Yet public silences, taboos, and overt affirmations of credulity concerning communism may well have coexisted with, and indeed nurtured, the discreet symbolism of routinized affirmations of social closure, both in the home and among private as indeed public networks. The grandmother domesticating the teaching of French to a group of children would not be simultaneously engaged in overt political propagandism. Many such grandmothers became decorated *Soviet* pedagogues, going through the motions of whatever reaffirmations of regime propaganda were inflicted upon them via central directives, perhaps even coming to believe in the promise of the Bolshevik project. The very act of teaching French itself constitutes an emblematic statement of group identity, making political-oppositional statementship redundant and, of course, dangerous in a totalizing polity. Indeed, as Tchuikina poignantly observes, group affirmation would be carried out in silences – a sign of one's own people (*svoi*) transcended the materiality of the speech act.[75] Private survival tactics in response to group threat thus naturally coexisted with the affirmation of the political edifice in the public domain. The cultivations of the private realm in turn reinforced people's status and aided their reinvention as particular types of Soviet employees and citizens, since the estatist society boasted not only superior human capital and an expanded range of choice in the labor market but the *confidence* of belonging.

The Family Gathering

Group affirmations of insularity that served a status-enhancing role outside of the home were also practiced in the form of *the family gathering*. Special occasions, by dint of being rare, celebratory, and ritualistic, play a nontrivial role in the transmission of symbolic capital. These could be later reflected on in the process of the mature self-placement of the adult. These are also the

---

[74] For an example of this angle, see Hellbeck, *Revolution*.

[75] "Descendants of the old elites based on barely discernible [*neulovimyye*] signs recognized each other in school and following that – in higher educational establishments and at workplace. If they began to interact, and even visit each other's homes, it was appropriate not to ask questions concerning 'politically significant' topics, especially social origin, arrests and exiles. Aristocratic identity [*dvoryanskaya identichnost'*], if one possessed one, was an inner, intimate feeling, which one tended not to discuss [*ne prinyato*].

'With close friends we did not talk at all. It was part of our upbringing. So we never learned truly to talk. It just turned out to be the case later that our close circle [*blizkiye lyudi*] understood everything without words anyway. Put differently, the very choice of a friend determined the development of the individual's attitude towards reality. Without a word spoken, actually.'

A unifying thread had been world outlook, interest in culture, ways of perception and discussion, leisure pursuits. Aside from that, a sign of '*svoikh*' [our own] would be silence with regard to particular topics." Tchuikina, *Dvoryanskaya pamyat'*, 113.

occasions that bring together in one safe, private, space members of a wider familial network, whether local or transregional, one that also diversifies the family's reach into that of the public. The domestic affirmations of broader social ties that provided possibilities for the expansion of mental cartographies beyond the locality also served group-affirming roles in other ways. As noted in Chapter 2, mainstream assumptions have painted a portrait of the decimation of local societies, not least because of the migration, population movement, and resettlement of the ostensible "quicksand" society. The contrasting angle taken here sensitizes us to the cross-regional and cross-national multiplexity of ties as channeling unarticulated and often articulated cognitive signposts and anchors that are simultaneously backward- and forward-looking. Estates most vulnerable to witch hunts are a case in point. It was precisely the vulnerability in one locality of some of the highest-status and best-educated strata that forced relocation elsewhere; and this enabled the, at times, spectacular reinvention of the fallen aristocrat, merchant, or clergyman as the bona fide cultural literatus of Soviet Russia.

Growing up, the future entrepreneur Vladimir Sherstnev vividly recalls gatherings of the extended family, including magnificent and momentous visits from metropolitan and Samara-based relations. These included an Uncle Tolya Plotnikov, a professor from St. Petersburg, and an Aunt Ol'ga Plotnikova, reportedly a "polyglot," who was "fluent in five languages" and was "corresponding with the entire world."[76] Unlike Uncle Tolya, Aunt Ol'ga remained in Samara, where she continued to reside in a desirable bourgeois district – around what became the Revolution Square – in an "enormous three-bedroom apartment." What especially caught the child's imagination was the giant fish tank in Aunt Ol'ga's home. "Nowhere else have I seen such an enormous fish tank, the size of a sofa ...! A fish tank, like a swimming pool, and several of those at that. In it swam exotic fish, and god knows what."[77] Aunt Ol'ga was much like an exotic fish herself, since it is in her dwellings that Sherstnev would be exposed to the strange and evocative semantics and tastes of the extra-Soviet realm. "There," he marvels, "for the first time in my life I tasted Camembert ... Camembert in 1965 or 1963? And she had it all."[78]

Bringing together the metropolitan glitterati and locally based – but transnationally connected – aunts and uncles, the family gatherings also provided ritualized affirmations of an unbroken, as it were, chain of distinction linking pre-Soviet Samara's public figures with status roles within Soviet society. Sherstnev conveys the subtleties of these consanguine affirmations, which were pregnant with meaning even when facts were obscured behind silence and taboo. It was on him, the latest in a direct and

---

[76] Interview, ZK, 2017.   [77] Ibid.

[78] Interview, ZK, 2017. Tragically, she committed suicide in 1969 as an act of defiance against state attempts to remove her from her apartment when the authorities were expanding a grocery shop in the building. Baranov et al., *Istoriya Samarskogo kupechestva*, 166.

unbroken line of descendants of Samara's first mayor, and not Vovka Shein, that the metropolitan and local relations bestowed the halo of distinction. The boy felt spoilt with attention and even pampered; but why? "I thought – why do they dote on me so much, why are they caring [*opekayut*] for me like this – "Voloden'ka, Voloden'ka" – it was not like this at all with Vovka Shein, my distant cousin [*troyurodnyy brat*]."[79]

Artifactual Exposure

Likewise, an exposure to artifacts that were evocative of the past became instrumental not only in shaping cultural sensibilities, in a Bourdieusian sense, but in providing ancestry goalposts. It was these that the present-day protagonist could lean on in order to "make sense" of their family's past, essentially mapping one's pre-communist social position onto the society of the present. Telling – and contrasting – artifactual tapestries emerge in the recollections of high-status groups and those lower down the social rungs within our broad category of the educated estates. The piano, as an artifact, a symbol of status, belonging, and loss, runs through the letters, memoirs, and recollections of the aristocrat, merchant, and cultivated *meshchanin*; and it has deep roots in Russian literary classics as the core around which images of bourgeois sensibilities and social identities are constructed.

Consider the example from a literary classic, the autobiographical novel *Engineers* by the noble Garin-Mikhaylovskiy, who made his home in pre-revolutionary Samara. The novel thus captures the multifunctional essence of the piano – as an instrument of the quick subjective placement of the bride-to-be; a family *essential*; a source of bliss for the newlyweds beginning their life together; and as a treasured inheritance to be passed on to the next generation. In the novel, the budding professional Artemiy (Tyoma) Kartashev falls in love with the relation of a *guberniya* official, Adelaida (Delya) Borisovna, "a young lady," we are told, "who had completed a gymnasium course abroad."[80] "One evening," Kartashev went for a stroll along the sea and only returned home at dusk. The transparent, fine windows of their apartment were open, and Kartashev heard someone playing the grand piano. The music was gentle and soft and the sounds virtually flowed – and straight into the soul. Who was it playing like this?[81] When Kartashev finally gets around to proposing to his muse, the grand piano is one of the first items purchased for the newlyweds' frugal family home:

And so, they decided to arrange their future family nest as modestly as possible . . .
    You know what – suggested Kartashev – let us purchase *only the essentials for now* . . .

---

[79] Ibid.; also discussed in ibid., 166.   [80] Garin-Mikhaylovskiy, *Studenty*; *Inzhenery*, 233.
[81] Ibid., 236.

And so, they went to buy furniture, beds, kitchenware. All purchases were of modest cost, and only the grand piano Kartashev kept insisting must be purchased not for 300 rubles, as Adelaida Borisovna was suggesting, but 750.

He maintained:

– There, in Troyanov Val [future family home], all our entertainment will consist of music, your playing is so majestic . . .
– But even on this, . . . the cheap piano – I shall play just as well – it is so petit, elegant, the tone is lovely, and the assurance that it is inexpensive, would add to the pleasure.
– No, you know, Delya, inexpensive means not solid enough, whereas the grand piano is bought for life, and if it is a good one, *it would be passed on to our children. Considering that we will only live together for some twenty-five years* . . .
Kartashev was making swift calculations in his head.
– . . . then it would come to roughly 9,000 days, and 450 rubles would come to five kopeks per day of extra costs only . . . Five kopeks! So, every day, to return this money, we shall make some savings in our budget to the value of five kopeks.
Adelaida Borisovna eventually gave in, and they bought the expensive grand piano.[82]

The piano and the musical sheet invariably feature as indispensable ingredients in the tapestry of the happy childhood of the noble and among privileged segments of urban estates alike. Just as invariably, it is an accompaniment to the privations of the aristocrat, the cultivated merchant, and the wealthier *meshchanin*.[83] Faced with the Bolsheviks' appropriation of her home, Aref'yev's young and defenseless widow, Ol'ga Ivanovna, who had been given one night to vacate the plush apartments on the Boulevard of Nobles, scrambles to salvage the piano:

Before that, perhaps to make sure that the order is received without obstruction, [the soldiers] tore with bayonets several paintings and dumped them on the floor, having smashed them, as they did the collections of porcelain statues . . . The frightened Ol'ga, having hired two horse-drawn carts . . . left the flat that same night. On one of the coaches was the piano with keys made of white and black ivory and bronze candelabra, as well as numerous collections of musical scores, while on the other one – everything that they managed to fit from the household items.[84]

The piano occupies a particularly privileged place in the fond childhood recollections of Sergey Golubkov, Ol'ga Konovalova's grandson. "In the old house on Osipenko street in which my childhood passed, there stood a small cabinet grand piano 'Schroeder.' Mother and grandmother frequently played together. My mother loved Chopin very much."[85] As a little boy, Sergey

---

[82] Ibid., 464 (emphases added).   [83] Tchuikina, *Dvoryanskaya pamyat'*, 68, 71–2, 133, 153.
[84] Thereafter, the Old Bolshevik Valerian Kuybyshev – after whom the region and regional capital Samara were renamed – made Aref'yev's home his private residence, appropriating the family's remaining valuables. Myakisheva, "Istoriya," 153–54.
[85] Golubkov, *Portfel'*, 78.

loved to sift through the ancient musical score sheets. Our house was very old and decrepit by then, and miserably freezing and dull in the winter, and one sadly had to put on layers and layers of clothes to keep warm, and so *the two deities of our household – the fireplace and the grand piano – warmed the soul and improved the spirits.*[86]

Golubkov's reference to the piano as a "deity" is a telling representation of the cultivated estates' veneration of the immaterial and as something that distinguishes what Thorstein Veblen terms "vulgar practicality" from that approximating the occult, the ethereal, the "high," the "noble," and the "worthy";[87] and it is this artifact that constituted one marker of the social gradations between those who are initiated and those who are not when, in Soviet Russia, the noble, the merchant, and the *meshchanin* played the instrument simply to make ends meet.[88] "Vulgarly useful" it may have become,[89] as a source of income for the Konovalovas, the Golitsyns, and the Trubetskoys,[90] but nevertheless it was an important social signifier of the initiations of the past.

   Much as the piano represents a symbol of holding on, having to part with the instrument signifies the drama of letting go; both, nonetheless, are reaffirmations of continuity in social place. A would-be straightforward transactional act involving the seller and buyer is impregnated with the tragedy of meaning for both. In Golubkov's discussion of the subject of the Schroeder baby grand – a reconstruction from the reminiscences of his grandmother Ol'ga – our only record of the transaction in the 1920s is that the seller "was sobbing so very bitterly" as she let go of the instrument and that, as a result, "they [grandmother's family] were buying this grand piano with a heavy heart."[91] We do not know the seller's name. With some imagination, we may speculate that she may have been one of the Neklutin youngsters, as they too mourned the loss of a deity-like object roughly at that time. "I heard that they sold your piano for 800 rubles," wrote a relation to Polia Neklutin in America.[92] The transaction may be endowed with a social meaning within the subtleties of the heterogenous fortunes of the merchant magnate *lishentsy* as opposed to the less ideologically conspicuous but high-status *meshchane*. The latter perhaps had greater access to income-generating possibilities within the pop-up sphere or were lucky, like Konovalova, to marry a would-be organization man, what with the secure income and perks.[93] Just as much, however, the transaction symbolizes the belongingness of the latter-day

---

[86] Ibid., 78 (emphasis added).   [87] Veblen, *Theory of the Leisure Class*, 395, 391.

[88] Bourdieu highlights consecratory and initiatory "rites" as distinguishing social groups with lasting consequences. Bourdieu, *Language*, 117.

[89] Veblen, *Theory of the Leisure Class*, 399.

[90] For Soviet professional trajectories of aristocrats, see Smith, *Former People*; and Golitsyn, *Zapiski*.

[91] Interview, October 25, 2018.   [92] Letter, June 8, year unclear, NC, f_16.

[93] A "solid income" and *domrabotnitsa* (housekeeper). Golubkov, *Portfel'* 28–30.

wealthiest merchant and the cultivated *meshchanka* alike in the aesthetic fields of estatist society, since their shared perception of the instrument transcends the materiality and fleetingness of actual ownership. Indeed, the Golubkovs would also one day part with the Schroeder baby grand, "somehow also very painfully."[94] The artifactual visual and auditory snapshots of the lost but treasured family relic remained nevertheless encoded in Sergey's memory. "Mother was so upset [when the piano was sold]. *Because it was the soul of the house*. I even have a poem about this."[95]

The piano in our protagonists' accounts thus maps continuities in social identity, even when the artifact is tragically pawned, sold, and discarded, and even when it is vulgarly relied on to make ends meet. Nowhere does one find explicit references to the musical instrument as a symbol delineating the social space of the noble, merchant, or upper-status *meshchanin*. In fact, the contrast would be precisely between the injunction-like, "soft disciplining"[96] aspect of Soviet state policies on culture concerning the aesthetics of everyday life – tablecloths, lampshades, flowerpots[97] – that is, this is what cultured people ought to do, and the unarticulated practice dimension of the internalization of the more elaborate symbols of refinement, such as the musical instrument as an identity marker – "this is what we all do." Obvious as it may appear in Bourdieu's France, this reaction is by no means predictable in a coercive context. Indeed, a rational response may have been to plebeianize or *sovietize* one's tastes, if only to survive, and dissolve into the inconspicuousness of the proletarian–peasant masses. The extreme case of Soviet Russia thus presents us with theoretical insights extending far beyond this state, to contexts where impulses to social erasure may be far milder and more benign.

Heterogeneity in the artifactual aspect of familial imprint on social identities emerges when we consider the domestically embedded possibilities and instrumentalizations among the lower to middling trading and *rentier* families of the *meshchane*. Where, in Golubkov's household, the routinization and affirmation of familial-social identity revolved around Olen'ka's presence, in Kobozeva's extended family, it was around Uncle Misha, whose *meshchane* family continued to reside in a two-story home in the old part of Samara that was typical of their pre-revolutionary lifestyle. Whereas, for the Golubkovs, the Schroeder baby grand piano filled the silences in the decrepit wooden home with the waltzes of Chopin, Uncle Misha's indulgence was the "cruel romance" (*zhestokiy romans*) vocal act performed to the guitar. Like the *meshchanstvo*, an academically neglected genre, it remained intrinsic to the subculture of the lower urban strata. Here, mournful pathos-filled ballads, often set in exotic locations, spin themes of tragic love, seduction, forced marriage, betrayal,

---

[94] Interview, October 25, 2018.   [95] Ibid. (emphasis added).
[96] Volkov, "Kontseptsiya," 208; and Dunham, *In Stalin's Time*.
[97] Volkov, "Kontseptsiya," 213.

abandonment, incest, and murder.[98] "Cruel romance," explains Kobozeva, "is not something written to the lyrics of poets, not the creation of magnificent composers, not even the gypsy romance-type songs, these are the kinds of urban [songs] to be performed with a harmonica, a guitar. This had been common also among the *meshchane* families." Inside Uncle Misha's guitar were "the obligatory stickers of cupids, roses." The performance, from the memory of Zoya as a child attending family gatherings at Uncle Misha's with her mother, unfolded thus:

> My mother was a striking brunette... We used to visit this *meshchane* family. He [Uncle Misha] would fall on one knee, with his little moustache, in a straw hat, as he was supposed to [according to the genre], and would sing to her: "Who is there in the mauve beret, speaking to the Spanish Ambassador" ... So, there was that pose, the affectation, the tearfulness.[99]

Much as the sticker-studded guitar and the cruel romance embody the lethargy in the reproduction of vulgarity that characterized the cultural tastes of the lower-status *meshchane* milieus, so does the impulse to delineate one's social space vis-à-vis those of a lower status. Symbolic and material-artifactual possibilities helped consolidate familial and group public identities from within the home. Absent the piano, the family would produce and display a status substitute that would consolidate the claim of the bona fide imperial burgher as opposed to the parvenu – in Kobozeva's household, the Tretyakovskaya Art Gallery tome. The album entered the family's possession as one of her great-grandfather's trophies, acquired either as a gift from a company manager to employees or during an assignment as a traveling salesman for his firm;[100] and it has occupied pride of place in the lounge ever since, through the tremors of the downfall of the Romanovs, the prosaic Soviet decades, and the post-Soviet glut of commercial print production.[101] Again, the innocuous object symbolizes the unbroken chain of *Bürgertum* stretching back to pre-revolutionary Russia. It is the old album, not the widely available new compilations of paintings from the *Soviet* gallery, that is most treasured; as are the periodicals to which ancestors subscribed, notably the *Vokrug sveta* (*Around the World*) magazine, copies of which were bound and preserved in the family library;[102] and the massive metal-clad framed photographic album complete with pictorial and written affirmations of the family's expansive cartographic horizons, captured in postcards from exotic locations.[103]

---

[98] See Trostina, "Zhestokiy romans." See also Yagubov, "'Zhestokiy' romans i gorodskaya ballada." One song in the genre is M. Isakovskiy's and M. Blanter's "Ogonyok": youtube .com/watch?v=Hy-Ro-LCTYY (accessed May 7, 2020).

[99] Interview, October 5, 2016.   [100] Ibid.

[101] The Gallery in Moscow houses Russian art assembled by the merchant philanthropist (*kupets-metsenat*) Pavel Mikhailovich Tretiakov; it opened to the public in 1881. On history, see Norman, "Pavel Tretiakov."

[102] Kobozeva, "Dialogichnost' khronotopov," 144; and interview, October 5, 2016.

[103] Author observations and interview, June 19, 2017.

These narrowly cultural-familial aspects of group affirmation are nontrivial from the perspective of extensions into the possibilities of public arenas under communism. Although cultural capital may not be straightforwardly causally linked to our other variable of interest – the bourgeois values that support a politically liberal system – it is inseparable from other aspects of the transmission of legacies that give rise to a middle class. Cultural capital would have certainly facilitated engagements in the pop-up sphere of the nascent Soviet labor market and, by extension, the transition of the educated estates and their children into the high-status *new* intelligentsia. It also facilitated navigation into "parking orbits" or "hiding places" of employment outside of the "cadre" route.[104] In Szelényi's analysis, in what is similar to my conception of the museum society haven, this trajectory spares our protagonists from incorporation into the party-managerial nomenklatura.[105] Anneta Bass, for instance, for many years the director of the Samara Art Museum (*Khudozhestvennyy muzey*), could be superficially bracketed under the rubric of a functionary in the cultural sphere. In the 2000s, shortly before her death, she received a state award from President Putin. Yet, much like the many other custodians of provincial cultural treasures, Bass, the granddaughter of a Samara merchant tea trader who, in the 1940s, attended the prestigious School No. 15 – the former KWG – became a celebrity countercultural figure. She is credited with salvaging the old and amassing a treasure trove of new, modern art for the museum. In fighting to secure an appropriate building to house the precious – and precarious – collections, she made enemies among the establishment.[106] Bass thus emerges as a custodian of the pre-revolutionary cultural icon – the Samara Museum – and of the traditions of the museum society. A close friend, Boris Kozhin, wrote:

It is impossible to even imagine how many people Anneta helped when she was director of the museum. She used to hide people in this museum. If a person would have strained relations with the powers that be, if he had not been given a chance to work (usually, young people), she would take this kind of a person into the museum. [She] would occupy them with brochures, teach them to become tour-guides. And so, he would quietly work in the museum . . . and she did it more than once – many people are grateful to her for that.[107]

---

[104] Szelényi, *Socialist Entrepreneurs*, 19.
[105] The intelligentsia were particularly resentful of political interference in their work: "The proportion of the intelligentsia who spontaneously cited the effects of political interference in the work situation was more than three times that among the kolkhozniks." Inkeles and Bauer, *Soviet Citizen*, 107.
[106] Kozhin, *Rasskazyvayet*, 181–89; and Aleksandr Ignashov "Anneta Bass, 1930–2006." *Samarskiye sud'by*, May 2007, 16–23, 17–18.
[107] Ibid., 185. Even if few intellectuals challenged the political authority in the 1970s, "the 'social resonance' of the intellectuals' activities was often tremendous, generating chain reactions with diverse consequences." Shlapentokh, *Soviet Intellectuals*, 57.

STORYTELLING IN SOCIAL SELF-PLACEMENT

To discern how living descendants instrumentalize their ancestry in the process of their social identity construction, the optics of "story-telling"[108] – or, to paraphrase George Herbert Mead, of the narrative embedding of the past in the present – may be deployed.[109] Rather than highlighting the contextual-familial dynamics of status preservation – the kin group's "armor" as it situates itself in society,[110] as well as in Stalin's Russia, as it defends itself from the vagaries of Soviet policy on class – the emphasis here is on present-day individual reconstructions and understandings of ancestry, in turn legitimizing the public personae, statuses, and roles. I am sensitive to the tension inherent in distinguishing between the structural underpinnings of this process and the less tangible instrumental dimension, which endows our heroes with the agency to engage in a *quest* of constructing one's fortune out of both the memory relics of the past and the surroundings of the present. Abbott notes the challenges of this kind of analysis: "Our problem is how to allow each side free play, neither romanticizing freedom nor worshipping determinism, accepting both the objective reality of social behavior and the subjective revisions that transform it."[111] The subtleties of self-placement may be a far cry from late imperial Russia's "walls" that "segregated" the various *sosloviya*,[112] and yet the process of delineating an individual's social space – in discourse, performance, and verbally reproduced scripts, or in the treasuring of an artifact – is by its nature simultaneously exclusionary, for inclusion is often inscribed in the form of juxtaposition.[113] Three narrative tropes in particular reaffirm social place in ways characteristic of a wide variety of settings, while also reflecting the peculiar Soviet historical experience: the *cosmopolitan bourgeois*, the *dynastic professional*, and *strategic ambivalences*.

The Cosmopolitan Bourgeois

The subtle allusions to a *cosmopolitan bourgeois* pedigree, whether urban or rural, speak to the estatist sensibilities, tastes, and exposure predating the 1917 watershed. Professor Kobozeva's narratives about her ancestry accentuate the

---

[108] Tilly, *Stories.*   [109] Mead, "The Nature of the Past," 204.
[110] Halbwachs, *On Collective Memory*, 59, 122–23.
[111] Abbott, *System of Professions*, 321. On contingency derived from temporally and spatially complex experiences – "states of consciousness … that … are alive and therefore constantly changing" – transcending what we understand as the temporal present, see Bergson, *Time and Free Will*, 196, 175–221. Bergson juxtaposes our attempts to measure and parcel out temporal frames with the human inner psychological experiences of time and space, and of memory: "That under the influence of the same external conditions I do not behave to-day [sic] as I behaved yesterday is not at all surprising, because I *change*, because I *endure*." Ibid., 209 (emphasis in original). Bergson exposes a "misunderstanding," namely "the illusion through which we confuse succession and simultaneity, duration and extensity, quality and quantity." Ibid., 240.
[112] Rieber, *Merchants*, 279.
[113] On classificatory aspects of language and practice, see Bauman, *Modernity*, 1–3.

FIGURE 7.3 Fathers and sons
Mikhail Nikanorovich Kashin (center) with parents. Nikanor (father) hailed from among the peasant estate of Vladimir *guberniya* and served as pilot (*lotsman*) in an association (*artel'*) of ship haulers. Kobozeva annotations. Note: The father's clothing and beard betray the social difference between the two generations.
Source. ZKPC, Image 174.1

family's refinements as opposed to those lacking the trappings of the "urban species" of the bourgeois, to use the French historian Ernest Labrousse's designation[114] – the bona fide peasant, in mentality, lifestyle, and outlook. The social place of Kobozeva's urban forbears, whose photographic images are presented in Figures 7.3 and 7.4, is delineated with reference to the troves of

---

[114] Labrousse, "New Paths," 68.

FIGURE 7.4 Mikhail Nikanorovich Kashin
Manager of the Samara office of the Brothers Krestovnikov Trading House, peasant by
estate (right), Kokand, 1917.
Source. ZKPC, Image 170, Kobozeva annotations

postcards that her great-grandfather, the traveling salesman Mikhail
Nikanorovich Kashin, sent home when on his many commissions across the
Russian Empire:

Even when he [great grandfather] travels across Russia, around the Empire, from different places he sends postcards to his family. I have been always amazed at this, the culture

of writing. This, a peasant-cum-urban family ... These little postcards [*otkrytochki*] speak [thus] about the family, firstly that these are urban dwellers, who habitually write letters; there is a certain warmth in relationships, expressed in these postcards timed to different holidays.[115]

The discourse of style of writing in the postcards of *meshchane* testifies to the presence of a certain ethos of an urban citizen [*gorozhanin*], relatively well educated, one espousing religious and family values, one ... open to learning about the outside world ... but one drawing confidence from the circle of family and friends.[116]

Tamara Vasil'yevna Polezhayeva, a professor from a dynastic family of academics in Samara, knows little about her ancestors' estate, bar that the family belonged to the rural intelligentsia well before the Revolution and only moved to Samara City after 1917, though most, before collectivization, in what Polezhayeva considers to be a lucky escape. Not only is her great-grandfather presented as a book worm passionate about drama but also her grandfather is described as a polyglot, fluent in three foreign languages – as recorded in tsarist police records of surveillance over him.[117]

Language – *how* one speaks,[118] to whom one wishes to confide, what is spoken, and what is left unsaid – also appears as a subtle status marker. We learn from Professor Sergey Golubkov that his grandmother, the cultivated Ol'ga Nikolayevna, easily established a rapport with the fallen aristocrats and other notables who were discreetly reinventing their lives in the quaint old quarters of Samara:

Grandmother could pursue interesting conversations with intelligent people. A few phrases and mutual understanding ensued and mutual interest of the interlocutors ... I remember her [grandmother] telling me about visiting the barrister [*advokat*] Vitelius, who lived on one of the streets adjacent to ours ... She went there to see him to get some consultation. They ended up talking, and the barrister confided to her about his father – a high profile St Petersburg dignitary from the pre-October [pre-1917] times, pictured on I. Ye. Repin's famous painting "Ceremonial Sitting of the State Council." It must be said that on our topsy-turvy [*nekazistyye*] little streets one encountered those who were called "former people." And grandmother knew the family stories of many of them.[119]

The Dynastic Professional

The *dynastic professional* narrative characterizes the urban intelligentsia's linear reconstructions of educational and professional milestones and the accumulation of achievement, status, influence, and stature; these are consistent with sociologists' findings about middle-class aspirational groups in diverse contexts. They contrast with cyclical stories characteristic of "subordinate"

---

[115] Interview, October 5, 2016.   [116] Kobozeva, "Dialogichnost' khronotopov," 144.

[117] Interview, ZK, 2017, name changed.

[118] On "legitimate" language of dominant groups, see Bourdieu, *Language*, 53.

[119] Golubkov, *Portfel'*, 32–33.

groups, the less-educated, and, particularly, rural inhabitants – a repetitive circle of births, marriages, deaths, births, marriages, and deaths.[120] The claims to a dynastic pedigree by several generations of medics, teachers, and university educators is of special interest here, for they take us to the pre-revolutionary origins of these "dynasties."

Daniil Popov identifies education as the path that links his career choices to those of his distinguished ancestor, Valerian Dmitriyevich Tikhovidov, who combined veterinary practice with university instruction. Daniil points out that Tikhovidov's daughter taught special needs children and that both of Daniil's parents are educators. At the time of the interview, Daniil was embarking on doctoral-level research following his graduation from Samara's prestigious Aviation Technology Institute.[121] Tikhovidov's university credentials feature in the strivings of the great-great-grandson:

The life trajectory of Valerian Dmitriyevich is an example for me. I have someone to measure up to [*mne yest' na kogo rovnyatsya*]. This is a self-made man [*chelovek kotoryy sdelal sebya sam*]. In-spite of life's challenges, he completed his studies at university, managed to become a good specialist. His destiny taught me not to give up in the face of obstacles, to strive to attain my goals and to be in every deed a professional.[122]

Likewise, a family pedigree in engineering runs as a thread linking the achievements of multiple generations of the family of Ol'ga Lyakhovskaya, beginning with the credentials of her father, the ship Captain Lyakhovskiy, and extending to those of her first husband, the merchant Pyotr Aref'yev, as well as her second husband, whose life inspired their son to embark on an engineering path.[123] Aref'yev's son Mitya, from his first marriage, who in all probability entered the Chemistry Faculty at the University of St. Petersburg,[124] is also appropriated to construct an unbroken professional-dynastic pedigree. Ol'ga Ivanovna's second husband, Nikolay Vasil'yevich Maliyev, we learn, became a civil engineer following his pre-revolutionary training in the Moscow Transport Engineering School and worked on "constructing dams and bridges" in Soviet Russia.[125] Their only son, Yuriy Nikolayevich (Yurochka) Maliyev (b. 1922), pursued a doctorate, becoming a "favorite professor to not one, but many generations of students" at Samara's Aviation Institute. Finally, Yuriy's stepson Kirill, representing at least the third generation of technical specialists, trained to become a ship navigator (*shturman-rechnik*) and was presented to family friends as a custodian of the long family tradition of stewardship of ships on the river Volga.[126]

A recent Russian Academy of Sciences Institute of Sociology study, albeit preoccupied with the conservation and transmission of human capital in

[120] See Connerton, *How Societies Remember*, 18–20.
[121] Popov, Daniil, "Vernost' professii," 2012; interview, June 19, 2017.
[122] Popov, Daniil, "Vernost' professii," III Annual Essay Competition "Family History-2011," Tolyatti.
[123] Myakisheva, "Istoriya," 142.   [124] Ibid., 152.   [125] Ibid., 154–55.   [126] Ibid., 154–55.

Samara during the Soviet period, likewise found dynastic narratives in discussions of the choice of school, university, and profession. The study surveyed engineering dynasties working in the region's core industrial fields of petrochemicals and aerospace and covering at least three generations. Spanning the period from the 1950s onward, it therefore encompasses Yurochka Maliyev's generation of professionals; he would have completed a doctorate, commenced his professional career, and started a family roughly in the period covered in the study. The engineering profession in Soviet Russia has had its ups and downs in the hierarchy of prestige and income. It nevertheless became an important source of professional capital and dynastic identity in post-communist Russia. Says one dynastic interviewee:

I never wavered in the choice of profession. I did not choose the institute. I knew where to go. I was the only one in my class applying to the mechanical faculty in the poly-technical institute. Everything was somehow natural [*vsyo bylo kak-to samo soboy*]. It was clear for a long time. *And after the specialized mathematics school it was kind of easy to gain entry.* And in the process of studying at the institute I obtained the advice of both father and uncle... No, the mathematical school I did not choose myself. Here it was the parents' effort [*roditeli postaralis'*].[127]

Another respondent speaks to the question of the transfer of professional capital acquired in the Soviet state-run economy into resources (and job experience) that were usable in a new economic context, converting a "family calling" (*semeynoye delo*) into a "family business" (*semeynyy biznes*):[128]

At first, it didn't matter that my father is an engineer. And as I was growing up, over time, increasingly, I began to understand that he truly is a smart person, and I can learn a lot [from him] ... He has a wealth of experience and can advise on many questions of an applied nature. Although he comes from the oil sphere, not machine building. But even so, the applied side plays a role. The first temporary work was at Neftemash [oil and gas and machine building] ... The second temporary job was at my father's place of work – processing requirements documents.[129]

Strategic Ambivalences

In storytelling as an act of social self-placement, subtle discursive boundaries vis-à-vis social outsiders, notably the illiterate peasant as well as the proletariat, are also discernable. This observation is not entirely self-evident considering that, for seventy years, the educated groups shared communal dwellings, the office, the shop floor, and indeed intermarried with those engaged in manual occupations. Let us not forget too that the Soviet Union prized and celebrated manual work not only in discourse but also, if we consider the skilled factory workforce, when it comes to pay. I discern these juxtapositions in how

---

[127] Kolesnikova, "Inzhenernyye dinastii," 107 (emphasis added).   [128] Ibid., 108.
[129] Ibid., 107.

respondents distinguish their forbears from new rural entrants into the city, and how they make sense of traces of their own peasant and proletarian roots.

Eclecticism in the de facto social trajectories of respondents' forbears in and of itself constitutes a fertile terrain for delineating one's cultivated status of urban bourgeois as distinct from the ideologically glorified peasant–proletarian identity. I refer to the process of legitimizing an otherwise socially undesirable plebeian trajectory as *strategic ambivalences*. The circumstances of ancestors lacking the formal trappings of higher education are presented as driven by the privations of the era and are set against their aesthetic credentials. Repression in these narratives legitimizes happenings otherwise inexplicable from the point of view of the history of the family's strivings. Strange occurrences in reverse mobility are juxtaposed with "evidence" elevating one above the social group to which one would be now ascribed by dint of a demise in their education or profession. Conversely, even the triumphs associated in the narrators' minds with Soviet state policies would be linked to past signifiers that prepared one for anointment into the post-revolutionary intelligentsia. The descent into a proletarian occupation is juxtaposed with the ethereal qualities that excavate one from the status demotion that resulted from the repressive Moloch. The professional and educational horizons are charted out with reference to subtle denigrations of the *proletariat* and *proletarian occupation* in narratives about ancestors' occupational trajectories. Alternatively, celebratory as they may be, accounts of an uncle or grandfather at the furnace are laced with caveats about temporality, digression, and deviation from what would have been in the past and what would constitute in the future a desirable occupation. The father who is engaged in a "proletarian" occupation but who does not swear, or one who is a factory worker but paints, becomes the symbolic element of status armor; and the descent into a proletarian occupation is not represented in terms of striving and aspiration to embrace a social class constructed as the proletarian vanguard of society but as a downfall, one explicable only in the context of Stalinist privations, repressions, and discrimination.

Zoya Kobozeva legitimizes proletarian aspects of her grandfather's biography with reference to the privations of early post-revolutionary Samara. Born in 1916 and the only son in the family, Boris Mikhaylovich "used to say: 'I always wanted to get an education, but I was forced in those difficult years of the twenties-thirties to support the family, and so I went to the FZU [factory-enterprise vocational *uchilishche*] school."[130] The professional downfall of her aspirational grandfather is set against his and the extended family's aesthetic sensibilities, for "in this family, everyone was artists, everyone did drawing";[131] and "he [grandfather] worked all his life at a machine building plant, but he used to do oil paintings. So, all along *he had an urge toward*

---

[130] Interview, June 19, 2017.   [131] Interview, October 5, 2016.

aesthetics, he would even carve the frames himself. But he rose only to the level of constructor ... my grandfather did." [132]

These juxtapositions of the biographical zigzags that the Soviet regime inflicted on an otherwise ascendant pre-revolutionary social trajectory are also found in the family remembrances of the veteran Samara pedagogue Ol'ga Il'yinishna Kuzmicheva. Ol'ga Il'yinishna was born in 1923 into a *meshchane* family who had been running a tailoring business in the town of Buzuluk. Kuzmicheva recalls that her mother Nina Vasil'yevna Shadrina's numerous attempts to enter the medical school in Soviet Samara were unsuccessful. Rejections were based on origin: "She carried the well-known in the city family name of a property owner [*sobstvennik*], and her wealthy uncle also owned a shop." [133] Only many years later, as a married "mature student" with a school-aged child, did Shadrina manage to gain a place in the evening classes of the Pedagogical Institute's historical faculty, following which she pursued a successful career as a history teacher in primary and secondary schools. [134] The state-thwarted aspirations are set against Nina Vasil'yevna's stellar pre-revolutionary education and the phenomenal erudition of her father. Although Kuzmicheva's mother grew up providing a helping hand as a seamstress in the family's tailoring workshop, we are told that she managed to complete the gymnasium before the Revolution and even received a "gold medal" for outstanding academic performance. [135]

The Samara entrepreneur and theater buff Mikhail Ivanovich Korostelyov [136] presents us with the life paradox of his grandmother Yelena Vladimirovna Petrova, who "never worked anywhere a day in her life," something atypical for the female sex in the Soviet labor market. A highly cultivated woman, Yelena Vladimirovna's refinement is attributed to attendance of an elite secondary school (*uchilishche*) for girls, an establishment that the respondent insists was as close as it gets to approximating Samara's "sole school for refined ladies [*blagorodnykh devits*]." Yelena Vladimirovna's education was evident from her comport. "I have never heard from her a swear word, she never raised her voice, addressed everyone like this – Grishen'ka, Mishen'ka, Yurochka – she stood out in both the way she presented herself and in dress, a very cultured woman." Grandmother's "upbringing had been partially reflected in my father. Although he worked all his life as factory worker, not once in my life did I hear a swear word coming from his mouth." The respondent's facetious admission that the continuities in pre-revolutionary refinement "were disrupted in me, for I can easily swear" masks the resumption of the trajectory of educational and professional aspiration and attainment that was temporarily reversed with his

---

[132] Interview, June 19, 2017 (emphasis added). Kobozeva also mentions the *dacha* (country house) where the family spent summers. Ibid. On the cultural, social status, and estate aspects of *dachi*, see Lovell, *Summerfolk*, esp. 86–117.

[133] Kuzmicheva, "Iz semeynoy khroniki," 157.   [134] Ibid., 157–58.   [135] Ibid., 157.

[136] Name changed. Interview, ZK, February 22, 2017.

parent's factory employment. Despite the swearing, Mikhail Ivanovich did not pursue his father's proletarian route. In his spare time away from his work as a manager in the construction industry, he is a well-known philanthropist, supporting the local theater. "Petty shopkeepers" his ancestors may have been, of whom he possesses photographs dating to the 1880s, but Korostelyov is quick to point out that these traders belonged to the merchant estate and are therefore likely to have been materially well-off.[137]

Yevgeniy Borisovich Bogomolov,[138] the Samara documentary filmmaker, historian, and artist, expresses "surprise" that his father became an artist. He had patchy formal education, growing up as he did during and after the war. Subsequently, in the late 1950s and 1960s, he attended art school where he studied with a legendary Samara-based painter. Bogomolov became a highly regarded artist and was already a leading figure in Samara's cultural circles in the Soviet period. He converted his fame into material capital after the collapse of communism when opportunities for selling art to connoisseurs opened up at home and abroad.[139] Bogomolov's grandfather had been reportedly "an ordinary peasant *muzhik*, who used to drink and swear." Grandmother is also presented as "an entirely ordinary, simple woman," her engagements in the Soviet educational sphere mentioned *en passant* but in ways that strongly accentuate distinction from the uneducated peasant masses: "The only aspect [worth noting] – [father's] mother had been literate. And mother was valued for … Here in Samara earlier there were many from among new arrivals [*prishloye naseleniye*], who used her services because she possessed high literacy."[140] Bogomolov makes it clear, in what is historically accurate, that even grandmother's rudimentary education would set her apart from the less fortunate peasants migrating to Samara in search of factory work or other manual labor. Whatever rudiments of education granny possessed would have elevated both the family's symbolic status and their material well-being whether through her *sluzhba* as a public sector employee, as a participant in the pop-up enlightenment campaigns, or as a private instructor.

CONCLUSION

In this chapter, I analyzed survey data, interviews, memoirs, and other documentary sources in search of familial drivers of status *inheritance* and intergenerational persistence in the stratification derived from the imperial estates beyond the first demographic cohort of Soviet-born citizenry. Survey data provided some tentative evidence of links between self-reported educated estates ancestry and professional-occupational placement in Soviet and post-Soviet Russia. Drawing on theorizing into collective memory, I then analyzed the ways in which social values, preferences, and boundaries were reproduced, maintained, and protected within families whether in an agential, purposeful

---

[137] Ibid.   [138] Name changed.   [139] Interview, ZK, 2017.   [140] Interview, ZK, 2017.

sense or as habitual practice. This chapter has also benefited from Bourdieu's theorizing into the engines of social distinction, while contributing insights into precisely how social lethargy operates in repressive, socially uprooting contexts. Cultural, symbolic, and material remnants of material capital(s) were all evidently combined to restore and patch up the punctured and truncated "fields" of estatist, delineated and circumscribed, social interaction. Yet the ways in which status had been and is being reaffirmed are very peculiar to the communist experience – for our respondents have had to deal with the consequences of social disgrace and their families' downfall – something unlikely to have been experienced en masse by the Bourdieusian bourgeoisie. We have yet to more fully explore the implications of repression and being uprooted in terms of social resilience and persistence, and it is to these questions I turn in Chapter 8.

8

Society in Space

The picturesque village [*selo*], located by the Volga and surrounded by oak groves, fields – this is my little motherland, my Yekaterinovka. Here lived several generations of my ancestors.

School essay on family history[1]

WIFE: "They [Soviet authorities] tried to send my husband [to work somewhere else in another village]"
HUSBAND: "And they failed."

Villagers, Pestravka[2]

In Fyodor Dostoevsky's *Demons*, an arson attack consumes the entire quarter of wooden dwellings in Zarech'ye, the outskirts of an unnamed town, in flames and multiple grisly murders are perpetrated on one night;[3] and it is during this night that the Governor's wife gathers the top layers of provincial society for an elaborately planned evening of highbrow entertainment. Space in this provincial city mirrors society, as the aristocratic quarter of Madam von Lembke's *soirée* contrasts with the shabby dwellings on the outskirts of town, what with their dim and unpaved dirt roads, feral dogs, deranged fallen women, and wayward criminals. The evening does not go to plan, for, unbeknownst to Madam von Lembke, a group of conspirators inspired by radical socialist ideas lure the uninvited parvenu, the merchant wives, and the *meshchane* to the high society event. A night of drinking and debauchery ensues; the town's outskirts, in the persons of Zarech'ye inhabitants, invade the genteel homes of the

---

[1] Participant, V Annual Essay Competition "Family History-2013," Tolyatti.
[2] Interview, Pestravka, June 21, 2017.
[3] Also translated as *The Possessed*. On the influence on Soviet intellectuals, see also Shlapentokh, *Soviet Intellectuals*, 94.

provincial aristocracy. Meanwhile, Zarech'ye's abandoned homes are torched. Social disorder – as the clique of radicals hoped – leads to the embarrassment and downfall of the provincial powers that be.[4] Dostoevsky's *Demons* anticipated the orgy of violence and destruction that flowed from the revolutionary ideals of nineteenth-century radical socialists. *Demons* also portrayed a society in flux, but one in which the marker of the estate continued to divide groups and to categorize them in space.

One and a half centuries later, space continues to mirror fissures in society, those that cleave the worlds of rural and urban dwellers; and within cities, those of the outer rim of working districts and the decorous homes of Russia's new bourgeoisie. The spatial dimension of Soviet modernization has often been invoked as pivotal to the reconfiguration of social relations, ties, and bonds. Here, as with other aspects of knowledge production on the Soviet project, to paraphrase James Scott, the historian and the social scientist "saw," as it were, like the Soviet state.[5] The bird's-eye view of policies apparently reconfiguring society in space overlooked both the appropriative logic of the Bolsheviks' developmental strategy and the inner rationality of social resilience. Inertia, manifested in both state policy and the social responses to it – for better or worse – like the underlying conservative moral of Dostoevsky's *Demons*, will come to triumph against Utopia.

Up to this point, I have only tangentially touched on Soviet industry. Yet this is precisely the domain that is often invoked in discussions of the socially transformative, indeed highly coercive, and spatially uprooting aspect of the Soviet Union's state-directed modernization.[6] Even if we accept elements of social resilience in the skills, know-how, and values of communities, we cannot deny the vastness and the magnitude of the Soviet industrial giants; the speed at which the state went about developing industries, rail, petrochemical, and other infrastructures; and the socially transformative consequences of these schemes in space. Stephen Kotkin's book *Magnetic Mountain* captures the sheer scale and ambition of some of the mega-projects.[7] Stalinist repressions, epitomized notoriously in the vast Gulag conglomerate of coerced labor settlements, also underline the urgency to explore how repression undermined, obliterated, or transformed the social fabric of a place. Not only were people moved at random but directives were promulgated setting curbs on victims' freedom of relocation after their release.[8] Even when coercion was not involved, many were commandeered to develop one or another industrial frontier as part of Soviet job placements; and many simply escaped, ran away, or disappeared for good,

---

[4] Dostoevsky, *Besy*, 8–9.   [5] Scott, *Seeing Like a State*.
[6] See, for instance, Hill and Gaddy, *The Siberian Curse*.   [7] Kotkin, *Magnetic Mountain*.
[8] Discussion in Tomila Lankina and Alexander Libman, "The Jekyll and Hyde of Soviet Policies: Endogenous Modernization, the Gulag and Post-Communist Support for Democracy." Paper presented at the Annual Meeting and Exhibition of the American Political Science Association, San Francisco, August 31 to September 3, 2017 (unpublished).

in an impulse to survive, to save their family, and against the odds of privations, coercion, and repression.[9] What do these legacies do to the social structure? The argument I develop in this chapter is that we discern social reproduction not only *despite* but, in some ways, *because of* communist industrial strategy. Whether inside or outside of the Gulag, Soviet industry relentlessly appropriated both the hardware – the infrastructures of modernity – and the software – the human resources in pedagogy, medicine, research, public enlightenment, and engineering. In turn, social mechanisms of relationships of status and closure converged with the state's developmentalist and survivalist imperatives. Unpacking these channels of resilience even when set against the most coercive aspect of Soviet planning provides additional credence to the argument that Russia had not been the purported melting pot that annihilated the society of estates.

The chapter continues as follows. I begin by performing systematic cross-regional statistical analysis to demonstrate that Soviet industries and high-tech knowledge hubs built on tsarist Russia's industrial heritage. Next, to back up my argument about the merits of anchoring an analysis of industry in the prior developmental and social ecosystem of a place, I provide illustrative vignettes of appropriations in Samara's consumer services, strategic armaments, and petrochemicals. I also discuss an aspect of Soviet state development that has invited the naïve observer to assume a *de novo* approach to the Soviet project, namely the establishment of "brand new" cities like Tolyatti. Based on a discussion of societal distinctions within Samara City, I then explore how even large-scale population movements followed the logic of social closure.

STATISTICAL ANALYSIS

How do we reconcile path-dependency in spatial aspects of economic development with repressions?[10] In what Alexander Libman and I have

---

[9] Edele, *Stalinist Society.*

[10] Although volumes have been written on the purges, there are few systematic regional statistics. An exception is Zhukov and Talibova, "Stalin's Terror." On the challenges of gathering systematic and complete data on repressions even with the archival materials now open to scholars, see Khlevniuk, *History of the Gulag*, 287–327. Rigby provides some evidence of the implications of repressions for regional party cadre for select regions only. Rigby, *Communist Party Membership*, 207–8. On national- and Soviet republic-level statistics, see Ellman, "Soviet Repression Statistics"; and Rosefielde, "Documented Homicides." Academic accounts, which are more transparent about the demographic realities of the Soviet state than popular books, indicate that, however ghastly, "repression *mortality* (excluding famine, war and disease mortality, and repression survivors) was only a modest part of the demographic history of the USSR." Ellman, "Soviet Repression Statistics," 1164 (emphasis in original). Robert Conquest's work has been criticized for overstating repression casualties because of the nature of the target readership: "He [Conquest] is a writer on Soviet affairs for the general public." Ibid., 1157. For detailed critiques, see ibid., 1155–58. The Great Purge had the most horrific toll on the general citizenry and the party. Ellman provides a "reasonable minimal estimate" of

conceptualized as the "Jekyll-and-Hyde" faces of Stalinist modernization,[11] the co-optation of tsarist Russia's qualified cadre went hand in hand with repressions targeting those same groups, beginning with the Shakhty affair that blacklisted engineers in the 1920s and culminating with the so-called Doctors' plot immediately preceding Stalin's death. Territorial cleansing is a known facet of repressions: many *lishentsy* were exiled to other regions;[12] and whole communities, in the Samara region the *Wolgadeutsche*, were forcibly displaced.[13]

There is now considerable historical evidence linking the origins of the Gulag to Soviet developmental imperatives.[14] The notorious archipelago provided slave labor where it was most needed, on large industrial and infrastructural sites. Were these coercive projects divorced from the industrial-economic ecosystems in existence before the camps were set up? My research collaborator Alexander Libman and I investigated covariation between pre-revolutionary human capital and the location of Gulag labor camps. We employed the dataset compiled by Tatiana Mikhailova based on documentary sources from Memorial, an NGO that has scrupulously assembled records of Stalinist crimes,[15] and located camps in present-day *rayony* using their geographic coordinates. Consistent with recent historical scholarship on the utilization of penal labor to service the war effort and industrialization, we found that spatial patterns of Gulag location – the topography of repressive institutions,[16] and not just of cooptation – were linked to tsarist-era human capital.[17] Furthermore, Table 8.1 indicates that those

950,000 deaths, with the "upper bound" estimated at 1.2 million. Ibid., 1154–55. In January 1938, the Soviet Union's population was roughly 160,294 million. Rosefielde, "Documented Homicides," 329. Khlevniuk provides an illustration of the scale of repression in one temporal snapshot. In 1937, according to the January census, the Soviet Union population of those aged sixteen and over was slightly above 100 million. He estimates that, in the early 1930s, roughly one-sixth of all adults were subjected to different forms of persecutions and repression. Khlevniuk, *History of the Gulag*, 304. Yet these horrific statistics also imply that, in that time frame, roughly five-sixths of the adult population were not shot, incarcerated, exiled, deported, or arrested, even if severely psychologically affected. This record makes analysis of social-structural resilience meaningful, even assuming the massive population compositional shifts in space.

[11] Lankina and Libman, "Jekyll and Hyde."   [12] Alexopoulos, *Stalin's Outcasts*.
[13] Conquest, *Nation Killers*.
[14] See, for example, Tatiana Mikhailova, "Gulag, WWII and the Long-run Patterns of Soviet City Growth." Munich Personal RePEc Archive, No. 41758, September 9, 2012. Available online at: ideas.repec.org/p/pra/mprapa/41758.html (accessed November 9, 2020); and Applebaum, *Gulag*.
[15] "Mikhailova, "Gulag."
[16] In what corroborates our account, other scholars found that tsarist railroad networks gave localities an "advantage" as a provider of forced camp labor. See Zhukov and Talibova, "Stalin's Terror," 274 and 275n13.
[17] We may also conjecture that citizens residing close to the camps were more aware of repressions. See Natalia Kapelko and Andrei Markevich, "The Political Legacy of the Gulag Archipelago," October 30, 2014. Unpublished manuscript. Available online at: dx.doi.org/10.2139/ssrn.2516635 (accessed January 1, 2021). Relatedly, when interviewing Soviet refugees in the early 1950s, scholars found that being arrested or the arrest of a family member markedly increased

TABLE 8.1 *Difference in average pre-revolutionary characteristics of districts (literacy and share of specific estates) with and without a Gulag camp (t-test)*

	No gulag	Gulag	Sig. difference of means
literacy	17.712	20.165	***
nobility	0.823	1.160	***
clergy	0.509	0.625	***
merchants	0.181	0.241	***
meshchane	5.955	6.603	*
peasants	78.566	70.210	***
foreigners	0.764	2.043	***

Note. * $p<0.1$; ** $p<0.05$; *** $p<0.01$.
Source. Analysis based on Tomila Lankina and Alexander Libman, "The Jekyll and Hyde of Soviet Policies: Endogenous Modernization, the Gulag and Post-Communist Support for Democracy." Paper presented at the Annual Meeting and Exhibition of the American Political Science Association, San Francisco, August 31 to September 3, 2017 (unpublished) and Lankina and Libman, "Two-Pronged Middle Class"; reproduced and expanded with permission of coauthor.

estates conceptualized here as educated – a good proxy for both the institutional and the human dimension of expertise – are significantly more likely to feature in areas designated as camp settlements.[18] Camps were situated in the vicinity of developed industrial infrastructure and facilities and, of course, where software in the persons of engineers, technicians, and scientists of imperial training were present. The Gulag thus tended to enhance and consolidate extant, pre-communist, spatial variations in industrial development.

To provide additional quantitative evidence that Soviet modernization policies relied on extant human capital as part of the agenda of industrialization, data for territories marked as "closed cities" were also analyzed. These were nationally designated territories originating at least in the 1940s and endowed with special status. Nonresidents were denied access to these towns, which helped advance the Soviet nuclear project and research related to the military-industrial complex. The Soviet government made decisions on the location of secret cities in a centralized fashion. The Russian authorities declassified these sites after the fall of the Soviet Union.

To assess the extent to which preexisting developmental infrastructures mattered for decisions to endow cities with the status of a closed entity we

respondents' hostility to the Soviet system. Inkeles and Bauer, *Soviet Citizen*, 266. See, however, Zhukov and Talibova, "Stalin's Terror." The authors find negative consequences of exposure to Stalin-era repression for post-communist electoral participation.
[18] Shearer, "Soviet Gulag," 724.

TABLE 8.2 *Secret cities: comparison of historical characteristics (literacy and share of specific estates, t-test)*

	No secret city	Secret city	Sig. difference of means
literacy	17.817	24.133	***
nobility	0.851	1.096	
clergy	0.514	0.806	***
merchants	0.186	0.259	**
meshchane	5.973	8.040	***
peasants	77.665	80.809	
foreigners	0.889	1.022	

Note. * $p<0.1$; ** $p<0.05$; *** $p<0.01$.
Source: Analysis based on Lankina and Libman, "Jekyll and Hyde"; "Two-Pronged Middle Class"; reproduced and expanded with permission of coauthor.

created a binary variable for districts with a secret city.[19] Comparing their historical characteristics with those of other *rayony* in Table 8.2, we observe striking patterns. The placement of these clandestine operations clearly had not been random, as the target districts featured comparatively high literacy and populations from the educated estates before the Revolution. Again, as with the Gulag, purposeful, state-led policies exploited and enhanced the developmental edge of some areas, while leaving others behind. Moreover, given what we know about the Bolsheviks' reliance on a skilled cadre, these policies would have had the effect of conserving elements of the pre-revolutionary social structure.

UNPACKING APPROPRIATIONS

The Zhigulyovskiy Beer Plant

Archival and other qualitative materials provide some texture to the appropriative dynamics in industry and their implications for social resilience. One nonstrategic enterprise, the Zhigulyovskiy Beer Production Plant, provides a good starting point. The plant continued production in the Soviet period and has thrived in the post-Soviet market economy of Samara. This case goes beyond illustrating the crafting of the mythologies about the *sovietness* of Soviet industry, since it supplies an example of the preservation of complex economic ecosystems that went beyond the primary objective of catch-up in heavy industry.

[19] Lankina and Libman, "Jekyll and Hyde."

The Bolshevik regime had never been entirely immune to sensitivity toward the consumer tastes, wants, and preference of Soviet citizens, not least due to the imperative of filling the state's coffers. Samara supplies but one, albeit a highly poignant, sketch of the scores of light industries that were appropriated. These were removed from or, to the extent that they were meant to keep workers happy and productive and revenue flowing, only tangentially connected to the objectives of the five-year plan, the electrification of the nation, or the space project. Samara had been home to one such industry that produced and cherished the quintessentially *Soviet* beer brand. A website dedicated to the celebration of Soviet beer begins thus: "Soviet beer ... For some reason, one instantly imagines Zhigulyovskoye and Zhigulyovskoye only, as though nothing else existed."[20] "The 'Zhigulyovskoye' beer was a truly people's brand, known to the entire Union. And its taste was familiar to the overwhelming majority of the male population of the country," claimed another authoritative account. The 22 kopeks for half a liter of tap beer notwithstanding – for comparison, the popular berry ice-cream bar was 7 kopeks[21] – it always enjoyed high demand.[22] "The most sought after bottled beer was again 'Zhigulyovskoye.' It had a spirit content of 2.8 percent and was tangy [*yadryonoye*], with a pleasant taste."[23] The Russian blogosphere has also continued to celebrate this quintessentially "Soviet" brand, for, as a Viktor Leonov writes, "many people continue to remember Soviet beer with a smile on their face. Back then they knew how to brew genuine, tasty beer. Especially liked was the 'Zhigulyovskoye,' the most popular and famous."[24]

The "legend" surrounding this brand illuminates as much the sensory sophistication of the Soviet food industry chief Anastas Mikoyan as it does the appropriative instincts of Soviet planners. According to one account, a certain "Venskoye" beer, a product of the Zhigulyovskiy plant, took the coveted top prize in the agricultural exhibition in Moscow. Mikoyan took a special liking to this beer but inquired as to the "bourgeois" labeling. "Let us rename it after your plant as 'Zhigulyovskoye'!," he is reported to have said.[25] The discarded Venskoye (Viennese) label is itself evocative of the origins of the brand, conceived in the von Vakano breweries and owned by Samara's distinguished Russified industrialists and philanthropists of Austrian origin. Before Bolshevik appropriation, the factory, which opened in 1881, had

---

[20] Pavel V. Yegorov, "Pivo v SSSR" (www.пи.BO.ru), March 8, 2014. Available online at: nubo.ru/pavel_egorov/pivo_sssr.html (accessed May 11, 2020).

[21] The ice cream still features on Russian culinary websites. See "Yedim doma" (eating at home): edimdoma.ru/retsepty/25349-morozhenoe-za-7-kopeek (accessed May 11, 2020).

[22] See *Strana SSSR: Vsyo o Sovetskom soyuze* (Country USSR: Everything about the Soviet Union): strana-sssr.net//статьи/сделано-в-ссср/советский-пищепром/пиво-в-советском-союзе.html (accessed May 11, 2020).

[23] Ibid.   [24] Ibid. See page discussion thread.

[25] According to other accounts, Mikoyan took note of the beer when he visited the plant in Samara. See "Pivo."

already become the leading supplier of beer throughout the Middle Volga region and other *gubernii*.[26]

What made Zhigulyovskoye the nation's favorite beer is the peculiar flavor, derived from a special brewing process using Viennese malt. The "secret" ingredient of success, hitherto imported, was over time substituted with a homegrown extract, but the recipe remained essentially the same. Alcohol production continued to function unscathed during the NEP years, and it is those years that count as the "official birth of the Soviet spirits industry." In 1922, the government introduced an alcohol licensing regime, leaving the production process intact but regulating and taxing it. Zhigulyovsokoye was the most famous imperial brand, but many others followed suit in the rebranding exercise, basically remaining the same alcohol beverages.[27] If anything, it is the post-Soviet era that is associated with the *erosion* of the original brand. This is when failing Soviet food and beverage industries adapted hitherto unknown technologies that substituted the natural ingredients and production process of the bygone era with the carcinogenic chemistry of America's junk food industry. Consequently, the "quintessentially soviet" Zhigulyovskoye brand so fondly reminisced about on the Russian blogosphere is that very same Viennese beer, reproduced through the seven decades of Soviet rule. The Soviet state, paradoxically, appears here as one faithfully preserving and cherishing the bygone regime's heritage, not one building the edifices of important production industries from scratch.

As anecdotal as this digression may appear to the reader, in this analysis the wholesale appropriation of the "shell" of a prosperous company, of the chain of supply (Zhigulyovskoye remained the most widely distributed beer much like the von Vakano product had been before 1917), of the technology, ingredients, and recipe of production, also speaks to the question of social path-dependencies in space. In my analysis, the emphasis on the appropriative side of the Soviet industrial strategy goes beyond illuminating structural continuities, since an appropriated ecosystem transcends the material-artifactual foundations of development. Here, again, the human resources that made the continuous and vast operation possible would be the same pre-revolutionary brewers and other industry specialists. The beer enterprise illuminates the normal side of the hundreds of industries, unscathed by the high-profile cases of "wreckers" among doctors, engineers, and scientists.

---

[26] The plant was also a pioneer in modern technology, notably electrification. Other entrepreneurs sought to emulate it and set up rival beer production facilities in Samara. Savchenko and Dubinin, *Rossiyskiye nemtsy*, 84, 88, 90.

[27] "Pivo."

The Sergiyevskiy Munitions Plant

The Sergiyevskiy Munitions Plant, presently "OAO 'Polimer'" in the city of Chapayevsk,[28] captures the appropriative dimension of Soviet policy in the strategic industries. The plant, located roughly 43 kilometers southwest of the regional capital Samara, had been founded in 1910 and in 1912 was named the Samara Sergiyevskiy Plant of Explosive Materials; it became tsarist Russia's leading center of munitions production.[29] It also proved pivotal to the Soviet Union's war effort against Nazi Germany and the postwar armaments industry. "During the Great Patriotic War," states the Russian-language Wikipedia page for the town and plant, "the Chapayevskiy [Sergiyevskiy] plant No. 15 was one of the few enterprises in the country where the entire range of explosive materials required for our army was being produced, which made a big contribution to the Victory of the Soviet people in its struggle against Hitler's fascism."[30] Soviet propagandists were keen to present this military-industrial giant as a product of the wartime evacuation of industries vulnerable to German attack to the provincial hinterland of Samara. Like scores of other production facilities across the country, an appropriated industrial giant in fact continued to function in a virtually uninterrupted fashion from its opening in 1911 all the way until the collapse of the Soviet Union; it remains operative today. By the time of the Bolshevik Revolution, thousands of workers were employed in the sprawling plant. Thereafter, it continued to expand; many engineers and skilled employees were retained despite class-based recriminations about their bourgeois origins and repressions targeting leading specialists in 1928–29. In the early 1920s, the factory was renamed Trotsk after Leon Trotsky, and later, when the Old Bolshevik fell into disfavor, it became known as the Chapayevsk factory. That scarce public records exist on the inner workings of Sergiyevskiy and other such plants beyond the 1920s and 1930s is itself testimony to their pivotal role in production for Soviet defense. The erstwhile Sergiyevskiy turned Plant No. 15 exemplifies the phenomenon of the "secret" city built around the extant hardware and human software.[31] The

---

[28] OAO stands for *otkrytoye aktsionernoye obshchestvo* (open shareholding society). Valeriy Yerofeyev, "Samarskiy zavod vzryvchatykh veshchestv," *Istoricheskaya Samara* (Historical Samara). Available online at: историческая-самара.рф/каталог/самарская-промышленность/самарский-завод-взрывчатых-веществ.html (accessed May 11, 2020).

[29] The plant had R&D operations and infrastructure for the medical care of staff as well as for leisure pastimes (a library and theater). Local Samara merchants bid for contracts for construction work, compensating low costings with cheap labor, mostly seasonal peasant workers from surrounding villages. Schools and vocational training were also expanding to meet the demand for skilled technicians. Documentary history available from Chigrinyov, *Ocherki*. A brief historical note is available from Yerofeyev, "Samarskiy zavod."

[30] See the Wikipedia entry for "Chapayevsk": ru.wikipedia.org/wiki/чапаевск (accessed May 31, 2020).

[31] The estimate for the number of employees in 1916 is 5,110, including workers in the construction of supplementary facilities and warehouses. By autumn 1917, residents, including families

facility's successive waves of rebranding and eventual anonymization on Russia's map go some way toward explaining the mythologization of the *sovietness* of the Bolsheviks' industrial project.

Archival sources add texture to general territorial patterns of reproduction of the cadre along with the appropriated industrial infrastructure in future secret facilities. The materials that I possess on the facility's personnel only cover the 1920s. Nevertheless, they go some way toward illuminating patterns of resilience in human resources and hierarchies of expertise, in evidence even as repressions unfolded. The difficulty of unpacking continuities in the embeddedness of the social structure within strategic industries is evident from a slice of documentary personnel records that straddle the late imperial and early post-revolutionary periods. In the years immediately preceding the Bolshevik takeover in Samara, personnel records, including applications for job hire, staff recommendations for promotion, and so on, continued to feature references to one's estate. Low-paid manual laborers not only habitually featured as "peasant" but many maintained attachments to the village:

Tsyganov S. P., peasant from Simbirskaya guberniya, plasterer.

V. V. Churakov, peasant, carpenter.

Aleksey Yakovlev Boltonogov, peasant, master (worker).[32]

I hereby humbly request Your High Excellency [*Vashe Vysokoblagorodiye*] permission for a three-week break, to visit my motherland, Vyatskaya *guberniya*, Yelabuzhskiy *uyezd*, Kozel'skaya *volost'*, village of Yakovlevo for managing my estate [*khozyaystvo*].[33]

I have the honour to humbly request You, Your High Excellency for a break to visit my Motherland, the village of Tsarkovnoye in Vitebskaya *guberniya* for at least 18 days to procure warm clothes and shoes, since a miserable and cold weather is approaching, and for work at the plant I do not have anything besides the work military clothing, which has become very shabby. Am in military service since 28 March 1916.[34]

Less frequently, among the skilled blue-collar workforce, we find references to *meshchanin* and perhaps one simultaneously deriving rent from an urban property, which is a challenge to Bolshevik portrayals of employees in class terms. A joiner, the Buguruslan *meshchanin* M. F. Petrov, was, for instance, spotted distributing leaflets for the Social-Democratic Party.[35] The white-collar

---

of workers at Sergiyevskiy and others servicing it, numbered 55,525, with 30,000 workers at the Sergiyevskiy plant, the Tomylov artillery warehouse, the Ushakov plant, and *zemstvo* phosphates plant. Chigrinyov, *Ocherki*, 26, and in the same volume in the chapter "Nakanune."

[32] Listings of military conscripts and staff. SOGASPI, f. 700, op. 1, d. 156, l. 4; and of free lancers (*po vol'nomu naymu*). TsGASO, f. 700, op. 1, d. 222, l. 1.

[33] Lists of employees under the authority of the plant's architect; certificates for 1916. TsGASO, f. 700, op. 1, d. 168, l. 29.

[34] Ibid., l. 63.

[35] Correspondence with Samara *guberniya* gendarmery management concerning hiring and dismissals of workers, 1915. TsGASO, f. 700, op. 2, d. 14, l. 19.

workforce appears with accolades corresponding to the Petrine Table of Ranks, which we know blended with the estate structure:

Kollezhskiy registrator Grigoriy Vankhal'skiy, clerk ... Roman Catholic, received education in the Kiev military feldsher college ... reliable ... superb mental skills ... impeccable morals, good family man, does not consume alcoholic beverages, does not smoke, does not play cards ...[36]

Head doctor of the Sergiyevskiy Samara plant of explosive materials, *Kollezhskiy sovetnik*, Pavel Sheffer ... is of modest tastes, reserved in matters of alcoholic beverages and impeccably honest. Scientifically educated in all branches of medicine, has excellent familiarity with eye diseases and wide knowledge of medical literature.[37]

Moreover, staff would go some lengths toward verifying a noble pedigree:

I request Your High Excellence [*Vashe Prevoskhoditel'stvo*] to inform me of the origins of a worker at the plant, a Mikhail Matveyevich Spasskiy, since according to the notification from the Samara nobles' representative assembly, he is not listed among the nobles of the City of Samara.[38]

Following the Bolshevik Revolution, existing employees became "comrades";[39] there is no record of immediate wholesale purges of "bourgeois" staff, although white-collar employees, management, and indeed the Soviet of Worker Deputies at the enterprise voted to enthusiastically endorse the State Duma and Provisional Government in the wake of the "bourgeois" February Revolution of 1917.[40] Even before the Bolsheviks established power in Samara, discussions and directives featured the authorization of the amalgamation "into one combined town" of settlements comprising the Sergiyevskiy plant, the Tomylovskiy artillery warehouse, the Ushakov Chemical Plant, the Samara *zemstvo* phosphates settlement, and the Vladimirskiy settlement, as well as workers engaged in construction on the sites – altogether thousands of people. While many in the settlements were soldiers, stationed and working at the facilities temporarily, others were established residents with families dwelling in barracks or apartments.[41] These records corroborate not only the argument about social appropriation but also the administrative fusion between extant infrastructure,

---

[36] Personal characteristics on *sluzhashchiye*, 1911. TsGASO, f. 700, op. 3, d. 1, 1912, l. 2.

[37] Ibid., l. 8. Sheffer, who had a degree as a Doctor of Medicine from the Imperial Kazan University, supervised several medics and feldshers. Medical care was free for plant workers while every doctor's visit to builders was charged to the contractor at 20 kopeks per visit. Sheffer lobbied to establish free treatment for eye diseases in the factory's clinics. Chigrinyov, *Ocherki*.

[38] Correspondence concerning hiring and dismissals, 1914. TsGASO, f. 700, op. 2, d. 14, l. 83.

[39] Protocols, 1917–18. TsGASO, f. 700, op. 5, d. 13, l. 19.

[40] On the State Coup (*perevorot*) of 1917, March 2, 1917. TsGASO, f. 700, op. 6, d. 1, ll., 1, 3, 7, 9, 12, 55.

[41] The papers include "Lists of electors of individuals, residing in apartments and barracks [*kazarmy*] in the vicinity of the Sergiyevskiy plant." TsGASO, f. 700, op. 5, d. 138, ll. 1, 3, 45–82. On discussions about establishing a new administrative settlement, see Chigrinyov, *Ocherki*.

skills, human capital, and "new" strategic facilities and would-be "secret" R&D and production settlements.

One early documentary record of the wave of repressions in the 1920s is a 1924 Samara *guberniya* "top secret" GPU file containing a survey of "politically untrustworthy" cadre working at the Trotsky Plant. The exercise in class vigilance resulted in recommendations to dismiss thirty-four workers.[42] The response of the plant manager, a certain A. Ya. Kustov, was to defend, and advocate the retention of, most of the employees. Kustov couched his objections in terms of the difficulties of finding replacements for qualified staff and to the unfair and unfounded allegations. "Obsequiousness" (*podkhalimstvo*) and a fondness for alcoholic beverages were some of the unjust allegations that he cited. These, he claimed, had nothing to do with production and work quality but perhaps more to do with personal rivalries and animosities between workers. Delaying tactics were also deployed as appeals were made to return to the issue in the future: "The practical implementation of the protocol would lead to complete disruption of the administrative-technical and managerial apparatus of the plant, which has to be regarded as unacceptable at a time when the plant is expanding its production program," pleaded Kustov. Workers facing dismissal included those like O. K. Yurvelin, a specialist working on the production of capsules, described as "one of a very limited number of specialists available in Soviet Russia, for military plants an exceptionally necessary person." An S. I. Fomichev was defended on the grounds that his "conscientiousness at work need not be qualified as obsequiousness." A comrade V. Ya. Gerasimov, a "specialist-chemist," could not possibly be dismissed; "he has been learning the capsule specialism for two years and complaints about his productivity could be only explained with reference to his short record of practical experience." The accountant comrade R. V. Kurganov inherited "abysmal" (*v sovershenno zapushchennom vide*) levels of accounting on taking up his post in 1923; he is credited with "bringing it [bookkeeping] to a satisfactory level, taking initiative and expending energy in carrying out reforms in accounting." Kurganov had not been spotted at work in a state of inebriation, though, admittedly, he had been so sighted "outside of the workplace." Then there was a certain comrade, A. N. Silant'yev, "a talented constructor, familiar with all the equipment at the plant, which had been built with his direct participation. His replacement would damage production." The manager recommended only two employees for immediate dismissal, while an additional nine staff were to be laid off "in the future," when trained specialists could be found to replace them.[43] Kustov may not have succeeded in saving the entire cohort of tsarist staff facing the ax. The apparently successful defense of his technocratic charges nevertheless speaks to

---

[42] Protocol, session of Commission on review of plant personnel named after Comrade Trotsky, June 11, 1924. SOGASPI, f. 1, op. 1, d. 968, ll. 99–101.

[43] Protocol. SOGASPI, f. 1, op. 1, d. 968, ll. 102, 102, ob. Kustov's response appended as "Special Opinion" based on protocol of April 2, 1924 of session of Personnel Review Commission.

the sociologist Max Weber's conviction – perhaps not entirely unwarranted even in Soviet Russia – that "generally speaking, the highest-ranking career official is more likely to get his way in the long run than his nominal superior, the cabinet minister, who is not a specialist."[44] Kustov, here, emerges as the precursor to the generic portrait of the Factory Manager in Joseph Berliner's classic account of the savviness, inventiveness, and ingenuity of the industry operative navigating the Orwellian world of unrealistic production quotas in Stalin's Soviet Union.[45]

Kustov's appellations to the authorities would not have necessarily fallen on deaf ears, since the technocratic arms of the party and state bureaucracies, as indeed the leading national-level cadre of so-called Old Bolsheviks, tended to be socially embedded in the highly educated layers of tsarist society. Consistent with patterns discussed in Chapter 4 concerning the vertical ties linking the provincial and metropolitan professional, the historian Sheila Fitzpatrick has proposed the term *semeistvennost'*. A concept that we could loosely translate as familism, it describes patronage favoring those who had fallen into disfavor on ideological grounds.[46] The metaphor of "family" protection may characterize a situation where party and administrative apparatchiks salvage an employee amid a bureaucratic muddle involving different agencies. Familism also captures attempts by the more fortunate members of a given social circle, who may have found their way into a managerial position in an enterprise, party, or Soviet bureaucracy, to rescue a less privileged associate from a pending dismissal or arrest. New evidence indicates that such survivalist dynamics were far more widespread, even at the height of the Great Terror, than had been hitherto assumed.[47] The examples given here also illustrate that it was not just vertical ties between a superior and employee that were at work but also horizontal forms of support where peers rallied in defense of a fellow worker.

The Petrochemicals Industry and the Gulag

The petrochemicals industry is another window into the appropriative aspects of Soviet development in space. It also illuminates the ways in which even the most brutal repressions epitomized by the Gulag mirrored relational aspects of the social structure within Soviet institutions. The emergence of Samara as one of the RSFSR's regional energy hubs is usually contextualized as the wartime evacuation of industries threatened by the advancing forces of the Third Reich. Between June 1941 and the early months of 1942, German forces carried out what came to be known as the blitzkrieg series of attacks on Russia's western regions, inflicting severe casualties on Soviet forces. By July 1942, the advancing German troops, determined to obtain access to the strategic energy reserves of the Caucasus, were mounting an assault on Russia's Southern Front. Faced with the prospect of imminent annexation of the oil fields, Russia began the

---

[44] Weber, *Economy and Society*, 1:224.   [45] Berliner, *Factory and Manager*.
[46] Described also as "family circles." Fitzpatrick, "Two Faces," 25.   [47] Golitsyn, *Zapiski*.

liquidation of operative oil rigs. It is at this time that Hitler was notoriously presented with a birthday cake decorated with a map of the Soviet Caucasus.[48] The Soviet government evacuated Russia's administrative capital, Moscow, and much of the industrial production to Samara. As German forces advanced toward the Caspian energy basin, frantic operations began to secure alternative sources of energy and transit routes. On April 7, 1942, the Soviet government endorsed the country's first major pipeline project, and in a short time span completed the 165-kilometer-long gas artery linking the Middle Volga towns of Buguruslan, Pokhvistnevo, and Samara.[49]

An economic-social ecosystem perspective taken here would place these initiatives in the wider temporal context of the development of Russia's industrial frontier. Already in the 1840s, Russian and European scientists were organizing geological expeditions with the aim of finding fossil fuels in the Middle Volga region. In the late nineteenth century, the syndicate of the Nobel Brothers' oil giant, as well as British and Belgian major oil enterprises, set their eyes on expanding oil fields beyond the Caspian Sea Basin and developing the oil and gas deposits in the Middle Volga.[50] The exigencies of the global energy market, however, put a break on imminent extraction. Emissaries of the Nobel Brothers Petroleum Production Company ostensibly went as far as bribing village communes and elders with large sums of cash to resist extraction, thereby sustaining high oil prices.[51] After the Bolsheviks took power, they set up a government department charged with the urgent exploration of oil in the Volga-Urals region.[52] These explorations built on the foundations of studies by imperial scientists and geologists like Ivan Mikhaylovich Gubkin. Gubkin and other members of the old scientific cadre were called on to facilitate exploration in the 1920s. In 1935–36, precise locations of oil and gas deposits and other minerals valuable for the chemical industry were eventually discovered in the Orenburg *oblast*.[53] By the time Russia was at war with Germany, extraction and the "Second Baku" boom, had already begun.[54] To achieve the mammoth task of developing energy extraction and transportation arteries, more "islands" were added to the Gulag archipelago, and more native and outside workers were mobilized to service both the highly technical aspects of oil exploration and the backbreaking manual labor of digging pipeline trenches, laying railway tracks, and constructing other infrastructure for alternative energy supply routes.[55]

---

[48] Blinova et al., *Rossiya*, 10.   [49] Ibid., 14.   [50] Ibid., 1–2.   [51] Ibid., 2.   [52] Ibid., 3.
[53] Ibid., 4–7.   [54] Ibid., 7.
[55] A special agency, *Upravleniye osobogo stroitel'stva NKVD SSSR* (Directorate of Special Construction of the USSR NKVD) managed the complex of camps known as Bezymyanlag, which were to facilitate the development of the aerospace and motor industries. Bezymyanlag had been part of a larger camp complex, including Samarlag, established in 1937 to construct a hydroelectric dam. With some 36,761 inmates in 1939, Samarlag is estimated at the time to have been the second largest in European Russia. Bezymyanlag likewise became one of the biggest in the Gulag system, in 1940–41 "hosting" more than 100,000 penal laborers. Exact

Recent historiography on the camps and forced labor that manned the pipeline work sheds light on the ways in which the know-how associated with pre-Soviet explorations and technical training was brought to bear on this effort. Declassified NKVD and industry files contain agonizing requests from operatives charged with delivering the construction plan to superiors running the Gulag operation in Moscow to make more "rational" use of and to engage, whether incarcerated or freely employed (*vol'nonayomnyye*), "qualified builders ... engineers and technicians."[56] In the Bezymyanlag network of camps on Samara's outskirts, skilled incarcerated cadre were promised "perks for conscientious labor"; and camp managers were instructed to provide "cash premiums" and an "enhanced diet" for "excellent workers."[57] These patterns were evident early on in the process of setting up the notorious slave labor settlements. Osokina writes that, during the period of acute food shortages in the 1930s, knowledgeable cadre in sought-after occupations *within* the Gulag system often enjoyed a better lifestyle, perks, and diet than did those *outside* of the penal institutions who lacked the requisite knowledge and expertise.[58]

A volume of memoirs by Gulag laborers from among the Volga Germans "conscripted" into the so-called *trudarmiya* (labor army) in wartime Samara provides a window into these mechanisms of reproduction in the knowledge economy within the Gulag's coercive context. Although confined to one ethnic community, the memoirs corroborate accounts of the relatively privileged position of scientists and other skilled professionals within the Gulag, most famously portrayed in Aleksandr Solzhenitsyn's novel *The First Circle*.[59] Skilled German professionals were in high demand, much as they had been in tsarist Russia. It had not been uncommon before the Revolution for European investors to favor German and other European engineers over ethnic Russians.[60] Many highly skilled ethnically German engineers were deported along with the other *Wolgadeutsche*, only to find themselves dispatched as part of the *trudarmiya* to Buguruslan, the frontline of intensified gas exploration, as technical specialists spared the manual labor of digging pipeline trenches. Others, who had cut their teeth as industry specialists in the Baku oil fields were promptly commandeered to Samara. One urgent report detailed a long list of preposterous mismanagement (*vopiyushchiye bezobraziya*) that greeted ethnic German camp laborers sent to Buguruslan – from lack of roofs, to an absence of matrasses on beds, to the patchy provision of hot meals and low bread rations.[61] The authorities in Moscow took note. While sanctioning thorough checks of these individuals with a view to assessing their "political

numbers of inmates fluctuated over the war period as laborers were moved between different colonies depending on industrial priorities. Zakharchenko and Repinetskiy, "Ispol'zovaniye truda," 790–91.

[56] Ibid., 792–93.   [57] Ibid., 793.   [58] Osokina, *Our Daily Bread*, 64–65.
[59] For recent academic treatment of the topic, see Siddiqi, "Scientists."
[60] Rieber, *Merchants*, 223.
[61] Letter marked "top secret," to NKVD. Cited in Blinova et al., *Rossiya*, 57–58.

trustworthiness and biographical details" and ensuring "incessant monitoring and control ... preferably by someone from the ranks of communists or the Komsomol," one directive read:

Among the mobilized German men and women, working in the enterprises and construction facilities of Narkomneft' [People's Commissariat for Oil Industry], there is a significant number of qualified workers with specialties in short supply, as for instance, locksmiths, metal turners, electricians, joiners, carpenters, tractor operators, drivers and so forth. And yet, these qualified workers, whom Narkomneft' badly needs, often are not used in accordance with their specialism and are engaged as lowly manual workers [*chernorabochiye*], because the heads of construction sites and enterprises do not allow them access to existing plants, equipment and facilities.

In consultation with NKVD of the USSR, Narkomneft authorizes access to repair and construction works of qualified workers from amongst the mobilized Germans on the territories of oil exploration, working plants, equipment, and facilities.[62]

The life story of one German deportee, Ferdinand Ferdinandovich Wiegand, provides an illustration of the status trappings of those with sought-after skills within the Gulag. Wiegand gained experience constructing oil rigs on the Nobel oil fields in Baku in the 1920s. A successful professional, as a free man Wiegand had been commandeered to Buguruslan to advise the Buguruslan Oil Trust and had even enjoyed a stint serving as a representative to the Supreme Soviet of the Republic of Azerbaijan. These accolades did not spare Wiegand and his family from the consequences of the infamous Deportation Decree. His son Eduard was sent to a foster home and his wife relocated to the district of Kungur in the Urals and forced to fell trees in a labor camp. Wiegand himself, initially deported to Kirov in 1941 where he was to engage in manual work on a rifle plant, was promptly commandeered to Buguruslan. Here, among other inmates, he found fellow Baku oil rig specialists (*Bakintsy-vyshkari*) A. Verfil and P. Mast. Wiegand came to supervise the work of an oil rig brigade comprised of fellow ethnic Germans, sharing the same barracks and seeking to "carry on with their life, to stick to each other, side by side." Here, they applied the techniques developed by other distinguished German engineers of the Baku vintage ("Who does not know the famous Kerschenbaum crane?").[63] When Wiegand proposes an ingenious engineering method to transport an existing rig to another location, a reward ensues: "A sack of wheat barley [*psheno*], potatoes and a smoked bream." Family reunion quickly follows. Wiegand's wife is permitted to return from Kungur and his son Eduard from the foster home. Although Eduard, who attended a local Tatar-language school along with other local kids, is refused entry into a *tekhnikum* (vocational college), he spent his spare time "hanging out at the rigs that were being constructed by his father." In 1953, Wiegand was transferred from the camp's site to the city of Buguruslan where he pursued a career as an instructor in a technical school. Eduard followed in his father's

---

[62] Letter marked "secret," to heads of oil plants, May 8, 1943. Ibid., 60. [63] Blinova et al., 20.

footsteps, working as an oil rig specialist.[64] Wiegand's biography is not uncommon for skilled *trudarmeytsy*. Many met their spouses from among fellow German inmates. German youth were encouraged to pursue technical training and continued to work in the area in the same specialty as their parents after their release from the camps.[65]

Recent historiography on the Gulag corroborates the *trudarmeytsy's* experiences. Scholars have questioned Solzhenitsyn's metaphor of an archipelago conjuring images of islands of colonies isolated from each other and the rest of society. Instead, they are now highlighting the fluidity between life inside and outside these institutions and camps. The language of "revolving doors, porous boundaries, mirror images, and continuums" has been used to characterize them.[66] The historian David Shearer writes: "In some instances, it seems as if the physical boundaries among camps, colonies, and 'free' society begin to blur into nonexistence. People seemed to circulate in and out of and through the Gulag system on a regular basis, as they did through the supposedly rigid system of spatial organization of Soviet socialism."[67] Inmates often had freedom to leave the premises. Even after release, many remained in the vicinity of the camps either because they continued to work there as salaried employees or due to the pull of family attachments.[68]

Stripped of their coercive foundations, the energy exploration and pipeline construction projects represented continuity with the old regime's developmental and social ecosystems. There and then, too, skilled technical specialists – rail and electric engineers, scientists, geologists, and cartographers – were dispatched to yet another technological frontier where they would temporarily, and sometimes for good, settle and make their homes.[69] Such was the destiny of the noble Garin-Mikhaylovskiy, whose autobiographical novel, *Engineers*,[70] conveys the quest of his real-life ascent from a junior assistant engineer facilitating cartographic mapping as part of the railway development in the southwestern reaches of the Russian Empire to his eventual long-term sojourn in the Samara *guberniya* where he left his mark as a brilliant, successful, and dashing literary figure and engineering professional.[71]

[64] Ibid., 19–20. Already in the 1950s, scholars found that "whether or not there was a political arrest in the family, even when it led to a sentence to forced labor, the educational level attained by the children was substantially the same as in families which did not experience an arrest." Further, "such facts argue strongly what experience everywhere has taught us, namely that differences in opportunity and ability to pay for education will not alone explain differential educational attainment." Inkeles and Bauer, *Soviet Citizen*, 149.

[65] Blinova et al., 27, 29, 48–49.

[66] Shearer, "Soviet Gulag," 711. See also other papers in the special issue.   [67] Ibid., 718.

[68] See the discussion in Khlevniuk, "Gulag," 490; and memoirs in Blinova et al., *Rossiya*.

[69] On engineers' employment patterns in imperial Russia, see Rieber, *Merchants*.

[70] Garin-Mikhaylovskiy, *Studenty; Inzhenery*.

[71] Valeriy Yerofeyev, "Garin-Mikhaylovskiy Nikolay Georgiyevich," *Istoricheskaya Samara*. Available online at: историческая-самара.рф/каталог/самарская-персоналия/г/гарин-михайловский-николай-георгиевич.html (accessed May 31, 2020).

PATTERNS OF POPULATION MOVEMENTS: "NEW" CITIES

The relentless industrial appropriations were characteristic of state policy in developed industrial hubs like Samara. To what extent do insights about continuities in the social structure in space apply to another well-publicized and highly mythologized dimension of state policy, the construction of new cities – those ostensibly populated with an eclectic mishmash of enthusiastic youth from across the Soviet Union's vast reaches? Tolyatti, the region's newest and most artificial city, is a good place to begin in illustrating the dynamics of social reproduction alongside social change in space. Tolyatti's population growth is extreme even by Soviet standards. In what significantly exceeds the Russia-wide average for the same period, the city's population has grown by a magnitude of *fifty-eight times* over the last sixty years.[72] As late as 1950, Stavropol'-na-Volge, around which the new city developed, remained a sleepy provincial backwater, better known for its fermented mare's milk (*kumys*) spas and healing sanatoria founded by local merchants at the end of the nineteenth century. The town's handful of enterprises had a workforce totaling only 750 people.[73] When the first gigantic industrial construction commenced in the area in 1951 – on what was at the time Europe's largest dam, the Kuybyshevskaya – Stavropol' had a population of only 11,896. The dam project resulted in the transfer, in 1953, of the entire town, including 300 buildings, 18 kilometers above the hydroelectric station. The new settlement, including encampments of laborers mobilized to work on the dam, constituted the core of the future city, which, by 1958, numbered some 70,000 workers engaged at rubber, phosphorus, and other chemical production plants. The construction of the Volga Automobile Plant (*Volzhskiy avtomobil'nyy zavod*, VAZ) in 1966–67 resulted in a further influx of workers, bringing the city's population to 162,000. In 1984, Tolyatti registered the birth of its 600,000th resident.[74] This was also a project typical of other new cities in that young workers from across the country streamed there; and, while many departed after their contracts ended – two out of three in the years 1950–56 – others stayed on and increasingly so as the town expanded its social infrastructures such as kindergartens, schools, parks, and other facilities.[75]

Nevertheless, researchers analyzing the city's demographics and migration patterns found significant correspondence between the intensity of labor migration and the origins of workers. One study found that "the lower the

[72] Adayevskaya, "Dinamika," 6.

[73] Ibid., 1. The "koumiss stations" (*kumysniki*) were popular with the middle class from the late 1800s, spurring a large service infrastructure. Sunderland, *Taming*, 197–99.

[74] Adayevskaya, "Dinamika," 1, 2, 3. Foreign tourists were fed a steady diet of information about the "newness" of Tolyatti: "There are no monuments of the distant past. Here the dynamic pulse of the present day is beating." The dam was a major stop on the tourist route. Kirsanova, "Organizatsionnyye," 29–30.

[75] Adayevskaya, "Dinamika," 3.

distance [from Tolyatti], the more intensive the process of migration."[76] More than 70 percent of all migrants arriving from rural areas reportedly resided in the same or neighboring administrative *rayon*. The establishment of VAZ, while expanding the "geography of arrivals," did not change this pattern. Most newcomers were from the surrounding villages; rural workers tended to be stability-oriented, putting down roots and starting families in Tolyatti.[77] Many migrants found it hard to integrate within the urban environment, leaving a rural imprint on the "urban culture of Tolyatti."[78] Newcomers, young Komsomol idealists of an impressionable, marriageable, age, would often wed men and women from the area.[79]

Although Soviet planners proudly reported that forty-two nationalities from across the Soviet Union enthusiastically labored in the Avtograd (automobile city) in the late 1960s,[80] a recent ethnic breakdown for Tolyatti in fact closely mirrors that of Samara and the surrounding Middle Volga *oblasti*. Some 83 percent residents are ethnically Russian and 3.8 percent, 3.6 percent, 3.6 percent, and 2.5 percent are Tatars, Mordovians, Chuvash, and Ukrainians, respectively, while the remaining population is made up largely of Belorussian, Bashkir, Armenian, German, and Jewish communities.[81] According to the 2010 census data for the Samara region, Russians comprise 85.6 percent of the population; 4.1 percent, the next largest group, are Tatars; followed by Chuvash at 2.7 percent, and Mordovians at 2.1 percent; while Ukrainians comprise 1.4 percent of the regional population.[82] Tolyatti's ethnic makeup also matches designations of groups considered "native to" and "historically rooted in" Samara in ongoing discussions among regional historians and ethnographers.[83]

Those relocated from old Stavropol'-na-Volge to new Tolyatti participated in the process of reconstituting the old communities and social ties that had bound them in their previous place of residence. Daniil Popov recalls talking to elders in Tolyatti who still remembered his great-great-grandfather Valerian Dmitriyevich Tikhovidov, who, for many years, was employed in Stavropol' as a veterinary specialist. "When homes were moved from old Stavropol' to the new town, the people also moved. I spoke to some [people] who still remembered him [Tikhovidov]."[84] Daniil's family helped maintain the threads that linked old Stavropol' to new Tolyatti by contributing artifacts from the Tikhovidov family archive to the local historical museum.[85] Popov laments the dire job situation forcing young people to leave Tolyatti: "Many aspire to move, to Kazan, Moscow, or at the very least to Samara."[86] Yet, while getting encouragement from his parents to pursue his dreams, even if it involves

---

[76] Ibid., 2, 3.   [77] Ibid., 4.   [78] Ibid., 5.   [79] Interview with a descendant, ZK, 2017.
[80] Adayevskaya, "Dinamika," 2.   [81] Ibid., 5.
[82] Data available from Chudilin et al., *Natsional'nyy sostav*, 12.
[83] Russians, Tatar, Chuvash, Mordovians, Ukrainians, Kazakhs, Belarussians, Bashkirs, Germans, Jews, Mari. Kolesnikova, "Istoriya poyavleniya," 137.
[84] Interview, June 19, 2017, Samara.   [85] Ibid.   [86] Ibid.

relocating to the nation's capital, Popov admits: "Although I can easily leave, what is holding me here? I started my scientific career here and have found what I like."[87] The construction of new cities thus did not represent something akin to the process of filling a new urban container with people lacking ancestral ties to the locality. Within-region migration had been a significant feature of population movements in the *oblast* during the Soviet period.[88]

Together with a colleague, Andrey Aref'yev from Metrikum, a Samara-based organization that tracks the ancestry of wealthy Russian clients, I aggregated the location details of the movements of dozens of families that are captured in the genealogical essays of secondary school children from Tolyatti and the surrounding rural areas. We should, of course, interpret these data with caveats. They only include current residents in the Samara *oblast* whose families either were already in the region before the Revolution or moved during the Soviet period, usually after World War II. The Google map that aggregates the movements of several generations of family members allows us to visualize these patterns. To capture the rationale for the population movement of individuals, we have distinct lines designating movements of military/ wartime servicemen; population migration before 1917; movements after 1990; and movements of repressed family members through the Soviet period. We included data from the 126 essays entered in the competition for the year 2013 and covering 126 extended families. Separate maps aggregate entries for small groups of families, so the image does not look too cluttered.[89] In exploring patterns that could be visualized when we look at these maps, as expected, we observe a typical trajectory of a Soviet family scattered across Russia, from Europe, to Siberia, to the Far East, and to Central Asia. At the same time, we see a dense cluster corresponding to Samara and other Middle and Lower Volga territories. While many people traveled or were exiled, forcibly resettled, or conscripted as soldiers, most family members encompassing three to five generations stayed in the native region or in the vicinity of it. In Figure 8.1, I present one illustrative map for a small number of families. The map shows a dense cluster corresponding to Samara and the Middle Volga regions. We also observe movement to the western reaches of the Soviet Union and the neighboring Central European countries, largely reflecting the wartime service of family members.

These patterns are consistent with what we know about migration in Soviet and post-Soviet Russia from other sources. In regions like Samara, with a developed petrochemicals industry, rural dwellers often acquired jobs in nearby industrial urban hubs. Migration took the form of step-by-step

---

[87] Ibid.
[88] Reportedly more so than in neighboring Ulyanovsk and Penza regions. Mal'tsev, "Osobennosti." On returnees to the region from among the post-revolutionary émigrés, see "Poslevoyennaya reemigratsiya."
[89] Giovanni Angioni created clean digital map images.

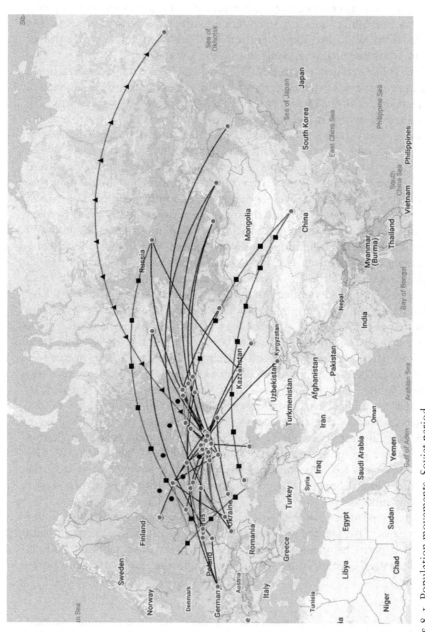

FIGURE 8.1 Population movements, Soviet period

Legend: ▲ Repressed family members

● Population migration before 1917

■ Movement of wartime/military servicemen

Compiled by the author from a sample of genealogical essays by Tolyatti pupils.

movement, from village to small town, within the same region. Recent Russia-wide surveys from the Levada polling agency corroborate patterns of low interregional mobility, with citizens who do move doing so within their native region. In 2019, only 13 percent of surveyed citizens reported moving within the last five years for a period of between a few months and more; of these, 55 percent moved within their home region.[90]

SAMARA CITY OLD AND NEW

Having established that Soviet industry largely mapped onto tsarist-era structural and human capital development in space, I now unpack the implications of this convergence for relations among social groups. For every "bourgeois" specialist enjoying relative privilege within an industrial giant or an exploration project, inside and outside the Gulag, there were scores of poorly educated and socially marginal strata who lacked such trappings of status, overwhelmingly of peasant origin. To what extent did the grinding mill of Soviet industrialization blur the estatist boundaries between groups? In answering this question, I am sensitive particularly to "cognitional" distinctions or attitudes toward social "others" within urban society and between urban and rural residents. Because spatial positioning is itself a reflection and marker of social identity, these cognitional patterns help explain resilience in the reproduction of the social structure in space. Following Benno Werlen, I regard social space as something that transcends the objective physical distance between individuals and social units as well as encompassing subjective constructions of space and the day-to-day decisions and preferences concerning social gravity, inclusion, and exclusion.[91] "Social space," in other words, is not identical to "geometrical space," as Sorokin illustrates using the analogy of king and servant.[92] In Bourdieu's conceptualization, "*space of relations* ... is just as real as a geographical space, in which movements have to be paid for by labour, by effort and especially by time (to move upwards is to raise oneself, to climb and to bear the traces or the stigmata of that effort)."[93] Time is thus intricately linked to social space considering the variable longevity of traversing the distances separating groups from others endowed with higher economic, cultural, or social capital.[94] I situate Samara's "space of relations" in the pre-Soviet social structure even when set against the developmental cataclysms intrinsic to the Soviet project.

---

[90] Representative survey of 1,625 urban and rural residents, conducted between April 18 and April 23, 2019, in 137 settlements in 50 regions. The most mobile category is youth aged 18–24. Discussion available online at the Levada Center website: levada.ru/2019/05/29/vnutrirossijs-kaya-migratsiya/ (accessed May 13, 2020).

[91] Werlen, *Society*, esp. discussion in chap. 1 (1–21). [92] Sorokin, *Social Mobility*, 3.

[93] Bourdieu, *Language*, 232 (emphasis in original). [94] Ibid., 232.

The subtle social distinctions could be illustrated with reference to spatial positioning and social gravity or separation in the context of large-scale wartime and postwar migration to Samara City. Scores of industries, as well as the shop floor, managerial, specialist engineering, and R&D workforce, were hastily evacuated to the region and city from western and northern parts of Russia as German forces advanced. Migration for the purposes of manning industrial facilities continued in the 1950s and 1960s. Much of the infrastructure was pegged to the vast industrial settlement of Bezymyanka located some 18 kilometers from the city center, eventually becoming part of Samara's urban sprawl.[95] The magnitude of the population movement that accelerated after the war was such that Bezymyanka in population terms eventually swamped "old" Samara.

Although Bezymyanka became synonymous with evacuated industry and a new workforce who lacked roots in the region, the migrant community constituted itself in space according to the estatist logic of social closure and in ways that transcended the "newcomer" versus "old families" social identity that might characterize otherwise broadly socially similar groups.[96] The historical part of Samara acquired the characteristics of a "parasitic" city,[97] where the pedigree bourgeoisie became an unwitting accomplice to the socially exploitative and stratification maintenance relationships vis-à-vis the rural migrant, the supplier of manual labor for industrialization projects. The precipitous pace of urbanization far exceeding that of imperial Russia resulted in parallel worlds, a "dual society" of the patrician old bourgeoisie and the "folklike" communities of rural marginal groups.[98] The spatial, cultural, and value separateness between the bourgeoisie and the rural newcomer led to a dualism in the types of urban culture observed in other rapidly developing contexts, a far cry from the assumed socialist melting pot.[99]

Bezymyanka came to be overwhelmingly inhabited with blue-collar workers – welders, builders, electricians, and many laboring in factories, constituting the Bezymyanlag Gulag outpost that expanded after the war. Multiple generations of workers lived in ramshackle barracks and, eventually, "modern" Soviet-era tower blocks in the vicinity of plants and factories. Many individuals circulated between rural farm and factory work or rural residence and training in the city. This life of rural–urban–rural rotation represented continuity with pre-communist practices of peasants becoming seasonal rural workers in towns, referred to as *otkhodniki*, who substituted the plow for lifelong factory labor but retained extended family ties in their villages. We

[95] A district named after the adjacent Bezymyanka River. Burlina, "Gorod Bezymyanka," 59. Bezymyanka literally means "without a name." Author note. See also semiotics of the district naming in Ilivitskaya, "Bezymyanka," 95.
[96] Elias and Scotson, *Established and Outsiders*, xvi–xvii.
[97] On this, see Hoselitz, *Sociological Aspects*, 198.
[98] Reference to the gulf between the rural migrant and the long-term urban resident. Ibid., 176.
[99] Ibid., 178, 179.

already discussed this pattern when drawing on the personnel records from the Sergiyevskiy Munitions Plant. David Hoffmann's classic account of this phenomenon is captured in the reference to Moscow as a "peasant metropolis," but the analysis concerned migratory processes in the 1920s, 1930s, and early 1940s.[100] Here, well into the second decade of the twenty-first century, when interviews in Bezymyanka were conducted for this project, researchers found families of a peasant-worker background, something that consolidated the distinct "proletarian" identity of this urban district. Some social mobility, of course, occurred. Many individuals obtained higher education and pursued white-collar occupations. Yet when researchers sought to tease out the nuances of social mobility, they found that tertiary specialties were often based on vocational qualifications.

The social identity as a "proletarian" quarter is intriguing given that scores of highly trained professionals – leading scientists, engineers, academics, and other, mostly technical, intelligentsia – relocated to Bezymyanka in the 1940s, 1950s and 1960s. They supplied the skills required to sustain the cutting-edge ferrous metals, machine building, and aviation industries. Furthermore, like the peasant-worker from another region, the newcomer engineer was an outsider to Samara. Would the shared outsider status trump the subtle differences in education, professional attainment, and cultural values derived from estate origins between the urban intelligentsia and "proletarian" workforce? Interviews with descendants of the "new arrivals" that comprised the technical and scientific intelligentsia – individuals lacking pre-revolutionary roots in Samara – indicate that many moved to "old" Samara where they molded with the social milieu of homologous social groups, while their children attended schools and mingled with the offspring of aspirational nobles, merchants, and *meshchane* of vintage Samara. The historical inner core of old mansions and quaint wooden houses discreetly reproduced the social character over the tremors of the new Bolshevik order, much like the Bezymyanka districts of "new" Samara came to be associated with proletariat and, in post-communist Russia, déclassé elements. The hemorrhage of the intelligentsia segment of wartime Bezymyanka evacuees and their descendants in turn reinforced the working-class character of this outlying district, however much Soviet ideologues strove to mythologize it as a heroic industrial and wartime frontier. The eventual phasing out and closure of the camps that constituted Bezymyanlag only exacerbated the socioeconomic deprivation in the district.[101] Consistent with patterns of the Gulag and post-Gulag economies elsewhere, many low-skilled inmates continued to reside near the camp, holding on to low-paid jobs as laborers. Many were saddled with mobility restrictions, so much so that the word muzzle (*namordnik*) came to be applied to the social predicament of these former camp inmates.[102]

---

[100] Hoffmann, *Peasant Metropolis.*
[101] See the discussion of research by Larisa G. Ilivitskaya in Burlina, "Gorod Bezymyanka," 58–61.
[102] Lankina and Libman, "Jekyll and Hyde."

Bezymyanka's status as a working quarter, as distinct from the prestigious districts of "old" Samara along the Volga River, became deeply embedded in perceptions of the space separating this district from the rest of Samara. "In Bezymyanka," as the local saying goes, "they take the bus and say: 'We are going to the city.'" The Samara-based cultural historian Larisa Ilivitskaya writes:

New outskirts will be settled, new micro-districts will emerge, but in the mentality of urban residents Samara continues to be divided into two poles: The City and Bezymyanka ... The City is mythologized as an embodiment of everything good, light, successful, prestigious (more expensive housing, brighter and cleaner streets, cultural and educational level of the population is higher and so forth). Bezymyanka, in turn, is ascribed the opposite characteristics.[103]

"For the old town," comments Ilivitskaya, Bezymyanka became something of an "alien body, artificial, even dangerous."[104] The chasm, according to another regional scholar, was not one separating the old-timer from the migrant but one impregnated with the connotations of social status and class. "Imprinted in the mentality of city dwellers," writes the Samara historian Yaroslav Golubinov, "has been the division of Kuybyshev [Samara] into two large parts, practically independent microcosms: the old town ... and Bezymyanka, the industrial, closed district. *Urban dwellers from the respective districts have felt more of a sense of alienation from each other than they did from the new arrivals.*"[105] The sheer number of industry evacuees in the 1940s and 1950s may have vastly outnumbered long-established families. Yet the intelligentsia segment of Bezymyanka naturally gravitated toward the refined "old"-town society, organically enmeshing themselves within the city's social stratification.

Natalya Borisovna Ivanova,[106] a professor of history in Samara, comes from a family of "new" Samara engineers of the postwar migration wave. Rather than maintaining a residence in Bezymyanka, where the technical intelligentsia contributed to the know-how aspect of the vast industrial operation, Natalya Borisovna grew up in a prestigious riverside inner-city district. Ivanova invokes proximity of the elite residence to the Volga, which provided "a completely different quality of life... this means a lot to the mentality of the people who live here."[107] In her school, children of Samara's pedigree estatist groups studied alongside the offspring of the "new arrival" intelligentsia. Childhood recollections of the jazz impresario Vadim Yakovlevich Bunin,[108] a second-generation representative of "new" Samara's engineering and technical elite, indicate that social ties naturally transcended the circles of the "new arrival" intelligentsia to embrace "old" Samara, but the fluidity of social interaction was simultaneously confined within the bounds of the "creative" marker of social

---

[103] Ilivitskaya, "Bezymyanka," 96.   [104] Ibid., 96.
[105] Golubinov, "Obraz," 57 (emphasis added).   [106] Name changed.
[107] Name changed. Interview, June 22, 2017.   [108] Name changed.

position. "*We were interesting to them* ... That is, us, people working in the creative sphere ... [of old and new Samara] *and they were interesting to us.*"[109]

Unlike Bezymyanka, which, in the words of the historian Mikhail Mikhaylovich Tsaritsyn,[110] became "proletarian through and through,"[111] the "old" Samara homes constituted part of a peculiar bourgeois microcosm. Here, fallen aristocrats, merchants, or latter-day *meshchane*, who held on to the material artifacts and cognitive markers of past lives, now mingled with post-revolutionary and postwar bourgeois arrivals, the *Soviet* technical intelligentsia, professoriate, and creatives, in fact likely sharing similar origins with the imperial-era educated estates-derived bourgeoisie. Many were housed in the new "Stalin architecture" mansions designed exclusively for the upper echelons of party nomenklatura and elite professionals and, as such, out of the reach of the less well-connected "indigenous" intelligentsia. The high-status segment of the Samara "new arrivals" nevertheless shared the same space, both geographically and in a social sense, with "old" Samara. Geographically, this space was the city's inner core, by the spectacular promenade on the banks of the Volga River. Socially, this space was being constituted in the process of routine interaction among those who were, in Bunin's words, "interesting to each other."[112] The material characteristics of the childhoods of Professor Golubkov, a descendant of "old" Samara's Polish nobles and *meshchane*, and of Professor Ivanova, representing "new" Samara, may have vastly diverged – Golubkov grew up in a freezing and decrepit wooden house in historical Samara; Ivanova was the daughter of Leningrad intelligentsia, who was raised in a Stalin mansion and attended the nomenklatura-studded school. Both, though, occupy the symbolically more prestigious geographic space by the riverside; and both, socially, represent the middle class or even elite of Samara society.

The cognitive status barriers are accentuated if we consider the identities of those who had seemingly traversed the social barrier between micro-districts and estates. Aleksandr Ivanovich Kapustin,[113] a young graduate of Samara University's Historical Faculty, is employed as a researcher at the Modern Museum, a leading repository of historical knowledge on Samara. In an interview for this project, Kapustin alludes to the fact that he is not representative of the "old" city's intelligentsia, for he is Bezymyanka "born and bred." His maternal grandfather "first worked on one of the Bezymyanka factories and then on the Progress Plant all his life until pension." Kapustin's father, who was not born in Samara, obtained a job at the Metallurgical Plant after graduating from university. "My parents have always been there and only there and have not moved anywhere else," says Kapustin. The respondent's maternal relations have deeper roots in Samara but only in the sense of having

---

[109] Interview, June 22, 2017 (emphasis added).   [110] Name changed.
[111] Name changed. Interview, ZK, 2017.   [112] Name changed. Interview, June 22, 2017.
[113] Name changed.

arrived in the city "sometime before the war, can't say exactly when. They too lived in Bezymyanka. But *these were all workers, that is, precisely the people who were supposed to be living in those districts.*"[114] Kapustin thus posits the disjuncture between his origins and the position he occupies as a bona fide urban *intelligent*, apologizing, as it were, for encroaching on the cultural sanctum of "old" Samara:

RESEARCHER: "Please tell me, Aleksandr Ivanovich, do you consider yourself a native Samarovite?"
KAPUSTIN [HESITANTLY]: "More yes, than no, but I am simply in this situation – I have always lived and continue to live on the outskirts of Samara"
RESEARCHER: "Specifically?"
KAPUSTIN: "Metallurg, Bezymyannyy … *rayon*"
RESEARCHER: "Well, that is not an outlying district"
KAPUSTIN: "How so? It is the outskirts [*okraina*], because after all there is a certain cultural identity there, which is a bit, in my opinion, different from that in the center. That is, *there is historical Samara, one that emerges in people's imagination, that is, precisely the Samara we talk about in the Museum*, not that it doesn't have any relation whatsoever, but has quite an indirect relation to what one can see there. So yes, of course I am a native Samarovite, but my formative years as an urban dweller took place there, on the outskirts, so perhaps I possess somewhat different cultural roots than those who lived and grew up here in the center, so to speak."[115]

Here, as in Bourdieu's allusion to the social theorizing of Erving Goffman, Kapustin, as it were, knows his place. This awareness, considering his work as museum curator, among Samara's intelligentsia, represents a form of "class unconscious" – "the sense of the position one occupies in the social space" – and not the actual position.[116] The cognitive anchor remains Bezymyanka's "proletariat," allegedly a "cultural identity" distinct from "old" Samara's and internalized through upbringing in that district. "The sense of one's place," writes Bourdieu, "as the sense of what one can or cannot 'allow oneself,' implies a tacit acceptance of one's position, a sense of limits ('that's not meant for us') or – what amounts to the same thing – a sense of distances, to be marked and maintained, respected, and expected of others."[117]

Kapustin's subtle confession of being an interloper in the middle class of "old" Samara could be contextualized in what would be "typical" – as distinct from his a-typical intergenerational social trajectory when set against the life stories of other residents in Bezymyanka. The statements that follow later in this section from respondents illustrate the social positioning of evacuees to Bezymyanka who tended to come from "dynastic" families of workers, from rural parts of Samara and European Russia, and from families that had been poorly educated or were even barely literate. Their professional careers included

[114] Interview, ZK, 2017 (emphasis added).
[115] Name changed. Interview, ZK, 2017 (emphasis added).
[116] Bourdieu, *Language*, 235. Precise work not cited.   [117] Ibid., 235.

elements of social mobility like university instruction, often in the form of evening or part-time courses, followed by white-collar work. Nevertheless, whether educational opportunities were seized to progress into white-collar occupations or not, the broader intergenerational pattern was one of precarity, reverse mobility, and embeddedness in the proletarian milieus of the Bezymyanka-based construction or factory workforce. An interview with Marina Grigor'yevna Sidorova,[118] an eighty-one-year-old retiree from among Samara's Soviet-era factory workforce, illustrates these trajectories. The respondent's parents transitioned from a village in Voronezh into factory labor in Samara during the Soviet period. She continues to live in Bezymyanka and thus describes her life story:

In Samara . . . I lived from the time of the war. Dad had been evacuated here together with the aviation plant . . . Dad worked at the factory. I attended school, completed studies, went to work at the factory [Aviation] and simultaneously applied to study at the evening division of the Aviation [institute] . . . Then, when I was in the third year of the institute, I moved to work at the Scientific-research institute of aviation materials and worked there practically until pension.

When asked about her parents' education, Marina Grigor'yevna reported that her father had "primary schooling, he had been a worker all his life . . . a respected welder. Mother had been a housewife. All her life." And what about her children?

The son completed practically nothing, it was in the middle of *perestroika*, because he came back from the army, did not [apply to] study anywhere [university], got a job at the factory, and then it got so bad that he was sent somewhere to work at some construction site . . . then he got married, so anyway, did not go to study anywhere. Now works as a repairman in construction, there, on the construction site . . . I also have a grandson, his son, he also somehow got around to working together with dad. My daughter completed a communications *tekhnikum*, so worked at the post office, then it turned out she didn't like it very much, so she mainly ended up staying home on maternity leave.[119]

Anna Ivanovna Serova, another respondent whose husband had also been a worker in the aviation industry, describes her family trajectory as "typical." Like her, many employees at the Aviation plant were evacuees from the

[118] Names of all Bezymyanka respondents have been changed. The sample of interviewees is small; findings and impressions from this part of the research are tentative, though supported with corroborating secondary evidence. Researchers had trouble accessing interviewees who had worked on Bezymyanka's plants. In the segments quoted in this section, respondents mention some of Bezymyanka's industrial giants in the aerospace, aviation, and metals industries, including those evacuated during World War II and part of Bezymyanlag, as well as segments of Samara-based armaments plants built in the imperial period, such as the Maslennikov plant for the production of pipes. A concise summary of Bezymyanka's industries is available on Wikipedia, "Безымянка (rayon)": ru.wikipedia.org/wiki/Безымянка_(район) (accessed December 28, 2020).

[119] Name changed. Interview, AA, December 2018.

Voronezh region. Together with other families of newcomers, the family received temporary space in the barracks in the vicinity of their employment site. "And so, we [Anna Ivanovna and her future husband] met there. He was a worker. Simultaneously, because at that point he had not finished his schooling, he completed an evening school, then he went to [study at] the *tekhnikum*, then worked on the shopfloor ... So, there we are. A typical working family."[120]

Another Bezymyanka resident, Irina Aleksandrovna Smirnova, after completing middle school and vocational courses, worked as a tram driver and then for twenty years in a laboratory at the Maslennikov Plant before layoff and retirement. Originally from the Sergiyevskiy district in Samara, Irina Aleksandrovna recalls that her grandfather had been "literate," while her mother had "perhaps one year of schooling." The extended family, including her daughter, who attended a pedagogical institute, continues to dwell in Bezymyanka.[121]

A retiree born in the Alekseyevka village of Samara reports that both of her parents hailed from Samara villages and ended up working in a munitions (*sernyy*) plant. After completing ten years of schooling, in 1955, at age sixteen, she obtained a job at the Progress Plant, to "help [her] parents," where she worked with some brief interruptions until 1991. What about her parents' education? "Mother had been illiterate, and father? He could read. *So, in short, the parents were so to speak... illiterate.*"[122] Both parents were of peasant stock. Her husband? He too worked at the Progress Plant. Her daughter? Married to a helper of a machinist; she is also on a measly monthly salary of 7,000 rubles (roughly $107),[123] despite completing studies at the Polytechnic Institute and working as a statistician for a "Moscow organization" in Samara.[124] The family of Nina Antonovna Lapina, another elderly woman from the Privolzhskiy micro-district in Bezymyanka, moved during wartime evacuation after her aunt enticed others from the extended family to join her in Samara. This family too hailed from rural areas. Lapina's father had been a circus showman, while her mother's education had been limited to seven years of school; the aunt who worked at the factory had four years of schooling.[125] Nina Antonovna herself, however, went on to complete higher education.

These accounts are supported by sociological studies of rural–urban migrations and mobility carried out by Novosibirsk scholars in the 1960s. Tatyana I. Zaslavskaya and her collaborators, in researching the process of "escape" to the city – usually a town or regional center within the same *oblast* – found that a large proportion of migrants did not substantially improve their educational level, while professional occupations stagnated or even showed

---

[120] Name changed. Interview, AA, December 2018.   [121] Interview, AA, December 2018.
[122] Interview, AA, December 2018 (emphasis added).   [123] Currency converter, March 4, 2020.
[124] Interview, AA, December 2018.   [125] Interview, AA, December 2018.

a tendency for regress into lower-skilled jobs as compared to those that characterized the migrant's employment in the *kolkhoz*.[126] Our interviews illustrate how, even when opportunities opened up for rural workers to abandon the collective farm, the family scripts were already circumscribing professional paths – and indeed the cognitive sense of belongingness or of being an outsider – of children stepping into the world beyond their family and village.[127] The narrative of "escape" captures the essence of the aspiration. Where the scions of Samara's long-established intelligentsia were programmed to enter the medical school, the collective farm escapee found refuge in the sanctum of the quasi-vocational teacher training institute or the medical school churning out nurses.

Natalya Mikhaylovna Ivanova is a history graduate who works in one of Samara's museums.[128] Ivanova, whose family comes from a Mordovian village, thus narrates the educational trajectory of her grandmother:

IVANOVA: "I think that my great grandmothers and great grandfathers were all illiterate, absolutely … But my grandmother went to school, and so did grandfather. They completed seven years, grandmother even with distinction. She was then encouraged to obtain further education, she studied in a medical *tekhnikum*, in Ulyanovsk, in Simbirsk as it was called before. But back then before the war professional education was paid for, so one had to pay a bit. And so, she studied there for only one semester. For as much as she could pay. And so, she returned. She did not have [the money]. So only seven grades. And so, my parents – that is the first generation. Though hang on. Grandfather also got higher education, for sure … Yes, he had higher education. But of a correspondence kind, he did not have a student life. Yes, one could say he is the first among us."[129]

RESEARCHER: "Were there any family traditions that would influence the choice of education of your own children? Is there [professional] continuity?"

IVANOVA: "Well, when my parents left [the village] they did not have that many options, since they left after the eighth grade. Accordingly, it was either a medical *uchilishche* for women, or a pedagogical *uchilishche*. And so, they put my mother, in her head-scarf, having literally tied together a knapsack [*uzelochek*], in her house slippers [*tapochki*], on a truck. And so, she arrives, comes out into the city, her face is all black, washes her face at the first tap she could find and goes around asking if anyone would take her as a temporary lodger [*na postoy*]. She gains entry [into the *uchilishche*]. By the way there had been colossal competition to gain a place in these pedagogical colleges because all the village girls went there … Actually, there was not much choice, and [in any case] she did not have any idea about a professional choice. But in her case somehow it worked out well. She then finished the institute and all her life worked in a school, as director, and in general realized herself fully …

---

[126] Discussed in Matthews, *Class and Society*, 205–7.
[127] THPSSS in 1950–51 revealed extremely low regard for rural jobs and peasants' perceptions of being exploited, at the bottom of the social ladder, and looked down upon by "city intelligentsia." Engineers, to give one poignant example, enjoyed higher professional esteem than factory managers. Inkeles and Bauer, *Soviet Citizen*, 78–79.
[128] Name changed. [129] Name changed. Interview, ZK, 2017.

Otherwise, the programming [*ustanovka*] among all was the same – leave the village, that was the first, since ... without a passport – they only started giving out passports in the 1960s – [the urge was] to escape in one way or another. As for my parents' generation, the general stipulation was to obtain higher education ... but they did not understand [*vnikali*] much at all, this was of course about thirty years ago, one had to simply come and say: 'Mother, I got a place at university.' 'Ok, well done, sit down, let's have tea.' Where you go, where you manage to get a place, they did not concern themselves with details at all. The main thing was that you study, and that's it."[130]

The scripted foundations of education were thus couched in aspirational – "The University" – and simultaneously circumscribed terms – nobody cared where exactly you ended up; all girls went to the teacher training college. The longing to escape among generations of rural dwellers in turn conditioned the acute awareness of position within Samara society after the flight from the dreaded *kolkhoz* had been successfully accomplished.[131] Tellingly, Ivanova communicates the legend of her mother's arrival into the city in the 1970s in terms not dissimilar to those that discursively distinguished the "old" Samara residents from peasant migrants of the 1930s.[132] Soviet authorities, concerned professionals, and the press derided the latter as "new urbanites" and an "outside element" (*prishlyy element*);[133] and their residential barracks were reported as "repositories of dirt and social pathology,"[134] of "lice and bedbugs."[135]

The cognitive distinctions, the "knowing one's place" that we discerned in the interview with the Samara museum employee, speak to the obstacles that those overcoming social barriers face in joining the ranks of the high-status social groups. Indeed, we also find rootedness of social identities in rural or worker milieus, and a sense of intergenerational attachment to them, which discourages social trespassing. Social agency is also powerfully at work, however. Genuine ancestral affection for the native village encouraged many to return or, indeed, to defy the state's injunction to be commandeered to some far-away outpost, as the statements of interviewees for this project that I placed at the start of this chapter illustrate. This, of course, typifies patterns of social mobility in other contexts not limited to Russia. For us, it helps illuminate how the legacy of the imperial social structure did not simply disappear in the furnaces of Bolshevik class policy but continued to find embodiment in social

---

[130] Name changed. Interview, ZK, 2017.

[131] The passport regime, set up in December 1932, made most rural workers ineligible for internal passports. Travel outside of the village for more than one month required authorization from the village Soviet. Matthews, *Class and Society*, 53–54. "The chairmen of village Soviets are traditionally reluctant to issue these passes, or *spravki* as they are called, and getting one is recognized as a major hurdle in village life. Overcoming it may absorb the energies of the rustic mind for a long period." Ibid., 54.

[132] Klimochkina, "Povsednevnaya zhizn'," 84.   [133] Ibid., 194, 92.   [134] Ibid., 189.

[135] Cited in ibid., 189.

barriers – material and cognitive – as, indeed, in the potent agency of the citizen, whether rural or urban, many decades later.[136]

CONCLUSION

This chapter has further developed the argument about institutional and social path-dependencies by addressing head-on the question of social persistence and resilience *despite* the forced and repressive elements of Stalinist industrial strategy as well as the more benign state-driven modernization in the decades that followed. What emerges from statistical analysis is that even the most coercive features of Soviet development were pegged to extant infrastructures of modernity (the hardware) as well as the human dimension (the software) of Soviet planning. I also continued to explore the theme of social agency but through the prism of implications for social configurations in space. The highly skilled "new arrivals" from the wave of postwar migrants to the city, initially housed in the proletarian district of Bezymyanka, eventually anchored themselves in "old" Samara, among the intelligentsia with roughly similar estate origins. By contrast, the granddaughter of peasants joining the factory workforce would speak of multiple generations of blue-collar employees and would continue to identify with and reside in the workers' quarters. Those of a worker background who "escaped" the "proletarian" district and pursued a white-collar occupation continued to self-identify in contrasting ways with the descendant of a wealthy merchant family with roots in "old" Samara going back three or four generations. As Bourdieu writes, "if the objective relations of power tend to reproduce themselves in visions of the social world which contribute to the permanence of those relations, this is ... because *the relations of power are also present in people's minds in the form of the categories of perception of those relations.*"[137] The caveat that my research adds to these assumptions is that the "visions" of the social world do not immediately shift with completely reconfigured relations of power in the realm of politics and in society. Ideologically celebrated and cheered on, the peasant and proletarian strata remained cognitively lower down in the hierarchy of social relations, much as they had been under the monarchical, capitalistic, order. Furthermore, as we have seen, even the targeted campaigns of social uplift are rife with possibilities of symbolic and indeed physical violence against the least advantaged groups in society,[138] with the regime itself becoming the most notorious perpetrator. It is true, as this chapter has

---

[136] For evidence corroborating the urban/rural and small/large town divide in social mobility elsewhere in Russia, see Shkaratan and Yastrebov, "Sravnitel'nyy analiz," 21.

[137] Bourdieu, *Language*, 235–36 (emphasis added).

[138] Concepts derived from Bourdieu's work. An example of symbolic violence is intimidation through modes of language associated with superior status groups rather than through overt acts of intimidation. Ibid., 51.

demonstrated, that the developmentally appropriative logic of communism in practice meant that the professional and expert bourgeois, who was hounded, robbed of their possessions, and violently attacked – the erstwhile aristocrat, merchant, clergyman, or *meshchanin* – often found themselves re-catapulted into positions of esteem. Yet herein lies the *dis-leveling* logic that would not escape even the most benign campaign seeking to *level* a social order, under both a democratic and a tyrannical regime alike.

In Chapter 9, I turn to exploring how the historically conditioned matrices of social relationships impinge on the choices, preferences, and values of Russia's various social groups across time and in space. I analyze the relationship between the legacies of the territorial distribution of the pre-communist bourgeoisie and the spatial variations in democratic quality across Russia's territories; and I discern variations *within* the present-day middle class derived from the differential origins of the substrata that comprised it in late imperial and Soviet societies.

9

The Two-Pronged Middle Class: Implications for Democracy across Time and in Space

It is October and the *volontyory* (volunteers) have gathered for their end-of-season brainstorming session. Here, they will go over the goals achieved and budgets spent and formulate the new agenda for the next season, when the gray-blue winter hues over the Zhigulyovskiye Mountains will give way to the emerald greens over the embankment of the mighty Volga. After the session is over, they will move to the completed "site," an object of physical after-work labor in the evenings and weekends, when the volunteers gather to renovate pre-revolutionary architectural relics. This time it is the house of *meshchanka* Pavlova, a decaying but now restored mansion in old-town Samara. As the group forms a semicircle in front of the house, photographs are taken, and a champagne cork flies up to the low-key and discreet cheers of the volunteers and the odd passerby. It is the end of the working week; they will now walk along a few streets of the old town in the moonlit atmospheric fog to have a drink or two.[1] Quiet, restrained, and dignified, this group eerily evokes the fictional, speechless society of Andrey Zvyagintsev's film *Loveless* where the nameless *volontyory* search the scorched urban wasteland to find any signs of life of Alyosha, a boy who disappears from his family home. As in *Loveless*, the Samara *volontyory* step into the void left by the omnipresent and simultaneously disengaged state. They are participants in the Tom Sawyer Fest, a movement that has spread across the urban terrain of Russia, counting hundreds of activists and followers. It is an effort to restore the decrepit, decaying, and vanishing dignity of urban living in the Russia of old.[2] It is a reenactment of the museum society, one whose preoccupation with the conservation of a bygone era's culture, art, and heritage is simultaneously re-

---

[1] Interview with Yevgeniy Niktarkin, Tom Sawyer Fest activist, and Zoya Kobozeva, as well as author observation of celebrations, October 24, 2018.

[2] On the social infrastructure and architecture of pre-revolutionary Samara, see Reka, "Gorodskaya sotsial'naya infrastruktura."

constitutive of the bonds among the cultivated class; and it is a world apart from the least privileged at the bottom of society in the working quarters of Bezymyanka just a few miles away.

For some in the Generation X in Samara, the 1980s evoke the democratic promise of Gorbachev's perestroika; for others, it is the *furagi* (see Figure 9.1). A movement of the urban underclass, *furagi* embodied the separation, the marginality, and the disengagement of the factory worker from the haves of "old" Samara. Distinguished by their oversized capes (*furazhki-furagi*), tight trousers, and cropped heels, the *furagi* straddled the criminal underworld and the factory youth – those who maintained an identity, lifestyle, and social space distinct from the old town in mythology and fact. The *furagi* congregated in the broken squares of the concrete jungle of Bezymyanka to the blasting of the *magnitofon* and the guitar; many succumbed to the gang, as Andrey Olekh describes in his fictionalized accounts of Bezymyanka.[3] Curiously, just as the Soviet Empire was about to disintegrate, their political statement, if they had one, was to embrace the ideology, symbols, and declared goals of communism.[4] The *furagi* would disappear from the urban scene, along with the democratic promise of the 1980s, but the social cleavage distinguishing the factory laborer from the "old" Samara citizen would not, as indeed that between a member of the intelligentsia and a village girl from the *mikrorayon* (micro-distict).

The two social configurations are extremes, the political scientist's neat partitioning of a far more complex, fluid, intermarried, socially transgressive, and multilayered society. For every scion of an unbroken chain in the estatist background of the pre-revolutionary bourgeoisie, there would be one who would rise from a modest background with the help or in spite of Soviet state policy; and for every engaged, active, discerning, and autonomous protagonist in the crypto-public sphere, there may be scores of others, conforming, passive, politically and civically disengaged, from an eclectic tapestry of backgrounds.[5] The story told in the previous chapters shines deliberate light on social reproduction and adaptation. I have therefore spared the reader the repetition of the narrative of the intermingling of the social classes and the genesis of a new *Soviet* value system and culture, of social change, uplift, and transformation. These assumptions are not entirely inaccurate. They have, nevertheless, in my view sadly towered over the voluminous literature on communism to the neglect of the unsung bourgeois discreetly reenacting the society of the past and, along with it, the social, structural, and institutional microcosms crowding out others within a community, a neighborhood, or a town. In what follows, I test what is essentially a *probabilistic* pattern of various social configurations shaping

[3] Olekh, *Obmen i prodazha*.
[4] Andrey Artyomov, "Furagi–domotkannaya subkul'tura rabochikh okrain," *Drugoy gorod*, December 29, 2013. Available online at: http://drugoigorod.ru/furagi/ (accessed May 18, 2020).
[5] For a discussion of soul-searching among intellectuals about their ambivalent relations with the regime, see Shlapentokh, *Soviet Intellectuals*, 98–104.

FIGURE 9.1 The Bezymyanka *furagi*
Photos are present-day reconstructions using actors; the original idea of a nostalgic
brand and reconstruction of the subculture of the *furagi* is based on recollections of
Samara old-timers and developed by Michael Al'kov, pers. comm. with Z. Kobozeva and
M. Al'kov, November 18, 2020
Source. Photo by Yelena Zagorodneva. Andrey Artyomov, "Furagi"

Russia's post-communist politics – the likelihood of a particular trajectory,
a process, an outcome that does not rule out the possibility of alternative or
parallel pathways. I first explain how unpacking the genesis, resilience, and
political orientations of the multilayered stratum of the educated estates

nuances ongoing debates about the interaction between distinct sets of legacies associated with pre-communist and communist regimes. Next, I present analysis that systematically extrapolates the insights from the dissection of the reproduction of the social structure to explain variations in subnational democratic processes in Russia.

REVISITING THEORIES OF SOCIAL STRUCTURE AND DEMOCRACY

My theory and analysis are sensitive to two aspects of social closure that I link to democratic outcomes. One concerns the bifurcation *between* distinct social groups, or classes, if we deploy materialist categories of group formation and identity, as I have discussed in Chapter 1. I have argued that the origins of the fissure between the hitherto privileged highly educated estates, on the one hand, and the illiterate or poorly educated rural and worker masses of overwhelmingly peasant estate origin, on the other, lie in pre-communist society. This cleavage endured in space and within society because of both social resilience and communism's relentlessly appropriative logic. The second aspect of social divisions, which I more fully tease out in this chapter, concerns bifurcations *within* communist and post-communist middle classes, here conceptualized in a stylized way as consisting of two prongs: one nurtured relatively "autonomously" in the bosom of pre-communist capitalist development and another emerging out of "hegemonic" policies of communist industrialization and social uplift. I hypothesize that both sets of processes contribute to within-nation and cross-national variations in democratic outcomes in post-communist societies. In what follows, I remind the reader of the logic behind the argument.

I have argued that the origins and nature of the pre-communist bourgeoisie are appropriately situated in imperial Russia's estate structure and the "critical juncture" of the 1860s Great Reforms. Progressive in intent, these reforms had the effect of consolidating the chasm between the would-be bourgeoisie of nobles, clergymen, and urban estates and the vast swathes of the illiterate peasantry. The latter were deprived of access to universal schooling just as serfdom was being abolished and new citizenship rights promulgated. By the time of the Bolshevik Revolution, not only did Russia possess a muscular middle class but this broad and admittedly fluid stratum had been institutionally incorporated into what I call "infrastructures" of modernity – the professions, educational institutions, and charitable, civic, and local governance bodies. These institutions retained an autonomous or quasi-autonomous character vis-à-vis the state. They also, however, reflected the wider societal bifurcations, notably the cleavage between the superbly educated proto-bourgeoisie, which encompassed a small share of the population, including a segment of peasant upstarts – often of state rather than manorial estate origin – and the overwhelmingly illiterate or poorly schooled former serfs, who comprised the masses. At the start of this chapter, I tried to capture these enduring bifurcations using the stylized reference to the civil society of "old"

Samara, enacting a public sphere against the background of Putin's autocracy and the working quarters' Bezymyanka *furagi*.

What are the expectations and state of knowledge concerning pre-communist legacies as drivers of democratic variations between and within formerly communist states; and those pertaining to interaction between legacies associated with distinct regimes? This knowledge would help verify that the causal mechanisms explored here and centered on the pre-communist social structure are not capturing other legacies. I distinguish between legacies that are grouped under the rubrics of (1) *structural legacies*, which include broad patterns of development such as industrialization and urbanization, among and within states, and predating communist state-led development; (2) those that Alberto Simpser and colleagues refer to as *cognitional*,[6] in my analysis centered on value orientations nurtured within pre-communist societies but also those pertaining to cultural socialization and characterizing distinct ethnic and religious communities and their institutions and values; and (3) the so-called *coalitional* dynamics driving macro-level political change.[7]

Structural Legacies

My analysis speaks to two strands of literature on the structural bundle of legacies in post-communist countries. One set of arguments pertains to the straightforward persistence of legacies of development; these are broadly in sync with the appropriative logic described in this book. Consistent with Jason Wittenberg's theorizing into a legacy as an "instantiation" of the same broad phenomenon across time periods associated with distinct regimes, development, and, by extension, democracy,[8] legacies would be straightforwardly attributable to the "prime mover" effect of initial conditions at the time of, respectively, the Revolution in Russia or the communist takeovers elsewhere in Europe. In analyses accounting for these legacies, pre-communist development is conventionally captured employing urbanization, GDP, or industry statistics. Structural legacies so defined and measured, however, as I discuss later in this section, have tended to produce ambivalent results, leading scholars to problematize the notion of a legacy as a straightforward "instantiation" of the same broad phenomenon.[9]

Correspondingly, a second strand of theorizing has highlighted that interaction of a legacy associated with a distinct regime or political, economic, or social order with those of another one may lead to perversion, distortion, or undermining of a legacy that we would normally associate with a specific long-

---

[6] Simpser et al., "Dead but Not Gone."   [7] Ibid.

[8] Jason Wittenberg, "What Is a Historical Legacy?" University of California at Berkeley, March 25, 2012, 9.

[9] Lankina et al., "Appropriation and Subversion," 232.

term outcome.[10] Structural legacies are a case in point. On the one hand, we would expect the reproduction of spatial patterns of development to augment the maturation of a "modern" urban constituency in industrial conurbations. This would be logical, since such conglomerates attract a large educated white-collar workforce. On the other hand, production facilities incorporated to serve the communist industrialization drive could become, to use Rosenfeld's apt characterization, "incubators" of a state-dependent and pliant workforce,[11] whether of managers, engineers, or shop-floor workers. Here, we would not be seeing the straightforward reproduction of a legacy and its expected effects as postulated in Wittenberg's framework. Rather, we would observe what Stephen Kotkin and Mark Beissinger, in another influential essay on legacies, discuss as a process of permutation or complete transformation of a legacy such that the effects are different from those that we would observe absent interaction with the legacies of the distinct, communist, regime.[12] Still others have argued that communist modernization and the carnage accompanying it purged society of its pre-modern characteristics, a process ostensibly conducive to democracy in some post-communist countries.[13]

   These conflicting expectations are mirrored in ambivalent, if not outright odd, results peculiar to post-communist countries: urbanization, for instance, in some studies has tended to *negatively* covary with democracy.[14] Furthermore, the fact that communist regimes tended to build on extant industrial infrastructure makes it difficult to disentangle the effects of pre-communist development from the legacies of communist industrial strategy. Alexander Gerschenkron wrote about the perils of the late industrializer experience, namely the state's propensity to take the lead in developing mega-industries.[15] Soviet industrial strategy, Gerschenkron argued, only "magnified and distorted out of all proportion" the preoccupation with oversized industry giants.[16] The social-structural perspective that I take in this book would hopefully inject nuance into how we make sense of these potentially conflicting dynamics. If the hypothesized legacy of the estates-derived bourgeoisie matters for understanding the social structure during communism and now, we would expect this variable to significantly covary with democratic quality over and above the legacies associated more narrowly with the Soviet-period modernization strategy.

---

[10] Kotkin and Beissinger, "Historical Legacies."
[11] Rosenfeld, "Reevaluating," 637. See also Frye et al., "Political Machines."
[12] Kotkin and Beissinger, "Historical Legacies," 7–9.
[13] Kopstein and Bernhard, "Post-Communism," 379.
[14] Lankina and Libman, "Soviet Legacies." Survey research on Russia has found that living in a larger city may reduce support for the current regime (respondents were pooled from the 1992–2007 New Russia Barometer surveys), though the effect is moderate. Education, however, emerges as an unreliable predictor of trends in regime support. Rose et al., *Popular Support*, 89.
[15] Gerschenkron, *Economic Backwardness*, 20.   [16] Ibid., 28.

The analysis in the preceding chapters and studies by other authors allow us to begin to unpack plausible causal mechanisms. Building on Rosenfeld's work, we may conjecture that pre-communist social legacies could be consequential for the types of jobs that individuals opt into.[17] Likewise, extending insights from Kelly McMann's research into post-communist economic autonomy as a driver of regional political openness in regions like Samara, we may conjecture as to where exactly this autonomy comes from, historically speaking. This may help take emphasis away from the temporally proximate drivers of the observed variations, adding refinements to causal assumptions concerning persistence in spatial gradations of national and subnational openness.[18] The embourgeoisement of educated estates may well have engendered a high human-capital professional class whose employment aspirations and possibilities would transcend large state-dependent public sector and industry occupations. While my account does not negate the comparatively high state dependencies of the middle class in imperial Russia and underdeveloped Eastern European peripheries,[19] I have highlighted that even the otherwise formally state-incorporated professions and the civil service constituted islands of a quasi-sovereign public sphere, a legacy that would persist. While many individuals working in such islands would be "appropriated" into the party-cadre route, becoming the regime's ideological spokespersons, others would eschew becoming victims of such "subversion" of their autonomy, deliberately opting into less ideologically and morally tainted jobs or career trajectories. Another channel distinct from that of human capital narrowly defined is the entrepreneurial ethos and values of the merchant–*meshchane* stratum that encourages risk-taking and "speculation" pursuits during communism and the entrepreneurship following the collapse of socialist state planning. Path-dependency in the location and expansion of industrial hubs meant that, even within one city, mega-industries coexisted with diverse and plural employment ecosystems. These constellations too derive from the peculiarities of pre-communist development, as I have demonstrated. Indeed, as Gerschenkron writes, in Russia, reduced government involvement in industry in 1907–14 "greatly" altered "the character of the industrialization process."[20] "Russian industry had reached a stage where it could throw away the crutches of government support and begin to walk independently."[21] The Neklutin papers

---

[17] Rosenfeld, *Autocratic Middle Class*.
[18] Samara and Ul'yanovsk are the contrasting Russian cases in the study. McMann, *Economic Autonomy*.
[19] I am grateful to Jeff Kopstein for highlighting this aspect of middle-class variations in Russia and elsewhere in Europe.
[20] Gerschenkron, *Economic Backwardness*, 21. On "autonomous" impulses in enterprise and banking after 1909, even if facilitated by "induced" state policies, see also Crisp, *Studies*, 33–34.
[21] Gerschenkron, *Economic Backwardness*, 22. For debates among economic historians concerning the accuracy of Gerschenkron's assumptions about the take-off of Russian capital and the reduced state role in the years leading up to World War II, see Davies, "Changing Economic

allude precisely to the kinds of smaller-scale light industries before the Revolution and during the NEP that Gershenkron argued had weak foundations during the earlier phases of Russia's industrialization – from grain production, to textiles, to small-scale food manufactures – but enjoyed fast growth in the years preceding World War I.[22] Finally, one's estate heritage could nurture value orientations via the intergenerational familial and broader social network channels. These would have the effect of building resilience against the otherwise citizen-remolding legacies of socialization in state-controlled industries or other sites of employment. In other words, exploring how the legacies of social structures work in post-communist contexts sheds light on complementary sources of resilience. Citizens may eschew employment with state-controlled industries or sectors limiting personal choice and autonomy; or they may exhibit orientations of scrutiny and autonomy even when exposed to the workplace arenas of political and peer pressures.

Finally, structural legacies as understood here transcend industrial development to embrace professional and civic institutions, which I have argued served as hubs of enactment of social agency and initiative during communism. These were indirectly consequential to industrial and more broadly capitalist development. Industry and trading hubs generated wealth that diffused, via philanthropy, into arenas like the museum society and fed the demand- and supply-side of the service sector of medical, educational, and other professionals. The museum society specifically would not lose its relevance as an

Systems," 3–4. I concur with Diane Davis (not to be confused with Davies above) that the literature on late developing states has relatively neglected the small entrepreneur segment of the middle class while focusing on capitalists, the state, and laborers. Davis, *Discipline*, 26. Indeed, scholars usually eschew discussing Gerschenkron's insights into the indigenous light industry producers and traders in tsarist Russia. Further, as Davis writes, those working as small producers or providers of services in the informal economy "have fallen off the conceptual map" because scholars "tend to use frameworks of class categories drawn from study of the developed world." Ibid., 38. Moreover, bundling such economic sectors with categories of popular or working classes is also problematic: "To recognize that urban artisanal work and street vending entail entirely different kinds of activities than does working in a factory, however, and that the former folk may have autonomy, more access to property, and a different set of economic and political priorities than factory workers or other wage laborers, is to be aware that their interests and actions may be quite different – and perhaps more similar to those characteristically called the middle class." Ibid., 40. The assumption that many artisans transition into factory work as their jobs become obsolete, which Davis highlights and critiques, is not borne out if we take the social trajectories of many *meshchane* small producers, *rentier*, and services providers transitioning into the professional stratum, due to an ability to pay for education, and not into factory workforce. In other words, they remain committed to "reinvestment" (a distinction from subsistence that Davis notes), except they will be investing in education/human capital, not expansion of production per se. Ibid., 41–42, 45.

[22] Other economic historians have agreed that, unlike the mostly foreign-owned, state-controlled, capital goods industries, consumer goods production in late imperial Russia had a predominance of "freely-competing Russian firms." See Davies, "Changing Economic Systems," 2. Here, we see an element of spontaneous non-state-led development within the state-led process of late industrialization of a capitalist market economic system.

autonomous or quasi-independent public space in the communist period, much like how today art galleries, university faculties, and think tanks constitute islands of oppositional engagement in Putin's autocracy, as they do in Orbán's Hungary or Xi's China.[23] These would be distinct from arenas of "collectivization of the middle class"[24] in the less skills-intensive large public sector bureaucratic and services spheres. These legacies are, of course, related to the cognitional dimension of social persistence.

Cognitional Legacies

Sensitive as my analysis is to the intergenerational transmission of value orientations via familial, social, and professional networks, it echoes theorizing into the so-called cognitional sets of legacies.[25] Cultural-religious variables specifically may arguably nurture democracy-conducive values or, in the case of ethnic minorities of pre-communist Empires, engender anti-communist sentiments.[26] In some of imperial Russia's territories, specific ethno-religious communities constituted sizeable shares of the urban estates of the *meshchane* and merchants. Many Jews were ascribed to *meshchane* status in the Pale of Settlement, for instance; and, in Samara, Old Believer merchant families were successful in banking, trade, and enterprise. In discussions of interaction with communist-period legacies, certain cultural-cognitional legacies have been construed as generating *resistance* to the otherwise deleterious influences of communist socialization.[27] Individual cultural identities and values are

---

[23] Although Xi's intensification of the crackdown on dissent, particularly in Hong Kong, warrants qualifiers.

[24] Expression used with reference to white-collar low-level employees in Weimar Germany. Speier, *German White-Collar Workers*, 44. In Weimar Germany, "old nobility" and "old wealth" continued to find reflection in professional choice and rank. Ibid., 80.

[25] Simpser et al., "Dead but Not Gone."

[26] The cultural underpinnings of democratic variations in post-communist societies have formed the bulk of studies of pre-communist legacies. Where studies of Central Europe have highlighted the legacies of religion, religious institutions, or the emergence of a national consciousness, Central Asianists have explored the role of clan, kinship, and other social structures predating nation building. Research on nationalism in fact contains many insights that resonate here (notably, the Bolsheviks' reliance on indigenous elites – the khans, the mullahs, the princes) in the process of incorporating "native" societies into Soviet modernity; or the role of nationalist intellectuals in a variety of contexts, from Central Asian states to Hungary, in crafting narratives of nationhood and statehood and in shaping pro- or anti-communist and, by extension, pro- or anti-democratic attitudes and proclivities. Yet these insights have not percolated into discussions of the social structure outside of the narrower question of nation building. On religious legacies, see Pop-Eleches and Tucker, *Communism's Shadow*; Wittenberg, *Crucibles*; Lankina, "Religious Influences." See also Brubaker, *Nationalism*; Giuliano, "Who Determines"; Gorenburg, *Minority Ethnic Mobilization*; Laitin, "Language and Nationalism"; Darden and Grzymala-Busse, "Great Divide"; Bunce, "National Idea." On Central Asia, see, Collins, *Clan Politics*; Junisbai, "Tale of Two Kazakhstans"; and, on the Caucasus, Derluguian, *Bourdieu's Secret Admirer*.

[27] Pop-Eleches and Tucker, *Communism's Shadow*.

regarded either as a product of socialization in pre-communist schools,[28] or in families and local communities,[29] or as reproduced and supported in surviving faith infrastructures – churches or religious community associations.[30] In the statistical analysis, I include 1897 census data on religion to ensure that estates do not simply proxy for cultural-religious values. Demonstrating that the institution of the estate matters for democratic voting patterns in the early 1990s, and that its significance goes over and above the complementary ethno-religious sources of influence on political trajectories of post-communist societies, corroborates the argument concerning this important channel of persistence.

Coalitional Legacies

To the extent that social structure has featured in the literature on legacies, the tendency has been to couch discussions in the language of coalitional dynamics driving democratization or regime change.[31] Barrington Moore's monograph on the social origins of democracy and dictatorship;[32] the many works that it spurred;[33] and indeed research projects in the historical sociology tradition concerned with democracy and autocracy in Europe[34] have been broadly written in this vein. The focus in this research is on social groups that become powerful enough to organize and effect major shifts in national-level representative institutions, political suffrage, or taxation and redistributive arrangements.[35] Scholars have also highlighted cleavages within groups and between them as well as other social actors that hamper impulses toward parliamentary democracy.[36] In an influential monograph, Ben Ansell and David Samuels highlight aspects of social structures that are particularly relevant to the argument advanced in my study. Contrary to implicit assumptions in leading research into the role of the bourgeoisie in driving democratic change, they contend that the strata near the top of income distribution, with their incentives to press for democracy, embrace a wide spectrum of social groups – from shopkeepers to large industrialists – the *petite* and the *grande bourgeoisie*, as well as white-collar employees.[37] In their account, even the innkeeper and small

---

[28] Darden and Grzymala-Busse, "Great Divide."

[29] Leonid Peisakhin, "Long Run Persistence of Political Attitudes and Behavior: A Focus on Mechanisms." Paper presented at the Conference on Historical Legacies and Contemporary Politics, Juan March Institute, Madrid, June 14–15, 2013.

[30] Wittenberg, *Crucibles.*

[31] For an overview of the literature, see Simpser et al., "Dead but Not Gone."

[32] Moore, *Social Origins.*

[33] See, for example, Boix, *Democracy and Redistribution*; Acemoglu and Robinson, *Economic Origins.*

[34] Luebbert, *Liberalism.*

[35] See Boix, *Democracy and Redistribution*; Acemoglu and Robinson, *Economic Origins.*

[36] Luebbert, *Liberalism.*   [37] Ansell and Samuels, *Inequality,* 39.

business owner is far wealthier than the "typically poor" median voter. This would mean, say, that the *meshchane* encountered on the pages of this book – the proprietor of a hair salon, the caterer, the *rentier* – whose descendants are the professoriate, the creatives, the businessmen – would fit into the higher income category, relatively speaking. This group attended elite schools or professional training courses, obtained white-collar jobs, and owned property, often large enough to generate rent. They were a small slice of imperial Russian society, however. According to Acemoglu and Robinson's well-known account, the size of the bourgeoisie matters, for "a relatively large and affluent middleclass acts as a buffer between the rich and the poor ... By ensuring that policies are not too far from those preferred by the rich, it discourages the rich from using repression and makes democracy more likely."[38] In response, Ansell and Samuels have observed that the middle class, whether defined culturally or in income terms – and one that is associated with groups between the landed elites and the poor – "earn between twice and ten times the average," far more than the "median voter" who "always earns less than average."[39] They underline the near universal smallness of the bourgeoisie or middle class, bar a handful of outliers, across Europe at the start of the twentieth century, let alone in peripheral, "backward," nations like Russia – even with their wide conceptualization of this stratum. Contradicting the argument of Carles Boix,[40] which presupposes economic equality as driving democratic change, they also write: "In a developing autocracy the middle class is, historically speaking, almost never located in the actual middle of the income distribution. It is found in the upper two deciles of a country's income distribution, or even in the top decile."[41] Although the emphasis is on rising inequalities as indicative of development engendering a bourgeoisie, this observation is broadly relevant to my study in that the smallness of the bourgeoisie as a proportion of the population, or the apparent material modesty or even semi-squalor of the *petit bourgeois*, does not necessarily disbar this social segment of property owners and tax-paying public from effecting democratic change via an articulation of preferences in the electoral arena; organized forms of social engagement pressing for change; or coalition with other, more powerful actors. My argument is precisely that imperial Russia already possessed the so-called bourgeoisie, small, but sizeable enough, and certainly more sizeable than one that emerges even from the social tables presented in the work of Ansell and Samuels.

Let us now extrapolate these arguments to present-day autocracies and illiberal regimes with a legacy of communist planning. Where my account differs from that of Ansell and Samuels is in the emphasis on the manipulability of what they refer to as the relatively poor "median voter." The size of the underprivileged mass is consequential in present-day illiberal regimes with communist legacies. Communist planners created or enhanced

---

[38] Acemoglu and Robinson, *Economic Origins*, 258.   [39] Ansell and Samuels, *Inequality*, 39.
[40] Boix, *Democracy and Redistribution*.   [41] Ansell and Samuels, *Inequality*, 34.

mega-industrial conglomerates where social services provision revolved around these hubs, something that helps autocrats now solidify their popular support base. In turn, the smallness of the bourgeoisie–middle class undermines its ability to engender effective defiance of autocratic rule. The "median voter" may indeed be politically inert,[42] but the "action" at the top of the income distribution pyramid that Ansell and Samuels refer to may not be enough to effect democratic change in communist legacy settings. The inert and manipulated workforce would continue to deliver support for an anti-democratic regime, while the small middle class would be electorally and institutionally too weak to tip the balance in favor of reform. My sociological account of inequalities underscores the educational gap at the pivotal junctures of the 1860s and 1917, dividing the small bourgeoisie and the underprivileged masses, with implications for the inevitably long catch-up period between old and new middle-class groups. We already know that these processes engendered spatial and within-regional variations in the presence of public engagement spaces and employment sites that educated groups populated, colonized, and gravitated toward. Did the educated estates already represent a democracy-supportive constituency in late imperial Russia? Electoral statistics capturing the vote share for the pro-democracy Constitutional Democrats Party (*kadety*), which I present in the following section, allow us to begin to unpack how the proto-middle class influenced voting outcomes. The data allow us to evaluate the assumption that the bourgeoisie expressed democratic preferences and orientations at the start of the twentieth century.

STATISTICAL ANALYSIS

Mapping the Estate Structure in Imperial Russia

I start with a descriptive exercise accentuating the contours of imperial Russia's spatial palette of estate constellations based on 1897 census data. Figures 9.2–9.5 aggregate district-level data over current regional administrative boundaries. The shades denote present-day regional borders and share of estates as captured by

---

[42] The authors consider that "action" occurs at the top 20 percent of income distribution. Ibid., 14. In my view, Ansell and Samuels erroneously calculate the size of Russia's middle class at the turn of the twentieth century at just 4 percent. The social table that they provide has no mention of estates, which would have been one indicator of middle-class status. Ibid., 30, table 2.4 for 1904; and discussion, 29–30. The category of "servants" alone comprises 4.2 percent. Yet, while servants were often of a peasant background, many servants in wealthy households were *meshchane* with high cultural aspirations and middle-class lifestyles. This may not be *Bildungsbürgertum* but *Bürgertum* nonetheless. The study's social table is based on Steven Nafziger and Peter Lindert, "Russian Inequality on the Eve of the Revolution." Williams College Working Paper, 2011. For a more up-to-date version, see the September 2012 draft (Working Paper No. 18383), 35, table 3. Available online at: nber.org/papers/w18383 (accessed November 9, 2020).

density, while dark lines are boundaries of the much larger imperial-era *gubernii*. Let us begin with the nobility estate at the apex of Russia's formal social hierarchy (Figure 9.2). As expected, we see a significant concentration of nobles in the imperial capital of St. Petersburg – 10 percent in the St. Petersburg *uyezd*. Unsurprisingly, there is a large concentration of nobles in districts surrounding Moscow – 5.77 percent. A less obvious pattern is the sizeable presence in pockets of territories in the Far East and Siberia. These featured large concentrations of exiled nobles of Polish ancestry; in these sparsely populated lands, the nobility stood for imperial authority on the periphery – the governor's office and other civil servants as well as political exiles. The Khabarovskiy district, then part of Primorskaya *oblast*, features proportionally the second-largest population of nobles after St. Petersburg, at 5.9 percent. Many nobles also congregated in the southern territories of the Voysko Donskogo region (nearly 4 percent); the Vladikavkaz district (nearly 4 percent) of Terskaya *oblast*; and in the Irkutsk district of Irkutstk *guberniya* in Siberia (3.68 percent). In the Omsk district of Akmolinskaya *oblast*, 5.27 percent of the population were registered as nobles. Individuals dispatched to the sparsely inhabited Far Eastern territories or the Caucasus as civil servants or as political exiles represented a distinct social demographic of the highly educated strata.[43] The writer Fyodor Dostoevsky,

Nobility

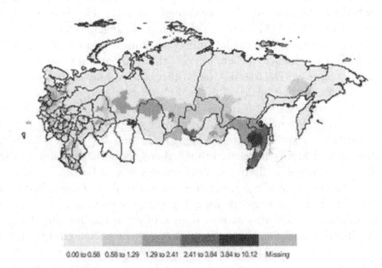

0.00 to 0.58   0.58 to 1.29   1.29 to 2.41   2.41 to 3.84   3.84 to 10.12   Missing

FIGURE 9.2 Historical share of nobility in *rayony*

---

[43] For a documentary and eyewitness account of the lives of educated political exiles in Siberia, see Kennan, *Siberia*, 1; and Dostoevsky, *Zapiski*, 3

Clergy

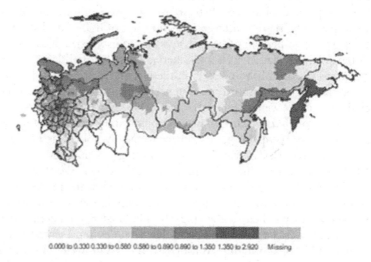

0.000 to 0.330 0.330 to 0.580 0.580 to 0.890 0.890 to 1.350 1.350 to 2.920   Missing

FIGURE 9.3 Historical share of clergy in *rayony*

exiled to Siberia for his youthful spell of oppositional activism, promptly embedded himself in the local high society. He befriended the public prosecutor, Baron Alexander Yegorovich Wrangel, a scion of "one of those Russian-German aristocratic families of Baltic origin that, under Nicholas I, staffed the higher echelons of the bureaucracy and the army."[44] Simultaneously, Dostoevsky like other exiles may have indirectly diffused knowledge in what he described as the cultural desert of Siberia.[45]

The clergy estate constituted a mere 0.5 percent of the empire's population (Figure 9.3). Unsurprisingly, in a country steeped in religion, with the Russian Orthodox Church enjoying state patronage, the clergy shows fairly even distribution across districts, though there are some outliers. In the Far East, the Komandorskiy district in Primorskaya *oblast* had the highest population share of clergy, at 2.9 percent. In Petropavlovskiy *okrug* (district), in present-day Kamchatskiy *kray* (region), the clergy constituted 1.85 percent of the population. Again, this pattern is an artifact of the low population density at the frontier and the proportional strength of social groups associated with

---

[44] Frank, *Dostoevsky*, 228.

[45] Dostoevsky's protagonist writes: "In Siberian towns one often meets teachers from amongst the exiled settlers; the local citizens are not squeamish [toward these people] [*imi ne brezgayut*]. They mostly teach the French language, so important in life, and without them [these teachers] about which [French language] in the distant parts of Siberia one would not have any idea." Dostoevsky, *Zapiski*, 3:6 (author's translation). See also discussion in Lankina, "Boris Nemtsov," 50–51.

Merchants

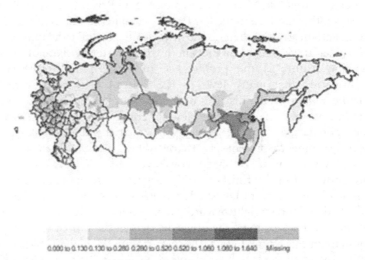

0.000 to 0.130 0.130 to 0.280 0.280 to 0.520 0.520 to 1.060 1.060 to 1.640 Missing

FIGURE 9.4 Historical share of merchants in *rayony*

imperial power on the periphery. The top ten districts by population share of clergy are also overwhelmingly urban and correspond to historical cities of Arkhangel'sk, Yaroslavl', Dmitrovsk, Kaluga, Vologda, Kostroma, and Tver'.

Let us now visualize the distribution of the urban estates. Barely 0.2 percent of imperial Russia's population belonged to the merchant estate (Figure 9.4). Out of the more than 400 districts, only three featured more than 1 percent of merchants – the Moscow (1.6 percent) and St. Petersburg (1.3 percent) districts in the respective *gubernii*, and Rybinskiy (1.05 percent) *uyezd* in Yaroslavskaya *guberniya*. Among the top ten districts by merchant share are also Kaluzhskaya, Amurskaya, Astrakhanskaya, Akrhangel'skaya, Terskaya, and Kazanskaya *gubernii*. Of these, the Kaluzhskiy district (like Rybinsk in Yaroslavskaya *oblast*) now forms part of the Central Federal District, while other territories are in the North, Southern Russia, or Far East. Old Believers, known as incubators of entrepreneurial activities, constituted sizeable populations in several of the top ten merchant regions. In Blagoveshchensk in Amur *oblast*, where the share of merchants was 0.8 percent, almost 12 percent of citizens were listed as belonging to the Old Believer community; and, in Kaluga, where the share of merchants was 0.86 percent, 4.9 percent of residents were Old Believers. Old Believer communities were also sizeable in Astrakhan (2.22 percent) and Moscow *uyezdy* (2.04 percent).

The *meshchane* estate forms sizeable chunks of the population in many territories (Figure 9.5). Districts with the largest share are historical towns that mostly correspond to present-day regional capitals or major cities, namely Rostov, Astrakhan, Tula, Tsaritsyn (Volgograd), Novorossiysk, St. Petersburg, Kaluga, Pyatigorsk, Moscow, and a district in Bryansk (Novozybkovskiy). The west, south, Siberia, and the Far East have higher densities of the concentration of this urban stratum than do the historically Black Earth lands in central parts of Russia. If we analyze districts in the top quarter by share of *meshchane*, one striking feature is the prominence of western and southern territories. Considering that many Jews in the Pale of Settlement were ascribed to the *meshchane* estate, districts with some of the highest concentrations of the *meshchane* also had sizeable Jewish communities. Nearly 10 percent of the population of the Velizhskiy district in Vitebskaya *guberniya*, corresponding to present-day Pskov *oblast*, and as much as 16 percent in Mstislavskiy *uyezd* of Mogilyovskaya *guberniya*, a Jewish *mestechko* presently part of the Khislavichskiy district, a *rayon* of the same name in the Smolensk region, were Jewish. The *meshchane*'s complex social demography, which does not straightforwardly correspond to Russia's religious map, is illustrated if we examine the other districts in the top 50 (out of 424 districts) by share of this estate. In fact, the district with the highest share of *meshchane*, at nearly 30 percent, is Rostov *uyezd*, in imperial Russia part of the Voysko Donskogo region with a large population of Cossacks and presently in Rostovskaya *oblast*. Jews constitute a modest 3.5 percent population share here, though it is larger than in most districts where it tended to be below 1 percent.

Meshchane

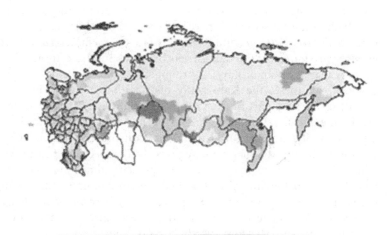

0.01 to 4.16   4.16 to 8.96   8.96 to 14.96   14.96 to 20.77   20.77 to 29.25   Missing

FIGURE 9.5 Historical share of *meshchane* in *rayony*

Several districts in the top fifty *meshchane* havens also prominently feature Old Believers. As a community, as I have discussed with reference to Samara, Old Believers had been conspicuous in merchant entrepreneurship and likely moved between *meshchane* and merchant status as rural occupations were abandoned in favor of the trades and business in towns. In the Saratov *uyezd* on the Volga River, where 19 percent of the population were *meshchane*, nearly 5 percent of the population were Old Believers. In the Samara *uyezd*, where 13 percent residents were *meshchane*, 6 percent of *uyezd* dwellers identified as Old Believers. Protestants also formed sizeable population shares in several top *meshchane* districts. Nearly 9 percent of the population, or almost one in ten residents, in the St. Petersburg district, were of the Protestant faith in 1897. In the Saratov district, home to a sizeable community of Volga Germans, more than 6 percent of the population were Protestants. In the Tsarskoye selo district of St. Petersburg *guberniya*, 29 percent, nearly one in every three, residents were Protestants.

To what extent do these statistics simply capture the urban/rural divide, the chasm between the peasantry and the rest of society? Further, how can we ensure that they do not simply reflect the stark human capital variations between the established European core and the newly conquered peripheries where nomadic frontier populations exhibited literacy rates in the single digits? Consider the following corroborating statistics. In the Kamyshinskiy *uyezd* of the then Saratovskaya *guberniya*, 95 percent of the population belonged to the peasant estate in 1897. Yet literacy in this district, at 38.3 percent, far exceeded the average for rural Russia. In this district, 30.47 percent of residents belonged to the Protestant faith; 9.68 percent were Catholics; and 2.57 percent were Old Believers. The Saratov, Samara, and Tsaritsyn (Volgograd) districts, which featured sizeable *meshchane* and merchant communities, absorbed the human capital from rural areas populated by Volga Germans. The size of the proto-bourgeois estate would thus, to a certain extent, be derived from the constellations in the cultural demographics of local societies.

The statistics presented in Table 2.1 in Chapter 2 for European Russia, that is, excluding districts in present-day Dagestan and some other North Caucasus territories exhibiting Russia's lowest literacy rates, also illustrate contrasting literacy rates of peasants and *meshchane* in rural areas. Note that, as the data in Table 9.1 show, in 1897, only 51 percent of the population ascribed to the urban estates resided in towns, while the rest, 49 percent, lived in villages. In 1917, 56 percent of those ascribed to the urban estates who resided in rural areas were literate, as compared to peasants residing in rural areas, at 32 percent literacy. Urban peasants were more literate than their rural counterparts – at 64 percent, but this figure is lower than the literacy levels for those ascribed to the urban estate living in towns and boasting a literacy rate of 73 percent. The literacy differences between urban peasants and *meshchane* may not appear large. Indeed, the fact that urban peasants had double the literacy rate of rural peasants underscores the significance of an urban effect in elevating human

TABLE 9.1 *Distribution of population by estate between towns and villages in European Russia, nineteenth century (%)*

	1802	1857	1897
Nobility			
Town	48	32.9	57.6
Village	52	67.1	42.4
Clergy			
Town	11.1	11.1	28.5
Village	88.9	88.9	71.5
Urban estates			
Town	59	50.2	51
Village	41	49.8	49
Peasant			
Town	3.4	2.5	6.7
Village	96.6	97.5	93.3
Military			
Town	21.9	20.9	
Village	78.1	79.1	
Others			
Town	20.6	11.9	28.4
Village	79.4	88.1	71.6

Note. Includes territories outside of present-day Russia.
Source. Mironov, *Rossiyskaya imperiya*, 1: 850: table V.15.

capital. At close to 10 percent, the variations between urban peasants and the urban estates nevertheless nuance the simple urban–rural paradigms of social modernization processes in imperial society. Furthermore, as noted in Chapter 2, considerable self-selection characterized peasant society on the move, with those more enterprising, literate, and numerate exhibiting a greater propensity to relocate to the city and indeed better chances of acquiring gainful employment there.

A summary of the impressionistic palette of the spatial distribution of estates in imperial Russia is in order here. Some estates were better represented in specific districts – aristocrats in St. Petersburg or *meshchane* in Rostov. Already we see patterns of the distribution of estates with high literacy rates in frontier territories outside of the core lands of European and Central Russia. These tapestries were, of course, intrinsic to the *longue durée* of economic development, population movements, and the taming of the frontier. As discussed in Chapter 2, the frontier

TABLE 9.2 *Correlation coefficients between shares of the educated estates*

	Nobility	Clergy	Merchants	*Meshchane*
Nobility	1.000			
Clergy	0.239***	1.000		
Merchants	0.710***	0.386***	1.000	
Meshchane	0.559***	0.204***	0.685***	1.000

Note. *** significant at 1% level.

came to shape society, but society already entered the frontier equipped with a set of values, skills, and faiths – often of a nonmainstream and even a persecuted kind – or, as in the case of nobles, equipped with human capital and educational credentials vastly superior to those of the masses in the overwhelmingly illiterate rural society. Table 9.2 provides basic statistics for correlation in the district-level distribution of the estates. Merchants and *meshchane* correlate with the other educated estates of the nobility and clergy not formally in the "urban" estate category. These patterns reflect the embourgeoisement of individuals ascribed to the two estates, particularly the nobility, who flocked into urban professions and pursuits, abandoning the life of the country squire or the priest. These trends are clear if we look at dynamic data provided by Mironov for 1802–97 in Table 9.1.

While the socioeconomic and religious profile of territories is itself a convincing explanation of spatial modernization variations – something that we know from earlier literature – the previous chapters have suggested how the institution of the estate channeled extant skills, aspirations, and values and indeed helped nurture and engender new ones. This perspective has allowed us to discern elements of the estate as contributing to the genesis of "bourgeois" human capital and inclinations in the political sphere, as well as the resources, networks, and values facilitating social initiative.

Key Outcome Variable of Democracy and Measures

Following the discussion presented so far, I expect the past social structure to shape democratic processes and outcomes at subnational and, ultimately, national levels. Specifically, I have highlighted how the social legacy of the high human-capital bourgeoisie contributes to the development of diverse employment ecosystems, which reduce the significance of large state-dependent workforces in shaping electoral outcomes. The heritage of a semi-free public sphere also shapes attitudes conducive to the genesis of plural social spaces that serve as a check on state authority. The bourgeois legacy also operates at the level of individual values: a better educated stratum possesses not only greater autonomy but also a more discerning mindset when navigating the political landscape.

Choice of Democracy Measures

I draw on Dahl's *Polyarchy* to identify the various dimensions of the key outcome variable, democracy. Dahl's baseline condition for a democratic political system are institutional guarantees for citizens to be able to formulate and signify heterogenous preferences and to have them "weighted equally in conduct of government."[46] These guarantees include the right to vote; the right of political leaders to compete for support; the availability of alternative sources of information; and free and fair elections. Yet democracy is meaningless unless institutional guarantees are honored in practice. Citizens may enjoy the right to vote, elections may be held regularly, and freedom of expression may be enshrined in the constitution, but ballot-stuffing may be rampant, journalists harassed, and chunks of the electorate uninformed and indifferent to these injustices. Furthermore, Dahl raises the possibility that the practice of democracy may vary across a country's subnational units. Subnational variations in political processes have been long acknowledged as important barometers of the health of a national democracy[47] and, most prominently in Robert Putnam's study of Italy, have been linked to historical peculiarities of local "civic traditions" dating back centuries.[48] As Dahl observes, whether institutional guarantees are provided or not, "social characteristics" like a weak middle class, low levels of educational attainment, and "an authoritarian political culture" may hinder competitive politics.[49] Dahl therefore captures both the supply-side of democratic institutions, as enshrined in laws, and the demand-side of a populace able to take full advantage of the right to signify preferences as well as to hold politicians to account.

The subnational research design allows me to hold constant national-level institutional frameworks governing these rights while teasing out subnational variations in the actual practice of democratic contestation. Yet even for the national, let alone the subnational, level, operationalizing and measuring the various aspects of citizen opportunity and agency in the electoral arena present notorious challenges. Fortunately, there are measures of some of the key aspects of the democratic process that have been validated in different subnational settings. I believe these measures help evaluate three important facets of Dahl's ideal-type democratic system: (1) the extent to which citizens exercise their right to vote in free and fair elections and thereby are able and willing to

---

[46] Dahl, *Polyarchy*, 3. Parts of the discussion in this chapter are reproduced with the permission of publisher from Lankina and Libman, "Two-Pronged Middle Class."

[47] For summaries of the literature, see Snyder, "Scaling Down"; Giraudy, "Varieties"; Behrend and Whitehead, *Illiberal Practices*; Lankina and Getachew, "Geographic Incremental Theory."

[48] Putnam et al., *Making Democracy Work*.   [49] Dahl, *Polyarchy*, 74.

hold politicians to account; (2) the extent to which political leaders can compete for support; and (3) freedom of expression or availability of alternative sources of information. I bracket the electoral dimensions under the rubric of "democratic competitiveness" and the availability of information as "media freedom." For reasons of space constraints, the analysis in the sections that follow presents the main results from a more expanded set of tests, including those related to multiple electoral cycles in Russia, reported in a paper coauthored with Alexander Libman. Readers interested in seeing the full set of regressions, results, and robustness checks are advised to consult the Supplementary Appendices and the large ancillary Online Appendices.[50]

To evaluate the competitiveness aspects of the democratic process, we draw on measures of electoral participation and competition deployed in earlier studies.[51] One such measure is the *effective number of candidates* (ENC); this captures the degree to which citizens' preference heterogeneity is reflected in votes for candidates in a competitive race. A higher ENC implies that a larger number of contestants received a sizeable share of the votes. Since this indicator could overestimate electoral competitiveness where voter participation is modest and where a large measure of ENC could emerge accidentally and would mask general apathy and a lack of interest in politics, we also, second, compute a *generic index of democratic competitiveness* based on a simple formula that Tatu Vanhanen developed to study national-level democratic variations.[52] The *Vanhanen index* (VI) is based on two indicators: participation (electoral turnout) and competition (share of the vote for any candidate except the contestant with the highest share of votes, in our case Yeltsin or Zyuganov). High VI values correspond to more competitive races. The index requires elections to be characterized by two features: lack of dominance of a single political force and high turnout. Thus, where local enterprises or regional political machines are instrumental in mobilizing electorates, even if turnout is high, the VI value would be small due to a modest share of nonwinning candidates. Robustness tests include several other electoral indicators, which help overcome the shortcomings of the two main democratic competitiveness proxies.

To capture *rayon*-level variations in competitiveness, we employ data from the first round of the 1996 presidential contest. Despite noted electoral irregularities, the elections are considered more competitive than subsequent electoral races, if only because the political landscape had been more "fluid" if not "chaotic."[53] The opposition candidate, Communist Party (KPRF) leader

---

[50] The data analysis here is based on Lankina and Libman, "Two-Pronged Middle Class." Analysis and discussion reproduced with permission from Alexander Libman. Parts of the paper are reproduced and reprinted with permission from Cambridge University Press.

[51] Petrov, "Regional Models"; Saikkonen, "Electoral Mobilization."

[52] Vanhanen, "New Dataset." For applications, see Lankina and Libman, "Soviet Legacies"; Beer and Mitchell, "Comparing Nations and States"; Lankina and Getachew, "Mission or Empire."

[53] Reisinger and Moraski, *Regional Roots*, 4.

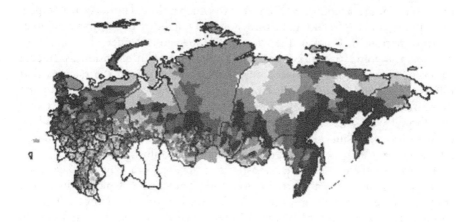

Effective number of candidates, 1996

0.000 to 2.310 2.310 to 2.943 2.943 to 3.533 3.533 to 4.126 4.126 to 5.962   Missing

FIGURE 9.6 Effective number of candidates (ENC), 1996 elections, first round

Gennadiy Zyuganov, posed a genuine threat to the incumbent Boris Yeltsin. Furthermore, already in 1996, Russia's regions featured variations in electoral competitiveness.[54] Figures 9.6 and 9.7 present the spatial structure of both the measures.

There are potential issues in employing the VI and ENC measures to the subnational level. In small jurisdictions, low VI values could be associated not with weak competitiveness but with strong partisan preferences. In the United States, in some "red" or "blue" districts, candidates dominate elections for decades. In such contexts, low VI values and low ENC may signal strong partisan loyalties. Unlike in the United States or other developed nations, where geographic patterns of electoral preferences are often stable, or emerging democracies like Ukraine with strong identity-based polarization of the electorate, in Russia, since the 1990s, citizen preferences for parties or candidates have been comparatively volatile. Scott Gehlbach describes

[54] Hale, "Explaining Machine Politics." In further checks reported in Lankina and Libman, "Two-Pronged Middle Class" (supplementary appendix 3.8), we employ data for the 1995 parliamentary elections. The elections exhibited extremely high levels of political fragmentation, with forty-three parties running. The results fully confirm our findings. In the supplementary appendix 3.8, we also analyze the 2012 presidential race coinciding with authoritarian consolidation. Although we find some evidence of a *meshchane* legacy, it is weaker and less robust. We interpret this result with reference to consolidated authoritarianism.

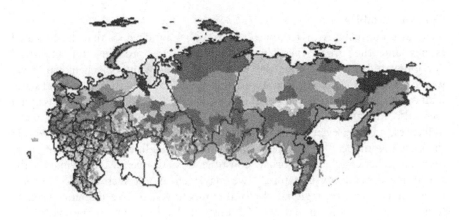

Vanhanen index, 1996

0.00 to 27.46 27.46 to 36.81 36.81 to 44.78 44.78 to 57.17 57.17 to 79.93 Missing

FIGURE 9.7 Vanhanen index (VI), 1996 elections, first round

fundamental shifts in Russian electoral geography in 1991–96;[55] and Rinat Menyashev demonstrates that voting for the United Russia (UR) pro-Kremlin party in the 2000s is positively correlated with support for the opposition KPRF in the 1990s.[56] Thus, in Russia, we are less likely to encounter the issue of territories with strong and persistent preferences for candidates in the same way that we would in the US electoral context. Nevertheless, we also consider regional differences in overall political pluralism and democratic freedoms in the 1990s.[57] While these variations have been generally explored at the *oblast* rather than *rayon* level,[58] the literature has generated useful quantitative proxies for the 1990s. We employ one appropriate indicator, namely *media independence and freedom*. As noted, this measure captures another important facet of democracy, namely freedom of expression or the availability of alternative sources of information.

---

[55] Gehlbach, "Shifting Electoral Geography," 381–82.

[56] Rinat Menyashev, "Consumer Cooperatives and Liberal Idea in Russia." Higher School of Economics Working Paper No. WP BRP 05/EC/2011, December 5, 2011, 7. Available online at: papers.ssrn.com/sol3/papers.cfm?abstract_id=2002129 (accessed November 9, 2020).

[57] Gel'man, "Regime Transition"; Hale, "Explaining Machine Politics"; Stoner-Weiss, *Local Heroes*; Tertytchnaya et al., "Electoral Protests"; Lankina and Tertytchnaya, "Protest."

[58] On the electoral aspect, see, however, Clem and Craumer, "Urban-Rural"; Clem, "Russia's Electoral Geography."

Control Variables

Structural controls. As noted, one concern that I anticipate is that the educated estates and the urban *meshchane* specifically are proxying for industrial development before and after the Revolution. Following Gerschenkron,[59] we would associate such late industrial catch-up development with state-led and state-financed mega-industries. In imperial Russia, a large chunk of industries and capital were also foreign owned.[60] The Bolsheviks appropriated and expanded mega-industries, creating even larger industrial conglomerates. Classic modernization theorizing would lead us to expect that such industrial hubs would nurture more discerning, better educated, urban constituencies. Conversely, drawing on the workforce dependency literature,[61] we may well expect such legacies to have detrimental effects on regional electoral competitiveness. We therefore need to find a way to isolate the effects of industrial development on the eve of the Revolution from the social dimension of the maturation of the proto-middle class engaged in professional occupations or civic pursuits outside of industries.

While accurate *uyezd*-level measures of industrial output are not available from imperial sources, the 1897 census contains employment structure data, which we leverage as a plausible proxy for pre-1917 spatial aspects of industrialization and which allows us to compute the share of *uyezd* population employed in industries, including railways and postal services. The data cover mining; fiber, wood, metals, and food processing; ceramics; chemical industry; fumigation and brewing; paper production and printing; production of jewelry, watches, fine instruments, clothing, and textiles; construction; production of ships and coaches; and postal, telegraph, telephone, and railroad services. Unsurprisingly, we observe significant spatial variations in the distribution of industry before the Revolution. In present-day *rayony*, in 90 percent of imperial territories corresponding to them, less than 30 percent of the population were employed in industry; by the end of the nineteenth century, only 1 percent boasted an industrial employment share of more than 50 percent; agricultural employment exceeded 70 percent of the population in 50 percent of territories.

In addition to the aforementioned variable capturing pre-revolutionary industrialization, we augment the regressions with a set of contemporaneous controls for *rayon* geographic location – latitude and longitude – and developmental levels – urbanization, housing, and doctors per capita. We are aware that developmental indices may include post-treatment variables, which themselves are influenced by historical legacies. Our goal here is to understand

---

[59] Gerschenkron, *Economic Backwardness*.

[60] Rieber, *Merchants*. Although "highly productive foreign-owned firms may promote technological catch-up of local firms." Giovanni Peri and Dieter Urban, "Catching-up to Foreign Technology? Evidence on the 'Veblen-Gerschenkron' Effect of Foreign Investments." National Bureau of Economic Research Working Paper No. 10893, November 2004, 1. Available online at: nber.org/papers/w10893 (accessed May 16, 2020).

[61] Frye et al., "Political Machines."

the extent to which the estates variable is mediated by contemporary development, something that could also be driven by other historical factors, or has a distinct effect on democratic competitiveness.

Cognitional controls. As discussed, I am conscious of the fact that estate data may also be capturing the "cognitional" dimension of values or indeed the social status of the empire's distinct ethno-religious communities. Thus, *meshchane* may be proxying for the Jewish community, and merchants for Old Believers and Jews. These groups are associated with social mobility, professional employment, entrepreneurial values, and, in the case of Old Believers, structures of mutual credit and social support that facilitate enterprise.[62] Protestants and Catholics often boasted superior human capital and colonized the professions. In the metropolitan and regional centers, many nobles were of western and central (Poles) European ancestry; and many lesser nobles from these European communities were *meshchane* or merchants who acquired honored citizen status. We account for human capital or cognitional legacies linked to these ethno-religious communities and isolate their effects from the legacies of the estate as a proxy for embourgeoisement of Russian society by controlling for population shares of Catholics, Protestants, Jews, and Old Believers.

Discussion of Main Results

I first discuss the main results with the most sizeable educated estate of the *meshchane* and then report findings for the educated estates combined. Table 9.3 demonstrates that, regardless of the model, a greater share of *meshchane* is associated with high competitiveness.[63] For instance, in a *rayon* with a 30 percent share of *meshchane* compared to one with no *meshchane*, there would be 0.45 more effective candidates. Note that the average ENC in

---

[62] See Blackwell, "Old Believers"; and Buss, "Economic Ethics." Buss provides a useful discussion of disagreements in the literature on Old Believers, notably in the writings of Weber and Gerschenkron. These debates concerned the decisive role of doctrinal factors (similarity or dissimilarity with doctrines of Russia's official church) versus the Old Believers' pariah status, in what would be similar to that of Jews, in accounting for their economic success. Ibid., 449–550. Blackwell points out that "partly as a result of their tradition of religious study and disputation, [they were] highly articulate." Blackwell, "Russian Entrepreneur," 18. He also discusses how the French observer of Russia, Anatole Leroy Beaulieu, in the 1880s, even before Weber, characterized dissenting groups like Old Believers, among others, as "progenitors of an entrepreneurial spirit." Ibid., 23. "Entrepreneurship," writes Blackwell, "wherever it appears, is the result of material arrangements, but it is also a state of mind, a view of the world, a type of personality, motivation, and ideology." Ibid., 21.

[63] All regressions include *oblast* fixed effects to capture possible political dependencies between *rayony* nested in a larger *oblast* such as *oblast* governor policies or economic dependencies; and to reduce the impact of unobserved heterogeneity. We start with a model without control variables, a potentially revealing reduced-form equation in that, by introducing controls, we risk blocking some of the causal paths between independent and dependent variables, thereby boosting significance levels of the estimated coefficients. Lenz and Sahn, "Achieving Statistical Significance."

TABLE 9.3 *Regressions, share of meshchane and democratic competitiveness in 1996 (rayon-level), OLS*

Dep. var.:	VI	ENC	VI	ENC	VI	ENC	VI	ENC	VI	ENC
Meshchane	0.136***	0.0153***	0.148***	0.0114***	0.186***	0.0153***	0.190***	0.0154***	0.0993**	0.00742**
	(0.0386)	(0.00264)	(0.0438)	(0.00311)	(0.0489)	(0.00337)	(0.0494)	(0.00338)	(0.0506)	(0.00340)
Industrial employment			-0.0129	0.00421**	-0.0197	0.00348**	-0.0217	0.00363**	-0.0169	0.000698
			(0.0239)	(0.00172)	(0.0241)	(0.00174)	(0.0243)	(0.00172)	(0.0255)	(0.00183)
Old Believers					0.0416	0.00321	0.0432	0.00354	0.0364	0.00262
					(0.0330)	(0.00245)	(0.0334)	(0.00232)	(0.0334)	(0.00205)
Catholics					-0.0652	-0.00567	-0.0525	-0.00503	0.0801	-0.0131
					(0.262)	(0.0206)	(0.262)	(0.0208)	(0.232)	(0.0193)
Protestants					-0.0241	-0.000527	-0.0246	-0.000447	-0.0523	0.00331
					(0.0635)	(0.00531)	(0.0637)	(0.00538)	(0.0629)	(0.00558)
Jews					-0.385**	-0.0418***	-0.386**	-0.0395***	-0.255	-0.0297***
					(0.182)	(0.0125)	(0.182)	(0.0125)	(0.180)	(0.0115)
Latitude							0.136	0.0215*	0.0524	0.0211
							(0.162)	(0.0127)	(0.180)	(0.0143)
Longitude							-0.0293	0.00850	0.0322	0.0133**
							(0.0667)	(0.00636)	(0.0619)	(0.00623)
Urbanization									0.0292***	0.00585***
									(0.00697)	(0.000423)

(continued)

	(1)	(2)	(3)	(4)	(5)	(6)	(7)	(8)	(9)	(10)
Housing									0.000	0.000
									(0.000)	(0.000)
Doctors per capita									0.0000	0.000
									(0.000)	(0.000)
Constant	34.55***	3.946***	34.53***	3.953***	42.38***	3.815***	43.14***	0.458	27.27**	1.365
	(4.471)	(0.0199)	(4.472)	(0.0201)	(0.992)	(0.107)	(16.23)	(1.396)	(13.24)	(1.033)
R^2	0.430	0.579	0.430	0.580	0.432	0.583	0.435	0.585	0.474	0.646
N	2,064	2,064	2,064	2,064	2,063	2,063	2,060	2,060	1,780	1,780

Note: * $p<0.1$; ** $p<0.05$; *** $p<0.01$. Robust standard errors in parentheses. All regressions control for *oblast* fixed effects. The sample size decreases with the inclusion of housing and doctors per capita due to missing values. ENC, effective number of candidates; VI, Vanhanen index.

Source: Data and analysis based on Lankina and Libman, "Two-Pronged Middle Class"; analysis reproduced and expanded with permission of coauthor.

1996 is equal to 3.32, with 5.96 being the *rayon* maximum. The effects hold even when data for urbanization, housing, and doctors per capita are included in the regressions as developmental proxies and when controlling for the pre-communist population share of industrial employment. Because we are aware that cross-sectional regressions do not allow us to fully eliminate omitted variable bias, we introduce a battery of controls.[64]

The regression results in Table 9.4 corroborate the positive relationship between democratic competitiveness and the generic educated estates, including the nobility, clergy, and merchants, in addition to the *meshchane*. The coefficients of the key explanatory variable of the educated estates remain positive and statistically significant across all models, showing substantial stability despite the gradual transition from reduced to extended model specifications. Nonetheless, the addition of the other educated estates causes a slight decrease in the magnitude of coefficients if compared to models involving the *meshchane* alone. Indeed, a 30 percent increase in the share of the educated estates would produce, on average, 0.39 more effective candidates, instead of 0.45 solely with *meshchane*. The behavior of the other regressors is largely comparable to the *meshchane* models. While urbanization appears to play a positive, but rather limited, role in influencing democratic competitiveness, the other two proxies for development – housing and doctors per capita – appear to have no impact.

The results hold when Catholics, Protestants, Jews, and Old Believers are controlled for, which emerge as insignificant apart from the Jews variable. Counterintuitively, given what we know about comparatively high literacy and the schooling of imperial Russia's Jewish populations, the variable emerges as significantly and negatively related to democratic competitiveness. We interpret this result with reference to persistent anti-market effects that scholars found in the Pale of Settlement,[65] or to wartime population displacement, which had catastrophic demographic effects on the Jewish population.[66]

---

[64] Note that omitted variable bias should be rather large to invalidate our results. For the specification without control variables, bar the *oblast* dummies, 44.48 percent of the estimator should be due to bias to invalidate it. We use the module KONFOUND to follow the Frank methodology in Stata. Frank, "Impact."

[65] Grosfeld et al., "Persistent Antimarket Culture."

[66] If we drop the top 0.5 percent *rayony* with a large share of Jewish populations from our sample, the coefficient loses significance while there is no effect on the significance of the *meshchane* coefficient. The observed effect could be an artifact of a handful of *rayony* with comparatively large Jewish communities, that is, exceeding 7 percent of a district's total population, and it may be driven by idiosyncratic factors. In future research, we may extend the argument about anti-market legacies to tease out how anti-Semitism in regions where many Jews were in the *meshchane* or merchant estates and were successful tradesmen or entrepreneurs may drive support for right-wing "patriotic strong-men" political forces in present-day *rayony*. Relatedly, we need to understand better the effects of persecution of Jews in the *meshchane* category on broader developmental outcomes; persecution and discrimination may wipe out the potential effect of high human capital. Teasing out the relevant causal mechanisms would involve both nuanced qualitative and quantitative *rayon*-level analysis. I am grateful to Otto Kienitz for encouraging me to think more about the possible causal mechanisms.

TABLE 9.4 *Regressions, share of educated estates and democratic competitiveness in 1996 (rayon-level), OLS*

Dep. var.:	VI	ENC	VI	ENC	VI	ENC	VI	ENC	VI	ENC
Educated estates	0.120***	0.013***	0.134***	0.010***	0.166***	0.013***	0.168***	0.013***	0.094**	0.006**
	(0.034)	(0.002)	(0.038)	(0.003)	(0.043)	(0.003)	(0.043)	(0.003)	(0.044)	(0.003)
Industrial employment			-0.017	0.004**	-0.024	0.003*	-0.025	0.003**	-0.020	0.001
			(0.024)	(0.002)	(0.024)	(0.002)	(0.025)	(0.002)	(0.026)	(0.002)
Old Believers					0.046	0.003	0.047	0.004*	0.039	0.003
					(0.033)	(0.002)	(0.034)	(0.002)	(0.034)	(0.002)
Catholics					-0.129	-0.011	-0.118	-0.010	0.046	-0.015
					(0.263)	(0.021)	(0.264)	(0.021)	(0.232)	(0.019)
Protestants					-0.009	0.001	-0.009	0.001	-0.044	0.004
					(0.064)	(0.005)	(0.064)	(0.005)	(0.063)	(0.006)
Jews					-0.373**	-0.040***	-0.372**	-0.038***	-0.255	-0.028***
					(0.177)	(0.012)	(0.177)	(0.012)	(0.175)	(0.011)
Latitude							0.135	0.021*	0.052	0.021
							(0.163)	(0.013)	(0.180)	(0.014)
Longitude							-0.024	0.009	0.035	0.014**
							(0.067)	(0.006)	(0.062)	(0.006)
Urbanization									0.029***	0.006***
									(0.007)	(0.000)
Housing									0.000	0.000
									(0.000)	(0.000)

(continued)

Overall, the results indicate that the legacies of the social structure, specifically the share of educated estates conceptualized as constituting the old proto-bourgeoisie and the proto-middle class, significantly affect subnational democratic competitiveness These findings tie in with the process-centered analysis pursued in the previous chapters, which underlined the educated estates' superior human capital and embeddedness in professional institutions and occupations. These legacies of human capital and autonomous values and resources facilitate navigation in the post-communist employment, occupational, and civic arenas. I attribute the observed relationship between democratic competitiveness and social structure to the complex processes that morphed the society of estates into the stratification configurations in Soviet Russia. Conversely, areas with a historically weak presence of the proto-bourgeois estates, even when benefiting from large-scale Soviet industrial development and urbanization, do not exhibit similarly high levels of democratic competitiveness.

The results also allow us to begin to distinguish the structural underpinnings of development from the social dimension of legacies. Urbanization, as noted, has produced ambiguous results in cross- and within-national analyses of the drivers of variations in democracy in post-communist contexts. As I have argued throughout this book, urban areas before the Revolution not only concentrated well-institutionalized and densely networked professional institutions but also engendered other arenas of public and civic activism. Yet, as Grigore Pop-Eleches and Joshua Tucker argue,[67] following Ken Jowitt,[68] cities had also been subjected to communist penetration and indoctrination more thoroughly than rural areas.[69] This is also the argument made in a study

---

[67] Pop-Eleches and Tucker, *Communism's Shadow*, 126.

[68] Jowitt, *New World Disorder*, 81–82.

[69] Educated professionals also tended to join the Communist Party for career reasons, something that arguably dampened their pro-democracy orientations. Lankina et al., "Appropriation and Subversion." Yet many became "lay" party members outside of the managerial and party leadership structures. The state had also been comparatively lenient in enforcing the requirement of party membership in skills-intensive jobs. Citing Rigby's work, I write in an earlier paper: "For instance, while in 1947, a mere 17 percent of engineering professors were CPSU members, 58 percent of professors in the social sciences and philosophy possessed CPSU membership cards." Lankina, "Boris Nemtsov," 57. See also Rigby, *Communist Party Membership*, 444–45. According to Churchward, most Soviet intellectuals eschewed holding bureaucratic positions or opted for only "minor ones"; office holding, not party membership, defined "we" (intellectuals) versus "they" (establishment). Churchward, *Soviet Intelligentsia*, 14. There was also a perception among intellectuals that those "recruited into the apparatus are generally the most socialized and the most conformist." Ibid., 133. Others discuss "the more radical political behavior" of professionals and intellectuals in the natural sciences and the technical intelligentsia; these groups had a "lower proportion of bogus and mediocre intellectuals among them – the result of the State's promotion of talentless and obedient people in the social sciences literature, and the arts." Shlapentokh, *Soviet Intellectuals*, 6. Finally, interviews with Soviet refugees revealed that "party" versus the "nonparty people" had been a key base of social differentiation, with "party people" regarded with disdain and as under-deserving of their privileges. Inkeles and Bauer, *Soviet Citizen*, 300–1, 312. Nevertheless, the party "believers" were distinguished from the "nonbelievers," arguably a majority among members joining for career purposes. Ibid., 328.

TABLE 9.4 (continued)

Dep. var.:	VI	ENC	VI	ENC	VI	ENC	VI	ENC	VI	ENC
Doctors per capita									0.000	0.000
									(0.000)	(0.000)
Constant	34.536***	3.948***	34.513***	3.954***	42.130***	3.799***	42.271***	0.388	27.098**	1.362
	(4.471)	(0.019)	(4.472)	(0.019)	(1.004)	(0.105)	(16.266)	(1.399)	(13.261)	(1.034)
R^2	0.431	0.579	0.431	0.581	0.433	0.584	0.435	0.586	0.474	0.646
N	2,064	2,064	2,064	2,064	2,063	2,063	2,060	2,060	1,780	1,780

Note: * $p < 0.1$; ** $p < 0.05$; *** $p < 0.01$. Robust standard errors in parentheses. All regressions control for *oblast* fixed effects. The sample size decreases with the inclusion of housing and doctors per capita due to missing values. ENC, effective number of candidates; VI, Vanhanen index.

Source: Data assembled by Lankina and Libman and based on Lankina and Libman, "Two-Pronged Middle Class," analysis reproduced and expanded with permission of coauthor.

of subnational electoral processes in Ukraine.[70] Many towns and cities feature mega-industries that are now associated with workforce dependencies among blue-collar workers and with a state-reliant white-collar stratum.[71] Studies of post-communist employment possibilities and choices, nonetheless, indirectly corroborate our call to discern intergenerational human capital patterns as something that potentially reduce state dependencies, even within the mega-industrialized settings that we associate with communism. As Gerber and Hout find in their analysis of intergenerational mobility spanning the late Soviet and post-Soviet periods, social origins became even more significant in the context of transition to a market economy than had been the case earlier. Those more advantaged, if we take the criterion of late Soviet period social origin – such as the offspring of professionals – enjoyed better opportunities for obtaining the highest paid and highest status jobs as "proprietors," including of firms employing staff, as compared to those who enjoyed preferential treatment in higher education and job placement in the Soviet period but who did not come from privileged family backgrounds.[72] Moreover, downward mobility in practice often means a precarious and vulnerable life situation, leading to increased electoral dependencies. Superior social capital, as measured by the resort to personal ties and networks when seeking employment, particularly among educated residents of large urban areas, facilitated employment in the private sector and is associated with higher salaries, as Gerber and Mayorova find.[73] In another study, Gerber finds that better education is associated with greater chances of self-employment in post-Soviet Russia. In turn, self-employment is correlated with greater support for market reforms and higher incomes, particularly for those running firms with employees:

As expected, respondents from more elite occupational class backgrounds are more likely to enter self-employment . . . This implies that, in the absence of an entrepreneurial class, the professional/managerial class provides its offspring with motivation, social capital, and/or particular skills that facilitate becoming self-employed.[74]

---

[70] Lankina and Libman, "Soviet Legacies."

[71] Frye et al., "Political Machines"; Hale, *Patronal Politics*; Rosenfeld, *Autocratic Middle Class*.

[72] Gerber and Hout, "Tightening Up," 683, 696–97. For a critique of the findings concerning change in "origin-destination" trends, see Bessudnov, "Effects," 164–65; and Yastrebov, "Intergenerational." Yastrebov employs data for cohorts born before 1951 and finds that "changes in the pattern of occupational mobility remained surprisingly invariant to the changes in historical and institutional context." Yastrebov, "Intergenerational," 2. In communist Hungary, scholars likewise found that many party members, who also had skilled professional backgrounds, took advantage of earlier connections in the party-managerial apparatus to become successful private entrepreneurs. Róna-Tas, "Second Economy," 77.

[73] Gerber and Mayorova, "Getting Personal," 896–903.

[74] Gerber, "Paths to Success," 26. Furthermore, Gerber finds: "Contrary to our prediction, having a parent who was a cadre in the KPSS effectively prevents Russians from entering either form of self-employment [with or without employees]: the negative direct effect is strong enough to outweigh any other variable. Perhaps Communist Party cadres remained convinced ideological opponents of capitalist institutions and socialized their children to disdain private enterprise.

Most importantly for my study, "self-employment opportunities represent yet another characteristic that has come to vary across regions in post-Soviet Russia."[75] The persistence of a social-structural legacy – and regional variations therein – help us situate sources of resilience against authoritarianism even within urban milieus that would have experienced intense forms of "hegemonic" industrial planning, as well as within rural areas that had sizeable segments of the "educated" estates before the Revolution and would be brought into the fold of communist industrialization.

Democratic "Coalitional" Legacies

As noted, class- or social structure-based analyses of the genesis, maturation, and resilience of democracy have centered on "coalitional" politics involving, among other aspects, an impulse to expand the social reach of national representative institutions. To the extent that Russia has featured in these analyses, scholars have tended to accentuate the infirmities of the indigenous bourgeoisie and industrial class in the "backward" empire. Electoral statistics allow us not only to interrogate these assumptions but to further explore the validity of the claim that the urban estates specifically represented a proto-bourgeoisie, by considering both the criteria of property ownership, lifestyle, and human capital and conventional expectations about orientations toward the political realm. Again, here the emphasis is on the bourgeoisie with a small "b," already vested with an interest in securing rule of law, stability, and constitutional limits on monarchical power and, importantly, endowed with the educational credentials that allow for a discerning attitude and awareness when exercising political choices. In other words, the focus here is on the electorate rather than on powerful groups engaged in pressing for change at the national level. If it can be demonstrated that, on the eve of the Bolshevik Revolution, the urban estates were more likely to vote for parties favoring democratic reforms, then the validity of the claim that the estate as a social legacy shapes long-term political regime contours could be enhanced further. In some influential studies of post-communist politics elsewhere in Europe, political cleavages that emerged in pre-communist elections were found to exhibit puzzling levels of persistence.[76] Again, these patterns provide additional validation of the hypothesized social legacy.

Here, therefore, results of a further test are presented, performed at the *oblast* level due to data availability issues. Electoral data for the territorial patterns of

---

Given the widespread cynicism toward Soviet ideology during the final decades of Soviet power, however, another thesis is more plausible: the offspring of KPSS cadres were probably geared toward pursuing opportunities through organizational careers as professionals or managers ... Having a parent who was a KPSS member, but not a paid cadre, has no net effect on entry to self-employment." Ibid., 26.

[75] Ibid., 32.   [76] Wittenberg, *Crucibles*.

representation of deputies affiliated with the *kadety* in the Russian Empire's elected assembly, the State Duma, are employed. The *kadety* are most strongly associated with a liberal alternative to the monarchy, a party attacked by the monarchist factions; the left-leaning Socialist Revolutionaries (*esery*); and the so-called social democrats, including their Bolshevik faction. These data should be interpreted as suggestive evidence, considering the known variations in electoral laws and political configurations that changed between the four Dumas. Specifically, as Tzar Nicholas II faced pressures coming from the *kadety* for wholesale constitutional reform, curia for the representation of different estates and social groups were altered, which led to drastically lower representation of the party in the Third and Fourth Dumas. The deputies also confronted pressures for an uncompromising stance toward the monarchy coming from the radical elements within the party itself; from parties that the *kadety* sought out as allies within the Duma like the agrarian socialists, because the *kadety* lacked absolute majority; and parties and constituencies outside the Duma, notably the socialists (Social-Democrats and Socialist-Revolutionaries) who decided to boycott inaugural elections to the First Duma (though not the Second) and a share of whose vote went to the *kadety* as a result. The objective is not to idealize the Constitutional Democrats – or to deny the fact that the social makeup of the representatives of this party changed in the successive Dumas – but to capture the party's general orientation as a staunch advocate of parliamentary democracy enjoying the robust support of the urban intelligentsia.[77]

I compiled the data from the *Encyclopedia of the State Duma of the Russian Empire, 1906–1917*.[78] This comprehensive source allows work with statistics for all the four legislative assemblies constituting tsarist Russia's brief experience with representative democracy that were elected between 1906 and 1912.[79] In Table 9.5, the positive and significant association between the regional population share of *meshchane* and the aggregate number of *kadety* representatives elected from that territory (correlation coefficient of 0.228) is indicative of the persistent effect of subnational political variations that had already been observable as the monarchy acceded to demands for representative democracy in the early twentieth century. Let us now examine individual Duma compositions separately – for the First Duma: April 27 to July 8, 1906; the Second: February 20 to June 3, 1907; the Third: November 1, 1907 to June 9, 1912; and the Fourth: November 15, 1912 to October 6, 1917. The share of *meshchane* is positively and significantly correlated with the number of *kadety*

---

[77] See Pipes, *Russian Revolution*, 146–52, 160–65, 179–83, 247–48, 250–58, 542–43. For an overview of the positions of leading figures in the party, see Burbank, *Intelligentsia*, esp. chap. 3 (113–69). "The party," writes Burbank, "reflected its Western prototypes; it attempted to include and resolve tactically the interests of many groups and individuals rather than to represent any one of them." Ibid., 114.

[78] Ivanov et al., *Gosudarstvennaya Duma*.   [79] Ibid.

TABLE 9.5 *Correlation between share of* meshchane *and number of representatives of the* kadety *party (oblast-level)*

Corr. coefficients	Aggregate reps Kadety	Duma (1)	Duma (2)	Duma (3)	Duma (4)
Meshchane	0.228**	0.057	0.196*	0.086	0.307***

Note. * p<0.1; ** p<0.05; *** p<0.01.
Source. Here and in Table 9.6 data assembled by Lankina and Libman and based on Lankina and Libman, "Two-Pronged Middle Class"; analysis reproduced and expanded with permission of coauthor.

TABLE 9.6 *Correlation between share of educated estates and number of representatives of the* kadety *party (oblast-level)*

Corr. coefficients	Aggregate reps Kadety	Duma (1)	Duma (2)	Duma (3)	Duma (4)
Educated estates	0.2247**	0.0790	0.1971*	0.0645	0.2859**
Nobility	0.1227	0.0758	0.0903	0.0097	0.1567
Clergy	0.1341	0.1940*	0.2186*	−0.1193	−0.0179
Merchants	0.1890*	0.0679	0.1828	0.0658	0.2058*
Meshchane	0.2276**	0.0572	0.1957*	0.0860	0.3073***

Note. * p<0.1; ** p<0.05; *** p<0.01.
Source. Lankina and Libman, "Two-Pronged Middle Class."

representatives in the Second and Fourth Duma. For the First and Third Duma, the correlation is still positive but insignificant. Considering the educated estates together in Table 9.6, we obtain similar results: positive correlation coefficients, which are higher – and statistically significant – with the aggregate number of representatives and with the Second and Fourth Duma.[80] Breaking down the educated estates, we observe positive and significant coefficients for the clergy in

[80] Numbers of faction deputies varied in the course of the Duma term due to fluidity in factional allegiance, notably this concerned deputies from among nonaffiliated independents, the Cossack group and the Muslim faction; the *kadety* party itself was known for factional discipline. Ibid., 282. The data I provide here are based on ibid. The Second Duma had far fewer representatives in the *kadety* faction (124) than the First, which had 178 *kadety* deputies (data are for faction size at the end of the Duma session) out of a total of 478; the Duma overall had a more left-leaning character than the First Duma because the socialists did not boycott it like they did the First Duma. Ibid., 109–12; 446–52. The Third Duma was formed according to new electoral legislation, which also applied to the Fourth Duma and served to increase numbers of landowners and other wealthy citizens. The Duma featured even fewer deputies in the *kadety* faction toward the end of the session (52). The Fourth Duma had a similar composition by the end of the last session (53 *kadety*). Wealthy landowners, according to the new election amendments applied to the Third and Fourth Dumas, obtained a proportional increase in the weight of their voice based on the new system of curia. Ibid., 618–24; 676–82; Kiryanov and Lukyanov, *Parlament.* For

the First and Second Duma and for merchants in the Fourth Duma. We also observe positive but not statistically significant correlation coefficients for the nobility. In particular, the results for merchants suggest that the wealthier entrepreneurial stratum, which was more robustly represented in the Fourth Duma due to altered formal property criteria for selection, tended to vote for the *kadety*.

The primary occupation profiles of *kadety* members in the four Dumas can also be instructive. The bulk of members – roughly 66 percent in the First Duma; 50 percent in the Second; 58 percent in the Third; and 76 percent in the Fourth – came from the "middling" strata of entrepreneurs, professionals, and those with leadership experience in local civic affairs, joining the more eminent intelligentsia of progressive jurists, journalists, and professors. Heads of local elected bodies (*gorodskoy golova*) feature in all of the four Dumas, as do *zemstvo* officials; landowners from outside the aristocratic estate – peasants and Cossacks with sizeable landholdings; mid-level *chinovniki*; as well as primary and secondary school teachers, doctors, and veterinarians. Peasant entrepreneurs and small business owners are likewise found among the *kadety*.[81] Additional qualitative evidence concerning the middling propertied strata – the urban electorate and *meshchane* specifically – illuminates political preferences some months later, after the Bolshevik coup. One eyewitness account is available from Georgiy (George) Konstantinovich Guins, a leading jurist in the Provisional Government. Guins played a major role in the Provisional Government's anti-Bolshevik operations in Omsk, in Siberia, alongside Constantine Neklutin, before emigrating to China and then the United States.[82] He thus describes the political orientations of citizens in Siberia during the Civil War,[83] where the Reds and Whites were fighting a battle to win hearts and minds; he distinguishes the political orientations of members of the social strata in Siberia from those of urbanites at the bottom of the social rung, the "plebs":[84]

The urban mass regarded bolshevism differently [from newly settled peasants]. The nationalization of houses, inventory-taking of horses, searches, confiscation of valuables – all this armed against Bolsheviks the well-off strata of the urban population. The *meshchanstvo* in Siberia, just as much as peasant-old-timers, had been used to a calm, "good" life, generosity, [*khlebosol'stvo*], drink [*vypivka*], affluence [*dostatok*].[85]

---

a discussion of factional composition, fluidity, and change for each of the Duma sessions for the *kadety*, see Ivanov et al., *Gosudarstvennaya Duma*, 282–89.

[81] Ivanov et al., *Gosudarstvennaya Duma*, 282–89.

[82] Guins describes Neklutin as a "modest young man ... impartial and business-like" and known as "de facto and acknowledged leader of the trade-industrial class in Samara." Guins, *Sibir'*, 334–35.

[83] Ibid., 5. In the years 1948–54, Guins taught international law at Berkeley. Ibid., 642.

[84] Ibid., 29.   [85] Ibid., 28.

In terms of the *meshchane*, whom Guins contrasts with the peasant and worker masses who embraced Bolshevism: "An uprising against Bolshevism could consume only the surface – the urban *meshchanstvo*, but this element is the least reliable in battle."[86] The *meshchane* as a group are thus characterized as inherently conservative and stability oriented whose moderation would make them an unreliable ally in the Civil War. Yet, as the conflict progressed, Guins observes: "The top layers of the village, significantly fortified and conscious, together with the city *meshchanstvo* are more decisively moving away from the revolution."[87] The political orientations of this semipolitical inert mass, who lacked the political capital and substantial wealth to mobilize an anti-Bolshevik response, mattered significantly in the context of the "coalitional" dynamics that involved the big players in the Revolution, since the "true bourgeoisie: representatives of industrial, financial and land capital – were absorbed with plans of a [anti-Bolshevik] rebellion everywhere, inside and outside the country ... preparing an armed uprising."[88]

Robustness Tests

The peasantry as a residual group. One possible concern is that, rather than capturing the bourgeoisie per se, what the analysis reveals is a more straightforward mechanism of urban/rural divide,[89] or indeed the relative absence of peasant populations rather than the presence of specific estates.[90] We performed additional tests corroborating that the results are not driven by a lower share of peasants in districts (see Online Appendix 1 [OA1]).

Population displacement: placebo test of the human capital persistence hypothesis. A major challenge in analyses of the human dimension of legacies is dealing with the issue of the geographical and structural underpinnings of development.[91] My analysis has underlined the dilemmas involved in distinguishing the social transmission mechanism from the structural inheritance one, given the appropriative logic of Bolshevik developmentalism. We have yet to more conclusively distinguish between structural factors that the Bolsheviks inherited and the social aspect of persistence – a variant of a dilemma

---

[86] Ibid., 48.   [87] Ibid., 42.   [88] Ibid., 46.
[89] Some of the effects could be associated with serfdom. See Buggle and Nafziger, "Slow Road from Serfdom."
[90] Zaslavsky, "Contemporary Russian Society."
[91] See Grosfeld et al., "Persistent Antimarket Culture"; Acemoglu et al., "Reversal of Fortune"; Glaeser et al., "Do Institutions Cause Growth?"; Charnysh, "Diversity"; and John W. McArthur and Jeffrey D. Sachs, "Institutions and Geography: Comment on Acemoglu, Johnson and Robinson (2000)." National Bureau of Economic Research Working Paper No. 8114. Cambridge, Massachusetts, February 2001. Available online at: nber.org/papers/w8114 (accessed November 9, 2020).

famously summarized in the "people" versus "institutions" debate among economists.[92]

Acemoglu and colleagues suggest a useful strategy for isolating the effects of specifically social – or cognitional[93] – legacies from those of other aspects of development. Analyzing the implications of the Holocaust in the Western Pale of Settlement, they find that those territories most affected also suffered from the worst developmental and democratic consequences because of the decimation of the professional and enterprising middle class.[94] However horrific the targeted repressions of the "former people" were, the closest the Soviet regime came to social cleansing was the removal of scores of aristocrats from Leningrad to provincial capitals or their exile to Siberia in the 1930s. The mass stratum from among which the foot soldiers of the Soviet public sector and the professions emerged, as noted in Chapters 4 and 5, were, however, not aristocrats but *meshchane* or lesser nobles of modest means who were inconspicuous and therefore escaped deportations. Furthermore, we cannot replicate Acemoglu and colleagues' test with data capturing the decimation of the Jewish community: territories affected by the Holocaust are largely outside of present-day Russia.

I locate legacies of ethnic cleansing in the tragic fate of German and other European settlers in the Middle Volga, Siberia, and the Caucasus who were deported to Central Asia. Although Stalin's "killing of nations" affected other ethnic groups,[95] the settlers' high human capital makes this community comparable to the Jewish community. German and Dutch Mennonite farms were regarded as exemplars of efficient and innovative production;[96] Germans were prominent in the trades and entrepreneurship,[97] as well as in the urban professions.[98] The 1937 "Stalin" census revealed, shortly before deportation, that Protestants were considerably more literate than those who self-identified as Russian Orthodox.[99] Importantly, former German settlements did not become ghost towns where normal economic activity ceased. They were repopulated with mostly ethnic Russian migrants from neighboring and other areas. While we may well find a long-term effect of German settlers,[100] the result would be less likely

---

[92] Glaeser et al., "Do Institutions Cause Growth?"   [93] Simpser et al., "Dead but Not Gone."
[94] Acemoglu et al., "Social Structure." See also Akbulut-Yuksel and Yuksel, "Long-Term Direct and External Effects."
[95] Conquest, *Nation Killers*.
[96] On German and Mennonite agricultural practices and emulation by native communities, see Moon, *The Plough*, 209–11, 184–87.
[97] Savchenko and Dubinin, *Rossiyskiye nemtsy*.
[98] Vesnina, "Chastnyye"; Dahlmann and Tuchtenhagen, *Zwischen Reform und Revolution*.
[99] Zhiromskaya et al., *Polveka*, 100.
[100] The Germanic communities may well have diffused specific values to neighboring populations, or their know-how and infrastructures like schools, clinics, or veterinary facilities continued to drive development, in which case we would expect the developmental legacies to persist. Alternatively, their decimation, consistent with theorizing into social dislocation, may undermine the otherwise positive legacies or have other implications for monitoring and enforcement of social order. Treyger, "Migration"; Foa and Nemirovskaya, "State Capacity."

considering the thoroughness of ethnic cleansing. The historical record therefore makes this group suitable for our placebo test.[101] My assumption is that specific territorially concentrated communities' intergenerationally reproduced human capital and attitudes constitute a legacy, rather than any geographical or other structural variables per se. I therefore expect to see no correlation between the presence of these communities in specific territories in 1897 and developmental outcomes after they were deported in the Soviet period. We test these assumptions in what follows.

For this part of the analysis, I created a dataset with statistics on thousands of imperial Russia's German settlements from Diesendorf's compendium,[102] to my knowledge the most up-to-date and comprehensive source.[103] We created two variables: a binary variable for *rayony* where a German settlement had been located and one capturing the number of ethnic Germans residing in them. As anticipated, the results presented in OA2 show that the presence of German settlers is positively related to literacy rates in 1897 but that there is no correlation between German settlements and education in post-Soviet Russia. We also run regressions discerning the impact of German settlements on post-communist electoral competitiveness. For the German settlements binary variable, no effect is observed in any of the specifications. For the size of the German settlements, we do find some positive relationship with democratic competitiveness. This effect disappears entirely, however, if we exclude the five outlier districts with very high populations of ethnic Germans, four in Saratov *oblast* and one in Volgograd *oblast*. In these five districts, the population exceeds the mean in the sample by almost 100 times! Thus, while some legacies may have survived in territories with a high population share of Germanic settlers, for the rest of Russia no effect is observed. The lack of systematic evidence of German settler influence on Soviet-period development or competitiveness contrasts with the effect of the educated estates and specifically the *meshchane* – social strata that, as a group, were not targeted for repressions. It also demonstrates that we do not find a significant effect for *any* high human-capital group in tsarist Russia but only for specific estates construed as constituting a bourgeois legacy.

The Old and New Middle Class: Illustrative Examples

Although I highlight the appropriative dimension of communist state-led modernization, the findings call for a conceptual differentiation between two channels of genesis of the educated middle class in autocracies – one engineered in the context of state-led development and another emerging outside or prior to it and, while adapting to the new political order, carrying a distinct set of

---

[101] I thank Volha Charnysh for suggesting conceptualizing this as a placebo test.
[102] Diesendorf, *Die Deutschen Russlands*.
[103] I am grateful to Daniel Fitter for help with compiling the dataset.

values.[104] I do not dispute the Bolsheviks' success in nurturing new educated groups from among the largely illiterate or poorly educated peasant and worker strata. The data that I have at hand allow me to ascertain the democratic consequences of the state-engineered middle class, as compared to those of the bourgeoisie pedigree. One way to better tease out the differential effects of legacies of pre-communist "organic" and communist-period state-engineered "induced" types of modernization, would be to compare democratic processes in two regions with similar education levels but with variable social-structural legacies.

Employing the 2003 census data, we selected two predominantly ethnically Russian *oblasti* with similar education levels: Yaroslavl in Central Russia and Volgograd in the Lower Volga area. The share of university degree holders is 17.4 and 17.5 percent in Yaroslavl and Volgograd, respectively. Founded in the eleventh century, Yaroslavl is one of the oldest cities of Northwestern Rus, a core area of the future Russian state. Volgograd, originally Tsaritsyn and later renamed Stalingrad, is significantly younger, founded at the end of the sixteenth century. While in territories comprising present-day Yaroslavl *oblast* the population share of *meshchane* was 12.2 percent, in Volgograd it constituted a mere 3.7 percent.

Furthermore, Volgograd experienced two socially shattering events in recent history. Territories comprising the present-day Volgograd *oblast* featured numerous German settlements; several districts formed part of the Volga German Autonomous Soviet Socialist Republic. The deportation of *Wolgadeutsche* devastated the social fabric of the respective districts. Volgograd was also on the frontline during World War II, with the 1942–43 Battle of Stalingrad considered a pivotal turning point. The battle resulted in the city's almost complete destruction. Because Stalin did not order the immediate evacuation of civilians as German forces were advancing, only a small fraction of the original population of roughly half a million people survived. The influx of migrants during postwar reconstruction would have further created a social discontinuity effect. By contrast, Yaroslavl *oblast* had not been a site of a major battle or suffered Nazi occupation.

If differences are observed in the two regions' voting patterns in 1996, this would provide further support for the argument advanced here. Yaroslavl *oblast* is indeed politically more competitive than Volgograd.[105] The VI score for Yaroslavl and Volgograd *oblasti* is 48.3 and 43.1, and the ENC is, 4.0 and 3.7, respectively. The *oblast* level-score for media independence is 1.6 times higher in Yaroslavl than in Volgograd. Thus, even though Soviet modernization provided a boost to overall education levels by engendering a new middle class, which was distinct from the "old" bourgeoisie, we observe variations in democratic competitiveness.

---

[104] Note: We do not claim that the observed relationships would hold for every region; statistical analysis reveals probabilistic trends.

[105] On Yaroslavl's democratic political culture, see also Hahn, "Yaroslavl' Revisited." In OA3, I report additional analysis employing data for age of cities.

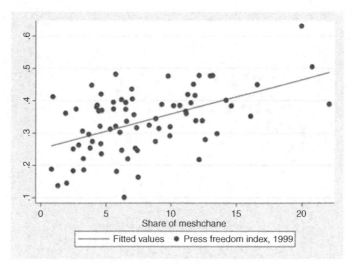

FIGURE 9.8 Share of *meshchane* and press freedom index

Another way to illustrate the significance of the pre-communist social structure is to compare covariation between *oblast*-level indices of democratic variations like press freedom – which, as mentioned, is an important barometer of the quality of democratic processes – and the distribution of the educated estates, with covariation between democracy indices and generic measures of human capital and the occupational profile of regions. We employ the 1999 Russian regional press freedom index developed by the Institute of Public Expertise (IPE). The index measures freedom of access to information, ease of news production, and distribution. I generate graphs demonstrating covariation between the *meshchane*/educated estates and regional press freedom indices, and those where, instead of *meshchane*/educated estates, I employ measures of the share of doctors and engineers, respectively, with a university degree and a generic measure of degree holders in the regional workforce. Figures 9.8 to 9.12 illustrate that past social structure is a more robust predictor of democratic outcomes than are indices capturing generic proxies for a middle class.[106]

---

[106] In OA5, we perform analysis with the outliers of Moscow and St. Petersburg removed and the results hold. See the subsection "Supplementary Analysis for the Appendix: Press Freedom." Comparisons within the Samara region are also instructive. In the 1995 relatively competitive State Duma elections, of the nine Samara City districts, only two registered a vote of below 6 percent for the politically liberal Yabloko Party, with the "old" Samara Leninskiy district registering 10 percent. In the newer industrial giant of Tolyatti, the three city districts registered a far lower vote for Yabloko of 5.7, 5.4, and 5.3 percent. By contrast, the highest percentage of all Samara City districts obtained by the populist-patriotic Liberal Democratic Party (LDPR) of Vladimir Zhirinovsky was 10.4 percent, while in the three districts of Tolyatti, the party garnered 16.9, 18.8, and 16.1 percent. McFaul and Petrov, *Politicheskiy*, 833. Leading political geographers have conceptualized a vote for

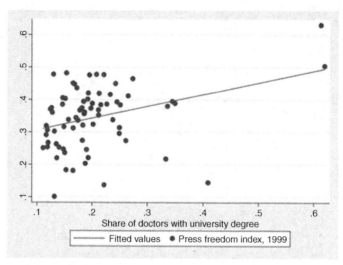

FIGURE 9.9 Share of doctors and press freedom index

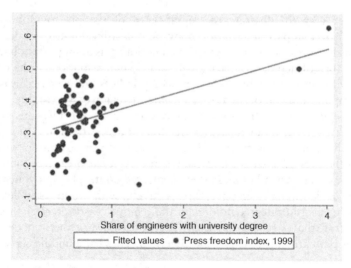

FIGURE 9.10 Share of engineers and press freedom index

Yabloko and the party leader Grigory Yavlinsky in the 1990s as "liberal." The vote for Zhirinovsky and his party is conceptualized as being on the "national-populist" spectrum. Turovskiy, "Kontseptual'naya elektoral'naya karta." Note that, nationally, in 1995, Yabloko obtained 6.9 percent of the vote, which means that, even within one of Russia's most industrialized and developed cities (Tolyatti), the vote for the liberal party was below the national average. By contrast, LDPR's national vote in 1995 was 11.2 percent. Ibid., 201–2. This shows that Tolyatti registered support for the party significantly higher than the national average, while Samara support was below the national average.

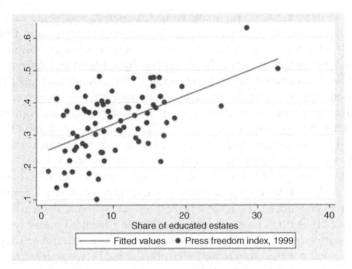

FIGURE 9.11 Share of educated estates and press freedom index

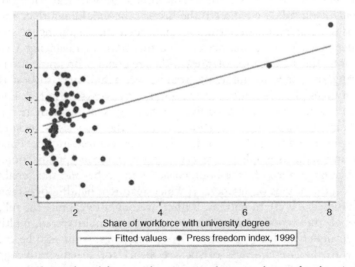

FIGURE 9.12 Share of workforce with university degree and press freedom index

CONCLUSION

The analysis presented here has augmented the previous chapters' qualitative and quantitative forensics concerning the reproduction of the legacies of the estates-derived bourgeoisie with systematic analysis of the social drivers of subnational democratic variations. Both the regional/district and individual-level Levada survey microdata analyzed in Chapter 7, with some caveats, are remarkably consistent in corroborating the argument advanced in this book. The estates-derived bourgeoisie did not simply disappear following the apocalyptic perturbations wrought on society by a Marxism-inspired leveling project. The decimation of capital spectacularly failed to abolish inequalities in Russia; elements of the social structure persisted; and the Soviet-engineered white-collar professional stratum remained socially distinct from the pre-revolutionary bourgeoisie. These social legacies continue to shape the human capital and the aspirations and values of Russian citizens as well as the ways in which they position themselves within the arenas of professional and more broadly civic and public life. Moreover, they have influenced democratic processes at the subnational and ultimately national levels. They explain why some regions engender a Tom Sawyer Fest as the symbolic descendant of the museum society of times past, while others exhibit a dormant public sphere; and why even within one region, citizen proclivities for civic activism or support for an oppositional political sphere may sharply diverge between districts.

These findings bring new insights to ongoing polemics about the social-political consequences of communist developmentalism. Extending Rosenfeld's work into heterogeneity within the middle class – employment within the state institutions or outside – we discern the historical conditioning that transcends communism of differential opportunities and proclivities in joining the structures of state dependency in the first place.[107] Furthermore, in advancing McMann's research into the significance of present-day regional economic autonomy in engendering resistance to autocratic trends, we, again, may suggest that we look for sources of variation in the pre-communist ecosystems of economy, the public, and civic spheres.[108] Broadly, our findings call for a more sustained research agenda into the interaction between the legacies associated with distinct regimes and the political orders, some far removed in time. Finally, the material and data assembled here cry out for a reconceptualization of the democratic significance of "the bourgeoisie" and go beyond the "coalitional" polemics on the origins of democracy, which feature a handful of established – and overstudied – Western nations. Rather, we ought to capture the full, trans-generational, trans-epoch, adaptive aspects of these multilayered, multifaceted strata even under the least "bourgeois" of all regimes, while also beginning to grapple with the consequences of such resilience for social stratification and inequalities beyond the obvious significance for democracy. How much confidence do we have, however, that our insights indeed cross over to other communist legacy settings? This is a question that I now turn to in the final chapter.

---

[107] Rosenfeld, *Autocratic Middle Class.*   [108] McMann, *Economic Autonomy.*

The Bourgeoisie in Communist States: Comparative Insights

> I was very annoyed, because I knew that if you were holding a flag it was impossible to leave the procession, because it would be very suspicious if you disappeared down a side street ... However, by a lucky accident, I was able to escape from the procession because we marched down a small alley and there was a toilet with an open door. And I went in with the intention of leaving the flag there and going out. That was a lovely moment, as when I went in, there were already a load of other banners there, so I wasn't the first person who had gone into the toilet with a flag and came out through another door without one. Having left my flag behind, I disappeared into a side street.
>
> Participant of a 1952 May parade in Hungary, reminiscences[1]

The above quotation is a metaphorical expression of the side streets of social resistance to communism. Yet how do we predict the parade goer who will disappear into an alley and ditch the flag? Moreover, how do we know whether the emblematic repository of the discarded flag is not but an island in a sea of conformist procession in a fractured society? In this chapter, I discuss how the preceding analysis has wider, portable, comparative implications for understanding the drivers of variations in the shades of authoritarianism and illiberalism in other communist-legacy countries. I structure the chapter as follows. I first sketch out an analytical framework for the comparative analysis of two new cases, Hungary and China. The section also delineates the limitations in scope and restrictions in applications to the universe of communist states and beyond. I then proceed to analyze each case in some depth with reference to the key variables of interest. A final section concludes with reflections on the utility of the framework for understanding social inequalities and the long shadow of pre-modern societies in effecting democratic vulnerabilities and resilience in the present-day illiberal world.

[1] Quoted in Mark, "Discrimination," 520.

CHARTING A COMPARATIVE FRAMEWORK

Motivating the case selection, I draw on Acemoglu and Robinson's framework of parceling out distinct paths of political development and identifying the original drivers nudging countries toward peculiar democratic trajectories,[2] an approach broadly consistent with Mill's method of difference.[3] The selected cases of Hungary and China, in addition to Russia, share the legacies of communist rule, repressions, and targeted persecutions of the bourgeoisie, that is, a broad set of factors that are ruled out, as it were, as the key explanandum. We may place these cases on a continuum of political illiberalism. China would be classed as a consolidated autocracy that failed to democratize during the third – also referred to as the fourth – wave of democratization.[4] Russia democratized in the 1990s but moved decisively into the camp of electoral authoritarian regimes in the 2000s. Recently, Hungary has been added to the list of comparative referents for the scholar of twenty-first-century illiberalism.

The cases represent three possible historical pathways to post-communist political outcomes. One is a path from a weakly professionalized feudal society to communism and then to capitalist autocracy. This is what we find in China, where the bourgeoisie never developed to the same extent as in Russia and could not constitute a similarly potent force for latent resistance to communist social engineering projects. Here, far larger swathes of the would-be communist middle class were of a "new" variety, overwhelmingly of peasant origin, that is, peasant occupational status, at the time of Mao's Revolution. Russia exhibits the second path of a revolution in a robustly professionalized and organizationally incorporated society that nevertheless retained a feudal-corporate character. Here, even after far-reaching land reforms, large swathes of the illiterate peasant society remained distinct from the estates-derived bourgeoisie, groups that were further incentivized to professionalize following loss of income and land. A policy sequencing perspective attunes us to the fact that reforms of antediluvian feudal institutions were not accompanied by simultaneous universal schooling, which would have eased the social mobility of newly liberated peasants.[5] This is the path leading to post-communist democratic breakthroughs followed by electoral autocracy. Democratic resilience would have a pronounced spatial-regional dimension, and even within regions the liberal impulse would be generally confined to a small middle class of professionally autonomous and habitually privileged

---

[2] Acemoglu and Robinson, *Economic Origins*, 1–14.
[3] On application of the method in comparative historical studies, see Faletti and Mahoney, "Comparative."
[4] Huntington, *Third Wave*. Some scholars have argued that democratization in communist Europe in the late 1980s ought to be considered a distinct phase. See Brown, "Transnational Influences," esp. 181–86.
[5] On a policy sequencing perspective, see Faletti and Mahoney, "Comparative."

urbanites. Russia's heritage middle class would nevertheless be far larger than the equivalent group in China if we take as its defining characteristic its origins in pre-communist estatist-bourgeois milieus, rather than its present-day position on the income scale or white-collar occupational status. Finally, Hungary illustrates a third stylized path of illiberal democracy. Like in Russia, the estatist society of post-feudal aristocrats and urban bourgeoisie had been sharply cleaved from the rural–worker masses well into the 1940s. Here, however, unlike either in Russia or in China, the mid-nineteenth-century agrarian and tax reforms that incentivized the professionalization of the gentry went hand in hand with the introduction of universal schooling. Further, a combination of historical shocks led to the *over-* not *under-* production of the educated estatist society. The pedigree bourgeoisie had been proportionately of a significantly larger magnitude than their equivalent in Russia, and far bigger than in China, even though ultimately Hungary remains a highly bimodal society where the professional middle class has its origins largely among the latter-day aristocracy, the country squire, and the urban "pariah" industrialist.

Scope and Extensions of the Framework

In terms of scope, I expect these patterns to apply across communist societies, but with some caveats. The perspective here is sensitive to the social and not just institutional aspect of the legacy. Institutions alone – notably in the professions – would not suffice to ensure the survival of the bourgeoisie in similar ways and to similar extents across communist states. In small nations like Estonia, Stalinist purges decimated pre-communist elites while the Holocaust engulfed the professional class across the Baltic states and Central Europe. As I discuss in the section "Social Structure, Bifurcation, and Illiberalism," countries like Poland and Czechoslovakia compare favorably with Hungary – they exhibit less pronounced patterns of persistence in social stratification under communism. Again, the Holocaust-induced social displacement and wartime population movement and territorial annexations partially account for these patterns.[6] The previous chapter has argued that devastation of entire communities like the Volga Germans essentially wipes out the effect of past social structure. Yet, as Hungary's case illustrates, even as scores of Jewish professionals perished in concentration camps, embeddedness in institutions of private industry and the professions sheltered many others.

In addition, insights are here applied, derived from the Russia case, to consider the catastrophic event – global wars, civil strife, famine, and other calamities prejudicing the social legitimacy of communist regimes – as a social *dis-leveler*. The analysis is attuned to variations in this dimension of the

---

[6] I am grateful to Grigore Pop-Eleches for raising this point and encouraging me to think about scope restrictions.

potentially corrosive pressures on regime legitimacy to reengage the bourgeoisie in Hungary and China.[7] Thus, while the Soviet regime confronted Nazi aggression in 1941, China's revolution occurred after the war, taking away the incentive apparently at work in the Soviet Union to boost popular morale and engage a wide swathe of professionals in the backbreaking war mobilization and armaments production effort. Hungary experienced a communist takeover after World War II, but Soviet occupation stripped the country of vital industrial infrastructure, making reliance on the old bourgeoisie an imperative for (re)industrialization.[8] In China, the shock to regime legitimacy did not come from fighting an external war but from de-Stalinization in Soviet Russia. Fears of a repeat of this scenario encouraged Mao to step up the attacks on "capitalists" at home, intensifying communist *leveling* policies.[9]

Finally, in proposing a new lens with which to analyze the historical-social drivers of regime variations in communist countries, I am cautiously optimistic that my insights transcend these regimes. Thus, a landmark study noted that, in non-communist states like West Germany, contemporary social bifurcations could be linked to Otto von Bismarck's social policy and even earlier, to policies and institutions in pre-unification Germany, a reminder of the "the long shadow of history" in shaping society in the present.[10] Among the most cited studies in comparative democracy, however, few have integrated sociological insights into the *longue durée* and path-dependencies of social bifurcation in the way proposed in this book – sensitive as my analysis is to the democratic implications of decisions made at the juncture at which late feudal societies give way to modern knowledge-professional economies. Even in the historically informed studies of democratic and authoritarian pathways, the professionalization of latter-day landowners, artisans, or entrepreneurs has remained in the shadows. Put bluntly, one would be hard-pressed to find "the professions" as a category accorded pride of place alongside conventional class actors.[11] This omission is puzzling in the context of growing threats to

---

[7] I here draw on Faletti and Mahoney, "Comparative," 229.

[8] Békés et al., *Soviet Occupation*, 159.

[9] Mao was particularly exercised about the possibility of the resurrection of the bourgeoisie, which he made clear in numerous speeches and writings invoking the Soviet Union as an example of this scenario. See Schram, "Classes," 41–42.

[10] Erikson and Goldthorpe, *Class Mobility*, 175.

[11] For instance, scholars have discussed power dynamics involving landlords, peasants, and entrepreneurial bourgeoisie, the latter encompassing urban commercial entrepreneurs and industrialists: Moore, *Social Origins*; the distribution of assets among elites and taxation (land, hydrocarbons): Boix, *Democracy and Redistribution*; coalitional dynamics involving liberal and sociodemocratic forces in interwar Europe: Luebbert, *Liberalism*; incentives of "citizens" versus "elites" concerning taxation and potential to rebel: Acemoglu and Robinson, *Economic Origins*; working-class movements: Rueschemeyer et al., *Capitalist Development*; and conflicts and relative bargaining strength between old economic groups like landed elites and new rising industrial elites, financial bourgeoisie, the middle class, and urban working classes: Ansell and

illiberalism that stem from social inequalities that are perceived to be deeply entrenched and intractable. This book's analysis of the processes of adaptation and professional incorporation of the latter-day aristocracy, clergy, and urban burghers helps nuance these accounts while raising new questions and paradoxes for democracy in present-day unequal societies. We find that the educated and habitually aspirational bourgeois of a heritage variety, incorporated into the professions and other autonomous spaces of a quasi-public sphere, provides a buffer against encroachments on illiberalism. Simultaneously, however, in many societies where a particular combination of policies and sequences had been at work during the nineteenth century's major agrarian and social reforms, the professional bourgeoisie is an unwitting accomplice to the deep social chasm separating it from the habitually left-behind. This is a threat not a boon to liberalism, given the potential for social conflicts to engender support for autocratic strongmen among both the privileged few and the masses. Table 10.1 provides a summary of key historical differences between the three cases. What follows is a more in-depth discussion of Hungary and China and the insights they bring to bear on the question of the historical conditioning of democratic pathways despite the shock of communism.

CASES

Hungary: Introduction

In social science speak, Hungary represents an interesting "puzzle" for the scholar of democracy. Not only did Hungary's political liberalization in the 1980s contribute to the demise of communism in Europe but the country had also witnessed the first truly mass anti-communist popular uprising in 1956, brutally suppressed by the Soviet Union. The uprising ushered in decisions of the reformist government of Imre Nagy to restore multiparty elections; reconstitute political parties of the pre-1948 era; and politically sideline Communist collaborators. Likewise, when in the late 1980s and early 1990s Hungary experienced a peaceful transition to a multiparty parliamentary democracy, it was hailed as a beacon of democratic reconstruction, drawing half of all the Western investment going to post-communist Europe. Yet the

Samuels, *Inequality*. Research on more recent democratic transitions has focused on contingent elite pacts and leadership. O'Donnell et al., *Transitions*; Linz and Stepan, *Problems*. These works also discuss the role of the generic middle class but not in the same way I propose to analyze it from the perspective of professional-institutional status, resources, and human endowments engendering autonomy. For summaries of these debates, see Boix, *Democracy and Redistribution*; and Mahoney, "Knowledge." I also go beyond capturing specific actors and incentives in one time snapshot and regard the bourgeoisie as a resilient intergenerational category, embedded in professional institutions, and possessing specific value orientations pegged to modern knowledge economies.

TABLE 10.1 *Legacy of the bourgeoisie and political regime pathways (devised by author)*

Countries	Regime type, 2020	Universal primary education, 1800s	Reform sequencing	Social structure	Professions and autonomous public sphere	Social bifurcation, key elements	Communist social change	External shocks and regime legitimacy
Hungary	Illiberal democracy	Yes	Liberal reforms: simultaneity of agrarian reforms with universal schooling; agrarian reforms incomplete	Relatively large and highly educated professional stratum; professional overproduction; strong cleavage between professional society and peasants/workers	Strong	Gentry/aristocracy, bourgeoisie, peasantry	Reproduction of estatist bourgeoisie despite, and after a period of a spell of, witch hunts	World War II Soviet occupation and industrialization imperatives after communist takeover
Russia	Electoral autocracy	No	Liberal reforms: agrarian reforms not accompanied by rolling out of universal schooling; agrarian reforms incomplete	Relatively small but highly educated professional stratum; strong cleavage between professional society and peasants/workers	Strong	Gentry/aristocracy, estates-derived bourgeoisie, peasantry	Reproduction of estatist bourgeoisie despite, and after a period of a spell of, witch hunts	Civil War, famine, economic ruin, 1917–1930s; Nazi Germany invasion and war, 1941–45
China	Autocracy	No	NA	Nascent professional class, strong cleavage between landlord and peasant; social status linked to literati examination systems and position in state bureaucracies	Weak	Landlords, peasants, small merchant stratum, historically weak/nonexistent urban estate	Narrow temporal window of reproduction of small professional stratum; comparatively high extent of class vigilance; policy change in late 1970s	Khrushchev's de-Stalinization campaign in the 1950s putting pressures on legitimacy of nascent regime in China; revolution happens after World War II

euphoria did not last very long. In the early 1990s already, signs of creeping authoritarianism emerged, manifested in ham-fisted attempts to control the media; reconstructed communist parties enjoyed revival at the polls;[12] and the gradual descent into illiberalism continued. Freedom House ranked Hungary as Free in 1990, yet by the start of the second decade of the 2000s, it stood at the authoritarian precipice, eventually descending into Partly Free status. "In Hungary," wrote the think tank, "Prime Minister Viktor Orbán has presided over one of the most dramatic declines ever charted by Freedom House within the European Union."[13] Although observers have tended to highlight leadership factors in the undermining of democratic institutions, Orbán's spectacular ascent may also be located in the social legacies of inequality, and the concomitant resentment of the "cosmopolitan bourgeoisie," something that Orbán tapped into to boost his appeal.

The Contours of the Late Feudal Social Structure

Like imperial Russia, the Hungary of the Austro-Hungarian Empire had been a rigidly bifurcated society. The medieval structure of the estates conditioned social privileges based on ascription to the nobility, clergy, burghers, and subject serfs; the system was altered in the mid-nineteenth century with the unveiling of constitutional reforms.[14] An estimated 5 percent of the population,[15] and as much as 12–13 percent among Magyars, were nobles,[16] a figure significantly exceeding the proportion of nobles elsewhere in Europe, bar Poland and Spain.[17] The nobility exhibited substantial heterogeneity in possession of assets like land and, before the 1848 Revolution, serfs.[18] The Hungarian historian László Péter distinguishes between the small minority of 300 or so titled families – princes, counts, barons – as the magnate class possessing aristocratic wealth, power, and legal status and dominating the diet's Upper House and the Roman Catholic church hierarchy; the roughly one-third of the *bene possessionati* of provincial gentry endowed with land as a royal donation, controlling country life, and constituting the dominant faction in the diet's Lower House – these groups became the revolutionary vanguard in 1848;[19] and the more than two-thirds of the poor "sandalled nobles," before 1848 residing on peasant plots or as landless "armalists" with a noble coat of

[12] Crampton, *Eastern Europe*, 298–301, 442–45.
[13] *Freedom in the World 2019: Democracy in Retreat*. Available online at: freedomhouse.org /report/freedom-world/freedom-world-2019 (accessed May 21, 2020).
[14] Péter, *Hungary's Long Nineteenth Century*, 310.   [15] Ibid., 307.
[16] Hoensch, *History*, 36. Hoensch estimates the nobility's overall population share at 6 percent. Ibid., 36.
[17] In eighteenth-century France, by comparison, there were an estimated 180 commoners to a noble, and the ratio was higher in Bohemia. Péter, *Hungary's Long Nineteenth Century*, 307n6.
[18] Ibid., 307–8.   [19] Ibid., 310.

arms who tended to move into the professions or help service the wealthy estates.[20] As with the "life" noble of tsarist Russia following the Petrine reforms, the administrative service would be rewarded with a title but without substantial land.[21] While the abolition of serfdom deprived scores of landholders of economic lifeline, others reinvented themselves as managers of estates that together comprised more than a third of Hungary's cultivable land. The erstwhile landlords also engaged in public service, banking, industry, and entrepreneurship.[22] At the same time, the royal grant of a noble title lubricated the ascent of the aspirational indigenous and assimilated groups of non-Magyar origin. As Péter writes,

In the age of capitalist entrepreneurship the ability of the Hungarian social system to absorb rising groups survived intact by generating new layers of hereditary nobility. And so it was that university professors and successful merchants (with German *lateiner* or Jewish middle class backgrounds) took great pride in being granted the patent of nobility by the king, and likewise bankers in the conferment of the title of baron on their families.[23]

The nucleus of the professional stratum and entrepreneurial bourgeoisie exhibited pronounced spatial variations due to complex legacies of imperial conquest and tutelage. In the eighteenth century, most nobles of Transdanubia, where their population share averaged 5.41 percent, resided in territories that had not been occupied by the Ottoman Empire in the sixteenth century. In Eastern Hungary's counties of Szabolcs, Szatmár, and Borsod, 13 percent, 14 percent, and 15 percent, respectively, of the population were nobles. In the 1840s, half of Hungary's nobility were concentrated in an estimated eleven counties.[24]

Estate and Social Cleavages after Liberal Reforms

Following the 1848 Revolution, a constitutional monarchy was formally established; civil equality proclaimed; hereditary privileges undermined; and the estates system underwent gradual transformation.[25] De facto, nobles retained preeminence in government and the professions until the collapse of the Dual Monarchy and, to a significant extent, the interwar period – in what Gale Stokes terms "aristocratic bureaucratism."[26] The implementation and consequences of liberal reforms broadly mirrored processes in Russia. Péter

---

[20] Ibid., 308–9.
[21] Many "armalists" reportedly lived in "abject poverty" and were even illiterate. Ibid., 309.
[22] Hoensch, *History*, 36–37.   [23] Péter, *Hungary's Long Nineteenth Century*, 313–14.
[24] Ibid. See 307n7.
[25] Hoensch, *History*, 36.; Péter, *Hungary's Long Nineteenth Century*, 309–10. More than 9 million serfs were freed in Hungary and Croatia. Ibid., 310n15.
[26] Stokes, "Social Origins," 30. An 1885 Law on the Upper House restricted membership to nobles paying at least 3000 fl. of land tax per year, which deprived 72–74 percent of the House members of their hereditary right although the figure was not considered to be "excessively high." Péter, *Hungary's Long Nineteenth Century*, 308n8.

notes, "Legal equality in Hungary was introduced so carefully that the social status of the titled nobility, and even of the ordinary nobility, was not undermined."[27] Taxation was made "equal and proportionate" but the legal status of a noble remained;[28] a juridical fog characterized the rights and status of former serfs; it remained unclear whether the emancipated serf became the legal owner of the plot of land the family cultivated; the system of royal land donation remained in place as a noble's privilege; and the landed estate, while proudly claiming to have voluntarily sacrificed property in the name of emancipation, did not publicize the financial compensation received from the state.[29] "Emancipation payments imposed on the peasants," notes Péter, "dragged on for many decades after the 1870s. All in all, legislation on legal equality and property rights was piecemeal and fragmentary rather than general and comprehensive."[30]

Both the top layer of aristocrats and the better-off gentry were in a good position to colonize and engender the modern professions; their status in the hierarchy of nobility before the liberal reforms influenced their futures in the social structure of modern Hungary. Take the large group of lesser nobles or gentry. Habitually active in local affairs, toward the end of the nineteenth century, in what is not dissimilar to the embourgeoisement of Russia's nobility, they came to colonize white-collar administrative occupations in their provinces. Although many were impoverished, even pauperized, as Hungary modernized scores reinvented themselves as clerks, industry managers, and supervisors of large land estates; others joined the sprawling state apparatus.[31] Faced with loss of material wealth, they were incentivized to leverage their human capital to populate the professions and civil service. Simultaneously, town burghers hitherto engaged in commerce, and those non-noble groups who had acquired wealth in the context of capitalist development, could be ennobled thereby enjoying the symbolic status of the upper elite. These groups' educational investments allowed them to join the ranks of professional bourgeoisie just as the empire was crumbling and the old structure of estates became obsolete.[32]

Hungary's *fin de siècle* modernization coincided with the rise of urban bourgeoisie of German, Czech, and Jewish origin. These groups accounted for a significant proportion of the urban middle class and included artisans and small tradesmen concentrated in medieval centers of commerce, as well as new would-be large traders, bankers, and industrialists suffusing wealth through risk-taking and capital accumulation.[33] The noble joined the merchant and the enterprising upstart from among the clergy or entrepreneurial peasantry in a competitive race to acquire modern education. The entrepreneur and the professional were overwhelmingly comprised of these hitherto privileged

[27] Péter, *Hungary's Long Nineteenth Century*, 313.   [28] Ibid., 310.   [29] Ibid., 310–12.
[30] Ibid., 313.   [31] Held, "Is History," 5.   [32] Hoensch, *History*, 37–38.
[33] Cornelius, "Education," 131; Hoensch, *History*, 37–38.

native, or habitually educated and aspirational, assimilated groups of non-Magyar origin. These processes of embourgeoisement of Hungarian society were highly spatially uneven. "Towns in Hungary appeared late," writes Péter, "they were few and small, economically weak and, since they were led by German burghers, socially isolated."[34] Beyond Budapest, a few regions blossomed as centers of industry and commerce, while others remained semi-feudal – isolated, left behind, and steeped in rural tradition.

Educational Reforms Accompanying Liberalization

Hungary's transition from a feudal society and embourgeoisement that took off in the second half of the nineteenth century is, nonetheless, different from cognate developments in Russia around that same time in important respects. The 1868 Education Law promulgated under the Education and Culture Minister Baron József Eötvös mandated compulsory education for children aged six to twelve. A network of elementary schools under state authority was to be created, parallel to the confessional schools run by the Catholic Church and other religious authorities. Consequently, a dramatic expansion of schooling occurred in the period leading up to World War I. Between 1867 and 1914, illiteracy among those aged six years and older, 90 percent of whom benefited from schooling, fell from 55 percent to 31 percent.[35] In a study comparing the long-run effects of education on post-communist democratic outcomes, Hungary is listed as a "highly schooled" society.[36] Magyarization of school instruction accompanying the rolling-out of universal education disadvantaged non-Magyar minorities, notably in university admissions. Nevertheless, as is evident from this cursory discussion, while feudalism and the "caste" system of noble privileges were slow to disintegrate, even as radical constitutional reforms were promulgated, Hungary experienced significantly further-reaching educational reforms than had been the case in post-emancipation Russia.

While developing a system of universal rudimentary teaching for the masses, Eötvös's educational reforms also embraced an "unashamedly elitist" system of secondary pedagogy modeled on the German high school. The *gymnasium* (*gimnázium*) taught classics, Greek, Latin, mathematics, and the sciences. Like in Russia, which likewise embraced the German gymnasium, it featured superbly educated pedagogues, including would-be members of the Hungarian Academy of Sciences and university professoriate.[37] Another German import were the *real gymnasium* (*reálgimnázium*) and the *real school* (*reáliskola*), with the former providing instruction in modern languages in addition to Latin and the latter more focused on exposure to arithmetic, modern languages, and the natural sciences. Hungary's first *gimnázium* for girls opened in 1896.[38] The

---

[34] Péter, *Hungary's Long Nineteenth Century*, 305.   [35] Hoensch, *History*, 46–47.
[36] Darden and Grzymala-Busse, "Great Divide," 94.   [37] Frank, "Teaching," 370.
[38] Ibid., 370.

gimnázium in turn constituted a springboard into higher education and, for the very lucky, access to training in the technical and classical subjects taught by the European-trained *éminence* of the Budapest scientific elite. The University of Budapest maintained strong ties with a network of prestigious gymnasia: high school teachers were expected to pursue scientific research and top teachers were invited to give lectures to university students.[39] Science, rationality, and enlightened thought and action permeating gymnasium instruction became the natural ally of anointments into the modern profession. Insofar as this ethos contrasted with the often conservative, "hostile to innovation" mentality of the ruling regime,[40] it is very similar to the Russian gymnasium in engendering anti-establishment critical thought.

In what accentuates both Russia's and Hungary's distinction from China, the university system also developed between the last quarter of the nineteenth century and 1914. On the eve of World War I, 16,300 students attended the Budapest Technical University (founded in 1872), the University in Kolozsvár (Cluj) (1872), and Debrecen or Pressburg (Bratislava) (1912), aside from the main university in Pest. Law, medicine, the humanities, and divinity studies enjoyed high popularity. Simultaneously, as many as 22 percent of undergraduate students opted for natural and technical subjects or economics.[41] Meanwhile, the establishment around that time of teacher training institutions – like the institute attached to the University of Budapest – provided professional-pedagogic training to the aspiring *gimnázium* instructor.[42] Secondary schools and the university system in turn built on the much longer tradition and architecture of existing Jesuit and Lutheran schools and specialized learning centers dating back to the eighteenth century.[43]

Social mobility made some inroads into the higher educational sector, but the proportion of students of worker and peasant backgrounds remained minuscule, at less than 3 percent. The nobility remained overrepresented in the student pool, constituting roughly half of the student body. The rest of the student population largely drew on urban bourgeoisie, with many students of Jewish backgrounds.[44] Here, as with the merchant class in Russia, the impulse to acquire wealth via industriousness and entrepreneurial pursuits would be in the next generation displaced with an appetite for knowledge and professional careers outside of business, and indeed for engagement in the vibrant public sphere of the *Belle Époque*.[45] Over- not undersupply characterized staffing in the burgeoning bureaucratic apparatus and the professions as thousands of cultivated aristocrats and gentry deprived of land-derived income sought gainful employment, competing with the aspirational new bourgeoisie.[46] "Bread to the people, jobs to the lawyers," was how one radical press outlet commiserated with the predicament of the educated liberal public of the former landowning ilk.[47]

[39] Ibid., 369–70.   [40] Ibid., 357.   [41] Hoensch, *History*, 47.   [42] Frank, "Teaching," 369.
[43] Ibid., 372–75.   [44] Hoensch, *History*, 47.   [45] Frank, "Teaching," 359.
[46] Janos, *Politics of Backwardness*, 93–94.   [47] Cited in ibid., 93.

High-skilled professions became part of an organic structure of aspirations and milestones for the middle class. Let us consider in brief medicine and engineering to appreciate the scale and extent of the demand- and supply-side of professionalization. Engineering became an established profession as Hungary industrialized rapidly in the last quarter of the nineteenth century. In a span of forty-five years, between 1869 and 1913, Hungary's railway network increased from a total of 2,736 kilometers to 21,798 kilometers, spurring growth in the iron industry and engineering, much like railway expansion did in the same period in the Russian Empire.[48] According to Hungary's 1910 census, of the 456,470 employees in mining, industry, and metallurgy, 5.2 percent, or nearly 24,000, were white-collar employees, slightly more than one-fifth of whom were engineers and other technically skilled workforce.[49] Although lower middle class in social origin, engineering represented a structured avenue to social mobility, particularly for Jews of modest means facing discrimination, and one with a developed sense of professional organization, ethos, and autonomy.[50]

In medicine, so developed had been medical provision and so extensive the roster of medical personnel by the interwar period that it invited the Health Section of the Secretariat of the League of Nations to make enviable comparisons with other emerging Western social democracies. Invoking the public health memorandum of Dr. Alexander De Dobrovits, Councilor in the Royal Hungarian Central Statistical Office, the League reported: "Though the population of Hungary is now only seven to eight million, the account of its health administration is longer and more elaborate than that relating to Germany." The report went on to enumerate the complex tapestry of agencies – from institutions charged with caring for the sick to those with authority over campaigns against epidemics, temperance, child welfare, and palliative care. The Minister of Labor and Social Welfare, we are told, has charge of no less than fourteen departments, "including sickness, workers' and disability insurance, war victims' relief, poor relief, housing, and child welfare." The web of agencies with medical and clerical staff permeated counties and localities; public hospitals, clinics, and pharmacies coexisted with private ones; and training, degree progression, and certification of diplomas were carefully monitored and regulated. These public institutions coexisted with civic associations – from temperance societies, to professional bodies, to nationally federated leagues uniting various associations.[51]

Social Gulf between the Estatist Bourgeoisie and Peasantry

The overwhelming mass of society well into the first half of the twentieth century not only remained rural but remained peasants. Despite the

---

[48] Schulze, "Economic Development," 82.   [49] Péteri, "Engineer Utopia," 85.   [50] Ibid., 86.
[51] TBMJ, "Public Health."

comprehensive education reforms providing for basic schooling, the peasantry retained its pre-modern character, detached from urban bourgeois society – and one with all but a rudimentary experience of the market. Hungary's conservative elites, including the Roman Catholic Church, the country's single largest landholder,[52] successfully resisted land redistributions. As Andrew Janos writes, quoting the patrician aristocrat Count István Bethlen de Bethlen, the premier in 1921–31,

"Land," as he [Bethlen] put it with infuriating logic, "[did] not belong to the 'people' nor to those who till[ed] it, but to those under whose name it appear[ed] in the land register." If one accepted the demagoguery of reformers, then, by the same logic, factories belonged to the workers, and apartment houses to their tenants. Anyway, land redistribution schemes violated the sanctity of private property, and if it was all right to expropriate his land, Bethlen argued, then one might as well expropriate his watch, coat, and pants.[53]

Until the 1940s, deference, status, and social boundaries were ascribed depending on one's position, indeed, status by birth, in the social hierarchy of the estates.[54] From the dawn of Hungary's electoral politics and through the period of interwar democracy, a poorly educated, economically dependent, and deeply traditional rural society constituted the backbone of elaborate political machines delivering votes to contending parties. The same electoral tricks that lubricate Putinism and Orbánism in the twenty-first century characterized the manipulation machines of the turn of the nineteenth and twentieth centuries and the interwar era. Taxes and fines were levied selectively to procure electoral obeisance, and if that would not suffice, "local authorities could resort to still more effective administrative means, such as manipulating the voter register, putting recalcitrant villagers under a health quarantine, or declaring bridges unsafe for passage to prevent the voters of the opposition from reaching the appointed polling place."[55] "As long as they remained peasants," writes Janos, "the lower classes of rural Hungary were to be citizens only in name."[56] The degree of citizen compliance varied and showed contrasting intensity across Hungary's subnational counties and electoral precincts, however. The so-called open boroughs counteracted the "rotten boroughs," with Budapest and other developed urban centers serving as "models of political probity."[57]

These bifurcations are corroborated in ethnographic-educational projects that the Hungarian intelligentsia embarked on as part of the Hungarian Folk College Movement of 1938–48.[58] Across the target communities, the well-meaning metropolitan bohemians find not only a society with only rudimentary education but one where, at a cognitive level, the cleavage separating the peasant from the urban bourgeois remained deep and

---

[52] Cornelius, "Education," 139.   [53] Janos, *Politics of Backwardness*, 229.
[54] Cornelius, "Education," 132.   [55] Janos, *Politics of Backwardness*, 97.   [56] Ibid., 233.
[57] Ibid., 99.
[58] The folk schools were dissolved after the communist takeover. Cornelius, "Education."

entrenched. "Servile," "conscious of its inferiority,"[59] "passive" and "apathetic"[60] are some of the epitaphs that came out of these encounters. One youth student leader thus commented on the target community: "It's difficult to get them to sit down. They have gotten used to getting orders from the gentleman in trousers [the term used for members of the upper- classes][61] which they have to accept standing, dutifully, with cap in hand."[62] A local student attending the sessions thus commented on his own society:

At that time there was *such a caste system in Hungary that quite sharp boundaries divided one caste from another – the aristocracy from the middle farmers, the middle farmers from the smallholders and the smallholders from the agrarian workers or cotters. In the village itself the intellectuals kept separate, and contact between two castes happened only in official matters.* It was a great experience when we came into direct contact with intellectuals [urban student activists].[63]

Writes Deborah S. Cornelius of the communities targeted for this project to "educate talented peasant youth":[64]

Ironically, this agrarian population, believed to retain the ancient roots of Hungarian culture, formed the most backward and poorly educated layer of society. In 1930 the agrarian population constituted 4.5 million of the total population of 8.7 million, but half of the land under cultivation was still in the hands of 7,500 large estate owners ... Hungary remained a land of large estates, upon which the vast majority of the agrarian population were dependent for employment.[65]

Furthermore,

The peasantry were at the very bottom of the social pyramid, since they completely lacked any feudal privileges. Law and custom granted broad rights to the large estates to supervise and regulate the life of the rural proletariat. These included the right to use corporal punishment, as well as the power to use any laborer of the locality to work on the estate at harvest time, or other time of need, and to determine the amount of wages, which were paid in kind. The rank and class of each individual was clearly revealed by clothing, behavior, manners, and speech. The booted peasant, painfully conscious of his lowly status, assumed a posture of inferiority and submission in his contacts with the upper classes. He took his position for granted and never thought to rebel against it.[66]

While the "village explorers" noted that most rural youth were pining to abandon the village, the vistas that they were "dreaming" were "careers as chimneysweeps, janitors, porters, garbage collectors, and conductors in the quasi-mythical city."[67] Although by 1930, close to 90 percent of the population were literate, and newspaper readership and general enlightenment increased, "this,"

---

[59] Ibid., 131.   [60] Ibid., 134.   [61] Clarification original.
[62] Cited in Cornelius, "Education," 133.   [63] Cited in ibid., 138 (emphasis added).
[64] Ibid., 130.   [65] Ibid., 131.
[66] Ibid., 132. A Hungarian bishop titled his lecture on the social gap in 1939 "The Great Chasm." Ibid., 141.
[67] Janos, *Politics of Backwardness*, 241.

observes Janos, "did not mean that there was a greater 'insight into the social mechanism,' or a real appreciation of the complexities of modern society ... Parliament was, at best, a distant place where educated people conducted their own business at the expense of the peasantry."[68] Writing in 1981, in what eerily anticipates the rise of Orbánism, Janos thus characterizes the political sensibilities of rural voters: "Clearly, the peasants had very little faith in any system that offered piecemeal solutions through legislative bargaining and bickering. Rather, *they expected their salvation from a strong leader blessed with prophetic gifts and standing above the petty squabbles of parties or the tedium of administrative minutiae.*"[69]

Hungary's Precarious Interwar Democracy and the Professions

Hungary's liberal traditions nevertheless moderated authoritarianism in the interwar period, even as defeat in World War I, leftist revolutions in 1918 and 1919, and the rightist counterrevolution of 1920 threatened to bring about the menace of fascism that engulfed neighboring Germany and Italy. Until 1944, it remained a parliamentary democracy – flawed, but featuring liberal opposition and moderate social democratic parties.[70] Hungary's professions constitute an interesting test of our theory of institutions of a modern knowledge society as both drivers of a quasi-public sphere and as engines of the reproduction of social structure. On the one hand, a picture emerges of a developed network of institutions comprising the liberal professions, public and private; featuring active associational life; and constituting powerful lobbies vis-à-vis the state. Institutionally, I regard this record as conducive to the reproduction of islands of social autonomy under communism. If we explore the value dimension of the professional society embedded in these institutions, a mixed picture emerges. The historian Maria Kovács identifies professions such as medicine and engineering as hotbeds of Hungary's interwar illiberalism – and as pressure groups for discriminatory anti-Jewish legislation that fed into Nazi persecutions during the brief occupation by Hitler's forces in 1944.[71] Simultaneously, Kovács paints a nuanced picture of fissures, struggles, and cleavages within and among liberal professions.

Hungary's interwar professional class featured extraordinary overcrowding. This situation became worse as the Treaty of Trianon deprived Hungary of rural territories, leaving districts with significant concentrations of professionals serving a shrunken clientele. The deterioration of material fortunes and degradation of professionals during the 1920s and the Great

---

[68] Ibid., 241.   [69] Ibid., 242 (emphasis added).

[70] Kovács, *Liberal Professions*, xviii–xix. Others, however, emphasize the lasting anti-democratic effects of the short-lived Soviet republic, which arguably "caused a widespread distaste among virtually the entire political class not only for communism and socialism, but also for liberal democracy." Polonsky, *Little Dictators*, 47.

[71] Kovács, *Liberal Professions*, 87, 94–95.

Depression years were such that medical trainees worked as tram drivers and conductors or shoveled snow. Universities, hitherto providing a supply of trained professionals to 18 million people, now catered to 8 million. In engineering, 47.5 percent of all practicing professionals in the 1920s were migrants to Budapest from "dismembered" territories. Medical doctors numbering 4,500 now served less than half of their prewar clientele.[72] Kovács thus characterizes the "striking anomaly" of professions: "By the end of the 1920s, Hungary, a small and relatively impoverished country, had the highest number of lawyers and medical doctors relative to population anywhere in Europe."[73] A quarter of all students at Hungarian universities came from "dismembered" lands in 1920–25.[74]

In medicine, occupational overcrowding spurred the emergence of the far-right MONE, the nativist anti-Jewish National Association of Hungarian Doctors. Founded in 1919, it advocated racialized quotas in admissions to medical schools and professional practice, as well as the expansion of public healthcare to guarantee jobs. Discriminatory legislation and preferential public employment engendered a cleavage – a form of "structural segregation" – between private and public medicine. In 1930, four-fifths of salaried public sector medics were Christian; two-thirds of Christian medics were public sector employees; while three-fourths of Jewish doctors practiced medicine privately.[75] Yet, Kovács writes, the Christian medics' embrace of the welfare system meant that "doctors [became] prisoners of a poor clientele that had no means to keep the doctors afloat without state assistance,"[76] something that the Great Depression only exacerbated.[77] Intra-professional fissures also emerged in the late 1930s as Hungary reacquired some of the territories lost consequential to the Treaty of Trianon, in Transylvania. Here, the shortage of medics had been more acute; consequently, the government, despite pressures from MONE, sought to water down Jewish quotas so that young doctors from Budapest would be able to practice there. Institutional and civic pluralism within Transylvania, where Jews allied with Magyars against discriminatory Transylvanian legislation, also constituted a check on illiberalism in the professions. "We are being swamped by letters from church dignitaries, politicians, members of the high elite and even magnates to protect and preserve the practice of Jewish doctors," wrote one Chamber of Doctors functionary.[78]

In engineering, where pressures to secure jobs in a situation of postwar precarity had been likewise acute, similar battles raged. Support for the 1919 Communist revolution among a proportion of professionals led to fissures whereby the "nonsocialist bulk of the profession" encouraged "reassertion of traditional, nontechnocratic values of professional life … demand[ing] an explicit demonstration of the profession's place in capitalist economy on the

---

[72] Ibid., 52–53. [73] Ibid., 53. [74] Ibid., 53. [75] Ibid., 69. [76] Ibid., 70. [77] Ibid., 85.
[78] Cited in ibid., 124.

side of the business enterprise."[79] Even against the background of militant anti-Semitism, such a position invited moderation considering that Jews owned 88.9 percent of financial institutions and constituted 57.9 percent of those self-employed in commerce.[80] Because many engineers were embedded in Jewish-run commercial enterprise, engineering featured arenas of institutional pluralism and oppositional impulse. Whether in medicine or in engineering, even before the imposition of communism, state-directed de-professionalization engendered cleavages between the superbly trained and socially well-regarded professionals and those serving as Magyar "straw men" to fulfill a quota and practice a trade.[81]

Finally, the legal profession remained virtually immune to the interwar politics of illiberalism. In the 1920s, and until the mid-1930s, the Chamber of Lawyers became allied with "Budapest's old-style, pre-war liberal forces."[82] "Exceptional among the professions," writes Kovács, was "the conservatism of the legal certification process, which involved years of apprenticeship after graduation from law school, [and] also worked to discourage a massive inflow of the young cohorts of politically radical students so typical of the interwar period."[83] Even as the government sought to introduce discriminatory provisions in hiring and practice, lawyers of left and liberal persuasions united to resist them and to clamor for professional autonomy.[84] Here long-established professional standards; training that was out of reach to the less privileged strata; and gatekeeping sheltered the profession against overcrowding. Furthermore, like engineers, lawyers sat on boards, assumed advisory roles, and practiced within private corporations, many Jewish-run, and found discriminatory laws abhorrent.

Thus, pre-communist Hungary's professions, much like medicine or gymnasium pedagogy in imperial Russia, featured not only a record of institutionalized and territorially dense autonomous spaces but also impulses to resist, water down, or obstruct state encroachments on autonomous social action. Ultimately, however, the professions remained sites of the embedding of privileged society – overwhelmingly of Magyar aristocratic pedigree as well as burghers of German, Czech, and Jewish origin originating within the artisanal, merchant, or urban professional milieus of *fin de siècle* Hungary.

Social Cleavages during Communism

Prior to communist rule, both Hungary and Russia thus possessed a well-developed network of what I term infrastructures of modernity. They were also blessed with a software of modern bourgeoisie or proto-bourgeoisie comprised of the habitually well-educated, well-networked, civically engaged nobles who were eagerly embracing the modern profession, as well as the new

---

[79] Ibid., 70–71.   [80] Ibid., 71.   [81] Ibid., 114, 115.   [82] Ibid., 97.   [83] Ibid., 110.
[84] The Justice Ministry later assumed control over the chamber. Ibid., 100.

entrants to the middle class comprised of the native and assimilated merchant, entrepreneurial, and industrial strata. These groups, along with the few peasant upstarts, constituted the core of what I conceptualize as the old bourgeoisie, in an intergenerational sense. Even as scions of the old bourgeoisie continued to colonize the professions in communist Hungary, the country's social structure exhibited characteristics of a less bifurcated society than in Russia, insofar as basic literacy and universal education were widely accessible decades before the communist takeover. Yet the rudimentary education had been nonetheless inferior to the trajectories of members of Hungary's privileged estates who benefited not only from habitual cultivation in the family home but from modern university-level and postgraduate professional training.

The historian James Mark draws attention to Hungary's status as "unique in central-eastern Europe."[85] The bourgeoisie found itself a target of more sustained forms of persecution and exclusion than in Czechoslovakia, for instance, in the years immediately following the communist takeover. Paradoxically, the pre-communist middle class, he writes, "achieved upward mobility in large numbers in a system which officially endorsed their marginalization."[86] The communist state divided the pre-communist privileged groups into categories of the "x-class" and "intellectuals." The "x-class" bracketed the offspring of landowning aristocrats; proprietors of factories, small enterprises, real estate, and apartments; managers, politicians, policemen, and old-regime military; as indeed any wealthy individual. The "intellectuals" comprised anyone whose parents had completed tertiary education and were employed as technical or professional intelligentsia after 1948 – these strata were also persecuted but to a lesser extent than the "x-class."[87] Within one fell swoop, Hungary thus stigmatized vast swathes of professionals and entrepreneurs – Russia's equivalent of the propertied *meshchanin*, merchant, clergyman, wealthy aristocrat, and indeed the intellectual who often came from the same stigmatized groups. Notably, citizenship restrictions applied to university admissions – a severe blow since, among Hungary's bourgeoisie, "going to university was considered a normal ... practice."[88] Yet, by 1952, as Hungary confronted the acute shortage of qualified cadre to implement large-scale industrialization, university restrictions were loosened if not entirely abandoned and other witch hunts moderated. Communist functionaries registered their alarm at the trend: "One 1956 party report highlighted that approximately half the cultural intelligentsia and 60–70 per cent of professionals were still taken from the families of the old middle and upper classes."[89]

The significance of the old professional class in accommodationist and reformist dynamics at the highest echelons of power is alluded to in Anna Seleny's study of the demise of Hungarian communism:

---

[85] Mark, "Discrimination," 502.   [86] Ibid., 502.   [87] Ibid., 503.   [88] Ibid., 505.
[89] Ibid., 504

East European state socialist systems are said to have collapsed in 1989. The Hungarian case, however, suggests a different formulation … [as] the Hungarian socialist system began transforming itself almost from its inception, and by 1989 was a hybrid produced by forty years of accommodation and compromise among the social, economic, political, and ideological forces it had suppressed or fostered.[90]

Scholars, academic economists, sociologists, and other experts were invited to partake in reformist debates of high-level "expert commissions"; and they were pivotal to the process of repackaging "scientific" socialism to drape the discreet policies of economic marketization and liberalization. During brief periods of conservative retrenchment, experts were branded as "foes";[91] at other times, "the 'foe' became 'friend' and 'helper' in official rhetoric and law."[92]

A Columbia University oral history project that included interviews with Hungarian immigrants also uncovered the same kinds of adaptations that were widespread in Russia among the bourgeoisie of various shades and gradations. Exclusion from university would be compensated with private schooling whereby the family drew on the services of another hounded "bourgeois" – a first-rate teacher unemployed because of her social background.[93] Prevarications, spells of blue-collar jobs, outright lies on CVs, and other mechanisms of resistance secured the reinvention, indeed rejuvenation, of the persecuted bourgeoisie as Hungary's professional class. Although there were communist party joiners, for others, as one respondent reported, "it was much more important that we could look at ourselves in the mirror in the morning."[94]

Recent studies of the privileged estates' adaptation after the communist takeover in Hungary also reveal subtle and more overt forms of resistance to communism. Echoing findings from statistical analysis of Russia concerning variations among the various estates in market values and oppositional proclivities, these attitudinal gradations were shaped by nuances of the pre-communist social structure. The conservative gentry segment reportedly eschewed active resistance. "Rather than resort to direct confrontation," writes Mark, "they saw the quiet, private maintenance of pre-Communist bourgeois and religious values as the most appropriate response to Communist power. Churchgoing was particularly popular, as it allowed conservatives to articulate their values 'discreetly.'"[95] The urban bourgeoisie and their descendants more actively espoused a liberal agenda of social resistance.[96] Still others embraced the metaphorical side "alley," pursuing technical subjects at university rather than

[90] Seleny, "Property Rights," 27. By contrast, in China, "technocrats" replaced "revolutionaries" only in 1976–81, after the "disasters of the Great Leap Forward and Cultural Revolution." Ibid., 33.
[91] Ibid., 35, 41, 46, 55.
[92] Ibid., 55. See also Róna-Tas, "Second Economy." "The best scholars on this topic [second economy] in Hungary were strongly involved in pushing for the legalization of private activities, and so it was imperative for them to argue that the second economy had few undesirable political side effects." Ibid., 80.
[93] Mark, "Discrimination," 507.   [94] Ibid., 508.   [95] "Society," 969.   [96] Ibid., 970–71.

those impregnated with ideology like the humanities.[97] Resilience also took the form of an "unspoken bargain between the old middle class and the state: they would be allowed limited educational and workplace opportunities as long as they confined themselves to narrow professional ambitions and remained politically inactive."[98]

Social Structure, Bifurcation, and Illiberalism

The preceding discussion has alluded to patterns of colonization of university places, professions, and other white-collar occupations by the old bourgeoisie, their children, and grandchildren in communist Hungary. More persecuted in the early years following the imposition of communist rule than, for instance, in communist Czechoslovakia, Hungary's bourgeoisie, according to sociological scholarship comparing the two countries, retained its predominant status as professional intelligentsia to a greater extent. In Czechoslovakia, those of worker background showed higher levels of social mobility. Poland and East Germany were apparently also more successful at resisting the colonization of higher education and the professions by the formerly privileged groups.[99] Explanations as to why this may be the case range from wartime decimation of large swathes of pre-communist bourgeoisie in Poland – 77 percent as compared to 10 percent for Hungary for that period by some estimates[100] – and in East Germany to the flight of many middle-class students to the Federal Republic.[101] Czechoslovakia's social trajectory furthermore had been arguably already on a distinct path in the early nineteenth century. Industrialization had made greater headway in the Czech lands, engendering a larger, more educated, and muscular working class, consequently making the bifurcation between the feudal agrarian society and the urban bourgeoisie less pronounced.[102] In their landmark cross-national sociological study, Robert Erikson and John Goldthorpe find Hungary repeatedly appearing "as having the lowest fluidity levels in transitions between classes within the non-agricultural sector," something they attribute to "the markedly hierarchical character of social relationships."[103] By contrast, similar

---

[97] "Discrimination," 512.   [98] Ibid., 519.
[99] On Poland, see Erikson and Goldthorpe, *Class Mobility*, 161–62.
[100] Mark, "Discrimination," 502. Citing Kovács and Örkény, "Promoted Cadres," 151.
[101] Mark, "Discrimination," 502.
[102] In contrast to Hungary, rural dwellers were also early on freed from dependencies on lords and brought into relations of capitalist production, notably in the textile industry. On this, see Stokes, "Social Origins," 37–39. Communist managers, the middle class, and the current business elite have, however, been heavily drawn from families of the pre-communist entrepreneurial bourgeoisie. Andrle, "Buoyant Class," 821.
[103] Erikson and Goldthorpe, *Class Mobility*, 153. As Stokes discusses, Romania, Serbia, and Bulgaria also exhibited lower levels of social bifurcation than Hungary: less dominant landlord/noble estates (in Serbia and Bulgaria destroyed by Ottoman rulers and landlords, who were in turn eventually displaced after nationalist uprisings and Russian intervention) and more emancipated, educated (in Serbia and Bulgaria consequential to nationalist drives), and

to patterns observed in Russia, "relatively high fluidity" is observed in "mobility between the farm sector and both the skilled and nonskilled sections of the industrial working class."[104] In other words, mobility encompassed movement between rural manual and industrial blue-collar workforce. A typical pattern would be peasants becoming factory workers and the latter returning to villages as workers servicing mechanized production.[105] Nevertheless, this does not mean that the latter-day peasant turned non-agricultural factory worker, skilled or unskilled – Hungary's "post-peasants" and "semi-proletarians"[106] – showed a strong intergenerational tendency of movement into the white-collar professional stratum. Fluidity between the working class and intelligentsia was found to be significantly higher in Poland than in Hungary.[107] Erikson and Goldthorpe argue that, while in Hungary following the 1956 uprising the regime sought accommodation with the old bourgeoisie, in Poland wartime social displacement led to a different outcome. In the latter,

around a third of all Poles with secondary or higher education were killed, and post-primary educational institutions were almost totally destroyed ... [and accordingly] large sections of the population were more or less coerced into mobility, both occupational and geographical, as the result of enemy occupation, deportation, and the destruction of the economy, and then in 1945 through the shifting of the national frontiers some 150 to 200 miles to the west.[108]

Consequently, "in the post-war period policies directed towards shaping new hierarchies and patterns of mobility were able to work in Poland on a social structure already greatly 'loosened' and, one may suppose, *with much reduced powers of resistance.*"[109]

The bourgeoisie emerged as a carefully and strategically selected target of Orbán's attack on the institutions of liberal democracy, much like westernized liberals have featured in Putin's witch hunts. In 2014, in a speech to ethnically Hungarian citizens in the Transylvanian region of Romania, "Prime Minister Viktor Orbán declared that Hungary had abandoned the liberal principles of societal organisation ... Orbán reasoned that as liberalism promotes the selfish interests of – often unpatriotic – individuals, only an illiberal democracy can devotedly serve the general interest of the whole nation."[110] At the same time, the illiberal message found fertile soil among not just rural strata but also many

economically empowered smallholder-type peasantries feeding into the middle class in the interwar period. Stokes, "Social Origins," 59, 61–62, 64. On Romania, see also Janos, "Modernization and Decay."

[104] Erikson and Goldthorpe, *Class Mobility*, 153.
[105] Szelényi found urban inequalities in Hungary rising in 1950–68, specifically in housing access. The state opted for "social merit" criteria of rewarding elite groups to attract skilled professionals to provincial towns. Szelényi, *Urban Inequalities*, 72–76.
[106] Erikson and Goldthorpe, *Class Mobility*, 154. [107] Ibid., 161–62. [108] Ibid., 162.
[109] Ibid., 162 (emphasis added). [110] Bíró-Nagy, "Illiberal Democracy," 36.

underpaid public sector and other white-collar employees habitually underprivileged in Hungarian society. While to the outside world the migration crisis in Europe and resultant rise in xenophobia have appeared to dominate electoral choices, analysts of Hungarian politics highlight domestic issues – rising inequalities, precarity, and the issue of the left-behind voter vulnerable to both material inducements and populist appeals.[111]

Education plays a pivotal role in shaping social bifurcation and polarization. Studies have highlighted that university degree holders were among the largest "winners" of the transition process, with very few "losers" registered among this category in studies of the fortunes of the various groups after 1989. By contrast, those with the least education, including citizens with only primary or vocational training, fared especially poorly. Unsurprisingly, survey evidence shows that educated citizens were more supportive of democracy after 1989.[112] One study charted the fortunes of the aristocracy in particular – a stratum that was expected to have all but disappeared under the weight of persecutions and expropriations. Although many emigrated, those who stayed quietly reinvented themselves as professionals and in the post-communist period were significantly likely to attain a high status, albeit one outside of the core of the political elite.[113] "Their prosperity," writes the author, "is visible also once [sic] considering the material dimensions of their living conditions (car, dimension of domicile, weekend house, jewelry, family valuables representing the past)." Furthermore, "Those results are especially remarkable because the analyzed group's parents and grandparents were not allowed to study at university and to get a corresponding job or position until the 1960s."[114] As in our Samara study, a spell of reverse mobility did not appear to in any way disadvantage subsequent generations. The aristocrat essentially resumed the pre-communist social trajectory of embourgeoisement fueled by habitual expectations of learning, cultivation, and professional achievement. Although the older generation would often have to forgo university studies, their children and grandchildren eagerly embraced higher education and the professions – but shunned the party-nomenklatura route of social advancement. Often eschewing direct participation in politics, respondents with an aristocratic pedigree in post-communist Hungary were supportive of parliamentary democracy and tended to espouse a conservative mindset that is characteristic of the center-right. In what is not dissimilar to Russia when it comes to the genesis of the middle class out of the ashes of the estates, the pedigree aristocrat more readily socialized and found common ground with the lower-status former gentry than they would in *ancien régime* Hungary. Common values – embodied in infatuation with foreign languages, refinement, and education – shaped associative ties as much as the *unsereiner* ("one of ours, our sort") identity of the fellow aristocrat.[115]

---

[111] Ibid., 32–34.   [112] Ibid., 33–34.   [113] Kézdy, "Descendants," 13.   [114] Ibid., 17.
[115] Ibid., 17–18, 20–21.

As in Russia, islands of liberalism serving as a check against authoritarianism are found in developed urban centers with a historically strong presence of the entrepreneurial and professional middle class. Jason Wittenberg finds persistence of the "backwardness" effect in Hungary's electoral politics in evidence already in the 1990s: "The less 'modern' a settlement ... the greater the congruence between pre- and postcommunist support for the Right," he finds.[116] As András Bíró-Nagy notes, Budapest emerged as the winner in transition; urban areas fared better than rural; and some territories, notably the rural parts of Hungary's Great Plain, became social laggards as low-skilled populations, those with but a few years of primary schooling, in particular entered a spiral of joblessness and poverty.[117] It is precisely the left-behind voter who would be vulnerable to workplace pressures or material inducements in elections. One account illustrates the resort to banal tactics in the arsenal of electoral manipulation that is characteristic of economically vulnerable electorates, urban or rural: "

"Two people from Fidesz came knocking on every door in our apartment building," a middle-aged woman from the working class district of Csepel told me ... less than a week before the election. "They asked every householder who they intended to vote for. If they replied Fidesz, they were given a box of foodstuffs."[118]

Summary

Rather than regarding Hungary's social structure as a product of the vagaries of post-communist transition or spatially uneven communist industrialization, I have contextualized it in the embourgeoisement and professionalization of Hungarian society following the mid-nineteenth century's liberal reforms. This juncture set some social groups on a trajectory of advancement and privilege that may show superficial variations under the distinct regimes that ruled Hungary in the twentieth century but that essentially preserved the relational characteristics of the social gulf between the aristocracy/gentry, burghers, and the rural and urban proletariat. During communism, institutional embeddedness in a vast hydra of well-developed modern professions and associations aided social adaptation and autonomy. In turn, the communist regime quietly shed its own ideological proclamations on social uplift, forced as it was to rely on the bourgeoisie to proceed with postwar reconstruction and industrialization. Historically better educated than Russia, and benefiting from the industrial development of Habsburg Austria's territories and markets, Hungary acquired the mantle of illiberalism, not consolidated autocracy.

---

[116] Wittenberg, *Crucibles*, 215. As measured by pre-1945 housing stock.

[117] Bíró-Nagy, "Illiberal Democracy," 33.

[118] Stephen Pogány, "Hungary's Lost Democracy," *Social Europe*, April 13, 2018. Available online at: socialeurope.eu/hungarys-lost-democracy (accessed May 20, 2020).

China: Introduction

China's wide discrepancy between meteoric economic change since the late 1970s and political stagnation has baffled observers. "Despite more than two decades of rapid socioeconomic changes, the core features of a Leninist party-state remain essentially unchanged ... The Polity IV Project consistently rates China as one of the most authoritarian political systems in the world," writes Minxin Pei.[119] Other international rankings have been likewise extremely unflattering: "On 'voice and accountability,' China was ranked 186, ahead only of failed states and the most repressive countries; it was comparable to Angola, Belarus, Vietnam, Saudi Arabia, and Afghanistan. China was behind most former Soviet-bloc states and major developing countries, including Russia, Ukraine, India, and Mexico."[120]

Social defiance of the communist autocracy is not uncommon in China. From environmental activism, to the emergence of the legal profession as a champion of the rule of law, to meaningful local participatory governance, to investigative journalism, and to everyday forms of resistance, China has featured many of the same hubs of discontent that constitute challenges to the authoritarian resilience-building strategies of rulers in Moscow or Budapest.[121] Yet astute observers have also noted a deeply particularistic nature of Chinese protest: "So long as Chinese popular protests target 'men' rather than 'principles,' a revolutionary challenge to the legitimacy of the regime remains unlikely," writes Elizabeth Perry.[122] Contrasts between Tiananmen – and its "anticlimactic outcome" – and the East European uprisings have also been made. "China [was] pictured as devoid of the institutional stage upon which the revolutions of 1989 were played out elsewhere in the communist world."[123] As Europe's post-communist regimes began to converge

---

[119] Pei, *China's Trapped Transition*, 4–5. For a historical summary of China's democratic experiments, see Nathan, *China's Transition*, 64–65.

[120] World Bank governance studies covering the 1990s and early 2000s. Pei, *China's Trapped Transition*, 5.

[121] See essays in O'Brien, *Popular Protest*; Chen, *Social Protest*; Nathan, *China's Transition*, 77–79; Plantan, "Tale of Two Laws"; and Repnikova, "Critical Journalists." In addition, in a large country, province-level variations in openness and democratization are highly likely, making national-level generalizations problematic. See Goodman, "Can China Change?" On Russian protest, see Smyth, *Elections*; Tertytchnaya and Lankina, "Electoral Protests"; Robertson, *Politics of Protest*; Smyth and Oates, "Mind the Gaps."

[122] Perry, "Permanent Rebellion?" Pre-Maoist China arguably featured more coordinated and widespread intellectuals-led activism. Ibid., 210–11. Unlike Russia, China also lacks an organized political opposition. See Koesel and Bunce, "Diffusion-Proofing," 95.

[123] Perry and Fuller cited in Wakeman, "Civil Society," 110. Scholars discussing Tiananmen and its aftermath also note weak evidence of cross-class coalitions between students, workers, and private entrepreneurs. Perry and Fuller, "China's Long March," 668. "Students, peasants, workers, and private entrepreneurs all organize on behalf of their own interests, but this activity has yet to coalesce into a 'public sphere' in which citizens cooperate in defining alternatives to state authority." Ibid., 679; and Chen writes: "The [Chinese] middle class as a whole is even less supportive of democratic principles and institutions in these areas than is the lower class," Chen, *Middle Class*, 77.

on the scale of authoritarianism, edging closer to China, scholars have embarked on a quest to identify similarities, not differences, among these cases. Researchers are now looking for clues in the contingencies of authoritarian resilience-building strategies of leaders, rather than searching for deep historical sources of variation.

If Hungary and Russia are countries with historically pronounced chasms between the *archaic* estates-derived *modern* bourgeoisie and the poorly educated rural masses, China is one where the entrepreneurial bourgeoisie and professional strata in a modern sense were only beginning to emerge at the start of the twentieth century. The gulf had not been between an estates-derived burgher and a poorly schooled rural peasant but between the latter and the old-style country gentleman. Peasants, not proletarians, became the unlikely allies in a Marxist revolutionary uprising; and by many accounts, communist China's white-collar professional stratum did not derive en masse from the minuscule pre-communist *Bürgertum*, since the nascent bourgeoisie would not have rooted itself to the same extent in modern institutions of learning, science, culture, and the professions as it did in Russia and Hungary. In China, it was rural society that took over the infrastructures of modernity over the course of communist rule.

The Contours of the Imperial Social Structure

The sociologist Hsiao-Tung Fei paints a portrait of late imperial Chinese society not dissimilar in very general terms to *ancien régime* Russia. The decaying court presided over an overwhelmingly rural society – some 80 percent of the population. Imperial China had also been undergoing profound change, but the social structure of the Qing era in important ways channeled the gelling of something approximating the social and class structure of Western societies and which began to take shape during the Republican period. The gentry – and the educated strata were overwhelmingly drawn from this group – increasingly gravitated toward the modern professions; and the peasant, while likewise escaping the buffalo and the plow in droves, would be far less likely than the country gentleman to pursue advanced learning and embrace human capital–intensive occupations. Dynamic urban centers of trade and commerce developed around treaty ports; though foreign-run, these were nurturing a new comprador class of mixed origin, not dissimilar to Russia's *raznochintsy*, and one whose values remained detached from the vast population of traditional rural society.[124]

Beyond these broad similarities, Russia and China featured major differences in the structure of pre-modern society as well as the substance and pace of development on the eve of revolutionary change; and these differences are even

---

[124] Fei, "Peasantry and Gentry." Like in Russia, subnational political economies variably affect social challenges to the regime in the post-Mao era. See Hurst, "Mass Frames."

more pronounced in the China–Hungary comparative dyad. Late Qing China remained a feudal empire sharply fractured into the gentry and peasant strata. Beyond the foreign representatives-run treaty ports, with their Western-owned industries and commerce, much of the indigenous economic activity – rural and industrial – remained confined to the countryside. In a classic account of the historical origins of democracy in modern states, Barrington Moore argues that "Imperial Chinese society never created an urban trading and manufacturing class comparable to that which grew out of the later stages of feudalism in Western Europe, though at times there were some starts in this direction."[125] Furthermore, "towns," writes Fei, "in traditional China are not founded on manufacturing or commerce. In China the chief industries, such as textiles, are mainly peasant occupations."[126] As William T. Rowe writes, in Europe, "which underwent structural changes in the economy from agriculture to manufacture, the areas of greatest population growth were major cities and the surrounding countryside. In China it was the reverse."[127]

Where, for the Russian and Hungarian gentry, industry, commerce, and a profession in the city were replacing the leisured lifestyle of the country gentleman, for the Chinese gentry-scholar the locus of social power and esteem remained "the big-family (or the house) system and the clan."[128] Where in Russia and Hungary, the peasant found a commercial outlet in the towns, in "most parts of China the periodical market takes the place of the town ... the permanent town has no place in the traditional rural economy."[129] The Chinese small town, as portrayed by Fei, barely made inroads into the specialized professional occupations as a lifestyle choice. As Fei muses,

Tea houses, big gardens, and magnificent residences are ... the paraphernalia of the gentry. From morning until nightfall, the leisured gentlemen gather in the tea houses to amuse themselves in sipping tea, in listening to the storytellers, in talking nonsense, in gambling, and in smoking opium. It would appear to a New Englander that such a town is no better than a concentration camp of voluntary deserters from life.[130]

Such a portrait of gentry idleness – which Fei likens to "medieval feudalism in western Europe"[131] – may find parallels in the Russian writer Goncharov's character of Oblomov, or in Gogol's Chichikov, the acquirer of serf "dead souls," but that was the gentry of Russia's mid-nineteenth century not the early twentieth.

Successive waves of revisionist historiography have questioned Fei's account of a "backward" empire in decay and his simplistic binary of the decadent gentry and the antiquated peasant as constitutive of the Chinese social structure, urban and rural. Rowe highlights the acceleration of the *embourgeoisement* and the fusion of literati and merchants "into a hybrid gentry-merchant class"

[125] Moore, *Social Origins*, 174.   [126] Fei, "Peasantry and Gentry," 6.
[127] Rowe, *China's Last Empire*, 91.   [128] Fei, "Peasantry and Gentry," 5.   [129] Ibid., 6–7.
[130] Ibid., 7.   [131] Ibid., 7.

in the post-Taiping era.[132] The gentry of pre-revolutionary China were increasingly embracing occupations like law, medicine, and commerce, which required training that transcended the classic learning preparing one for royal service and then dignified retirement into the country estate. Although toward the beginning of the twentieth century, one group of what became essentially a "bifurcated" gentry "continued to stress the primacy of classical education and long-established gentry roles in society," the so-called new-style gentry tended to "embrace more cosmopolitan educational and social agendas."[133] It is from these ranks that many of the late Qing era's "modern schoolteachers, bankers and investors in industrial, mining, and transportation enterprises, white-collar professionals in law, medicine, and journalism, and a new Chinese intelligentsia" emerged.[134] It is these men who also "made up the core of the local and provincial representative assemblies."[135] Further, Rowe's more up-to-date analysis highlights important changes in China's urban life in the late Qing era. Urban centers were reportedly heaving with philanthropy; a network of charitable institutions – like the merchant-run "benevolent halls" – provided shelter, care, and schooling for the urban poor;[136] and, in a country where sheer size precluded effective state penetration, merchant guilds and nascent self-governing bodies comprised of gentry and notables often assumed "quasi-governmental powers."[137]

Rowe's own account, however, also underlines the late embrace and institutionalization of modern forms of urban self-governance and the significance of state fiat in both the perpetuation of institutions that fundamentally shaped social relations – the 1,000-year state-run examination system – and their eventual reform. "Bureaucratic" not "entrepreneurial capitalism" characterized China's late nineteenth-century industrialization.[138] When the scholar-official Feng Guifen called for self-government reforms, his "call for the election of local subofficials – in effect a move toward representative self-government – was not derived from any foundational notion of natural rights, social contract, or popular sovereignty but instead arose from a perceived need to enhance the 'wealth and power' of the state."[139] The first municipal council was only established in 1905, in Shanghai,[140] a far cry from the nobility- and merchant-run local governance structures and the public sphere characteristic of Samara and other Russian cities well before that

---

[132] Rowe, *China's Last Empire*, 213. On the Chinese social structure, see Kuhn, "Chinese Views" and other essays in the volume. Thus, one finds estate-like categories of scholars who do "brain" work unlike those working with their hands; the former being the ruling group/the state, while the latter are the ruled. Ibid., 21.

[133] Rowe, *China's Last Empire*, 274. [134] Ibid., 274. [135] Ibid., 274.

[136] On philanthropy, see ibid., 119–21, 132, 213. [137] Ibid., 213.

[138] In what scholars liken to "state-owned enterprises of the Maoist era ... planning and oversight were conducted by state officials, while day-to-day management was left in the hands of private merchants." Ibid., 214.

[139] Ibid., 216. [140] Ibid., 213.

date. Moreover, a careful dissection of the evidence that Rowe provides, and other historical records, led critics to interrogate notions of an incipient public sphere, civil society, and autonomous urban governance by merchants and other notables.[141]

Education and the Professions

In late Qing China, the civil service exam remained virtually the sole route to literati status. As it became obsolete, the literati served in the state bureaucracy, tutored pupils privately, or taught at the local school; they also engaged in the ghostwriting or proofreading of bestselling books.[142] A few pursued occupations that even Rowe's sympathetic account characterizes as "incipient" in their development, notably medicine, law/litigation, or hydraulic engineering.[143] Even as shoots of trade and enterprise were emerging, many merchants continued to aspire to literatus status via the examination route, some going so far as to "castrat[e] themselves in order to become eunuchs and enjoy a position close to the throne."[144] In contrast to Russia and Hungary, China evidenced far less intergenerational fusion between aristocratic–merchant human and material capital, modern training, and the professions, something that in the former two countries would engender the development of not only the professions as sites of autonomous social action but also viable hedging strategies encompassing both private and public occupational as well as service sectors. The millennium-old system of recruitment into the bureaucratic and social elite in the form of the state-run civil service examination was only scrapped in 1905. "In its place, the court decreed the establishment of Western-curriculum schools in all localities." In 1904, in an empire of roughly 415 million people,[145] there were only 4,000 such schools, their student body estimated to be a mere 92,000 – or only 0.022 percent of the population. The first decade of the twentieth century witnessed a dramatic rise in schools and pupil numbers. Even so, the

---

[141] Many of Rowe's Hankou merchants (also referred to as Hankow) reportedly came from comprador backgrounds, often sojourners with primary residence or trade in treaty ports and working for foreign companies. The ostensibly locally initiated activities to coordinate the work of guilds and merchant civic activism came consequential to the fiat of imperial state representatives on the ground; and the purported tribune of the local public opinion and public sphere, the *Shenbao*, "which Rowe associated with the rise of an urban reformist elite that would presumably constitute China's new public sphere ... [had been] founded by an Englishman named Ernest Major, [and] was published in Shanghai, not Hankou." Wakeman, "Civil Society," 128. Hankou, classed in Rowe's account as a "city," itself was more of "an entrepot: a city of mixed origins inhabited by immigrants and sojourners." Ibid., 117. All these characteristics we could contrast with the merchant milieus, governance, and civic activism of Samara merchants, rooted in the city.

[142] Rowe, *China's Last Empire*, 112–13.   [143] Ibid., 113.   [144] Moore, *Social Origins*, 175.
[145] World population cartogram for 1900. Available online at: http://i.imgur.com/we6EIjI.png (accessed May 22, 2020).

estimated 52,000 schools encompassed a total of only 1.5 million pupils in 1909.[146] The gentry elite – beneficiaries of the examination system – only reluctantly and belatedly accepted the change and began adapting to the new system.[147] "Many members of the traditional gentry fought hard against it, and the hapless classically educated scholar, cast adrift after a lifetime of intense study, with his career aspirations suddenly snatched away from him, became a stock character in both reformist and popular fiction."[148] At the time of the Communist Revolution, in 1949, an estimated 70–80 percent of a population of roughly 500 million remained illiterate; and only a quarter of school-age children were enrolled in primary educational institutions, usually confined to provision of four to six years of schooling. Progression to secondary schools was also low – fewer than 10 percent of primary school attendees went on to pursue secondary education, which remained largely confined to the cities.[149]

[146] Figures as cited in Rowe; percentages calculated by author. Rowe, *China's Last Empire*, 260.
[147] Isolated literati were compared to the Russian intelligentsia in the sense of their social conscience and "profound" impact on the political sphere. Goldman, *China's Intellectuals*, 2. Yet, unlike the Russian intelligentsia, these "scholar-bureaucrats" operated from within state power. "Because the literati were members of the ruling elite," writes Goldman, "those who dissented were often close to the centers of power." Ibid., 3. Further, in contrast with Russian intelligentsia's embeddedness in legally sanctioned sites of occupational-civic domains, "since the rights of groups were never institutionalized, the literati lacked a corporate entity or autonomous organization with sufficient power to exert influence." Also, "since dissenting literati groups had only ideological justification and no institutional standing, they were unable to gain a hearing unless they had allies in positions of authority." Ibid., 4. In Goldman's account, literati become only influential when rival factions from within state power enlisted them in struggles with political rivals, whether in Qing or Mao's China. Ibid., 6–7. Indeed, "unlike China, the major way to express dissent in the Soviet Union is to go outside the system, to the underground or the foreign press. In the People's Republic, although underground writings have become increasingly important, the major method to get a hearing for divergent ideas in the 1960s and 1970s was, as in traditional times, through alliances with factions in the establishment. As in the past, this procedure had the characteristics of a quasi-official form of dissent." Ibid., 10.
[148] Rowe, *China's Last Empire*, 260. Still others, "a surprising number of long-established elite families adapted rather quickly to this revolutionary event, having even already taken the precaution of sending at least one promising son to a Western school before the axe fell on the examination system. Menfolk in this class retrained themselves to become Western school instructors or to enter other new and promising careers. With these kinds of adaptations, the 'gentry' – originally a product of the examination system – managed to survive the abolition of that system by a generation or two at the very least." Ibid., 260.
[149] Pepper, "Education and Revolution," 847–48. One study comparing the democratic attitudes of citizens in China, Australia, Germany, Great Britain, the United States, Austria, and Italy found: "By far the most intolerant group… were the Chinese illiterates." Nathan, *China's Transition*, 169. The landmark survey – "the first valid national-level sample survey on the political behavior and attitudes of the general populace ever done in a communist country" – was carried out in 1990. Ibid., 154; see also ibid., 196–97 for description of the survey. In the sample, 25.7 percent (!) of respondents were illiterate and 30 percent were educated at or below primary level only. Ibid., 158. Nevertheless, Chinese respondents were "substantially less likely to hold democratic orientations than people of the same educational levels elsewhere." Ibid., 171.

The modern professions were slow to emerge. Although the general contours of professionalization in China paralleled developments in Russia and Hungary – including when it comes to the role of occidental capital, inspiration, and models for the professions – China was a latecomer to these processes. In engineering, for instance, foreign investment in large infrastructure projects attracted non-native professionals; eventually, there would be state-led native investment into infrastructure and concomitant professional training; an engineer trained in native specialized schools supplemented and displaced the trainee of a Western engineering college. Professional associations emerged, as did periodicals debating issues in the craft; eventually a labor market surfaced that prized and rewarded the professional on a mass scale. Yet milestones associated with the establishment of the modern profession, demand for it, and the charting of educational trajectories streaming professional aspiration from a very young age are not to be found in the late eighteenth and early-to-mid nineteenth centuries, as in Hungary and Russia, but in the first quarter of the twentieth century. Take railroads: "In terms of professional training," writes Köll, "Chinese railroad engineering did not emerge until the late 1910s when railroad engineering institutes were established and began to produce engineers with expertise in railroad technology, geological sciences, bridge and tunnel construction, and so forth."[150] "An additional problem," according to Köll, "was the lack of vocational training to prepare Chinese employees for work on the railroads in the capacity of conductors, engine drivers, and signalers through basic technical and on-the-job training."[151] At the juncture between the end of the Qing Empire and the establishment of the Republic in 1911, several specialized training centers were established, specifically the Shanghai-based Imperial Polytechnic Institute, the Imperial University of Shanxi at Taiyuan, the Tangshan-based Engineering and Mining College, and the Imperial Beiyang University at Tianjin.[152] Yet, as late as 1920, a small handful of trained engineers continued to comport themselves like Chinese literati. One Western hydraulics engineer "stated with surprise that 'young Chinese engineers did not climb trees to put up flags' but instead used their own hired porters and instrument bearers. This attitude did not begin to change until engineering developed into an established discipline in Chinese universities and a profession with social prestige."[153]

When it comes to the law and jurisprudence, the Republican era not only ushered in occupational development but also featured professional impulses against state encroachments of the kind that I discerned in Hungary and Russia. A rigorous tiered structure of local nominations and exams, while reminiscent of the anointments into the literati, configured expectations and aspirations for an entirely different, modern, system of professional learning. "Empowered, differentiated, and emancipated" is how one revisionist scholar characterizes the emerging native legal profession of the Republican era modeled on the

---

[150] Köll, "Making of the Civil Engineer," 154.   [151] Ibid., 154.   [152] Ibid., 163.
[153] Ibid., 157.

jurisprudence of Meiji Japan.[154] These shoots of incipient autonomy were nipped in the bud, however, even before the establishment of the People's Republic of China (PRC) as the "insistent ideological and political intrusions of the aggrandizing Guomindang eroded this fragile arrangement and prefigured its PRC collapse."[155] Domestic strife and war with Japan put severe strains on the continuity of the legal examination system, thereby further hampering the development of a sizeable autonomous professional bourgeois stratum out of the ashes of the literati and the country squire. In 1946, there were only 737 provincial, branch, and local courts across China and 3,297 judges trained according to the reformed system of law and jurisprudence.[156] Law professionals were subjected to increasing "partification," something that already in the Guomindang period undermined the promise of professional autonomy.[157] The development of China's legal profession could be usefully contrasted with that of Hungary. For the latter, after 1848, if there was one chief guardian of the freedoms of parliamentary democracy, it was the judiciary. "Many of these institutions," writes Janos, "of course, had deep roots in the local soil, but after 1848 they were brought up to prevailing international standards: laws were codified, courts were separated from the other branches of government, and juries were drawn from the voting registers rather than from the ranks of the local nobility."[158]

Higher education statistics are also telling in the Russia–Hungary–China comparison. Most of China's top modern universities appeared at the very end of the nineteenth and beginning of the twentieth century. By that time, Russia had half a dozen established higher institutions of learning with a pedigree of close to 100 years, and, if we include St, Petersburg University, 200 years. Furthermore, in Hungary, as noted in the section "Educational Reforms Accompanying Liberalization," prior to the outbreak of World War I, in 1914, 16,300 students were already studying at several metropolitan and provincial universities.[159] Taking the population of Hungary in 1914 into account (some 21 million people), 16,300 students attending *higher educational institutions* represents 0.077 percent of Hungary's population – more than three times the number of pupils attending modern schools *below the university level* in China in 1904 as a share of total population.

China and Russia exhibited general similarities of semi-isolated status in the percolation of enlightenment and other developments associated with modernization and the genesis of liberalism in Western societies, in contrast to Hungary, which was tied to the wider European realm via its Austrian tutelage. Yet, while in China it is mostly the "conservative gentry" corps that exhibited some of the characteristics of the equivalent Western middle classes in matters of education,[160] in Russia a far more sizeable medley of state peasants, merchants, and *meshchane* were joining the noble and the clergyman as the

[154] Tiffert, "Chinese Judge," 115.   [155] Ibid., 115.   [156] Ibid., 138, table 4.10.
[157] Ibid., 143.   [158] Janos, *Politics of Backwardness*, 103.   [159] Hoensch, *History*, 47.
[160] Fei, "Peasantry and Gentry," 13.

educated professional men and women. Where in China the foreign missionary represented an alien incursion, in Russia a Western cultural-religious imprint in the provinces had long been embedded and indigenized in the fabric of urban societies, diffusing professional knowledge, schooling, and expertise. Where in China the aspiration for a modern Western-style education emerged from among the compradors of treaty ports, and where on the eve of the Communist Revolution only the second generation of gentry exhibited elements of a modern professional class, in Russia it had been organically nurtured within the modernizing estate structure of late tsarist society. By the start of the twentieth century, not only did a Russian adolescent with a family background of a noble, clergyman, merchant or urban *meshchanin* pedigree vaguely aspire to an occupation but for him – and increasingly for her – the path would already be precisely charted out and structured, from the home to the schooling system that streamed pupils into internships, higher institutions of learning, and the professions. Professional institutionalization thus went hand in hand with what Stinchcombe calls "spontaneous" cognitive aspirational maps. Where in China the native gentry had no say in the governance of the most dynamic centers of industry and commerce – the treaty ports – the Russian merchant, alongside the aristocrat, engaged in running elaborate institutions of elected urban self-rule.

Social Adaptation under Communism

We may thus distinguish China from both Hungary and Russia if we consider the late and very weak embourgeoisement-cum-professionalization of the society of native aristocrats, feudal lords, and literati. In Russia and Hungary, by the end of the nineteenth century and certainly well before the 1917 Revolution and the 1948 communist takeover, respectively, in the two states the aristocrat and the feudal lord became the civil servant, the professor, the medical consultant, and the engineer laboring in well-established professional institutions modeled on, networked with, and all but indistinguishable from those in the more developed parts of Europe. The elite society thus incorporated provided a buffer against social change. It would also be too powerful to decimate – and too valuable an asset – in the broader modernization drive.

In China, there existed hardly any incorporated bourgeoisie of this kind; and the feudal lord and literatus would be a supine and vulnerable target in the class-based "destratification" campaigns.[161] The peasant became Mao's ally and beneficiary in the fight for a communist future. China's old society, attracting the wrath of the Cultural Revolutionaries in the early 1960s, manifested itself more in the revival of "superstition," the building of temples, the resurrection of the popular folk ballad, the invocation of spirits to the burning of incense, and the discreet resurrection of the Three Character Classic in the village school – "a

---

[161] Chen, *Middle Class*, 46.

simple text used before liberation to teach children Confucian values"[162] – than in the quiet reconstitution of the vast network of autonomous professional spaces of the organization men and women or those of the museum society. While the peasant world remained steeped in medieval superstitions in Hungary and Russia alike well into the first half of the twentieth century, it coexisted with a parallel world of a comparably large stratum of the modern networked, skilled, institutionalized, and autonomous professional – rural and urban. Unlike in Russia or Hungary, China's minuscule old bourgeoisie did not transition into the privileged segment of the communist middle class as a mass stratum and failed to engender the human capital, educational credentials, and professional independence typically characteristic of this group.[163]

One study, by Bian and colleagues, systematically analyzed the social composition of the Chinese Communist Party and managerial apparatus in the decades following the Revolution.[164] Party membership is, of course, more of an indicator of the "cadre" route, which I distinguish from the professional trajectory of adaptation seen in estatist society. Yet it provides one indication of the general differences in the profiles of the white-collar middle classes in China and Europe's communist states. The authors highlighted pronounced variations between China and Central Europe's communist countries in education, a key indicator of social background. Furthermore, they singled out differences between Hungary, the Soviet Union, and China in particular:

Unlike in Hungary or the former Soviet Union, in China education did not become a criterion for party recruitment following the Communist revolution. Instead, only after the introduction of economic reforms in the late 1970s did individuals with higher education begin to be favored. This shift was consistent with the regime's new demands for human talents to modernize its economy.[165]

Prior to that shift, not only did education emerge as of scant importance as a criterion for party membership but the correlation between these two variables emerges as *negative* for some years. For many years, the Chinese

---

[162] Dikötter, *Cultural Revolution*, 31.
[163] Policies of "re-stratifying" society were abandoned or curtailed by the late 1950s. China initially, in 1956, adopted the Soviet wage system, with salary grades, bonuses, and prizes for "exceptional performance." "The Chinese," however, "were never very happy with this imported system, and began to soften some of its harder material aspects soon after its adoption." Parish, "Destratification," 87. The Cultural Revolution in 1966 ended perks until the 1970s. Ibid., 87. By the early 1970s, China was "slightly more equal than the average socialist state." Ibid., 89. "Under Stalin," by contrast, "in the 1930s and 1940s, Russia was a highly inegalitarian society ... While the Soviet Union was becoming more equal in the 1960s, China moved even faster to avoid the more inegalitarian aspects of the Soviet model and to adopt reforms of its own to become one of the most egalitarian socialist states." Ibid., 89.
[164] Bian et al., "Communist Party Membership." [165] Ibid., 833.

Communist Party drew on uneducated peasants, whereas in Russia, to a significantly higher extent, it drew on the old, educated, society.[166]

If one considers professional embeddedness of the bourgeoisie as a buffer against communist absolutism, the engineering profession is a case in point. Much like in Soviet Russia, pre-communist hubs of academic and professional excellence were appropriated to serve the country's developmental drive and the fabrication of a new cadre of "red engineers." As Joel Andreas notes, before the Cultural Revolution, the small old bourgeoisie continued to colonize the ranks of the professoriate and to feed sons and daughters into elite engineering institutions like Tsinghua University (TU). Here, these strata, the holders of cultural capital, would mingle with the children of the revolutionary cadre, the bearers of political capital, engendering a new generic technocratic elite. Yet, as the Cultural Revolution dawned, the pool of an educated "proletarian" cadre emerged as being so paltry that peasant adolescents with only a few years of primary schooling would be admitted.[167] Andreas makes it clear that it was because of the paucity of peasants and proletarians with even a rudimentary education, rather than a desire to completely scrape the bottom when it comes to educational credentials, that drove party ideologues to admit poorly trained peasants into the elite engineering schools: "In 1970, only about 10 percent of the eligible age group had graduated from junior middle school and only about 3 percent had graduated from senior middle school."[168] While the general contours of appropriation of bourgeoisie following the relaxation of class vigilance under Deng echo the zigzags in class vigilance observed in Russia, we also find a far narrower scope for the appropriation of the educated and professionalized strata before the Cultural Revolution, and in the late 1970s, as witch hunts subsided.[169] Andreas cites a survey that employed the communist

---

[166] Three distinct periods of cadre policy and recruitment were 1949–65, 1966–78, and 1979–93. In the first period, education did not significantly affect, or only marginally positively affected, the likelihood of membership; in 1966–78, it became *negatively* correlated with joining the CCP; only for 1979–93 is there a positive association between education and membership. Ibid., 810–12, 825.

[167] Andreas, *Red Engineers*, 206–7.   [168] Ibid., 207.

[169] Parish writes: "The pre-1949 order was never thoroughly inverted even in the first years of the regime. Capitalist parents from the 1930–49 generation were hindered in getting and keeping the best jobs. But their children regained part of their lost advantage in the 1950s and continued it into the 1960s." Parish, "Destratification," 102. The Cultural Revolution put an end to this practice: "Academic excellence was to be abandoned since it selected careerists and people of bad class origin." Ibid., 103. Consequently, as Martin Whyte notes, we observe an overall "gearing down" effect. Thus, male educational attainment, as measured by mean years of schooling, fell in the 1950s and early 1960s even as female education slightly rose. Whyte, "Sexual Inequality," 213, 214, figure 1. The difference with Russia was both one of kind (nature of the bourgeoisie and context nurturing it) and extent (size of the bourgeois stratum), even if there were broadly similar processes of adaptation. "The Chinese pattern is distinctive," writes Parish, analyzing Chinese data for the 1960s, which contrasts with global patterns of parental influence on occupational status. "The reshaping of the social order in China ... was more than just apparent; it was real, with old inequalities being drastically reduced and with education, occupation, and income levels being brought down at the same time." Parish, "Destratification," 107.

regime's new class categories; here, the share of "old" elites was estimated based on family status immediately preceding the 1949 Revolution. The categories of "landlords" and "rich peasants" – the rural elites – comprised 4.3 percent of China's population, while the "old urban elite" of "capitalists," white-collar employees, and independent professionals together comprised a minuscule 1.4 percent of the population (of these, 0.2 percent were "capitalists" and 1.2 percent white-collar or independent professionals). Out of an adult population of close to 400 million, only 185,000 people (less than 0.05 percent) had a college degree in 1949.[170]

The bulk of China's professionals thus emerged from within the peasant milieus of Mao's Cultural Revolution China, and not from a much more sizeable stratum of the pedigree expert. Chen goes so far as to state that, consequential to Maoist policies, "the pre-1949 middle class ceased to exist."[171] In its place an entirely new middle class emerged in the post-Mao era. Such accounts, nevertheless, leave out the question of why other communist states like Russia differed from China in the scope and extent of proletarianization and peasantification in the professions – something that I attribute to the feudal estates-derived bourgeoisie that was densely enmeshed in professional institutions, possessed a vested intergenerational interest in preserving them, and leveraged institutionally-embedded resources to pursue status advantages. We may also look at variations in the timing and nature of external shocks with the potential to affect regime consolidation and legitimacy. In Soviet Russia, famine, epidemics, and war with Nazi Germany prompted a U-turn in reliance on experts. By contrast, in China during the later years of the Cultural Revolution, the menace of the restoration of capitalism by the post-Stalin "revisionist renegade clique" provoked just the opposite policies of attempted extermination of capitalists.[172]

Of course, one straightforward explanation for the variations in class policy in China and Soviet Russia would be the role of leadership, an argument that I consider less persuasive.[173] Stalin, like Mao, may have been a tyrant but there was something about Russia's society that have pushed him to reverse the policy of "specialists-baiting" early on. Overemphasizing Mao's leadership or Deng's

---

[170] Andreas, *Red Engineers*, 62–63, and data in 63, table 3.1.   [171] Chen, *Middle Class*, 48.

[172] Andreas, *Red Engineers*, 135. Shlapentokh distinguishes between Stalin's repression of thousands of intellectuals, punctuated with statements of admiration, respect, and support for them, and Mao's attacks on the intelligentsia "as a group." Further, hostility toward intellectuals "was manifested in even more conspicuous and cruel ways during the Cultural Revolution." Shlapentokh, *Soviet Intellectuals*, 10, 18. Nathan contrasts Soviet and Chinese academic dissidents' discourses on human rights; the latter emerge as lacking a "firm idea of human rights as something inherent and inalienable." Nathan, *China's Transition*, 85. The contrast with Taiwan is also instructive. Here, geopolitics and intricacies of class structure, affinities, and alliances helped the bourgeoisie. Davis, *Discipline*, 192.

[173] Contingency and leadership, of course, also matter. On the merits and limitations of the "strong leader" approach to explaining policy choices and ability to push them through, see Brown, *Myth of Strong Leader*.

policy choices may take away from an appreciation of the underlying social dynamics driving these decisions, and indeed the societal undercurrents and institutions imposing boundaries and constraints as to what leaders can or cannot achieve.[174] In China, there had hardly been any bourgeoisie and professionally incorporated and networked middle class to serve as discreet and subtle custodians of established institutions, or to impress on the revolutionary regime that their services were indispensable to the modernization of the country. Nor would there be the same kind of record of spatial and societal islands of a highly educated and politically discerning bourgeoisie that would provide a relatively robust check on authoritarian consolidation and resilience in the late twentieth and early twenty-first centuries. Not only does China's new middle class owe its origins to the class and welfare policies of the communist state but, whether in the private or public sector, it continues to be embedded in structures of state patronage and dependency, disincentivizing potentially confrontational policies vis-à-vis the political regime.[175] Chen's recent dissection of China's *new* middle class summarizes the broad orientations of this stratum: "Most members of the middle class do not appear to support democratization and democracy in China, in large part due to their close and dependent relationship with the current party-state."[176]

---

[174] Thus, in explaining why China failed to democratize, Pei focuses on policy decisions and deliberations of the senior party elite, invoking "Deng's own hostility toward democracy" as making "a dramatic democratic breakthrough unlikely, if not impossible." Pei, *China's Trapped Transition*, 57. In the conclusion, Pei writes: "While it is true that economic growth and modernization can create favorable conditions for the emergence of liberal political regimes, China's slow movement toward political openness in spite of twenty-five years of rapid economic growth suggests that the choices of its ruling elites are the real determinants of democratization." Ibid., 207. Nathan summarizes nine sets of proposed "inconclusive" causes of China's democratic failures: ideology, national security problems, militarism, political culture, underdevelopment, the "peasant mass" issue, flaws in institutions, democrats' moral failures, and elite transactions theory – but not the bourgeoisie or professions. Nathan, *China's Transition*, 66–76.

[175] See Chen, *Middle Class*; Wright, *Accepting Authoritarianism*. Neither the state-engendered elite strata nor the newly rising middle class from among farmers and private sector employees have constituted a prospective challenge to the regime due to reliance on the party-state for welfare. Ibid., 3. Also, "[t]he wide gulf between the rich and poor has bred divergent lifestyles and interests that have limited any potential feeling of common cause or trust between the upper and lower 'classes.'" Ibid., 3. Further, unlike in "early developers" and nonsocialist legacy states, citizens and entrepreneurs expect state paternalism. Ibid., 28–29, 31–34.

[176] Chen, *Middle Class*, 90. At least half of the middle class are estimated to be public sector employees, including in state-owned enterprises. Ibid., 94. Chen finds significant negative correlation in survey responses between state employment and support for democracy. Ibid., 115. While those from the nonstate-sector middle class are more likely to protest and organize, the state-dependent middle class tend to participate in official channels like elections. Ibid., 137, 139. Higher education positively correlates with democratic values, an "inconsistency," Chen argues, that "deserves a separate and more thorough study." Ibid., 116.

CONCLUSION

This chapter has completed the journey of uncovering the reproduction of the bourgeoisie under the weight of some of the twentieth century's most brutal socially transformative dictatorships. Emerging as it did out of the ashes and bifurcations of the feudal *Ständestaat*, the nascent bourgeoisie had been superbly endowed with reserves most prized in the context of new knowledge-based economies – a combination of assets that could pay for education as well as the human capital pedigree and cultivation that would make access to education facile, habitual, and routinized. While Hungary had been more advanced than Russia, and certainly more ahead than China, in bestowing universal public education on the masses, even these far-reaching measures would fail to bridge the chasm between the distinct prongs of a bimodal society. As the revolutionary era dawned, Russia and Hungary would have already been saturated by the hydra of a well-institutionalized, well-networked, autonomous professional strata overwhelmingly of aristocratic, gentry, burgher, and clergy stock. Truncating the hydra as part of the most visible high-profile witch hunts would spectacularly fail to annihilate the autonomous educated substratum. To account for the intergenerationally self-reproducing dynamics of social resilience and persistence, I invoked Bourdieusian perspectives on intangible drivers of social distinction and Stinchcombe's logic of cognitive maps, which habitually structure the role models and the heroes to emulate in erecting life's educational-professional milestones. These reverberated across the ideological super-impositions that touted the qualities of the would-be-new heroes and new role models of the revolutionary regimes. The privileged estatist bourgeoisie became the silent custodian of institutions and values that nurtured the democratic promise of post-communism, much as it remained the unwitting accomplice to the seemingly *ad perpetuum* gulf that cleaved it from the latter-day illiterate peasant society. More broadly, the sociological exploration of these mechanisms of social reproduction would hopefully invite the reader to ponder on the effectiveness of redistributive justice solutions as a panacea against social inequalities. *Society*, not *capital*, in the twentieth and twenty-first centuries, perhaps proffers some answers as to why social justice has proven to be such an elusive goal.

Afterword

The drive from Samara to the village of Tyagloye Ozero takes two hours. The hustle and bustle of the city quickly gives way to a green mass of forest. Slowly, the trees recede, shrinking to low-lying shrubs and then fading completely into the flatness of the Russian steppe – an immense, mute, empty space unimaginable just a short time ago. On and on and on, the sense of time dissolves into the unchanging beauty and silence of emptiness. After what seems like an eternity of evenness and expanse, some signs of settlement – a few cottages scattered here and there. Then, finally, the signboard of Tyagloye with its brooding dark lake. So remote and yet still alive. There is a kindergarten and a school, some small children chasing geese on the empty road, and the haunting call of the rooster. Wooden houses, some freshly painted, some decaying, but a dignified neatness and order throughout – hardworking (*rabotyashchiye*), not wealthy (*zazhitochnyye*), is how the locals prefer to describe themselves. I picture my father, sitting on that unpaved road outside his home, his first memory of his mother reaching out to him when he was four: "Volodya." Born to parents still confined to the Far Eastern Gulag, the newborn was ushered to the steppes, into the bosom of his grandmother. Here, he first heard from her the commandments of the Bible.

Tyagloye Ozero was originally a settlement of Molokans,[1] who, from at least the beginning of the nineteenth century, found a haven here to practice their faith and to thrive. Local elders still know on which side of the road and village the Molokans and the Orthodox Christians lived, and which families are descended from which faith. American Baptists preached here in the 1920s, converting many Molokans to their denomination. Lankin remains one of the most common surnames; even the district mayor is a Lankin – a descendant of

---

[1] Molokans were a Christian sect whose traditions, especially their consumption of milk (*moloko*) during fasting periods, did not conform to those of the Russian Orthodox Church, which regarded them as heretics.

early settlers. One, my great-grandfather, ran the village shop, his camel transporting goods to and from the markets, perhaps near and perhaps far and wide.

This is the story of one family, but it is also a narrative of twentieth-century Russia. Already at the outset, a few impressionistic snapshots raised a myriad of questions. How did this village survive – in particular, how did its community, faith, and traditions remain seemingly intact for so long? How was it that people were meeting, falling in love, and starting families in the Gulag?[2] And why do some villagers still practice their ancient faith? How were American Baptists able to roam the steppes of the Soviet Union in the 1920s apparently unhindered? How is it that these villagers still stubbornly bear the imprint – and genes – of the settlers of a bygone era? How can we reconcile their resilience with the legacies of the Gulag and with the communist project itself, which displaced, decimated, and bathed its peoples in blood? Was the Gulag what we think it was, if love, marriage, and even careers in geology, cartography, and pedagogy were found within its oppressive confines? And, finally, does the entire Soviet project live up to what we have come to think of it?

My book has sought to make sense of some of these dilemmas by looking at the bigger picture of social structures and social resilience. If families survive, adapt, and carry on, so too do their society's patterns of stratification: the situation in which Russians found themselves at the dawn of communism shaped how and where they continued to live. The imperial estate was like the Procrustean bed that bent and molded the free citizen and the subject – significant even as an incentive to escape from the clutches of serfdom. I have demonstrated how the estate structured both the market and the professional and organizational dimensions of the Russian bourgeoisie. Remote and distant, even Tyagloye became engaged in trade, credit, and commercial relationships, linking this far-away corner of the governorate to markets in Central Asia. Here, sober, enterprising Molokans, free well before the 1861 emancipation that reshaped the peasant world of European Russia, instilled grammar in their children, barely one generation away from the *meshchanstvo* of Samara. The faraway modesty of the rural entrepreneur's village shop, however, set him apart socially from the well-heeled merchants of urban Samara. The latter, sharing a high school desk with the aristocrat would, if he survived the bloodbath of repression, join organization men and the best and brightest of academia, the arts, and the world of theatre and film. Connected, networked, and engaged, these thespians of the museum society, organization men and women, and the pop-up cultural brigade were also equipped with the skills, tools, and capital needed to retain their independence from the state, even when rooted in its structures. Statistically, there were few such people – but then, how

---

[2] For example, my paternal grandparents – my grandfather was a geologist and my grandmother an accountant – met as Gulag "inmates" and, on their release, got married and lived happily thereafter for decades.

many were needed to become curators of provincial art museums, directors of local opera houses, or rectors of typical mid-sized towns' universities, or indeed even Moscow or Leningrad? The remaining bulk of professionals, of the middling sort, as I have argued, would have descended from the urban and rural *meshchane*, as well as the educated village entrepreneur, the artisan, and the rural intelligentsia. Together, they became the middle class and the professional-cultural elite, umbilically linked to their origins among the educated free, or relatively free, estates of Russia's *ancien régime*.

In embarking on this project, I had much to work with as regards the downfallen high-profile aristocracy or the collectivized peasantry. Yet I sought in vain to find any trace of discussion concerning the post-revolutionary fate of the clergy, the *meshchane,* or the institutions of the estate – buried as they had been in narratives of the grand revolutionary rupture. Nor were wider class theories, unable to shed the baggage of Marxism, helpful in making sense of the trans-epochal, trans-generational, multilayered complexity of social occupations and relationships that I found in the stories of individual families living through the Revolution. Recent polemics on social injustice, centered as they have been on redistributive solutions to inequality, have done little to address the question of how it survived the worst of the twentieth century's conflagrations. If anything, they have skirted and swept the issue under the carpet: if we assume – as do recent "rock star economist" works on inequality defined in purely monetary terms – that the twentieth century was the great leveler, then we have nothing to decipher and explain. Yet my research makes clear not only society's capacity to resist the pressures of de-stratification but also the built-in logic of inequality in the socioeconomic policies themselves, for no attempt to educate, elevate, and dignify can succeed without the enabling, didactic, persona of the expert – the teacher, the medic, the propagator of culture to the masses, and, yes, the professor. Yet, in Marxist analyses in particular, the knowledge bearer, the intellectual, and the specialist have remained in the shadows as "class" actors of sorts in their own right.[3] As Alvin Gouldner bitingly observes, accounting for the "invisible" group[4] – often doubling as the public critic of ills in society – as simultaneously the symbol, the practitioner, and the embodiment of intractable inequalities would place the intellectual in the uncomfortable position of "account[ing] for *themselves.*"[5] Gouldner formulates this dilemma as that of the "cameraman."[6] The cameraman who draws our gaze to urgent social problems observes, reveals, and interrogates yet

---

[3] I do not analytically distinguish the intelligentsia from the generic middle class, entrepreneurial, or other high-status groups: the purported self-ascribed disregard for materialism or preference for high-minded pursuits do not negate this group's material, social, and cultural distinction from the peasant and worker strata.

[4] Gouldner, *Future of Intellectuals*, 11.

[5] That is, as a class that does not feature as such in Marxist analysis. Ibid., 58 (emphasis in original).

[6] Ibid., 9.

remains hidden behind the camera and, as such, beyond the scrutiny of class relations – we therefore never clamor for his revolutionary downfall – nor, of course, would he clamor for his own fall from the pedestal of social esteem.

Russia's estate structure fused with modern processes of the organizational development and professionalization of the middle class to produce, on the eve of the Revolution, many such cameramen, solidly incorporated into institutions of learning, the professions, and the arts and embodying an active, concerned, and discerning public. The long path that separated these groups from those least advantaged goes all the way back to the tiered and titled system of estates and rank, which only further privileged those already educated and already partly free at the time of the nineteenth century's emancipatory reforms that did little to establish a solid foundation of accessible schooling. The communist regime's relentlessly appropriative logic unavoidably led to the reincorporation of this estatist educated society of professionals and entrepreneurs into an elite layer or *prosloyka*. Many older members of this cohort, due to their background or because they had made known their distaste for Bolshevism, suffered repression. However, those barely out of the gymnasium were the equivalent of the lucky generation, born in the right place at the right time and into the right social position.[7] Educated to perfection in imperial schools of the highest caliber, often privately, they were too young to have tarnished themselves with a political stance but old enough to join the ranks of the relatively privileged middle class. Soviet citizens in name, this and the older generation absorbed all the values of the social milieus of their childhood, adolescence, and upbringing, all far removed from the drumbeats of the revolutionary new dawn. Discreetly and quietly, they persevered in transmitting these values to their children and grandchildren; and they used established institutions of the professions, the arts, and academia as platforms to procure, retain, and safeguard their autonomy as individuals, entrepreneurs, professionals, and citizens.

The book, of course, cannot satisfactorily address all the important conceptual questions that the analysis of one country may have raised. One avenue for further research would be to more precisely embed the merchant-trading-*meshchane*, lesser aristocracy, and clergy-type strata within comparable social categories in other settings; and we need a fuller exposition of the social possibilities of these groups going beyond the focus in earlier literature on their role in the grand coalitional dynamics during revolutionary strife. That would involve comparing the Russian estate with cognate feudal institutions in, say, England and France and tracing the relevant groups' fortunes against the relational tapestries of the social structure in the respective national contexts. The superior human capital of, for example, the clergyman or country gentleman-scholar in eighteenth- and nineteenth-century England or France may carry similar potential for conversion of old knowledge into the modern

---

[7] Gladwell, *Outliers*.

professional economies of twentieth-century Europe, much as it did for the clergyman, *meshchanin*, or provincial merchant in Russia. Russia is, of course, distinct from states conventionally featuring as templates for analyses of historical origins of social democracy via enfranchisement not only because of the "backwardness" aspects – and perpetuation of serfdom long after it disintegrated elsewhere – but also because of the far more sustained, ideologically sanctioned, and fanatical execution of the vision of a classless society. Look at the Communist Manifesto of Marx and Engels and you would recognize just how far and to the letter the Bolsheviks went in their *intention* to achieve communism, fantastical as it may seem to the present-day scholar rereading this famous treatise. Yet the excesses of communism also make Russia a useful background case of an outlier that suggests the plausibility of the social mutation of the educated feudal estates into the modern professional in far more benign leveling contexts.

The Hungarian and, of course, Russian cases also suggest that, in future research, we should pay more attention to the interaction of the mechanisms outlined in this book with land inequality. One extension of the analysis would be to examine the question of reform sequencing and synchronicity during peasant emancipation and agrarian restructuring. Russia's failure to supply a wide, quality, and all-encompassing education to peasants before or after emancipation significantly hampered social mobility, as I have showed. Social inequalities mutated from being land-based to human capital–derived. Even in Hungary, the rolling out of universal schooling did not end the rigid social bifurcation because of the partial nature of agrarian reform and perpetuation of quasi-feudal economic relationships in the countryside as late as the interwar period. Yet questions of education opportunity during important processes of agrarian change are just as pertinent, say, in England where capitalist relations permeated the countryside and feudalism disintegrated much earlier but where enclosures not only pushed peasants off the land but left them destitute, leaving them with no choice but to flee to the industrial urban slums and send their children to the factory, not the school.[8] And this, I conjecture would also shape the probability of which groups would become the middle class in a modern sense of a skilled white-collar professional variety.

Finally, the tension between the historically reproduced autonomous professionally incorporated stratum and the feudalism-originating inequitable distribution of human capital raises new questions for democratic theory. The totalizing aspect of information control in Soviet Russia made it hard to trace preferences and values concerning the political system and regime in the same systematic way as it was possible to do for the inequality aspect of my analysis. As I have shown, not only were surveys charting trajectories in social stratification conducted by sociologists in Soviet Russia but the state asked for

---

[8] Marx's account is persuasive on enclosures and their connection to social degradation and educational opportunity. Marx, *Capital*, 1:628–29, 877–95.

this information. No such comparable evidence is available across the communist decades for popular political values that would allow us to extrapolate democratic preferences, beyond the tiny handful of high-profile dissidents and the eclectic memoir and diary literature. Nevertheless, I have tried to infer these from the structures of autonomy and active public sphere embedded in the institutions of the estate, the professions, and education in imperial and Soviet Russia. Cross-regional analysis also suggested covariation between the educated estates and democratic preferences in imperial, and in post-communist, Russia. However, we are left with a cognate, broader, set of questions intrinsic to social bifurcation even if a large social segment has the autonomy, human capital, and values to challenge and scrutinize political authority. A country that has an intergenerationally resilient, educated, professional bourgeoisie that survives the twentieth century's most brutal leveling dictatorships may have the seeds of democratic promise; but the inequities intrinsic to the resilience of privilege within the knowledge segment of the demos in Russia and elsewhere may well also shatter faith in democracy's ability to deliver social justice, leading to anger, vulnerability to populist appeals, and social resentment of those left behind.

The limitations and unanswered questions aside, I hope that the perspective presented here does much to question long-established paradigms about what the communist project really meant in terms of shaping the fabric of society. Not only does it excavate the *longue durée* of the sources of grievance among the habitually left-behind that take us back to serfdom, the ennoblement of the aristocracy, religious schism, or the frontier – a pessimistic, deterministic, dead end; it also provides a glimmer of hope as to the regenerative capacity of the free and autonomous society of the Russia that I love.

Supplementary Appendices

A ARCHIVAL SOURCES

The bulk of the archival materials comes from the Central State Archive of Samara Oblast (*Tsentral'nyy gosudarstvennyy arkhiv Samarskoy oblasti*, TsGASO) and the Samara Oblast State Archive of Social-Political History (*Samarskiy oblastnoy gosudarstvennyy arkhiv sotsial'no-politicheskoy istorii*, SOGASPI). They include official documents, correspondence, and statistical records of local party, soviet, and government branch bodies charged with implementing state policy in Samara. TsGASO materials are sourced from collections (*fond*) R81: Executive Committee of the Samara *guberniya* Soviet of Worker, Peasant, and Red Army Deputies (SWPRAD); R353: SWPRAD Executive Committee's Division of People's Education of Samara Guberniya; R558: Samara Scientific Local Knowledge Society of the Middle Volga Region; R828: The Middle Volga *kray* SWPRAD in Samara City; and R2344: SWPRAD Division of Management of the Executive Committee of the Samara Uyezd in Samara City. Papers covering the brief period of KOMUCH rule in Samara are sourced from R3931: Bureau for Public Enlightenment of KOMUCH in the City of Samara. The TsGASO Syzran branch *fond* R187 containing materials for the Executive Committee of the Syzran City Soviet of Deputies of Workers was also consulted.

The SOGASPI materials were sourced from *fond* 1 containing papers of the Samara *guberniya* Committee of the All-Union Communist Party of Bolsheviks (VKPb) in Samara City, including protocols of sessions of party organs; materials of public enlightenment bodies; papers of commissions for purges of Soviet bodies of "alien" elements; papers of Soviet, professional, cooperative, and public organizations; information notes of the Samara *guberniya* division of OGPU concerning political sentiments of particular groups of citizens; and reports on antireligious propaganda and activities of religious organizations. These materials are valuable for understanding the processes and limits of policy implementation and changes in policy concerning estates and classes in the 1920s and 1930s.

In addition, I assembled materials concerning two leading public and professional figures whose careers span the pre- and post-revolutionary periods, sourced from the Khardina and Kavetskiy archives, from TsGASO, *fond* 300, and TsGASO, *fond* R4135, respectively. The Khardina papers cover regulations concerning the gymnasium that A. Khardina founded in Samara; day-to-day administrative matters, including admission of students, staff salary payments, and communications with exam and supervisory boards; and memoirs written by and about former pupils who became successful professionals in Soviet Russia. The materials also cover Khardina's post-revolutionary professional career. The Kavetskiy papers mostly cover the professional career of Samara's leading medic and medical dynasty spanning the late 1800s and the Soviet period and as such allow us to trace the reproduction of professional institutions and networks. Materials concerning the operation of a leading agency soliciting, processing, and managing foreign currency transfers in the 1930s, Torgsin, were assembled from TsGASO, *fond* 1078. These cover letters between various Soviet agencies, reports, and estimates of earnings from transfers; they also provide a window into perceptions of how past estate structure continued to matter as a signifier of social wealth in the various regions in the 1920s and 1930s.

Finally, an extensive collection of materials comes from the Constantine Neklutin archive, deposited with the Cammie G. Henry Research Center at Northwestern State University of Louisiana.[1] These materials – letters, bank account details, records of remittances to Soviet Russia, documents, photographs, essays, mementoes, and communications with other émigrés – cover the period from the 1800s to the late 1970s, allowing us to trace social mobility, social networks, and the material, educational, and professional fortunes of a large family of merchants, many of whom stayed in Soviet Russia. The materials were deposited by the US-based descendants of Constantine, who emigrated to America in the early 1920s. This is not a well-known archive, and, as far as I am aware, I am the first scholar of Russian politics to have accessed it.

B THE 1897 CENSUS

Overview

The 1897 census was the first census that covered the entire territory of the Russian Empire. Since at least the 1850s, census data were collected in isolated provinces (*gubernii*). The census was unprecedented in that it generated systematic socioeconomic data comparable across Russia's territories. It took at least a year for the census bureau to process these records, employing the latest computational techniques. These were adapted from the more advanced

---

[1] Information available from: library.nsula.edu/collections/ (accessed November 1, 2020).

industrialized European states in which regular population surveys had become the norm by the end of the nineteenth century.[2]

Census Data Analyzed

The census data help us ascertain the drivers of developmental and specifically human capital as well as political variations as they relate to the estate, in the imperial and post-communist periods. As units of analysis, I chose the *uyezd* level, which is roughly translated as "district." In some regions referred to as *okruga*, *uyezdy* were the next unit of administration below the regional, *gubernii* level. It is the unit most closely corresponding to present-day Russia's districts, or *rayony*, in that it often encompasses a town of local significance and surrounding rural areas. Many of the *uyezd* center towns have retained their status as *rayon* centers in present-day Russia – in what reflects their significance then and continued importance as a local hub of commerce, industry, or services now – despite the many administrative perturbations in the Soviet and post-Soviet periods. For each of the variables employed in the analysis, the data are *uyezd* averages – that is, they are based on statistics for both urban and rural areas in an *uyezd*.

Only districts that are now in Russia – and, of course, only those administratively part of imperial Russia at the time of the 1897 census – are in the imperial dataset. For instance, only districts of Turgayskaya *oblast* (Kustanayskiy and Aktyubinskiy *uyezdy*), much of which is now part of Kazakhstan, that are now administratively part of Russia, in Orenburg *oblast*, are analyzed; and territories of the region of Tyva, which became a Russian protectorate in 1914, or Kaliningrad, which Russia annexed from defeated Germany in 1945, are not in the dataset. The objective is to capture as faithfully as possible present-day Russia's geographical palette of territories surveyed in the 1897 census, without including the vast empire's other lands, say, in present-day Poland, which might affect our results. The total number of observations in the dataset corresponding to the *uyezdy* is 423.

C   DISTRICT MATCHING

To ensure inter-temporal observational equivalence, I matched *uyezdy* – administrative units below the *guberniya* level – with Russia's current *rayony* – administrative units below the region level. The *rayony* are third-order administrative entities within Russia's regions and include subdivisions of large cities (*gorodskiye rayony*).[3] Along with cities that have a special independent status, *rayony* correspond to the roughly 2,700 territorial

---

[2] Troynitskiy, *Obshchiy svod*. For an overview of the planning, issues, and challenges in the design and execution of the census, see Safronov, "Iz istorii."
[3] Clem et al., "Urban-Rural."

electoral commissions.[4] As the political geographers Ralph S. Clem and Peter R. Craumer note, *rayony* vary considerably in territorial size and population.[5]

Matching *uyezdy* with *rayony* is an imperfect solution, given the many administrative changes that Russia's territories experienced over the Soviet and post-Soviet periods, but one that enables us to roughly map statistical data for imperial districts onto current Russia's administrative *rayony*. I here note the difficulties involved in this exercise. For many districts, particularly those in historically more developed European parts of Russia, matching districts was relatively straightforward, since they retain the names of the original *uyezdy*, which in turn often correspond to major regional towns and surrounding rural areas. Even in such instances, however, the original *uyezd* had often been carved up, its territories straddling several *rayony* of a given region, or multiple regions, in present-day Russia. For most *uyezdy*, we thus have multiple *rayony* in the post-Soviet district-level dataset. If more than one *uyezd* covered a particular present-day *rayon*, I chose a matching *uyezd* based on the historical presence of an important town. In other words, the *uyezd* would be assigned to a *rayon* based on which *rayon* ended up with an important *uyezd*-level town or *uyezd* center. In Siberia and the Far East, many *uyezdy* covered large territories and had been subdivided into multiple *rayony* as part of Soviet-era administrative reorganizations that began in the early 1920s and continued through the Soviet period. In practice, this means that, in the dataset combining pre-Soviet, Soviet, and post-Soviet data, one *uyezd* appears multiple times for several *rayony*. Accordingly, although the imperial dataset covers roughly the same territory as present-day Russia (excluding Kaliningrad and Tyva), there are 423 observations, corresponding to *uyezdy*, and roughly 2,000 observations in the post-Soviet dataset, corresponding to post-Soviet *rayony*.

The 1897 census also has data for *volosti*, the smaller administrative units below the *uyezd* level. Employing *volosti* in lieu of *uyezdy* data would not make sense, however. Many *volosti* would have been engulfed by the larger, historically significant, *uyezd* towns. Employing statistics that average out data for the *uyezd* in my view far more accurately captures the wider processes of modernization characteristic of a given territory – in that it includes statistics for both the *uyezd* urban centers and surrounding rural areas – than if we were to employ *volost*-level data. Matching *volosti* with present-day sub-*rayon* districts would have been a far more daunting – if not an impossible task – than the already formidable one of matching *uyezdy* with present-day *rayony*.

The main sources of information for matching districts were Wikipedia entries for present-day *rayony*. These entries often list the *uyezd* that the present-day *rayon* formed part of at the time of the 1897 census. Each of the

---

[4] Ibid., 382.
[5] Clem, "Russia's Electoral Geography," 397; and Clem et al., "Urban-Rural," 382.

Wikipedia entries was cross-checked with other sources, notably other historical records about the district history obtained from either official websites of municipalities; historical maps listing administrative status of towns; or other online and print materials.

Subjectivity is unavoidable in ensuring inter-temporal observational equivalence between the two datasets. Nevertheless, I am not aware of historical atlases that would systematically map and document administrative changes over time for Russia. For another project, I perused one such atlas when performing historical analysis of the drivers of human capital and democratic variations in Indian districts and am aware that scholars of other contexts face similar hurdles.[6] In India, too, many districts were subdivided into multiple units over time, and the best solution that scholars could find in dealing with this issue was to assign colonial-era district data to the multiple districts into which a particular unit was subdivided after independence.[7]

D   INTERVIEW QUESTIONNAIRE

[Note that all questions are nonpolitical; the main objective of this part of the project is to ascertain cognitive aspects of the reproduction of the social structure and to gather additional material on adaptations of families. Only the last question is phrased such that it opens up the possibility of discussing political orientations if the respondent is comfortable and willing to make such a digression.]

Questionnaire (English Translation)

Intelligentsia, Samara

Please tell us a little about yourself: profession, where you studied and in what years. Do you consider yourself a native (indigenous to) of Samara? What does it mean to you to be a Samarovite (regional identity)?

Please tell us what you know about the previous generations of your family who lived in Samara (here and hereafter we are referring to the city and region) and the Volga region – we are interested in the pre-revolutionary period and post-revolutionary years:

- From which regions of the Russian Empire did they move to Samara or the Volga region, when, under what circumstances (peasant settlements, cantonists, religious settlements, etc.)?
- in what places did they live (settlement, city, etc.)?
- do relatives still exist in these settlements?

---

[6] Lankina et al., "Mission or Empire," 3.   [7] See Banerjee et al., "History," 1199.

Please tell us what you know about the social status of the members of the previous generations of your family who lived in Samara:

- Estate (peasants, *meshchane*, merchants, etc.)
- material status (property ownership, etc.)
- social status
- examples of participation in the economic life of the province or district (agriculture, commerce, trades, etc.)
- examples of occupations and professions

Please tell us what you know about the social activities (obshchestvennaya deyatel'nost') of the previous generations of your family who lived in Samara before the Revolution:

- Charity
- public organizations
- religious organizations

Please tell us what you know about the education of the previous generations of your family who lived in Samara:

- In which schools and educational institutions did they study before the Revolution
- have family stories or documents survived

Please tell us how the Revolutionary turn of 1917 affected the fate of the previous generations of your family who lived in Samara:

- Continuity or vice versa, break in the profession or educational process
- examples of professional adaptation in new conditions; have they managed to keep their job and social status?
- repressions
- the trajectory of the family after repressions (if they were in the family): rehabilitation, restoration of work, return to the previous place of residence, etc.

Speaking about the Soviet period, please tell us in more detail about the choice of study and career of the previous generations of your family who lived in Samara:

- Have the skills and vocational orientations of previous generations been passed on to the new generation and how?
- what was the impact of party stipulations (*partiynyye ustanovki*) about social mobility and general education on mobility in your family? Were there any "promoted" (*vydvizhentsy*) members from the workers' and peasants' strata in the family?
- and vice versa, what do you think was the influence of attitudes in your own family on the choice of education and profession of children?

– did the family talk about the pre-revolutionary generations of your family or did it keep silent (*umalchivalos'*)?

Please tell us about specific artifacts preserved in your family that are evocative of the past of your ancestors (books, photos, household items, letters, etc.).
Please tell us about your family's religious affiliation:

– If applicable, how were religious traditions preserved in the family during the Soviet period?
– were there religious repressions?
– the degree of influence of religious identity on the family's values and attitudes
– the degree of influence of religious identity on family attitudes in the field of education
– the degree of influence of religious identity on the upbringing of children

How did your family react to the changes associated with the crisis and collapse of the Soviet system?

– Participation in social activities of the *perestroika* period and after
– emigration of family members abroad or migration to other regions of Russia
– loss of work, or vice versa, finding a new profession or new ways of self-realization

Please tell us about you and the new generation in your family

– Do the children live in Samara?
– what do children do now?

How typical is your family history for Samara in your opinion? And how typical is Samara (city and region) of Russia?
As a representative of science and culture of Samara, how would you characterize the development or state of these areas after the collapse of the USSR and now, in recent years, specifically in Samara? Are there positive or negative changes?

E ILLUSTRATIVE GENEALOGIES

All three genealogies are based on published memoirs and supplemented with information from personal interviews, email clarifications to the author, and additional sources. The figures illustrate patterns of pre-revolutionary and Soviet-period mobility, education, occupations, and professional trajectories of the educated estates, including of would-be *meshchane* of rural origins who often intermarried with *meshchane* as fellow long-term urban dwellers even when maintaining their ascription to the peasant estate.

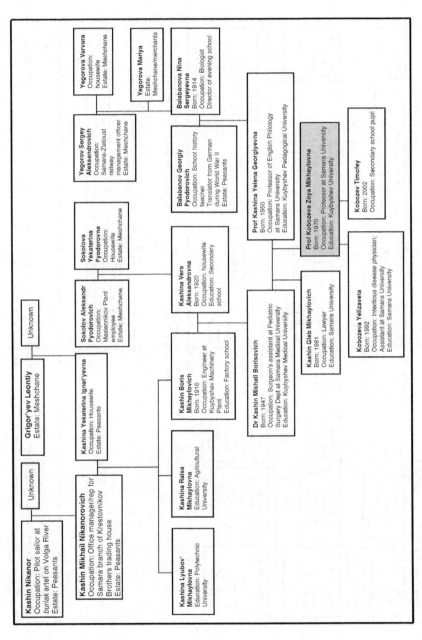

FIGURE A.1 Kobozeva genealogy

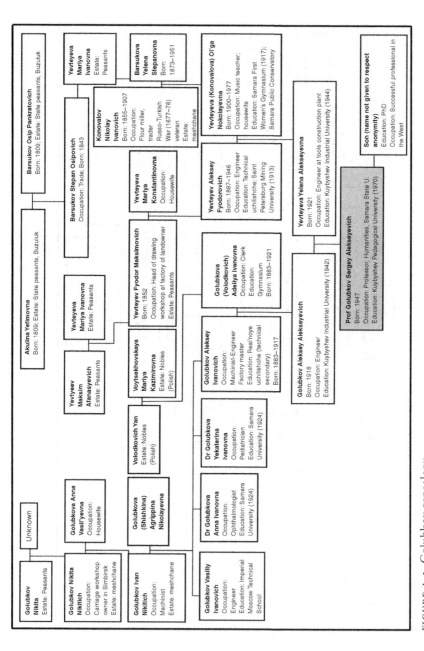

FIGURE A.2 Golubkov genealogy

Golubkov writes that the Barsukovs transitioned from state peasant to the *meshchane* estate, then to merchant status, and back to *meshchane* as material fortunes soured. Email correspondence with author, November 7, 2020.

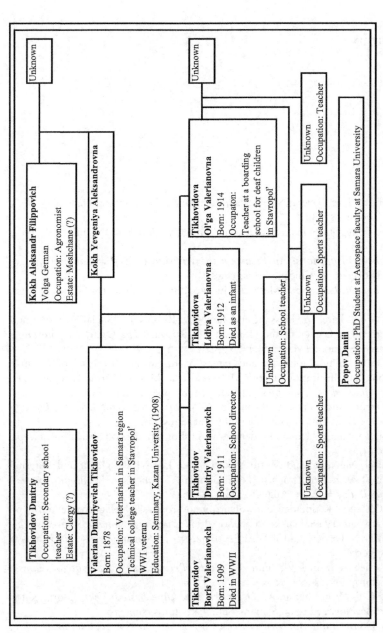

FIGURE A.3 Tikhovidov genealogy

Bibliography

Abbott, Andrew. "Life Cycles in Social Science History." *Social Science History* 23, no. 4 (Winter 1999): 481–89.

——— "Status and Status Strain in the Professions." *American Journal of Sociology* 86, no. 4 (January 1981): 819–35.

——— *The System of Professions: An Essay on the Division of Expert Labor.* Chicago, Illinois: University of Chicago Press, 1988.

——— *Time Matters: On Theory and Method.* Chicago, Illinois: University of Chicago Press, 2001.

Acemoglu, Daron, Tarek A. Hassan, and James A. Robinson. "Social Structure and Development: A Legacy of the Holocaust in Russia." *The Quarterly Journal of Economics* 126, no. 2 (May 2011): 895–946.

Acemoglu, Daron, Simon Johnson, and James A. Robinson. "Reversal of Fortune: Geography and Institutions in the Making of the Modern World Income." *The Quarterly Journal of Economics* 117, no. 4 (November 2002): 1231–94.

Acemoglu, Daron, and James A. Robinson. *Economic Origins of Dictatorship and Democracy.* New York: Cambridge University Press, 2006.

Adayevskaya, Tatyana I. "Dinamika demograficheskoy situatsii v Tolyatti." *Kontsept*, no. 7 (2014): 1–7.

Akbulut-Yuksel, Mevlude, and Mutlu Yuksel. "The Long-Term Direct and External Effects of Jewish Expulsions in Nazi Germany." *American Economic Journal: Economic Policy* 7, no. 3 (August 2015): 58–85.

Aleksushin, Gleb V. "K tipologii dorevolyutsionnoy rossiyskoy blagotvoritel'nosti (po materialam Samary i Samarskogo kraya)." In *Neizvestnaya Samara: Sbornik statey*, edited by N. V. Iyevleva and T. F. Aleksushina, 17–35. Samara: Detskaya kartinnaya galereya, 2007.

Aleksushin, Gleb V., and Vladimir L. Sinin. *Pervyy vek Samarskogo tennisa.* St. Petersburg: Liki Rossii, 2013.

Aleksushina, T. F. "Von Vakano A." In *Samarskoye kupechestvo: Vekhi istorii*, edited by Ye. P. Barinova, 224–43. Samara: Samarskiy universitet, 2006.

Alexopoulos, Golfo. *Stalin's Outcasts: Aliens, Citizens, and the Soviet State, 1926–1936.* Ithaca, New York: Cornell University Press, 2003.

Alliluyeva, Svetlana. *Letters to a Friend*, translated by Priscilla Johnson. London: Hutchinson of London, 1967.

Alliluyeva, Svetlana I. *Doch' Stalina: Posledneye interv'yu, sbornik*. Moscow: Alistorus, 2013.

Altshuler, Mordechai. *Soviet Jewry since the Second World War: Population and Social Structure*. New York: Greenwood Press, 1987.

Aminzade, Ronald. "Historical Sociology and Time." *Sociological Methods and Research* 20, no. 4 (May 1992): 456–80.

Andreas, Joel. *Rise of the Red Engineers: The Cultural Revolution and the Origins of China's New Class*. Stanford, California: Stanford University Press, 2009.

Andrle, Vladimir. "The Buoyant Class: Bourgeois Family Lineage in the Life Stories of Czech Business Elite Persons." *Sociology* 35, no. 4 (November 2001): 815–33.

Anfimov, Andrey M., and Avenir P. Korelin, eds. *Rossiya 1913 god: Statistiko-dokumental'nyy spravochnik*. St. Petersburg: Blits, 1995.

Ansell, Ben W., and David J. Samuels. *Inequality and Democratization: An Elite-Competition Approach*. Cambridge: Cambridge University Press, 2014.

Applebaum, Anne. *Gulag: A History of the Soviet Camps*. London: Allen Lane, 2003.

Armstrong, John A. "Socializing for Modernization in a Multiethnic Elite." In *Entrepreneurship in Imperial Russia and the Soviet Union*, edited by Gregory Guroff and Fred V. Carstensen, 84–103. Princeton, New Jersey: Princeton University Press, 1983.

Assmann, Aleida. "*Memory, Individual and Collective*." In *The Oxford Handbook of Contextual Political Analysis*, edited by Robert E. Goodin and Charles Tilly, 210–24. Oxford: Oxford University Press, 2011.

Astafyev, Ya. U., and V. N. Shubkin. "Sotsiologiya obrazovaniya v SSSR i Rossii." *Mir Rossii* no. 3 (1996).

Attias-Donfut, Claudine, and Sara Arber. "Equity and Solidarity across the Generations." In *The Myth of Generational Conflict: The Family and State in Ageing Societies*, edited by Sara Arber and Claudine Attias-Donfut. ESA Studies in European Societies, 1–21. Abingdon: Routledge, 2007.

Aven, Pyotr. *Vremya Berezovskogo*. Moscow: AST, 2017.

Baboreko, Aleksandr K. *I. A. Bunin: Materialy dlya biografii (s 1870 po 1917)*. Moscow: Khudozhestvennaya literatura, 1967.

Bahry, Donna. "Politics, Generations, and Change in the USSR." In *Politics, Work, and Daily Life in the USSR: A Survey of Former Soviet Citizens*, edited by James R. Millar, 61–99. New York: Cambridge University Press, 1987.

Bailes, Kendall E. *Technology and Society under Lenin and Stalin: Origins of the Soviet Technical Intelligentsia, 1917–1941*. Princeton, New Jersey: Princeton University Press, 1978.

Bakhtin, Mikhail. *Problems of Dostoevsky's Poetics*, translated by Caryl Emerson. Theory and History of Literature, Vol. 8. Minneapolis: University of Minnesota Press, 1987.

Balzer, Harley D. "Conclusion: The Missing Middle Class." In *Russia's Missing Middle Class: The Professions in Russian History*, edited by Harley D. Balzer, 293–319. Armonk, New York: M. E. Sharpe, 1996.

  Russia's Missing Middle Class: The Professions in Russian History. Armonk, New York: M. E. Sharpe, 1996.

Banerjee, Abhijit, and Lakshmi Iyer. "History, Institutions, and Economic Performance: The Legacy of Colonial Land Tenure Systems in India." *The American Economic Review* 95, no. 4 (September 2005): 1190–213.

Baranov, V. S., A. V. Mikheyeva, Vladimir G. Sherstnev, and Galina S. Sherstneva. *Istoriya Samarskogo kupechestva: Dinastii Plotnikovykh-Sherstnevykh XIX-nachala XX vv.: Istoricheskiy ocherk*. Samara: OOO "Kniga," 2012.

Barinova, Ye. P. "Blagotvoritel'naya deyatel'nost' Samarskogo kupechestva." In *Samarskoye kupechestvo: Vekhi istorii*, edited by Ye. P. Barinova, 315–20. Samara: Samarskiy universitet, 2006.

Bartlett, Rosamund. *Chekhov: Scenes from a Life*. London: Free Press, 2004.

Bauman, Zygmunt. *Modernity and Ambivalence*. Oxford: Polity Press, 2004.

Baviskar, Amita, and Raka Ray. "Introduction." In *Elite and Everyman: The Cultural Politics of the Indian Middle Classes*, edited by Amita Baviskar and Raka Ray, 1–23. London: Routledge, 2011.

Bayly, Christopher A. *The Birth of the Modern World, 1780–1914: Global Connections and Comparisons*. Malden, Massachusetts: Blackwell Publishing, 2004.

Becker, Seymour. *Nobility and Privilege in Late Imperial Russia*. Dekalb: Northern Illinois University Press, 1985.

Beer, Caroline, and Neil J. Mitchell. "Comparing Nations and States: Human Rights and Democracy in India." *Comparative Political Studies* 39, no. 8 (October 2006): 996–1018.

Behrend, Jacqueline, and Laurence Whitehead, eds. *Illiberal Practices: Territorial Variance within Large Federal Democracies*. Baltimore, Maryland: Johns Hopkins University Press, 2016.

Békés, Csaba, László Borhi, Peter Ruggenthaler, and Ottmar Traşcă. *Soviet Occupation of Romania, Hungary, and Austria, 1944/45–1948/49*. Budapest: Central European University Press, 2015.

Bell, Daniel A. "After the Tsunami: Will Economic Crisis Bring Democracy to Asia?" *The New Republic* 218, no. 10 (March 1998): 22–25.

Bellin, Eva. "Contingent Democrats: Industrialists, Labor, and Democratization in Late-Developing Countries." *World Politics* 52, no. 2 (January 2000): 175–205.

Bergson, Henri. *Time and Free Will: An Essay on the Immediate Data of Consciousness*, translated by F. L. Pogson. Mansfield Centre, Connecticut: Martino Publishing, 2015.

Berliner, Joseph S. *Factory and Manager in the USSR*. Cambridge, Massachusetts: Harvard University Press, 1957.

Bessudnov, Alexey. "The Effects of Parental Social Background on Labour Market Outcomes in Russia." In *Education, Occupation and Social Origin: A Comparative Analysis of the Transmission of Socio-Economic Inequalities*, edited by Fabrizio Bernardi and Gabrielle Ballarino, 150–67. Cheltenham: Edward Elgar, 2016.

Bian, Yanjie, Xiaoling Shu, and John R. Logan. "Communist Party Membership and Regime Dynamics in China." *Social Forces* 79, no. 3 (March 2001): 805–41.

Bim, Alexander S., Derek C. Jones, and Thomas E. Weisskopf. "Hybrid Forms of Enterprise Organization in the Former USSR and the Russian Federation." *Comparative Economic Studies* 35, no. 1 (April 1993): 1–37.

Bíró-Nagy, András. "Illiberal Democracy in Hungary: The Social Background and Practical Steps of Building an Illiberal State." In *Illiberal Democracies in the EU:*

The Visegrad Group and the Risk of Disintegration, edited by Pol Morillas, 31–44. Barcelona: Barcelona Centre for International Affairs (CIDOB), 2017.

Blackwell, William. "The Russian Entrepreneur in the Tsarist Period: An Overview." In *Entrepreneurship in Imperial Russia and the Soviet Union*, edited by Gregory Guroff and Fred V. Carstensen, 13–26. Princeton, New Jersey: Princeton University Press, 1983.

Blackwell, William L. "The Old Believers and the Rise of Private Industrial Enterprise in Early Nineteenth-Century Moscow." *Slavic Review* 24, no. 3 (September 1965): 407–24.

Blinova, O., V. Mavrinskiy, S. Frank, and L. Perukhina, eds. *Rossiya, odnu sud'bu s toboy my razdelili. (O vklade nemtsev-trudarmeytsev v delo razvitiya neftyanoy i gazovoy promyshlennosti Orenburzh'ya i Samarskoy oblasti)*. Buguruslan: Orenburzh'ye, 2012.

Boix, Carles. *Democracy and Redistribution*. Cambridge: Cambridge University Press, 2003.

Boldyrev, N. I. *Rol' shkoly i sem'yi v vospitanii detey*. Moscow: Uchpedgiz, 1954.

Boone, Catherine. *Political Topographies of the African State: Territorial Authority and Institutional Choice*. Cambridge: Cambridge University Press, 2003.

Bourdieu, Pierre. *Distinction: A Social Critique of the Judgement of Taste*, translated by Richard Nice. London: Routledge Classics, 2010.

    Language and Symbolic Power, translated by Gino Raymond and Matthew Adamson. Cambridge: Polity Press, 2014.

    The Logic of Practice, translated by Richard Nice. Cambridge: Polity Press, 1990.

    The State Nobility, translated by Lauretta C. Clough. Cambridge: Polity Press, 1996.

Bourdieu, Pierre, Craig J. Calhoun, Edward LiPuma, and Moishe Postone. *Bourdieu: Critical Perspectives*. Chicago, Illinois: University of Chicago Press, 1993.

Bourdieu, Pierre, and Jean-Claude Passeron. *The Inheritors: French Students and Their Relation to Culture*, translated by Richard Nice. Chicago: University of Chicago Press, 1979.

    Reproduction in Education, Society and Culture, translated by Richard Nice. 2nd ed. London: Sage Publications, 1990.

Bradley, Joseph. *Voluntary Associations in Tsarist Russia: Science, Patriotism, and Civil Society*. Cambridge, Massachusetts: Harvard University Press, 2009.

Braudel, Fernand. *On History*, translated by Sarah Matthews. Chicago, Illinois: University of Chicago Press, 1982.

Brooks, Jeffrey. *When Russia Learned to Read: Literacy and Popular Literature, 1861–1917*. Princeton, New Jersey: Princeton University Press, 1988.

Brown, Archie. *The Myth of the Strong Leader: Political Leadership in the Modern Age*. London: The Bodley Head, 2014.

    The Rise and Fall of Communism. London: The Bodley Head, 2009.

    Seven Years that Changed the World: Perestroika in Perspective. Oxford: Oxford University Press, 2007.

    "Transnational Influences in the Transition from Communism." *Post-Soviet Affairs* 16, no. 2 (April–June 2000): 177–200.

Brubaker, Rogers. *Nationalism Reframed: Nationhood and the National Question in the New Europe*. Cambridge: Cambridge University Press, 1996.

Buggle, Johannes C., and Steven Nafziger. "The Slow Road from Serfdom: Labor Coercion and Long-Run Development in the Former Russian Empire." *The Review of Economics and Statistics* 103, no. 1 (March 2021): 1–17.

Bulgakov, Mikhail. *Sobach'ye serdtse*. Moscow: Azbuka-Klassika, 2012.

Bunce, Valerie. "The National Idea: Imperial Legacies and Post-Communist Pathways in Eastern Europe." *East European Politics and Societies and Cultures* 19, no. 3 (August 2005): 406–42.

Bunin, Ivan. "Zhizn' Arsen'yeva." In *Sonechnyy udar: Roman, povesti, rasskazy*, 299–638. Moscow: Eksmo, 2014.

Burbank, Jane. *Intelligentsia and Revolution: Russian Views of Bolshevism, 1917–1922*. New York: Oxford University Press, 1986.

  Russian Peasants Go to Court: Legal Culture in the Countryside, 1905–1917. Bloomington: Indiana University Press, 2004.

Burds, Jeffrey. *Peasant Dreams and Market Politics: Labor Migration and the Russian Village, 1861–1905*. Pittsburgh, Pennsylvania: University of Pittsburgh Press, 1998.

Burlina, Yelena Ya. "Gorod Bezymyanka: Prostranstvennyy razlom." In *Polifoniya gorodskikh prostranstv: Internatsional'nyy nauchno-issledovatel'skiy al'manakh. Obzory i kontseptsiya*, edited by Yelena Ya. Burlina, 56–61. Samara: Mediakniga, 2014.

  "Iz istorii staroy Samarskoy sinagogi." In *Evrei provintsial'noy Rossii*, edited by Yelena Ya. Burlina, 34–48. Samara: Terem, 1992.

Burlina, Yelena Ya. ed. *Yevreyi provintsial'noy Rossii*. Samara: Terem, 1992.

Burlina, Yelena Ya. "Imya?... Interv'yu starykh samartsev." In *Evrei provintsial'noy Rossii*, edited by Yelena Ya. Burlina, 118–36. Samara: Terem, 1992.

  "Staryye semeynyye al'bomy." In *Evrei provintsial'noy Rossii*, edited by Yelena Ya. Burlina, 49–59. Samara: Terem, 1992.

  "Ya uchilas' v Yevreyskoy shkole." In *Evrei provintsial'noy Rossii*, edited by Yelena Ya. Burlina, 77–89. Samara: Terem, 1992.

Buss, Andreas. "The Economic Ethics of Russian-Orthodox Christianity: Part II–Russian Old Believers and Sects." *International Sociology* 4, no. 4 (December 1989): 447–72.

Capoccia, Giovanni, and R. Daniel Kelemen. "The Study of Critical Junctures: Theory, Narrative, and Counterfactuals in Historical Institutionalism." *World Politics* 59, no. 3 (2007): 341–69.

Capoccia, Giovanni, and Daniel Ziblatt. "The Historical Turn in Democratization Studies: A New Research Agenda for Europe and Beyond." *Comparative Political Studies* 43, no. 8–9 (June 2010): 931–68.

Chamberlain, Lesley. *Lenin's Private War: The Voyage of the Philosophy Steamer and the Exile of the Intelligentsia*. New York: St. Martin's Press, 2006.

Channon, John. "Tsarist Landowners after the Revolution: Former Pomeshchiki in Rural Russia During NEP." *Soviet Studies* 39, no. 4 (October 1987): 575–98.

Charnysh, Volha. "Diversity, Institutions, and Economic Outcomes: Post-WWII Displacement in Poland." *The American Political Science Review* 113, no. 2 (May 2019): 423–41.

Checkel, Jeff. "Ideas, Institutions, and the Gorbachev Foreign Policy Revolution." *World Politics* 45, no. 2 (January 1993): 271–300.

Chen, Jie. *A Middle Class without Democracy: Economic Growth and the Prospects for Democratization in China*. New York: Oxford University Press, 2013.

Chen, Xi. *Social Protest and Contentious Authoritarianism in China*. New York: Cambridge University Press, 2014.

Chibber, Vivek. *Postcolonial Theory and the Specter of Capital*. London: Verso, 2013.

Chigrinyov, Mikhail S. *Ocherki po istorii goroda Chapayevska 1909–1918*. Samara: Ofort, 2010.

Chudilin, G. I., N. Ye. Fomina, and G. V. Bakina, eds. *Natsional'nyy sostav naseleniya Samarskoy oblasti (po dannym Vserossiyskoy perepisi naseleniya 2010 goda): Statisticheskiy sbornik*. Samara: Samarastat, 2013.

Churchward, L. G. *The Soviet Intelligentsia: An Essay on the Social Structure and Roles of Soviet Intellectuals during the 1960s*. London: Routledge and Kegan Paul, 1973.

Clark, Gregory. *The Son Also Rises: Surnames and the History of Social Mobility*. Princeton, New Jersey: Princeton University Press, 2015.

Clem, Ralph S. "Russia's Electoral Geography: A Review." *Eurasian Geography and Economics* 47, no. 4 (2006): 381–406.

Clem, Ralph S., and Peter R. Craumer. "Urban-Rural Voting Differences in Russian Elections, 1995–1996: A Rayon-Level Analysis." *Post-Soviet Geography and Economics* 38, no. 7 (1997): 379–95.

Clowes, Edith W., Samuel D. Kassow, and James L. West, eds. *Between Tsar and People: Educated Society and the Quest for Public Identity in Late Imperial Russia*. Princeton, New Jersey: Princeton University Press, 1991.

Cohen, Stephen F. *The Victims Return: Survivors of the Gulag after Stalin*. London: I.B. Tauris, 2012.

Collier, David, James Mahoney, and Jason Seawright. "Claiming Too Much: Warnings About Selection Bias." In *Rethinking Social Inquiry: Diverse Tools, Shared Standards*, edited by Henry E. Brady and David Collier, 85–102. Lanham, Maryland: Rowman & Littlefield, 2004.

Collier, David, and Gerardo L. Munck. "Critical Junctures and Historical Legacies." *Qualitative and Multi-Method Research* 15, no. 1 (Spring 2017): 1–47.

Collier, Ruth Berins, and David Collier. *Shaping the Political Arena: Critical Junctures, the Labor Movement, and Regime Dynamics in Latin America*. Notre Dame, Indiana: University of Notre Dame Press, 2002.

Collins, Kathleen. *Clan Politics and Regime Transition in Central Asia*. New York: Cambridge University Press, 2006.

Confino, Michael. "The Soslovie (Estate) Paradigm: Reflections on Some Open Questions." *Cahiers du Monde russe* 49, no. 4 (October–December 2008): 681–704.

Connerton, Paul. *How Societies Remember*. Cambridge: Cambridge University Press, 2014.

Conquest, Robert. *The Great Terror: A Reassessment*. London: Pimlico, 2008.

———. *The Nation Killers*. London: Sphere Books, 1972.

Conrad, Sebastian. *What Is Global History?* Princeton, New Jersey: Princeton University Press, 2016.

Conway, Martin A. "The Inventory of Experience: Memory and Identity." In *Collective Memory of Political Events: Social Psychological Perspectives*, edited by James W. Pennebaker, Dario Paez, and Bernard Rimé, 21–45. New York: Psychology Press, 2008.

Cornelius, Deborah S. "Education for a New Peasant Leadership: The Hungarian Folk College Movement, 1938–1945." In *Hungary's Historical Legacies: Studies in Honor of Steven Béla Várdy*, edited by Dennis P. Hupchick and R. William Weisberger, 130–45. Boulder, Colorado: Columbia University Press, 2000.

Crampton, R. J. *Eastern Europe in the Twentieth Century – and After*, 2nd ed. London: Routledge, 1997.

Crisp, Olga. *Studies in the Russian Economy before 1914*. London: Macmillan Press, 1976.

Dahl, Robert A. *Polyarchy: Participation and Opposition*. New Haven, Connecticut: Yale University Press, 1971.

Dahlmann, Dittmar, and Ralph Tuchtenhagen, eds. *Zwischen Reform und Revolution: Die Deutschen an der Wolga, 1860–1917*. Essen: Klartext, 1994.

Darden, Keith, and Anna Grzymala-Busse. "The Great Divide: Literacy, Nationalism, and the Communist Collapse." *World Politics* 59, no. 1 (October 2006): 83–115.

David-Fox, Michael. *Revolution of the Mind: Higher Learning among the Bolsheviks, 1918–1929*. Ithaca, New York: Cornell University Press, 1997.

Davies, Robert W. "Carr's Changing Views of the Soviet Union." In *E. H. Carr: A Critical Appraisal*, edited by Michael Cox, 91–108. Basingstoke: Palgrave Macmillan, 2000.

"Changing Economic Systems: An Overview." In *The Economic Transformation of the Soviet Union, 1913–1945*, edited by Robert W. Davies, Mark Harrison, and Stephen G. Wheatcroft, 1–23. Cambridge: Cambridge University Press, 1994.

Davis, Allison, Burleigh B. Gardner, and Mary R. Gardner. *Deep South: A Social Anthropological Study of Caste and Class*, abridged ed. Phoenix Books series. Chicago, Illinois: University of Chicago Press, 1969.

Davis, Diane E. *Discipline and Development: Middle Classes and Prosperity in East Asia and Latin America*. New York: Cambridge University Press, 2004.

de Vries, Jan. *The Industrious Revolution: Consumer Behavior and the Household Economy, 1650 to the Present*. New York: Cambridge University Press, 2008.

Dennison, Tracy. *The Institutional Framework of Russian Serfdom*. New York: Cambridge University Press, 2011.

Derluguian, Georgi M. *Bourdieu's Secret Admirer in the Caucasus: A World-System Biography*. Chicago, Illinois: University of Chicago Press, 2005.

Diesendorf, Viktor F., ed. *Die Deutschen Russlands: Siedlungen und Siedlungsgebiete: Lexikon*. Moscow: ERD, 2006.

Dikötter, Frank. *The Cultural Revolution: A People's History, 1962–1976*. London: Bloomsbury Press, 2016.

Ding, X. L. "Institutional Amphibiousness and the Transition from Communism: The Case of China." *British Journal of Political Science* 24, no. 3 (July 1994): 293–318.

Djilas, Milovan. *The New Class: An Analysis of the Communist System*. San Diego: Harcourt Brace Jovanovich Publishers, 1983.

Dobson, Richard B. "Communism's Legacy and Russian Youth." In *The Social Legacy of Communism*, edited by James R. Millar and Sharon L. Wolchik. Woodrow Wilson Center Series, 229–51. Washington, DC: Woodrow Wilson Center Press, 1994.

Dolgopyatov, A. V. "Domovladeniye meshchan gorodov Moskovskoy gubernii v kontse XIX-nachale XX v.: Stoimost', struktura, osobennosti." *Vestnik Tambovskogo gosudarstvennogo universiteta* 12, no. 80 (2009): 344–49.

Dostoevsky, Fyodor M. *Besy*. In *Sobraniye sochineniy v dvenadtsati tomakh*, Vols. 8–9. Moscow: Pravda, 1982.

Zapiski iz myortvogo doma. In *Sobraniye sochineniy v dvenadtsati tomakh*, Vol. 3. Moscow: Pravda, 1982.

Dower, Paul Castañeda, Evgeny Finkel, Scott Gehlbach, and Steven Nafziger. "Collective Action and Representation in Autocracies: Evidence from Russia's Great Reforms." *The American Political Science Review* 112, no. 1 (February 2018): 125–47.

Dowler, Wayne. "Merchants and Politics in Russia: The Guild Reform of 1824." *The Slavonic and East European Review* 65, no. 1 (January 1987): 38–52.

Dunham, Vera S. *In Stalin's Time: Middleclass Values in Soviet Fiction*, updated ed. Durham, North Carolina: Duke University Press, 1990.

Dunning, Thad. "Contingency and Determinism in Research on Critical Junctures: Avoiding the 'Inevitability Framework.'" *Qualitative and Multi-Method Research* 15, no. 1 (2017): 41–47.

Edele, Mark. *Stalinist Society, 1928–1953*. Oxford: Oxford University Press, 2011.

Ekiert, Grzegorz, and Stephen E. Hanson. "Time, Space, and Institutional Change in Central and Eastern Europe." In *Capitalism and Democracy in Central and Eastern Europe: Assessing the Legacy of Communist Rule*, edited by Grzegorz Ekiert and Stephen E. Hanson, 15–48. Cambridge: Cambridge University Press, 2003.

Eklof, Ben. *Russian Peasant Schools: Officialdom, Village Culture, and Popular Pedagogy, 1861–1914*. Berkeley: University of California Press, 1986.

Eley, Geoff. "On Your Marx: From Cultural History to the History of Society." In *The Politics of Method in the Human Sciences: Positivism and Its Epistemological Others*, edited by George Steinmetz, 496–507. Durham, North Carolina: Duke University Press, 2005.

Elias, Norbert. *The Civilizing Process: Sociogenetic and Psychogenetic Investigations*, translated by Edmund Jepcott, rev. ed. Oxford: Blackwell Publishing, 2000.

Elias, Norbert, and John L. Scotson. *The Established and the Outsiders: A Sociological Enquiry into Community Problems*, 2nd ed. London: Sage Publications, 1994.

Ellman, Michael. "Soviet Repression Statistics: Some Comments." *Europe-Asia Studies* 54, no. 7 (November 2002): 1151–72.

Elster, Jon, Claus Offe, and Ulrich K. Preuss. *Institutional Design in Post-Communist Societies: Rebuilding the Ship at Sea*. Cambridge: Cambridge University Press, 1998.

Emmons, Terence, and Wayne S. Vucinich, eds. *The Zemstvo in Russia: An Experiment in Local Self-Government*. New York: Cambridge University Press, 1982.

Engel, Barbara Alpern. *Mothers and Daughters: Women of the Intelligentsia in Nineteenth-Century Russia*. New York: Cambridge University Press, 1987.

Erikson, Robert, and John H. Goldthorpe. *The Constant Flux: A Study of Class Mobility in Industrial Societies*. Oxford: Clarendon Press, 1992.

Escribà-Folch, Abel, Covadonga Meseguer, and Joseph Wright. "Remittances and Democratization." *International Studies Quarterly* 59, no. 3 (September 2015): 571–86.

Evans, Peter B., Dietrich Rueschemeyer, and Theda Skocpol. *Bringing the State Back In*. New York: Cambridge University Press, 1985.

Ewing, Thomas E. *The Teachers of Stalinism: Policy, Practice, and Power in Soviet Schools of the 1930s*. New York: Peter Lang, 2002.

Fainsod, Merle. *How Russia Is Ruled*, rev. ed. Cambridge, Massachusetts: Harvard University Press, 1963.

Faletti, Tulia G., and James Mahoney. "The Comparative Sequential Method." In *Advances in Comparative-Historical Analysis*, edited by James Mahoney and Kathleen Thelen, 211–39. Cambridge: Cambridge University Press, 2015.

Fei, Hsiao-Tung. "Peasantry and Gentry: An Interpretation of Chinese Social Structure and Its Changes." *American Journal of Sociology* 52, no. 1 (July 1946): 1–17.

Fernandes, Leela. "Hegemony and Inequality: Theoretical Reflections on India's 'New' Middle Class." In *Elite and Everyman: The Cultural Politics of the Indian Middle Classes*, edited by Amita Baviskar and Raka Ray, 58–82. London: Routledge, 2011.

Field, Mark G. *Doctor and Patient in Soviet Russia*. Cambridge, Massachusetts: Harvard University Press, 1957.

Figes, Orlando. *Peasant Russia, Civil War: The Volga Countryside in Revolution, 1917–1921*. London: Phoenix Press, 2001.

The Whisperers: Private Life in Stalin's Russia. London: Allen Lane, 2007.

Finkel, Evgeny. *Ordinary Jews: Choice and Survival during the Holocaust*. Princeton, New Jersey: Princeton University Press, 2017.

Finkel, Evgeny, Scott Gehlbach, and Tricia D. Olsen. "Does Reform Prevent Rebellion? Evidence from Russia's Emancipation of the Serfs." *Comparative Political Studies* 48, no. 8 (July 2015): 984–1019.

Fitzpatrick, Sheila. "Afterword: The Thaw in Retrospect." In *The Thaw: Soviet Society and Culture during the 1950s and 1960s*, edited by Denis Kozlov and Eleonory Gilburd, 482–91. Toronto: University of Toronto Press, 2013.

"Cultural Revolution as Class War." In *Cultural Revolution in Russia, 1928–1931*, edited by Sheila Fitzpatrick, 8–40. Bloomington: Indiana University Press, 1978.

Education and Social Mobility in the Soviet Union, 1921–1934. Cambridge: Cambridge University Press, 1979.

Tear Off the Masks! Identity and Imposture in Twentieth-Century Russia. Princeton, New Jersey: Princeton University Press, 2005.

"The Two Faces of Anastasia: Narratives and Counter-Narratives of Identity in Stalinist Everyday Life." In *Everyday Life in Early Soviet Russia: Taking the Revolution Inside*, edited by Christina Kiaer and Eric Naiman, 23–34. Bloomington: Indiana University Press, 2006.

Foa, Roberto Stefan. "Modernization and Authoritarianism." *Journal of Democracy* 29, no. 3 (July 2018): 129–40.

Foa, Roberto Stefan, and Anna Nemirovskaya. "How State Capacity Varies within Frontier States: A Multicountry Subnational Analysis." *Governance* 29, no. 3 (July 2016): 411–32.

Foner, Philip S. *History of the Labor Movement in the United States: The T.U.E.L. to the End of the Gompers Era*, Vol. 9. New York: International Publishers, 1991.

Frank, Joseph. *Dostoevsky: A Writer in His Time*. Princeton, New Jersey: Princeton University Press, 2010.

Frank, Kenneth A. "Impact of a Confounding Variable on a Regression Coefficient." *Sociological Methods and Research* 29, no. 2 (November 2000): 147–94.

Frank, Tibor. "Teaching and Learning Science in Hungary, 1867–1945: Schools, Personalities, Influences." *Science and Education* 21, no. 3 (March 2012): 355–80.

Freeze, Gregory L. "The *Soslovie* (Estate) Paradigm and Russian Social History." *The American Historical Review* 91, no. 1 (February 1986): 11–36.

Frieden, Nancy Mandelker. *Russian Physicians in an Era of Reform and Revolution, 1856–1905*. Princeton, New Jersey: Princeton University Press, 1981.

Frye, Timothy, Ora John Reuter, and David Szakonyi. "Political Machines at Work: Voter Mobilization and Electoral Subversion in the Workplace." *World Politics* 66, no. 2 (April 2014): 195–228.

Furaker, Bengt. "Review Essay: The Intelligentsia as a Class under Capitalism and Socialism." *Acta Sociologica* 25, no. 4 (October 1982): 455–67.

Gaddis, John Lewis. *We Now Know: Rethinking Cold War History*. Oxford: Oxford University Press, 1997.

Gagkuyev, R. G., ed. *Kappel' i kappelevtsy*. 3rd rev. ed. Moscow: Russkiy put', 2010.

Garin-Mikhaylovskiy, Nikolay. *Studenty; Inzhenery*. Leningrad: Khudozhestvennaya literatura, 1988.

Gehlbach, Scott. "Shifting Electoral Geography in Russia's 1991 and 1996 Presidential Elections." *Post-Soviet Geography and Economics* 41, no. 5 (2000): 379–87.

Gel'man, Vladimir. "Second Europe-Asia Lecture. Regime Transition, Uncertainty and Prospects for Democratisation: The Politics of Russia's Regions in a Comparative Perspective." *Europe-Asia Studies* 51, no. 6 (September 1999): 939–56.

Gel'man, Vladimir, and Cameron Ross, eds. *The Politics of Subnational Authoritarianism in Russia*. Farnham: Ashgate, 2010.

Gelman, Vladimir, Sergei Ryzhenkov, and Michael Brie. *Making and Breaking Democratic Transitions: The Comparative Politics of Russia's Regions*. Lanham, Maryland: Rowman & Littlefield, 2003.

Gerber, Theodore P. "Market, State, or Don't Know? Education, Economic Ideology, and Voting in Contemporary Russia." *Social Forces* 79, no. 2 (December 2000): 477–521.

"Paths to Success: Individual and Regional Determinants of Self-Employment Entry in Post-Communist Russia." *International Journal of Sociology* 31, no. 2 (Summer 2001): 3–37.

Gerber, Theodore P., and Michael Hout. "Educational Stratification in Russia during the Soviet Period." *American Journal of Sociology* 101, no. 3 (November 1995): 611–60.

"Tightening Up: Declining Class Mobility during Russia's Market Transition." *American Sociological Review* 69, no. 5 (October 2004): 677–703.

Gerber, Theodore P., and Olga Mayorova. "Getting Personal: Networks and Stratification in the Russian Labor Market, 1985–2001." *American Journal of Sociology* 116, no. 3 (November 2010): 855–908.

Gerring, John. "Case Selection for Case-Study Analysis: Qualitative and Quantitative Techniques." In *The Oxford Handbook of Political Methodology*, edited by Janet M. Box-Steffensmeier, Henry E. Brady, and David Collier, 645–84. Oxford: Oxford University Press, 2010.

Gerschenkron, Alexander. *Economic Backwardness in Historical Perspective: A Book of Essays*. Boston, Massachusetts: The Belknap Press of Harvard University Press, 1962.

Getmansky, Anna, and Thomas Zeitzoff. "Terrorism and Voting: The Effect of Rocket Threat on Voting in Israeli Elections." *American Political Science Review* 108, no. 3 (August 2014): 588–604.

Gilligan, Michael J., Benjamin J. Pasquale, and Cyrus Samii. "Civil War and Social Cohesion: Lab-in-the-Field Evidence from Nepal." *American Journal of Political Science* 58, no. 3 (July 2014): 604–19.

Gilman, Nils. *Mandarins of the Future: Modernization Theory in Cold War America.* Baltimore, Maryland: Johns Hopkins University Press, 2003.

Ginzburg, Carlo. *Clues, Myths, and the Historical Method*, translated by John Tedeschi and Anne C. Tedeschi. Baltimore, Maryland: Johns Hopkins University Press, 2013.

Giraudy, Agustina. "Varieties of Subnational Undemocratic Regimes: Evidence from Argentina and Mexico." *Studies in Comparative International Development* 48 (March 2013): 51–80.

Giuliano, Elise. "Who Determines the Self in the Politics of Self-Determination? Identity and Preference Formation in Tatarstan's Nationalist Mobilization." *Comparative Politics* 32, no. 3 (April 2000): 295–316.

Gladwell, Malcolm. *Outliers: The Story of Success.* London: Penguin Books, 2009.

Glaeser, Edward L., Rafael La Porta, Florencio Lopez-de-Silanes, and Andrei Shleifer. "Do Institutions Cause Growth?" *Journal of Economic Growth* 9, no. 3 (September 2004): 271–303.

Glassman, Ronald M., William H. Swatos, Jr., and Peter Kivisto, eds. *For Democracy: The Noble Character and Tragic Flaws of the Middle Class*, Contributions in Sociology, Vol. 105. Westport, Connecticut: Greenwood Press, 1993.

Goldman, Merle. *China's Intellectuals: Advise and Dissent.* Cambridge, Massachusetts: Harvard University Press, 1981.

Golitsyn, Sergey. *Zapiski utselevshego: Roman v zhanre semeynoy khroniki.* 2nd ed. Moscow: Nikeya, 2016.

Golubinov, Yaroslav A. "Obraz volzhskogo goroda: Ot krayevedeniya k regionalistike." In *Gorod i vremya*, edited by Yelena Burlina, Larisa Ilivitskaya, and Yuliya Kuzovenkova, 54–60. Samara: Samara Book Publishing House, 2012.

Golubkov, Sergey A. *Portfel' moyego deda: Memuarnyye ocherki, esse, stikhotovoreniya.* Samara: Nauchno-tekhnicheskiy tsentr, 2010.

Goncharenko, K. P. "Kupecheskaya dinastiya Shikhobalovykh v Samare." In *Samarskoye kupechestvo: Vekhi istorii*, edited by Ye. P. Barinova, 307–15. Samara: Samarskiy universitet, 2006.

Goodman, David S. G. "Can China Change?" In *Consolidating the Third Wave Democracies: Regional Challenges*, edited by Larry Diamond, Marc F. Plattner, Yun-han Chu, and Hung-mao Tien, 250–56. Baltimore, Maryland: Johns Hopkins University Press, 1997.

Gorenburg, Dmitry P. *Minority Ethnic Mobilization in the Russian Federation.* Cambridge: Cambridge University Press, 2003.

Gorky, Maxim. *M. Gorky: Izbrannoye.* Moscow: Khudozhestvennaya literatura, 1989.

Goskomstat. *Rossiyskaya Federatsiya v 1992 godu: Statisticheskiy yezhegodnik.* Moscow: Respublikanskiy informatsionno-izdatel'skiy tsentr, 1993.

Gould, Roger V. "Uses of Network Tools in Comparative Historical Research." In *Comparative-Historical Analysis in the Social Sciences*, edited by James Mahoney and Dietrich Rueschemeyer, 241–69. Cambridge: Cambridge University Press, 2003.

Gouldner, Alvin W. *The Future of Intellectuals and the Rise of the New Class: A Frame of Reference, Theses, Conjectures, Arguments, and an Historical Perspective on the Role of Intellectuals and Intelligentsia in the International Class Contest of the Modern Era.* London: Macmillan, 1979.

Graham, Loren R. *The Ghost of the Executed Engineer: Technology and the Fall of the Soviet Union.* Cambridge, Massachusetts: Harvard University Press, 1993.

The Soviet Academy of Sciences and the Communist Party, 1927–1932. Princeton, New Jersey: Princeton University Press, 1967.

Gramsci, Antonio. *Selections from Prison Notebooks*, translated by Quintin Hoare and Geoffrey Nowell Smith. London: Lawrence and Wishart, 1986.

Granovetter, Mark S. "The Strength of Weak Ties." *American Journal of Sociology* 78, no. 6 (May 1973): 1360–80.

Grenfell, Michael, ed. *Pierre Bourdieu: Key Concepts.* 2nd ed. London: Routledge, 2012.

Grosfeld, Irena, Alexander Rodnyansky, and Ekaterina Zhuravskaya. "Persistent Antimarket Culture: A Legacy of the Pale of Settlement after the Holocaust." *American Economic Journal: Economic Policy* 5, no. 3 (August 2013): 189–226.

Grzymala-Busse, Anna. "Time Will Tell? Temporality and the Analysis of Causal Mechanisms and Processes." *Comparative Political Studies* 44, no. 9 (September 2011): 1267–97.

Guins, Georgiy K. *Sibir', soyuzniki i Kolchak: Povorotnyy moment russkoy istorii, 1918–1920 (Vpechatleniya i mysli chlena Omskogo Pravitel'stva).* Moscow: Ayris Press, 2013.

Habermas, Jürgen. *The Structural Transformation of the Public Sphere: An Inquiry into a Category of Bourgeois Society*, translated by Thomas Burger. Cambridge: Polity Press, 2008.

Hacker, Jacob S., Paul Pierson, and Kathleen Thelen. "Drift and Conversion: Hidden Faces of Institutional Change." In *Advances in Comparative-Historical Analysis*, edited by James Mahoney and Kathleen Thelen, 180–208. Cambridge: Cambridge University Press, 2015.

Hahn, Jeffrey W. "Yaroslavl' Revisited: Assessing Continuity and Change in Russian Political Culture since 1990." In *Political Culture and Post-Communism*, edited by Stephen Whitefield. St. Antony's Series, 148–79. New York: Palgrave Macmillan, 2005.

Halbwachs, Maurice. *On Collective Memory*, translated by Lewis A. Coser. Chicago, Illinois: University of Chicago Press, 1992.

Hale, Henry. "Explaining Machine Politics in Russia's Regions." *Post-Soviet Affairs* 19, no. 3 (July/September 2003): 228–63.

Hale, Henry E. *Patronal Politics: Eurasian Regime Dynamics in Comparative Perspective.* New York: Cambridge University Press, 2015.

Hanley, Eric, Natasha Yershova, and Richard Anderson. "Russia-Old Wine in a New Bottle? The Circulation and Reproduction of Russian Elites, 1983–1993." *Theory and Society* 24, no. 5 (October 1995): 639–68.

Hanson, Stephen E. "The Leninist Legacy and Institutional Change." *Comparative Political Studies* 28, no. 2 (July 1995): 306–14.

Hardy, Jeffrey S. *The Gulag after Stalin: Redefining Punishment in Khrushchev's Soviet Union, 1953–1964.* Ithaca, New York: Cornell University Press, 2016.

Hartley, Janet M. *Siberia: A History of the People.* New Haven, Connecticut: Yale University Press, 2014.

The Volga: History of Russia's Greatest River. New Haven, Connecticut: Yale University Press, 2021.

Haxthausen, August von. *Studies on the Interior of Russia*, translated by Eleanore L. M. Schmidt. Chicago, Illinois: University of Chicago Press, 1972.

Held, Joseph. "Is History the Enemy of Hungarian Democracy? Musing about the Past and Present." In *Hungary's Historical Legacies: Studies in Honor of Steven Béla Várdy*, edited by Dennis P. Hupchick and R. William Weisberger, 1–23. Boulder, Colorado: Columbia University Press, 2000.

Hellbeck, Jochen. *Revolution on My Mind: Writing a Diary under Stalin*. Cambridge, Massachusetts: Harvard University Press, 2006.

"Working, Struggling, Becoming: Stalin-Era Autobiographical Texts." *Russian Review* 60, no. 3 (July 2001): 340–59.

Herrera, Yoshiko M. *Mirrors of the Economy: National Accounts and International Norms in Russia and Beyond*. Ithaca, New York: Cornell University Press, 2010.

Hildermeier, Manfred. "Was war das Mescanstvo? Zur rechtlichen und sozialen Verfassung des unteren städtischen Standes in Rußland." *Forschungen zur osteuropäischen Geschichte* 36 (1985): 15–53.

Hill, Fiona, and Clifford G. Gaddy. *The Siberian Curse: How Communist Planners Left Russia Out in the Cold*. Washington, DC: Brookings Institution Press, 2003.

Hirsch, Marianne. *Family Frames: Photography, Narrative and Postmemory*. Cambridge, Massachusetts: Harvard University Press, 1997.

Hoensch, Jörg K. *A History of Modern Hungary 1867–1994*, translated by Kim Traynor, 2nd ed. London: Longman, 1996.

Hoffmann, David L. *Peasant Metropolis: Social Identities in Moscow, 1929–1941*. Ithaca, New York: Cornell University Press, 1994.

Hoselitz, Bert F. *Sociological Aspects of Economic Growth*. New York: The Free Press, 1965.

Hough, Jerry F., and Merle Fainsod. *How the Soviet Union Is Governed*. Cambridge, Massachusetts: Harvard University Press, 1979.

Hout, Michael, and Thomas A. DiPrete. "What We Have Learned: RC28's Contributions to Knowledge about Social Stratification." *Research in Social Stratification and Mobility* 24, no. 1 (2006): 1–20.

Howlett, Michael, and Klaus H. Goetz. "Introduction: Time, Temporality and Timescapes in Administration and Policy." *International Review of Administrative Sciences* 80, no. 3 (September 2014): 477–92.

Hunter, Floyd. *Community Power Structure: A Study of Decision Makers*. Chapel Hill: University of North Carolina Press, 1953.

Huntington, Samuel P. *The Third Wave: Democratization in the Late Twentieth Century*. Norman: University of Oklahoma Press, 1991.

Hurst, William. "Mass Frames and Worker Protest." In *Popular Protest in China*, edited by Kevin J. O'Brien, 71–87. Cambridge, Massachusetts: Harvard University Press, 2008.

Hutchinson, John F. "Politics and Medical Professionalization after 1905." In *Russia's Missing Middle Class: The Professions in Russian History*, edited by Harley D. Balzer, 89–116. Armonk, New York: M. E. Sharpe, 1996.

Ilic, Melanie J. "The Forgotten Five Percent: Women, Political Repression and the Purges." In *Stalin's Terror Revisited*, edited by Melanie Illic, 116–39. New York: Palgrave Macmillan, 2006.

Ilivitskaya, Larisa G. "Bezymyanka: V poiskakh samoidentifikatsii." In *Gorod i vremya*, edited by Yelena Burlina, Larisa Ilivitskaya, and Yulia Kuzovenkova, 95–99. Samara: Samara Book Publishing House, 2012.

Inkeles, Alex. "Social Stratification and Mobility in the Soviet Union: 1940–1950." *American Sociological Review* 15, no. 4 (August 1950): 465–79.

Inkeles, Alex, and Raymond A. Bauer. *The Soviet Citizen: Daily Life in a Totalitarian Society.* Cambridge, Massachusetts: Harvard University Press, 1959.

Isaac, Larry W., and Larry J. Griffin. "Ahistoricism in Time-Series Analyses of Historical Process: Critique, Redirection, and Illustrations from U.S. Labor History." *American Sociological Review* 54, no. 6 (December 1989): 873–90.

Ivanov, B. Yu., A. A. Komzolova, and I. S. Ryakhovskaya, eds. *Gosudarstvennaya Duma Rossiyskoy imperii, 1906–1917: Entsyklopediya.* Moscow: ROSSPEN, 2008.

Iversen, Torben, and David Soskice. *Democracy and Prosperity: Reinventing Capitalism through a Turbulent Century.* Princeton, New Jersey: Princeton University Press, 2019.

Janos, Andrew. "Modernization and Decay in Historical Perspective: The Case of Romania." In *Social Change in Romania, 1860–1940: A Debate on Development in a European Nation,* edited by Kenneth Jowitt, 72–116. Berkeley, California: Institute of International Studies, 1978.

Janos, Andrew C. *The Politics of Backwardness in Hungary, 1825–1945.* Princeton, New Jersey: Princeton University Press, 1982.

Jarausch, Konrad H. "The German Professions in History and Theory." In *German Professions, 1800–1950,* edited by Geoffrey Cocks and Konrad H. Jarausch, 9–24. New York: Oxford University Press, 1990.

Jarausch, Konrad H., and Kenneth A. Hardy. *Quantitative Methods for Historians: A Guide to Research, Data, and Statistics.* Chapel Hill: University of North Carolina Press, 1991.

Johnson, Dale L., ed. *Middle Classes in Dependent Countries.* Beverly Hills, California: Sage Publications, 1985.

Jowitt, Ken. *New World Disorder: The Leninist Extinction.* Berkeley: University of California Press, 1993.

Junisbai, Barbara. "A Tale of Two Kazakhstans: Sources of Political Cleavage and Conflict in the Post-Soviet Period." *Europe-Asia Studies* 62, no. 2 (March 2010): 235–69.

Kabytov, P. S., Ye. P. Barinova, and S. S. Selivestrov. *Zhizn' i sud'ba Aleksandra Naumova.* Samara: Izdatel'stvo As Gard, 2013.

Kadushin, Charles. *Understanding Social Networks: Theories, Concepts, and Findings.* Oxford: Oxford University Press, 2012.

Kahan, Arcadius. "Notes on Jewish Entrepreneurship in Tsarist Russia." In *Entrepreneurship in Imperial Russia and the Soviet Union,* edited by Gregory Guroff and Fred V. Carstensen, 104–24. Princeton, New Jersey: Princeton University Press, 1983.

Kalyagin, Andrey V. "Komitet chlenov Vserossiyskogo uchreditel'nogo sobraniya v Samare: Nachalo i konets (iz vospominaniy)." *XX vek i Rossiya: Obshchestvo, reformy, revolyutsii. Elektronnyy sbornik,* part 1, issue 1, 2013.

Kalyvas, Stathis N. *The Rise of Christian Democracy in Europe.* Ithaca, New York: Cornell University Press, 1996.

Kaplan, Vera. *Historians and Historical Societies in the Public Life of Imperial Russia.* Bloomington: Indiana University Press, 2017.

Kavetskaya-Mazepa, Natalya. *O moyom ottse i blizkikh yemu lyudyakh.* Kiev: DIA, 2006.

Kennan, George. *Siberia and the Exile System.* 2 vols. London: Forgotten Books, 2012.

Kézdy, Éva Sztáray. "The Descendants of Former Aristocratic Families in Hungary at the Turn of the 21 Century." *Acta Universitatis Sapientiae – Social Analysis* 9, no. 1 (2019): 9–27.

Khlevniuk, Oleg. "The Gulag and the Non-Gulag as One Interrelated Whole." *Kritika: Explorations in Russian and Eurasian History. Special Issue: The Soviet Gulag: New Research and New Interpretations* 16, no. 3 (Summer 2015): 479–98.

Khlevniuk, Oleg V. *The History of the Gulag: From Collectivization to the Great Terror.* New Haven, Connecticut: Yale University Press, 2004.

King, Gary, Robert O. Keohane, and Sidney Verba. *Designing Social Inquiry: Scientific Inference in Qualitative Research.* Princeton, New Jersey: Princeton University Press, 1994.

Kirsanova, Irina A. "Organizatsionnyye i ideologicheskiye aspekty ekskursionnoy raboty s inostrannymi turistami v Kuybyshevskoy oblasti v 1960-e-1980-e gody." *Vestnik samarskogo gosudarstvennogo universiteta* 5, no. 106 (2013): 26–31.

Kiryanov, I. K., and M. N. Lukyanov. *Parlament samoderzhavnoy Rossii: Gosudarstvennaya Duma i yeyo deputaty, 1906–1917.* Perm: Izdatel'stvo Permskogo universiteta, 1995.

Kizhner, D. M., and I. V. Chernova. "Tomskiye melamedy: Nachal'noye obrazovaniye v natsional'nykh traditsiyakh." In *Materialy VII Mezhdunarodnoy nauchno-prakticheskoy konferentsii "Istoriya, pamyat', lyudi,"* edited by M. S. Makarova, 293–304. Almaty: IP Volkova Ye. V., 2015.

Klimochkina, Aleksandra Yu. "Povsednevnaya zhizn' rossiyskogo provintsial'nogo goroda 1930-kh gg. (Na materialakh Srednego Povolzh'ya)." PhD thesis, Samara State University, 2007.

Klinova, Marina A. "Spekulyatsiya i fartsovka v SSSR 1960-kh-1980-kh gg.: Vektory sovremennogo istoriograficheskogo osmysleniya." In *Ural industrial'nyi: Bakuninskiye chteniya,* edited by Vasiliy V. Zapariy, 78–83. Ekaterinburg: URFU, 2014.

Kobozeva, Zoya M. "Dialogichnost' khronotopov: 'Meshchanskiy mirok' v 'kupecheskom tsarstve' provintsial'noy Samary." *Vestnik Samarskogo gosudarstvennogo universiteta* 7, no. 73 (2009): 139–46.

——— "Gorod i meshchane: V poiskakh utrachennogo raya." In *Gorod i vremya,* edited by Yelena Burlina, Larisa Ilivizkaja, and Julia Kuzovenkova, 49–53. Samara: Samara Book Publishing House, 2012.

——— "Meshchanskaya povsednevnost' provintsial'nykh gorodov Rossii vo vtoroy polovine XIX-nachale XX vv." PhD thesis, Samara State University, 2014.

——— *Meshchanskoye sosoloviye Samary v prostranstve vlasti i povsednevnosti (vtoraya polovina XIX – nachalo XX v.), ili "rasskaz o dushe s povinnostyami."* Samara: Samarskiy universitet, 2013.

——— "Samarskaya meshchanka gulyala po XX veku." *Istoriya v podrobnostyakh* 11, no. 29 (2012): 72–77.

Koch, Fred C. *The Volga Germans in Russia and the Americas, from 1763 to the Present.* University Park: Pennsylvania State University Press, 1977.

Koesel, Karrie J., and Valerie J. Bunce. "Diffusion-Proofing: Russian and Chinese Responses to Waves of Popular Mobilization against Authoritarian Rulers."

In *Citizens and the State in Authoritarian Regimes: Comparing China and Russia*, edited by Karrie J. Koesel, Valerie J. Bunce, and Jessica Chen Weiss, 87–113. Oxford: Oxford University Press, 2020.

Kohli, Atul. *State-Directed Development: Political Power and Industrialization in the Global Periphery*. Cambridge: Cambridge University Press, 2007.

Kolesnikova, Lyubov' A. "Istoriya poyavleniya i formirovaniya etnicheskikh obshchin, traditsionno prozhivayushchikh v Samarskoy oblasti." *Vestnik Samarskogo gosudarstvennogo universiteta* 7, no. 73 (2009): 131–38.

Kolesnikova, Yelena M. "Inzhenernyye dinastii: Resurs sotsial'noy mobil'nosti i formirovaniya gruppy." *Vestnik Nizhegorodskogo universiteta imeni N. I. Lobachevskogo* 2, no. 42 (2016): 104–10.

Köll, Elisabeth. "The Making of the Civil Engineer in China: Knowledge Transfer, Institution Building, and the Rise of a Profession." In *Knowledge Acts in Modern China: Ideas, Institutions, and Identities*, edited by Robert Culp, Eddy U, and Wen-hsin Yeh, 148–73. Berkeley: University of California, Berkeley, 2016.

Konrád, George, and Iván Szelényi. *The Intellectuals on the Road to Class Power: A Sociological Study of the Role of the Intelligentsia in Socialism*, translated by Andrew Arato and Richard E. Allen. Brighton: Harvester Press, 1979.

Kopstein, Jeffrey. "Review Article: Postcommunist Democracy: Legacies and Outcomes." *Comparative Politics* 35, no. 2 (January 2003): 231–50.

Kopstein, Jeffrey, and Michael Bernhard. "Post-Communism, the Civilizing Process, and the Mixed Impact of Leninist Violence." *East European Politics and Societies and Cultures* 29, no. 2 (May 2015): 379–90.

Kordonskiy, Simon G. *Soslovnaya struktura postsovetskoy Rossii*. Moscow: Institut fonda "Obshchestvennoye mneniye," 2008.

Kotkin, Stephen. *Magnetic Mountain: Stalinism as a Civilization*. Berkeley: University of California Press, 1997.

Kotkin, Stephen, and Mark R. Beissinger. "The Historical Legacies of Communism: An Empirical Agenda." In *Historical Legacies of Communism in Russia and Eastern Europe*, edited by Mark R. Beissinger and Stephen Kotkin, 1–27. New York: Cambridge University Press, 2014.

Kotsonis, Yanni. "'Face-to-Face': The State, the Individual, and the Citizen in Russian Taxation, 1863–1917." *Slavic Review* 63, no.2 (Summer 2004): 221–46.

Kovács, Mária M. *Liberal Professions and Illiberal Politics: Hungary from the Habsburgs to the Holocaust*. Washington, DC: Woodrow Wilson Center Press, 1994.

Kovács, Maria M., and Antal Örkény. "Promoted Cadres and Professionals in Post-War Hungary." In *Economy and Society in Hungary*, edited by Rudolf Andorka and László Bertalan, 139–52. Budapest: Karl Marx University of Economic Sciences, 1986.

Kozhin, Boris A. *Rasskazyvayet Boris Kozhin*. Samara: Metida, 2013.

Kracauer, Siegfried. *Die Angestellten*. Frankfurt am Main: Suhrkamp Verlag, 2017.

The Mass Ornament: Weimar Essays, translated by Thomas Y. Levin. Cambridge, Massachusetts: Harvard University Press, 1995.

Kreuzer, Marcus. *The Grammar of Time: Using Comparative Historical Analysis to Investigate Macro-Historical Questions*. New York: Cambridge University Press, in press.

"The Structure of Description: Evaluating Descriptive Inferences and Conceptualizations." *Perspectives on Politics* 17, no. 1 (March 2019): 122–39.

"Varieties of Time in Comparative Historical Analysis." In *The Oxford Handbook of Time and Politics*, edited by Klaus H. Goetz. New York: Oxford University Press, 2019.

Kryshtanovskaya, Olga, and Stephen White. "From Soviet Nomenklatura to Russian Elite." *Europe-Asia Studies* 48, no. 5 (July 1996): 711–33.

Kuhn, Philip A. "Chinese Views of Social Classification." In *Class and Social Stratification in Post-Revolution China*, edited by James L. Watson, 16–28. New York: Cambridge University Press, 2010.

Kuz'min, Vladimir Yu. *Zdravookhraneniye Samarskoy gubernii v pervyye gody sovetskoy vlasti: 1918–1922 gody*. Samara: Parus, 2001.

Kuz'minykh, S. V., I. Ye. Safonov, and D. A. Stashenkov. *Vera Vladimirovna Gol'msten: Materialy k biografii*. Samara: Ofort, 2007.

Kuzmicheva, Ol'ga I. "Iz semeynoy khroniki." In *Neizvestnaya Samara: Sbornik statey*, edited by N. V. Iyevleva and T. F. Aleksushina, 157–61. Samara: Detskaya kartinnaya galereya Samary, 2007.

Labrousse, Ernest. "New Paths Toward a History of the Western Bourgeoisie (1700–1850)," translated by Arthur Goldhammer and others. In *Histories: French Constructions of the Past*, edited by Jacques Revel and Lynn Hunt, 67–74. New York: The New Press, 1995.

Laitin, David D. "Language and Nationalism in the Post-Soviet Republics." *Post-Soviet Affairs* 12, no. 1 (January 1996): 4–24.

Lankina, Tomila. "Boris Nemtsov and the Reproduction of the Regional Intelligentsia." *Demokratizatsiya: The Journal of Post-Soviet Democratization* 24, no. 1 (Winter 2016): 45–68.

Lankina, Tomila, and Lullit Getachew. "Mission or Empire, Word or Sword? The Human Capital Legacy in Post-Colonial Democratic Development." *American Journal of Political Science* 56, no. 2 (April 2012): 465–83.

Lankina, Tomila V., and Alexander Libman. "Soviet Legacies of Economic Development, Oligarchic Rule and Electoral Quality in Eastern Europe's Partial Democracies: The Case of Ukraine." *Comparative Politics* 52, no. 1 (October 2019): 127–76.

"The Two-Pronged Middle Class: The Old Bourgeoisie, New State-Engineered Middle Class and Democratic Development." *American Political Science Review* 115, no. 3 (August 2021): 948–66.

Lankina, Tomila V. *Governing the Locals: Local Self-Government and Ethnic Mobilization in Russia*. Lanham, Maryland: Rowman & Littlefield, 2004.

"Religious Influences on Human Capital Variations in Imperial Russia." *Journal of Eurasian Studies* 3, no. 1 (January 2012): 10–19.

Lankina, Tomila V., and Lullit Getachew. "A Geographic Incremental Theory of Democratization: Territory, Aid, and Democracy in Post-Communist Regions." *World Politics* 58, no. 4 (July 2006): 536–82.

Lankina, Tomila V., Alexander Libman, and Anastassia Obydenkova. "Appropriation and Subversion: Pre-communist Literacy, Communist Party Saturation, and Post-Communist Democratic Outcomes." *World Politics* 68, no. 2 (April 2016): 229–74.

Lankina, Tomila V., and Katerina Tertytchnaya. "Protest in Electoral Autocracies: A New Dataset." *Post-Soviet Affairs* 36, no. 1 (2020): 20–36.

LaPorte, Jody, and Danielle N. Lussier. "What Is the Leninist Legacy? Assessing Twenty Years of Scholarship." *Slavic Review* 70, no. 3 (Fall 2011): 637–54.

Ledeneva, Alena V. *Russia's Economy of Favours: Blat, Networking and Informal Exchange*. Cambridge: Cambridge University Press, 1998.

Lenz, Gabriel S., and Alexander Sahn. "Achieving Statistical Significance with Control Variables and without Transparency." *Political Analysis* (2020): 1–14.

Lerner, Daniel. *The Passing of Traditional Society: Modernizing the Middle East*. Glencoe, Illinois: The Free Press, 1958.

Levitt, Peggy. *The Transnational Villagers*. Berkeley: University of California Press, 2001.

Lewin, Moshe. "Society, State, and Ideology during the First Five-Year Plan." In *Cultural Revolution in Russia, 1928–1931*, edited by Sheila Fitzpatrick, 41–77. Bloomington: Indiana University Press, 1978.

Libman, Alexander, and Anastassia V. Obydenkova. "CPSU Legacies and Regional Democracy in Contemporary Russia." *Political Studies* 63, no. 1 (suppl.) (August 2015): 173–90.

Linz, Juan J., and Alfred Stepan. *Problems of Democratic Transition and Consolidation: Southern Europe, South America, and Post-Communist Europe*. Baltimore, Maryland: Johns Hopkins University Press, 1996.

Lipset, Seymour Martin. "Some Social Requisites of Democracy: Economic Development and Political Legitimacy." *American Political Science Review* 53, no. 1 (March 1959): 69–105.

Lipset, Seymour Martin, and Richard B. Dobson. "The Intellectual as Critic and Rebel: With Special Reference to the United States and the Soviet Union." *Daedalus* 101, no. 3 (Summer 1972): 137–98.

Lipsky, Michael. *Street-Level Bureaucracy: Dilemmas of the Individual in Public Services*. New York: Russell Sage Foundation, 1980.

Lovell, Stephen. *Summerfolk: A History of the Dacha, 1710–2000*. Ithaca, New York: Cornell University Press, 2003.

Luebbert, Gregory M. *Liberalism, Fascism, or Social Democracy: Social Classes and the Political Origins of Regimes in Interwar Europe*. New York: Oxford University Press, 1991.

Lyubzhin, A. I. *Istoriya russkoy shkoly imperatorskoy epokhi*, Vol. 2. Moscow: Nikeya, 2016.

Mahoney, James. "Knowledge Accumulation in Comparative Historical Research: The Case of Democracy and Authoritarianism." In *Comparative Historical Analysis in the Social Sciences*, edited by James Mahoney and Dietrich Rueschemeyer, 131–74. Cambridge: Cambridge University Press, 2003.

Makitrin, K. M., and Ye. P. Barinova. "Samarskoye kupechestvo: Demograficheskaya kharakteristika." In *Samarskoye kupechestvo: Vekhi istorii*, edited by Ye. P. Barinova, 40–57. Samara: Samarskiy universitet, 2006.

Mal'tsev, Aleksey A. "Osobennosti poslevoyennykh migratsiy v sel'skoy mestnosti Srednego Povolzh'ya (1946–1955 gody)." *Vestnik Samarskogo gosudarstvennogo universiteta* 5, no. 79 (2010): 84–86.

"Poslevoyennaya reemigratsiya naseleniya v Sredneye Povolzh'ye (1945–1951 gg.)." *Izvestiya Samarskogo nauchnogo tsentra Rossiyskoy akademii nauk* 12, no. 6 (2010): 113–15.

Mannheim, Karl. "The Problem of Generations." In *The New Pilgrims: Youth Protest in Transition*, edited by Philip Altbach and Robert S. Laufer, 101–36. New York: McKay, 1972.

Mark, James. "Discrimination, Opportunity, and Middle-Class Success in Early Communist Hungary." *The Historical Journal* 48, no. 2 (June 2005): 499–521.

"Society, Resistance and Revolution: The Budapest Middle Class and the Hungarian Communist State 1948–56." *The English Historical Review* 120, no. 488 (September 2005): 963–86.

Martin, Terry. *The Affirmative Action Empire: Nations and Nationalism in the Soviet Union, 1923–1939.* Ithaca, New York: Cornell University Press, 2001.

Marx, Karl. *Capital: A Critique of Political Economy, Vol. 1: The Process of Production of Capital,* translated by Ben Fowkes. London: Penguin Classics, 1990.

Capital: A Critique of Political Economy, Vol. 3: The Process of Capitalist Production as a Whole, translated by David Fernbach. London: Penguin Classics, 1991.

Marx, Karl, and Friedrich Engels. *The Communist Manifesto with Selections from The Eighteenth Brumaire of Louis Bonaparte and Capital by Karl Marx.* New York: Appleton-Century-Crofts, 1955.

Maton, Karl. "Habitus." In *Pierre Bourdieu: Key Concepts,* edited by Michael Grenfell, 48–64. London: Routledge, 2012.

Matthews, Mervyn. *Class and Society in Soviet Russia.* London: Allen Lane, 1972.

"Elitism in Postcommunist Russia: Some Interim Comments." In *The Social Legacy of Communism,* edited by James R. Millar and Sharon L. Wolchik. Woodrow Wilson Center Series, 309–28. Washington, DC: Woodrow Wilson Center Press, 1994.

Privilege in the Soviet Union: A Study of Elite Life-Styles under Communism. London: George Allen & Unwin, 1978.

McFaul, Michael, and Nikolai Petrov, eds. *Politicheskiy al'manakh Rossii 1997,* Vol. 2. Moscow: Moscow Carnegie Centre, 1998.

McMann, Kelly M. *Economic Autonomy and Democracy: Hybrid Regimes in Russia and Kyrgyzstan.* New York: Cambridge University Press, 2006.

McMann, Kelly M., and Nikolai V. Petrov. "A Survey of Democracy in Russia's Regions." *Post-Soviet Geography and Economics* 41, no. 3 (April–May 2000): 155–82.

Mead, George Herbert. "*The Nature of the Past.*" In *G. H. Mead: A Reader,* edited by Filipe Carreira da Silva, 204–9. Abingdon: Routledge, 2012.

Migdal, Joel S. *State in Society: Studying How States and Societies Transform and Constitute One Another.* New York: Cambridge University Press, 2009.

Mills, C. Wright. *White Collar: The American Middle Classes,* 50th anniversary ed. New York: Oxford University Press, 2002.

Mironov, Boris N. *Rossiyskaya imperiya: Ot traditsii k modernu,* Vol. 1. St. Petersburg: Dmitriy Bulanin, 2014.

Rossiyskaya imperiya: Ot traditsii k modernu, Vol. 2. St. Petersburg: Dmitriy Bulanin, 2015.

Rossiyskaya imperiya: Ot traditsii k modernu, Vol. 3. St. Petersburg: Dmitriy Bulanin, 2015.

Sotsial'naya istoriya Rossii perioda Imperii (XVIII–nachalo XX v.). Genezis lichnosti, demokraticheskoy sem'yi, grazhdanskogo obshchestva i pravovogo gosudarstva, rev. 3rd ed., Vol. 1. St. Petersburg: Dmitriy Bulanin, 2003.

Moon, David. "Peasant Migration, the Abolition of Serfdom, and the Internal Passport System in the Russian Empire, c. 1800–1914." In *Coerced and Free Migration: Global Perspectives,* edited by David Eltis, 324–57. Stanford, California: Stanford University Press, 2002.

The Plough That Broke the Steppes: Agriculture and Environment on Russia's Grasslands, 1700–1914. Oxford: Oxford University Press, 2013.

Moore, Barrington, Jr. *Social Origins of Dictatorship and Democracy: Lord and Peasant in the Making of the Modern World.* Boston, Massachusetts: Beacon Press, 1993.

Morris, Jeremy. "The Informal Economy and Post-Socialism: Imbricated Perspectives on Labor, the State, and Social Embeddedness." *Demokratizatsiya: The Journal of Post-Soviet Democratization* 27, no. 1 (Winter 2019): 9–30.

Morris, Jeremy, and Abel Polese. "Informal Health and Education Sector Payments in Russian and Ukrainian Cities: Structuring Welfare from Below." *European Urban and Regional Studies* 23, no. 3 (July 2016): 481–96.

Mousnier, Roland, Jean-Pierre Labatut, and Yves Durand. "Problems of Social Stratification," translated by Arthur Goldhammer and others. In *Histories: French Constructions of the Past*, edited by Jacques Revel and Lynn Hunt, 154–58. New York: The New Press, 1995.

Munting, Roger. "Lend-Lease and the Soviet War Effort." *Journal of Contemporary History* 19, no. 3 (July 1984): 495–510.

MVDRF, and MYuRF. *Prestupnost' i pravonarusheniya, 1991: Statisticheskiy sbornik.* Moscow: Finansy i statistika, 1992.

Myakisheva, Ye. Yu. "Istoriya v otkrytkakh." In *Neizvestnaya Samara: Sbornik statey*, edited by N. V. Iyevleva and T. F. Aleksushina, 140–56. Samara: Detskaya kartinnaya galereya Samary, 2007.

Nafziger, Steven. "Did Ivan's Vote Matter? The Political Economy of Local Democracy in Tsarist Russia." *European Review of Economic History* 15, no. 3 (December 2011): 393–441.

Nathan, Andrew J. *China's Transition.* New York: Columbia University Press, 1997.

Neklutin, Konstantin N. *Ot Samary do Siettla.* Samara: Samarskiy Dom Pechati, 2011.

Norman, John O. "Pavel Tretiakov and Merchant Art Patronage, 1850–1900." In *Between Tsar and People: Educated Society and the Quest for Public Identity in Late Imperial Russia*, edited by Edith W. Clowes, Samuel D. Kassow, and James L. West, 93–107. Princeton, New Jersey: Princeton University Press, 1991.

Nove, A. "Is There a Ruling Class in the USSR?" *Soviet Studies* 27, no. 4 (October 1975): 615–38.

O'Brien, Kevin J., ed. *Popular Protest in China.* Cambridge, Massachusetts: Harvard University Press, 2008.

O'Donnell, Guillermo A. *Modernization and Bureaucratic Authoritarianism: Studies in South American Politics.* Berkeley: Institute of International Studies, University of California, 1973.

O'Donnell, Guillermo A., Philippe C. Schmitter, and Laurence Whitehead, eds. *Transitions from Authoritarian Rule: Comparative Perspectives: Prospects for Democracy*, Vol. 3. Baltimore, Maryland: Johns Hopkins University Press, 1986.

Olekh, Andrey. *Obmen i prodazha.* Moscow: Eksmo, 2018.

Orlovsky, Daniel. "The Lower Middle Strata in Revolutionary Russia." In *Between Tsar and People: Educated Society and the Quest for Public Identity in Late Imperial Russia*, edited by Edith W. Clowes, Samuel D. Kassow, and James L. West, 248–68. Princeton, New Jersey: Princeton University Press, 1991.

Orren, Karen, and Stephen Skowronek. "Beyond the Iconography of Order: Notes for a 'New Institutionalism.'" In *The Dynamics of American Politics*, edited by

Lawrence Dodd and Calvin Jillson, 311–30. Boulder, Colorado: Westview Press, 1994.

Osokina, Elena. *Zoloto dlya industrializatsii: Torgsin.* Moscow: Rosspen, 2009.

Osokina, Elena A. *Our Daily Bread: Socialist Distribution and the Art of Survival in Stalin's Russia, 1927–1941,* translated by Kate Transchel and Greta Bucher. Armonk, New York: M. E. Sharpe, 2001.

Parish, William L. "Destratification in China." In *Class and Social Stratification in Post-Revolution China,* edited by James L. Watson, 84–120. New York: Cambridge University Press, 2010.

Parkin, Frank. "System Contradiction and Political Transformation." *European Journal of Sociology* 13, no. 1 (May 1972): 45–62.

Pearson, Thomas S. *Russian Officialdom in Crisis: Autocracy and Local Self-Government, 1861–1900.* Cambridge: Cambridge University Press, 1989.

Pei, Minxin. *China's Trapped Transition: The Limits of Developmental Autocracy.* Cambridge, Massachusetts: Harvard University Press, 2008.

Pepper, Suzanne. "Education and Revolution: The 'Chinese Model' Revised." *Asian Survey* 18, no. 9 (September 1978): 847–90.

Perry, Elizabeth J. "Permanent Rebellion? Continuities and Discontinuities in Chinese Protest." In *Popular Protest in China,* edited by Kevin J. O'Brien, 205–15. Cambridge, Massachusetts: Harvard University Press, 2008.

Perry, Elizabeth J., and Ellen V. Fuller. "China's Long March to Democracy." *World Policy Journal* 4, no. 3 (Fall 1991): 663–83.

Péter, László. *Hungary's Long Nineteenth Century: Constitutional and Democratic Traditions in a European Perspective: Collected Studies.* Leiden: Brill, 2012.

Péteri, György. "Engineer Utopia: On the Position of Technostructure in Hungary's War Communism, 1919." *International Studies of Management and Organization* 19, no. 3 (Fall 1989): 82–101.

Petrov, Nikolai. "Regional Models of Democratic Development." In *Between Dictatorship and Democracy: Russian Post-Communist Political Reform,* edited by Michael McFaul, Nikolai Petrov, and Andrei Ryabov, 239–67. Washington, DC: Carnegie Endowment for International Peace, 2005.

Petrova, Yaroslavna I. "Likbez kak sotsial'nyy proyekt (na materialakh Samarskoy gubernii 1920–1930-e gody)." *Zhurnal issledovaniy sotsial'noy politiki* 5, no. 4 (2007): 519–40.

Pierson, Paul. *Politics in Time: History, Institutions, and Social Analysis.* Princeton, New Jersey: Princeton University Press, 2004.

"Power and Path Dependence." In *Advances in Comparative-Historical Analysis,* edited by James Mahoney and Kathleen Thelen, 123–46. Cambridge: Cambridge University Press, 2015.

Piketty, Thomas. *Capital in the Twenty-First Century,* translated by Arthur Goldhammer. Cambridge, Massachusetts: The Belknap Press of Harvard University Press, 2014.

Pipes, Richard. *The Russian Revolution 1899–1919.* London: The Harvill Press, 1997.

Pitelina, Natalya A. "Fenomen kommunal'noy kvartiry v povesti I. Grekovoy 'Vdoviy parokhod.'" *Vestnik Pskovskogo gosudarstvennogo universiteta* 3 (2008): 86–91.

Plantan, Elizabeth. "A Tale of Two Laws: Managing Foreign Agents and Overseas NGOs in Russia and China." In *Citizens and the State in Authoritarian Regimes: Comparing China and Russia,* edited by Karrie J. Koesel, Valerie J. Bunce, and Jessica Chen Weiss, 167–90. Oxford: Oxford University Press, 2020.

Polanyi, Karl. *The Great Transformation: The Political and Economic Origins of Our Time*, 2nd ed. Boston, Massachusetts: Beacon Press, 2001.

Polonsky, Antony. *The Little Dictators: The History of Eastern Europe since 1918*, 1st ed. London: Routledge and Kegan Paul, 1975.

Pop-Eleches, Grigore. "Communist Development and the Postcommunist Democratic Deficit." In *Historical Legacies of Communism in Russia and Eastern Europe*, edited by Mark R. Beissinger and Stephen Kotkin, 28–51. New York: Cambridge University Press, 2014.

"Historical Legacies and Post-Communist regime Change." *The Journal of Politics* 69, no. 4 (November 2007): 908–26.

Pop-Eleches, Grigore, and Joshua A. Tucker. *Communism's Shadow: Historical Legacies and Contemporary Political Attitudes*. Princeton, New Jersey: Princeton University Press, 2017.

Pravilova, Ekaterina. *A Public Empire: Property and the Quest for the Common Good in Imperial Russia*. Princeton, New Jersey: Princeton University Press, 2014.

Przeworski, Adam, Michael E. Alvarez, José Antonio Cheibub, and Fernando Limongi. *Democracy and Development: Political Institutions and Well-Being in the World, 1950–1990*. New York: Cambridge University Press, 2000.

Putnam, Robert D. *Our Kids: The American Dream in Crisis*, 1st ed. New York: Simon & Schuster, 2015.

Putnam, Robert D., Robert Leonardi, and Raffaella Y. Nanetti. *Making Democracy Work: Civic Traditions in Modern Italy*. Princeton, New Jersey: Princeton University Press, 1993.

Pykhalov, Igor' V. "Obrazovaniye v Rossiyskoy imperii: Fakty i mify." *Terra Humana* 2 (2011): 196–200.

Raeff, Marc. *Origins of the Russian Intelligentsia: The Eighteenth Century Nobility*. New York: Harcourt, Brace & World, 1966.

Ramer, Samuel C. "Professionalism and Politics: The Russian Feldsher Movement, 1891–1918." In *Russia's Missing Middle Class: The Professions in Russian History*, edited by Harley D. Balzer, 117–42. Armonk, New York: M. E. Sharpe, 1996.

Reisinger, William M., and Bryon J. Moraski. *The Regional Roots of Russia's Political Regime*. Ann Arbor, Michigan: University of Michigan Press, 2017.

Reka, Anastasiya V. "Gorodskaya sotsial'naya infrastruktura dorevolyutsionnoy Samary." PhD thesis, Samara State University, 2009.

Repnikova, Maria. "Critical Journalists in China and Russia: Encounters with Ambiguity." In *Citizens and the State in Authoritarian Regimes: Comparing China and Russia*, edited by Karrie J. Koesel, Valerie J. Bunce, and Jessica Chen Weiss, 117–36. Oxford: Oxford University Press, 2020.

Reyfman, Irina. *How Russia Learned to Write: Literature and the Imperial Table of Ranks*. Madison: University of Wisconsin Press, 2016.

Ribot, Jesse C., Ashwini Chhatre, and Tomila Lankina. "Introduction: Institutional Choice and Recognition in the Formation and Consolidation of Local Democracy." *Conservation and Society* 6, no. 1 (2008): 1–11.

Rieber, Alfred J. *Merchants and Entrepreneurs in Imperial Russia*. Chapel Hill: University of North Carolina Press, 1982.

Rigby, T. H. *Communist Party Membership in the U.S.S.R., 1917–1967*. Princeton, New Jersey: Princeton University Press, 1968.

Political Elites in the USSR: Central Leaders and Local Cadres from Lenin to Gorbachev. Aldershot: Edward Elgar, 1990.

Rimé, Bernard, and Veronique Christophe. "How Individual Emotional Episodes Feed Collective Memory." In *Collective Memory of Political Events: Social Psychological Perspectives,* edited by James W. Pennebaker, Dario Paez, and Bernard Rimé, 131–46. New York: Psychology Press, 2008.

Robertson, Graeme B. *The Politics of Protest in Hybrid Regimes: Managing Dissent in Post-Communist Russia.* Cambridge: Cambridge University Press, 2011.

Rogers, Douglas. *The Old Faith and the Russian Land: A Historical Ethnography of Ethics in the Urals.* Ithaca, New York: Cornell University Press, 2009.

Róna-Tas, Ákos. "The Second Economy as a Subversive Force: The Erosion of Party Power in Hungary." In *The Waning of the Communist State: Economic Origins of Political Decline in China and Hungary,* edited by Andrew G. Walder, 61–84. Berkeley: University of California Press, 1995.

Rose, Richard, William Mishler, and Neil Munro. *Popular Support for an Undemocratic Regime: The Changing Views of Russians.* New York: Cambridge University Press, 2011.

Rosefielde, Steven. "Documented Homicides and Excess Deaths: New Insights into the Scale of Killing in the USSR during the 1930s." *Communist and Post-Communist Studies* 30, no. 3 (September 1997): 321–31.

Rosenfeld, Bryn. *The Autocratic Middle Class: How State Dependency Reduces the Demand for Democracy.* Princeton, New Jersey: Princeton University Press, 2021.

"Reevaluating the Middle-Class Protest Paradigm: A Case-Control Study of Democratic Protest Coalitions in Russia." *American Political Science Review* 111, no. 4 (November 2017): 637–52.

Roshchina, Yana. "Intergeneration Educational Mobility in Russia and the USSR." In *The Asian Conference on Education 2012: Conference Proceedings,* 1406–26. Osaka: The International Academic Forum, 2012.

Rowe, William T. *China's Last Empire: The Great Qing.* Cambridge, Massachusetts: The Belknap Press of Harvard University Press, 2009.

RSFSR (Central Statistical Bureau of). *Narodnoye khozyaystvo SSSR za 60 let (Yubileynyy statisticheskiy yezhegodnik).* Moscow: Statistika, 1977.

Ruane, Christine. *Gender, Class, and the Professionalization of Russian City Teachers, 1860–1914.* Pittsburgh, Philadelphia: University of Pittsburgh Press, 1994.

Rueschemeyer, Dietrich, Evelyne Huber Stephens, and John D. Stephens. *Capitalist Development and Democracy.* Cambridge: Polity Press, 1992.

Ryadchenko, Yelena A. "Samarskiy publichnyy muzey v sotsiokul'turnom razvitii regiona: Istoriya sozdaniya i formirovaniye kollektsii." *Voprosy muzeologii* 2, no. 4 (2011): 75–81.

Ryndzyunskiy, Pavel G. *Krest'yane i gorod v kapitalisticheskoy Rossii vtoroy poloviny XIX veka.* Moscow: Nauka, 1983.

Safronov, A. A. "Iz istorii podgotovki pervoy vseobshchey perepisi naselenuya Rossiyskoy imperii 1897." *Dokument. Arkhiv. Istoriya. Sovremennost',* no. 1 (2001): 211–31.

Saikkonen, Inga A.-L. "Electoral Mobilization and Authoritarian Elections: Evidence from Post-Soviet Russia." *Government and Opposition* 52, no. 1 (January 2017): 51–74.

Savchenko, I. A., and S. I. Dubinin. *Rossiyskiye nemtsy v Samarskom kraye: Istoriko-krayevedcheskiye ocherki.* Samara: Samara University, 1994.

Schacter, Daniel L. "Memory Distortion: History and Current Status." In *Memory Distortion: How Minds, Brains, and Societies Reconstruct the Past*, edited by Daniel L. Schacter, 1–43. Cambridge, Massachusetts: Harvard University Press, 1997.

Scheidel, Walter. *The Great Leveler: Violence and the History of Inequality from the Stone Age to the Twenty-First Century*. Princeton, New Jersey: Princeton University Press, 2017.

Schimpfössl, Elisabeth. *Rich Russians: From Oligarchs to Bourgeoisie*. Oxford: Oxford University Press, 2018.

Schippan, Michael, and Sonja Striegnitz. *Wolgadeutsche: Geschichte und Gegenwart*. Berlin: Dietz, 1992.

Schram, Stuart R. "Classes, Old and New, in Mao Zedong's Thought, 1949–1976." In *Class and Social Stratification in Post-Revolution China*, edited by James L. Watson, 29–55. New York: Cambridge University Press, 2010.

Schulze, Max-Stephan. "Economic Development of Austria-Hungary's Machine-Building Industry, 1870–1913." PhD thesis, London School of Economics and Political Science, 1993.

Schuman, Howard, Robert F. Belli, and Katherine Bischoping. "The Generational Basis of Historical Knowledge." In *Collective Memory of Political Events: Social Psychological Perspectives*, edited by James W. Pennebaker, Dario Paez, and Bernard Rimé, 47–77. New York: Psychology Press, 2008.

Scott, James C. *Seeing Like a State: How Certain Schemes to Improve the Human Condition Have Failed*. New Haven, Connecticut: Yale University Press, 1998.

   Weapons of the Weak: Everyday Forms of Peasant Resistance. New Haven, Connecticut: Yale University Press, 1985.

Seleny, Anna. "Property Rights and Political Power: The Cumulative Process of Political Change in Hungary." In *The Waning of the Communist State: Economic Origins of Political Decline in China and Hungary*, edited by Andrew G. Walder, 27–60. Berkeley: University of California Press, 1995.

Seregny, Scott J. "Professional Activism and Association among Russian Teachers, 1864–1905." In *Russia's Missing Middle Class: The Professions in Russian History*, edited by Harley D. Balzer, 169–95. Armonk, New York: M. E. Sharpe, 1996.

SGSC. *Pamyatnaya knizhka Samarskoy gubernii na 1916 god*. Samara: Samarskiy gubernskiy statisticheskiy komitet, Samarskaya gubernskaya tipografiya, 1916.

Sharonova, Viktoriya G. "Russkaya emigratsiya v Khan'kou (Kitay)." *RSM* 4, no. 89 (2015): 218–24.

Shearer, David R. "The Soviet Gulag–an Archipelago?" *Kritika: Explorations in Russian and Eurasian History. Special Issue: The Soviet Gulag: New Research and New Interpretations* 16, no. 3 (Summer 2015): 711–24.

Shkaratan, Ovsey I., and Gordey A. Yastrebov. "Sravnitel'nyy analiz protsessov sotsial'noy mobil'nosti v SSSR i sovremennoy Rossii." *Obshchestvennyye nauki i sovremennost'* 2 (2011): 5–28.

Shlapentokh, Vladimir. *Soviet Intellectuals and Political Power: The Post-Stalin Era*. London: I.B. Tauris, 1990.

Shubkin, V. N., V. I. Artemov, N. P. Moskalenko, N. V. Buzukova, and V. A. Kalmyk. "Quantitative Methods in Sociological Studies of Problems of Job Placement and Choice of Occupation [Part I]." *Soviet Sociology* 7, no. 1 (1968): 3–24.

Siddiqi, Asif. "Scientists and Specialists in The Gulag: Life and Death in Stalin's Sharashka." *Kritika: Explorations in Russian and Eurasian History. Special Issue:*

The Soviet Gulag: New Research and New Interpretations 16, no. 3 (Summer 2015): 557–88.

Sidel, John T. *Republicanism, Communism, Islam: Cosmopolitan Origins of Revolutions in Southeast Asia.* Ithaca, New York: Cornell University Press, 2021.

Silver, Brian D. "Political Beliefs of the Soviet Citizen: Sources of Support for Regime Norms." In *Politics, Work, and Daily Life in the USSR: A Survey of Former Soviet Citizens,* edited by James R. Millar, 100–41. New York: Cambridge University Press, 1987.

Simpser, Alberto, Dan Slater, and Jason Wittenberg. "Dead but Not Gone: Contemporary Legacies of Communism, Imperialism, and Authoritarianism." *Annual Review of Political Science* 21, no. 1 (May 2018): 419–39.

Sinyavsky, Andrei. *Soviet Civilization: A Cultural History,* translated by Joan Turnbull. New York: Arcade, 1988.

Skocpol, Theda. *States and Social Revolutions: A Comparative Analysis of France, Russia, and China.* Cambridge: Cambridge University Press, 1991.

Slater, Dan. *Ordering Power: Contentious Politics and Authoritarian Leviathans in Southeast Asia.* Cambridge: Cambridge University Press, 2010.

Slezkine, Yuri. *The House of Government: A Saga of the Russian Revolution.* Princeton, New Jersey: Princeton University Press, 2017.

Smith, Alison K. *For the Common Good and Their Own Well-Being: Social Estates in Imperial Russia.* New York: Oxford University Press, 2014.

Smith, Douglas. *Former People: The Last Days of the Russian Aristocracy.* London: Pan Macmillan, 2013.

Smyth, Regina. *Elections, Protest, and Authoritarian Regime Stability: Russia 2008–2020.* New York: Cambridge University Press, 2020.

Smyth, Regina, and Sarah Oates. "Mind the Gaps: Media Use and Mass Action in Russia." *Europe-Asia Studies* 67, no. 2 (March 2015): 285–305.

Snyder, Richard. "Scaling Down: The Subnational Comparative Method." *Studies in Comparative International Development* 36, no. 1 (Spring 2001): 93–110.

Snyder, Timothy. *Bloodlands: Europe between Hitler and Stalin.* London: Bodley Head, 2010.

Sontag, Susan. *On Photography.* London: Penguin Books, 1979.

Sorokin, Pitirim. *Social Mobility.* New York: Harper & Brothers Publishers, 1927.

Sorokin, Pitirim A. *A Long Journey: The Autobiography of Pitirim A. Sorokin.* New Haven, Connecticut: College and University Press Services, 1963.

Man and Society in Calamity. Westport, Connecticut: Greenwood Press, 1968.

Speier, Hans. *German White-Collar Workers and the Rise of Hitler.* New Haven, Connecticut: Yale University Press, 1986.

Speranskiy, Mikhail M., ed. *Polnoye sobraniye zakonov Rossiyskoy imperii (1649–1825), Vol. 6: 1720–1722, laws 3480–4136.* St. Petersburg: Tipografiya II otdeleniya Sobstvennoy Yego Imperatorskogo Velichestva kantselyarii, 1830.

Starr, S. Frederick. *Decentralization and Self-Government in Russia, 1830–1870.* Princeton, New Jersey: Princeton University Press, 1972.

"Local Initiative in Russia before the Zemstvo." In *The Zemstvo in Russia: An Experiment in Local Self-Government,* edited by Terence Emmons and Wayne S. Vucinich, 5–30. New York: Cambridge University Press, 1982.

Stinchcombe, Arthur L. *Constructing Social Theories.* Chicago, Illinois: University of Chicago Press, 1987.

Stokes, Gale. "The Social Origins of East European Politics." *East European Politics and Societies* 1, no. 1 (1986): 30–74.

Stokes, Susan C. "Political Clientelism." In *The Oxford Handbook of Comparative Politics*, edited by Carles Boix and Susan C. Stokes, 604–27. Oxford: Oxford University Press, 2007.

Stoner-Weiss, Kathryn. *Local Heroes: The Political Economy of Russian Regional Governance*. Princeton, New Jersey: Princeton University Press, 1997.

Sunderland, Willard. *Taming the Wild Field: Colonization and Empire on the Russian Steppe*. Ithaca, New York: Cornell University Press, 2004.

Suris, L. M., ed. *V. I. Lenin i VeCheKa: Sbornik dokumentov, Part I, 1917–1919*, Vol. 1. Moscow: DirectMedia, 2017.

Szelényi, Iván. *Socialist Entrepreneurs: Embourgeoisement in Rural Hungary*. Cambridge: Polity Press, 1988.

Urban Inequalities under State Socialism. Oxford: Oxford University Press, 1983.

Tarrow, Sidney. "'The World Changed Today!' Can We Recognize Critical Junctures When We See Them?" *Qualitative and Multi-Method Research* 15, no. 11 (2017): 9–11.

Tavrina, A. M. "Obraz geroya-obyvatelya v russkoy romanticheskoy povesti kontsa 20kh-nachala 40kh godov XIX veka." *Uchyonyye zapiski Orlovskogo gosudarstvennogo universiteta*, no. 5 (2012): 251–57.

TBMJ. "Public Health Services in Hungary." *The British Medical Journal* 2, no. 3379 (October 1925): 616.

Tchuikina, Sofya A. *Dvoryanskaya pamyat': "Byvshiye" v sovetskom gorode (Leningrad, 1920–30-e gody)*. St. Petersburg: European University at St. Petersburg, 2006.

Teckenberg, Wolfgang. "The Social Structure of the Soviet Working Class: Toward an Estatist Society?" *International Journal of Sociology* 11, no. 4 (Winter 1981/2): 1–163.

Tertytchnaya, Katerina, Catherine E. De Vries, Hector Solaz, and David Doyle. "When the Money Stops: Fluctuations in Financial Remittances and Incumbent Approval in Central Eastern Europe, the Caucasus and Central Asia." *The American Political Science Review* 112, no. 4 (November 2018): 758–74.

Tertytchnaya, Katerina, and Tomila V. Lankina. "Electoral Protests and Political Attitudes under Electoral Authoritarianism." *The Journal of Politics* 82, no. 1 (January 2020): 285–99.

Thelen, Kathleen. "How Institutions Evolve: Insights from Comparative Historical Analysis." In *Comparative Historical Analysis in the Social Sciences*, edited by James Mahoney and Dietrich Rueschemeyer, 208–40. Cambridge: Cambridge University Press, 2003.

How Institutions Evolve: The Political Economy of Skills in Germany, Britain, the United States, and Japan. New York: Cambridge University Press, 2004.

Thompson, E. P. *The Making of the English Working Class*, new ed. London: Penguin Books, 2013.

Tiffert, Glenn D. "The Chinese Judge: From Literatus to Cadre, 1906–1949." In *Knowledge Acts in Modern China: Ideas, Institutions, and Identities*, edited by Robert Culp, Eddy U, and Wen-hsin Yeh, 114–47. Berkeley: University of California, Berkeley, 2016.

Tikhomirov, M. N. "Samara v moyey zhizni." In *Klassika samarskogo krayevedeniya: Antologiya*, edited by P. S. Kabytov and E. L. Dubman, 20–78. Samara: Samara University, 2006.

Tilly, Charles. *Durable Inequality*. Berkeley: University of California Press, 1999.
    Stories, Identities, and Political Change. Lanham, Maryland: Rowman & Littlefield,
    2002.
Timasheff, Nicholas S. *The Great Retreat: The Growth and Decline of Communism in
    Russia*. New York: E. P. Dutton & Company, 1946.
Tolstoy, Aleksey N. *Khozhdeniye po mukam: Trilogiya*. Moscow: Khudozhestvennaya
    literatura, 1990.
Treadgold, Donald W. *The Great Siberian Migration: Government and Peasant in
    Resettlement from Emancipation to the First World War*. Westport, Connecticut:
    Greenwood Press, 1976.
Treyger, Elina. "Migration and Violent Crime: Lessons from the Russian Experience."
    Georgetown Immigration Law Journal 27, no. 2 (Winter 2013): 257–310.
Tromly, Benjamin. *Making the Soviet Intelligentsia: Universities and Intellectual Life
    under Stalin and Khrushchev*. Cambridge: Cambridge University Press, 2015.
Trostina, M. A. "Zhestokiy romans: Zhanrovyye priznaki, syuzhety i obrazy." In
    *Novyye podkhody v gumanitarnykh issledovaniyakh: Pravo, filosofiya, istoriya,
    lingvistika (Mezhvuzovyy sbornik nauchnykh trudov)*, 197–202. Saransk:
    Mordova State University, 2003.
Trotsky, Leon. *The Revolution Betrayed: What Is the Soviet Union and Where Is It
    Going?*, translated by Max Eastman. Mineola, New York: Dover Publications,
    2004.
Troynitskiy, N. A., ed. *Pervaya vseobshchaya perepis' naseleniya Rossiyskoy imperii,
    1897 god: Samaraskaya guberniya*, Vol. 36. St. Petersburg: Ministry of the Interior,
    1904.
Troynitskiy, N. A., ed. *Obshchiy svod po imperii rezul'tatov razrabotki dannykh
    pervoy vseobshchey perepisi naseleniya, proizvedyonnoy 28 Yanvarya 1897 goda*,
    Vol. 1–2. St. Petersburg: Tipografiya N. L. Nyrkina, 1905.
Turovskiy, Rostislav F. "Kontseptual'naya elektoral'naya karta postsovetskoy Rossii."
    Politiya no. 4 (Winter 2006): 161–202.
van Leeuwen, Marco H. D., and Ineke Maas. "Historical Studies of Social Mobility and
    Stratification." *Annual Review of Sociology* 36, no. 1 (August 2010): 429–51.
Vanhanen, Tatu. "A New Dataset for Measuring Democracy, 1810–1998." *Journal of
    Peace Research* 37, no. 2 (March 2000): 251–65.
Veblen, Thorstein. *The Theory of the Leisure Class*. New York: Penguin Books, 1994.
Vesnina, S. G. "Chastnyye tovarishcheskiye russko-nemetskiye uchilishcha
    v nemetskikh koloniyakh Povolzh'ya: Materialy Rossiysko-Germanskoy
    nauchnoy konferentsii. Anapa, 22–26 sentyabrya 1994 g." In *Rossiyskiye nemtsy
    na Donu, Kavkaze, Volge*, edited by Ye. A. Sherwud, 323–28. Moscow:
    Mezhdunarodnyy soyuz nemetskoy kul'tury, 1995.
Vishnevskiy, Anatoliy. *Serp i rubl': Konservativnaya modernizatsiya v SSSR*, 2nd ed.
    Moscow: State University Higher School of Economics, 2010.
Vishnevskiy, Anatoliy G. *Demograficheskaya modernizatsiya Rossii, 1900–2000*.
    Moscow: Novoye izdatel'stvo, 2006.
Volkov, Vadim V. "Kontseptsiya kul'turnosti, 1935–38: Sovetskaya tsivilizatsiya
    i povsednevnost' stalinskogo vremeni." *Sotsiologicheskiy zhurnal* 1, no. 2 (1996):
    203–21.
Voslensky, Michael. *Nomenklatura: Anatomy of the Soviet Ruling Class*, translated by
    Eric Mosbacher. London: The Bodley Head, 1984.

Wakeman, Frederic, Jr. "The Civil Society and Public Sphere Debate: Western Reflections on Chinese Political Culture." *Modern China* 19, no. 2 (April 1993): 108–38.

Wawro, Gregory J., and Ira Katznelson. "Designing Historical Social Scientific Inquiry: How Parameter Heterogeneity Can Bridge the Methodological Divide between Quantitative and Qualitative Approaches." *American Journal of Political Science* 58, no. 2 (April 2014): 526–46.

Webb, Sidney, and Beatrice Webb. *Soviet Communism: A New Civilization*, 3rd ed., 3 vols. London: Longmans, Green, 1947.

Weber, Max. "'Churches' and 'Sects' in North America: An Ecclesiastical and Sociopolitical Sketch," translated by Peter Baehr and Gordon C. Wells. In *The Protestant Ethic and the "Spirit" of Capitalism and Other Writings*, edited by Peter Baehr and Gordon C. Wells, 203–20. New York: Penguin Books, 2002.

"Class, Status and Party," translated by H. H. Gerth and C. Wright Mills. In *Class, Status, and Power*, edited by Reinhard Bendix and Seymour Martin Lipset, 21–28. New York: The Free Press, 1967.

Economy and Society: A New Translation, translated by Keith Tribe. Cambridge, Massachusetts: Harvard University Press, 2019.

Economy and Society: An Outline of Interpretive Sociology. Vol. 1, translated by Ephraim Fischoff, Hans Gerth, A. M. Henderson et al. Berkeley: University of California Press, 2013.

Economy and Society: An Outline of Interpretive Sociology. Vol. 2, translated by Ephraim Fischoff, Hans Gerth, A. M. Henderson et al. Berkeley: University of California Press, 2013.

Wirtschaft und Gesellschaft: Die Stadt, Vol. 5. Tübingen: J. C. B. Mohr (Paul Siebeck), 2000.

Wirtschaft und Gesellschaft: Gemeinschaften, Vol. 1. Tübingen: J. C. B. Mohr (Paul Siebeck), 2009.

Wirtschaft und Gesellschaft: Herrschaft, Vol. 4. Tübingen: J. C. B. Mohr (Paul Siebeck), 2009.

Werlen, Benno. *Society, Action and Space: An Alternative Human Geography*, translated by Gayna Walls. London: Routledge, 1993.

Wheatcroft, Stephen G. "Doctors and the Revolution in Russia." *Bulletin of the Society for the Social History of Medicine* 34, no. 5 (June 1984): 19–24.

Wheatcroft, Stephen G., and Robert W. Davies. "The Crooked Mirror of Soviet Economic Statistics." In *The Economic Transformation of the Soviet Union, 1913–1945*, edited by Robert W. Davies, Mark Harrison, and Stephen G. Wheatcroft, 24–80. Cambridge: Cambridge University Press, 1994.

White, Stephen. "Soviet Political Culture Reassessed." In *Political Culture and Communist Studies*, edited by Archie Brown, 62–99. Basingstoke: Macmillan, 1984.

Whyte, Martin King. "Sexual Inequality under Socialism: The Chinese Case in Perspective." In *Class and Social Stratification in Post-Revolution China*, edited by James L. Watson, 198–238. New York: Cambridge University Press, 2010.

Whyte, William H. *The Organization Man*. Harmondsworth: Penguin Books, 1961.

Wirtschafter, Elise Kimerling. *Social Identity in Imperial Russia*. Dekalb, Illinois: Northern Illinois University Press, 1997.

Wittenberg, Jason. *Crucibles of Political Loyalty: Church Institutions and Electoral Continuity in Hungary*. New York: Cambridge University Press, 2006.

Wright, Erik Olin. *Understanding Class.* London: Verso, 2015.

Wright, Teresa. *Accepting Authoritarianism: State-Society Relations in China's Reform Era.* Stanford, California: Stanford University Press, 2010.

Yagubov, Boris A. "'Zhestokiy' romans i gorodskaya ballada: Genezis i funktsionirovaniye." *Filologicheskiye nauki. Voprosy teorii i praktiki* 3, no. 21 (2013): 215–19.

Yastrebov, Gordey. "Intergenerational Social Mobility in Soviet and Post-Soviet Russia." Basic Research Program Working Paper 69/SOC/2016. National Research University Higher School of Economics, 2016.

"Kharakter stratifikatsii rossiyskogo obshchestva v sravnitel'nom kontekste: Ot vysokikh teoriy k grustnoy real'nosti." *Vestnik obshchestvennogo mneniya* 4, no. 110 (October–December 2011): 19–31.

Yurchak, Alexei. *Everything Was Forever, Until It Was No More: The Last Soviet Generation.* Princeton, New Jersey: Princeton University Press, 2006.

Zakharchenko, A. V., and A. I. Repinetskiy. "Ispol'zovaniye truda zaklyuchyonnykh i industrializatsiya Kuybyshevskoy oblasti nakanune i v gody Velikoy otechestvennoy voyny." *Izvestiya Samarskogo nauchnogo tsentra Rossiyskoy akademii nauk* 8, no. 3 (2006): 789–800.

Zakharova, Larissa. "Soviet Fashion in the 1950s–1960s: Regimentation, Western Influences, and Consumption Strategies." In *The Thaw: Soviet Society and Culture during the 1950s and 1960s,* edited by Denis Kozlov and Eleonory Gilburd, 402–35. Toronto: University of Toronto Press, 2013.

Zaslavskaya, R. M. *Yeshchyo odno posledneye skazaniye...,* 2nd ed. Moscow: Medpraktika-M, 2015.

Zaslavsky, Victor. "Contemporary Russian Society and Its Soviet Legacy: The Problem of State Dependent Workers." In *Social Change and Modernization: Lessons from Eastern Europe,* edited by Bruno Grancelli. De Gruyter Studies in Organization, 45–62. Berlin: De Gruyter, 1995.

Zerubavel, Eviatar. *Hidden Rhythms: Schedules and Calendars in Social Life.* Chicago: University of Chicago Press, 1981.

Time Maps: Collective Memory and the Social Shape of the Past. Chicago, Illinois: University of Chicago Press, 2004.

Zhiromskaya, Valentina B., I. N. Kiselyov, and Yu. A. Polyakov. *Polveka pod grifom sekretno: Vsesoyuznaya perepis' naseleniya 1937 goda.* Moscow: Nauka, 1996.

Zhukov, Yuri M., and Roya Talibova. "Stalin's Terror and the Long-Term Political Effects of Mass Repression." *Journal of Peace Research* 55, no. 2 (March 2018): 267–83.

Zinov'yev, Aleksandr. *Gomo sovetikus.* Moscow: Tsentrpoligraf, 2000.

Zubok, Vladislav. *The Idea of Russia: The Life and Work of Dmitry Likhachev.* I.B. Tauris, 2017.

Zhivago's Children: The Last Russian Intelligentsia. Cambridge, Massachusetts: The Belknap Press of Harvard University Press, 2011.

Index

(includes select bibliographic references)